OUT OF THE ABYSS™

RAGE of DEMONS™

GREEN RONIN
PUBLISHING

CREDITS

This book was a collaboration between Wizards of the Coast and Green Ronin Publishing. Members of the Green Ronin creative team are marked with an asterisk.

Story Creators: Christopher Perkins, Adam Lee, Richard Whitters

Story Consultants: R.A. Salvatore, Troy Denning

Lead Adventure Designer: Steve Kenson*

Designers: Cam Banks,* Walter Ciechanowski,* Alex Melchor,* Christopher Perkins, Chris Pramas,* Robert J. Schwalb,* Matt Sernett, Rodney Thompson, Ray Winninger*

Managing Editor: Jeremy Crawford

Editors: Scott Fitzgerald Gray, Christopher Perkins, Tom Cadorette*

Additional Proofreading: Peter Lee, Sean K Reynolds

Producer: Greg Bilsland

D&D Lead Designers: Mike Mearls, Jeremy Crawford

Art Directors: Hal Mangold,* Kate Irwin, Shauna Narciso

Cover Illustrator: Tyler Jacobson

Interior Illustrators: Empty Room Studios, Sam Burley, Olga Drebas, Wayne England, Ilich Henriquez, David Hueso, William O'Connor, Claudio Pozas, Jasper Sandner, Craig Spearing, Bryan Syme, Carlos Nuñez de Castro Torres, Francis Tsai, Anthony Waters, Richard Whitters, Ben Wootten, Kieran Yanner

Cartographers: Jared Blando, Mike Schley

Graphic Designer: Emi Tanji

Project Management: Neil Shinkle, John Hay

Production Services: Cynda Callaway, Jefferson Dunlap, David Gershman

Brand and Marketing: Nathan Stewart, Liz Schuh, Chris Lindsay, Shelly Mazzanoble, Hilary Ross, John Feil, Laura Tommervik, Greg Tito, Kim Lundstrom, Trevor Kidd

Playtesters: Robert Alaniz, Jay Anderson, Bill Benham, Stacy Bermes, Anthony Caroselli, Krupal Desai, Frank Foulis, Jason Fuller, Gregory L. Harris, Justin Hicks, Yan Lacharité, Jonathan Longstaff, Matt Maranda, Shawn Merwin, Lou Michelli, Mike Mihalas, Karl Resch, Kyle Turner, Arthur Wright, Keoki Young

FOREWORD

To get myself in the mindset of telling an Underdark-themed story set in the Forgotten Realms, I went back and read *Exile* by R.A. Salvatore, one of my favorite Drizzt novels. It tells the story of the dark elf's initial ascent to the surface world. Along the way, Drizzt encounters weird Underdark characters, including a deep gnome with hammers for hands, a pech (a small earth creature) polymorphed into a hook horror, and a crazy wizard with a *Daern's instant fortress*.

After reading the book again, I was reminded of *Alice's Adventures in Wonderland* and *Through the Looking Glass*. That's when I decided that our Underdark tale was going to draw inspiration from Lewis Carroll's works. We would paint the Underdark as an insanely wondrous domain into which our heroes must descend.

First, we needed a villain as deranged as the Queen of Hearts. Lolth was an obvious choice, as was Zuggtmoy. In researching the latter, I was reminded of the Demon Queen of Fungi's ongoing feud with Juiblex. That's when it occurred to me that we could be bold and tell an Underdark story featuring not just one demon lord, but several of them. Maybe even *all* of them.

We knew that our demon-infested tale would have two Drizzt novels as bookends, so we asked R.A. Salvatore to help us break the story. We also asked Troy Denning, another one of our talented authors, to join us, since he was writing a novel about Orcus. Out of those discussions came the Rage of Demons storyline, which we presented to the folks at Green Ronin. *Callooh, callay!* They agreed to collaborate with us on a D&D adventure—this book you now hold in your hands. Have fun with it, and may the stories of your players' harrowing exploits be as wonderful and unforgettable as any great novel!

Christopher Perkins
June 2015

ON THE COVER

Tyler Jacobson illustrates Demogorgon, the Prince of Demons, rampaging through Menzoberranzan after being ripped from the Abyss by the drow archmage Gromph Baenre.

620B2439000001 EN
ISBN: 978-0-7869-6581-6
First Printing: September 2015

9 8 7 6 5 4   (includes corrections)

C E

Contents

CHAPTER 1: PRISONERS OF THE DROW

Deep beneath the surface of the world lies the Underdark, a realm of endless labyrinthine tunnels and caverns where the sun never shines. The Underdark is filled with races and creatures too numerous to count or list, and foremost among these are the dark elves—the drow. Hated and feared even by their fellow dwellers in darkness, the drow raid other settlements in the Underdark as well as the surface world, taking prisoners back with them. Rendered unconscious with drow poison, then collared and shackled, these prisoners are eventually sold as slaves or entertainment in the dark elves' subterranean cities.

The adventurers have all had the misfortune of falling to such a fate. Captured by the drow, they are prisoners at one of the dark elves' outposts, awaiting transportation to Menzoberranzan, the City of Spiders. Whether they came into the Underdark seeking knowledge or fortune, or were just in the wrong place at the wrong time, they were ripe prey for a drow raid.

The setup of *Out of the Abyss* is such that the characters need have no connections with events in the Underdark, or with each other, prior to the start of the adventure. They can meet and get to know each other as prisoners of the drow. Players who would like their characters to have a stronger Underdark connection can choose from the background options in appendix A.

"Prisoners of the Drow" assumes the characters start at 1st level, and that they will achieve 2nd level (if not 3rd) by the end of this chapter of the adventure. Given the challenges of the adventure and the dangers of the Underdark, you can start the characters at a higher level (2nd or 3rd) to make things a bit easier for the players.

ESCAPE!

The characters' goal in this chapter of the adventure is straightforward: escape from the drow outpost of Velkynvelve, with an eye toward escaping from the Underdark. However, this goal is complicated by the adventurers' lack of familiarity with their surroundings. Even if the prisoners can get away from the drow, where will they go and how will they survive?

RESTRAINTS

All the drow's prisoners, including the characters, wear iron slave collars along with manacles connected to iron belts by a short length of chain. This leaves the prisoners restrained, but doesn't affect their movement or speed.

In addition to being manacled, spellcasters don't have any spell components or focuses, initially limiting their spellcasting ability. (Wizard characters don't need their spellbooks to cast spells, but will be unable to change their prepared spells without them. As such, give wizard characters some leeway in determining which spells they had previously prepared before being captured.) Moreover, spellcasting isn't possible inside the slave pen because of its magical wards (see area 11).

Slipping out of manacles requires a successful DC 20 Dexterity check, while breaking them requires

a successful DC 20 Strength check. A character can unlock the manacles using thieves' tools with a successful DC 15 Dexterity check. The manacles have 15 hit points. The iron collars can be broken with a successful DC 20 Strength check. The collars have 12 hit points. A character who fails a check to break a collar, break a set of manacles, or escape from a set of manacles can't attempt checks of that kind again until he or she finishes a long rest. A character can still use the Help action to aid another character, however.

THE ADVENTURE BEGINS

The characters begin the adventure in the slave pens of Velkynvelve. Stripped of everything but their underclothing, they are at the mercy of the dark elves and in the company of other prisoners, many of who aren't what they seem.

> Captured by the drow! You wouldn't wish this fate upon anyone, yet here you are—locked in a dark cave, the cold, heavy weight of metal tight around your throat and wrists. You are not alone. Other prisoners are trapped in here with you, in an underground outpost far from the light of the sun.
>
> Your captors include a cruel drow priestess who calls herself Mistress Ilvara of House Mizzrym. Over the past several days, you've met her several times, robed in silken garments and flanked by two male drow, one of whom has a mass of scars along one side of his face and neck.
>
> Mistress Ilvara likes to impress her will with scourge in hand and remind you that your life now belongs to her. "Accept your fate, learn to obey, and you may survive." Her words echo in your memory, even as you plot your escape.

Assume that each player character has been a prisoner in Velkynvelve for 1d10 days. (Roll separately for each character.) The characters spend most of this time locked in the slave pen, emerging occasionally under heavy guard to perform menial chores for their captors' amusement (see "Hard Labor").

Feel free to play out any interaction between the drow, the player characters, and the other prisoners. This is an opportunity to reveal who the characters are and to flesh out their backgrounds and personalities through roleplaying, even as you introduce some of their fellow prisoners. Ilvara's newest consort, Shoor, wants to impress his mistress, while Jorlan, her former consort, sullenly does his duty but casts a curious eye over the prisoners. Any hostile move is met with poisoned crossbow bolts from the drow, and possibly a strike from Ilvara's scourge or a *ray of sickness* spell. The giant spiders attack and poison anyone who attacks the drow. The drow don't kill any of the prisoners (leaving them unconscious at 0 hit points) but have no compunction about beating them.

IN THE SLAVE PEN

Velkynvelve's slave pen is closed with a heavy iron gate bolted into the stone. See area 11 for more information about the slave pen, including options for opening or breaking through the gate.

The prisoners are provided with clay chamber pots, and one of the duties of slaves is to empty them into the pool during their shift. There are no other comforts in the slave pen. Prisoners must sit or lie on the stone floor, and are fed only once each day—a thin mushroom broth served in small clay bowls passed through gaps in the bars of the gate.

SCAVENGED POSSESSIONS

The player characters have not been idle during their captivity. Have each player roll a d20, and add the number of days (1d10) that player's character has been imprisoned in Velkynvelve. The result determines what, if anything, the character has in his or her possession when the adventure begins.

SCAVENGED POSSESSIONS

Result	Item
2–9	—
10–12	A gold coin
13–15	A living **spider** the size of a tarantula
16–18	A 5-foot-long strand of silk rope
19–21	A flawed carnelian gemstone worth 10 gp
22–24	A rusted iron bar that can be used as a club
25–27	A flint shard that can be used as a dagger
28–30	A hand crossbow bolt coated with drow poison (see "Poisons" in chapter 8 of the *Dungeon Master's Guide*)

FELLOW PRISONERS

The characters are held with ten other prisoners, captured during various raids and likewise awaiting transportation to Menzoberranzan. Some can expect to be sold as slaves, while others await death at the hands of the drow or their pets. Regardless of what they might think of the adventurers—and each other—outside the slave pens, all the NPCs have good reason to cooperate in order to escape and survive.

PRISONERS OF THE DROW

Buppido	Talkative and cunning derro
Prince Derendil	Quaggoth who claims to be a cursed elf prince
Eldeth Feldrun	Shield dwarf scout from Gauntlgrym
Jimjar	Deep gnome with a gambling problem
Ront	Orc bully
Sarith Kzekarit	Drow accused of murder
Shuushar the Awakened	Kuo-toa hermit and mystic
Stool	Myconid sprout
Topsy and Turvy	Deep gnome wererat twins

BUPPIDO

A male **derro**, Buppido is surprisingly gregarious and talkative, demonstrating a keen mind and a disarming manner. This pleasant facade conceals the soul of an insane killer. Buppido secretly believes he is the living incarnation of the derro god Diinkarazan—an avatar of murder offering bloody sacrifices to create a path of carnage through the Underdark for his people to follow to glory. He rationalizes any setbacks (including his capture and imprisonment) as part of his "divine plan." His killings are carefully ritualized, following an exacting process of cutting open the victims and arranging their organs.

Although mad, Buppido is cunning and capable of hiding his true nature to serve his own ends. Because he believes he is a god, he is convinced that he can't be killed (or at least that the death of his mortal form means nothing to him), so he is completely fearless. He assumes everything is part of his divine plan, and enthusiastically participates in any plot to escape from the drow so he can continue his holy work. Buppido is happy to consider his fellow prisoners allies until such time as he no longer needs them, or becomes convinced that the omens point toward the need for one or more of them to be sacrificed to his greater glory.

PRINCE DERENDIL

This hulking **quaggoth** is the most menacing-looking prisoner in the slave pens, and the other prisoners give him a wide berth. If any of the characters speak to him, however, the quaggoth replies in urbane Elvish. He explains that he is not, in fact, a quaggoth, but a gold elf prince polymorphed into quaggoth form by a curse. He claims to be Prince Derendil of the kingdom of Nelrindenvane in the High Forest. His crown was usurped by the evil wizard Terrestor, who trapped him in this form and exiled him from his people.

Although Derendil behaves like the highborn prince he believes himself to be, he responds to stress—and particularly threats—like a quaggoth: violently tearing foes limb from limb and rending their flesh with sharp claws and teeth. He comes back to himself only after battle, or when someone reinforces his "true identity" to snap him out of it. Derendil laments that he is

slowly but surely losing himself to the savagery of his quaggoth form.

In fact, Derendil is simply mad, touched by the delusions of the demon lord Fraz-Urb'luu. The kingdom of Nelrindenvane doesn't exist, and all of "Derendil's" recollections and personality are an illusion created by the Demon Prince of Deception. The quaggoth refuses to believe the truth, and any incontrovertible evidence as to his real nature sends him into a murderous rage.

ELDETH FELDRUN

A female shield dwarf **scout** from Gauntlgrym, Eldeth is high spirited and proud of both her heritage and her people's achievement in reclaiming the ancient dwarven kingdom; she suggests Gauntlgrym as a destination to escape from the Underdark. Eldeth is stubborn and hates the drow and all other "corrupt dark dwellers" such as the derro and duergar.

Eldeth wants to get back home, but she is also defiant and self sacrificing—and therefore among the most likely prisoners to perish before getting the opportunity. If that happens, Eldeth asks a character she trusts to promise to carry word of her fate back to her family in Gauntlgrym, along with her shield and warhammer if they are recovered. This might win the characters the approval of Eldeth's kin when they later visit Gauntlgrym.

JIMJAR

A male deep gnome **spy**, Jimjar is a feckless rogue with a devil-may-care attitude, a fondness for coin, and an obsession with betting on virtually anything and everything. Once he knows the characters, Jimjar regularly offers them bets on things from their own efforts ("I bet you ten gold you can't get past that sentry without being seen") to the outcomes of random events ("I bet you twenty gold this tunnel is the right way"). He sometimes uses betting to goad others into doing things, but characters can easily turn the tables knowing that Jimjar finds it difficult to refuse a wager. His behavior is unusual for the dour deep gnomes, and others of his kind (including Topsy and Turvy) find Jimjar annoying at best, and unstable and potentially mad at worst.

Jimjar is always true to his word, and he manages to keep exact track of his debits and credits in his head,

JIMJAR   RONT   SARITH KZEKARIT

paying up on his bets (or demanding payment) as soon as possible. He's not above pocketing a little extra coin when no one is watching, and he has an amazing ability to secret significant wealth on his person.

Jimjar feels as though there's something odd about the twins Topsy and Turvy, but he keeps his opinion to himself unless asked. He does his best to get along with everyone, although some find his gregariousness and constant wagers grating.

RONT

A male **orc** from the Iceshield tribe, Ront fled from the slaughter of a band of orcs at the hands of the dwarves, falling down a shaft and wandering in the Underdark before being captured by the drow. He's ashamed of his cowardly act and knows that Gruumsh, the god of the orcs, is punishing him. But he also doesn't want to die, or at least not in drow captivity. Ront is mean, stupid, and hateful, but he also knuckles under to authority and threats. He especially hates Eldeth, as his tribe is at war with her people.

Ront engages in threatening behavior and bullying toward the other prisoners unless someone stands up to him.

SARITH KZEKARIT

A male **drow**, Sarith is sullen and keeps to himself, rebuffing attempts to talk to him. He is disgraced by his imprisonment but is resigned to his fate, since there doesn't appear to be anything he can do about it. Sarith is accused of murdering one of his fellow drow warriors in a fit of madness, but he has no memory of it. He varies between believing the whole thing is a setup to discredit and destroy him, and fearing that it is all true—which, in fact, it is. He is being held until he can be sent back to Menzoberranzan as a sacrifice to Lolth and an example to others.

Unknown even to the other drow, Sarith is infected with tainted spores from myconids corrupted by Zuggtmoy, the Demon Queen of Fungi. The initial infestation of the spores caused Sarith's bout of madness, and his health and sanity continue to deteriorate as the spores grow within his brain.

SHUUSHAR THE AWAKENED

A **kuo-toa**, Shuushar is likely to be one of the more unusual creatures any of the adventurers have met. The aquatic hermit is a calm and peaceful presence. He is aware of his people's well-deserved reputation for madness, and claims to have spent a lifetime in contemplation and solitary meditation to overcome that legacy. He appears to have been successful, exuding an aura of enlightened balance. Shuushar is even calm and accepting of his current imprisonment, merely saying that it is what it is, and who can say what end it might eventually lead toward?

Although Shuushar is by far the most sane, stable, and honest of the adventurers' fellow prisoners, he is also the most useless to their immediate goals. The kuo-toa hermit is a complete pacifist. He doesn't fight or cause harm to any other creature, even refusing to defend himself or others. He gladly accompanies the party if permitted to do so, however, helping them in any way he can other than violating his most sacred vow.

Shuushar is familiar with Sloobludop, the kuo-toa town near the Darklake, and has navigated the twisting routes of the Darklake for many years. He hopes to share his enlightenment with his fellow kuo-toa, although he isn't aware of recent events in Sloobludop (see chapter 3 for details).

STOOL

Stool is a **myconid sprout** captured by Sarith Kzekarit. Stool is lonely and frightened, wanting only to return to its home in Neverlight Grove. If befriended by the characters, Stool gladly offers to guide them to its home, promising them sanctuary with its folk, although it isn't aware of the dangers posed by Zuggtmoy's influence on the myconids (see chapter 5).

Stool uses rapport spores to establish telepathic communication with other creatures, and it does so to communicate with characters who are kind and friendly toward it. The myconid will also help establish communication with Underdark denizens with whom the characters don't share a language. Once it becomes attached to one or more of the adventurers, Stool behaves somewhat like an enthusiastic and curious younger sibling, sticking close to the characters and asking all kinds of questions.

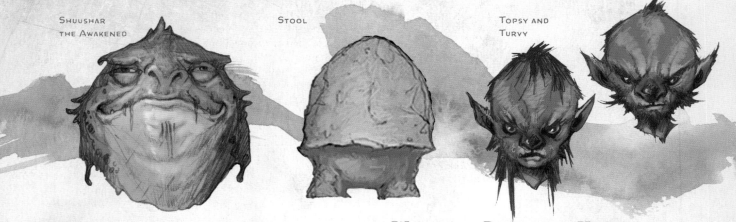

TOPSY AND TURVY

Twin deep gnomes, Topsy and her brother Turvy
are originally from Blingdenstone in the Underdark.
They were captured by the drow while out gathering
mushrooms in the tunnels near their home. Like most
other svirfneblin, Topsy has a stringy mop of hair while
Turvy only has a few tufts of hair atop his otherwise
bald head. Topsy is by far the more social of the two.
Turvy constantly mumbles and mutters darkly, with
Topsy repeating or translating what her brother says.

Topsy and Turvy hide the fact that they are **wererats**.
Infected with the curse of lycanthropy, neither deep
gnome has entirely embraced it yet, and they struggle
to control their wererat instincts and urges. They are
fearful of what potential allies might do if they learn
the truth, and are looking out for each other and their
own survival. With their transformations controlled by
the unseen cycle of the moon, you can use the twins'
impending change as a wild card in the adventure.
They've been prisoners for less than a month, meaning
the full moon is coming.

A MOTLEY CREW

The other prisoners who manage to escape with the player
characters are likely to become their companions for a
substantial part of the adventure, so it is good to lay the
groundwork for those relationships early on. Some of
the NPCs might not survive the initial escape attempt.
Others might be lost to the dangers of the Underdark—or
might reveal their true colors and betray the party. A few
could become true companions. Keep in mind the other
prisoners have their own personalities and goals, but are
generally willing to cooperate for their own benefit. Their
knowledge of the Underdark should encourage the player
characters to keep them around at least initially.

Since managing such a large cast of NPCs can be quite
involved, enlist the aid of the players if you wish, having
each of them take on the role of managing one or more of
the party's companions. The player generally decides what
that NPC is doing, with the knowledge that you, as Dungeon
Master, can overrule them as needed by the story. Not only
does this make the secondary characters easier to manage,
it helps the players get to know them and strengthens the
bonds between the NPCs and the adventurers.

WHAT THE PRISONERS KNOW

Allow the characters to freely mingle and interact with
their fellow prisoners or even the drow guards, although
the guards rarely talk to the "surface-dweller scum." Of
all the prisoners, only Eldeth and Jimjar speak fluent
Common. The others speak Undercommon (or at least
understand it). Ront knows some Common, while
Derendil speaks Elvish. Stool's rapport spores can
establish telepathic communication to allow everyone
to speak freely. The guards aren't observant enough
to notice.

You might wish to consult the social interaction rules
in the *Dungeon Master's Guide*, in which case the other
prisoners are initially indifferent toward the characters.
Handle the interactions using roleplaying, Charisma
checks, or a balance of the two as best suits your group
and the way the adventure unfolds.

The characters can learn the following things from
talking with their fellow prisoners, some of who have
been captives of the drow for a tenday or two:

- There are nineteen drow at the outpost, including
  Ilvara, Shoor, and Jorlan, as well as another priestess
  named Asha. There are also a dozen quaggoths and a
  number of giant spiders.
- Three drow guards watch the slave pen from the
  hanging guard tower across the rope bridge, visible
  through the locked gate.
- The cell has some sort of antimagic effect on it (see
  area 11 for details).
- Jorlan the drow warrior suffered disfiguring injuries
  recently. Before then, he seemed more in Ilvara's
  favor. Now Shoor seems to have displaced him.
- Jorlan used to have a wand that shot globs of sticky
  material able to trap targets. Now Shoor carries it, as
  another sign of their change in status.
- It might be a matter of days or tendays before a contin-
  gent from Menzoberranzan arrives to take prisoners
  back to the drow city.

Additionally, the drow Sarith Kzekarit knows
the following:

- A gray ooze lives in the pool. It's harmless, feeding off
  waste unless disturbed.
- A supply patrol from Menzoberranzan is a few days
  overdue, which is unusual.

Hard Labor

The drow divide their prisoners into three roughly equal-sized groups and put them to work for a third of the day, supervised by the quaggoths. Their menial tasks include filling and hauling water barrels, operating the lift, cleaning any or all parts of the outpost (whether they need it or not), emptying chamber pots, food preparation and service, washing dishes, and laundry. The prisoners are also given cruel or pointless tasks to occupy them, and for the dark elves' amusement. Such labors include moving or stacking rocks, coiling ropes, and organizing supplies, with prisoners forced to redo work that doesn't meet the drow's arbitrary standards.

Characters might or might not work together, depending on how the drow split them up. Prisoners known to be friendly to each other are usually kept apart, and no more than two or three prisoners are allowed to work at a single task at once.

The drow and quaggoths are cruel and capricious, but also somewhat bored and looking for amusement. The quaggoths are poor conversationalists, hateful and mistrustful toward the prisoners. The drow are more inclined to talk, if only to boast of their superiority. Characters might trick them into dropping useful bits of information, such as how long the journey to Menzoberranzan is expected to take, or that the outpost is relatively close to the Darklake.

Bad Dreams

The characters' sleep in the slave pen is troubled and fitful, filled with strange dreams and disturbing images. Dark shadows seem to move and reach out toward them as the characters wander lost through endless mazes of tunnels. Oily tentacles slide to brush up against them, while a great buzzing and howling rises in the distance. Suppurating wounds burst open in clouds of spores or crawling masses of maggots or insects. At least one or more of the characters should wake in a cold sweat from these nightmares after every rest, feeling as though something is out there in the dark depths—something far worse than the drow.

You need not explain the cause of these dreams and images at this time. Characters can chalk them up to the conditions in the slave pen, or to the aftereffects of drow poison, but they are omens of what is happening in the Underdark. Spellcasters, particularly clerics and warlocks, might be most prone to these dreams, but they can visit any or all of the characters.

Fight!

Most of the other prisoners aren't looking for trouble, and even killers such as Buppido are careful to bide their time. Still, both Derendil and Ront have quick tempers, and Sarith the drow is prone to bouts of violence as Zuggtmoy's spores take over his mind. It's possible the characters could provoke a fight. If they do, some of the prisoners (including the deep gnomes) egg on the fighters while others keep their distance or even try to break up the brawl.

Any violent conflict draws the attention of the drow guards, who initially order any prisoners to stand down from a fight, threatening them with hand crossbows from outside the gate. If necessary, they shoot prisoners with poisoned crossbow bolts to incapacitate them. (See chapter 8 of the *Dungeon Master's Guide* for information on drow poison.) The guards let any fight play out for their own amusement as long as the prisoners don't seem likely to actually kill one another.

Feeding Time

If a prisoner becomes too much trouble, or if the drow need to mete out a lesson on the price of disobedience, they make a gruesome spectacle of feeding a malcontent to the giant spiders in the webs beneath Velkynvelve. Drow guards or quaggoth servants throw the bound prisoner over the edge into the webs, where the spiders quickly converge to bite the victim, injecting their venom. Once the victim is paralyzed, the spiders wrap their meal up in webbing.

This event is a convenient opportunity to get rid of one or more of the other prisoners before the escape attempt if you don't want them around. As well, you can drive home the cruelty and threat of the drow by eliminating an NPC with whom the characters have formed a bond.

The Drow

The garrison at Velkynvelve consists of twelve **drow**, five **drow elite warriors**, a junior drow priestess named Asha (use the **priest** stat block in the *Monster Manual*, but add the Fey Ancestry, Innate Spellcasting, and Sunlight Sensitivity features of the **drow** stat block), and the outpost's commander, a senior **drow priestess of Lolth** named Ilvara. The drow have the assistance of a pack of twelve **quaggoths** and six trained **giant spiders**.

Prominent Drow

Ilvara Mizzrym	Drow priestess and commander of the outpost
Asha Vandree	Junior priestess
Shoor Vandree	Drow elite warrior. Ilvara's lieutenant and lover, and Asha's distant cousin
Jorlan Duskryn	Maimed drow elite warrior. Ilvara's former lieutenant and lover.

Ilvara Mizzrym

The commander of Velkynvelve is an ambitious drow priestess looking to rise in the esteem of Lolth and her house. She considers command of a mere outpost a stepping stone in her ascension. The posting is beneath her, and she treats both it and her prisoners with contempt. But she also knows the posting is temporary, and she intends to wring every advantage from it in the meantime.

A member of a drow house with a long history as slavers, Ilvara is a cruel mistress who enjoys taunting and tormenting enemies and underlings alike. In addition to a scourge, she wields a *tentacle rod*. Although she has taken Shoor Vandree as her lover, Ilvara cares no more about him than she did about Jorlan Duskryn, the lover she discarded due to his crippling injuries.

ILVARA
MIZZRYM

ROLEPLAYING THE DROW

The drow are arrogant, cruel, and vicious, viewing their slaves as little more than livestock and treating them with cold disregard. Even the lowest drow understands the inferiority of other creatures, behaving toward the prisoners like sneering nobility. With their superiors, however, the drow are fawning sycophants with a passive-aggressive edge. The males defer to the females, the rank-and-file warriors defer to the elite warriors, and everyone defers to the priestess Ilvara.

Twithin the outpost, which shows in his swagger and the way he lords it over every other male in Velkynvelve, particularly Jorlan. Still insecure in his position, Shoor feels the need to demonstrate his skill and effectiveness to his mistress and to find ways to please her.

As Ilvara's lieutenant, Shoor carries a *wand of viscid globs* (see appendix B), which once belonged to Jorlan and is used to capture and restrain prisoners.

JORLAN DUSKRYN

Jorlan turned a talent for inflicting pain into skill as a warrior, and a certain roguish charm into a way to ingratiate himself with his female superiors. He quickly made himself useful to Ilvara Mizzrym as both the field commander of the Velkynvelve garrison and as her lover, enjoying all the benefits that came with both roles.

Jorlan thought that Lolth favored him, or at least that his charms had deflected her malice, until he had the misfortune of a run-in with a black pudding on an otherwise routine raid. Ilvara's healing magic saved his life but couldn't undo the terrible damage wrought by the ooze's acid. With his once-handsome face melted and scarred, and his sword hand twisted and missing two fingers, Jorlan was no longer the warrior he once was.

Ilvara relieved Jorlan of duty during his recuperation, replacing him with the young bravo Shoor Vandree. When she then took Shoor to her bed, Jorlan realized his recovery would never be sufficient to regain what he had lost. His heartbreak and loss has since become a virulent hatred for Ilvara and Shoor that slowly eats at him. Jorlan finds the idea of suicide or reckless self-destruction beneath him, however—unless he can find a way to take Ilvara and her new lover with him.

Jorlan knows full well that the sympathy the priestess Asha shows him is an attempt to manipulate him. But he's willing to play along for the time being, hoping to draw Asha closer and potentially use her against Ilvara when the time is right.

Because of his injuries, Jorlan has disadvantage on attack rolls, Dexterity checks, and Dexterity saving throws.

DROW WARRIORS

The remaining drow males garrisoning Velkynvelve are named Balok, Bemeril, Guldor, Honemmeth, Imbros, Jaezred, Jevan, Kalannar, Malagar, Nadal, Nym, and Sorn.

ASHA VANDREE

A junior drow priestess under Ilvara's guidance, Asha initially considered Ilvara an example to emulate. That changed after she saw how Ilvara treated Jorlan Duskryn, a seasoned drow warrior who was the commander's lover up until he was badly wounded. Ilvara discarded Jorlan without a second thought, showing Asha the foolishness of expecting any reward for loyalty.

Asha is ambitious enough to know she could assume command of the outpost if anything was to happen to Ilvara, but not courageous enough to challenge her superior openly. She also knows that she would have to impress her superiors in the City of Spiders for any such field promotion to become permanent. As such, Asha moves cautiously, fanning the fires of Jorlan's hatred while keeping her own hands clean of any plotting.

SHOOR VANDREE

This drow elite warrior has assumed the role of Ilvara's lieutenant and lover after the injuries suffered by his predecessor, Jorlan Duskryn. Shoor is relatively young and quite arrogant for a drow male, proud of his abilities and accomplishments. He is still flush with his success in winning the favor of Ilvara and advancing his position

VELKYNVELVE

The drow outpost is located high in a cavern, built 100 feet above the rocky floor. The outpost consists of a series of small caves in the cavern walls and four "hanging towers"—hollowed-out stalactites connected by walkways, stairs, and rope bridges. The towers are concealed by the thick webs of giant spiders stretched below them, so that only the lowermost parts of the stalactites are visible from the cavern floor.

With the small amount of dim light used in the outpost shielded from the cavern floor below, one might walk the entire length of the cleft without becoming aware of the outpost overhead, hidden in the darkness above the range of torches and lanterns. The giant spiders also serve as guards, dropping down on their web strands to prey upon creatures that find their way into the cavern. Similarly, drow warriors can drop to the cave floor on lines of spider silk to ambush enemies.

Three caves and two hanging towers surrounding a platform make up the main part of the outpost for the drow warriors. The largest of the hanging towers is reserved for the priestesses and the shrine of Lolth, while the other is a guard tower opposite the cave used to hold slaves. North of the slave pen is the den of the outpost's quaggoth servants. Watch posts lie at either end of the outpost, near the northern and southern entrances to the cavern.

1. Southern Watch Post

Near the southern passage from the cavern is an alcove used as a watch post.

Two **drow** are stationed here at all times, keeping watch over the passage and noting the approach of any creatures. The duty is long and dull, so the watchers are sometimes distracted. A successful Dexterity (Stealth) check made against the guards' passive Wisdom (Perception) score of 12 allows characters to pass unnoticed. Any light from the passage or the cavern below automatically draws the guards' attention, however.

The drow guards are under orders to report intruders immediately, and to keep them under observation. They take no other action unless ordered or unless they see signs of a significant threat. In that case, they blow a high, shrill note on a warning trumpet to alert the whole outpost.

2. Barracks

Stone steps lead from the watch post to a 1-foot-thick platform of zurkhwood (see "Fungi of the Underdark" earlier in this chapter) extending between two of the hanging towers and into three adjoining caverns.

The two southernmost caves serve as barracks for the rank-and-file drow warriors of the outpost. Six warriors dwell in each barracks, each set up with a pallet, a small zurkhwood chest for holding personal possessions and equipment, and a side table. Spider silk rope webbing on the cavern walls is set with hooks for hanging lanterns and other items, but the barracks are rarely lit.

One **drow** is present in each of the barracks caves at any time, resting in a meditative trance. A resting drow rises at any significant light or noise, ready to attack.

Velkynvelve: General Features

The following features apply throughout the outpost.

Light. The interior spaces of the outpost are dimly illuminated by lanterns containing phosphorescent fungi, while the exterior is dark.

Sound. A small waterfall pouring into the cavern creates a constant background noise, negating the cave's tendency to amplify and carry sounds. Checks made to hear things in the cavern are made normally.

Stairs. These 5-foot-wide stairs are carved into the stone sides of the cavern between several of the cave entrances.

Bridges. Bridges of spider-silk rope connect the walkways to the guard tower and the entrance to the priestess's tower. The swaying bridges are difficult terrain for non-drow.

Falling. A creature pushed off the stairs, a bridge, or the edge of a platform must attempt a DC 10 Dexterity saving throw. On a failure, the creature falls, landing in the webs stretched beneath the outpost. On a successful save, a creature grabs hold of the edge and hangs there until it can climb back up with a DC 10 Strength (Athletics) check made as part of its movement. A failed Strength check means the creature is unable to move and must check again, while failure by 5 or more means a fall to the webs.

Webs. The dense webs of giant spiders kept by the drow conceal the outpost from below. A creature falling into the webs becomes restrained. As an action, a restrained creature can attempt a DC 12 Strength check to break free from the webs. The webs can also be attacked and destroyed (AC 10, 15 hp per 10-foot section, vulnerability to fire, and immunity to bludgeoning, poison, and psychic damage). Each foot of movement in the webs costs 1 extra foot, and any creature other than a spider that enters the webs or starts its turn there must succeed on a DC 12 Strength or Dexterity check to avoid becoming restrained. Any movement in the webs attracts the attention of the giant spiders, which attack and feed on trapped creatures.

A creature falling from the webbing to the cavern floor takes 10d6 bludgeoning damage.

Treasure

The equipment of the resting drow is stored under his pallet: a shortsword, a hand crossbow with a case of 20 hand crossbow bolts, a chain shirt, and a 100-foot coil of silk rope with a small grappling hook at the end.

Each of the six chests in each barracks contains a flask of drow poison used to treat crossbow bolts (see "Poisons" in chapter 8 of the *Dungeon Master's Guide*). One flask has enough poison to treat 20 bolts. Each chest also contains two sets of clothing and 1d4 items from the Trinkets table in chapter 5 of the *Player's Handbook*.

3. Main Hall

This cave serves as a gathering and eating place for the drow warriors of the outpost. It has four circular tables carved from zurkhwood, each surrounded by five chairs. Part of the hall is used as a food preparation and storage area, containing stocks of dried and fresh fungi, dried fruits, cheeses, preserved meat, and a few clay jars of spices. A heavy iron brazier provides heat for cooking along with dim light, but much of the food is served cold.

At any time, there is a 25 percent chance that 1d4 **drow** are in the main hall eating or entertaining themselves with dice or card games. If any drow are present, 1d4 **quaggoths** are also on hand, serving and cleaning. If there are no drow in the main hall, there is a 25 percent chance that a lone **quaggoth** is here performing its duties.

Treasure

There is nothing of value in the main hall apart from what the drow have on them, but characters can loot the larder for the equivalent of up to 30 days of rations, limited by what they can carry. Each day of rations for one character weighs 2 pounds.

4. Elite Barracks

The two hanging towers flanking the platform are the quarters of the elite warriors of the outpost, except for the commander's lieutenant (currently Shoor Vandree) who has his own quarters in the priestess's tower. Each hanging tower has two chambers, with a rope ladder running between the upper and lower chamber through a zurkhwood trapdoor. The elite warriors have finer furniture, including zurkhwood chairs and small tables around which they sit.

One off-duty **drow elite warrior** rests in one of the chambers here at any given time. There is a 50 percent chance that one **quaggoth** is also present, carrying out chores such as cleaning up or delivering water. Either reacts hostilely to intruders, but they might choose to flee and warn the outpost rather than attack, depending on the odds.

Treasure

The equipment of the resting drow warrior is stowed beneath his pallet: a shortsword, a hand crossbow with a case of 20 bolts, a chain shirt, and a 100-foot coil of silk rope with a small grappling hook at the end.

Each of the chests in the four chambers contains a flask of drow poison used to treat crossbow bolts. One flask has enough poison to treat 20 bolts. Each chest also contains two changes of clothing, 2d6 sp, 1d8 gp, and 1d4 items from the Trinkets table in chapter 5, "Equipment," of the *Player's Handbook*.

5. Lift

Attached to the edge of the barracks platform is a winch-and-basket device consisting of a large swinging arm that carries a thin cord of strong spider silk. The cord runs through a series of pulleys from a hand-cranked horizontal spool to a heavy woven basket suspended at the end. The basket is kept up on the platform except when it is in use.

Two **quaggoth** attendants remain by the lift to watch for a signal from below for the basket to be lowered. They are on guard in case anyone other than a drow or one of their own kind approaches.

Using the Lift

Up to four Medium creatures can fit somewhat snugly in the basket, which is swung out over the edge of the platform and lowered to the cavern floor below by turning the spool using attached handles. This requires a successful DC 18 Strength check, normally provided by two quaggoth servants (one of which makes the check while the other assists with the Help action). Once on the cave floor, the basket can be loaded with other passengers or up to 800 pounds of cargo, then lifted back up to the platform in the same way. It takes 4 rounds for the basket to move between the platform and the floor under normal operation.

6. Shrine to Lolth

A steep rope bridge leads from the walkway ledge to the uppermost level of the largest hanging tower, called the priestess's tower. The floor of this circular chamber is covered by dark silken mats with a pale web-strand pattern woven through them in silvery thread. In the middle of the chamber (at the center of the web) stands a broad pedestal carved from zurkhwood, with a 10-foot-high sculpted spider at its head. The carving is so lifelike that anyone initially entering the chamber and seeing it in dim light must succeed on a DC 12 Wisdom (Perception) check to recognize it. On a failure, a character mistakes it for a real giant spider.

This place is a shrine to Lolth, the drow's spider goddess, and also serves as quarters for Asha, the junior priestess. She tends the shrine, overseeing routine rituals and offerings to Lolth.

Roll a d6 when the characters enter the shrine to determine who they might meet.

Shrine Activity

d6	Activity
1–2	Asha is in the room alone, resting
3–4	Asha and 1d4 **drow** are engaged in worship
5–6	The shrine is empty

The back half of the chamber, behind the altar, is piled with a semicircle of pillows and cushions. Resting among these is a **giant spider** trained and kept by the priestesses. The cushions give the spider sufficient concealment to hide from anyone entering the tower from the front. A character must succeed on a Wisdom (Perception) check contested by the spider's Dexterity (Stealth) check to spot it before it moves.

Treasure

The altar is flanked by a pair of heavy silver candlesticks worth 25 gp each. They hold thick black candles, lit only when a ritual is being performed in the shrine.

The eight "eyes" of the spider statue are eight pieces of polished jet—four small ones worth 5 gp each and four larger ones worth 10 gp each. Any non-drow who possesses these gems falls under a curse from Lolth. All spiders and spiderlike creatures attack the bearer of the stones on sight, and such creatures have advantage on checks to detect the possessor of the stones. The curse lasts until all the stones are given into the safekeeping of a drow worshiper of Lolth or the gems are subject to a *remove curse* spell.

7. Ilvara's Quarters

A rope ladder leads down from the shrine into this chamber, which serves as private quarters to Mistress Ilvara, priestess of Lolth and commander of Velkynvelve.

Velkynvelve

15FT

BLANDO

velkynvelve side view

Inside, the walls are hung with black mesh resembling a spider's web, extending from a central spot on the ceiling out to the walls, then draped down like curtains. Thick, woven mats cover the floor, while a low platform is covered with cushions and pillows to make a broad, divan-like bed. One side of the chamber contains a small table and two chairs, while the other holds a small shrine to Lolth, draped in white silk. A heavy chest of black-stained zurkhwood sits at the foot of the bed.

Ilvara retreats to her quarters for privacy, rest, and meditation. Roll a d6. On 1–2, the priestess is here. On a roll of 1, Shoor Vandree is also here with her. Ilvara is furious if anyone dares to enter her quarters unbidden. If the characters catch her here, she casts *web*, *conjure animals*, or *insect plague* to bedevil them while she flees and calls for help. If Shoor is with Ilvara, he attacks to cover her escape.

Trap

The chest is locked, and Ilvara keeps the key in a hidden pocket on the inside of her belt. The lock is trapped with a poison needle tipped with drow poison (see "Poisons" in chapter 8 of the *Dungeon Master's Guide*), which is activated if any attempt is made to open the lock without the proper key. The victim takes 1 piercing damage and must succeed on a DC 13 Constitution saving throw or be poisoned for 1 hour. If the saving throw fails by 5 or more, the target is also unconscious while poisoned in this way. A successful DC 20 Intelligence (Investigation) check reveals the trap. A character using thieves' tools can make a successful DC 15 Dexterity check to disarm it. Picking the lock requires thieves' tools and another successful DC 15 Dexterity check.

Treasure

The side table holds a small silver-framed mirror worth 10 gp. The small shrine to Lolth is carved of zurkhwood and bone, and inlaid with semiprecious stones. It is worth 50 gp if the characters can find a buyer for it.

The chest contains a variety of silken garments and personal items. There is a silver chain headdress set with small onyx stones, worth 50 gp, and a drawstring bag containing two *potions of healing*. A small leather purse contains 24 gp, 30 sp, and a small moonstone worth 20 gp, while another purse is Ilvara's spare spell component pouch.

Additionally, the chest contains any valuables once held by the characters and NPCs, including any spellbooks, components, foci, and magic items lost to the adventurers.

8. Shoor's Quarters

The lowermost and smallest chamber of the priestess's tower belongs to the commander's lieutenant, the leader of the elite warriors of the outpost. Shoor Vandree, Ilvara's current favorite, is the present occupant. The area's former occupant, Jorlan Duskryn, has been displaced to the elite barracks after his recent injuries.

The chamber contains cushions laid out across floor mats, a small carved table with two chairs, and a sturdy zurkhwood chest.

Shoor spends most of his off-duty time in Ilvara's quarters, attending to his mistress or awaiting her. Unless you wish him to be found here, his quarters are unoccupied.

Trap

The chest is locked, and Shoor keeps the key in his belt pouch. The lock is trapped with a poison needle trap identical to the one in Ilvara's quarters.

Treasure

The table holds a pewter pitcher and a pair of matched goblets, worth a total of 1 gp.

The chest contains Shoor's personal items and clothing, as well as a small purse containing 20 gp, a black velvet mask stitched with silver thread in a spiderweb pattern (worth 25 gp), a set of bone dice engraved with Elvish characters (worth 10 gp), a small black velvet bag containing a spider-shaped onyx brooch (worth 50 gp), and a flask of strong, syrupy blue liquor (worth 10 gp). The liquor leaves anyone who drinks it pleasantly poisoned for 1d4 hours.

9. Waterfall

Water vents through a crack in the ceiling near the eastern wall between the stalactites of the priestess's tower and the guard tower, creating a small waterfall that pours down to the cavern floor and forms a natural pool (see area 14). Quaggoths gather small barrels of water from the head of the waterfall to serve the outpost's needs.

The water makes the stone wall within 10 feet of it difficult to scale. Any creature attempting to do so has disadvantage on checks made to climb. Any character who falls lands in the pool below, taking no damage.

10. Guard Tower

The fourth hanging tower, connected by rope bridges to the slave pen and the walkway alongside the priestess's tower, serves as a guard tower for observing the cavern, the western passage, and the slave pen.

The lower chamber of the tower is occupied by two **drow** and one **drow elite warrior** on guard duty. It contains a zurkhwood table and three chairs, a smaller side table, and spider-silk webbing set with hooks for hanging equipment.

As at the watch posts, guard duty here is a dull affair, and the guards are usually distracted enough (talking or passing the time with dice games) that prisoners can move or act unnoticed with a successful Dexterity (Stealth) check contested by the guards' passive Wisdom (Perception) score.

The tower's upper chamber stores extra arms and armor for the outpost. Characters who gain entrance to the armory can easily loot it (see "Treasure").

Treasure

The contents of the armory include the following:

- 6 chain shirts
- 6 suits of studded leather armor
- 6 shields
- 6 hand crossbows

- 20 cases of hand crossbow bolts, each case containing 20 bolts
- 6 shortswords and 10 daggers
- 6 bags of caltrops (20 caltrops per bag)
- 4 100-foot-long coils of silk rope
- 2 building hammers (not usable as weapons)
- 2 bags of iron spikes (10 spikes per bag)

11. SLAVE PEN

This cave is built to hold captives until they are sent to Menzoberranzan to be sold as slaves.

The gate to the slave pen is kept locked. A character using thieves' tools can pick the lock with a successful DC 20 Dexterity check. A character using makeshift tools can attempt the same check but has disadvantage. A lock-picking attempt might draw the attention of the guards, requiring a Dexterity (Stealth) check contested by the guards' passive Wisdom (Perception) score to carry it off without notice. Each of the guards on duty in the other areas of the outpost has a key to the gate hanging from a belt ring. Breaking the gate's lock and forcing it open requires a successful DC 20 Strength check.

MAGICAL WARDS

The drow have placed powerful wards on the slave pen to inhibit spellcasters and shield the area against scrying attempts.

Spells cast within the slave pen have no effect, and any slot or magic item charge expended to cast such a spell is consumed. The wards don't suppress or negate spell effects that originate outside the slave pen. For example, a creature under the effect of an *invisibility* spell remains invisible when it enters the slave pen.

Creatures inside the slave pen can't be targeted by any divination magic or perceived through magical scrying sensors.

12. QUAGGOTH DEN

Beyond the slave pen and down a set of stone steps, this cave is used as a den by the dozen quaggoths that serve the drow of Velkynvelve. The interior is littered with nest-like mounds of debris and the scattered bones of the quaggoths' past meals.

These servants of the drow use the den only to sleep and eat, with 1d4 **quaggoths** resting here at any given time. The quaggoths attack any creature that comes into their den that isn't a drow, a spider, or one of their kind. They don't initially attack unknown quaggoths or drow on sight, but they know all those assigned to the outpost and will question strangers. Derendil and Sarith's status as prisoners is known to them.

13. NORTHERN WATCH POST

This small alcove just past and below the quaggoth den has the same features as the watch post at area 1.

Two **drow** are stationed here on watch, typically hating that duty for its proximity to the quaggoth den, the slave pen, and the pool.

14. POOL

Water pouring down from the waterfall at area 9 forms a 20-foot-deep pool before flowing out into an underground river that travels several miles before spilling into the Darklake. Since the drow take the water they need from the top of the waterfall, they use the pool to dump waste and garbage. Although this fouls the surface of the pool, the constant flow keeps the water beneath the surface clear.

A **gray ooze** lurks in the pool's shallows, blending perfectly with the dark, wet stone. It feeds on the waste dumped into the pool, along with the occasional creature that finds its way into the cavern or falls into the pool.

The inhabitants of Velkynvelve remain unaware that the recent arrival of the demon lord Juiblex in the Underdark has made this ooze particularly aggressive and malevolent. In addition to attacking any creature in the pool, the ooze surges up to 10 feet out of the pool to attack creatures at its edge. When it does so, creatures within 30 feet of the ooze telepathically sense a voice cry out, "Flesh for the Faceless Lord!"

MEANS OF ESCAPE

Unless they want to spend the rest of their lives as drow slaves, the characters should quickly begin looking for ways they can escape. Though the task will not be easy, the characters can take advantage of certain opportunities if they use their heads.

ACQUISITIONS

One or more of the characters might have useful items in their possession (see "Scavenged Possessions"), and working outside the slave pen creates new opportunities for the characters to acquire and hide small items, including makeshift weapons or tools, or even lift a key to the slave pen from a guard. What they can acquire depends on the work they do and where they go. Use the description of the different locations throughout the outpost as a guide to opportunities. Taking something without being noticed requires a successful Dexterity (Sleight of Hand) check contested by the Wisdom (Perception) checks of any active observers, or using an observer's passive Wisdom (Perception) score as the base DC. A prisoner that fails the check is commanded to relinquish the item, on pain of death.

What equipment and treasures the characters claim during their escape depend on how much of the outpost they are able to explore before fleeing. For some characters, it might be a fun challenge to escape into the Underdark with little more than the clothes on their backs. For others (including spellcasters who need spellbooks or components), consider placing the party's captured equipment (normally in Ilvara's quarters) in an alternate location if the characters are intent on escaping without exploring all of the outpost, such as the elite drow barracks (area 4) or the armory (area 10).

Jorlan's Gambit

When the initial contact between the adventurers and the other prisoners has been played out, Jorlan Duskryn arranges to bring the prisoners their food during his guard duty. (Shoor delights in giving Jorlan such menial work). Standing at the gate to the slave pen and passing in bowls, he mutters to the nearest character: "If I could give you a means to escape from here, would you take it?"

If the answer is affirmative, Jorlan quickly and quietly proposes to leave the gate to the slave pen unlocked, as well as to create a distraction during the changing of the guards on duty. He tells the characters about the armory, located in the chamber above the guard post in the hanging guard tower in front of the slave pen. The escapees can jump down into the webs below, then over the edge into the pool, making their escape from there.

Jorlan doesn't particularly care if the prisoners actually escape, which is why he doesn't offer any further help or warn them about the gray ooze in the pool. It suits him just as well if the prisoners are killed during their attempt to flee. He simply wants to create an embarrassing incident for Shoor and Ilvara.

Jorlan furtively glances around as he speaks quickly to the characters. If they question him or ask for changes to the plan, he insists it is all he can do. If they accept, he is true to his word, leaving the gate unlocked close to the next guard shift change and delaying the replacement guards for a few minutes.

A Flight of Demons

During a guard change, the prisoners hear a horrible droning buzz echoing through the cavern, followed by inhuman shrieking. Alarm horns sound out as four **chasme** demons pursue a pair of **vrock** demons into the cavern from the northern passage. The demons swoop and buzz around, initially ignoring other creatures as both groups savagely assault each other. The demons' arrival catches all of the drow off guard.

The drow rush to defend the outpost from a possible attack. The demons initially buzz past the hanging towers, leaving the walkways and caverns out of range of the effects of their droning and screeching. However, drow and quaggoths in the towers are close enough to be affected. The aerial battle eventually circles around the platform and the towers of the elite warriors as the demons savagely tear into each other.

The drow move to engage the demons and defend the outpost, leaving the characters with an opportunity to escape. You can combine this event with Jorlan's offer to leave the gate unlocked, making it easy for the characters to slip away. Alternatively (or if they refuse Jorlan's offer), the characters can use the distraction to engineer their own breakout, then decide how to get down to the cavern floor and where to go after that.

Describe the chaos of the demon attack and the drow's response as the escaped prisoners try to flee. The characters can follow Jorlan's suggestion to drop into the webs and then dive into the pool, possibly dealing with a giant spider or two and the gray ooze along the way. Alternatively, they can look for another way down. Reaching the lift requires getting past the drow clustered on the platform and then attempting to operate it during the attack, which might prove difficult.

If you want to provide an additional challenge for the characters, a **vrock** tumbles almost in front of them as they reach the cavern floor or move toward their chosen exit. The demon is badly wounded, but even with only 11 hit points remaining and having expended its spores and stunning screech abilities, it is still quite dangerous. It screeches at the characters, but if they do nothing to threaten it for 1 round, the demon takes wing and launches itself back into the fight overhead.

If the adventurers take on the fallen vrock and defeat or escape from it, award them a quarter of its usual XP value, or 575 XP, given its weakened state.

If Jorlan is alive when the demons attack, he might use the distraction to free the prisoners (as described in "Jorlan's Gambit"). Any character who asks Jorlan about the demons gets a stern reply: "The demons are not my doing. Fight them at your own risk."

Leaving Velkynvelve

The characters have three choices for leaving Velkynvelve: the north, west, and south passages.

North Passage

This leads toward Menzoberranzan (see chapter 15) and, eventually, Blingdenstone (see chapter 6). Most of the characters' fellow prisoners discourage travel toward the drow city, and the deep gnomes suggest Blingdenstone as a route out of the Underdark. The party can also follow a circuitous route westward toward the Darklake (see chapter 3).

West Passage

This leads most directly toward the Darklake (see chapter 3), although the party could eventually veer south toward Gracklstugh (see chapter 4).

South Passage

This leads toward the duergar city of Gracklstugh (see chapter 4), following a south-westerly route. Characters might need to pass under the battling demons, but the cavern floor is well out of range of their droning and screeching. The demons locked in combat ignore the escaping prisoners, with the possible exception of a fallen vrock (see "A Flight of Demons").

Whichever route the characters take, chapter 2 covers their passage through the Underdark toward their eventual destination.

XP Awards

In addition to the XP awards earned for overcoming the creatures in this chapter, escaping from Velkynvelve earns the characters a special award of 150 XP (divided equally among all party members).

CHAPTER 2: INTO DARKNESS

Once the adventurers escape from Velkynvelve, they'll want to escape the Underdark. Already miles beneath the surface, they must make their way through an endless maze of passages and caverns, avoid pursuit by the drow, and find a route to the world above—all the while dealing with the dangers of the Underdark and struggling to find the resources they need to survive.

This chapter presents guidelines for the characters' travels between the various Underdark locales detailed in the other chapters of *Out of the Abyss*. Specific areas (including the Darklake region in chapter 3) offer modifications to these guidelines to suit those areas' particular qualities. This chapter also offers guidelines for the drow pursuit of the escaped prisoners, along with additional encounters you can place along the adventurers' route as they travel.

WHERE TO GO?

The players' first question upon escaping from Velkynvelve is likely, "Where do we go next?" The adventurers must find a way out of the Underdark and back to the surface world. Their NPC companions have destinations of their own in mind, and are the ones best able to navigate the subterranean realms. As such, the adventurers will be dependent on their guidance. The NPCs can offer directions and suggestions as follows:

- Buppido knows how to reach Gracklstugh from the southern route out of Velkynvelve. He can also find a route to Gracklstugh from the Darklake. Buppido urges the characters to go to Gracklstugh to acquire better equipment, and out of a desire to return to his people. He also intends to murder the characters one by one along the way, believing them to be divine offerings delivered into his hands.
- Prince Derendil, the delusional quaggoth, can't offer any useful directions, but he gladly accompanies the party, eager to go to the surface world.
- Eldeth Feldrun is unfamiliar with this region of the Underdark and can't navigate, but she has a +5 bonus on Wisdom (Survival) checks and can help out in that regard.

- Jimjar can guide the party to Blingdenstone from the north route out of Velkynvelve. The svirfneblin city will give the characters access to the surface, although Jimjar is fine with visiting other interesting places along the way, as well as taking Stool back to its home.
- Ront is unfamiliar with the Underdark and can't navigate. He's willing to stick with the adventurers as long as they seek a destination that gets him back to the surface world.
- Sarith Kzekarit is the best potential guide in the group, but also the most deceptive. He can navigate to any region of the Underdark shown on the map, but will encourage the characters to travel to Neverlight Grove (see chapter 5). He claims to want to take advantage of Stool's offer of sanctuary, but it is actually the influence of Zuggtmoy's demon-tainted spores upon his mind.
- Shuushar can navigate through the Darklake once the party is within three miles of any part of it. He's willing to travel with the characters and guide them, and suggests visiting the kuo-toa town of Sloobludop to acquire boats. Shuushar wishes to return to his own people in hopes of guiding them to the enlightenment he has achieved.
- Stool can't navigate and has no knowledge of the local area, but it desperately wants to return home to Neverlight Grove, pleading with the characters to take it there. It claims that its people will be grateful and offer the party shelter and aid, and describes its sovereign as wise in the hidden ways of the Underdark.
- Topsy and Turvy can navigate to Blingdenstone, but they're reluctant to do so. As such, they are likely to support any suggestion that will not take them to their former home. Once they feel safer, they're likely to strike out on their own, just as they were before the drow captured them.

UNDERDARK TRAVEL

The Underdark is a vast network of caverns, tunnels, vaults, and passages stretching from one end of Faerûn to the other. Its physical features are even more varied than those of the surface world. Subterranean rivers, fungus fields, deep gorges, underground cities, yawning chasms—the adventurers will have to deal with all these features and more.

Much of the party's travel through the Underdark is handled abstractly, using the rules and advice in chapter 8, "Adventuring," of the *Player's Handbook*. The following specific guidelines apply to travel in the Underdark during this adventure.

TRAVEL PACE

Travel pace in the Underdark is significantly slower than for overland travel. Not only are the tunnels and passages often difficult terrain with uneven surfaces, but routes in the Underdark are rarely direct, and the characters must follow available passages and their various twists and turns, climbs and descents. Creatures that can burrow through solid rock (such as purple worms) move at their normal burrowing speed, but this isn't likely an option for the party.

UNDERDARK TRAVEL PACE

Pace	Miles Per Day	Effect
Fast	8	−5 penalty to passive Wisdom (Perception) scores; no foraging
Normal	6	—
Slow	4	Improved foraging, or able to use Stealth

A fast pace makes it harder to spot ambushes or items of interest and prevents the characters from foraging, while a slow pace allows the characters to travel stealthily enough to surprise or sneak past creatures they encounter, and improves their chances of successful foraging for food and water.

The Underdark Travel Times table shows the time to travel between the locations in chapters 1 through 6 of the adventure. These times assume that the party moves at a normal pace without stopping (other than for time spent resting or becoming lost). For a fast pace, reduce the travel times by one third; for a slow pace, increase them by one third.

UNDERDARK TRAVEL TIMES

Location	Velkynvelve	Sloobludop	Gracklstugh	Neverlight Grove	Blingdenstone	Menzoberranzan
Velkynvelve	—	8 days	28 days	36 days	30 days	26 days
Sloobludop	8 days	—	20 days	26 days	20 days	20 days
Gracklstugh	28 days	20 days	—	12 days	20 days	27 days
Neverlight Grove	36 days	26 days	12 days	—	16 days	24 days
Blingdenstone	30 days	20 days	20 days	16 days	—	8 days
Menzoberranzan	26 days	20 days	27 days	24 days	8 days	—

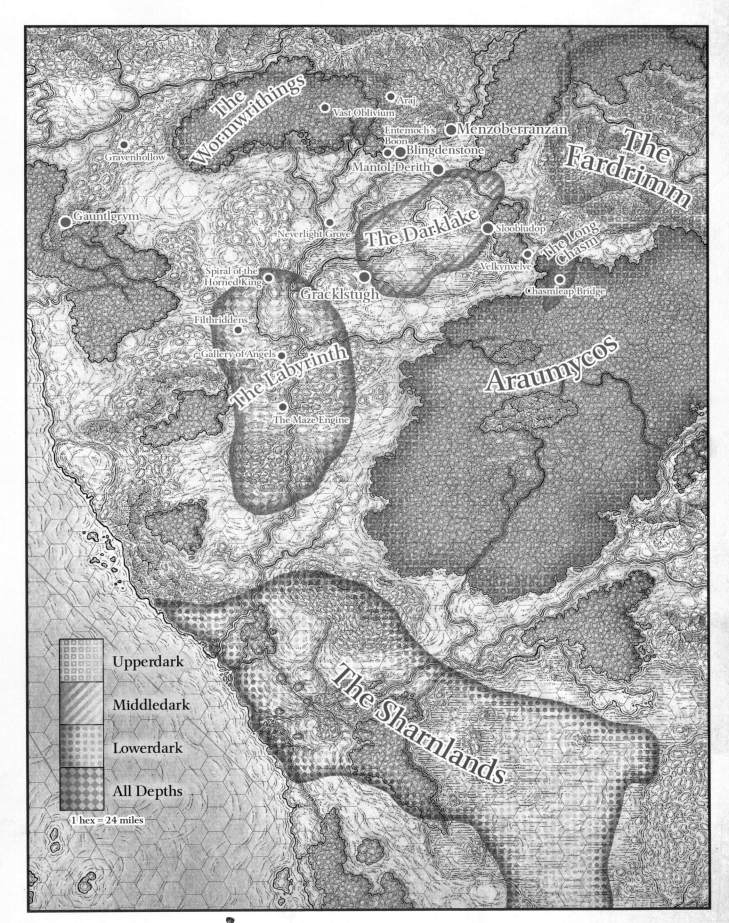

The Wornwrithings

Araj

Vast Oblivium

Gravenhollow

Entemoch's Boon

Menzoberranzan

The Fardrimm

Blingdenstone

Mantol-Derith

Gauntlgrym

Neverlight Grove

The Darklake

Slooblludop

The Long Chasm

Velkynvelve

Spiral of the Horned King

Gracklstugh

Chasmleap Bridge

Filthriddens

Araumycos

Gallery of Angels

The Labyrinth

The Maze Engine

Upperdark

Middledark

Lowerdark

All Depths

1 hex = 24 miles

The Sharnlands

Encounter Setup

When an encounter occurs during the adventurers' journey, a number of factors will play into its setup and potential difficulty.

Space and Marching Order

Ask the players to establish two marching orders for the characters—one for moving single file and one for moving two abreast. Then when an encounter occurs, roll a d6. On a roll of 1–2, the party is traveling through a narrow passageway, so position the adventurers in the single-file marching order. On a roll of 3–4, the characters are traveling through a standard passageway and can use the two-abreast marching order. On a roll of 5–6, the encounter occurs in a large open area, so allow the players to position the characters wherever they like.

Illumination

Roll a d6 to determine how an encounter area is illuminated. On a roll of 1–3, the area is dimly lit by the phosphorescent moss and lichen common in the Underdark, or by *faerzress* (see "*Faerzress*"). On a roll of 4–6, the area is dark except for whatever light sources the characters might have.

Noticing Threats

The passive Wisdom (Perception) scores of characters in the party count toward noticing hidden threats only if both the following conditions are met:

- The characters are able to see the threat (due to illumination or darkvision) or otherwise perceive it.
- The characters aren't engaged in other activities, including navigating or foraging.

A fast pace imposes a −5 penalty to passive Wisdom (Perception) scores to notice threats. You might also decide that only characters in a particular rank of the marching order are able to notice a specific threat.

Surprise

When an encounter occurs, determine if the adventurers or their foes are surprised, as normal. The adventurers can achieve surprise only if all the following conditions are met:

- The encounter occurs while the party is moving (not stopped or camped).
- The party elected the stealth option while moving at a slow pace.
- At least one party member is capable of noticing the threat and communicating it to the rest of the group.

Navigating

Becoming lost is a serious risk in the twisting tunnels of the Underdark, and travelers can wander in circles without knowing it. Creatures unfamiliar with a given region of the Underdark are automatically lost, wandering in a random direction for every 4 hours of travel until they encounter an area they are familiar with (which could be a very long time).

Even creatures that know the routes of the Underdark aren't immune. For each day of travel, and any time the characters set out again after finishing a short or long rest, the party's navigator makes a DC 10 Wisdom (Survival) check. If the party is moving at a slow pace, the navigator gains a +5 bonus to the check, while a fast pace imposes a −5 penalty. A failed check result means the characters become lost, wandering in a random direction for 1d6 hours before the navigator can make a new check to find the right path.

Mapping

A character not focused on any other task—including watching for danger while traveling—can record the group's progress through the Underdark and create a map of the route. Such a map can be a useful resource in later chapters of the adventure when the characters retrace their steps. Having a map allows the party to navigate that area without any chance of becoming lost.

Foraging

Unless they obtain a supply of food and water, the adventurers must forage to survive on their journey. Finding sustenance in the Underdark is difficult but not impossible. Characters can gather food and water if the party travels at a normal or slow pace. A foraging character makes a Wisdom (Survival) check. The DC is typically 15, but might be as high as 20 in some parts of the Underdark. Food and water requirements for characters are described in chapter 8, "Adventuring," of the *Player's Handbook*.

In addition to foraging, spells such as *create food and water* and *goodberry* can help provision the party, and there's always a chance for the characters to encounter others from whom they can buy or steal provisions. Additionally, many creatures the adventurers might meet and kill can be butchered, but the meat they yield spoils after a single day if uneaten. Eating spoiled meat might require a Constitution saving throw to keep the meal down, a Wisdom saving throw to avoid acquiring a level of madness from the awful experience (see "Madness" later in this chapter), or both.

Creature Food Yield

Creature Size	Food Gained
Tiny	1 lb.
Small	4 lb.
Medium	16 lb.
Large	32 lb.

The characters' need to forage and acquire supplies serves as a motivator to drive them to explore and visit different parts of the Underdark. The more desperate their need becomes—as levels of exhaustion rack up—the more risk players will likely be willing to take.

Time-Keeping

With no sunlight, visible sky, seasons, or weather in the Underdark, most characters can only track the passage of time based on their periods of rest. Most Underdark creatures do the same (if they care about timekeeping at all), unless there is a local means of keeping time.

FAERZRESS

An unusual magical energy the drow call *faerzress* pervades much of the Underdark. The origin of this mysterious arcane power is unknown. Legend claims it is an ancient elven magic dating back to the time when the dark elves were first exiled from the world above. The drow and other Underdark creatures use the properties of areas suffused with *faerzress* to protect their settlements.

Areas suffused with *faerzress* can range in size from a few dozen feet across to several miles in diameter, and feature the following effects:

- Areas suffused with *faerzress* are always filled with dim light.
- A creature in an area suffused with *faerzress* has advantage on saving throws against any divination spells. If a divination spell doesn't allow a saving throw, the caster must succeed on a DC 15 Constitution saving throw to cast the spell. Failing this save means the spell is wasted and has no effect.
- Any creature attempting to teleport into, within, or out of a *faerzress*-suffused area must succeed on a DC 15 Constitution saving throw. On a failed save, the creature takes 1d10 force damage and the teleportation attempt fails. Even if the save succeeds, the teleportation attempt can suffer a mishap as if the destination was known only by description, regardless of how familiar the destination actually is. See the table in the *teleport* spell for more information.
- Areas suffused with *faerzress* have become tainted by the chaos of the demon lords. When a spell is cast in a *faerzress*-suffused area, the caster rolls a d20. On a roll of 1, the spell has an additional effect, determined by rolling on the Wild Magic Surge table in chapter 3, "Classes," of the *Player's Handbook*.

Though *faerzress* can't be dispelled, its effects are temporarily suppressed in the area of an *antimagic field*.

EQUIPMENT

The equipment the characters have on hand will depend on what they were able to salvage or steal in their escape from Velkynvelve. Indeed, one of the primary reasons for the party to visit known settlements in the Underdark is to acquire proper equipment and provisions.

CRAFTING

Characters can use downtime during their travels to craft equipment, provided they are proficient with the necessary tools and have access to them (see "Downtime Activities" in chapter 8 of the *Player's Handbook*). Having to improvise tools doubles the crafting time, and some items require materials that are hard to find in the Underdark, including wood and other surface-world plants. Leather, bone, or zurkhwood (see "Fungi of the Underdark" later in this chapter) might substitute in some cases. Crafting can include modifying scavenged or salvaged items to fit other needs, such as creating a makeshift suit of armor from gathered pieces of armor and other materials.

COMPONENTS

Spellcasters might be without material components for their spells (see "Components" in chapter 10 of the *Player's Handbook*). They can acquire component pouches and spellcasting focuses from defeated enemy spellcasters, settlements, and traders, or they can craft such items during their downtime activities while traveling.

MADNESS

At the best of times, the Underdark is a bizarre, alien, and inhospitable world, but the influence of the demon lords has transformed it into a domain of madness and chaos. *Faerzress* acts as a catalyst, spreading the demon lords' madness throughout the Underdark.

Once the party escapes Velkynvelve and strikes out into the Underdark, begin taking into account the effects of demonic madness on the characters' sanity (see "Madness" in chapter 8 of the *Dungeon Master's Guide*). At various times in the adventure, characters will be called upon to make a saving throw to resist some madness-inducing effect. In addition, you can have one or more characters make a saving throw against madness whenever one of the following events occurs:

- The characters encounter or witness something particularly alien or disturbing (such as a demon lord).
- The characters stay in a *faerzress*-suffused area for a long time (eight or more consecutive hours).
- A character takes psychic damage, particularly in an area suffused with *faerzress*.

In *Out of the Abyss*, madness is measured in three levels:

MADNESS LEVELS

Level	Effect
1	Bout of short-term madness (lasts 1d10 minutes)
2	Bout of long-term madness (lasts 1d10 × 10 hours)
3	Bout of indefinite madness (lasts until cured)

A creature's madness level starts at 0. When the creature fails a madness saving throw, its madness level increases by 1, and the creature immediately suffers the level's effect (as determined by rolling on the Short-Term Madness, Long-Term Madness, or Indefinite Madness table in the *Dungeon Master's Guide*, as appropriate). When the effect ends, the creature's madness level doesn't change. Any time the creature's madness level increases, it suffers the effect of the new level.

If a creature with level 3 madness fails a madness saving throw, its madness level becomes 1. In this way, characters can potentially accumulate multiple forms of madness.

Bouts of short- and long-term madness can be cured as described in the *Dungeon Master's Guide*. Given the demonic source of the madness, *remove curse* and *dispel evil* are also effective as cures. A *greater restoration* spell or more powerful magic is needed to cure indefinite madness and also resets a creature's madness level to 0.

Death

Allowing the chips to fall where they may in combat emphasizes the challenging nature of this adventure. However, if the characters start falling just as fast, you might want to give the players some opportunities to return dead characters to life during the lower levels of their progress through *Out of the Abyss*.

- A *spell scroll* of *raise dead* can turn up among some treasure, either when it is needed or for the characters to save for later. A successful DC 15 spellcasting ability check is required for a lower-level character to use such a scroll.
- A strange *faerzress* effect can bring a fallen character back to life, but not without a cost. The restored character's madness level increases by 1 upon being restored to life (see "Madness" earlier in this chapter).
- If a fallen character's body is lost or left behind, the party's drow pursuers find it. The drow high priestess casts *raise dead* on the corpse so that the character can be questioned. The character might escape later, or can be reunited with the other adventurers in a later chapter of the adventure when the drow catch up to them.

If a player character is permanently slain, think about the ways a player might introduce a new character to the party in the midst of a journey through the Underdark.

- Convert one of the group's existing nonplayer character allies—including fellow escaped prisoners from Velkynvelve—into a player character. Drow, dwarf, and deep gnome characters are all easily playable. You can even allow a player to take control of a more unusual NPC until a new character can join the group. This is particularly suitable if the player has already been managing that NPC (see "A Motley Crew" in chapter 1).
- A creature encounter could reveal a potential new party member, such as a surface dweller lost in the Underdark or sent there to investigate rumors of strange happenings. An escaped slave from another Underdark settlement is another possibility.
- A monster encountered by the party might be holding other victims or hostages (a giant spider with a still-living victim wrapped up in its web, or troglodytes holding prisoners destined for their larder, for example). Once the monsters are defeated, a former captive might join the group.
- Characters might meet up with new party members in any of the Underdark settlements they visit during the adventure, particularly visitors or locals with a strong reason to leave in a hurry.

Fungi of the Underdark

The Underdark is home to a tremendous variety of fungi with a variety of different uses. Characters can encounter different examples of the Underdark's flora in their travels. Identifying a species of fungi and its potential uses requires a successful DC 15 Intelligence (Nature) check, but Underdark inhabitants are familiar with many of these species automatically.

Edible Fungi

Edible fungi provide food and water. Basic food and water requirements for characters are covered in chapter 8, "Adventuring," of the *Player's Handbook*.

Barrelstalk

A barrelstalk is a large, cask-shaped fungus that can be tapped and drained of the fresh water stored within it. A single barrelstalk contains 1d4 + 4 gallons of water and yields 1d6 + 4 pounds of food.

Bluecap

Dubbed the "grain of the Underdark," a bluecap is inedible, but its spores can be ground to make a nutritious, bland flour. Bread made from bluecap flour is known as sporebread or bluebread. One loaf is equivalent to 1 pound of food.

Fire Lichen

Pale orange-white in color, fire lichen thrives on warmth, so it grows in regions of geothermal heat. Fire lichen can be ground and fermented into a hot, spicy paste, which is spread on sporebread or added to soups or stews to flavor them. Duergar also ferment fire lichen into a fiercely hot liquor.

Ripplebark

Ripplebark is a shelf-like fungus that resembles a mass of rotting flesh. It is surprisingly edible. Though it can be eaten raw, it tastes better roasted. A single sheet of ripplebark yields 1d4 + 6 pounds of food.

Trillimac

A trillimac is a mushroom that grows to a height of four to five feet, and has a broad gray-green cap and a light gray stalk. The cap's leathery surface can be cut and cleaned for use in making maps, hats, and scrolls (its surface takes on dyes and inks well). The stalk can be cleaned, soaked in water for an hour, then dried to make a palatable food akin to bread. Each trillimac stalk provides 1d6 + 4 pounds of food.

Waterorb

A waterorb is a bulbous fungus that grows in shallow water. A mature waterorb can be squeezed like a sponge, yielding a gallon of drinkable water and a pound of edible (if chewy and somewhat tasteless) food.

Zurkhwood

Zurkhwood is a massive mushroom that can reach a height of thirty to forty feet. Its large grain-like spores are edible and nutritionally equivalent to 1d4 + 4 pounds of food, but zurkhwood is more important for its hard and woody stalks. Zurkhwood is one of the few sources of timber in the Underdark, used to make furniture, containers, bridges, and rafts, among other things. Skilled crafters can use stains, sanding, and polishing to bring out different patterns in zurkhwood.

EXOTIC FUNGI

The fungi species described in this section have strange properties but no nutritional value.

NIGHTLIGHT

A nightlight is a tall and tube-shaped bioluminescent mushroom that grows to a height of 1d6 + 4 feet and emits bright light in a 15-foot radius and dim light for an additional 15 feet. A nightlight that is uprooted or destroyed goes dark after 1 round. If a living nightlight is touched, either by a creature or an object, its light goes out until it is touched again.

NILHOGG'S NOSE

A Nilhogg's nose is a small mushroom that grants any creature that eats it advantage on Wisdom (Perception) checks based on smell for 1d4 hours. However, the creature suffers disadvantage on saving throws against effects based on smell for the same amount of time.

ORMU

A bioluminescent green moss that grows in warm and damp areas, ormu is particularly common near steam tunnels and vents. It sheds dim light in a 5-foot radius, and can be harvested, dried, and made into a phosphorescent powder or pigment.

TIMMASK

Also known as "the devil's mushroom," a timmask is a two-foot-tall toadstool with orange and red stripes across its beige cap. Uprooting or destroying a timmask causes it to expel a 15-foot-radius cloud of poisonous spores. Creatures in the area must succeed at a DC 14 Constitution saving throw or be poisoned. While poisoned in this way, the creature is under the effect of a *confusion* spell with a duration of 1 minute. When the spell effect ends, the poisoned condition also ends.

TONGUE OF MADNESS

Tongue of madness is an edible fungus that looks somewhat like a large human tongue. A creature that eats a tongue of madness must succeed on a DC 12 Constitution saving throw or compulsively speak aloud its every thought for the next hour. The effect can be ended with a *lesser restoration* spell or similar magic.

TORCHSTALK

A one- to two-foot-tall mushroom with a combustible cap, a single torchstalk burns for 24 hours once lit. There is a 1-in-6 chance that a torchstalk explodes when lit, bursting into a cloud of fiery spores. Creatures within 10 feet of an exploding torchstalk take 3 (1d6) fire damage.

Narrating the Journey

As the adventurers make their way through the Underdark, it helps to improvise descriptions of what they experience to add flavor to the journey. As you do, try to stress two key points.

First, the trek is long and arduous. The party is traveling underground, over incredibly difficult and rough terrain, without any of the comforts of the surface world. Food and water are scarce. The darkness never ends. The players should feel as though their characters are in peril throughout their travels, never knowing when something is set to leap at them from the shadows.

Second, the Underdark is an exotic, alien landscape unlike anything found on the surface world. Throughout its twisted passageways and impossibly large caverns, characters might find bizarre reminders of lost and forgotten civilizations, unearthly flora and fauna, and incredible geography. Little is as it seems, and much is difficult to explain, or even to describe.

Drow Pursuit

A party of drow from Velkynvelve pursue their escaped prisoners into the Underdark. The drow priestess Ilvara becomes increasingly obsessed with the adventurers, believing they are involved in some secret conspiracy, or perhaps some test of her worthiness. The longer the pursuit, the more determined she is to retake them and have the opportunity to teach them the error of defying her.

The drow party consists of Ilvara (**drow priestess of Lolth**), the **drow elite warriors** Jorlan and Shoor, and the junior priestess Asha Vandree (use the **priest** stat block in the *Monster Manual*, but add the Fey Ancestry, Innate Spellcasting, and Sunlight Sensitivity features of the **drow** stat block). The hunting party also includes four **drow** warriors who serve as forward scouts. If any of the drow NPCs did not survive chapter 1, replace them with newly arrived reinforcements from Menzoberranzan under the command of Ilvara, or another priestess of her caliber.

Narrow Escapes

If an encounter with the drow is going badly and you don't want the characters recaptured, you can always have fate intercede on their behalf with another encounter or event offering a distraction.

For example, a wandering stone giant, a purple worm, or a pack of savage gnolls whipped into a frenzy by Yeenoghu might show up just as the drow have the characters cornered, giving them a chance to run. Likewise, a minor earthquake (caused by instability from the demonic incursion or a wild magic surge) might cause a cave-in, cutting off a tunnel between the party and their pursuers, and dropping the pursuit level by 1 or 2.

Don't do this so often that the players feel they haven't earned it, but use it as an option to keep the pursuit going rather than coming to an anticlimactic conclusion.

Tracking the Party

The drow must track the party through the Underdark on foot, as there are no mounts available at Velkynvelve and Ilvara doesn't wait for an already-late relief detachment from Menzoberranzan to arrive. This limits how quickly the dark elves can move to catch up, since they must seek out signs of their quarry's passage, occasionally doubling back to pick up their trail again.

Pursuit Level

The closeness of the drow pursuit is measured by a pursuit level. It begins at 4, with the drow not far behind the characters. If the pursuit level reaches 5, the drow forward scouts catch up to them, and the drow leaders arrive not long thereafter (see "Catching Up"). If the pursuit level drops to 0, the party has eluded the drow until circumstances bring both factions into contact again (see "Eluding Pursuit").

Characters can increase or decrease the pursuit level in the following ways:

- Decrease the pursuit level by 1 for each day the party travels at a fast pace.
- Decrease the pursuit level by 1 if a character spends time covering up the party's trail that day, requiring a successful DC 16 Wisdom (Survival) check.
- Decrease the pursuit level by 1 each time the characters cross or traverse some feature that obscures their trail, such as a subterranean river.
- Decrease the pursuit level by 1 if the party splits into two or more groups. Each group becomes a separate party for purposes of determining random encounters and whether or not the group becomes lost.
- Increase the pursuit level by 1 each time the party has a random encounter with one or more creatures, unless the encounter is bypassed or avoided entirely.
- Increase the pursuit level by 1 for each day the adventurers travel at a slow pace.
- Certain terrain encounters increase or decrease the pursuit level. See the individual descriptions in the "Random Encounters" section.

The players might come up with additional ways of evading pursuit. Adjudicate these as you see fit. For example, if the characters convince a randomly encountered creature to let them pass by telling them about the wealthy drow following them, you might reduce the pursuit level by 1 as the drow are forced to deal with the encounter before they can resume tracking the party. Similarly, the adventurers could lay traps to slow down their pursuers, or they might convince a friendly creature to lie to the drow about which way the party went.

If you choose to skip over a few days of travel (as described under "Summarizing Travel" later in this chapter), the pursuit level doesn't change during that time.

Catching Up

When the pursuit level reaches 5, the drow forward scouts spot the party. At this point, the pursuit might become an encounter if the characters spot the drow and engage them. The characters might try to run, at which point a chase ensues (see "Chases" in chapter 8 of the *Dungeon Master's Guide*), or they might stand and fight. They might even try to set up some sort of ambush, since the front ranks of the party are likely out of sight of the drow when they first catch up.

If the adventurers flee and successfully escape, they lower the pursuit level to 4 and begin avoiding their pursuers again. If they fight the drow, run the encounter. The drow scouts focus on maintaining close pursuit and peppering the characters with poisoned hand crossbow bolts. After 1d6 + 4 rounds, the remainder of the drow party (Ilvara, Asha, Jorlan, and Shoor) catches up and joins the encounter.

ELUDING PURSUIT

If the adventurers lower the pursuit level to 0, the drow lose the trail unless circumstances allow them to locate the characters again. This might include the characters spending a day or more in a place where they are recognized, or where they talk openly about their escape from Velkynvelve. If the characters pass through an area watched over by drow scouts or spies, Ilvara will inevitably hear word of the characters' location. When this occurs, increase the pursuit level to 1 and begin tracking it again as the drow pick up the trail once more.

CAPTURE

The drow try to capture the escaped prisoners if at all possible, since Ilvara wants the pleasure of teaching them a lesson about disobedience. If the dark elves reduce any characters to 0 hit points, those characters are knocked out rather than dying (see "Knocking a Creature Out" in chapter 9 of the *Player's Handbook*). Even if one or more of the characters are accidentally killed, Ilvara is obsessed enough to cast *raise dead* to restore them to life (assuming the character's soul is willing to return).

Captured characters are disarmed, their hands bound with spider-silk rope, and gagged. The drow march them back to Velkynvelve unless Menzoberranzan is closer, in which case Ilvara takes them there instead. The characters will need to come up with a new plan of escape, ideally before Ilvara has the opportunity to torture them or sell them into slavery in the City of Spiders. If they escape her clutches again, the drow priestess continues her pursuit until she is dead or the party leaves the Underdark (see chapter 7).

RANDOM ENCOUNTERS

Each day of travel through the Underdark, check twice to see if the characters encounter anything unusual: once while they are traveling, and again while they are camped or resting. Roll a d20 and consult the Random Encounters table to determine what, if anything, they encounter. Characters might encounter special terrain, one or more creatures, or a combination of the two.

Any random encounter that occurs while the party is camped is automatically a creature encounter, in which case determine the encounter by rolling a d20 and consulting the Creature Encounter table.

RANDOM ENCOUNTERS

d20	Encounter
1–13	No encounter
14–15	Terrain (roll once on the Terrain Encounters table)
16–17	One or more creatures (roll once on the Creature Encounters table)
18–20	Terrain encounter featuring one or more creatures (roll once on the Terrain Encounters table, then roll once on the Creature Encounter table)

TERRAIN ENCOUNTERS

The Underdark contains dangerous hazards and wondrous terrain. Special terrain rules are explained after the table.

TERRAIN ENCOUNTERS

d20	Encounter
1	Boneyard
2	Cliff and ladder
3	Crystal clusters
4	Fungus cavern
5	Gas leak
6	Gorge
7	High ledge
8	Horrid sounds
9	Lava swell
10	Muck pit
11	Rockfall
12	Rope bridge
13	Ruins
14	Shelter
15	Sinkhole
16	Slime or mold
17	Steam vent
18	Underground stream
19	Warning sign
20	Webs

BONEYARD

The characters come upon an eerie cavern littered with countless bones of various creatures. Whether the site is a natural graveyard for some Underdark species or the former lair of a fearsome predator, the characters can potentially gather useful material for crafting among the bones.

When the party enters a boneyard, roll a d20 and consult the table to determine what creatures, if any, are present. The undead rise up out of the bones and attack when the first characters are halfway across the cavern.

BONEYARD ENCOUNTER

d20	Encounter
1–14	No encounter
15–18	3d4 **skeletons**
19–20	1d3 **minotaur skeletons**

Cliff and Ladder

A cliff 2d4 × 10 feet high blocks the party's passage, but a rolled-up rope ladder is visible at the top. If someone can climb the cliff—requiring a successful DC 15 Strength (Athletics) check—and toss down the ladder, the characters can proceed. Otherwise, they lose a day's travel finding another route. If the characters remove the ladder once they are at the top, they decrease the drow pursuit level by 1.

Crystal Clusters

The adventurers pass through a *faerzress*-suffused area containing fist-sized chunks of quartz that shed dim light in a 10-foot radius. A sharp blow to one of the crystals, including throwing it so it impacts a hard surface, causes it to burst in a 10-foot-radius flash of blinding light. Any creature within the radius must succeed on a DC 10 Constitution saving throw or be blinded for 1 minute. A creature blinded by this effect repeats the Constitution saving throw at the end of each of its turns. On a successful save, it is no longer blinded.

The characters can harvest up to twelve of the crystals in total, but taking the time to do so increases the drow pursuit level by 1.

Fungus Cavern

The adventurers stumble upon a cavern filled with fungi and mushrooms of all sizes and types. See "Fungi of the Underdark" and choose some interesting examples.

Gas Leak

The adventurers come upon a cavern with a dangerous natural gas leak. Any member of the party with a passive Wisdom (Perception) score of 14 or higher detects signs of the gas. The characters' travel pace for the day is slowed by half as they circumvent the area, but there are no ill effects. If the gas goes undetected, each character in the area must make a DC 12 Constitution saving throw, taking 5 (1d10) poison damage on a failed save, or half as much damage on a

successful one. Any open flames brought into the area cause the gas to explode. Each creature in the explosion must make a DC 15 Dexterity saving throw, taking 10 (3d6) fire damage on a failed save, or half as much damage on a successful one.

Gorge

The characters must make a difficult climb down a gorge 2d4 × 100 feet deep and up the other side, or find a way around it. Their travel pace for the day is slowed by half unless they come up with a plan to cross the gorge quickly.

High Ledge

The characters must walk along an 18-inch-wide ledge that skirts a ravine 2d6 × 10 feet deep. The party's travel pace for the day is slowed by half, and each character must succeed on a DC 10 Dexterity saving throw to avoid a fall. Precautions such as roping everyone together let each character make the save with advantage. Increase the pursuit level of the drow by 1.

Horrid Sounds

For hours, the party's travel is plagued by terrible shrieks, moans, and incoherent gibbering echoing through nearby passages, without any apparent origin. Each character must make a successful DC 11 Wisdom saving throw. On a failed save, the character's madness level increases by 1.

Lava Swell

As the party traverses a long and winding corridor, a tremor opens up a lava-filled fissure behind them. Each character must make a DC 10 Dexterity saving throw to avoid the lava swell, taking 21 (6d6) fire damage on a failed save. Decrease the drow pursuit level by 1.

Muck Pit

The adventurers must wade through a broad, 3-foot-deep pit of slimy muck. The muck is difficult terrain and characters have disadvantage on Dexterity saving throws while within it, but their travel pace for the day is slowed by half if they go around it.

Rockfall

As the adventurers make their way through a long, twisting cavern, a tremor sets off a rockfall. Each party member must attempt three DC 12 Dexterity saving throws, taking 10 (3d6) bludgeoning damage on each failed save. Any incapacitated creature not moved out of the area is buried under rubble, taking an additional 1d6 bludgeoning damage at the end of each of its turns until the creature is dug out or dead. Decrease the drow pursuit level by 1.

Rope Bridge

A ravine 2d4 × 10 feet wide and 2d4 × 10 feet deep cuts across the party's path, spanned by an old rope bridge. If the characters cut the bridge after they pass, the drow pursuit level decreases by 1.

RUINS

The adventurers come across a small ruin hidden in the Underdark. This might be the creation of a subterranean race or a surface ruin that collapsed and sank long ago. If the characters search the ruins, there is a 50 percent chance of them finding 1d4 trinkets (see chapter 5, "Equipment," of the *Player's Handbook*). Roll on the Trinkets table or choose appropriate ones.

SHELTER

The party stumbles upon a cave that is sheltered and easily defended. If the characters camp here, they can finish a long rest without any chance of an encounter while they are resting.

SINKHOLE

One random party member steps on and collapses a sinkhole, and must succeed on a DC 12 Dexterity saving throw to avoid falling into a 20-foot-deep pit and taking 7 (2d6) bludgeoning damage. Climbing out of the pit requires a successful DC 15 Strength (Athletics) check.

SLIME OR MOLD

As the adventurers pass through a small cavern, they encounter a patch of slime or mold. Roll a d6 and consult the table to determine what type of slime or mold is present (see "Dungeon Hazards" in chapter 5 of the *Dungeon Master's Guide* for details on these threats).

SLIME OR MOLD ENCOUNTER

d6	Encounter
1–3	Patch of green slime
4–5	Patch of yellow mold
6	Patch of brown mold

STEAM VENT

A hot steam vent erupts beneath a random party member, who must succeed on a DC 12 Dexterity saving throw or take 7 (2d6) fire damage.

UNDERGROUND STREAM

A waterway 2d4 × 5 feet wide cuts across the party's path. The stream is shallow and easily crossed, and the characters can drink and refresh their water supplies. Edible fish inhabit the stream, so that the DC of any foraging attempts for food in this area is reduced to 10. Crossing the stream reduces the drow pursuit level by 1.

WARNING SIGN

The characters enter a cavern dotted with stalagmites and stalactites. Those with a passive Wisdom (Perception) score of 11 or higher spot the following sigil carved into one of the stalagmites:

The sigil is a drow warning sign that means "Demons ahead!" Any non-drow creature that touches the symbol must make a DC 10 Wisdom saving throw. On a failed save, the creature's madness level increases by 1.

If the characters take a long rest within one mile of the warning sign, roll a d20 and consult the table to determine what, if anything, they encounter at the end of their rest.

WARNING SIGN ENCOUNTER

d20	Encounter
1–14	No encounter
15–16	1 invisible **barlgura**
17–18	3d4 **dretches**
19–20	1d2 **shadow demons**

WEBS

Sticky webs fills a passage (see "Dungeon Hazards" in chapter 5 of the *Dungeon Master's Guide*). The webs extend for hundreds of feet. Unless the characters come up with a plan for clearing the webs quickly, the party's travel pace for the day is halved as the characters are forced to cut their way through or find an alternate route.

Check for an encounter when the party enters the webs. On a roll of 1–2 on a d6, the characters encounter 1d4 **giant spiders** lurking among the webs.

CREATURE ENCOUNTERS

Keep the party's level in mind when fleshing out these encounters, and allow the characters to retreat from or avoid an encounter that is too great a challenge. Escape should come at a cost, however. Characters fleeing their camp to avoid a creature encounter might be forced to abandon food and water supplies, for example.

CREATURE ENCOUNTERS

d20	Encounter
1–2	Ambushers; reroll this encounter if the characters are resting
3	Carrion crawler
4–5	Escaped slaves
6–7	Fungi
8–9	Giant fire beetles
10–11	Giant "rocktopus"
12	Mad creature
13	Ochre jelly
14–15	Raiders
16	Scouts
17	Society of Brilliance
18	Spore servants
19–20	Traders

AMBUSHERS

One or more creatures attempt to ambush the party as it makes its way through the Underdark. Roll a d20 and consult the table to determine what the characters encounter.

AMBUSHERS

d20	Encounter
1–2	1 **chuul** lurking in a pool of water
3	1d6 **giant spiders** clinging to the walls or ceiling
4–5	1 **grell** floating near the high ceiling
6–9	1d4 **gricks** hiding in a crevice or fissure
10–15	1d4 **orogs** perching on ledges
16–17	1d6 **piercers** masquerading as stalactites
18–20	1 **umber hulk** bursting out of a nearby wall

If the ambush occurs in the monster's lair, there is a chance that characters searching the area find something of interest or value. Roll a d20 and consult the table below to see what, if anything, they find.

AMBUSHER LAIR DISCOVERIES

d20	Discovery
1–10	None
11–12	A humanoid skeleton or corpse clutching a salvageable, nonmagical weapon (your choice)
13–14	A humanoid skeleton or corpse wearing a salvageable suit of nonmagical armor (your choice)
15–17	1d6 50 gp gems
18–19	A humanoid skeleton or corpse carrying a random magic item (roll once on Magic Item Table B in chapter 7 of the *Dungeon Master's Guide*)
20	A monster hoard containing 2d6 50 gp gems and one or more random magic items (roll 1d4 times on Magic Item Table C in chapter 7 of the *Dungeon Master's Guide*)

CARRION CRAWLER

The characters encounter a **carrion crawler** scouring tunnels and caves for food.

There is a 25 percent chance that the crawler is domesticated and outfitted with a leather saddle and harness, though there's no sign of the rider. A character can approach and mount the carrion crawler without being attacked by succeeding on a DC 13 Wisdom (Animal Handling) check. While in the saddle and harness, a rider can remain mounted on the carrion crawler as it crawls across walls and ceilings.

ESCAPED SLAVES

These slaves have been wandering the Underdark since their escape from Gracklstugh or Menzoberranzan. They are scrounging for food and water. Roll a d4 and consult the table to determine what the characters encounter. Elf, dwarf, and human slaves are friendly; if given food and water they'll join the party. Goblin slaves are hostile and likely to attack.

ESCAPED SLAVES

d4	Encounter
1	1d2 moon elf **commoners**
2	1d3 shield dwarf **commoners**
3	1d4 human **commoners**
4	1d6 goblins

FUNGI

Roll a d6 and consult the table to determine what kinds of fungi the characters encounter.

FUNGI

d6	Encounter
1–2	1d4 **gas spores**
3–4	1d4 **shriekers**
5–6	1d4 **violet fungi**

There's a 25 percent chance that a gas spore carries a memory fragment from a dead beholder in its spores (see the gas spore's description in the "Fungi" entry of *Monster Manual*). This memory can be of anything you wish, or you can roll a d4 and consult the Beholder Memories table.

BEHOLDER MEMORIES

d4	Memory
1	A tense negotiation with drow, ending with the beholder agreeing to allow the drow safe passage through "the Vast Oblivium" in exchange for help ridding its lair of a deep gnome infestation
2	Chasing svirfneblin thieves through the tunnels of its domain to recover stolen gemstones
3	A fierce battle against a wizened drow archmage, ending with the beholder suffering a grievous injury
4	Spying on a drow ranger with two gleaming scimitars and a black, quadrupedal animal companion

GIANT FIRE BEETLES

The characters encounter 3d6 **giant fire beetles** scouring tunnels and caves for food. Characters in need of light sources can harvest the glowing glands of slain beetles.

GIANT "ROCKTOPUS"

This creature is a **giant octopus** that has evolved to live and thrive on land. It can alter its coloration to appear as a rock formation, and it tends to lurk in crevices and fissures, attacking smaller creatures that wander near. It has a walking speed of 20 feet and a climbing speed of 10 feet, loses its Hold Breath feature, and replaces its Underwater Camouflage feature with the following feature:

Camouflage. The octopus has advantage on Dexterity (Stealth) checks.

MAD CREATURE

The party encounters a creature driven insane by the influence of the demon lords. Roll a d4 and consult the table to determine what appears. Then roll on the Indefinite Madness table in chapter 8 of the *Dungeon Master's Guide* to determine the nature of the creature's madness. If cured of its madness, the creature behaves in accordance with its alignment.

Mad Creature

d4	Encounter
1	1 deep gnome
2	1 drow
3	1 duergar
4	1 stone giant

There is a chance that the mad creature has something of interest or value in its possession. Roll a d20 and consult the table below to see what, if anything, it has. The creature doesn't part with the item willingly.

Mad Creature Possessions

d20	Possession
1–10	None
11–13	A 10 gp gem
14–15	A gold ring worth 25 gp
16–17	An obsidian statuette of Lolth worth 100 gp
18–19	A random magic item (roll once on Magic Item Table A in chapter 7 of the *Dungeon Master's Guide*)
20	A random magic item (roll once on Magic Item Table B in chapter 7 of the *Dungeon Master's Guide*)

Ochre Jelly

As the characters move through a series of caves, they attract the attention of a **ochre jelly**. The ooze follows the characters, attacking when they stop to take their next rest. Characters in the back rank of the marching order who have a passive Wisdom (Perception) score of 14 or higher spot the ooze following them.

Raiders

This group of raiders from the surface ventured into the Underdark looking for riches and got lost. Roll a d6 and consult the table to determine what appears. The raiders are initially hostile toward the party, though clever characters might try bribing them for safe passage or information.

Raiders

d6	Encounter
1–2	1d6 human **bandits** and 1 human **bandit captain**
3–4	2d4 **goblins** and 1 **goblin boss**
5–6	1d6 **orcs** and 1 **orc Eye of Gruumsh**

There is a chance that the leader of the group has something of interest or value. Roll a d20 and consult the table below to see what, if anything, the leader of the raiders has in its possession.

Raider Leader Possessions

d20	Possession
1–5	None
6–10	2d6 10 gp gemstones in a pouch
11–14	2d6 50 gp gemstones in a pouch
15–17	1d4 torchstalks (see "Fungi of the Underdark")
18–19	1d4 waterorbs (see "Fungi of the Underdark")
20	A random magic item (roll on Magic Item Table B in chapter 7 of the *Dungeon Master's Guide*)

Scouts

Each of these groups is in the Underdark on a secret mission. Roll a d6 and consult the table to determine what appears.

Scouts

d6	Encounter
1–2	1 **drow**
3–4	1d4 **myconid adults**
5–6	1d6 shield dwarf **scouts**

The drow scout is searching for escaped slaves. If he spots the party, he'll attempt to avoid notice and take away information regarding the group's location (see "Drow Pursuit").

The myconid scouts are indifferent toward the party and unwilling to discuss their mission or their travels with the adventurers.

Shield dwarf scouts are friendly if the party includes one or more surface dwellers. They are willing to give the party a day or two's worth of food and water rations.

Society of Brilliance

The characters stumble upon a member of the Society of Brilliance, a sect of highly intelligent monsters that have banded together to solve all of the Underdark's problems. The society is investigating areas suffused with *faerzress* to ascertain whether it has something to do with what the society fears is some kind of "demonic incursion." Roll a d10 to determine which society member the characters encounter.

Society of Brilliance

d10	Encounter
1–2	Y the **derro** savant (see appendix C)
3–4	Blurg the **orog**
5–6	Grazilaxx the **mind flayer**
7–8	Skriss the **troglodyte**
9–10	Sloopidoop the **kuo-toa archpriest**

Every member of the Society of Brilliance has an alignment of neutral, an Intelligence of 18 (+4), and fluency in multiple languages including Dwarvish, Elvish, and Undercommon (although Grazilaxx prefers to communicate using telepathy). Its statistics are unchanged otherwise. Members are erudite and talkative, preferring diplomacy and debate over violence (though they defend themselves if attacked).

Each society member can cast the *teleport* spell once per day, but the intended destination must be within 30 feet of another society member. This teleport effect can be disrupted (see "*Faerzress*" earlier in the chapter), which is how society members sometimes end up in far corners of the Underdark, separated from their fellows.

Members of the Society of Brilliance are aware that paths to the surface world exist but haven't explored any of them (their concerns are with the Underdark, after all). If the characters seem intent on reaching the surface, a society member might suggest they look for a guide in one of the Underdark's larger settlements,

Y

BLURG

GRAZILAXX

SKRISS

SLOOPIDOOP

such as Blingdenstone or Gracklstugh. The society member can provide detailed verbal directions that characters can follow to reach whichever Underdark settlement they desire. However, the society member can't guarantee that the route is safe. If characters are searching for something else, the society member provides whatever assistance it can.

SPORE SERVANTS

One or more creatures killed and reanimated by Zuggtmoy's spores observe the characters as they pass by. The spore servants don't communicate and don't attack except in self-defense. Roll a d10 and consult the table to determine what the characters encounter.

SPORE SERVANTS

d10	Encounter
1–3	1d4 **drow spore servants** (see appendix C)
4–6	1d6 **duergar spore servants** (see appendix C)
7–8	1d4 **hook horror spore servants** (see appendix C)
9–10	1d8 **quaggoth spore servants**

TRADERS

These traders ply the tunnels of the Underdark, traveling from settlement to settlement. Roll a d4 and consult the table to determine what appears.

TRADERS

d4	Encounter
1	2d4 **deep gnomes**
2	2d4 **drow**
3	2d4 **duergar**
4	2d4 **kuo-toa**

Deep gnome and drow traders have a 50 percent chance of having half their number in **giant lizards** as mounts and pack animals. Duergar traders have a 50 percent

chance of having half their number in **male steeders** (see appendix C) as pack animals. If there are male steeders present, there is a 50 percent chance that the traders are escorted by a **duergar kavalrachni** astride a **female steeder** (see appendix C for both).

The traders carry goods worth 5d4 × 10 gp plus ten days of provisions per member of their party; they are willing to sell up to 20 percent of either. If drow traders see the adventurers and have the opportunity to report it, increase the drow pursuit level by 1.

SUMMARIZING TRAVEL

Instead of checking for random encounters every day, you can skip over or summarize parts of the characters' journey. Roll 1d6 + 1 for the number of days between encounters, with the usual chance of the encounter being a terrain encounter, a creature encounter, or both (as described under "Random Encounters"). For example, if roll a result of 4, you would tell the players: "You've been making your way through the tunnels and passages for four days ..." before describing the circumstances of the encounter to them.

With this approach, encourage players to describe what their characters do—or even see and experience—during the intervening time. In addition to downtime activities such as crafting, characters have plenty of opportunities for interaction. If the players are handling the roles of some or all of their nonplayer character companions (see "A Motley Crew" in chapter 1), ask them to elaborate on the activities of those characters as well, filling in details as you see fit. Players can also suggest and spin out stories about things their characters have experienced during the intervening time, including arduous climbs, swinging across gorges, or dodging piercers, and you can do the same. This additional storytelling aspect adds color and background to the journey while keeping the pace relatively brisk.

Set Encounters

You can use the following four encounters during the party's travels in the Underdark between the locations in chapters 3 through 7, inserting them as desired. They provide more detailed challenges for the characters, as well as giving them chances to encounter some potential allies. If the characters need an XP boost as they work through subsequent chapters, these encounters can help provide it.

The Silken Paths

The Silken Paths are a network of spider webs crisscrossing a 500-foot-deep, 2,000-foot-wide chasm that stretches for nearly five miles. The major strands of the webs are traversable but, due to the fact that old webs disintegrate over time and the giant spiders inhabiting the chasm are constantly spinning new ones, the Silken Paths are ever-changing.

The chasm has numerous passages at varying heights leading away from it. It is rare for a web strand to connect one opening with another on the same "level." Characters navigating the Silken Paths need to follow sloping strands as well as climb and cross over several strands to reach their intended destination. This is quite hazardous, but there simply isn't any easy way around the chasm. The characters can easily get lost in the mass of strands stretching across the chasm unless they have help.

The Web Runners

The Web Runners are a pair of thrill-seeking **goblins** named Yuk Yuk and Spiderbait. They have lived in the Underdark for as long as either can remember, with much of their time spent treasure hunting and surviving in the Silken Paths. The goblins are prone to daring (and often foolish) stunts. That either of them is still alive is a testament to their luck and skill. Modify their statistics as follows:

- Both goblins are neutral.
- Add Acrobatics +6 and Athletics +3 to the goblins' list of skills.
- The goblins have advantage on checks made to avoid being surprised.

The goblins notice the adventurers as they approach the Silken Paths and are willing to act as guides and helpers—for a fee, of course. They'll settle for 2 gp per day each, but Yuk Yuk (who does all the negotiating) is just as likely to ask for something flashy belonging to one of the characters. He might also ask for some unspecified favor, to be paid when the goblins and the adventurers get to wherever they're going and part ways. He might ask for first pick of any loot the party uncovers in the Silken Paths, and will expect and ask for a share of the treasure regardless.

Yuk Yuk and Spiderbait each carry a gourd of grease, which they apply to their feet so that they can "surf the webs." While sliding down webs, they move at twice their normal walking speed.

The Web Runners are as good as their word when it comes to their services, and they can teach the

YUK YUK AND
SPIDERBAIT

characters a thing or two. While they travel with the two goblins, the characters have advantage on checks made to avoid being surprised. The goblins know the Silken Paths well enough not to become lost in them.

If the adventurers make a good impression on the Web Runners and if the party's goals appear to offer interesting opportunities to do new and dangerous things, the goblins offer to stay on after crossing the Silken Paths, and to help guide the characters through the Underdark. The two won't leave the Underdark, however. Yuk Yuk will try to negotiate a suitable fee, but the goblins might simply tag along, content to earn any fair share of whatever the party acquires.

Silken Paths: General Features

As characters traverse the Silken Paths, keep in mind the following features.

Difficult Terrain. Any creature with a climbing speed can walk along the webs at that speed. For all other creatures, the webs are difficult terrain. Any creature that falls can potentially become entangled in the webs (see "Falling").

Falling. Whenever a creature takes damage while traversing the Silken Paths, or whenever the webs upon which it is walking break, the creature must make a DC 15 Dexterity saving throw. On a successful save, the creature manages to avoid a fall by grabbing nearby web strands. On a failure, the creature falls 1d10 × 10 feet. If the distance fallen is less than the distance to the chasm floor, the creature becomes entangled in webs and restrained; otherwise, it hits the floor and takes damage from the fall as normal. A restrained creature can make a DC 12 Strength saving throw at the end of each of its turns, freeing itself and ending the restrained condition on a success. Another creature can use its action to help a restrained creature within its reach, granting advantage on that creature's next saving throw to end the effect.

Light. The chasm is dark. Carrying a light source attracts hostile creatures, increasing the chance of an encounter to 1–3 on a d6.

Fire. Webs burn away when exposed to any attack or effect that deals fire damage. This causes several strands to break, and all creatures within 30 feet of the affected area must make a saving throw to avoid falling (see "Falling").

SILKEN PATH ENCOUNTERS

For every 500 feet the party travels through the webs, check for a random encounter by rolling a d6. An encounter occurs on a roll of 1 unless one or more party members are carrying light sources, in which case an encounter occurs on a roll of 1–3. Roll on the Silken Paths Encounters table or choose a suitable encounter when one occurs.

SILKEN PATHS ENCOUNTERS

d12	Encounter
1	Cocooned lightfoot halfling
2	1d4 **darkmantles**
3	1d4 **drow** and 1d4 **quaggoth** slaves
4–8	2d4 **giant spiders**
9	1 **mimic**
10	1 **spectator**
11–12	Web break

COCOONED HALFLING

The characters find a still-living lightfoot halfling cocooned in webbing. He is poisoned and paralyzed for the next hour.

Fargas Rumblefoot was a member of an adventuring band looking for a long-lost tomb when they were attacked by a pack of mad gnolls. Fargas escaped, got lost in the Silken Paths, and was attacked by the spiders. If rescued, he promises to show the characters the way to the tomb in exchange for a share of its treasures (see "Lost Tomb of Khaem" later in this chapter). Fargas is a chaotic good halfling **spy**. In addition to his armor and weapons, he carries a *potion of invisibility*.

DARKMANTLES

These subterranean hunters swoop down and attack the party.

DROW AND QUAGGOTH SLAVES

These hateful drow and their murderous quaggoth slaves are navigating the Silken Paths on their way through the Underdark. If Derendil is with the party, he can use an action to make a DC 15 Charisma check, turning the quaggoth slaves against their drow masters on a success. If the drow are disposed of, Derendil can repeat the check to turn the surviving quaggoths into his followers. Should Derendil perish, these quaggoths can't be controlled and fight to the death.

If any drow escape the encounter, increase the pursuit level of the party's drow pursuers by 1.

GIANT SPIDERS

Giant spiders are the most common inhabitants of the Silken Paths, and they are drawn to vibrations in the webs that indicate potential prey.

MIMIC

This creature pretends to be an iron chest entangled in the webs. When the characters draw close to examine it, the mimic attacks.

SPECTATOR

Freed from its service to a long-dead drow wizard, this mad aberration now floats through the web-filled chasm. It communicates with the characters telepathically, warning them about "demons rising in the dark." The creature becomes increasingly paranoid and convinced that the characters are themselves demons, come to bind it into servitude, at which point it attacks and tries to destroy them.

WEB BREAK

A strand of web under one randomly determined party member snaps. Each creature walking on that web strand must make a DC 15 Dexterity saving throw as described under "Falling" in the "Silken Paths: General Features" sidebar. Immediately check for another encounter after the saving throws are resolved.

HOOK HORROR HUNT

The characters enter an area where a band of gnolls lured to the Underdark by the demon lord Yeenoghu are hunting a mated pair of hook horrors. Having left guards at the main entrance to the lair (area 5), the gnoll pack lord has split its remaining hunters into two groups, both of which are attempting to flush out the hook horrors to win the right to tear them apart.

The adventurers wander into the area from a second entrance to the caverns (area 1) and become embroiled in the hunt. Whether they choose to avoid the hunting party, aid the hook horrors, or negotiate their way out of the situation is up to the players.

1. HOOK HORRORS

The characters hear clacking noises as they approach this point in the passageway. Suddenly, two **hook horrors** dash from the side passage, moving from area 2A toward area 3. The hook horrors attack only in self-defense and are more afraid of the giggling, rampaging gnolls than they are of the characters.

The gnolls are two chambers behind the hook horrors, reaching this point on the following round, unless the characters move toward them (in which case the two groups converge in area 2A).

2A. GNOLL HUNTERS

Four **gnolls** move into this area the round after the hook horrors move past the party, then follow their quarry into area 1 on the following round.

The gnolls can't resist attacking any other creatures that cross their path while shrieking "Sacrifices for Yeenoghu!" in their own tongue. (Even if no one in the party speaks Gnoll, the name of the demon lord is clearly recognizable.)

DEVELOPMENT

Sounds of combat or calls from the gnolls might attract their pack mates in areas 2B and 5.

The Hook Horror Lair

ONE SQUARE = 10 FEET

N

BLANDO

2B. Gnoll Hunters

The rest of the gnoll hunters race through these caverns in search of the hook horrors. Unless they are drawn elsewhere, four **gnolls** and a **gnoll pack lord** are here.

Treasure

The gnoll pack lord carries two bloodstones worth 50 gp each and a brown tourmaline worth 100 gp.

3. Cornered

The fleeing hook horrors make their way here, where they wait in ambush for any creatures that follow them. The passage is narrow enough that Medium creatures must move single file through it. The cave appears to be a dead end, and the hook horrors fight to the death against any creatures that enter.

Characters who take the time to search the cave spot a hole in the 10-foot-high ceiling (marked C on the map), which requires a successful DC 12 Strength (Athletics) check to climb up into. It leads to area 4.

4. Hook Horror Nest

The sandy floor of this cavern holds a clutch of four 1-foot-diameter eggs with rocky outer shells, all half-buried in a shallow pit. These are hook horror eggs, and any character that touches an egg can feel it trembling.

Each hour, there is a 10 percent chance that one of the eggs hatches. The infant hook horror that emerges imprints on the first creature it sees. It thereafter follows that creature around like its parent, demanding to be fed. If the characters manage to keep the hook horror alive, it eventually reaches adulthood after six months. Track its growth using the Hook Horror Maturation table.

Hook Horror Lair: General Features

As characters explore the hook horror lair, keep in mind the following features.

Light. The tunnels are completely dark, which doesn't hinder either the gnolls or the hook horrors.

Tight Passages. Tunnels marked "P" on the map are narrow enough that Large creatures such as the hook horrors must squeeze through them, spending 1 extra foot of movement for every foot of passage. Medium or smaller creatures can move through such areas normally.

GLABBAGOOL

THE OOZING TEMPLE: GENERAL FEATURES

As characters explore the Oozing Temple, keep in mind the following features.

Light. Except where specified otherwise, the tunnels and chambers are dark.

Air. The air is stale and perceptibly thin. The temple contains enough air for the oozes, plus 160 hours of breathable air for one creature, divided by the number of creatures present. For example, a party of four adventurers has 40 hours of air. Characters who are at rest and not undertaking activities such as moving or fighting consume half as much air.

Once half of the breathable air is consumed, the characters suffer one level of exhaustion (see appendix A of the *Player's Handbook*). For each additional 10 percent of the air used up, the characters suffer one additional level of exhaustion. At 90 percent, the characters are unable to move. When the air is used up, they die. Once the first level of exhaustion sets in, the characters become aware that they are running out of air, and know roughly how much they have left.

A lit torch or its equivalent uses up air as a character does. Briefer but hotter magical effects consume 1 hour of air per die of fire damage per round. For example, a *fireball* spell that deals 8d6 fire damage consumes 8 hours of air, while a *fire bolt* that deals 1d10 fire damage consumes 1 hour of air per use.

Water. In addition to running low on air, the characters become aware that the tunnels and chambers are filling with water flowing in from area 6. The water rises at a rate of 1 foot per hour, meaning most of the tunnels and chambers will be completely flooded within 10 hours. Areas filled with waist-deep water are difficult terrain for the characters. Once the water is over their heads, they have to swim.

HOOK HORROR MATURATION

Age	Size	Notes
Infant (up to 1 month)	Tiny	AC 10; 4 (1d4 + 2) hit points; speed 10 ft., climb 10 ft.; Str 9 (–1); no effective attacks; Challenge 0 (0 XP)
Young (1–3 months)	Small	AC 11; 11 (2d6 + 4) hit points; speed 15 ft., climb 15 ft.; Str 12 (+1); hook attacks are +3 to hit, have a reach of 5 ft., and deal 3 (1d4 + 1) piercing damage on a hit; Challenge 1/4 (50 XP)
Juvenile (3–6 months)	Medium	AC 13; 39 (6d8 + 12) hit points; speed 20 ft., climb 20 ft.; Str 15 (+2); hook attacks are +4 to hit, have a reach of 5 ft., and deal 5 (1d6 + 2) piercing damage on a hit; Challenge 2 (450 XP)
Adult (6+ months)	Large	See the *Monster Manual*

5. GNOLL CAMP

The gnolls have a small camp set up here to prevent the hook horrors from fleeing in this direction.

Three **gnolls** guard the camp and attack any creatures emerging from the tunnels that are not of their kind.

THE OOZING TEMPLE

A tremor causes a cave-in and traps the adventurers in a maze of tunnels with no obvious way out. With a dwindling air supply and water rising in the tunnels, the characters are forced to find a means of escape. Complicating matters, part of the maze belongs to a forgotten temple that now serves as the lair of servants of the demon lord Juiblex.

1. BOXED IN

As the characters make their way through a 10-foot-high tubular passage, a tremor shakes the area and drops part of the ceiling on them. Each party member must succeed on a DC 13 Dexterity saving throw or take 5 (1d10) bludgeoning damage from falling debris.

Once the dust clears, the characters realize that fallen rock has buried both ends of the passageway. However, a new passage has opened in one of the walls, offering a possible escape route. It's clear that the route the party was following has been permanently blocked by tons of rubble, and runs the risk of triggering another collapse if the characters attempt to dig out.

2. DRIPPING DEATH

Whether finished stone or rough rock, the walls of these 10-foot-high areas glisten with dark, dripping water.

Each of these keyed areas holds a **gray ooze** that pours through cracks in the ceiling to attack any creatures that enter.

ONE SQUARE = 5 FEET

3. GLABBAGOOL

This area contains the skeletal remains of a drow, along with a dark metal mace and a scattering of coins. However, the characters are quick to notice that these items appear to hover above the stone floor.

All the visible items are trapped within the body of a **gelatinous cube** named Glabbagool—or at least, that's what it has chosen to call itself. Unlike most gelatinous cubes, this monster has an Intelligence of 10 (+0) and telepathy out to a range of 60 feet (see the *Monster Manual* introduction for telepathy rules).

Juiblex's arrival in the Underdark has granted Glabbagool sentience and awareness. The ooze is genuinely curious about other creatures and wants to learn more about the world. It defends itself if attacked, but doesn't otherwise try to harm the characters, instead asking who they are, where they come from, and why they have come to the temple.

Other oozes won't attack Glabbagool, so it can block a passageway to help the adventurers fend them off. However, the cube can't safely move past characters in a passageway. Glabbagool might ask to accompany the adventurers if it likes or is intrigued by them. Unfortunately, the ooze's speed of 15 feet means

that characters accompanied by it can travel only at a slow place (see "Travel Pace" at the beginning of this chapter).

TREASURE

Glabbagool's body contains a mace along with 14 ep and the mostly digested body of a drow. It will disgorge the items for the characters if they win its trust.

The mace is a common magic item. While attuned the weapon, its wielder can use an action to make the head of the mace alight with green flame, or use an action to extinguish the flame. While the mace is "lit," it glows as brightly as a torch and deals an extra 1 fire damage on a hit.

4. PUDDING PITS

This chamber is divided into four hallways and floored with heavy flagstones, the walls carved with worn and faded bas-reliefs. These show strange, swirling shapes that might be waves, tentacles, or some combination thereof.

TRAP

The squares marked on the map have been undermined, leaving a 10-foot-deep pit beneath each one. A

THE LOST TOMB

LEVEL 1

1

LEVEL 2

2

3

LEVEL 3

4

5

ONE SQUARE = 10 FEET

BLANDO

successful DC 15 Wisdom (Perception) check enables a character to notice that the stone is weakened.

More than 50 pounds of weight on an undermined area causes it to collapse. A creature standing in the area must succeed on a DC 11 Dexterity saving throw to grab the edge of the pit, after which the creature must succeed on a DC 11 Strength (Athletics) check to scramble out. On a failed saving throw or a failed check, the creature falls into the pit and takes 1d6 bludgeoning damage.

At the bottom of each pit is a **black pudding**, which attacks any creature that falls in. If denied a victim, or if it devours a fallen creature quickly, the pudding climbs up the sides to attack any dangling creatures, or to move into the hallway in search of prey.

5. FOUNTAIN OF MADNESS

This room contains a stone fountain with a raised edge. The basin contains shallow, brackish water. At the center of the pool, the rubble of a broken statue rest atop a pedestal. All that remains recognizable are a pair of clawed stone feet clutching the pedestal's top. Carved into the walls are seven niches. Water seeps into one niche through a crack in the wall. The two niches that

flank it are empty. Strange, formless sculptures occupy the four remaining niches.

The "sculptures" are actually four **gray oozes** held in magical stasis. They liquefy and attack when any one of them is touched or damaged.

TREASURE
Hidden beneath the dark waters of the fountain are 112 sp, 41 gp, three green-gold bracelets worth 25 gp each, a drow *+1 dagger* (the hilt has a spider design), a *potion of greater healing*, and a vial containing *oil of slipperiness*.

6. WATER CHAMBER

Characters approaching this rough-walled cave hear the sound of pouring water. The water enters through cracks in the 10-foot-high ceiling. Given the rate at which the water flows in, the characters can easily conclude that the cracks were caused by the tremor they experienced, and it's only a matter of time before the water floods the entire complex.

The water rises at a rate of 1 foot per hour until the tunnels are completely flooded. However, chipping away at any of the cracks causes more of the ceiling to collapse, doubling the amount of water pouring into the complex but also revealing a diverted underground river that is the source of the water. Once the water level rises to the ceiling, the flow is slowed and the characters can swim upward for 30 feet to reach the water's surface. They find themselves in a larger cavern from which they can resume their journey.

DEVELOPMENT

If Glabbagool is with the party, the intelligent gelatinous cube floats upward as the water rises and squeezes through a crack in the ceiling to escape the flooded temple and remain with the characters.

LOST TOMB OF KHAEM

In ages past, at the height of Faerûn's great empires of magic, the half-elf sorcerer Brysis of Khaem was interred in a floating tomb. After the fall of the empire of Netheril and its flying cities, Brysis's tomb plummeted into a crevasse and wound up in the Underdark, where it has remained for centuries. The rise of the demon lords has awakened Brysis from the eternal sleep of death as a wraith, served by specters who were once her loyal retainers. Brysis yearns to accumulate enough life force to leave the confines of her tomb, to which her spirit is bound.

The adventurers might discover the tomb by accident or with the aid of Fargas Rumblefoot, the halfling from the Silken Paths encounter. Either way, when they're nearby, read the following to the players:

> A soft feminine voice sounds out in your mind suddenly, faint and distant.
>
> "Hello? Is someone there … ? Oh please, I need your help! I have been trapped in the dark for so long … so very long. Please, won't you help to free me?"

The characters receive an impression of the direction to the entrance of the tomb, but the mysterious voice doesn't respond to any queries. As they follow the voice, a narrow side passage takes them to a dirty marble wall with a deep-set door made of bronze-encased stone, green with age (see the "Lost Tomb of Khaem: General Features" sidebar).

1. ENTRANCE ROOM

A stone diorama stands to the right of the entrance, depicting the sorcerer Brysis Khaem as a Netherese noble in her prime, surrounded by attendants, slaves, and other trappings of wealth and power. A vista of fantastic floating cities covers the wall to the left of the entrance.

STAIRCASE AND LANDING

Across from the entrance, empty stone torch sconces flank a dusty staircase descending 20 feet to a landing. Set into the back wall of the landing is a Netherese calendar stone. Beyond this landing, the staircase resumes its descent, stopping at three more landings of bare stone and descending a total of 100 feet before arriving at area 2.

LOST TOMB OF KHAEM: GENERAL FEATURES

As characters explore the Lost Tomb of Khaem, keep in mind the following features.

Ceilings. Room ceilings are 15 feet high. The hallways connecting them are 10 feet high.

Doors. Each door in the tomb is a 10-foot-by-10-foot slab of solid marble encased in a thin layer of beaten bronze. The bronze has turned green with age. The door pivots on a central axis, creating narrow openings on either side while open. The door is also heavy and tight-fitting, requiring a DC 15 Strength (Athletics) check to open or close.

Light. Except as otherwise noted, the interior of the tomb is dark.

Chaotic Magic. The tomb was crafted during an age of high magic, and it has become suffused with *faerzress*. The ancient and chaotic energy now permeating the structure causes any spell cast within the tomb to trigger a roll on the Wild Magic Surge table in chapter 3, "Classes," of the *Player's Handbook*.

---

2. SHRINE

The stairs lead down to this shrine, where shreds of dusty tapestries lie scattered across the floor. Friezes on the walls are defaced with deep gouges, making them unrecognizable. An altar of pale gray marble stands gouged and cracked against one wall.

A successful DC 13 Intelligence (Investigation) check reveals that the damage to this room is relatively recent, and that the creatures that caused it left no tracks of any kind in the layer of dust on the floor.

3. SERVANTS' SARCOPHAGI

Four stone sarcophagi mark the resting places of Brysis's most faithful servants. The lid of each sarcophagus bears the sculpted image of a robed human figure in repose. Brysis's four servants have arisen at her command as **specters**. If anyone touches or otherwise disturbs a sarcophagus, all four specters emerge from their sarcophagi, howling in fury, and attack. The specters can pursue their prey beyond the confines of the tomb, if necessary.

Opening a sarcophagus lid requires a successful DC 17 Strength check and reveals treasure within (see "Treasure").

A character inspecting the northeast sarcophagus and succeeding on a DC 15 Wisdom (Perception) check notices that the sarcophagus is built on hidden stone rollers. It can be moved aside with a successful DC 10 Strength check to reveal a 4-foot-square hole in the floor, and in the ceiling of a similarly sized chamber directly below this one (area 5). If the characters move the sarcophagus but leave the chamber without exploring the tomb below, they hear the same telepathic voice that called out to them initially, saying, "Please! Don't leave! I'm here, below!"

TREASURE

Each sarcophagus contains mummified remains, the tattered remnants of ancient burial garments, and treasure of Netherese origin.

The northeast sarcophagus contains two gold bracelets worth 50 gp each and a ceremonial wand (nonmagical) made of chiseled ivory worth 25 gp.

The northwest sarcophagus contains an onyx ring worth 50 gp and a silver necklace set with two azurites and a carnelian worth 250 gp.

The southwest sarcophagus contains a ewer made of beaten gold worth 25 gp and a walking stick worth 75 gp. The walking stick is made of varnished yew with a golden handle shaped like a scorpion.

The southeast sarcophagus contains a gold censer with platinum filigree worth 250 gp.

4. FALSE TOMB

Stone blocks standing against the western and eastern walls are carved with niches, inside which rest a dozen clay canopic jars containing desiccated organs. These organs belong to Brysis's servants, who are entombed in area 4.

In the middle of the room rests a wide stone sarcophagus atop a black marble bier. The lid of the sarcophagus is inlaid with dust-covered mosaics depicting great floating cities high above a beautiful landscape. The lid of the sarcophagus looks incredibly heavy but is made lighter by an ancient spell that has survived to this day. The lid can be pushed aside with a successful DC 10 Strength check. The sarcophagus contains a life-sized statue of Brysis, sculpted and painted to make it appear that she is sleeping comfortably. The statue is affixed to the inside of the sarcophagus with *sovereign glue* and can't be moved. There is no treasure to be found.

TRAP

Opening the sarcophagus triggers a *magic mouth* spell that calls out in a booming voice, "You have disturbed the tomb of Brysis of Khaem! Accursed are you, most miserable of creatures!" Each creature in the room, whether it hears the booming voice or not, must make a DC 15 Charisma saving throw. On a failure, the creature is cursed with disadvantage on attack rolls and saving throws. The creature can repeat the saving throw after 24 hours have elapsed, ending the effect on itself with a successful save. Otherwise, a *remove curse* spell ends this effect, as does destroying the wraith in area 5.

If Brysis's wraith is destroyed, both the *magic mouth* and the curse on the sarcophagus cease to function.

5. TRUE TOMB

Brysis's true tomb is hidden below area 3 and has murals on the walls decorated with rich pigments and inlays of semiprecious stones. A gilded sarcophagus stands atop a stone bier along the west wall. An invisible stone chest rests at the foot of the sarcophagus. Characters searching the area thoroughly locate the chest. The chest becomes visible within an *antimagic field*, and a successful *dispel magic* (DC 19) also ends the *invisibility* effect.

Brysis of Khaem has arisen as a murderous **wraith**, bound to her tomb until she can steal enough life force to leave it. She arises from within the sarcophagus and attacks when creatures enter this chamber. She gloats about how the characters' deaths will free her from this prison, and how her victims will serve her even in death.

On initiative count 1 in the round in which Brysis attacks, the characters hear the telepathic voice that first called to them. "In the sarcophagus! I can help you!" See "Treasure" for more information.

TREASURE

The thin gold sheath covering Brysis's sarcophagus can be pried loose and is worth 250 gp. Inside the stone sarcophagus, lying atop Brysis's withered and mummified corpse, is a magic sword called *Dawnbringer* (see appendix B). This intelligent weapon is the source of the telepathic messages.

The stone chest is unlocked and contains the other treasures Brysis took with her into the afterlife: 4,000 sp, 1,200 gp, eleven zircons (worth 50 gp each), a *necklace of fireballs*, a *philter of love*, and a *potion of greater healing*.

Chapter 3: The Darklake

Though its name might evoke images of a single subterranean body of water, the Darklake is a network of underground rivers, natural tunnels, and canals that connect innumerable water-filled caverns and chambers. This vast waterway stretches over a hundred miles across, with ceilings that are miles high in some places and depths that are unfathomable.

Long ago, duergar engineers extended and widened many of the interconnecting passages of the Darklake. They also constructed locks for raising and lowering watercraft to different levels within it, opening up large portions of the network for travel. Many Underdark creatures are experienced in navigating the Darklake, including the kuo-toa—fishlike humanoids known for their insane obsession with unraveling the secret patterns of the Underdark. Still, better to trust a kuo-toa guide than attempt to traverse the Darklake alone and become lost within it forever.

The adventurers can use the Darklake to reach many destinations in the Underdark. More importantly, water travel makes it difficult for their drow pursuers to track them. The kuo-toa town of Sloobludop is located on the eastern edge of the Darklake, and is a potential source of watercraft and navigational aid. But as they seek out these resources, the characters learn of terrible powers loose in the Underdark—worse than the drow, the kuo-toa, or any other threat of this dark realm.

Traversing the Darklake

The adventurers need to find a way to cross the Darklake on the way to their ultimate destination—out of the Underdark and back to the surface world. They might attempt to find a guide or hire passage in Sloobludop, but other possibilities could also present themselves.

Modes of Travel

The adventurers might find different ways to cross the Darklake, depending on how long they traverse it and who or what they encounter along the way.

Since there is no wind in the Underdark, all water travel involves either rowing at 1½ miles per hour, or floating with prevailing currents at 1 mile per hour. Characters can work in shifts to row more than 8 hours per day, but crewing a boat for longer than that is considered a forced march (see chapter 8 of the *Player's Handbook*).

Boat

Most craft navigating the waters of the Darklake are zurkhwood vessels piloted by the kuo-tua or the duergar. These boats are equivalent to keelboats (see the Airborne and Waterborne Vehicles table in chapter 5 of the *Dungeon Master's Guide*).

The Darklake: General Features

The following features commonly apply to the Darklake region.

Darkness. True to its name, most of the Darklake exists in pitch blackness. The only light available is whatever the characters are able to provide.

Caves and Tunnels. The Darklake is a giant labyrinth of lakes, waterways, and canals that connect myriad caverns and chambers. Some of these caverns are massive, with immeasurably deep water and vaulted ceilings far outside the range of any light. Others are narrow, with only a few feet of space between the ceiling and the surface of the water. Some are completely submerged, navigable only by those able to breathe underwater.

Navigation. Without the sky or the stars to navigate by, any successful passage of the Darklake relies on one's familiarity with its intricate network of caverns, passages, and currents. Experienced navigators know how to find and read ancient duergar runes carved along the Darklake's tunnels, though most of these "road signs" are nearly worn away by the passage of time. Such knowledge is something that takes years, if not decades, of wandering the Darklake to acquire.

Those without the skill to navigate the Darklake (including the adventurers) must employ maps or guides. If the characters manage to acquire a map, they can make Wisdom (Survival) checks normally to avoid becoming lost.

Foraging. The characters can forage for food while traversing the Darklake, primarily by fishing and gathering edible fungi (see "Fungi of the Underdark" in chapter 2). Much of the water of the Darklake is unsafe to drink, making it important to seek out springs and other clean sources of water feeding into it.

Makeshift Raft

Characters can also construct makeshift rafts using materials at hand. For example, the cap of a giant zurkhwood mushroom can be hollowed out to make a coracle equivalent to a rowboat, but with half a rowboat's hit points (see the Airborne and Waterborne Vehicles table in chapter 5 of the *Dungeon Master's Guide*). This is a downtime crafting activity requiring one day's work per raft.

An even more makeshift craft might involve a character sitting in a floating barrel or other watertight container, either steering with a paddle or flowing with the current. Such a vessel has a speed of 1 mph, requires a crew of 1, allows for no passengers or cargo, and has AC 11, hp 20, and damage threshold 0.

Swimming

Swimming in the Darklake is a poor choice given the number of dangerous creatures inhabiting it. Check for a creature encounter each hour that characters are swimming, rather than every 4 hours of travel. A swimming character must succeed on a DC 10 Constitution saving throw for each hour of swimming or gain one level of exhaustion.

Characters not actively swimming but simply clinging to something that floats (including the wreckage of a boat or raft) can drift with the current at a speed of 1 mph. Check for creature encounters each hour that characters float in the water, and call for Constitution checks against exhaustion for every 8 hours of travel.

Other Options

Travelers can mix and match modes of travel, and a sizable party might need multiple boats or rafts. A creature with a swimming speed (including a polymorphed character) can travel without risk of fatigue for up to 8 hours, and can even serve as a mount for a creature smaller than it. Water-breathing (or nonbreathing) creatures can swim underwater or even walk across the bottom of shallow sections of the Darklake, but need darkvision or a source of light to see.

Random Encounters

Every 4 hours that the characters are on the Darklake, roll a d20 and consult the Darklake Random Encounters table to determine what, if anything, they encounter. If the characters aren't moving—anchored or ashore, for example—any encounter is automatically a creature encounter.

Darklake Random Encounters

d20	Type of Encounter
1–13	No encounter
14–15	Terrain (roll a d10 and consult the Darklake Terrain Encounters table)
16–17	One or more creatures (roll a d12 and consult the Darklake Creature Encounters table)
18–20	Terrain encounter featuring one or more creatures (roll a d10 and consult the Darklake Terrain Encounters table, then roll a d12 and consult the Darklake Creature Encounter table)

Darklake Terrain Encounters

Special terrain rules are explained after the table.

Darklake Terrain Encounters

d10	Terrain
1	Collision
2	Falls or locks
3	Island
4	Low ceiling
5	Rockfall
6	Rough current
7	Run aground
8	Stone teeth
9	Tight passage
10	Whirlpool

Collision

This terrain encounter occurs only if one or more party members are traveling by raft or boat, and there's a strong current. Have everyone aboard the vessel make a DC 13 group Dexterity check to avoid hitting a wall or other large obstacle directly ahead. If the group check succeeds, the collision is avoided. Otherwise, the vessel takes 2d10 bludgeoning damage from the collision, and everyone aboard must succeed on a DC 10 Strength or Dexterity saving throw to avoid falling overboard.

Falls or Locks

Any character with a passive Wisdom (Perception) score of 12 or better can hear the roar of a waterfall ahead. A successful DC 14 group Strength (Athletics) check is necessary to steer or swim away from the falls. Otherwise, the characters go over, falling 1d6 × 10 feet into a pool or river 1d6 × 5 feet deep. A creature swept over the falls must succeed on a DC 11 Dexterity saving throw or take 1d6 bludgeoning damage per 10 feet fallen. A successful save indicates that the creature avoids a hard landing in the water below.

There is a 50 percent chance that any waterfall area contains a duergar-built lock designed to traverse it, in which case there is no risk of going over the falls. It takes a successful DC 11 Intelligence (Investigation) check to figure out how to operate the lock. Once a lock is opened, it takes 1 hour for the water level to lower so the party can proceed.

ISLAND

A small island rises from the water ahead. An island with no hostile creatures makes a good place for the party to take a long rest. There is a 50 percent chance that the island has one or more types of fungi growing atop it (see "Fungi of the Underdark" in chapter 2). Otherwise, the island is barren rock.

LOW CEILING

The clearance of the cave or passage lowers suddenly to 3 feet above the water's surface. Each Medium character must succeed on a DC 10 Dexterity saving throw or take 1d4 bludgeoning damage from hitting the ceiling before the passage ends.

ROCKFALL

Loose rocks fall from the ceiling above. Each character must succeed on a DC 12 Dexterity saving throw or be hit by a chunk of falling stone for 2d6 bludgeoning damage. If the characters are traveling in a boat or raft, their vessel takes 2d6 bludgeoning damage for each successful save; in other words, each rock that misses a character hits the boat or raft instead. Roll the damage for each rock striking a vessel separately to see if it overcomes the vessel's damage threshold.

ROUGH CURRENT

The waters here are especially turbulent. If the characters are traveling by boat or raft, the crew must succeed on a DC 13 group Dexterity check to maintain control. If the group check fails, the vessel takes 2d6 bludgeoning damage, and each occupant must succeed on a DC 10 Strength or Dexterity saving throw to avoid falling overboard.

RUN AGROUND

This terrain encounter occurs only if one or more party members are traveling by raft or boat. The vessel hits a shallow area or sandbar and runs aground. The characters can push the vessel back into the water with a successful DC 10 group Strength (Athletics) check. While characters are pushing their boat free, there is a 50 percent chance that one or more creatures attack them; in this event, roll on the Darklake Creature Encounters table to determine what attacks.

STONE TEETH

This terrain encounter occurs only if one or more party members are traveling by raft or boat, and there's a strong current. Stalagmites jutting up from the bottom of a tunnel are hidden just below the waterline. Spotters must succeed on a DC 13 Wisdom (Perception) check to notice the "stone teeth," allowing the vessel's crew to attempt a DC 12 group Dexterity check to navigate through them. If the group check succeeds, the vessel passes through unscathed. Failure to notice or navigate through the stone teeth deals 6d6 piercing damage to the boat or raft.

TIGHT PASSAGE

The adventurers encounter an especially tight passage, requiring a successful DC 12 group Dexterity check to navigate a boat or raft through it. If the group check succeeds, the boat slips through. Otherwise, the boat gets stuck, requiring a successful DC 14 group Strength (Athletics) check to push it free. While characters are pushing their boat free, there is a 50 percent chance that one or more creatures attack them; in this event, roll on the Darklake Creature Encounters table to determine what attacks.

WHIRLPOOL

An underwater crevasse or drain creates a small vortex in this area, much like the whirlpool effect of the *control water* spell (save DC 14).

DARKLAKE CREATURE ENCOUNTERS

The sections that follow the table provide additional information to help you run each creature encounter.

DARKLAKE CREATURE ENCOUNTERS

d12	Encounter
1	1 aquatic **troll**
2	2d4 **darkmantles**
3	1d4 + 2 **duergar** in a keelboat
4	1 **green hag**
5	1 **grell**
6–7	1d6 + 2 **ixitxachitl** (see appendix C)
8	1d4 **kuo-toa** in a keelboat
9	1d4 **merrow**
10	3d6 **stirges**
11	1 swarm of **quippers**
12	1 **water weird**

AQUATIC TROLL

An aquatic troll swims up from the depths. It has the abilities of a normal troll, but can also breathe water and has a swimming speed of 30 feet.

DARKMANTLES

These creatures cling to the ceiling as the adventurers approach, cloaking themselves in darkness as they unfurl and attack. A creature in a boat or on a raft that tries and fails to detach a darkmantle from itself or another creature must succeed on a DC 10 Dexterity saving throw or fall out of the vessel and into the water.

DUERGAR

A keelboat crewed by duergar is traversing the Darklake on business. The gray dwarves parley with the adventurers—or attack them if the opportunity looks ripe to capture them and sell them as slaves in Gracklstugh. If the duergar surprise all the characters, they turn invisible, making it appear that their boat is abandoned so as to lure the adventurers on board before they attack.

Roll a d20 and consult the Duergar Keelboat Cargo table to determine what, if anything, the duergar are transporting in their keelboat.

Duergar Keelboat Cargo

d20	Cargo
1–10	None
11–13	1d20 × 100 pounds of unrefined iron ore
14–16	1d4 zurkhwood crates filled with mining tools
17–19	2d4 zurkhwood casks of harvested fungi (see "Fungi of the Underdark" in chapter 2)
20	A locked iron chest containing 3d6 × 100 gp and a random magic item (roll once on Magic Item Table B in chapter 7 of the *Dungeon Master's Guide*).

Green Hag

Nanny Plunk is a green hag who likes to taunt and lead travelers astray. She might instead bargain with the characters with her knowledge of the Darklake, especially if her life or freedom is at stake. If this encounter occurs again, it might be with Nanny or one of her sisters, Maven Delve or Dame Spiderwort.

Grell

A grell descends from the cavern ceiling, attempting to grab and paralyze one party member, then fly off with its victim.

Ixitxachitl

These creatures attack any party members in the water. Otherwise, they follow the party and wait for an opportunity to strike. If denied a meal for too long, they begin to gnaw on the hull of a boat or the underside of a raft, hoping to sink it (this tactic is ineffective against craft with a high damage threshold).

Kuo-toa

These kuo-toa pole a keelboat toward Sloobludop (or away from the town if it has been attacked; see the end of this chapter). If the characters have not been to Sloobludop, the kuo-toa might try to capture them and bring them there. See "The Day's Catch" for details.

Roll a d20 and consult the Kuo-toa Keelboat Cargo table to determine what, if anything, the duergar are transporting in their keelboat.

Kuo-toa Keelboat Cargo

d20	Cargo
1–15	None
16–17	1d4 nets; each net has a 50 percent chance of containing 3d6 dead, edible quippers
18–19	1d4 nets; each net has a 50 percent chance of containing 1d4 living **stirges**
20	1d4 pieces of broken, barnacle-encrusted statuary, each worth 50 gp; each weighing 1d4 × 5 pounds; and each depicting a weird alien creature, a long-forgotten god, or fragment thereof.

Merrow

These worshipers of Demogorgon have been driven into a frenzy by his arrival in the Underdark. They immediately attack, trying to capsize or wreck boats as they utter the war cry, "Blood and salt for the Prince of Demons!" in Abyssal.

A merrow can use its action to capsize a boat or raft within 5 feet of it. Anyone in the boat can thwart the merrow by using a reaction to make a Strength check contested by the merrow's Strength check. If the merrow wins the contest, the vessel capsizes.

Stirges

These stirges cling to the ceiling like bats. If the party is aware of the stirges, the characters can make a DC 13 group Dexterity (Stealth) check to slip past the stirges without disturbing them. If the group check succeeds, the stirges ignore the party. Otherwise, the stirges descend and attack the nearest party members.

Swarm of Quippers

A swarm of quippers keeps pace with the characters, attacking anyone in the water. If an hour passes and no meal has presented itself, the quippers stop following the party.

Water Weird

Bound to some long-lost site beneath the surface of the water, this neutral evil elemental rises to attack when the characters pass by.

Roll a d6 and consult the Weird Discoveries table to determine what the water weird is guarding.

Weird Discoveries

d6	Discovery
1–2	Sunken altar dedicated to a forgotten deity
3–4	Sunken statue with 500 gp black pearls for eyes; a thief who removes one or both gems becomes the target of a *contagion* spell (save DC 14).
5–6	Sunken, sealed sarcophagus containing a **mummy** and 1d4 art objects (roll on the 250 gp Art Objects table in chapter 7 of the *Dungeon Master's Guide*)

Sloobludop

Population: 500 kuo-toa

Government: The archpriest Ploopploopeen once ruled in the name of the Sea Mother, the goddess Blibdoolpoolp. He was recently challenged and displaced by his daughter Bloppblippodd, archpriest of Leemooggoogoon the Deep Father.

Defense: All kuo-toa rally to the village's defense, including whips and monitors serving the priesthood.

Commerce: The kuo-toa trade with various races of the Underdark near the Darklake, in addition to providing ferry service and navigation.

Organizations: Two major shrines and several other minor ones.

Sloobludop is a kuo-toa village on the eastern edge of the Darklake. From a distance, it looks like a massive tangle of reeds stretching up into the darkness, lit by glowing spots of phosphorescence. Upon closer approach, a series of rickety towers can be seen, lashed together by rope and plank bridges set in haphazard patterns. Even above ground, the kuo-toa build in line with their three-dimensional aquatic sensibilities, constructing their "great city" as if it were underwater.

Sloobludop simmers with religious fervor and sectarian tension. While many of the kuo-toa still worship the goddess Blibdoolpoolp, a faction has shifted its worship to Leemooggoogoon the Deep Father, a vision influenced by the manifestation of the demon prince Demogorgon from the depths of the Darklake. Initially, the archpriest of Blibdoolpoolp tolerated this—but then his own daughter declared herself an archpriest of Leemooggoogoon, and the cult began to grow.

SLOUCHING TOWARD SLOOBLUDOP

The characters can choose to go to Sloobludop for several reasons:

- They need a boat (and possibly a guide) to navigate the Darklake. Travel along the waterways of the Darklake is an excellent way to throw off their drow pursuers (see chapter 2 for details).
- Staying a short while in Sloobludop can provide a respite from pursuit, since the drow are reluctant to provoke the kuo-toa needlessly. Reduce the pursuit level by 1 while the characters consider their next move.
- The characters need supplies and equipment, and hope the kuo-toa might be willing to trade for whatever they can offer. Alternatively, the characters might try to steal what they need from the kuo-toa.
- Shuushar might point out any of the previous reasons, or wish to go to Sloobludop to rejoin his people, feeling he has important guidance to offer them.
- Shuushar might not be the only one with "higher guidance." One or more characters might experience dreams or visions guiding them toward

Sloobludop—not realizing that such dreams are simply further manifestations of the madness growing in the Underdark.

NOTABLE KUO-TOA IN SLOOBLUDOP

A number of important kuo-toa have the ability to influence the adventurers' fate in Sloobludop.

PROMINENT KUO-TOA

Ploopploopeen ("Ploop")	Archpriest of the Blibdoolpoolp the Sea Mother
Bloppblippodd ("Blopp")	Ploopploopeen's daughter, now calling herself the archpriest of Leemooggoogoon the Deep Father; demon tainted
Glooglugogg ("Gloog")	Ploopploopeen's son, kuo-toa whip, and loyal worshiper of the Sea Mother
Klibdoloogut ("Klib")	Kuo-toa whip and keeper of the altar of the Deep Father

SHUUSHAR CONNECTION

If Shuushar accompanies the party, the kuo-toa monk can be helpful in communicating with his people at Sloobludop. However, keep in mind that Shuushar is either a heretic or a holy man depending on which kuo-toa he's speaking to, and how they view things at that particular moment. The mysterious monk could serve as an ace in the hole to help the party out, or he could just as easily cause trouble with his stubborn refusal to acknowledge his fellow kuo-toa's religious obsessions

---

SLOOBLUDOP: GENERAL FEATURES

Sloobludop spreads out along the rocky shore of the waters of a broad cavern lake, with high fences of woven netting to the north and south of the village boundaries.

Light. Sloobludop's cavern is almost entirely dark except for a few spots of dim light from phosphorescent fungus and coral, or from glowing cave-fish glands. The kuo-toa recoil from areas of bright illumination, becoming hostile if bright light is brought among them.

Bridges and Platforms. Bridges and platforms are haphazardly strung throughout the city, connecting various levels of structures with each other as well as crisscrossing open spaces. Characters can move at a normal pace across the platforms and bridges, but this puts strain on their poor construction. Whenever one or more characters move at normal speed across a bridge or platform, roll a d6. On a roll of 1, a bridge flips or breaks to drop characters to the platform below, or a platform tilts to tip the characters into the water. These areas can be navigated safely by treating them as difficult terrain.

Language. None of the inhabitants of Sloobludop speak Common or any surface-world language, which might present a challenge for the characters. The fish-folk speak Undercommon, and Stool the myconid sprout can establish communication using its rapport spores if it is present. Shuushar the kuo-toa monk can also translate if he accompanies the party.

ROLEPLAYING THE KUO-TOA

Though the kuo-toa are mad, at least some of that madness comes from an utterly alien mind-set. Although amphibious air dwellers, the kuo-toa still largely behave as aquatic creatures. Thus, much of what they do on land is a bizarre approximation of life under the water.

Kuo-toa names are a long series of gargling syllables, and their voices have a bubbly, gargling quality. However, the kuo-toa communicate as much through gesture as speech. They have difficulty standing still, and are prone to quick, darting movements. They pace constantly, walking in circles around creatures talking to them. A kuo-toa priest speaking to a group of followers doesn't stand at a podium but wanders aimlessly while the crowd follows like a school of fish.

Kuo-toa prefer their leaders to be physically above their subordinates. (If no dais or platform is available for leaders, they have been known to literally stand on top of prostrate underlings.) However, leaders tend to dwell on the lowest levels of buildings because these are considered the safest areas in a settlement, due to their proximity to the water.

Since the kuo-toa are fishlike, they lack eyelids. This isn't only unnerving in conversation (a kuo-toa never blinks), but it also means that kuo-toa all look the same sleeping as awake—and virtually all kuo-toa sleepwalk, making things even more confusing. There is a 25 percent chance that any individual kuo-toa the party encounters in Sloobludop is sleepwalking, ignoring everyone around it and moving in a shuffling gait from place to place.

as anything other than "dangerous illusions," combined with his preference for nonviolent solutions.

THE DAY'S CATCH

When the adventurers come within an hour's travel of Sloobludop, they encounter a party of eight **kuo-toa** led by a **kuo-toa monitor**. The fish-folk immediately attack, but their tactics show that they are attempting to capture the characters. The kuo-toa leave any fallen opponents unconscious at 0 hit points, intending to bring them back to Sloobludop as live offerings to the Deep Father. They bind prisoners with tough cords of gut, each with 2 hit points and requiring a successful DC 17 Strength check to break.

THE ENEMY OF MY ENEMY

On the way to Sloobludop after the previous encounter, the characters run into another kuo-toa patrol, this one made up of six **kuo-toa** and two **kuo-toa monitors**, led by the **kuo-toa archpriest** Plooploopeen. If the characters are prisoners of the first kuo-toa patrol, the newcomers ambush them and fight to free the characters. Otherwise (or after the fight), Plooploopeen attempts to communicate in Undercommon, then casts *tongues* if none of the characters speak it. Read the following:

> "I am Plooploopeen, archpriest of the Sea Mother Blibdoolvpoolp. She answers my prayers by delivering you. Help us, and you will be rewarded for your service."

If the characters talk with Plooploopeen, the archpriest explains his intentions as the kuo-toa escort the party to Sloobludop. If the characters refuse, the kuo-toa attempt to capture them, as with the previous patrol.

Plooploopeen explains that the inhabitants of Sloobludop have lived in harmonious service to the will of the Sea Mother for some time. Oh, there were occasional "visionaries" who stirred up trouble (at this, he might cast a walleyed glance at Shuushar) but nothing of any great concern. A few weeks ago, Bloppblippodd, Plooploopeen's own daughter, experienced a powerful vision of "Leemooggoogoon the Deep Father," proclaiming him the new god of her people. She has backed up her claims with a great increase in her magical power, and new followers have flocked to her.

A KUO-TOAN KOAN

The kuo-toa are aquatic creatures. As such, they have no real need for the boats they use to ply the Darklake, even as boating remains a significant part of their culture.

It might well be that the kuo-toa's former masters—the mind flayers—used them as ferry pilots and navigators in the Underdark, and the fish-folk continue to do so out of habit or some deep-seated need. Certainly, their relative usefulness to the other races of the Underdark has served the kuo-toa well. Only the duergar have shown any interest in navigating the waters of the Darklake on their own, and not even they do it as well as the kuo-toa.

There is a persistent myth among the inhabitants of Sloobludop that the maze of tunnels, passages, and pools of the Darklake is a kind of meditation—a spiritual journey. Kuo-toa who navigate that maze long enough will awaken to a great revelation for their people. As with many of the strange beliefs of the kuo-toa, this one might only need time to become a reality.

"We are split in two," Ploopploopeen explains, "fighting among ourselves." The followers of the Deep Father have been making an increasing number of offerings on his altar—killing blood sacrifices then casting bloody chum into the waters of the Darklake, where it is consumed by ... something.

BAITING THE HOOK

The archpriest of the Sea Mother tells the characters he wants to use them as bait. The archpriest of the Deep Father needs humanoid sacrifices, and the party represents a prize collection in that regard. Ploopploopeen will offer the characters as a "token of peace and reconciliation" to get closer to the archpriest of the Deep Father—except the adventurers will not be helpless prisoners, but infiltrators. Ploopploopeen wants the characters to disrupt the upstart faction's rituals, allowing his true believers of the Sea Mother to cut off the head of the cult. The archpriest promises that the characters will be "well rewarded" for their aid.

If the characters refuse, Ploopploopeen tries to turn them over anyway, still using them as bait to get his own kuo-toa loyalists closer to his daughter's cult. However, he no longer depends on or supports the characters as allies, leaving them to survive on their own.

No matter whether the characters approach the final encounter as willing participants or prisoners, the kuo-toa make no effort to bind them or take their weapons, believing in the power of their superior numbers and the divine might of their competing gods.

1. GATE

Sloobludop is enclosed to the north and south by outer "walls" of heavy netting with sharp bone hooks woven into them. In the middle of each wall is a gate through which creatures can safely pass. Any creature wishing to crawl through the netting can do so with a successful DC 15 Dexterity (Acrobatics) check. On a failure, the creature takes 1d8 piercing damage and becomes restrained in the netting, requiring a successful DC 12 Strength check as an action to break free.

Stationed outside each gate are four **kuo-toa whips**. They confront anyone who approaches. Party members escorted by other kuo-toa can pass through the gate unchallenged. If the characters are unescorted, any kuo-toa they meet attempt to capture them. Roll a d20. On a 1–7, captives are taken to area 3. On an 8–18, captives are taken to area 4. On a 19–20, the guards are evenly split and immediately begin to brawl for the right to take the characters as prisoners.

2. DOCKS

A half-dozen kuo-toan keelboats are moored here. Although kuo-toa will negotiate terms for ferrying the characters across the Darklake, none leave without permission (see below). Party members can attempt to steal one or more of the boats, but doing so requires a successful DC 16 Dexterity (Stealth) check (and the kuo-toa are able to sense invisible creatures). The kuo-toa pursue any stolen boats, intending to capture the thieves as offerings to appease their gods.

Five groups of three **kuo-toa monitors** led by a **kuo-toa whip** patrol the platforms at the water's edge. They ensure no vessel enters or leaves without submitting to "auguries" to determine if a crew's actions are pleasing to the god of the hour—in this case, the Deep Father.

The auguries consist of a half-hour ritual, during which the whip casts bones, shells, and other tokens and reads the resulting omens. Roll a d20. On 1–8, the whip finds the omens favorable; on 9–18, he finds them unfavorable; and on 19–20, the auguries are unclear, and the whip feels the need to consult the archpriest of the Deep Father (area 4).

If the characters met or spoke with the archpriest of the Deep Father before coming here, the whip automatically refuses their request to leave.

3. SHRINE OF THE SEA MOTHER

When the characters arrive here, on their own or escorted, read the following to the players:

A nine-foot-tall statue stands here. Its body is roughly carved from some kind of wood in the shape of a humanoid female, its head and forearms formed from the severed head and claws of a giant albino crayfish. These parts are lashed on with strands of gut, and emit an overpowering stench of rotting shellfish. Shells, brightly colored stones, mushrooms, and rotting fish are piled at the statue's feet and strung in garlands around its neck. Four stern kuo-toa slowly circle the statue, alert and on guard, while a few others mill about, gazing up at the statue and bowing repeatedly while chanting.

All creatures that come here are expected to make an offering to the Great Sea Mother Blibdoolpoolp. A successful DC 13 Intelligence (Religion) check recalls that Blibdoolpoolp is a scavenger goddess, meaning that discarded and recovered items are worthy offerings—and the more personal the better. Regurgitating at the goddess's feet is considered a sincere show of faith (and a behavior faithful kuo-toa might display if the characters wait long enough).

Four **kuo-toa monitors** guard the statue at all times, and there are always 2d4 **kuo-toa** worshipers around it offering prayers. Currently the shrine is tended by Glooglugogg, a **kuo-toa whip** and son of Plooploopeen, the archpriest of the Sea Mother. The guards are wary of anyone, including other kuo-toa, due to recent tensions.

Plooploopeen claims a small hovel adjacent to the shrine, where he is attended by four **kuo-toa**. This is where he brings the characters if they are his "guests."

Treasure

The home of the archpriest contains a closet full of "offerings" taken from less fortunate travelers or culled from the depths of the lake. This includes 500 cp, 2,000 sp, 150 gp, 27 pp, a strand of matched pearls worth 1,000 gp total, two *potions of healing*, a *potion of water breathing*, and a *spell scroll* of *light*.

4. Altar of the Deep Father

When the characters visit the altar of the Deep Father, read the following to the players:

> The idol to Leemooggoogoon the Deep Father consists of a large hide cut roughly in the shape of a manta ray and stretched out on cords between two support poles. A dead, splayed-out manta ray is pinned to the center of the hide. Two dead octopuses are draped across the top, their tentacles pinned and artfully arrayed, their heads tied together and painted with red and blue pigments. The idol reeks of decay, and the broad stone altar below the idol is stained dark with blood.

Six **kuo-toa** work at the altar, cleaning up and arranging offerings. Klibdoloogut, a **kuo-toa whip** dedicated to the Deep Father, stands in front of the altar with two **kuo-toa monitors**. Offerings are usually living creatures killed on the altar, although an offering of one's own blood also satisfies the whip. Humanoids other than kuo-toa are immediately taken into custody to be brought before the archpriest of the Deep Father, who summarily condemns them to be sacrificed.

Bloppblippodd, a female **kuo-toa archpriest** of the Deep Father, lives on the bottom floor of a squat hovel near the altar. She is a bloodthirsty sadist absolutely assured that her divine vision will raise her in glory to rule her people. Bound and gagged against the far wall is a duergar prisoner (see "The Offering").

Treasure

Bloppblippodd's hovel contains wealth accumulated since her rise to power: 1,000 cp, 500 sp, 290 gp, an embroidered silk handkerchief with a spider design worth 25 gp, three azurite gems worth 10 gp each, a duergar-made bronze cup worth 25 gp, and a silver choker with a spider design worth 30 gp.

The Offering

If allowed to do so, Plooploopeen brings the characters to his quarters near the Shrine of the Deep Mother. There they meet Glooglugogg, who loudly tells his father in Undercommon that he sees no need for outsiders to be involved in sacred matters. The archpriest dismisses his son's concerns with a negligent wave, telling Glooglugogg that he must flow with the currents of the goddess's visions. The whip relents but throws the characters a hostile glare.

Within the hour, twelve **kuo-toa** led by a **kuo-toa monitor** arrive at Plooploopeen's quarters. The archpriest of the Sea Mother admits the monitor and informs him that he, his whip, and the prisoners will accompany them to see the archpriest of the Deep Father. They are escorted to the altar of the Deep Father near the docks, where Bloppblippodd awaits them. Describe the scene to the players as given in that area, then read the following boxed text; if none of the characters speak Undercommon, the exchange is gibberish to them, though Shuushar can translate.

The archpriest of the Sea Mother steps forward across the span of the altar toward the kuo-toa waiting for him there. "The time has come," he says, "for us to acknowledge your divine vision and welcome it. I have brought these as offerings." He gestures toward all of you, standing within a circle of guards behind him. "Will you not accept them?"

"You are wise, father," the younger archpriest replies. "I accept your offering in the name of the Deep Father. May their blood nourish and strengthen him!" A burbling cheer goes up from the surrounding kuo-toa, their fists raised in the air.

The followers of the Deep Father are already prepari to sacrifice a bruised and bedraggled **duergar** named Hemeth—an arms smuggler who was looking to cut a deal with one or both factions of the kuo-toa, but inst found himself captured for his trouble. He's willing to cooperate with the characters to save his own skin, a will even return the favor given the opportunity (see chapter 4, "Gracklstugh").

The Ritual

Kuo-toa parade around the altar in a wide circle as they chant. Part of their path sends them splashing and wading through the shallows of the Darklake. T characters quickly can't tell one faction of fish-folk fro the other, but they see the archpriest of the Sea Moth and his whip moving toward the altar.

Bloppblippodd calls for the sacrifices to be brough forth, and one **kuo-toa** per character jumps to do her bidding. They prod the characters with their spears t herd them toward a slight depression 20 feet from th altar, with a large grate at its center. The characters c see that the stonework of the depression is stained w the blood of innumerable sacrifices, and they can hea the gentle lapping of the Darklake coming up throug the grate. The chanting grows louder.

When the sacrifices are brought forward, Bloppblippodd gestures toward the altar, whereupon father suddenly attacks, striking her with his scepter Kuo-toa loyal to him surge forward to attack, while t guards that brought the characters forward stand in shock. They are surprised and can't move or take an action on their first turn of the combat, and they can' take reactions until that first turn ends.

As the two archpriests and their followers fight, th characters can intervene on either side or attempt to away during the melee.

On round 3 of the fight, characters notice kuo-toa crying out and flailing in the shallows of the Darkla Several are pulled under or strike at unseen foes beneath the surface. The water foams red with bloo

Dozens of **ixitxachitl** (see appendix C) are respons for the attacks in the water. They have been drawn by the kuo-toa ritual and feast on any creatures they can reach, including party members in the water. Th sudden frenzy sets a wave of panic through the kuo-t The young archpriest calls out "Leemooggoogoon!" just as her father strikes a final, fatal blow, dropping her before the profane altar. (If any character is also engaging the archpriest of the Deep Father, allow tha character to strike the final blow.)

Demogorgon Rises!

Although Bloppblippodd falls, the ritual still achieve terrible success. Read the following:

> Another sound rises above the burbling cries of the kuo-toa. The dark surface of the water farther out bubbles and begins to foam. A thick, oily tentacle bursts forth, followed by another. Then two monstrous heads break the surface, both resembling hideous, angry baboons with wickedly curved tusks. Both heads are attached to a single torso, and the monster's red eyes burn with bloodlust and madness. The creature rising from the Darklake must stand thirty feet tall or more, with water cascading down its back and shoulders. Upon reaching its full height, the great demon throws back both its heads and roars!

The kuo-toa offerings and the fervor of his worshipers in the Darklake have drawn the attention of Demogorgon (see appendix D). Upon witnessing the rise of the Prince of Demons, each party member must succeed on a DC 13 Charisma saving throw or gain a level of madness (see "Madness" in chapter 2). The kuo-toa become incapacitated for 1d10 minutes, crying out "Leemooggoogoon!" over and over again.

Demogorgon wades toward Sloobludop, heads roaring and gibbering, tentacles flailing and smashing the water. In 4 rounds, he comes within reach of the shoreline and lashes out, smashing docks and sending bodies flying with each sweep of his tentacles. When the demon lord attacks, some kuo-toa recover their wits enough to flee, while others cower, paralyzed with fear.

Escaping the Demon Lord

Hopefully, the players exercise the better part of valor and flee as soon as they see the demon lord. If they confront him, they are almost certainly doomed. Fortunately for them, Demogorgon is focused on smashing the kuo-toa settlement and pays little heed to the puny creatures fleeing from him. The characters thus have a good chance of getting away if they act quickly. They might first need to deal with companions overcome by bouts of madness, however, and they need to decide how they intend to escape.

Escape by Land. Fleeing by land requires dodging terrified kuo-toa, and even fighting fish-folk driven to a killing frenzy against the characters for having drawn this doom down upon them. Roll a d20. On a 17–20, 2d4 **kuo-toa** attack the characters during their escape.

Escape by Water. The adventurers can steal boats from the docks and paddle them along the shore away from the attacking demon lord. The ixitxachitl attack anyone in the water, but most are occupied with slaughtering kuo-toa fleeing into the Darklake. A near miss from one of Demogorgon's tentacles might require each character to make a DC 10 Strength or Dexterity saving throw (player's choice), with failure indicating that the character has been thrown overboard by a wave.

Development

The adventurers end this chapter with a terrible realization: Demogorgon is loose in the Underdark! Initially, they might blame the kuo-toa ritual or the ixitxachitl. But as they learn more about what has happened, the need to escape the Underdark becomes even more urgent.

XP Awards

In addition to the XP awards earned for the creatures the party overcomes in this chapter, the characters earn 400 XP (divided equally among all party members) for surviving the encounter with the Cult of the Deep Father and their brush with the Prince of Demons.

CHAPTER 4: GRACKLSTUGH

Visitors to the duergar city of Gracklstugh are greeted by its hot and acrid air, followed by the angry red glare of the eternally burning smelters fueling the city's metal works, its clanging heart, and the forges kept alive by the flames of Themberchaud, the red dragon that holds the title of Wyrmsmith. Gracklstugh toils endlessly, its smiths churning out the best armor and weapons among the Underdark races. Those who do business here refer to Gracklstugh as "the City of Blades."

As merciless as it can be, Gracklstugh is a major bastion of civilization in the Underdark with active trade routes. For the characters, this means a potential chance to find a way back to the surface world—and just as importantly, to shake off the drow that pursue them. However, the adventurers will quickly realize that the power of the demon lords is a threat even here, getting an even closer glimpse of the Underdark's decay as the madness of the Abyss continues to spread.

Built within the walls of a deep cavern southwest of the Darklake, Gracklstugh is the commercial, political, and spiritual center of the duergar, all of whom look to the Deepking with respect. The city has an open shore

along the Darklake, while several caverns and pas[sages] connect Gracklstugh to other parts of the Underda[rk to] facilitate travel and trade.

The characters have a chance to witness and [help] shape events in the city that point toward the dang[er] Gracklstugh faces—and how unprepared the city [is for] it. But with each moment the characters spend in [the] City of Blades, they run the risk of having escaped [the] drow only to be enslaved by the duergar.

GOING TO GRACKLSTUGH

Despite its dangers, Gracklstugh does have a few [things] to offer ... or at least that's what some of the chara[cters'] fellow escapees tell them.

Buppido (see chapter 1) and Hemeth (see chap[ter] 3) are the only NPCs who actively suggest going [to] Gracklstugh. They know that duergar have no lo[ve for] the drow, and their draconian laws keep all foreig[ners] in check, which should provide some measure of [safe] sanctuary from drow pursuit. Gracklstugh is as g[ood] a place as any in the Underdark to sell stolen gea[r.]

buy more useful equipment. Additionally, the duergar trade actively with other subterranean and surface-dwelling races. Gracklstugh's Blade Bazaar might be the ideal place to find traders or explorers heading to the surface world.

If Buppido or Hemeth isn't with the party, others can provide the above information. Sarith resists plans to travel to the city at first, conscious of the low regard the duergar have for drow. He changes his mind quickly, however, as Zuggtmoy's spores drive him to seek a densely populated area where he can spread his contagion.

It's also possible the party arrives at Gracklstugh involuntarily. Duergar slavers scour the Underdark in search of new "merchandise," and they might deceive or outright capture the characters and bring them to their city's slave markets. The random encounters in chapters 2 and 3 can easily set up this scenario.

GRACKLSTUGH AND DROW PURSUIT

Taking refuge in Gracklstugh has its advantages. Each day they spend in the duergar capital, the characters can attempt a DC 16 group Dexterity (Stealth) check to move around cautiously, with success indicating that they avoid drawing attention to themselves. The characters can also attempt a DC 13 group Wisdom (Insight) check to assess the mood in the city, with success allowing them to avoid trouble before it starts. Characters who lie low for the day have advantage on this Wisdom check.

Success with either check reduces the party's pursuit level by 1 (see "Drow Pursuit" in chapter 2).

ARRIVING IN GRACKLSTUGH

The Darklake District is a likely entry point to the city for the characters, whether they arrive via the water or travel one of the many tunnels leading to the district's gates. Non-duergar arriving from tunnels that lead to other districts are stopped and escorted to the Darklake District under heavy guard, as every other district is normally off limits to outsiders, and trespassers risk being confronted by an invisible patrol of four **duergar**.

The party's fellow escapees know that trying to enter through the main entrances is a sure way to get enslaved, unless one of the characters is an epic liar who can convince the guards the party is a legitimate diplomatic or trade delegation. Anyone with a merchant or criminal background has heard rumors that the Zhentarim trade in the Underdark, but posing as Zhentarim has its own risks, as such claims are bound to be questioned. A character who is actually a member of the Zhentarim can buy the adventurers a couple of days inside the city before the duergar slavers start taking their measure.

Arriving by way of the Darklake Docks is easier and more discreet. If the characters are traveling by boat, Buppido can guide them to a deserted pier where they can dock quietly. He warns them that they have to keep a low profile and head directly to the only inn in the city devoted to outsiders. The Ghohlbrorn's Lair is frequented by merchants, mercenaries, and other foreigners who can offer information about traveling

Sweltering heat and cloying smoke cling to every corner of the duergar city, spewing from smelters housed inside massive stalagmites and stalactites. These protrude from the cavern's floor and ceiling like the teeth of some great maw.

Light. Gracklstugh's glowing forges and smithies operate continuously. Most of the city is dimly lit by a hellish red glow, with patches of darkness here and there.

Noise. The clanging and clacking of hammers and machinery echoes constantly throughout the city. Wisdom (Perception) checks made to listen in Gracklstugh have disadvantage.

Smoke and Haze. Despite vents dug into the walls and ceiling of the city's great cavern, fumes from smelters and forges linger at ground level (as does the gas tapped in Laduguer's Furrow). Visitors might contract the illness known as grackle-lung (see the Grackle-lung sidebar).

elsewhere in the Underdark—or perhaps even to the surface world.

RANDOM ENCOUNTERS

With routine patrols of heavily armed gray dwarves who can turn invisible, Gracklstugh is a relatively safe place for those who know where they belong and stay there. However, tensions are rising because of the influence of Demogorgon, and the characters have many opportunities to participate in events unfolding in the city. At the end of each long rest, roll a d20; on a roll of 17–20, an encounter takes place. Roll another d20 and consult the Random Encounters in Gracklstugh table; if the characters are outside the Darklake District, treat any entry marked with an asterisk as a "Duergar Patrol" encounter instead.

RANDOM ENCOUNTERS IN GRACKLSTUGH

d20	Encounter
1–2	Abusive duergar guards
3–4	Deep gnome merchant*
5–7	Derro rioters*
8–9	Drow emissary*
10–12	Duergar patrol
13–14	Mad duergar
15–16	Orc mercenaries*
17–18	Slave caravan
19	Steeder handlers
20	Themberchaud

ABUSIVE DUERGAR GUARDS

The characters come upon two **duergar** guards beating a duergar merchant and shouting accusations of heresy. Any Underdark native accompanying the party urges the characters not to intervene on the merchant's behalf, telling them this isn't their business and warning them that any interference might get them arrested or killed. Bystanders look a little surprised or concerned but don't intervene, not even to aid the unconscious merchant once the guards leave.

If the characters investigate the circumstances leading to the assault, bystanders tell them that one of the guards noticed a golden pin the merchant was wearing inside his collar. Though adornment for adornment's sake is something duergar society frowns upon, the guards' violent response was unnatural—a hint of the growing madness festering inside the City of Blades.

Deep Gnome Merchant

A female **deep gnome** named Ariana and her **earth elemental** bodyguard approach the party. Ariana aims to deliver a cargo of gemstones, but she can't find the duergar merchant she's supposed to meet. She assumes the characters are smugglers and tries to unload her goods: ten sparkly garnets worth 100 gp each. Ariana keeps the gems in a *bag of holding*, which isn't for sale.

The merchant whom Ariana is looking for was recently arrested and executed for selling stolen jewelry. You can decide whether Ariana's interest in the characters attracts the attention of a duergar patrol.

Subsequent occurrences of this encounter are with other deep gnome merchants who ignore the characters unless approached. They carry nothing of value.

Derro Rioters

A mob of **derro** (see appendix C) rampages through the streets. Five of them detach from the mob to attack the characters. Four duergar patrols (see "Duergar Patrol") arrive when the characters kill the last derro, but they simply nod at the characters before repressing the rest of the mob. Word quickly spreads that the characters helped the city guard control the unruly derro scum. At your discretion, give the characters advantage on checks

---

Roleplaying the Duergar and Derro

The gray dwarves are dour, joyless, and all business. They live by a simple but exacting code of law, honor, hard work, and seeing all non-duergar as lesser creatures. Duergar are ruthless but not unnecessarily cruel, and pragmatism drives their every decision. Though they treat the adventurers with contempt, their first thought is to enslave them or use them rather than kill them.

The duergar of Gracklstugh are beginning to suffer the effects of the arrival of the demon lords—and specifically the influence of Demogorgon. Many are developing tics, habits, and behaviors that fly against their core beliefs, including guards flaunting their corrupt behavior, the use of adornment for adornment's sake, and disloyalty to their clans. Of late, the folk of Gracklstugh have become increasingly more violent, abandoning their characteristic cunning and stoic pragmatism for wanton malice and petty displays of self-entitlement.

Unlike the disciplined duergar, the derro are sloppy, erratic, and utterly insane. Their temperament is fickle, and their speech hard to follow. The one guaranteed emotion they have when interacting with others is seething hatred, and they make no effort to hide it. Their eyes are shifty, their teeth grind, and they look as though they would rather be somewhere else. They hate everyone and everything, but surface-dwellers are particular targets of their loathing.

Their inherent insanity means that the derro suffer no ill effect from the demon lords' presence, their minds already too volatile and mercurial.

---

made to interact with any duergar in the city until s time as the benefit no longer seems appropriate.

Drow Emissary

A **drow** proudly wearing the insignia of a drow hou travels with an entourage of 1d4 + 1 **quaggoth** slav The drow is in Gracklstugh to retrieve a cargo of duergar metalwork and knows nothing about the r events in Velkynvelve. Roll a d6 and consult the Dr House Loyalty table to determine the house to whi drow is affiliated.

Drow House Loyalty

d6	House
1–2	House Baenre
3–4	House Faen Tlabbar
5–6	House Xorlarrin

House Faen Tlabbar and House Mizzrym are bitt rivals. If the drow emissary belongs to House Fae Tlabbar and the characters divulge that they are enemies or former prisoners of House Mizzrym, t drow warns the party about Xalith (see "Signs of Pursuit" later in the chapter).

House Baenre and House Xorlarrin are current of House Mizzrym. A drow emissary allied with H Mizzrym who knows that the characters are esca prisoners from Velkynvelve seeks out Xalith and v her that the characters are in Gracklstugh.

Duergar Patrol

A patrol consists of 1d4 + 2 **duergar**, all but two o whom are invisible. Invisible duergar can sneak u a character by making a Dexterity (Stealth) check advantage, contested by the character's passive W (Perception) score.

Mad Duergar

The characters encounter a **duergar** afflicted wit form of indefinite madness. Roll a d10 and consu the Mad Duergar table to determine what the par encounters.

Mad Duergar

d10	NPC
1–2	A merchant desperate to sell his wares, conv that his life depends on it.
3–4	A street sweeper who hounds the characters accusing them of being spies working for th
5–6	A cloaked guard who thinks he's Deepking H Steelshadow V drafts the party to help him s Themberchaud, convinced that the dragon i possessed by a demon lord.
7–8	A merchant who accuses the characters of t calls out for a duergar patrol to arrest them.
9–10	A weaponsmith convinced that one of the characters is a long-lost member of her clar who insists on giving the party food and she

Orc Mercenaries

These 1d4 + 1 **orcs** have come to Gracklstugh as caravan guards, and see the characters as a chance to bully some surface dwellers. The orcs try to goad the characters into striking first, then quickly stand down, knowing that a patrol (see "Duergar Patrol") will arrive 1d6 rounds after combat starts.

Slave Caravan

The characters come across a group of 1d4 + 1 **duergar** slavers herding unarmed slaves (roll a d12 and consult the Slaves table). The slaves wear iron collars and manacles similar to the ones worn by the characters in Velkynvelve (see "Restraints" in chapter 1).

Slaves

d12	Slaves
1–2	2d4 human **commoners**
3–4	3d4 shield dwarf **commoners**
5–6	2d4 strongheart halfling **commoners**
7–8	3d6 **goblins**
9–10	2d6 **grimlocks**
11–12	3d6 **kobolds**

Steeder Handlers

A group of 1d4 + 1 **duergar** teamsters herd a clutch of 2d6 **male steeders** (see appendix C). There is a 50 percent chance that 1d4 of the steeders attack nearby characters or bystanders. The duergar keep the rest of the clutch in check, but they clamor for the characters' arrest if even one of the arachnids is killed. A nearby patrol (see "Duergar Patrol") hears the teamsters' clamor and arrives 1d6 rounds later.

Secrets of Gracklstugh

Wary outsiders visiting Gracklstugh quickly learn the most important details of life in the city.

Unseen Sentries. The duergar power of invisibility plays a significant role in their society. The potential presence of unseen spies everywhere enforces honesty among duergar. Slaves rarely, if ever, talk or act against their masters, never knowing who might be watching.

A City Divided. Not only is the layout of Gracklstugh divided, so are its people. Nearly five hundred years ago, the derro launched a Uniting War against the Deepkingdom, but were swiftly crushed, and the survivors brought back to Gracklstugh in chains. Though their status as slaves was eventually set aside, the derro have always been second-class citizens, living in squalor and scrounging food and resources, even as their leaders on the Council of Savants live in secret opulence.

Frugal and Monolithic. The gray dwarves value efficiency, stoicism, and hard work, and these values are exemplified in their capital. Everything the duergar make or build has a purpose and function; the only aesthetic they value in architecture is imposing vastness, and even that is secondary to a building's structural function. The only ornamentations found in Gracklstugh are iconic representations of rank and function within duergar society, and the only music is the ceaseless rhythmic hammering in the forges. The duergar consider art a frivolous pursuit, and only rarely appreciate or create it.

Themberchaud

The **adult red dragon** is out on his regular rounds, keeping the city's forges aflame. Themberchaud has long been keeping his eye out for mercenaries in the city that could be bent to his service. If he spots the characters, he might take an interest in them. See "Themberchaud's Lair" for information on the Wyrmsmith's motivations and possible setups for an additional encounter with the red dragon.

Important NPCs

The characters might encounter one or more of the following NPCs during their stay in Gracklstugh.

Gracklstugh NPCs

Gorglak	Corrupt male duergar on duty at the gate where the characters first arrive in Gracklstugh
Xalith	Female drow scout charged with recapturing the characters for Ilvara
Errde Blackskull	Female duergar captain of the Stone Guard with a side quest for the party
Themberchaud	The city's Wyrmsmith, an adult red dragon with a possible mission for the party
Gartokkar Xundorn	Male duergar Keeper of the Flame with a side quest for the party
Ylsa Henstak	Female duergar merchant with a side quest for the party
Droki	Male derro courier in the employ of both the Gray Ghosts and the Council of Savants, and the subject of different possible side quests
Werz Saltbaron	Male duergar merchant with a mission for the party
Stonespeaker Hgraam	Male stone giant leader with a side quest for the party
Narrak	Male derro savant, junior member of the Council of Savants and leader of a cult dedicated to Demogorgon

Factions of Gracklstugh

The Deepkingdom is a feudal state with the Deepking as the absolute monarch, who passes the crown to descendants or relatives in his Steelshadow clan. Each clan is led by a *laird*, who rules over his or her own holdings and directs the clan in dedicating its efforts toward a particular trade or craft. A caste of priests called *thuldar* officiate all rituals and record the Deepkingdom's lore. However, ultimate political and religious power is held by the Deepking and the lairds.

Deepking Horgar Steelshadow V

Deepking Horgar V ascended to the throne in 1372 DR. He is a ruthless and canny ruler who engages in secret meetings with all the city's councils and clans to keep their members guessing what he's up to, hands out favors out of the blue, and lets it be known that he'll use any trick to maintain his hold on power. This includes hiring assassins through third parties to take care of potential troublemakers (see "Empty-Scabbard Killers," below). This strategy keeps all the city's factions at each other's throats and out of Horgar's way.

COUNCIL OF LAIRDS

This advisory body represents the interests of the different clans that have pledged allegiance to the Deepking. The lairds hold council to resolve disputes and discuss future plans. Each clan has its own holdings in Gracklstugh and specializes in a certain craft or service.

DUERGAR CLANS

Smithing	Clan Steelshadow (weaponsmiths), Clan Ironhead (weaponsmiths), Clan Thrazgad (armorsmiths), Clan Firehand (smelters), Clan Anvilthew (toolmakers)
Mercantile	Clan Thuldark (metalworks and jewels), Clan Henstak (food), Clan Muzgardt (brewers)
Mining	Clan Coalhewer (coal miners), Clan Xardelvar (gas miners), Clan Saltbaron (salt miners)
Other	Clan Parlynsurk (clothing manufacturers), Clan Hammercane (construction engineers), Clan Xundom (steeder breeders), Clan Burakrinwurn (dock operators), Clan Xornbane (scouts and prospectors), Clan Blackskull (stonemasons), Clan Bukbukken (farming), Clan Thordensonn (jewelers)

DUERGAR

COUNCIL OF SAVANTS

The Council of Savants is a circle of derro savants enjoy all the privileges and trappings of a governing body while the rest of their people live in squalor. O the best thirty-six savants are admitted into the cou and succession almost always includes an incumbe member's demise. The savants control members of some duergar clans through magic and guile, and a always looking for ways to expand their influence.

MERCHANT COUNCIL

The lairds and merchants who sit at this council m sure that trade and commerce flow smoothly. They employ slave labor to maintain trade routes in the dangerous Underdark, and are always open to hiri explorers to check out leads on potential new route Expendable outsiders hired as caravan guards alw take point and receive little aid or support from the caravan masters. Despite these unfair assignment the duergar always live up to their bargains, paying survivors as promised.

GRACKLSTUGH MILITARY

In addition to the clans' regular armies, Gracklstug trains specialized warriors whose oaths of service always supersede their original loyalties. See appe C for more information.

Stone Guard. This force of five hundred veteran warriors serves the Deepking as bodyguards, elite troops, and secret police.

Darkhafts. Members of the Deepking's secret c of psionic agents, the darkhafts often travel with d merchants as overseers and spies.

Kavalrachni. The vicious kavalrachni ride giant tarantulas known as steeders (see appendix C). M kavalrachni come from Clan Xundom.

Xarrorn. These specialists train with deadly fla lances forged in Gracklstugh. Most xarrorn come Clan Xardelvar.

GRACKLE-LUNG

The constant smog in Gracklstugh causes grackle-lung in living, breathing creatures, resulting in persistent, wracking coughs and the spewing of thick, black phleg Whenever a living, breathing creature finishes a long r in Gracklstugh, it must make a DC 11 Constitution sav throw. On each failed save, the creature gains one leve exhaustion as its airways become increasingly clogged creature that reaches level 6 exhaustion dies, as norm

A creature with one or more levels of exhaustion bro on by grackle-lung must succeed on a Constitution ch to take the Dash action. If the check fails, the action cannot be attempted. If the creature attempts to cast a spell with a verbal component, it must succeed on a Constitution check or be unable to complete the spell causing the spell to fail with no effect. The DC for each check is 10 + the creature's current exhaustion level.

If a creature's exhaustion level drops below 1, it no longer suffers the effects of grackle-lung and becomes immune to it for the next week. Duergar and derro are inured to grackle-lung, making Constitution checks ag it with advantage. Any spell or effect that cures diseas also cures grackle-lung, effectively removing all levels exhaustion brought on by the affliction.

Despite reports that the darkhafts and the Stone Guards have received about the growing crisis outside the city's walls, hubris and the onset of madness prevents them from mounting any sort of response or campaign, blind to the corruption that festers around them.

Clan Cairngorm

The stone giants of Clan Cairngorm lead quiet lives of art and contemplation in Gracklstugh. Although reclusive and averse to conflict, the giants have sworn an ancient oath of loyalty to the Deepking, and have been serving his line for as long as any can remember. This oath, however, was given only to the Steelshadow clan. If the throne passes to another dynasty, the stone giants will cease to be the city's allies.

The leader of the stone giants is Stonespeaker Hgraam, a priest of Skoraeus Stonebones, the god of his people. Hgraam is wise and knowledgeable. He has sensed that some great evil has broken into the Underdark, but isn't aware of the threat's danger or extent. The giants will rise to defend Gracklstugh if any demons dare to invade, but they are unaware of the danger creeping into the city from within.

Keepers of the Flame

This order of psionic clerics tends to Themberchaud's needs, enjoying great influence and helping Horgar V stay ahead of the machinations of the Council of Savants.

The Keepers of the Flame are currently distracted by their ongoing vendetta against the Gray Ghosts, who recently stole a valuable dragon egg that would have hatched Themberchaud's eventual successor. Complicating matters, Themberchaud himself is growing stronger and more resistant to the clerics' coaxing, appeasement, and psionic manipulation.

Themberchaud the Wyrmsmith

This adult red dragon keeps the city's smelters and forges ablaze, receiving treasure, free meals, and constant pampering in exchange. Themberchaud doesn't know that, like other Wyrmsmiths before him, he is doomed to be slain before he grows too strong, replaced by a new red hatchling. However, the line of succession was interrupted when the Gray Ghosts stole a red dragon egg from the Keepers of the Flame.

The Wyrmsmith is beginning to chafe under the Keepers' control. He now wonders why he is content with a mere trickle of gold and a paltry handful of slaves, when he could simply force the entire city to bend knee to him and give him everything he desires. For now, his actions are limited by how little he cares about the duergar and how much the Keepers speak "on his behalf." But he has begun taking an interest in the affairs of Gracklstugh and the opportunity to recruit new servants from outside the Keepers of the Flame, using his outings to rekindle forges and smelters as a means to keep an eye out for promising subjects.

Gray Ghosts

The Gray Ghosts are the only true thieves' guild in Gracklstugh and the Deepkingdom. Its members are duergar and derro outcasts, plus the odd escaped slave.

The Keepers of the Flame caught and executed the Gray Ghosts' previous leader, who stole their red dragon egg but never revealed its whereabouts. The relentless vendetta forced the thieves into hiding and restricted their activities, but they persevere thanks to the three renegade derro savants who are their current leaders: Uskvil and the twin sisters Aliinka and Zubriska.

Empty-Scabbard Killers

The *Forak-Erach-Naek* ("Empty-Scabbard Killers" in Common) are a folktale in Gracklstugh, their name derived from an ancient, obscure Dwarvish dialect. They are an order of psionic assassins practicing disciplines unknown to even the savviest derro or the wisest priest. More than a myth, these killers have been plying their trade for centuries, their motives unknown and their methods inscrutable.

The Empty-Scabbard Killers are **duergar soulblades** (see appendix C) who roam the streets of Gracklstugh searching for psionically gifted children to abduct and train. They also keep an eye out for worthy *calassabrak* (see below), offering them a chance to join a new community from which they can strike back at those who cast them out.

Life in the City of Blades

The duergar are called gray dwarves not only because of the color of their skin, but also because of their drab and joyless lifestyle. While they make no time for merriment, the duergar have a culture as rich and complex as any other, and nowhere is this so evident as in Gracklstugh.

Work never stops in the City of Blades, and the gray dwarves take pride in efficiency and perfection even as they abhor waste and carelessness. They are merciless masters to the derro and slaves who toil and suffer under them.

Strict Hierarchy

By appearance and bearing, all duergar know their place and where they belong. Whether as individuals, families, or entire clans, duergar below other duergar in the social order don't seek to bring their rivals down through intrigue and deceit. Rather, they roll up their sleeves and work harder to increase their prestige through the fruits of their labor.

All the honor and honesty the duergar apply among themselves doesn't apply to outsiders. The gray dwarves constantly try to manipulate contracts to take advantage of foreign merchants, looking for any excuse to enslave random visitors who appear weak or vulnerable— including adventurers.

Though they aren't moved by vanity, duergar are extremely proud of their work, and praising the quality of duergar crafting can sometimes help outsiders in their dealings with the gray dwarves.

Subsistence

Duergar clans use caverns under Gracklstugh and choice outlying caves to farm a variety of plants and fungi. These crops are complemented by meat from Underdark beasts and fish from the Darklake. Not even the duergar risk drinking water from the Darklake, however, and with clean streams in short supply, the people of Gracklstugh cover this scarcity with Darklake Stout, the signature ale brewed by the Muzgardt clan.

Outcasts

The bottom rung in Gracklstugh society is mostly occupied by the underclass of the derro. Enslaved by the duergar centuries ago, then freed, the derro aren't allowed to hold honest jobs, and their rights are hardly ever recognized by the duergar. Even slaves are held in higher regard. Derro scuttle about like vermin and are mostly confined to hovels built along the walls of Laduguer's Furrow in the West Cleft District and East Cleft District.

Another kind of outcasts are those duergar who dishonor their clans so grievously they are stripped of all but their lives: the *calassabrak*, meaning "the flawed who aren't to be trusted" in Dwarvish. They are shunned by other duergar, many eventually taking their lives rather than face an existence apart from family and clan. Those who live on become bitter and tough, with many leaving Gracklstugh as hermits or adventurers, or turning to crime and a life in the shadows. Members of both the Gray Ghosts and the Empty-Scabbard Killers include a significant number of calassabrak, no longer bound by oath, honor, and duty.

Religion

Duergar don't pray, but their religion is tightly woven into their everyday life. Deities worshiped in Gracklstugh include the following.

Laduguer. The patron of the duergar is a god of self-reliance, defense, and survival. His clerics have access to the War domain.

Deep Duerra. Laduguer's mortal daughter who then ascended, Deep Duerra is the goddess of cooperation and dominance. War is her domain as well.

Diirinka. The patron of the derro betrayed his twin brother Diinkarazan to escape with the secrets of magic. He embodies cruelty, insanity, and cleverness. His clerics have access to the Trickery domain.

Skoraeus Stonebones. Stone giants revere the King of the Rock, god of buried things, whose clerics can access the Knowledge and Life domains. Stonespe[...] Hgraam, a powerful spellcaster, is Skoraeus's only [...] priest in Gracklstugh.

Law and Order

Minor crime is relatively rare in Gracklstugh. The [...] duergar live by a strict code of honor, and their law[...] are few, simple, and practical. Both guards and re[...] citizens can be invisible and watching, which keep[...] any potential criminals and dissenters uncertain a[...] fearful. A laird may punish any member of his or h[...] clan who commits a crime, but offenses between c[...] are immediately brought before the Council of Lai[...] which resolves matters swiftly and harshly. The c[...] of punishment is simple. Because dishonor, mutila[...] and imprisonment are a waste of resources and c[...] weakness in society, a duergar who intentionally [...] commits any crime receives a death sentence. Accidental crime by a duergar is compensated by [...] or work equivalent to the damages. Derro, slaves [...] outsiders caught committing any crime can be ex[...] on the spot by any duergar present.

Gracklstugh

Population: 10,000 duergar, 2,000 derro, 50 sto[...] giants, and an unknown number of slaves (quag[...] grimlocks, orcs, shield dwarves, svirfneblin, an[...] kobolds and goblinoids)

Government: Absolute monarchy

Defense: Large standing army with specialized c[...] every duergar is trained for battle, and the citiz[...] the city create a formidable militia

Commerce: Weapons and armor of high quality; [...] fungi, molds, and exotic creatures for food; trac[...] across the Underdark and the surface world

Organizations: The Council of Lairds, the Coun[...] Savants, the Merchant Council, the Keepers of [...] Flame, Clan Cairngorm, the Gray Ghosts, and [...]

The cavern housing Gracklstugh is split in two b[...] rift called Laduguer's Furrow, after the duergar [...] god. The north half comprises Northfurrow Dist[...] where common workers and the clans devoted to [...] crafts make their home, and Darklake District, o[...] to foreigners and where the city's merchants eng[...] in trade with visitors. As befits a major settlemer[...] dangerous realm, Gracklstugh places no restrict[...] the weapons or gear characters can carry or trac[...]

Twelve stone bridges lead to Southfurrow Dist[...] and then farther south to Flowstone District. The[...] boroughs are reserved for the more prestigious c[...] and the largest smelters and forges Thembercha[...] ignites during his flights. The Wyrmsmith's lair a[...] cavern complex the stone giants of Cairngorm C[...] home both connect to these districts.

Welcome to the City of Blades

Entering the city is the first major hurdle the characters must surmount in Gracklstugh. Unless they heed Buppido's advice to arrive by way of the Darklake (or come up with the idea on their own), the characters reach one of the gates. (See "Arriving in Gracklstugh" earlier in this chapter.)

City Gates

The pragmatic nature of the duergar means that all Gracklstugh's entrance gates are similar in design, for ease of maintenance and the training of guards.

> The ground at your feet has been getting smoother and flatter, a welcome respite from the uneven passages to which you have grown wearily accustomed. Eventually, stone tiles become more noticeable, turning the path into a proper road. You can see spots of light in the distance, blue-white and too regularly placed to be phosphorescent mushrooms.
>
> The lights are proper lamps flanking two massive stone gates blocking the tunnel. Before you get a chance to examine the intricate carvings on the gates' surface, a harsh voice hisses from a slit on the cavern wall that was not there before.

> "State your names and business!" the voice orders in Dwarvish. Other similar slits open, revealing the tips of a dozen crossbow bolts. Behind you, a metallic din announces a group of six heavily armored dwarves appearing out of thin air, their swords leveled at you from behind sturdy metal shields.

When the characters first reached the road, six **duergar** watching invisibly started following them at a safe distance. Twelve more **duergar** soldiers are stationed in guardhouses concealed within the rocky walls of the cavern, all of them aiming heavy crossbows at the party.

The duergar are hostile, and the guard who spoke follows up on every answer the characters give. One character can take the lead in the interrogation by speaking for the party and making a DC 15 Charisma check (Deception and Persuasion apply; Intimidation or Performance are met with scorn). Depending on how believable the party's story is and how the other adventurers behave during the questioning, you might allow the character to make the check with advantage or impose disadvantage.

The guard grudgingly lets the characters pass if the check succeeds, and refuses them entrance if it fails. If the check fails by 5 or more, the guard gives the order to arrest the characters, announcing that they are now slaves of the duergar (see "Getting Captured" below).

The first time the characters are allowed inside the city or turned away from a gate, a secret door on the wall opens, revealing Gorglak, a **duergar Stone Guard** (see appendix C).

> "Well." The duergar removes his helmet, revealing the gray skin of his kind. He musses his white beard as he walks closer, switching to Common as he lowers his voice. There is a discomfiting glint in his eyes and his smile. "You are clearly lying. I ought to just send you to the slave pens, but ... you amuse me. What do you have that is worth your freedom?"
>
> The duergar waits for your answer, his gaze touching on each of you in turn as he smiles in anticipation.

If they are with the party, Topsy and Turvy, Sarith Kzekarit, Jimjar, and Buppido can whisper to the characters that few duergar are so blatantly corrupt as Gorglak seems to be. A successful DC 12 Wisdom (Insight) check lets a character notice that Gorglak is eying the adventurers' weapons (especially any drow

weapons or magic weapons they might have), an[d] there's something odd about his behavior. The n[...] creeping into Gracklstugh has made Gorglak ob[...] with rare weapons. He's willing to go to great ex[...] acquire new weapons of exquisite design for his [...] collection.

Offering Gorglak a worthy weapon for his coll[...] gets the characters through the gate. Any other [...] requires one of the characters to succeed on a D[...] Charisma (Persuasion) check, or Gorglak is ins[...] and has the party arrested. If the characters are [...] open about the negotiation, Gorglak has them a[...] and pretends he didn't say anything.

If Gorglak finds the characters' bribe appeali[ng, ...] refuses to accept it then and there, instead dire[...] them to find one Werz Saltbaron in the Darklak[...] and hand the bribe to him. Gorglak tells the cha[...] that he will check with Werz at the end of his sh[...] will find the characters and arrest them if they [...] paid by then.

Characters allowed through the gate are esco[...] the Darklake District by four **duergar** guards, [...] whom are invisible. Once the party reaches the [...] the district, the guards leave and return to the [...]

DARKLAKE DOCKS

Arriving at the Darklake Docks requires a combination of skill, ingenuity, and luck. Vigilance is a little more relaxed here because the guards at Overlake Hold can spot any obvious threat coming from the waters.

> After hours of tense navigation, you glimpse an orange glow in the distance. Soon you hear faint metallic echoes, growing louder as you come closer.
>
> Firelight illuminates massive columns with structures built around their bases. The cold air of the Underdark is becoming warmer even at this distance, and you can now see a variety of piers made from zurkhwood, stone, and plain rock jutting out along the edge of a huge cavern.

As the characters draw closer, they can see that the eastern docks are the least crowded. If Buppido is with them, he guides them to a natural rock pier on the eastern edge of the cavern. Otherwise, the characters must make a successful DC 14 group Dexterity (Stealth) check or a DC 15 group Wisdom (Survival) check to guide their boat safely and inconspicuously to an empty dock. If the group check fails, nearby guards notice the characters but don't immediately identify them as a threat. However, you can choose to impose disadvantage on any checks the characters make to remain inconspicuous during their first day in Gracklstugh.

GETTING CAPTURED

Even after making it inside the city, the characters must tread carefully, as the duergar use the slightest pretext to arrest them. Even trying to haggle with a duergar merchant might inspire a call for the guards to take the characters away. Getting caught stealing is punishable by death on the spot, but guards or the offended party might see some value in enslaving the culprits instead, so the characters can be shackled and shipped beyond the Darklake District. Resisting arrest is a truly bad idea; every duergar around is reinforcement.

If the characters get arrested, you can interrupt their transfer with a random encounter or lead them to other planned encounters. The "Rampaging Giant" encounter (which takes place in the Darklake District) is the most likely event to interrupt a prisoner transfer. Alternatively, an agent of the Keepers of the Flame can stop the guards before they take the characters to Overlake Hold (see "Themberchaud's Lair" for information regarding the keepers' interest in foreign mercenaries).

Possible offers of employment in the Blade Bazaar can also be turned into timely rescues for the adventurers. Otherwise, they end up in Overlake Hold, interrogated by Errde Blackskull.

DARKLAKE DISTRICT

The Darklake District gives an illusion of openness. The streets are relatively wide to allow for merchant carts and wagons to pass, and the buildings aren't as crowded around stalagmites as in the southern districts. Openness doesn't mean welcoming, however. The duergar who ply their trades here are wary of all the foreigners confined by law to this part of the city.

> A wave of heat slams against you as an acrid smog rises to choke the air out of your lungs. The Darklake spreads out beyond a jumble of buildings and streets, reflecting the lights of countless fires burning across the city within hollowed-out columns and stalagmites.
>
> Though the streets are crowded, you move easily within the surging throng of buyers, merchants, and slaves. You aren't the only outsiders here, as you spy drow, svirfneblin, derro, orcs, and other races in the crowds. The shouting of people blends with the sound of distant hammering to create a constant, distracting din.

Behind the forbidding walls separating the Darklake District from the rest of the city stand the docks, markets, and shops where Gracklstugh's commerce and trade are conducted. The many duergar merchants—along with drow, svirfneblin, orcs, and others—pay little attention to the characters unless they are looking to do business.

Guards posted at the gates make it clear to the characters that non-duergar are restricted to the Darklake District, and the characters have better luck asking other outsiders for directions rather than trying to engage the duergar locals. They are directed to the Blade Bazaar if they wish to sell anything they might be carrying with them. For gossip and a meal, the Shattered Spire tavern is recommended, while lodging for non-duergar can be had at the Ghohlbrorn's Lair inn.

At any point during which the characters move from point to point in the Darklake District, they can witness one or more of the following events.

RAMPAGING GIANT

This encounter triggers possible side quests through which the characters can learn about the influence of Demogorgon in Gracklstugh. You can use this event any time during the party's stay in the city. Holding it for later use gives characters a chance to notice the little things wrong among the duergar, while using it right away can help characters avoid being enslaved if they are arrested at any point during their visit.

> The rhythmic hammering of the city's forges is drowned for a second by a thundering roar and the sound of crumbling rock. Duergar and visitors alike turn to look as a two-headed, gray-skinned giant bursts through a gate, howling madly and lashing out left and right, littering the plaza with rock and stone debris. As he bellows, one of his swings connects with a duergar soldier, whose broken body flies through the air and crashes near you with a sickening crunch.

A stone giant from Cairngorm Cavern has succumbed to a demonic curse that has caused him to grow a disfigured second head. A successful DC 12 Wisdom (Insight) check reveals that the giant is crazed and terrified. Use the **stone giant** stat block with the following modifications:

- The giant has advantage on Wisdom (Perception) checks and on saving throws against being blinded, charmed, deafened, frightened, stunned, or knocked unconscious.
- The giant is unarmed. As an action, it can make two unarmed strikes (+9 to hit, reach 10 ft., one target). On a hit, the giant deals 13 (2d6 + 6) bludgeoning damage.

The rampage happens in a broad plaza, so there is plenty of space for the different combatants to maneuver.

The giant moves in the characters' direction and lashes out. Two **duergar** guards and two **duergar xarrorn** (see appendix C) respond to the giant's roaring, racing in to join the fight in the second round. They are well trained and do their best to help, but to avoid additional complexity during the encounter, assume that the duergar act at the end of the initiative order and deal a flat total of 10 damage to the giant each round.

Bystanders take cover at once, but **duergar** citizens are ready to jump in if the guards fail to contain the threat. The giant ignores characters attacking from range and attacks opponents in melee at random, including the duergar. Both the giant and the guards fight until they drop to 0 hit points.

DEVELOPMENT

Without the characters' help, the guards and assisting citizens bring down the stone giant with few casualties. If the characters are prisoners under escort when the giant attacks, the guards who engage the giant are their escort. The characters can use this chance to escape, or they can help, albeit with disadvantage on attack rolls if they are shackled. The duergar are pragmatists and release characters who help them deal with the giant's threat, but they attempt to arrest them again after the combat is over.

Once the crazed giant is put down, another stone giant comes through the shattered gate, but this one looks perfectly sane. He reaches the fallen giant at the same time as a squad of three **duergar Stone Guards** (see appendix C).

The guards who fought alongside the characters explain the situation, neither downplaying nor exalting the characters' actions. The characters can speak to the newly arrived giant while the duergar confer. The giant introduces himself as Dorhun, apprentice to Stonespeaker Hgraam. He reveals that the fallen giant's name is Rihuud, and that he was another of the Stonespeaker's apprentices. Rihuud was "communing with the stone" in Cairngorm Cavern when he went mad, sprouted a second head, and stormed out.

If the party was not previously arrested and didn't participate in the fight, the Stone Guards start questioning bystanders, who eventually point out the characters as new arrivals to the city.

If the characters knocked Rihuud unconscious in[stead] of dealing a lethal blow, a grateful Dorhun asks the[m] to visit Cairngorm Cavern before they leave the city [and] informing the Stone Guards of this. The importance of the Stonespeaker means that the Stone Guards [will] escort the party across the city to meet with him, t[hough] they don't hide their displeasure at doing so.

XP AWARDS

Divide 1,740 XP equally among the characters if th[ey] cooperate with the guards to defeat the two-heade[d] stone giant.

GUESTS OF THE STONE GUARD

Whenever circumstances see the Stone Guards de[velop] an interest in the party (including being arrested [or] witnessing the giant's rampage without taking pa[rt), the] characters are ordered to follow a squad of duerga[r to] Overlake Hold for further questioning.

From this point, the adventure can take differen[t turns] depending on how you want to proceed. Talk to th[e] players about their preference, or decide on your o[wn] what happens next:

- Gartokkar Xundorn intervenes on behalf of the Keepers of the Flame, which can lead to a meet[ing] with Themberchaud (see "Themberchaud's Lai[r").
- The characters can continue to Overlake Hold and meet with Captain Errde Blackskull (see "Overlake Hold").
- The drow scout Xalith approaches the Stone G[uard,] claiming the characters as escaped property of [her] mistress, Ilvara (see "Signs of Pursuit" in the "[Blade] Bazaar" section). The Stone Guards arrest the [char]acters and take them to Overlake Hold, pendin[g] negotiations with the drow. At this point, they a[lso] meet Captain Errde Blackskull.
- Droki (see "Droki" in the "Blade Bazaar" sectio[n) acci]dentally bumps into the patrol, creating a distra[ction] that allows the characters to escape.
- A successful DC 15 Charisma (Persuasion) ch[eck con]vinces the Stone Guards not to arrest the char[acters,] provided the characters agree to visit Overlake [Hold] once their business in Gracklstugh is conclude[d. The] party remains under watch at all times by an i[nvisible] **duergar Stone Guard** (see appendix C). If it se[ems] like the characters have done what they came [to do,] the invisible duergar reminds them to make go[od on] their promise to visit Overlake Hold.

BLADE BAZAAR

This marketplace is named after the most abund[ant] goods the duergar offer, but the shops here sell a[lmost] everything available in the city, along with stalls [run] by visiting merchants. The din of people arguing [prices] in Dwarvish, nearly drowns out the hammering [noise] from the city's forges, and the crowds here offer [a good] chance to slip away from pursuers.

Characters can unload some of the treasures [they] might be carrying. Nonmagical weapons, armor[, and] shields can be purchased in the Blade Bazaar.

MERCHANT MADNESS

Characters who look around the bazaar notice a number of odd things:

- A duergar merchant can't stop insulting customers when they are trying to sell something, but becomes a picture of politeness when they want to buy.
- A number of duergar merchants give different prices to buy or sell every time they are asked about the same items, and insist that the characters dealing with them are the ones changing their terms.
- A duergar merchant suddenly turns invisible in the middle of a transaction, but keeps speaking as if nothing has happened.
- A duergar merchant threatens to kill the characters as a haggling technique, then denies ever saying so.
- A duergar merchant constantly asks the opinion of a nonexistent twin brother, claiming that he is invisible.

YLSA'S DEAL

Ylsa Henstak is a female duergar member of the Merchant Council. She's a canny caravan master and prides herself on always arriving at her destination ahead of schedule. If the characters ask around for merchants who know how to reach the surface, they are directed to Ylsa. Though she has no caravans scheduled anytime soon, she does make the characters an offer.

Ylsa invites the characters into her well-guarded office, where she shows them a pile of coins and jewelry from all over the surface world. The hoard consists of 80 gp in mixed coinage, three gold rings worth 25 gp each, and two gem-inlaid necklaces worth 250 gp each. She has tracked the pieces to derro, who use them to pay for food. If the characters can figure out how the derro are getting surface currency and jewelry, Ylsa will provide the adventurers with directions for at least the next stage of their journey, including valuable advice on routes to Blingdenstone (see chapter 6) and the Wormwrithings (see chapter 12).

DROKI

Attentive characters can spot a curious figure darting between the stalls and shops of the Blade Bazaar. Every time they roam the market, they have a 20 percent chance to see a derro dressed in rags styled as an imitation of a fancy jacket, wearing a wide-brimmed hat with two tentacles from a displacer beast sewn into the hat's crown. A large satchel hangs from his shoulder, and he's always muttering to himself.

Duergar merchants glare scornfully at this derro, and none will discuss him with the characters. If a character asks about him in the Ghohlbrorn's Lair, a successful DC 12 Charisma (Persuasion) check yields up the name "Droki," and identifies the wily derro as a courier and supplier of goods who works for disreputable employers.

Catching **Droki** (see appendix C) is the objective of quests from Errde Blackskull (see "Overlake Hold") and Gartokkar Xundorn (see "Themberchaud's Lair"), but if the characters pursue the courier openly, he flees for the West Cleft District. Pursuing characters quickly lose sight of the derro as he vanishes into the crowd. See "Finding Droki" in the "Whorlstone Tunnels" section

DROKI

for more information on what Droki is carrying if the characters catch him.

SIGNS OF PURSUIT

If the characters arrive in Gracklstugh with a drow pursuit level of 3 or higher (see "Drow Pursuit" in chapter 2), Ilvara has already sent a party ahead of them, guessing correctly that the escaped prisoners might seek refuge with the duergar.

Characters with a passive Wisdom (Perception) score of 15 or higher spot six **drow** watching them in the Blade Bazaar. One of them is Xalith Masq'il'yr, a female drow allied with House Mizzrym. Any of the party's NPC companions who know the duergar well can guess that these drow won't want to attract the duergar's attention to their "lost property." Doing so would likely involve having to pay the gray dwarves a reward for the adventurers' capture. This gives the characters a chance to evade their pursuers, but they need to stay out of sight.

Xalith speaks to the duergar only if the characters are arrested. Otherwise, she sends a messenger to Ilvara and makes sure the characters don't go anywhere without her knowing. If the characters fail to lose themselves in the city (see "Gracklstugh and Drow

Pursuit" earlier in this chapter), their pursuit level increases by 1 every 1d4 days until Ilvara arrives.

Alternatively, the adventurers might decide to turn the tables on the drow. Characters might figure out a way to quietly neutralize Xalith and her squad, perhaps tricking them into damaging a duergar merchant's property or forcing them outside Darklake District, where even drow are forbidden to go. Doing so decreases the pursuit level by 2. However, if combat ever breaks out between the characters and the drow, a squad of five **duergar Stone Guards** (see appendix C) and five **duergar** warriors arrive within 1d4 rounds and arrest the lot of them (see "Getting Captured").

DARKLAKE BREWERY

This huge, ramshackle brewery is built of stone blocks stacked to make walls between the petrified stems of a small forest of gigantic mushrooms. Big copper vats steam within, filling the air with a heavy, yeasty stink. Dozens of copper kegs stand nearby, and burly gray dwarves swarm over the place, mashing fungus, mixing fermenting masses, and filling casks with freshly brewed ale. This complex is the workplace and home of Clan Muzgardt, the duergar clan in charge of brewing Darklake Stout and in control of the brewing and importation of other spirits. Non-duergar aren't welcome inside the brewery.

DARKLAKE DOCKS

These busy docks are used primarily by flat-bottomed rafts made of zurkhwood and lacquered puffball floats. Some of these ramshackle barges come with oars or paddle wheels. The rafts look ungainly, but each can carry tons of trade goods.

The characters land at the easternmost inlet if they arrive at Gracklstugh by way of the Darklake, near the Ghohlbrorn's Lair inn. If they instead arrived through a gate and successfully bribed Gorglak, they might come here looking for his contact, Werz Saltbaron.

ASSASSINS INTERRUPTED

The characters spot a male duergar merchant at the end of a pier. Suddenly, two invisible duergar appear next to him and stab him viciously with glowing swords. The assassins' faces are masked and hooded. The characters have 2 rounds to distract the two **duergar soulblades** (see appendix C) before they finish off the merchant.

The merchant is Werz Saltbaron. If the characters save him, he is grudgingly grateful and says he has no idea why the assassins targeted him. A successful DC 12 Wisdom (Insight) check suggests he's lying. He flees the scene, but not before telling the characters to meet him at the Shattered Spire the following day so he can reward them properly.

The characters have 1 minute to search the ass[...] before a patrol of four **duergar** arrives. The glow[...] weapons wielded by the assassins are nowhere t[...] found, but one of the assassins has a piece of fish[...] parchment bearing Werz's likeness drawn in cha[...]

ACCESS TO THE WHORLSTONE TUNNELS

Hidden next to the easternmost pier, a disabled [...] pipe is the Gray Ghosts' access point to a secret [...] cavern system beneath Gracklstugh (see "Whorl[...] Tunnels"). It takes a successful DC 15 Wisdom [...] (Perception) check to notice the pipe beneath pil[...] refuse. Within, loose bars block the 5-foot-wide [...] but removing them activates an alarm that warn[...] Gray Ghosts inside the caverns. A character can [...] the alarm's trigger—a thin wire connected to the [...] of one of the bars—with a successful DC 14 Wis[...] (Perception) check, and can disable it with a suc[...] DC 12 Dexterity check using thieves' tools.

Nearly 100 feet into the pipe, a hatch on the flo[...] opens into a rough-hewn well. A ladder extends [...] feet to another hatch on the floor, which leads to[...] in the Whorlstone Tunnels.

OVERLAKE HOLD

Dunglorrin Torune, which translates as Overlak[...] is a fortress and temple dedicated to Laduguer [...] into the heart of a massive stalagmite on the sh[...] Darklake. It is also the home of the Deepking a[...] center of government. Dunglorrin Torune bristl[...] forge chimneys from which smoke billows and l[...] from which catapults can hurl stones at waterbo[...] invaders. (If necessary, use the mangonel statis[...] chapter 8 of the *Dungeon Master's Guide*.)

CONSCRIPTED BY THE STONE GUARD

If the characters are arrested, they are taken to [...] hold's dungeons, where they receive a chance t[...] their freedom by serving the Stone Guard.

After waiting a long while in a dungeon cell carved [...] of impressively thick stone, you are taken to a dark [...] and met by an imposing female gray dwarf. She is [...] armored and bears an insignia you have not seen [...] other duergar. She is flanked by two Stone Guards [...] remain by the door.

"I am Captain Errde Blackskull, commander of t[...] Stone Guard," she says, giving each of you a calcu[...] look. "Let me start by saying you are worth nothin[...] here in Gracklstugh. Most of those in my comman[...] would sell you off in a heartbeat as the cheapest n[...] labor. However, I've learned to make much better [...] adventurers like you."

Search for Droki. Errde explains that her guards have been tracking the movements of a derro named Droki. Despite his presence in the Darklake District, the derro has managed to avoid capture, as if he somehow knows in advance where the duergar patrols will be—invisible or otherwise. All the Stone Guards know is that Droki lives in the West Cleft District, a place the duergar enter only in force and where their presence would likely provoke a chaotic uprising. Errde wants the characters to follow Droki, see what he does and where he goes, and report back. Or if they see an opportunity, seize him and either bring him in for questioning, or kill him and bring back evidence of his activities.

Errde's tone turns dark as she voices her suspicions that Droki is linked to a conspiracy involving the Council of Savants, and maybe even elements among the clan lairds. She describes in detail how discovering the conspiracy and purging the corrupt will earn her great favor with the Deepking. Errde swears (truthfully) that she will arrange for the characters to get safe passage out of Gracklstugh if they do as she asks.

Search for Corruption. Errde's suspicions of conspiracy have her looking for signs of corruption creeping among the people of Gracklstugh. She rewards the characters if they bring her evidence of such corruption that has escaped the eyes of her warriors. The characters can build a case if they witness odd events throughout Gracklstugh, such as some of the random encounters and the behavior of merchants in the Blade Bazaar. For every three such events they report, the characters can attempt a DC 15 group Charisma (Persuasion) check, but they only need to succeed once to convince Errde and complete this quest. Errde then promises to outfit the characters with supplies and gear when they leave Gracklstugh, from the Stone Guards' own armory. Each character can claim a total of 350 gp worth of equipment, including weapons, armor, and common potions and scrolls.

DEVELOPMENT

If the characters refuse Errde's offer after being arrested, they spend a few days imprisoned and then are sold back to the drow. Xalith and her squad meet up with Ilvara and then return to Velkynvelve, if the characters can't manage to escape from their captors.

If the characters accept Errde's offer, she gives them insignias allowing them to move as far south as Laduguer's Furrow without being accosted by guards. The adventurers need only to show the insignias discreetly when confronted, and should keep them hidden otherwise. They are then released without fanfare. Errde knows about the stone giants' invitation if the characters spared the two-headed giant's life, and advises the characters to heed it before looking for Droki.

The characters' pursuit level is reduced to 0 and remains so while they are in Errde's employ inside Gracklstugh. If they end their employment, the Stone Guards stop covering for them and their pursuit level increases as normal if Xalith is in town (see "Signs of Pursuit" in the "Blade Bazaar" section). Otherwise, it remains at 0 until some other action raises it again.

FLASHING BADGES

Working for either the Stone Guard or the Keepers of the Flame grants characters a degree of freedom in Gracklstugh, as they can show the insignia given to them by each faction if they are detained. At least one character in the party must succeed on a DC 14 Charisma (Persuasion) check to convince duergar not to detain the party any longer, but characters who show the insignia have advantage on the check.

THE SHATTERED SPIRE

A broken stalagmite juts out from the Darklake about forty feet from the shore, forming the foundation of a tavern built with fungi stalks in a manner similar to a log cabin. A bridge woven of rothé wool allows patrons to cross the water to visit.

MEETING WERZ

If the characters rescued Werz Saltbaron from the assassins (see "Darklake Docks"), he meets them at the Shattered Spire at the designated date and time. As modest thanks for saving him, he gives each character an obsidian gemstone worth 10 gp. He then offers them a job, delivering a sack full of raw gemstones (worth 100 gp total) to a svirfneblin named Kazook Pickshine in Blingdenstone, no questions asked.

Jimjar, Topsy, and Turvy know of Kazook Pickshine and can provide basic information about the gnome alchemist (see chapter 6). The deep gnomes also recognize that Werz's gems resemble empty *spell gems*, similar to those used in the defense of Blingdenstone. The gems, mundane in their current form, are actually raw stones used in the crafting of *spell gems*. Werz met Kazook in Mantol-Derith (see chapter 9), and the two have been trading recently behind their superiors' backs. He declines to mention this, though, deflecting any questions by mentioning that Blingdenstone is a good place to find a way out of the Underdark.

BAR FIGHT

While the characters are in the tavern, two **duergar** who had been just talking business suddenly fly into a rage and start brawling. If the characters don't intervene to stop the fight, other patrons do. No guards appear unless weapons or spells come out, and the fight stops as soon as any of the brawlers is restrained or knocked unconscious. Neither of the duergar remember why they started fighting.

THE GHOHLBRORN'S LAIR

This inn is the only establishment in Gracklstugh that accepts non-duergar guests. "Ghohlbrorn" means "bulette" in Dwarvish, and the inn is built inside a small cavern complex beneath the Blade Bazaar at the northern end of the Darklake District. Its halls are cold and damp. A central chamber serves as a dining room, branching out into different small, twisting halls along which the rooms are excavated. It's dark, cramped, and uncomfortable, but safe and defensible.

RUMOR MILL

The inn's dining hall gives characters a chance to mingle with non-duergar who are visiting Gracklstugh. Characters seeking information can, with a successful DC 10 Charisma (Persuasion) or Intelligence (Investigation) check, find out the following information, or you can simply roleplay their interactions with random patrons.

The general gist of the information is that trade routes out of Gracklstugh have become more dangerous recently. The fauna and more primitive denizens of the Underdark are all riled up about something. Among the tales told by the travelers, second-hand stories about demons attacking isolated settlements are common.

LADUGUER'S FURROW

Long ago, an earthquake split the cavern that houses Gracklstugh, leaving a rift nearly two hundred feet deep and five hundred feet wide. Laduguer's Furrow has a packed-gravel floor and extends roughly a quarter mile beyond the natural walls of the city in both directions. Each end of the rift has a steeply sloping floor, carved with a set of stairs and a wide ramp for both pedestrians and wagons. Vents along the walls release potent gases that sappers of Clan Xardelvar tap for industrial applications, including the crafting of the magical flame lances used by xarrorn warriors.

The chasm is Gracklstugh's main residential zone, with homes built on the top part of its north and south sides. Outsiders are normally forbidden from this area.

ABANDONED GUARDHOUSES

Near the western gate of Laduguer's Furrow, the duergar built a series of guardhouses to keep an eye on derro slaves living in the West Cleft. These were abandoned when Deepking Tarngardt, grandfather of the current monarch, liberated the derro, allowing them to spread from the West Cleft District into the East Cleft District. The guardhouses now stand empty, providing an ideal place to lie low and keep an eye on traffic in and out of the eastern derro boroughs.

GREAT GATES

The openings that Laduguer's Furrow creates in the walls of Gracklstugh's cavern are blocked by massive structures of bars and scaffolding, each set with several gates. Gates are guarded by two visible **duergar** soldiers and 1d4 + 3 invisible ones.

CHASING DROKI

If the characters decide to wait for Droki to enter the West Cleft or somehow follow him here, use the chase rules in chapter 8 of the *Dungeon Master's Guide*, adapting the results for urban complications to a cave full of hateful derro. If Droki loses them, the characters must resort to less convenient means of finding the Whorlstone Tunnels.

If the characters do manage to catch Droki in the West Cleft, he drops limp and babbles, but is suspiciously amenable and shows the characters the entrance to the tunnels. See the "Whorlstone Tunnels" section for how to roleplay Droki.

WEST CLEFT AND EAST CLEFT DISTRICTS

East and west of Laduguer's Furrow gates are ar that serve as home to Gracklstugh's unwanted de population. The West Cleft District was the origi abode for the city's derro slaves and remains a d and dangerous ghetto. The East Cleft District wa recently settled after the derro earned their freed though it is only slightly less rough than West Cl

The homes of the derro are mostly burrows ca into the walls and simple structures piled atop o another. The dirty and cluttered streets of both formed as dwellings spread and came together, as a product of planning. The derro population i greater and their tunnels extend much farther th the duergar believe. The derro are close to moun an insurrection, held back only by their own lac organization and by their leaders in the Council Savants having grown too used to their privilege foment rebellion.

ENTERING DERRO TERRITORY

The derro are automatically hostile toward anyc entering their warrens, especially surfacers.

> As you pass through the gates, the stench in the ai changes from acrid and metallic to fetid and repug the fires of industry replaced by squalor. The home this part of Gracklstugh are crudely carved from th or are just holes in the walls, arranged in no appar order. The chatter in the air is unnerving, with hun of derro muttering, screaming at each other, and otherwise reveling in their insanity. Those who spo look at you with a burning hatred.

At the end of each hour the adventurers stay in either derro area, there is a 25 percent chance **derro** (see appendix C) attack without warning characters kill any derro, the chance of anothe becomes 50 percent every half hour.

Sneaking through the senseless arrangemen burrows is relatively easy, as the derro are nor preoccupied with their own mad scheming to r group trying not to attract attention. The chara attempt a DC 10 group Dexterity (Stealth) chec success negating the need to roll for a possible the end of each hour or half hour.

Other means of subterfuge such as illusions, along the walls, or using flying or levitation ma automatically avoid detection, but invisibility o kind activates magical wards placed by derro s guard against duergar intrusion. When a ward in response to the presence of an invisible crea nearby derro fly into a frenzy, creating a chaoti meant to drive away invisible duergar patrols. make active Wisdom (Perception) checks cont the characters' Dexterity (Stealth) checks if a activated. Characters using *detect magic* actively can spot the invisible sensor of a ward before it activates. Otherwise, invisible characters encounter a ward every 15 minutes they move through derro territory.

Access to the Whorlstone Tunnels

Between a cluster of hovels in West Cleft lies the most well-used entrance to the Whorlstone Tunnels (see "Whorlstone Tunnels"). A narrow fissure in the chasm wall is hidden by scraps of cloth, gray sheets of canvas, and moldy boxes. The fissure is tall and wide enough for a Medium creature to squeeze through the first 10 feet, and then continues for 50 feet at an average 5 feet in width, with a gentle downward slope.

Ever since the foul irruption of the demon lords into the Underdark, the fissure is easier to find, as it sometimes leaks wisps of eerie fog created by *faerzress*. Otherwise, finding it requires careful searching and a successful DC 15 Wisdom (Perception) check. Each character can make this check at the end of each hour the party spends in the West Cleft warrens looking for the Whorlstone Tunnels' entrance.

Any attempt to question the locals without an effective means of disguise or manipulation, such as enchantment or illusion magic, is doomed to fail, as the derro are more likely to attack the characters than answer their questions. Even then, the derro are often incoherent, and a successful DC 15 Charisma (Persuasion) check is needed to obtain useful information. A successful DC 15 Charisma (Intimidation) check also works, but has a 50 percent chance of inspiring the derro to flee or attack.

Halls of Sacred Spells

The Halls of Sacred Spells comprise a temple of Diirinka carved into a stalagmite in Northfurrow District. Here, the derro Council of Savants meets and plots, living in luxurious quarters and hiding such opulence from their fellow derro. All areas of the Halls of Sacred Spells except the central worship chamber are forbidden to derro who aren't savants. Duergar don't enter this place, whose main doors are false and carved into the rock. The savants enter and leave using spells such as *dimension door* and *passwall*, while lesser derro access the worship chamber through secret tunnels from the West Cleft.

Cairngorm Cavern

A long tunnel opens in Southfurrow District, extending several hundred feet and into the home of the stone giants of Clan Cairngorm. The tribe is named after the ancient oath of fealty their ancestors swore to the bearers of the Cairngorm Crown, the traditional regalia of Deepkingdom monarchs. The giants lead simple, uncomplicated lives, and their dwellings reflect this.

The stone giants value their privacy, and duergar are normally not allowed inside Cairngorm Cavern. An exception is made for the Deepking, who holds meetings here with the giants' leader, Stonespeaker Hgraam, when necessary.

Audience with the Stonespeaker

If the adventurers helped stop the rampaging giant in the Darklake District (and especially if they didn't kill him), Hgraam is expecting them by the entrance to the Cairngorm Caverns. Though the stone giant is short on pleasantries, he gives the characters what information he can in response to their questions, including ways to return to the "dreamlands," as the stone giants call the surface world. Because he has never left the Underdark, the paths he knows have come to him only as whispers through the stone. As such, you can easily shape his advice to your players' plans.

Additionally, Hgraam gives the characters a warning:

> "Something evil stirs in the Underdark. The rock itself cries in pain and horror, and a madness creeps from the blackest depths. Pay heed to the signs surrounding you. A cave with two faces. Rock devoured, and the land overgrown. The pebble believes itself flesh. The earth rejects its wards, and the tunnels shake in fury. By these portents, you shall know of evil's presence and of evil's face. This is what the stones tell me."

This cryptic message refers to the demon lords and the madness their presence is spreading, but Hgraam has not deciphered it yet.

Treasure

As the characters prepare to leave, Hgraam calls for his apprentice Dorhun, who arrives bearing a polished crystal the length of a human forearm. Hgraam offers the crystal to the characters as a token of his gratitude, telling them it might be helpful in the future.

The *stonespeaker crystal* (see appendix B) resonates strongly with conjuration and divination magic. If the characters keep the crystal after escaping the Underdark, it will be of use if they return to deal with the demonic incursion, as it is linked to the mysterious library of Gravenhollow and has additional properties when used there (see chapter 11).

Themberchaud's Lair

At the far southeast corner of Gracklstugh's cavern, the entrance to Themberchaud's lair is guarded by the Keepers of the Flame. Not that anyone would be foolish enough to trespass into the Wyrmsmith's home, but ever since the Gray Ghosts stole a red dragon egg meant to hatch Themberchaud's successor, the Keepers aren't taking any chances.

For some time now, the Keepers have been actively seeking capable mercenaries in Gracklstugh and taking any opportunity to press them into service. If an agent of the order intervened in the characters' arrest (see "Getting Captured"), the leader of the Keepers of the Flame—Gartokkar Xundorn—is notified by magical messaging. He waits for the characters as they are brought to the dragon's cavern—but Themberchaud is watching too.

THEMBERCHAUD

The dragon speaks Dwarvish to its servants as the characters approach. Read the following:

> As the duergar priests lead you to a building carved from the stone just outside a huge cave entrance, the ground trembles slightly, and a thunderous voice echoes against every wall.
>
> "Gartokkar," the voice calls as a reptilian behemoth comes into view, it scales the color of lava, its bright yellow eyes glowing in the shadows of the cave before coming into the light. "You didn't say I was having surfacers for dinner today."
>
> The dragon chuckles at his own wit. His massive body gives the distinct impression that he is overweight, indicating eating habits that don't bode well.
>
> "Foreigners," the duergar priest says with great reverence, "meet the Father of Flame, the Everburning, and the Foundry's Heart—Themberchaud, the Wyrmsmith of Gracklstugh."

AGENTS OF THE WYRMSMITH

Like most of his kind, Themberchaud is vain and proud. He's pampered, but also restless. The **adult red dragon** has been aware for several years that his handlers are withholding things from him, but rather than demand disclosure, he has waited and observed. He wants agents of his own, and sees the interest of the Keepers in the adventurers as an opportunity.

The dragon demands to speak with the characters in private, with his nervous duergar handlers having no

choice but to acquiesce. When they escort the cha[racters] into the dragon's lair, Themberchaud is resting on mountain of gold. He tells the keepers to leave hir with the adventurers, hissing that any invisible lu[rkers] will be turned to ash. Once alone, he asks the cha[racters] their names, backgrounds, how they found thems[elves] in the Underdark, and the events that led them to Gracklstugh.

Themberchaud makes the characters an offer: his agents in Gracklstugh, and gain his protectic[on] first mission is to do whatever the Keepers of the ask them to—but to report to Themberchaud bef[ore] reporting to them.

The dragon doesn't wait for the characters to r[eply] since his ego can't accept the notion that anyone would refuse him. He assigns Gartokkar to be th[eir] liaison, orders badges of gold be given to them, a sends them off.

TREASURE

The characters might be tempted to inspect Themberchaud's hoard from where they stand, a dragon doesn't allow them to get closer than 60 front of him. The hoard consists of 3,000 pp, 20 45,000 sp, 150,000 cp, six 1,000 gp fire opals, t gp peridots, thirty 100 gp garnets, a gourd conta[ining] *of sharpness*, a *potion of flying*, a *potion of longe[vity]* a *potion of supreme healing*. The magic items a[re] under coins and not visible at a glance. One mu[st] through the coins to find them.

A character who tries to get closer receives a warning in the form of a growl, a stare, and claw clicking on the floor. Themberchaud uses his br[eath] weapon on any character who tries again, or wh[o] attempts to sneak past him and fails. Then he c carries on as if nothing happened.

A TASK FOR THE KEEPERS

When the characters are done with Themberch[aud] exit the lair to where Gartokkar waits to take th[em] the guard house where the Keepers of the Flam[e] watch. He darkly asks what business the drago[n] with them, but what the characters choose to te[ll] (and whether they intend to follow up on the dra[gon's] orders) is up to them.

The power of the Keepers of the Flame deriv[es] in equal measure from their psionic abilities, th[e] leadership of the Deepking, and their influence Themberchaud. They lost face when the Gray G[hosts] stole the valuable red dragon egg that would ha[ve] Themberchaud's replacement, and they have be[en] waging war on the thieves' guild ever since. Bu[t] the egg still lost and their control over Thembe[rchaud] waning, the Keepers are exploring all options i[n] war against the Gray Ghosts.

The psionic Keepers have sensed a great dis[turbance] in the Underdark—a phenomenon that Gartokk[ar] compares to a hole having been torn through th[e] The Keepers have no idea about the demonic i[ncursion] however, and even if the characters tell Gartok[kar] they know, he is fixated on the idea that the Gr[ay] are behind the disturbance, dismissing anything else as delusions, ignorance, or outright lies.

In his paranoia, Gartokkar wants the characters to confirm the Gray Ghosts' involvement and to bring back whatever powerful magic the thieves used to cause the disturbance. The Keepers have identified a Gray Ghost agent—a derro called Droki, who carries messages and supplies for the thieves' guild (see "Droki" in the "Blade Bazaar" section). Droki uses the West Cleft to contact his employers, and Gartokkar wants the party to follow this derro and locate the Gray Ghosts.

If the characters accept his offer, Gartokkar gives them a holy symbol of Laduguer after an acolyte arrives with gold pins featuring Themberchaud's profile. The symbol and the badges grant characters the right to travel beyond the Darklake District, though they are still limited from moving freely in the city (see the "Flashing Badges" sidebar). If they refuse, they are turned over to the Stone Guards for arrest and delivery to Overlake Hold.

WHORLSTONE TUNNELS

The Whorlstone Tunnels are a cavern system extending partially underneath Gracklstugh, away from the mines and passages the city's inhabitants use regularly. The derro savants who first found the tunnels didn't reveal their discovery to anyone, and to this day only a handful among the Council of Savants and the Gray Ghosts know about them.

The long, gently curving tunnels have relatively regular dimensions. They are known for their unusual rock formations and abundant patches of fungi, and for being suffused with *faerzress* (see chapter 2).

There are currently two factions using the tunnels for their own ends. The Gray Ghosts have an alchemical laboratory and a fungal garden supplying them with poisons, and the leaders of the guild conceal a secret in the form of a mysterious black obelisk in the farthest cave (see area 16). The other group is a budding cult of derro demon worshipers led by a renegade member of the Council of Savants. Sensing that the demon lords are somehow using *faerzress* to spread chaos and madness, the demon worshipers have begun conducting rituals to infect Gracklstugh. Intent on weakening the city and breaking the power of King Horgar Steelshadow V, the cultists plan to inflict a curse on the stone giants of Clan Cairngorm that causes them to grow second heads, driving them insane.

FAERZRESS-SUFFUSED FUNGI

The Whorlstone Tunnels are home to two unique kinds of *faerzress*-suffused mushrooms: bigwigs and pygmyworts. Any character who studies these mushrooms can identify their magical effects with a successful DC 15 Intelligence (Nature) check, an *identify* spell, or by trial and error. A single nibble of a mushroom alters a character's size by a few inches for 5 minutes, so characters foraging for food might discover the mushrooms' magic by accident. The size-altering effects of eating multiple bigwigs or pygmyworts aren't cumulative, although their durations are. These mushrooms lose their properties if they are taken outside the Whorlstone Tunnels for 1 hour or more.

BIGWIG

A bigwig is a four-inch-tall mushroom with a thin stem and a wide purple cap. A creature that eats one can choose to make a DC 12 Constitution saving throw to not be affected by the mushroom's magic. If the creature fails or forgoes the saving throw, it grows in size as though under the enlarge effect of an *enlarge/reduce* spell. The effect lasts for 1 hour. Ten minutes before the effect ends, the creature feels a tingling sensation, at which point it can sustain its current size by eating another wurple. The effect ends if the creature eats a pygmywort mushroom or is magically reduced to its normal size (using the reduce effect of an *enlarge/reduce* spell, for example).

PYGMYWORT

A pygmywort is a mushroom with a one-inch-long stem and a stubby blue cap with white dots. A creature that eats one can choose to make a DC 12 Constitution saving throw to not be affected by the mushroom's magic. If the creature fails or forgoes the saving throw, it shrinks in size as though under the reduce effect of an *enlarge/reduce* spell. The effect lasts for 1 hour. Ten minutes before the effect ends, the creature feels a tingling sensation, at which point it can sustain its current size by eating another pygmywort. The effect ends if the creature eats a bigwig mushroom or is magically enlarged to its normal size (using the enlarge effect of an *enlarge/reduce* spell, for example).

RANDOM ENCOUNTERS

As the characters explore the Whorlstone Tunnels, they can run into various creatures or hazards. Check for an encounter whenever the characters are moving along a stretch of tunnel or at the end of a long rest. Roll a d20 and consult the Whorlstone Tunnels Encounters table to determine what, if anything, they encounter.

WHORLSTONE TUNNELS ENCOUNTERS

d20	Encounter
1–10	No encounter
11–12	1 **carrion crawler**
13	Demon pack
14	1 **flumph**
15	1 **gray ooze**
16	1d4 moldy **quaggoth spore servants**
17	1d4 two-headed **grimlocks**
18	1 **swarm of insects** (centipedes)
19	1 **xorn**
20	Yellow mold

CARRION CRAWLER

There's a 50 percent chance that the carrion crawler is feasting on the putrid flesh of a dead grimlock and ignores the party unless disturbed. Otherwise, it is scouring tunnels for food and attacks the party on sight. It prefers to attack while clinging to the ceiling.

Demon Pack

This pack consists of a **quasit** leading 1d4 + 2 **dretches**. The quasit turns invisible and tries to escape when only two dretches remain; if it succeeds, the cultists in area 14 are alerted. Replace any subsequent demon pack random encounter with 1d4 **derro** (see appendix C).

Flumph

This creature telepathically asks the characters to rid the cave complex of the derro cultists (see area 14) because it knows what they're trying to do and wants to stop them. If the characters agree and seem friendly, the flumph offers to accompany them indefinitely. It will not willingly leave the Underdark, however.

Gray Ooze

There's a 50 percent chance that this ooze has psionic abilities (use the psychic variant of the gray ooze, as described in the *Monster Manual*).

Moldy Quaggoth Spore Servants

A patch of yellow mold (see "Dungeon Hazards" in chapter 5 of the *Dungeon Master's Guide*) covers each spore servant. Each time a spore servant is touched or takes damage, it releases a cloud of yellow mold spores until the mold patch is destroyed.

Two-Headed Grimlocks

The grimlocks living in the Whorlstone Tunnels keep to themselves, feeding on fungi and vermin. The derro have tried to enslave them, without much success. In a weird example of détente, members of the two races have learned to avoid one another. Each grimlock has sprouted a screaming second head, which has no effect on its statistics.

Whorlstone Tunnels: General Features

The following features are prevalent throughout the Whorlstone Tunnels.

Ceilings and Floors. The average ceiling height is 50 feet, dropping to 25 feet in narrow tunnels.

Narrow Tunnels. The narrowest tunnels are barely 2 feet wide at their widest points. A Tiny creature can move through these tunnels unimpeded, while a Small creature must squeeze to pass through them. Medium and larger creatures can't fit through these narrow passageways.

Faerzress. The Whorlstone Tunnels are suffused with *faerzress* (see "Faerzress" in chapter 2 for effects). *Faerzress* has also altered the physical appearance of the complex, creating spiral patterns on the walls and ceilings. These spirals are what give the complex its name. Because of these weird spiraling patterns, saving throws to resist *faerzress*-induced madness are made with disadvantage.

Foul Water. Water from the Darklake drips from stalactites and trickles through cracks in the walls, forming narrow streams and shallow pools throughout the Whorlstone Tunnels. Any creature that drinks the foul water must succeed on a DC 12 Constitution saving throw or become poisoned. The poisoned creature can repeat the saving throw at the end of each hour to end the effect.

Edible Fungi. Edible fungi (including pygmywort and bigwig) are abundant in the Whorlstone Tunnels. Characters can attempt DC 10 Wisdom (Survival) checks to forage here.

Xorn

This creature has been working its way through rock of the Whorlstone Tunnels, consuming vast amounts of *faerzress*-infused stone. The change *faerzress* brought on by the arrival of the demon has left the xorn confused and easily angered. It bargain for metal or gems to eat, and attacks if re If the adventurers feed the xorn and can commu with it, the creature can tell them that it sensed planar upheaval recently, though it knows nothin the demons or their spreading madness.

Yellow Mold

The characters notice a patch of yellow mold (se "Dungeon Hazards" in chapter 5 of the *Dungeon Master's Guide*) growing on something of interes determined by rolling a d4 and consulting the Be the Yellow Mold table. Tampering with the mold encrusted object causing the yellow mold to rele deadly spores.

Beneath the Yellow Mold

d4	Encounter
1	A humanoid skeleton wearing a *ring of wate* on one bony finger (no ring is found on sub occurrences of this encounter)
2	A closed zurkhwood chest containing 1d6 × and 1d6 50 gp gems
3	A humanoid skeleton in tattered leather arr carrying a rusted shortsword and one of th following: a rotted quiver holding 1d20 +1 a leather pouch containing 1d10 +2 sling ston zurkhwood case containing 1d4 +3 crossbow
4	A +1 shield (on subsequent occurrences of encounter, the shield is rusted and nonmag

Finding Droki

If the characters are on a quest to find Droki, re following boxed text when his path crosses with

> The dirty derro is easy to recognize: a pale face und a floppy hat fitted with two tentacle-like things that bob up and down in time with his brisk pace. He k muttering a repetitive series of phrases to himself different volumes, failing to notice you. "Droki is la They will be so angry! Stupid, stupid, stupid! Delay blocks, procrastination, obstructions, pfah! No tim rhyme, not mine! No! Time!"

Droki (see appendix C) has errands to perform characters can shadow him or chase him down the Darklake District and the derro territories him with abundant places to hide and paths do he can lose pursuers, and he knows them all. In Whorlstone Tunnels, however, the derro is dist ever-present threats, giving the party the best c to catch him. The characters can fight Droki by tunnels' entrance or follow him farther in, depending on their end goals. If they follow Droki, he goes to area 1a, eats a pygmywort mushroom, and disappears into a narrow tunnel (see the "Whorlstone Tunnels: General Features" sidebar).

Droki's route takes him all around the Whorlstone Tunnels, and he's too scatterbrained to notice anyone following him. Droki's route is marked with red arrows on the map of the Whorlstone Tunnels. He eats a pygmywort mushroom whenever he needs to navigate a narrow tunnel. As he approaches areas 7 and 8, he eats a bigwig mushroom, reverts to normal size, delivers the Gray Ghost parcel (see "Treasure"), and collects his payment from Lorthio the duergar alchemist (see area 8). Droki then heads north to area 9, where he sneaks quietly around the central pool so as not to disturb its occupant. Upon reaching area 11, he greets the derro there before eating another pygmywort mushroom and traveling through the narrow tunnel leading to area 12. He eats another bigwig and reverts to normal size before making his delivery to the cultists in that area. After visiting the cultists, Droki makes his way out of the Whorlstone Tunnels.

If the characters hinder or attack Droki, he screams in fright and knocks his feet together, activating his *boots of speed*. If a chase ensues, resolve the outcome using the chase rules in chapter 8 of the *Dungeon Master's Guide*. Droki has advantage in his Dexterity (Stealth) checks, as he knows the Whorlstone Tunnels well. If he loses the characters, he resumes his errands as if nothing had happened.

If Droki manages to escape, characters can pick up his trail by searching any area through which the derro passed and succeeding on a DC 15 Wisdom (Survival) check.

Roleplaying Droki

Droki hates everyone in general and surfacers in particular. He gnashes his teeth if he has to address the characters, taking every opportunity to be insulting and misleading. If the characters look through his satchel while he's still conscious, he throws an epic tantrum and becomes intractable until knocked unconscious.

Droki is also obsessed with things happening where and when they should. If he is captured before he runs his errands in the Whorlstone Tunnels, he constantly complains about the characters altering fate by delaying him, and a good tactic to pressure him is to threaten to hold him indefinitely. He prefers to escape than to fight, except if the characters take his satchel.

Treasure

Killing or incapacitating Droki gives the characters the chance to rummage through his belongings. He wears *boots of speed* and a hat that is one of a kind. He sewed two stuffed displacer beast tentacles to the hat in the hopes of them attacking his enemies on their own, a delusion he volunteers if the characters question him. The hat might be worth something to a collector of oddities, but is otherwise worthless.

Droki's satchel is made of stitched darkmantle hide and contains the following items:

- 1 gp and 10 sp
- A *spell scroll* of *see invisibility*
- Two *potions of healing*
- A worthless collection of dead vermin (spiders, centipedes, and the like) in various states of decomposition
- Pages of lizard-skin parchment held together between two leather covers from two different books. The pages are full of mad scribbles and arcane formulas, but a character proficient in Intelligence (Arcana) can study them for 1 hour to discover that they constitute a spellbook containing the *Tenser's floating disk* and *feign death* spells.
- A strange lump of black metal, which Droki intends to deliver to the Gray Ghosts (see below)
- A scroll in a copper tube and four small pouches containing stone giant toenail clippings and skin flecks, which Droki intends to deliver to the cultists (see below). Each pouch is tagged with a different name, and the scroll contains a list of names matching those on the tags, together with descriptions. One of the names is "Dorhun," with a description corresponding to Stonespeaker Hgraam's apprentice. The rest of the names belong to other stone giants of Clan Cairngorm.

The derro might have other items depending on whether he is allowed to make his deliveries and collect his payments, as follows.

Delivery to the Gray Ghosts. Droki intends to deliver the strange lump of black metal to the Gray Ghosts, receiving payment from Lorthio the alchemist (see area 8) in the form of a mithral medallion worth 125 gp. The medallion is a holy symbol of Laduguer, set with a carving depicting an arrow breaking on a shield. Characters not sanctioned by the Keepers of the Flame to carry the symbol will be arrested by the guards (see "Getting Captured") if they are caught with it in Gracklstugh.

Delivery to the Cultists. Droki intends to deliver the scroll and the pouches of stone giant toenail clippings and skin flecks (ritual components) to the derro cultists (see area 12). Droki is paid for this delivery with a *potion of invisibility* and an hourglass worth 50 gp.

XP Awards

Capturing the derro and taking him to Errde Blackskull earns the characters 150 XP each.

1. Entrance

The narrow corridor from the West Cleft opens into a long cavern lined with stalactites and stalagmites. Whater drips from the stalactites, forming small pools on the floor.

> The glow of *faerzress* casts an eerie soft light across this cavern, swirling into spiral patterns and casting dancing shadows from the jagged pillars lining the walls. The air smells and tastes slightly metallic, and the sound around you is strangely muted. The dripping of water makes no echo, as if you stood in open air.

This place offers many hiding places for characters to lay in ambush. *Faerzress* prevents sounds of combat from being heard outside in the West Cleft or farther into the tunnels.

If the characters wait here for Droki, he appears after 2d12 hours. In the middle of that wait, each character must make a DC 14 Wisdom saving throw. On a success, the character feels only a mild discomfort. A character who rolls a natural 20 on the save receives flashes of the future, gaining the benefit of the Lucky feat (see chapter 6, "Customization Options," in the *Player's Handbook*) until the start of his or her next long rest. If the character already has the Lucky feat, he or she gains an extra 3 luck points to spend. On a failed save, a character sees disturbing images within the shimmering *faerzress* light and has disadvantage on ability checks and saving throws until he or she finishes a short rest outside this area.

If the characters caught Droki in Gracklstugh and brought him here, they must make the saving throw at some point during their interrogation. Knowing the power of the cavern, Droki bides his time, giving nonsensical answers and hissing at the characters. He makes his move to escape after the characters make their saving throws, fleeing by the route described in the "Finding Droki" section.

DEVELOPMENT

If Buppido is with the party, he takes advantage of any distraction to slip away, taking refuge in area 1b.

1A. POOL BYPASS

A relatively small cave branches off the main tunnel. If the characters are shadowing Droki, read the following boxed text aloud to the players.

> Droki stands before a tall yet narrow crack in the wall. He stares at the crack for a moment, then leans down and rummages among the fungi, cackling with glee as he plucks a short mushroom and eats it whole. As he finishes the last bite, you see him shrink down to a doll's size, then run into the crack.

The far side of the small cavern has a narrow crack in the wall surrounded by patches of pygmywort and bigwig mushrooms (1d10 + 10 of each). The crack forms the entrance of a narrow, naturally-formed tunnel.

1B. BUPPIDO'S LAIR

The derro Buppido discovered the Whorlstone Tunnels months ago but never dared to explore beyond the first couple of chambers. He settled in this area and erected a grisly altar to himself, to support the delusion that he is a god.

If Buppido returns to Gracklstugh, he abandons the characters at the first opportunity and makes his way to this place. If he is here when the characters arrive, read the following boxed text aloud to the players. Modify the text as appropriate if Buppido isn't present.

> As you venture into the cavern, a stench of rotting r
> rises. The floor is carpeted with humanoid remains
> varying stages of decomposition, arranged in a spir
> pattern around the cave's center. An off-key hummi
> comes from a hunched figure working busily at
> something on the floor.
>
> "Oh, there you are!" The figure is Buppido. He w
> his hands on his vest and smiles viciously. "I didn't
> expect you to find me here, with my shrine nearly
> finished! And power! My faithful are finally honorin
> Are you ...? Yes. Yes, I sense that you are ready to r
> my truth into your hearts!"

The humanoid remains on the floor make the er cavern difficult terrain. Characters can identify remains as belonging to several derro, deep gno and goblins, as well as a couple grimlocks.

Buppido is a typical **derro** and attacks the cha regardless of their intentions. On his first turn, a bonus action to channel the power of this "shr raising six **skeletons** to aid him. The undead as from the remains on the floor to form shamblin mismatched bodies. Each skeleton has two sku although this has no effect on its abilities.

Buppido fights with insane confidence and se surprised if the party defeats him, screaming ir last words about the end of the world. The skele fight until destroyed even if Buppido is defeated

If Buppido was killed in Velkynvelve or at son point in the characters' travels through the Und replace him with a **carrion crawler** feeding on dead remains.

DEVELOPMENT

When the monsters are defeated, the **ghost** of a gnome named Pelek pokes its head up out of th blinks, and then emerges fully. The ghost is frie and tells the adventurers that Buppido killed hi too long ago, then chopped him into pieces to jo other body parts in the shrine. Pelek explains h was traveling from Blingdenstone when he fell Buppido. He knows little about the Whorlstone but he has observed a shrunken derro with a fu (Droki) entering and leaving the narrow tunnel doesn't know about the pygmywort mushroom

Pelek asks the characters to take one or mor of him to Blingdenstone and bury his remains so that his spirit can rest. It's impossible to tell body parts are his, and looking around is a gru task that speaks loudly to Buppido's madness. recalls that the strange magic that pervades th animated one of his severed hands, and it scutt through one of the narrow tunnels. (Character encounter it in area 13.) Pelek points out that c can recognize the hand because it was wearin obsidian ring. If the characters need more rea to Blingdenstone, Pelek adds that the svirfnebl live there know many ways to the surface.

GRACKLSTUGH:
THE WHORLSTONE
TUNNELS

14a

14

13

10

9

11

8

6

12

7

1a

2

5

1

1b

3

4

ONE SQUARE = 25 FEET

THE OBELISK

N

THE GRAY ALCHEMIST

14

8

7

6

GRAY
GHOST GARDEN

CULTIST PENS

THE DIRE DEN

SHRIEKER

12

PIT TRAP

10

ONE SQUARE = 5 FEET

BLANDO

TREASURE

Scattered around the floor are 10 gp, 11 sp, and a damp piece of lizard-skin parchment with the words "Worship Buppido" written in shaky Dwarvish.

2. DISEASED POOL

This pool is fed by a river that flows from the Darklake. The river carries many things from the subterranean lake, including the carcasses of countless creatures, fouling the pool (see the "Whorlstone Tunnels: General Features" sidebar).

> The tunnel slopes down to the edge of a large pool that fills the cavern ahead. The opposite shore is nearly one hundred feet away, but nothing can be seen beneath the surface of the black water.

The water is heated by a thermal spring and pleasantly warm. However, the pool is disease-ridden. Any creature that starts its turn in the water must make a DC 13 Constitution saving throw. On a failed save, the creature is infected with cackle fever (see "Diseases" in chapter 8 of the *Dungeon Master's Guide*). Gnomes are immune.

The characters can try to get around the pool without swimming it, by using magic or climbing along the walls. Climbing the slippery walls of the cavern requires a successful DC 13 Athletics check. On a failed check, a character falls into the water.

3. PARADE OF FOOLS

Myconids journeying through the Underdark were attracted to the enriched fungal life in the Whorlstone Tunnels and made a stop here. They are friendly, but there is something seriously wrong with them.

> The tunnel opens into a natural cave, wherein you see several fungal creatures dancing to a silent tune. Three of them stand five feet tall, while the others are half as tall. One of the small ones stands apart from the rest, its movements not nearly as frantic. Hunched nearby are two larger creatures that resemble apes covered with mushroom growths and yellow mold.

Characters who know anything about myconids know that myconids don't dance. If Stool is with the party, it points this out. This group is composed of three **myconid adults** and five **myconid sprouts**. Stool recognizes one of the sprouts—the one not dancing—as his buddy, Rumpadump (see "Development"). The ape-like creatures are two **quaggoth spore servants**, and each one is covered with a patch of yellow mold (see "Dungeon Hazards" in chapter 5 of the *Dungeon Master's Guide*). Whenever a quaggoth spore servant is touched or takes damage, it releases a cloud of yellow mold spores until its mold patch is destroyed.

The myconids are too swept up in their silent revelry to notice the characters. If the adventurers attack, the myconid adults fight fiercely while the sprouts ru[...] hide. The spore servants join the fray if either th[...] the myconids are threatened. Otherwise, they re[...] motionless.

If the characters try to communicate with the [...] myconids, they release rapport spores so that ev[...] can speak telepathically. The leader of the myco[...] is an adult named Voosbur, who speaks on beha[...] of the others. Sharing thoughts with these senti[...] mushrooms is an odd and strangely intoxicating experience (and feels quite different than the rap[...] the characters might have shared with Stool). Vo[...] happily tells the party how its "troupe" was attra[...] by the special mushrooms in these tunnels, and [...] the characters about the magical properties of th[...] pygmywort and bigwig mushrooms. Voosbur fu[...] explains that the myconids didn't wander into th[...] area, but arrived here by traveling "through the [...] dream." Voosbur describes "the Lady" as a pow[...] being that loves and guides all myconids. He off[...] share "the Lady's gift" with the characters, allov[...] them to travel "through the Lady's dream" as th[...] myconids do. Characters who accept the offer ga[...] Zuggtmoy's gift (see the sidebar).

If present, Stool tells the characters it has no [...] what Voosbur is talking about. Additionally, Sar[...] Kzekarit starts to act erratically, trying to warn [...] characters away from the myconids, but unable [...] off the influence of Zuggtmoy's spores.

The myconid sprout standing by itself is name[...] Rumpadump. It sends a subtle warning as a feel[...] distress through its own rapport spores in resp[...] Voosbur's offer, saying that the other myconids a[...] behaving right.

ROLEPLAYING RUMPADUMP

Rumpadump is as introverted as Stool is outgoi[...] preferring to hang back and not use its rapport [...] unless absolutely necessary. Whether Stool is p[...] not, Rumpadump can guide the characters to N[...] Grove (see chapter 5), where the sovereigns mig[...] of a way out of the Underdark. However, the my[...] sprout is worried that Voosbur's "strange spore[...] have infected the rest of the myconids back hom[...]

DEVELOPMENT

Voosbur takes no offense if the characters refus[...] his offer to teach them how to travel "the Lady's dream," simply bidding them farewell as the my[...] resume their dancing. If the characters have sh[...] Rumpadump any kindness, it asks their permiss[...] to join the party, especially if Stool is present. A[...] same time, Sarith breaks away from the party t[...] the myconids. The drow turns one last time to g[...] characters a look of terror and despair before h[...] loses all expression. He and the dancing mycon[...] enter a mushroom patch and use the *tree stride[...] granted by Zuggtmoy's blessing to vanish from [...]

XP AWARDS

Award 50 XP to each character if the party par[...] with the myconids.

4. Fungi Thicket

This tunnel juncture is blocked by a thicket of fungi. The thicket is an ecosystem unto itself, with its own challenges for those who wish to cross it.

> A dense fungi forest blocks your way, its tallest specimens growing some five feet high. Even as you assess the best way to pass through it, a hissing sound starts to rise—like uncounted tiny voices whispering in tongues you don't understand.

Although creepy, the hissing sound is harmless, caused by air whistling through perforated mushrooms in the thicket of fungi. The characters can cross this area by forcing their way through it, or by eating pygmywort mushrooms first to move through without disturbing the other fungi present. If the characters are chasing Droki, he uses the thicket to his advantage, eating a pygmywort to sneak his way across. At reduced size, he leaves no trail that normal-sized pursuers can follow.

Tiny creatures can move through the thicket at no penalty. For Small and Medium creatures, the thicket is difficult terrain. While in the thicket, Tiny and Small creatures have half cover against Medium creatures and can hide.

Creatures can negate the movement penalty by destroying the fungi before crossing the thicket. Each 5-foot-square area of fungi has AC 10 and 10 hit points. Any attack that deals fire damage has a 50 percent chance of igniting a torchstalk mushroom (see "Fungi of the Underdark" in chapter 2).

The first time a Small or larger character reaches the tunnel intersection, two **swarms of insects** (centipedes) emerge from nests under the thicket and attack. Two more **swarms of insects** (spiders) arrive on the second round of combat, plus another **swarm of insects** (centipedes) on the third round.

Treasure

The abundance of fungi in the thicket makes it easy to forage here. Among the common, inedible fungi are the following edible and exotic fungi, most of which are described in chapter 2:

- 1d6 barrelstalks
- 3d6 bluecaps
- 1d6 patches of fire lichen
- 1d6 nightlights
- 1d6 Nilhogg's noses
- 1d6 sheets of ripplebark
- 1d6 timmasks
- 1d6 torchstalks
- 1d6 tongues of madness
- 1d6 trillimacs
- 2d6 bigwigs (see *Faerzress*-Suffused Fungi")
- 2d6 pygmyworts (see *Faerzress*-Suffused Fungi")

Zuggtmoy's Gift

A myconid with Zuggtmoy's gift can, as an action once per day, release a 20-foot-radius cloud of demon-tainted spores. Any other creature within the area that isn't already "blessed" with Zuggtmoy's gift must make a Constitution saving throw, with a save DC of 8 + the myconid's Constitution modifier + the myconid's proficiency bonus. A creature that forgoes or fails the saving throw becomes infected. While infected with Zuggtmoy's gift, the creature gains the ability to cast a special version of the *tree stride* spell that has no components. This spell allows the infected creature to move through patches of mold and fungi instead of trees. Once it casts this spell, the infected creature can't cast the spell again until it finishes a long rest.

Any creature infected with Zuggtmoy's gift has disadvantage on attack rolls against plant creatures. In addition, whenever an infected creature finishes a short or long rest, it must make a DC 15 Wisdom saving throw. On a failed save, the creature lapses into a state of euphoric bliss. While in this state, the creature can't take actions, bonus actions, or reactions, and must use all of its movement to dance and twirl about. At the end of its turn, the creature can repeat the saving throw, ending the euphoric bliss effect on a success.

A *remove curse* or *greater restoration* spell rids a creature of Zuggtmoy's gift.

RUMPADUMP

5. Raucous Mesa

This chamber was sculpted by *faerzress* with the side effect of trapping sound.

> The glow of *faerzress* shifts across this chamber as if pushed by an unseen wind. It flows toward and around a large mesa and continues to spiral upward, but the ceiling of the cavern is too dark and high to see. You hear murmurs and whispers coming from atop the mesa, which grow louder as you approach. Its stacked levels resemble steps in a staircase, but a ramp running from top to bottom provides an easy way up.

Climbing the mesa reveals that its steps aren't concentric circles but the bands of a spiral, rising from the cavern floor to the mesa's top.

The west wall has a noticeable crack leading to a narrow tunnel, which can be used as a shortcut to area 7 if the characters are small enough to fit through it (see the "Whorlstone Tunnels: General Features" sidebar). Droki uses this narrow tunnel on his travels.

Characters at the top of the mesa hear the murmur of the chamber more clearly, and can recognize it as disparate sounds. They hear the rhythmic clank and roar of Gracklstugh's forges, the low rumble of Themberchaud's displeasure, the mad screaming of derro, and even hints and snatches of conversations. The *faerzress* in this place echoes the sounds produced in Gracklstugh above, creating a storm of noise.

A character can use an action to focus on spec[ific] sounds but must make a DC 12 Wisdom saving [throw,] taking 7 (2d6) psychic damage on a failed save, [or half] as much damage on a successful one. A characte[r who] fails the saving throw by 5 or more gains one lev[el of] madness (see "Madness" in chapter 2) as his or [her] mind is overwhelmed by what is heard.

A character who exceeds the saving throw DC [by 5 or] more can ask one question about Gracklstugh th[at can] be answered by overhearing any sound or conve[rsation] occurring within the previous tenday in the city [or] in the Whorlstone Tunnels. This can include dis[cerning] Droki's current location by following his insane mutterings.

A character can focus on the sound in the cha[mber a] number of times equal to his or her Wisdom mo[difier] (minimum 1). After that, the character no long[er has the] ability to tell sounds apart.

6. Dire Den

This small network of tiny grottos leads into on[e] of the dens of the Gray Ghosts, but it is the curr[ent] residence of a warped creature called the Spid[er King.] The characters must travel through narrow tun[nels to] reach this area (see the "Whorlstone Tunnels: [General] Features" sidebar).

> The glow of *faerzress* in these tunnels reveals stick[y] strands clinging to the walls. The strands become [more] dense as you move farther in.

The northeastern cave is the lair of the Spider [King, a] two-headed giant spider warped by demonic in[fluence] into a vaguely humanoid shape. This horrific cr[eature] uses the **giant spider** stat block with the follow[ing] modifications:

- The Spider King has 44 hit points, a passive [Wisdom] (Perception) score of 14, a Wisdom (Percept[ion) mod]ifier of +4, and the following saving throw b[onuses:] Constitution +3, Wisdom +2.
- Because of its two heads, the Spider King ha[s advan]tage on Wisdom (Perception) checks and on [saving] throws against being blinded, charmed, dea[fened,] frightened, stunned, and knocked unconsci[ous.]

The Spider King senses when intruders ent[er its] domain and can't be surprised by them. Along [with its] two normal **giant spiders** (its attendants), the [Spider] King waits in ambush. It moves to the entran[ce of its] chamber in an attempt to keep the characters [bottled] up, while the two giant spiders approach alon[g the walls] and ceiling, getting into position above creatu[res on the] floor. The Spider King and the giant spiders fi[ght to the] death, but they don't follow prey that flees.

Development

Sounds of combat here alert the duergar in a[rea 7.]

7. Gray Ghost Garden

The Gray Ghosts use this chamber to grow a variety of fungi for use in alchemical experiments.

Double doors blocks the western tunnel. The doors are made of thick zurkhwood and reinforced with crudely forged steel. The sturdy lock can be opened with a successful DC 15 Dexterity check using thieves' tools. A successful DC 20 Strength check will break the doors down.

> The smell of rot is strong in this room, coming from a large depression at the center, where dozens of fungi of many species grow. A barrel-shaped copper tank sits at the edge of the pit. Attached to the tank is a tall copper pipe that arcs over the pit. Crates line one wall.

Three **duergar** work here. They are members of the Gray Ghosts who have been assigned gardening duty. They attack as soon as they see intruders. If the characters arrive through the crack in the east wall (see "Fungi Pit"), they can hide among the fungi and try to catch the duergar by surprise. If the characters make a lot of noise in area 6 or force their way through the doors to the west, the duergar turn invisible and attack as soon as the characters arrive.

At the start of combat, two duergar use their Enlarge action while the third opens the valve on the copper tank and aims its nozzle at the characters. During the second round of combat on the same initiative count as the duergar, the **duergar alchemist** from area 8 joins the fight. If the other duergar fall, the alchemist turns invisible and tries to escape.

Fungi Pit

The pit is 5 feet deep and filled with various kinds of fungi. It is difficult terrain for Small and Medium creatures, and Tiny creatures have half cover while amid the fungi.

A crack in the east wall forms the mouth of a narrow tunnel that leads from the floor of the pit to area 6; see the "Whorlstone Tunnels: General Features" sidebar for more information on narrow tunnels.

The abundance of fungi in the thicket makes it easy to forage here. Among the common, inedible fungi are the following edible and exotic fungi, most of which are described in chapter 2:

- 1d6 barrelstalks
- 3d6 bluecaps
- 1d6 Nilhogg's noses
- 2d6 sheets of ripplebark
- 1d6 timmasks
- 1d6 torchstalks
- 2d6 trillimacs
- 2d6 bigwigs (see "*Faerzress*-Suffused Fungi")
- 2d6 pygmyworts (see "*Faerzress*-Suffused Fungi")

A character proficient and equipped with a poisoner's kit can also collect 1d6 doses of assassin's blood poison from the fungi pit (see "Poisons" in chapter 8 of the *Dungeon Master's Guide*).

Sprinkler Tank

The copper tank is a sprinkler used by the duergar to fertilize the fungi in the pit. The copper pipe that extends from the tank is 10 feet long and can be turned so that its nozzle points in any direction. The nozzle is pointed toward the pit by default.

Any creature can use an action to open or close a valve on the tank, releasing a cloud of pungent fertilizer that fills a 30-foot cube. The cloud grows 10 feet per side each round the valve remains open. The cloud has the same effect as a *stinking cloud* spell (save DC 12), but the effect ends 1d4 + 1 rounds after the valve is closed or the tank runs out of fertilizer. The tank contains enough fertilizer to spray for 10 rounds.

As an action or a bonus action, a creature can turn the pipe 90 degrees in any direction.

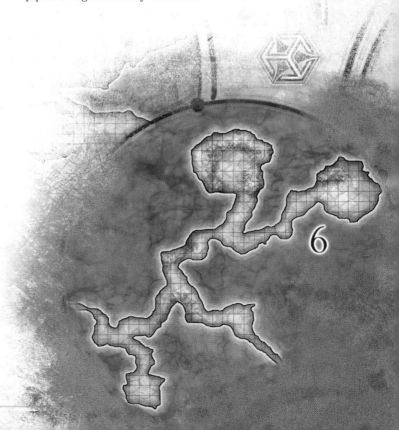

CRATES

The crates along the north wall are made of zurkhwood and stacked 5 feet high, and climbing on top of them costs 5 feet of movement. Most of the crates are empty, but four of them contain harvested, edible fungi. Each crate of fungi weighs 50 pounds, contains the equivalent of 20 days of rations, and can be sold in Gracklstugh or another Underdark settlement for 25 gp.

DEVELOPMENT

If the characters keep any duergar alive for questioning, it takes a successful DC 16 Charisma (Intimidation) check to gain an answer to a single question. The characters can ask only three questions total before the surviving duergar become incoherent and start frothing at the mouth—a form of madness brought on by demon-tainted *faerzress*. Any spell or effect that cures indefinite madness also restores a duergar's sanity (see "Madness" in chapter 8 of the *Dungeon Master's Guide*).

The duergar stationed here are tasked with protecting the fungi garden and helping the alchemist in his work. They use a trapdoor in area 8 to move between the Whorlstone Tunnels and the Darklake Docks in Gracklstugh. They have been ordered not to explore the rest of the Whorlstone Tunnels, though their leaders sometimes go farther into the tunnels on unknown business.

8. GRAY ALCHEMIST

The Gray Ghosts have claimed this cave as both a safe house and a laboratory, where their alchemists can work in relative peace and isolation.

> This area is surprisingly clean and orderly, split into two levels connected by a ramp made from zurkhwood planks. The upper level contains a fully furnished laboratory, while the lower level has two bunk beds. The wall of the lower level is set with a closed door.

Unless he is drawn to sounds of combat in area 7, a **duergar alchemist** (see the sidebar) named Lorthio Bukbukken works on the upper level of this area. Lorthio's laboratory contains a work table, a desk, a case of shelves lined with vials, and a dome-shaped oven. All furnishings are made of zurkhwood except the oven, which is made of stone.

DUERGAR ALCHEMIST

A duergar alchemist carries two vials of acid and two flasks of alchemist's fire. It uses the normal **duergar** stat block but replaces the Javelin attack option with the following attack options:

Acid Vial. *Ranged Weapon Attack:* +4 to hit, range 20 ft., one target. *Hit:* 7 (2d6) acid damage.

Alchemist's Fire. *Ranged Weapon Attack:* +4 to hit, range 20 ft., one target. *Hit:* 2 (1d4) fire damage at the start of each of the target's turns. A creature can end this damage by using its action to make a successful DC 10 Dexterity check to extinguish the flames.

The lower level is 10 feet below the laboratory contains two bunk beds and two small chests, a of zurkhwood (See "Treasure" below for informa the contents of the chests). The door is barred o side and has closed peepholes at dwarf's-eye he Opening the peepholes allows one to see into th beyond. The bar is easily lifted from this side, bu breaking down the door requires a successful D Strength check.

The room east of the door is empty except for ladder that climbs 60 feet to a stone trapdoor en in the ceiling. The trapdoor is unlocked, and ab narrow, spiraling tunnel leads to the Darklake I

DEVELOPMENT

Sounds of combat here alert the duergar in area use their Enlarge actions before heading this w

TREASURE

If the characters spend 1 hour ransacking the la can assemble two herbalism kits, one poisoner' ten healer's kits. In the (unlocked) zurkhwood c they find 1d6 vials of acid, 1d6 flasks of alchemi two *potions of healing*, one *potion of greater he* one *potion of fire breath*, and one *potion of psyc resistance*.

Depending on whether or not Droki delivered parcel and took his payment, the desk contains lump of black metal or a holy symbol of Ladugu of mithral (see "Finging Droki"). The desk also alchemical recipes scrawled in Dwarvish on to of parchment. A character who studies these so an hour and succeeds on a DC 15 Intelligence (check can piece together the formulas for craft of acid and flasks of alchemist's fire. The chara gather enough ingredients in the laboratory to of each. The character who knows the recipe a the proper ingredients can craft a vial of acid o alchemist's fire in 1 hour.

A character who searches the desk and succ a DC 12 Intelligence (Investigation) check also a letter hidden in a secret compartment. The le written in Dwarvish on a patch of lizard hide:

> I don't need your poison anymore. I'll deal with W Saltbaron myself. Bring me an elf blade, one with swirlies carved on the steel, and I'll forget you fail me. And I don't want to see any of your goons ne post. The captain is poking around, and I could u scapegoat.

If the characters capture Lorthio and question about the letter, he reveals one of the following information each time a character succeeds o Charisma (Intimidation) check:

- Gorglak is a warrior of the Stone Guard stat one of the outer gates near the Darklake Dis
- Gorglak is an avid collector of weird weapor
- Gorglak is easily bribed.

Presenting Gorglak's letter to Captain Errde Blackskull earns each character 50 XP for retrieving evidence of corruption within the ranks of the Stone Guard.

9. Fountain of Evil

Foul water from the Darklake spills into this cave, forming a pool. See the "Whorlstone Tunnels: General Features" sidebar for the effects of drinking foul water. The ceiling in this cave is 80 feet high.

> The chamber splits into two paths surrounding a large pool, filled by water trickling from stalactites along the ceiling. The western path forms a ramp above the pool's surface, while the eastern path runs level with the water and continues into a tunnel opening. The water turns darker toward the center of the pool, where it transforms from a gentle swirl into a churning vortex.

A **water weird** bound to the pool years has been corrupted by the demonic influence infecting these tunnels, turning it evil and giving it a dark hunger.

The western path slopes upward to a maximum height of 60 feet above the pool's surface. If the characters take this upper path, the water weird attacks them when they are 30 feet above the surface of the pool, as it was bound here to protect the path leading to area 16. The water weird can command the pool's water to erupt like a geyser, effectively lifting the water weird up to the characters' level and putting them within its reach. Any character the water weird successfully grapples is dropped in the pool, taking no damage from the fall. The pool is 30 feet deep in the middle and 5 feet deep near the shore.

If the characters follow Droki into this chamber, they see him sneaking carefully along the eastern path. They can attempt to follow him with a group Dexterity (Stealth) check contested by the water weird's passive Wisdom (Perception) score. If more than half the characters fail the check, the water weird notices them and attacks. If the characters are attacked by the water weird while following Droki, the wily derro realizes he's being shadowed and makes a run for it.

10. Cultist Pens

The insane derro cultists have been buying cave bears from Underdark hunters and smuggling them through Gracklstugh. For what purpose is anyone's guess.

A large gate made of iron bars blocks the northwest entrance and is usually locked. One of the derro cultists carries the key. The lock can be opened with a successful DC 15 Dexterity check using thieves' tools. A creature with a Strength of 20 or higher can force the gate open with a successful DC 25 Strength check.

> The first thing you notice as you enter the room is a heavy, unpleasant musk in the air, coming from cages assembled from scrap iron on both sides of the chamber. A spiral path circles into the center of the room, marked off by small stone pylons.
>
> Two derro stand by a large cauldron in front of a tent near the cave's center. Both are talking while apparently ignoring each other. In the cages, three hulking brown bears appear to be resting.

The two **derro** (see appendix C) are cultists. One of them is complaining about "the master" while the other talks about something he once fished out of the Darklake.

The three cave bears (use the **polar bear** statistics) are alert, despite appearances to the contrary. Characters hoping to sneak past them must succeed on Dexterity (Stealth) checks contested by the bears' passive Wisdom (Perception) score of 13. On their first turn, the cultists move to free the bears. Each cage is closed with a simple bolt that can be unlatched with an action. Once the first two bears are set free, the third bear breaks out of its cage on its own.

A crack in the south wall leads to a narrow tunnel that wends toward area 12. Medium and larger creatures are too big to fit through this narrow tunnel (see the "Whorlstone Tunnels: General Features" sidebar).

Spiral Path

This path helps to channel the ritual magic the cultists use to tame the cave bears. Though the ritual is currently inactive, the area radiates a faint aura of enchantment under the scrutiny of a *detect magic* spell.

Treasure

Inside the tent are two flea-ridden bedrolls, a zurkhwood bucket containing edible fungi (the equivalent of two days of rations), and a wineskin full of Darklake Stout.

11. Quasit Playground

Some of the cult's more powerful derro savants keep quasits as familiars, and the wee demons discovered this tunnel network. They use the tunnels as shortcuts to deliver messages across the areas of the Whorlstone Tunnels controlled by the cultists, or simply to hide from their duties. Shrinking down allows the characters to more easily navigate this area.

> The narrow tunnel is lit by the same dim, ambient light found throughout this complex. Ahead, you hear the high-pitched cackling of several creatures.

Four **quasits** are wrestling each other farther along in the tunnel. If they notice the characters, they attack.

When two quasits are reduced to 0 hit points, the two remaining ones turn invisible and flee. However, they make enough noise in doing so for the characters to follow them by sound. If any quasit escapes, the cultists in area 12 can't be surprised and prepare an ambush.

DEVELOPMENT

If the characters manage to capture and interrogate a quasit, the creature readily surrenders the name of Narrak—the derro savant leading the cultists in the Whorlstone Tunnels (see area 12). In exchange for its life, the quasit reveals that the cult plans to curse Gracklstugh's stone giants with madness as a means to sowing chaos in the city.

XP AWARDS

Each character earns a special award of 50 XP if the party learns of Narrak's plans from a quasit.

12. CULTIST HIDEOUT

Droki enters this cavern from the east, via a narrow tunnel that comes up through a crack in the cavern floor (see the "Narrow Tunnels" section of the "Whorlstone Tunnels: General Features" sidebar).

West of the cavern is a shrieker that serves as an alarm system (see "Fungi Patches") and a pit trap (see "Trap").

> The smell of brimstone and foul chemicals emanate
> from this large chamber. The light of campfires show
> a natural platform where five derro are droning a
> cacophonous chant. A two-headed dog stirs inside
> cage, while another derro nearby plays with a crossb
> and watches the dog nervously.
>
> A green glow rises suddenly from a magic circle a
> center of the platform, where a small humanoid sta
> is the focus of the chanting ritual. As you watch, a l
> sprouts from the statue's neck, enlarging and resha
> itself with each unholy verse to take the form of a
> second head.

Narrak, a derro savant, belongs to a fringe grou
the Council of Savants using demonology as a p
to power. Since the arrival of the demon lords, h
gathered and bullied several apprentices to part
in rituals aimed to sow chaos in Gracklstugh. N
knows the stone giants are a pillar of the Deepk
power, and that cursing them with Demogorgon
madness will be an appropriate first step towar
delivering the entire city to the demon lord.

The cage by the tunnel holds a **death dog**, wa
over by a nervous **derro** cultist. Atop the platfor
Narrak and four more **derro** cultists are perfor
a ritual around the statue at its center. (Statistic
Narrak and the derro can be found in appendix
cultists' chanting is punctuated with Narrak cal
the name "Demogorgon!") Also atop the platforr
comfortably in an fungi-filled alcove (and initial
the party's view), is Narrak's bodyguard—a fem;
named Grula-Munga.

When intruders appear, the cultists cease their chanting and take up positions along the edge of the platform as Grula-Munga rises to her feet and picks up her weapons. At the same time, the cultist standing next to the cage releases the death dog. Narrak continues his part in the ritual until the characters kill the death dog or one of the cultists, at which point he joins the battle. The door to the death dog's cage is held shut with a simple clasp and requires an action to open.

If any of the quasits escaped from area 11, they warn the cultists that intruders are near. Otherwise, the characters might catch the cultists by surprise. The quasits remain invisible and stay close to Narrak.

FUNGI PATCHES

Fungi is rampant throughout this area, growing in large patches on the floors and walls.

Two thick fungi patches grow by each wall in the western tunnel. Clinging to the north wall is a **shrieker** that party members can recognize with a successful DC 12 Intelligence (Nature) check. The shrieker starts screaming as soon as anyone comes within 30 feet of it.

The crack in the floor by the east wall is surrounded by a thick fungus patch that is difficult terrain for Small and Medium characters, and provides half cover for Tiny creatures. Growing among the common fungi are 2d6 bigwigs and 2d6 pygmyworts.

PLATFORM

The cavern floor rises to form a natural 5-foot-high platform. A glowing ritual circle dominates the top of the platform. Any non-derro that enters or touches the circle must succeed on a DC 13 Wisdom saving throw or gain one level of madness (see "Madness" in chapter 2). Whether the save succeeds or fails, the creature can't be affected by the circle in this way again. In addition, non-evil creatures within the circle have disadvantage on attack rolls and saving throws.

The statue within the ritual circle is 2 feet tall, weighs 100 pounds, and looks vaguely like a crouching stone giant with a lump on its neck where a second head is beginning to form. The statue is engraved with profane symbols, with the name "Dorhun" scribed in Dwarvish into its back. A successful DC 16 Intelligence (Arcana or Religion) check allows a character to recognize the profane symbols as being related to Demogorgon.

A search of the platform uncovers a similar but broken statue near a locked iron chest and a pile of books (see "Treasure" for more information on the chest and books). The broken statue is similar to the statue in the circle, except it has the name "Rihuud" carved into its back and its second head is fully formed. If Rihuud is dead, the broken statue turns to dust when the characters touch it. If the characters spared Rihuud's life, a successful DC 12 Intelligence (Arcana or Religion) check reveals that the second head is a conduit for the curse's magic, and that removing it and returning it to Stonespeaker Hgraam in Cairngorm Cavern will allow the elder giant to end Rihuud's curse.

TRAP

The tunnel west of this cavern contains a hidden pit (see "Sample Traps" in chapter 5 of the *Dungeon Master's Guide*). Debris conceals the lid, which is made of thin zurkhwood that breaks when a creature weighing 50 pounds or more steps on it. (A character of reduced size might not weigh enough to break the lid.) The pit is 10 feet deep, and its floor is covered by a patch of green slime (see "Dungeon Hazards" in chapter 5 of the Dungeon Master's Guide). Any creature that falls into the pit takes 1d6 bludgeoning damage and automatically fails its Dexterity saving throw to avoid the slime.

TREASURE

If the characters return the broken statue (or, at the very least, its second head) to Stonespeaker Hgraam, he gives them an emerald worth 500 gp as a reward, as well as his promise to vouch for them in anything they seek to accomplish in Gracklstugh.

Narrak has a key around his neck that opens the lock on the iron chest, which can also be picked with thieves' tools and a successful DC 17 Dexterity check. The chest contains a jar of *Keoghtom's ointment* and a small leather bag containing 45 gp and 15 sp.

The books have pages made from trillimac caps (see "Fungi of the Underdark" in chapter 2). They contain the mad scribblings of Narrak and his fellow derro savants. A character proficient in Arcana, Investigation, or Religion can spend 8 hours poring through them; subtract 1d4 hours if the character reads Dwarvish. At the end of this time, the character knows that the books outline two rituals: one that causes a one-headed creature to sprout a second head, and another that allows the grafting of a severed head onto a living creature. The notes fail to mention that the ritual's caster must be suffering from some form of madness to perform either ritual successfully.

Tucked in one book are two scrolls: one that bears a list of six stone giant names (including Rihuud's and Dorhun's) and another that is actually a letter written in broken Dwarvish:

> Narrak—
>
> Need more scrolls! Stonespeaker Hgraam has traps traps traps. But Droki is wily too and very small! I can hear talk, and in talk they say names, and I hear names and write names and give you names so you give me time. But you have to give me more scrolls. Magicky spelly scrolls!
>
> —Droki

XP AWARDS

Award 100 XP to each character for discovering Demogorgon's influence on the cultists.

The characters can complete a quest by turning over the books, scrolls, and letter to Errde Blackskull. Award 150 XP to each character when they deliver the items. If the characters ask Errde about Narrak, she tells them that he was a junior member of the Council of Savants.

13. DUMPING PIT

Victims of Narrak's experiments are dumped here. Exposure to the *faerzress* has begun to animate the corpses.

> This cavern is one enormous pit that reeks of death and decomposed flesh. The glow of *faerzress* is everywhere, seeming to flow like fog around dark shapes shambling across the pit floor. A single derro watches from atop a 15-foot-high ledge. A crack in the southeast wall of the pit leads to a narrow tunnel and is flanked by mounds of fungi and offal.

The pit is 15 feet deep, and the ledge that overlooks it is lined with pointy bits of scrap metal to make any climbing attempt perilous. A creature trying to reach the top of the ledge must succeed on a DC 12 Strength (Athletics) check. On a failed check, a creature takes 3 (1d6) slashing damage and remains in the pit. The pit's floor is difficult terrain due to the many corpses and body parts strewn around.

A single **derro** stands on the ledge overlooking the pit, which contains seven shambling **zombies**—three duergar and four grimlocks. The grimlock zombies are drawn to noise, while the duergar zombies attack any living creatures they see in the pit. Meanwhile, the derro uses its crossbow to take shots at any living creatures it sees.

A **crawling claw** wearing an obsidian ring on one stubby finger (see "Treasure") lurks amid the offal mounds. These mounds are difficult terrain to Small and Medium creatures, and the fungi growing atop them provide cover to Tiny creatures. The shriveled gray hand once belonged to Pelek the svirfneblin (see "Development").

The crack in the southeast wall between the mounds leads to a narrow, meandering tunnel, the floor of which is sunk below a foot of foul water. See the "Whorlstone Tunnels: General Features" sidebar for rules on narrow tunnels and foul water.

TREASURE

Faerzress has transformed Pelek's obsidian ring into a single-use magic item. When a living creature puts it on, the ring disappears, and the creature's skin becomes as hard as obsidian for the next hour. For as long as the effect lasts, the creature gains the benefit of a *stoneskin* spell.

DEVELOPMENT

If the characters capture and interrogate the derro, he talks willingly if they agree to spare him. He knows as much as the quasits in area 11.

Killing the crawling claw and burying its remains in Blingdenstone lays Pelek's spirit to rest (see area 1b).

14. OBELISK

The Gray Ghosts believe that the mysterious obelisk in this cavern is an important source of magical power,

and they are intent on rebuilding it. The obelisk [was] broken long ago. However, shards of the obelisk [that] appear throughout the Underdark are magically absorbed into it as soon as they touch its metal s[urface]. The leaders of the Gray Ghosts are obsessed wit[h] finding missing shards and completing this mon[ument,] but not even they know what will happen when t[he] obelisk is made whole again.

> After a steady upward climb, the tunnel opens into a huge, well-lit chamber. The glow of *faerzress* and bioluminescent fungi compete with shafts of white [light] that fall upon naturally formed shelves along the wa[lls] well as a rocky mesa at the center of the cavern. Cru[dely] formed ramps connect the different levels of the me[sa] up to the height of its two topmost tiers, which are [joined] by a sturdy bridge. Atop one of those tiers sits a larg[e] egg. Atop the other stands a 50-foot-tall obelisk ma[de of] smooth black metal with a few noticeable imperfec[tions,] as though small parts of it were somehow chipped [away.]
>
> A female derro stands close to the obelisk, gently patting and stroking its surface. The obelisk flashes once, the glow of *faerzress* around the cavern flaring [in] response. The derro squeals with glee as she snatch[es an] object up from the ground, then writes something in a small notebook.

The chamber is brightly lit, as if by sunlight. Th[e] sunlight is just a natural trick caused by crystal[s] reflecting and amplifying the light of the biolum[inescent] fungi growing on the walls. The characters rea[lize this] if they climb near the ceiling of the cavern, whe[re the] optical trick is easy to discern.

The different levels of the mesa are separate[d by] 10-foot-high cliffs. Climbing a cliff requires a su[ccessful] DC 12 Strength (Athletics) check. Pliinki, a ma[le] **derro** savant (see appendix C), stands atop of t[he] mesa. Hidden on a shelf above the cavern's ent[rance,] a **spectator** tasked with guarding this area see[s the] characters as soon as they walk 15 feet into the [cavern.] The spectator screeches an alarm and attacks, [killing] non-derro with glee. As it fights, it projects telep[athic] ramblings into the characters' minds, mostly de[scribing] how exciting it is to have intruders to kill and ho[w much] more exciting things will be when the obelisk is [whole.]

Pliinki shouts crass obscenities at the charac[ters in a] raspy voice while commanding the spectator to [kill] them. Both she and the spectator fight to the de[ath.]

OBELISK

Made from a black metal of alien origin, this m[onolith is] perfectly smooth except for the cracks and chi[pped] edges where it was splintered by some unknow[n force.] The obelisk is 15 feet per side at its base, stand[s 50 feet] tall, and tapers slowly to a pyramidal cap.

Any character proficient in Arcana can tell th[at the] obelisk's fractures are leaking quasi-magical en[ergy.] The character further understands that feedin[g] energy into the obelisk might activate its latent magic. Spending a spell slot of any level while touching the obelisk activates it and teleports everyone on the mesa to a location in the Underdark just outside the northwest gate of Gracklstugh.

The character who expended the spell slot knows the teleport effect can be repeated, but that this power is only temporary—a fluke due to the recent disruption of *faerzress* throughout the Underdark. Both the potency and the nature of the effect could change within a week or two, and this teleport effect likely bears no relation to the obelisk's actual purpose.

If the characters took the lump of metal from Droki or the Gray Ghosts, they notice the obelisk is made from the same material. If the lump is touched to the obelisk, it is instantly absorbed, repairing a crack on its surface.

Red Dragon Egg

The egg atop the northeast mesa is an unhatched dragon egg that the Gray Ghosts stole from the Keepers of the Flame. The 4-foot-tall, 3-foot-diameter egg weighs 180 pounds, and without fire to keep it warm, the egg can't hatch. If and when the egg does hatch, a **red dragon wyrmling** emerges and bonds with the first creature it sees.

Treasure

The derro savant carries a single gold coin, a stick of charcoal, and a battered notebook with pages made from trillimac (see "Fungi of the Underdark" in chapter 2). The coin is a shilmaer, an ancient gold coin traded among surface elves. The notebook contains Dwarvish writing, specifically a long list of random items, mostly coins and jewelry. There are no dates, but some entries appear in different handwriting. The last entry describes the "miraculous" appearance of the gold coin.

Development

If the characters capture and interrogate Pliinki, she laughs at their folly as she tells them that the Whorlstone Tunnels are nowhere near the surface. She believes the obelisk was hidden here by Diirinka, the derro god, and that it contains "unimaginable power." Pliinki and her fellow savants hope to harness the obelisk's power and use it to conquer Gracklstugh.

If the characters take the dragon egg to Themberchaud, he destroys it and rewards the party with a magical potion or oil plucked from his hoard. If the characters return the egg to the Keepers of the Flame, Gartokkar Xundorn promises them safe passage through Gracklstugh if they mention nothing about the egg to Themberchaud.

XP Awards

Taking the coin and the notebook to Ylsa Henstak in the Blade Bazaar fulfills her quest and earns the characters 100 XP each.

If the characters describe the obelisk to Gartokkar Xundorn, he assumes that is what the Gray Ghosts are using to wreak havoc in Gauntlgrym and dispatches a force to study it. Each character earns 100 XP for completing the task set for them by the Keepers. Award each character an additional 150 XP if the party

delivers the red dragon egg to either the Keepers or to Themberchaud.

14a. Fungi-Covered Doors

A set of double doors are hidden by a patch of fungi that includes 2d6 bigwigs and 2d6 pygmyworts. Characters west of the doors must succeed on a DC 15 Wisdom (Perception) check to notice the doors behind the fungi. The doors are fashioned from planks of zurkhwood and barred from the east side. A successful DC 20 Strength check allows a character to break through the doors, but this alerts the derro savant and the spectator in area 14.

Leaving Gracklstugh

The characters can gain the means to leave the city—and information to guide them on their journey—from a number of different sources, depending on the NPCs they interact with and the quests they undertake.

Errde Blackskull is true to her word, and she lets the characters leave the city freely if they fulfilled the tasks she set for them. Working for Themberchaud or the Keepers of the Flame leaves the characters in a position where they can at least avoid arrest in the city.

Deciding the next step for the characters depends on what information or quests the characters picked up in Gracklstugh. Heading for Neverlight Grove (see chapter 5) or Blingdenstone (see chapter 6) are the obvious next steps, as both places hold the promise of a route to the surface world. Alternatively, the characters can try their luck in the Labyrinth or the Wormwrithings.

Some of the quests the characters complete have the potential to change the power structure of Gracklstugh. For example, aiding Errde Blackskull and the Stone Guards might grant the characters the privilege of an audience with King Horgar Steelshadow V at some later time. If the characters press Errde, Gartokkar, or Stonespeaker Hgraam for a meeting with the Deepking, use the following section to run an encounter in the Deepking's palace.

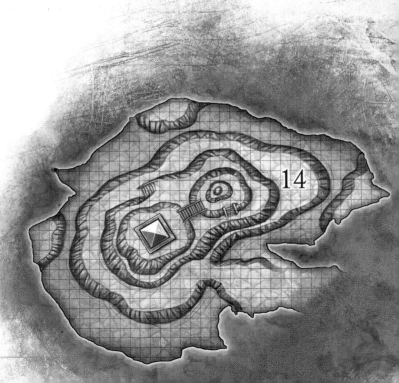

Hold of the Deepking

The Hold of the Deepking stands south of Laduguer's Furrow and north of Themberchaud's lair. When the characters first lay eyes on it, read the following boxed text aloud to the players.

> The Hold of the Deepking is a dark and foreboding edifice lodged between two great columns that rise up into thick clouds of smoke that conceal the cavern ceiling. Giant basalt braziers filled with molten lava bathe the palace facade in a hellish glow, and the thick stone walls bristle with iron turrets and battlements.

There appears to be no one guarding the palace, but this is an illusion. All of the palace guards are invisible, and characters who observe the palace for some time can hear duergar guards in heavy armor marching to and fro.

Two hundred invisible **duergar Stone Guards** (see appendix C) protect the palace and its king. Fifty stand at attention in perfect rows before the palace, ready to cut down anyone who approaches the palace gates unescorted. Another fifty watch from the turrets and battlements. One hundred more stand guard in the palace and comprise the Deepking's honor guard.

DEEPKING HORGAR
STEELSHADOW V

Audience with the Deepking

Characters who befriend Stonespeaker Hgraam complete quests for Errde Blackskull or Gartokk Xundorn can use their newfound influence to ga audience with the Deepking. Characters escorte palace by Hgraam, Errde, or Gartokkar are adm inside and led past rows of invisible duergar gua the Deepking's throne room.

> Lava pours down troughs cut into the black basalt of this vast hall. The heat is oppressive, and the air of sulfur. Thick black columns support the heavy ce and at the far end of the hall stands an iron throne a polished obsidian dais. A crowned duergar encas in armor sits on the throne. Next to him stands a r consort wearing a gown made of gold coins.

An invisible *wall of force* stands between the D dais and the characters. Whether the Deepking mind to fight the demon lords is up to you, altho many other duergar in the city, Horgar Steelsha has been touched by the demon lords' madness on the Indefinite Madness table in chapter 8 of *Dungeon Master's Guide* to determine Horgar's

If the characters attack the Deepking, use the statistics in the *Monster Manual* to represent hi the following modifications:

- Horgar is lawful evil.
- He speaks Draconic, Giant, and Dwarvish.
- He has AC 20 and wears *dwarven plate*.
- He has advantage on saving throws against p son, spells, and illusions, as well as to resist charmed or paralyzed.
- While in sunlight, he has disadvantage on att rolls, as well as on Wisdom (Perception) che rely on sight.
- He has the Enlarge and Invisibility action op **duergar** (see the *Monster Manual*).
- He wears *gauntlets of ogre power*, giving him Strength score of 19 (+4).
- He wields a *+2 warhammer* instead of a grea +8 to hit, reach 5 ft., one target. *Hit:* 10 (1d8 + bludgeoning damage, or 11 (1d10 + 6) bludge damage if used with two hands. While Horga enlarged, the damage increases to 15 (2d8 + (2d10 + 6) bludgeoning damage, respectively.

The Deepking's royal consort is a **succubus** guise of Shal, a female duergar. The succubus servant of the demon lord Graz'zt (see appendi Her only task is to make sure no one tries to ri of his madness. The gown she wears was a gift Horgar. It weighs 75 pounds and is worth 750

Development

If the characters expose the succubus as a fien and help restore Horgar's sanity, the Deepking friendly toward them and tries to set them aga drow, whom he blames for the spreading madr

Chapter 5: Neverlight Grove

Communities of myconids can be found throughout the Underdark. These intelligent, vaguely humanoid fungi lead lives of work and shared contemplation, providing shelter and safe passage to any who approach them peacefully.

The relative isolation of Neverlight Grove, its abundance of food and water, and the welcoming nature of its inhabitants might bring the characters here to rest, recuperate, and resupply. While in the grove, they can consult with the colony's myconid sovereigns about possible ways back to the surface world, while enjoying a much-needed respite from the brutal and harrowing conditions of the Underdark.

However, this particular myconid haven isn't as safe as it might appear. One of their sovereigns has fallen under the sway of Zuggtmoy, the Demon Queen of Fungi, who wasted no time building herself a stronghold in a colossal mushroom called Yggmorgus. There, she works on a malevolent scheme to claim all the Underdark as her domain. More and more myconids are slowly becoming unwitting thralls under her control, and characters who linger in Neverlight Grove might find themselves in great peril.

Going to Neverlight Grove

Because so few Underdark travelers have ever stumbled upon Neverlight Grove, it rarely appears on any maps. Nearly all the routes leading to it are dangerous and difficult to navigate, although many streams flow into and through the grove. If the characters enter the general area of the grove and stay close to—or travel along—these waterways, they eventually find their way

here. Alternatively, three of the party's companions can guide them to Neverlight Grove.

Stool, the characters' fellow prisoner from chapter 1, is a myconid sprout from the grove, captured by the drow before Zuggtmoy began exerting her influence over the myconids here. Although not knowledgeable about the Underdark, Stool has an innate sense of where its home lies and can guide the party toward it. Upon its return, Stool is greatly disturbed by the changes it encounters in the grove. It isn't well acquainted with either sovereign, but finds itself drawn toward Basidia.

The former drow prisoner Sarith Kzekarit might also become the party's guide, owing to his extensive knowledge of the Underdark. Though the party doesn't realize it, Sarith is infected with Zuggtmoy's spores, which now control his mind. He tries to steer the party toward Neverlight Grove, citing it as a place of safety in which the adventurers can decide their next move. In reality, he unknowingly leads the characters to become slaves of the Demon Queen of Fungi.

If the characters already visited Gracklstugh, Sarith might have gone with the infected myconids in the Whorlstone Tunnels, leaving Rumpadump with the party. A myconid sprout traveling with a troupe of infected myconids, Rumpadump has avoided infection and can also lead characters to the grove. He also expresses concern that the corrupted spores of its previous traveling companions might have also infected its home.

RANDOM ENCOUNTERS

Characters traveling to and from Neverlight Grove encounter evidence of Zuggtmoy's growing influence in the region. Whenever the party is within four days of Neverlight Grove, use the Encounters around Neverlight Grove table instead of the random encounter tables in chapter 2 to determine what, if anything, they encounter.

ENCOUNTERS AROUND NEVERLIGHT GROVE

d20	Encounter
1–8	No encounter
9–16	Fungi patch (see below)
17–18	1d4 nothics
19–20	1 chasme demon crawling on the ceiling or 1 vrock demon perched on a ledge (your choice)

FUNGI PATCH

If the characters are camped or resting, treat this encounter as "no encounter." Otherwise, the characters stumble upon a large fungi patch growing in a damp cave or tunnel. The fungi patch is difficult terrain and consists of many common but inedible species of giant fungi. Roll a d10 and consult the Fungi Patch Discoveries table to determine what else the characters find here.

See "Fungi of the Underdark" in chapter 2 for more information on edible and exotic species of fungi. Entries marked with an asterisk are further described after the table.

FUNGI PATCH DISCOVERIES

d20	Fungi or Creatures
1	1d6 barrelstalks
2	2d6 bluecaps
3	1d3 carrion crawlers
4	1d4 drow spore servants* (see appendix 1d4 quaggoth spore servants*
5	Fire lichen growing near a thermal vent
6	3d6 giant fire beetles
7	1d4 myconid adults*
8	1d6 nightlights
9	1 otyugh hidden under a mound of offal
10	Patch of brown mold (see "Dungeon Ha chapter 5 of the Dungeon Master's Guide
11	1d4 awakened zurkhwoods* (see appen
12	2d4 sheets of ripplebark growing on the
13	1d4 shriekers*
14	2d4 timmasks
15	1d6 tongues of madness
16	2d6 torchstalks
17	2d6 trillimacs
18	1d4 violet fungi
19	2d4 waterorbs growing near a freshwate
20	1d4 zurkhwoods*

Awakened Zurkhwoods. These giant anima mushrooms guard the fungi patch, attacking if are harmed or if the characters try to harvest a the fungi.

Drow and Quaggoth Spore Servants. These servants tend the fungi patch on behalf of the n and ignore the party unless attacked or interfer in which case they defend themselves.

Myconid Adults. These gentle creatures tend fungi patch and mind their own business, attac only in self-defense. If the characters establish communication with the fungus folk and ask fo directions to Neverlight Grove, the myconids of escort them to the grove and introduce them to exalted leader, Sovereign Phylo.

Shriekers. The shrieking of these fungi has percent of attracting a nearby chasme or vroc (your choice), which arrives 1d6 + 4 rounds late fights until killed.

Zurkhwoods. There is a 50 percent chance of the zurkhwoods has 1d4 + 4 stirges nesting The stirges are drawn to light sources.

ARRIVING AT THE GROV

While many passages lead to Neverlight Grove are little more than narrow fissures riven by tr of water. Only one natural tunnel is fit for relati easy travel by Medium creatures, formed by a underground stream and dimly lit by glowing l

Upon entering the cavern of the grove, chara leave the horrors of the Underdark behind. The themselves in a hidden enchanted place, strang alien but serenely beautiful. The access tunnel opens above the grove's main floor, providing t characters a panoramic view of a mushroom forest that covers every surface—including the ceiling—and illuminates the darkness with brilliantly colorful bioluminescent patterns.

On the other side of this exotic forest, the cavern narrows into a ravine. In a cavern beyond the ravine, a glimpse of a majestic mushroom tower can be seen, although the poor light and a rising mist makes it impossible to discern its details.

Drow Pursuit in Neverlight Grove

Though the characters don't know it yet, a drow scout patrol arrived in Neverlight Grove ahead of them, anticipating that the escaped adventurers might seek shelter among the myconids. Unfortunately for the drow scouts, an encounter with one of Zuggtmoy's servants led them to a grisly fate. See area 5, "The Garden of Welcome," for more information.

While the characters remain in Neverlight Grove, their pursuit level remains unchanged, as Ilvara waits to hear from the missing patrol. The drow pursuit resumes when the party leaves the grove. See chapter 2 for more information.

Important NPCs

The adventurers might interact with the following characters and creatures in Neverlight Grove.

Neverlight Grove NPCs

Sovereign Phylo	One of the two rulers of Neverlight Grove, in thrall to Zuggtmoy
Sovereign Basidia	The other ruler of Neverlight Grove, free of Zuggtmoy's influence and suspicious of Phylo
Loobamub	Leader of the Circle of Hunters, loyal to Basidia, with tasks for the party
Rasharoo	Leader of the Circle of Explorers and loyal to Basidia; knows of routes to the surface world
Yestabrod	Mutated leader of the Circle of Masters and Zuggtmoy's monstrous servant
Xinaya	Drow scout trapped in a horrible fate

A Day in Neverlight Grove

The myconid way of life is simple, contemplative, and cyclical. Myconids work for eight hours farming their fungi fields, scouting for resources, and maintaining their defenses. After their labors, they spend eight hours in telepathic communion with each other in what they call "melding." They then rest for eight hours before starting the cycle anew.

Many of the myconids in the grove are more extroverted than might be expected of their normally shy species. Characters who communicate with the myconids by way of their rapport spores note that the creatures seem to be preparing for a celebration of some sort, proclaiming "The day of joy is nigh!" and exhorting others to "Rejoice in the true union that will meld us all!" These are the myconids affected by Zuggtmoy,

and their behavior is cause for concern among the unaffected, including Sovereign Basidia and its allies.

Two Sovereigns

Myconid communities normally have only a single sovereign—the largest among them, who stands alone and outside of any circle (see below). Two years ago, Sovereign Basidia arrived in the grove with its two circles, and Sovereign Phylo welcomed the new myconids gladly, grateful for Basidia's offer to share the burdens of leading all the circles in the grove. The two sovereigns have been close friends ever since, sharing authority and responsibilities with no conflict. Each knows that an individual myconid has only so much time in the cycle of life, and that when both have passed, a single sovereign will take their place after their bodies are returned to nourish the soil.

SOVEREIGN BASIDIA

CIRCLES

The circles in Neverlight Grove are divided by specialized function, with each circle performing a specific role in the colony. Seven circles are present in the grove, each containing an average of twenty myconids—the Circle of Hunters, the Circle of Explorers, the Circle of Sowers, the Circle of Builders, the Circle of Growers, plus the recently formed Inner Circle and Circle of Masters. Each circle gathers around a circle mound—a pile of rocks and soil upon which mold, lichen, and mushrooms are encouraged to grow. The myconids of a circle gather around their own mound to meld and sleep.

After becoming enthralled by Zuggtmoy, Phylo decided the myconids would meld exclusively within their own circle, and only the circle leaders would meld with the other circle leaders and the sovereigns. Phylo asserted that this would make all the circles' meldings far more efficient, thereby making the tending of the grove that much easier. Most of the grove's myconids have gone along with this new and unusual concept, swayed by Phylo's claims that a higher level of communal harmony will be achieved.

Basidia believes that Phylo's separation of the circles is contrary to the unity and harmony of the myconid way of life, and that this segregation isolates individuals from the experiences of others outside their circle. Basidia has likewise expressed concern about the unnaturalness of the Inner Circle and the Circle of Masters. However, Basidia's views are either dismissed or ignored by Phylo and its allies, who zealously claim that exciting changes are coming for the grove.

A more recent development has Basidia even more disturbed when the adventurers arrive in Neverlight Grove. Yestabrod, the leader of the Circle of Masters, has not attended an Inner Circle melding for several days now, instead sending a representative (see Circle of Masters" in area 5). Times in Neverlig Grove are strange and worrisome indeed.

MELDING

Myconids share everything through melding. Ra spores carry a tiny bit of all myconids to the oth myconids in their circle, to be absorbed and resi within them, and creating a telepathic familial b When the myconids of a circle gather to meld, th their individual insights, fears, hopes, and drea Through the melding, all myconids join together the heart and soul of a colony.

ZUGGTMOY'S INFLUENCE

Initially weakened by the summoning ritual tha wrenched her from the Abyss, Zuggtmoy found way to Neverlight Grove, drawn by the strength fungal vitality. Upon her arrival, she quickly ass the situation, realizing the shortest path to gain of the grove would be to sway and corrupt its or sovereign to serve her until she recovered her st

After being welcomed to the grove by Phylo, Z melded with the sovereign in secret, seducing it the promise of a paradise for the mushroom foll Phylo would lead them to become her followers the Material Plane. Its mind completely lost insi demon queen's insidiously mad vision, Phylo be enthralled by the promise of plentiful soil and m perpetual rot, and beautiful transcendent drean be shared in a never-ending communal melding offered to the grove's folk as generous and wond gifts from the Lady of Decay.

Everyday melding has now become a subtle ideological war between supporters of the two sovereigns. Phylo is slowly convincing the mush folk to follow the new path. Basidia and its dwin supporters argue against the new way, even as t ground (and allies) each time the circles of the g share consciousness.

As more and more myconids unwittingly beco vessels for Zuggtmoy's spores, Neverlight Grove becomes a more extravagantly festive place. The contemplative joy of the mushroom folk's way of is being inexorably replaced by decadent, enrap euphoria—and the madness that euphoria hides

NEVERLIGHT GROVE

Population: 150 myconids and spore servants
Government: Organized circles ruled by larger
   specimens called circle leaders; even larger
   specimens called sovereigns rule the entire c
Defense: Spore servants and awakened zurkhw
Commerce: None
Organizations: Seven myconid circles;
   Zuggtmoy's servants

Myconids have lived in Neverlight Grove for unt generations, experiencing little or no change in lives until recently. Now their world is being alte faster than many of the fungus folk can keep up

---

ROLEPLAYING THE MYCONIDS

Myconids lead lives completely unlike the experiences of any surface dweller. The only things they have in common with humanoids are the need for sustenance, the desire to live, and the joy of socialization, although they practice each of these things in different ways than humanoids. Truly alien creatures, myconids have difficulty telling flesh-and-blood humanoids apart.

Myconids are innocent about matters of ethics and morality, their lives centered on living fully each day and worrying little about the future and nothing at all about the past. Despite the communal nature of their existence, they are individuals with their own unique interests and distinct personalities. They gravitate toward simple, shared joys, living by the wisdom and insight their melding provides. Because of their naive and sharing ways, as well as their fungal nature, they are extremely vulnerable to the corrupting influence of Zuggtmoy.

The myconids of Neverlight Grove are beginning to reel from the Lady of Decay's influence, with many blissfully welcoming her madness, while others bravely try to resist it. Myconids affected by Zuggtmoy abandon the growth of life as the core of their being in favor of decay and death. More horrifying is that they do so with childlike innocence, reveling in the corruption of all life with a sense of wonder and joy, unable to grasp the evil they have embraced.

with—as is their world view, twisted by the chaotic and corrupting influence of the Demon Queen of Fungi.

Upon her arrival in the Underdark, Zuggtmoy found Neverlight Grove and took up residence there. The myconids welcomed her, sealing their fate. Through telepathically shared dreams, corruption has taken root deep within the colony, warping the myconids' normally placid and peaceful nature into something restive and rapturous. A few realize what is happening and try to resist, but internal strife is alien to the myconids—they will not prevail without outside aid to save them.

1. FUNGAL WILDS

The myconids cultivate this stretch of wilderness as their first line of defense, creating a living palisade. Fungal creatures and wild Underdark beasts form a rich ecosystem here.

> Pale cream and beige stalks grow thick and tall, resembling a surface world forest. Fungi grow in profusion everywhere, and it's hard to find anything resembling a path between them. The giant caps of zurkhwood mushrooms obscure your view of the cavern's ceiling, but luminescent fungi there give off a shimmering aura. With each step taken on the soggy ground, a rank scent of decay rises around you.

CIRCLE OF HUNTERS

A circle mound sits at the edge of the wilds but still inside them. It belongs to the Circle of Hunters—myconids that pursue creatures in the wilds. In spite of their name, the hunters don't kill their prey, but merely track down creatures that have died near the grove. The hunters bring the remains of such creatures back to be reanimated by their sovereigns, until they are eventually allowed to rot and join the cavern's detritus bed.

Loobamub. The circle leader of the hunters, this tall and lean myconid shares Basidia's concerns about Phylo's new way, though it is still capable of resisting Phylo's corrupted meldings when it joins with the Inner Circle. Loobamub keeps its opinions to itself, but its wariness spreads to the other hunters when they meld, cementing their loyalty to Basidia. Loobamub redirects the spore servants and awakened zurkhwoods Phylo creates away from its circle's territory.

Loobamub is happy to enlist the party's aid in dealing with a few unwelcome monsters that have found their way into the fungal wilds. In particular, the circle leader asks the adventurers to kill a **grick alpha** and then take its carcass to Basidia for reanimation. A **shambling mound** is also exhausting the soil in the grove and needs to be put down for the good of the colony. These encounters can occur wherever you wish.

2. NORTHERN TERRACES

The terraces lining the northern walls are suffused with *faerzress*, and the myconids reserve these areas for cultivating certain fungi.

> Water trickling from the walls of this vast cavern are channeled into a crude but effective terraced irrigation system. A thick, sweet smell fills the air from the thousands of fungi of all colors and sizes, many glowing with a strange, inviting light.

CIRCLE OF BUILDERS

This circle is found in the middle terrace, but its members travel to the top and the edges of the cave to harvest the resilient fungi used in their craft.

Gasbide. The builders' circle leader is a pioneering would-be architect and a supporter of Sovereign Phylo. Already driven mad by Zuggtmoy's spores, Gasbide dreams of bizarre, elaborate structures no myconids would ever need, inspired by visions of Abyssal palaces.

NEVERLIGHT GROVE: GENERAL FEATURES

Visitors encounter the following features throughout Neverlight Grove.

Underground Marsh. Water trickles into the large cavern from many places, forming terraces, pools, and streams. This creates an underground marsh ideal for the growth of fungi and the myconids.

Abundant Fungi. Mushrooms, molds, and fungi grow in abundance in Neverlight Grove, creating a bizarre yet beautiful tapestry of color.

Quiet Cacophony. Myconids don't speak. They communicate telepathically by emitting their rapport spores. As a result, they live quiet lives. Strange music and singing echoes from the large cavern behind the grove, just loud enough to be noticeable.

Otherworldly Light. Luminescent lichen grows across the cavern and spreads to the larger mushrooms, bathing the grove in soft hues of yellow, blue, and violet. Dim light suffuses the entire grove and lends the grove a dreamlike quality.

Sentinel Mushrooms. To defend themselves, myconids have cultivated and guided the growth of awakened zurkhwoods (see appendix C) to serve as a kind of palisade around the grove.

Zuggtmoy's Spores. This malevolent disease is spread by myconids transformed by Zuggtmoy's demonic influence (see "Myconids" in appendix C).

A transformed myconid can release the spores in a cloud that fills a 10-foot-radius sphere centered on it, and the cloud lingers for 1 minute. Any flesh-and-blood creature in the cloud when it appears, or that enters it later, must make a Constitution saving throw. The save DC is 8 + the myconid's Constitution modifier + the myconid's proficiency bonus. On a successful save, the creature can't be infected by these spores for 24 hours. On a failed save, the creature is infected with a disease called the spores of Zuggtmoy and also gains a random form of indefinite madness (determined by rolling on the Madness of Zuggtmoy table in appendix D) that lasts until the creature is cured of the disease or dies. While infected in this way, the creature can't be reinfected, and it must repeat the saving throw at the end of every 24 hours, ending the infection on a success. On a failure, the infected creature's body is slowly taken over by fungal growth, and after three such failed saves, the creature dies and is reanimated as a spore servant if it's a type of creature that can be (see the "Myconids" entry in the *Monster Manual*).

If Gasbide interacts with the characters using rapport spores, it demands descriptions of surface-world structures, bristling with an excitement seldom seen in myconids. It asks for exasperatingly minor details such as the precise dimensions of bricks or the density of lumber. Gasbide reveals through the rapport that it dreams of building a fungal tower "even greater than Yggmorgus." It hopes to break through the Underdark to the surface world, possibly "with the aid of Araumycos." Gasbide has no conscious knowledge of what Araumycos is, sensing only that it is part of the great celebration to come. See "Yggmorgus" (at the end of this chapter) and chapter 16, "The Fetid Wedding," for more information.

CIRCLE OF GROWERS

The circle mound of the growers is on the top terrace, near the cavern wall. The growers are the colony's farmers, ensuring the soil beneath the pools remains fertile and tending the fungi there.

Hebopbe. The leader of the growers doesn't care much for Phylo's new ideas. But though it misses mass meldings, Hebopbe doesn't see Basidia's protests as worthy of concern. Hebopbe is infected by Zuggtmoy's spores, but isn't yet under her control.

3. CENTRAL BASIN

This depression in the cavern floor is the main part of the myconid colony. The central circle mound was only recently created, and is now a kind of "town square" where all the grove's myconids gather for mass meldings. These have become rare, however, reserved for when Phylo wants to stoke the myconids' enthusiasm for the celebration that only those infected by Zuggtmoy know about. This leaves the uninfected confused but happy that something joyous is about to happen.

> Beyond the mud and mushrooms that spread across the cavern, a large, clear pool sits in the midst of the fungal grove. A central mound seems to be the only dry spot in sight, though a small cliff rises above the cavern floor far across the clearing, with giant mushrooms visible in the distance. Bioluminescent fungi trace strange constellations along the cavern's ceiling and walls, showing the darkness of the ravine and a mist-shrouded smaller cavern beyond.

INNER CIRCLE

The central mound is the base of the colony's two **myconid sovereigns**, Phylo and Basidia. They hold court together with three **myconid adult** councilors named Brelup, Posbara, and Breberil. Ten **awakened zurkhwoods** (see appendix C) protect the mound and obey either of the sovereigns.

Sovereign Phylo. The sovereign towers above the other myconids, its multiple caps swaying with the sinuous shifting of its thick stalk as it moves. Once it spreads its rapport spores, Phylo welcomes the characters with honest enthusiasm—doubly so if they have returned Stool and Rumpadump to their home.

> "You are safe, friendly softers. You arrive at a wond[...] time, for Neverlight Grove is on the verge of some[...] great, something marvelous! Celebrate, as the day [...] joy is nigh!

Phylo invites the characters to stay as long as tl[...] inviting them to explore and enjoy the many del[...] of Neverlight Grove. He politely asks that they a[...] the eastern plateau because the Circle of Maste[...] preparing "a wondrous and glorious surprise" i[...] Garden of Welcome. Phylo offers to give them a[...] next day if they want. If Sarith is with the chara[...] he suggests they accept this offer, saying that k[...] on the sovereign's good side will help the party [...] long term. In truth, he is attempting to deliver t[...] adventurers to Zuggtmoy.

Phylo goes on about how "the Great Seeder" [...] beyond the garden can answer any questions tl[...] The sovereign describes this entity in favorable[...] using "she" and "her" as it does so. Because my[...] have no concept of gender, this unusual speech[...] further indication of Phylo's madness. Howeve[...] sovereign dodges any question about who the C[...] Seeder actually is, saying it is important for the[...] characters to experience her first hand.

Sovereign Basidia. A successful DC 12 Wisc[...] (Insight) check reveals that Sovereign Basidia i[...] uncomfortable with Phylo's behavior. Stool and [...] Rumpadump can easily discern that the harmo[...] between Phylo and Basidia is off. At the earlies[...] opportunity, Basidia volunteers to show the cha[...] around, or finds another opportunity to rapport[...] them privately.

When alone with the characters, Basidia war[...] about staying in Neverlight Grove too long. It te[...] another group of "softers" (the name myconids [...] fleshy creatures) arrived not too many cycles ag[...] accepted Phylo's offer. They were taken to the C[...] of Welcome and Basidia hasn't seen them since[...] has Phylo made any further mention of them (s[...] "Questions for the Sovereigns"). Basidia also te[...] characters that the Circle of Masters is taking [...] the carcasses the Circle of Hunters bring in, ar[...] sending groups of myconids outside the grove [...] telling anybody.

If Basidia rapports with Sarith or any other [...] myconid infected with Zuggtmoy's spores, it s[...] the alien nature of the demon lord's corruptio[...] can't identify Zuggtmoy's spores, but knows o[...] it has not encountered them before. This is un[...] Basidia tells the party, since most myconid so[...] recognize all spores produced by myconids th[...] the Underdark.

Questions for the Sovereigns. If the charact[...] ask the sovereigns to help them return to the s[...] world, both are apologetic that they know of no [...] routes. However, Basidia notes that during its [...] migration, the many travelers from the surface [...] world they encountered were mostly merchants[...]

BLANDO

their way to or from Blingdenstone, Gracklstugh, or Menzoberranzan.

If the adventurers ask the sovereigns about any drow in the area, Basidia tells them about a drow patrol that just recently arrived. However, Phylo immediately interrupts, telling the characters that the drow were here a few days ago, but left shortly after Phylo showed them the Garden of Welcome. A successful DC 12 Wisdom (Insight) check reveals that Basidia seems puzzled by Phylo's answer. If pressed, Basidia simply says it didn't know the drow had already left.

Quest: Into the Garden. Basidia offers to give the party a guided tour of all the circles in areas 1 through 4, where it introduces them to the respective circle leaders, pointing out which leaders support it, and which ones support Sovereign Phylo. Basidia uses this time away from Phylo to express its fear that Phylo has contracted some sort of "diseased spore." Basidia thinks that a clue to the spore's nature might be found in the Garden of Welcome. Basidia asks the characters to investigate the garden, fearing to do so itself in case it also falls victim to Phylo's disease.

As a sign of friendship, Basidia gives the characters a moldy scroll case containing a *scroll of protection against fiends*. Basidia promises an additional reward (see "Treasure") if the characters investigate the

Garden of Welcome on its behalf. Basidia can also brew potions out of the different molds and fungi in the grove, storing them in hollow gourd-like mushrooms. Basidia can craft a common or uncommon potion in eight hours, or a rare potion in two days.

Treasure

If the characters complete Basidia's quest, the myconid sovereign digs up a small box buried in the earth and gives it to them. The box contains curiosities Basidia has collected from dead travelers over the years. The box is unlocked, made of fine wood inlaid with silver, and worth 25 gp by itself. It contains three amethysts (100 gp each), four small diamonds (50 gp each), and one large diamond (500 gp).

If the characters kill the grick alpha, the umber hulk, or the shambling mound in the Fungal Wilds and bring the carcasses to Basidia, the sovereign rewards each character with a *potion of greater healing* stored in a hollow gourd-like mushroom.

Circle of Sporers

This circle mound is devoted to sporing new myconids. Freshly spored myconids are only a few inches tall and have no awareness, but they grow quickly into myconid sprouts.

4. Southern Terraces

The terraces along the southern rim of the ca[v]
narrower and not as fertile as the northern on[e]

> These terraces are quiet and calm. The only soun[d]
> here are soft, "ploopy" splashes as water drips fr[om]
> stalactites above onto the caps of oversized mush[rooms]
> sprouting from mushy earth.

Circle of Explorers

This circle is the smallest in Neverlight Grove,
merely the temporary home for restless mycon[ids]
brave the Underdark as scouts, patrols, and pa[rties]

Rasharoo. This circle leader is loyal to Basi[dia]
Frequent trips outside the grove have allowed [it]
to notice the changes in Phylo and the entire c[olony]
more sharply, and it now trusts nothing and n[o one]
except Basidia. Its paranoia isn't the product [of]
Zuggtmoy's corruption, however, but of the ris[ing]
madness gripping the Underdark from the int[rusions]
of the demon lords. If the characters demonst[rate]
sympathy with Basidia or if the sovereign is w[ith them,]
Rasharoo discloses it has a few escape plans [and]
has nutrient caches hidden along exit tunnels [in case]
Basidia decides it is better to abandon the gr[ove and]
return to a nomadic lifestyle.

Characters can climb the eastern corner of [this]
top terrace to reach area 5, and Rasharoo gla[dly]
helps them if they head to the Garden of Welc[ome at]
Basidia's request.

Developments

Among the myconids, Rasharoo and its circle [are the]
adventurers' best hope of finding a way back [to the]
surface. Rasharoo knows many promising pa[ths, but]
since myconids have no interest in the sunlit [world, it]
has never followed them all the way there. Th[e circle]
leader helps the characters only after they co[mplete]
Basidia's quest, assigning one of its explorer[s to guide]
the characters to their destination.

5. Garden of Welcome

Phylo has converted this unused terrace for [the]
new ideas that Zuggtmoy has inspired in it—[ideas that]
are "too incredible" for the rest of the colony [to grasp]
at once. This so-called garden is just a samp[le of the]
horrors that Zuggtmoy, the Demon Queen of [Fungi,]
intends to bring to the Underdark.

> This plateau rises higher than the other terrace[s and is]
> screened by a natural fence of soaring zurkhwo[od trees.]
> Muffled murmuring can be heard from atop th[e plateau.]

Yrberop. The circle leader is infected by Zuggtmoy's
madness. It is always swaying to music only it can
hear, but those in rapport with Yrberop can hear a faint
echo of its internal cacophony. Yrberop is enthusiastic
about Phylo's plan to spread the happiness brought by
the Great Seeder to everyone in the Underdark and
beyond. For that to happen, the colony needs many
more sprouts.

If the characters confer with Basidia, Stool, or
Rumpadump, these myconids tell them this push to
expand the population is unusual, given the balance
that the myconids have endeavored to maintain in
Neverlight Grove for so long.

Yrberop loses track of any conversation after a short
while and begins talking to the newly spored myconids
instead. Characters who communicate with Yrberop in
rapport and succeed on a DC 13 Wisdom (Insight) check
can make out some of the words and impressions in
the circle leader's lullaby. It sings of the Great Seeder
and "her" wedding to the Great Body, and how every
myconid is invited, bringing joy to all in the world below
and above.

Chuul Spore Servants. Behind the myconid breeding
grounds is a narrow path leading up to a plateau and
the Garden of Welcome (area 5). Two **chuul spore
servants** (see appendix C) guard this path. They don't
allow anyone to pass without Yrberop's permission,
which the circle leader doesn't grant, even at
Basidia's request.

Circle of Masters

The newest circle in the colony, the Circle of Masters is formed exclusively by myconids touched by Zuggtmoy. These myconids share Phylo's vision of happiness spread through Zuggtmoy's spores, experimenting on the carcasses brought to them by the hunters—or on live prisoners they hunt in their own expeditions outside the grove. Their mound lies at the center of an obscene garden.

Yestabrod. Mutated by Zuggtmoy's spores, the circle leader has become an abomination. No longer recognizable as a myconid, it looks like a fungal larva slithering along the ground. Mold and lichen grow in hypnotic patterns along its ringed stalk, and it puffs clouds of spores from a slit resembling a mouth. It can use this orifice to actually speak, rather than depending on rapport spores. It no longer attends melds with the other leaders, instead sending its representative.

Garden of Horror

As the characters enter the garden, they make a frightening discovery.

> The low muttering grows louder as you reach the top, turning into a symphony of moans, cries, and hisses. The only light comes from a few glowing mushrooms along the edge, but even in the gloom, you can't miss the source of the sounds. The heads of creatures of a dozen humanoid Underdark races peek from the ground, mold and fungi growing around them.
>
> One voice calls out loudly in Undercommon—a female drow fighting to speak. "Please ... for your gods of light . . . kill me!" She manages to stir within her living grave, raising a spider medallion half-embedded in the bloated growth that was once her hand. Half her face is rotten and pustulate, a bed for the sprouting of scores of tiny mushrooms. "The Great Seeder ... trap ... she's here ... the Lady of Decay ... Zuggtmoy ..."

The drow is Xinaya, a young acolyte of Lolth. She was leading a routine scouting patrol out of Velkynvelve before Ilvara contacted her with a *sending* spell. The patrol was ordered to search near the grove for the characters, anticipating that the escapees might seek shelter among the peaceful mushroom folk.

Upon her arrival, Xinaya made the mistake of accepting Phylo's invitation to visit the Garden of Welcome, where she and her patrol quickly became victims of the myconids' madness. She begs the adventurers to end her suffering and warn her people about the presence of the Demon Queen of Fungi in the Underdark, unaware of the madness that has already erupted in Menzoberranzan and throughout the Underdark (see chapter 15). Xinaya is too far gone to be saved, and any amount of damage kills her.

After the characters speak with Xinaya, **Yestabrod** appears (see appendix C). The master of the foul garden takes delight in toying with trespassers.

> The moans of the garden's victims suddenly take on a new tone of fear as something moves across the foul ground. A disgusting larval creature rises up before you, showing only vestigial fungal growths that hint that it might once have been a myconid.
>
> "Welcome, travelers." The aberrant myconid's voice gurgles and spits as it speaks both aloud and in your minds at once. "Are you here for the wedding rehearsal? Friends of the bride or her intended? No matter! Let the love of the Great Seeder embrace you as you become one with her chosen, the Great Body!"

As the garden comes alive with screams from its buried victims, Yestabrod raises two **drow spore servants** (see appendix C). At the same time, two **myconid adults** from the Circle of Masters emerge from the surrounding growth, all of the creatures following the circle leader as he attacks.

If Sarith Kzekarit (see chapter 1) is still with the party, he screams in agony as Yestabrod attacks. The characters can only watch as the drow's head splits open, releasing a cloud of infecting spores and turning him into another **drow spore servant** that joins the fight.

If Yestabrod is slain and there are still drow spore servants active, they go limp and stop attacking, at which point the myconids from the Circle of Masters attempt to flee.

Treasure

Xinaya's equipment is piled in a heap not far from where she was buried. Characters searching the pile find a suit of *+2 studded leather armor*, a *+2 shortsword*, and a *bag of holding* containing two *spell scrolls* (*remove curse* and *spider climb*), 40 days of rations, and 320 sp. The drow spore servants wear chain shirts and carry shortswords. All of the armor and weapons found here are of drow construction (see the "Drowcraft Items" sidebar in appendix B).

XP Awards

In addition to the normal creature XP for this encounter, the characters earn a special award of 1,000 XP (divided equally among all party members) for defeating Yestabrod and its minions.

Wedding Rehearsal

After the confrontation with Yestabrod, the characters can hear sound and movement from the cavern to the northeast. Read the following boxed text if the characters investigate.

Echoes spill from the misty cavern beyond, a cacophony of wheezing voices that wrap together like some kind of discordant music. The remaining heads planted in the Garden of Welcome begin to croak and groan, joining the horrible song.

Through the mist that shrouds the smaller cavern, you see the parade of creatures responsible for the melody. Their bodies are only vaguely humanoid, with clusters of luminescent lichen and tumescent growths forming chaotic patterns on their decaying flesh, their voices stabbing into your minds, both insane and gleeful in equal parts:

From rocky bed the toadstool rose,
From chaos dark, her love She shows.
Wish! Yearn! Laugh!
The Lady will be wed!
Crave! Hunger! Dance!
Her joyous spores will spread!
Youth is gone, beauty rots,
Araumycos and Zuggtmoy!
Joined together, heart to heart,
Becoming one 'til death do part!
Hail! Hail! Hail!

The entourage is composed of twelve **bridesmaids of Zuggtmoy** and six **chamberlains of Zuggtmoy** (see appendix C for both), all of which are lost in their own reverie. They are in the midst of conducting an obscene ritual of some sort—like a parody of a wedding ceremony.

Zuggtmoy's thralls make their way to Yestabrod's garden, attacking only if the characters stand in their way.

Any character reduced to 0 hit points in this encounter is knocked unconscious rather than killed. If all the characters are knocked unconscious, the party wakes up in a fungi-filled cave 1d6 + 4 miles away from Neverlight Grove, with or without their NPC companions (at your discretion). Their drow pursuit level decreases by 1, and each character is infested with Zuggtmoy's spores (see the "Neverlight Grove: General Features" sidebar).

DEVELOPMENT

If left alone, the thralls enact a mock wedding, with a chamberlain and a bridesmaid standing in for Araumycos and Zuggtmoy. Yestabrod, if alive, assumes the role of priest to preside over the vows. If Yestabrod is dead, three spore servants rise from the garden and carry its corpse, moving it like a puppet to play out the part of priest. At this point of the ceremony, any onlookers experience a vision.

The tableau of the mock wedding is replaced by a vision of the inside of a great tower. Spiraling stai[...] balconies are carved into its walls, with the interio[...] phosphorescent patches of mold growing in who[...] the center of the open space floats a humanoid fig[...] womanlike in form, but made entirely of fungi and mold. She is easily three times the height of the fu[...] bridesmaids that move up and down the spiraling [...] tending to their giant mistress. They croon a stra[...] soothing song as they weave the substance of the[...] figure into delicate lichen veils and a long, myceliu[...] like a bridal gown.

The vision ends when the ceremony does, afte[...] which the creatures file solemnly back to Yggm[...] Characters witnessing the wedding rehearsal a[...] the accompanying vision must succeed on a DC[...] Wisdom saving throw or gain one level of madn[...] "Madness" in chapter 2).

If the characters share their experience with [...] the sovereign leads the two circles loyal to it ou[...] Neverlight Grove before it is too late. Alternativ[...] characters can follow the wedding procession i[...] Yggmorgus and witness the further horrors wa[...] the Underdark if Zuggtmoy rises in power.

XP AWARDS

In addition to the XP gained for defeating Zugg[...] bridesmaids or chamberlains, each characters [...] 100 XP for witnessing the wedding rehearsal.

YGGMORGUS

When Zuggtmoy arrived in the Underdark, she [...] immediately drawn to Neverlight Grove and its [...] riches. She cultivated Yggmorgus, a mushroom [...] proportions, from the rich, rotting soil.

Conveniently secluded from the rest of the Un[...] Yggmorgus is a perfect base of operations for th[...] Demon Queen of Fungi. She has completely en[...] Phylo, and the hapless sovereign is growing a m[...] and spore servant army for her. Zuggtmoy has a[...] become aware of Araumycos, the largest fungal [...] form—and possibly the largest creature of any k[...] in the world. Araumycos is a vast fungus colony [...] a single mind, which fills the caverns and tunne[...] the Underdark in an area the size of the High F[...] Araumycos is so interwoven with the fabric of th[...] that control of it would grant Zuggtmoy nearly u[...] power in her new home.

Though Yggmorgus can't be seen clearly from[...] main cavern of Neverlight Grove, the unholy ligh[...] sounds there can be discerned and sometimes e[...] Characters who ask the myconids about it recei[...] responses. Sovereign Phylo and those loyal to it[...] state of near bliss when they speak about Yggm[...] if it was a paradise. Sovereign Basidia and its fo[...] give wary answers. Phylo's secrecy means that t[...] aren't sure what lies beyond the ravine.

GIANT MUSHROOM TOWER

The cavern around Yggmorgus is huge, and the giant mushroom nearly fills it from floor to ceiling.

> You have no clear reference to judge the towering mushroom's size at this distance. Thousands of smaller fungi cling to the main stalk, which itself splits into several lesser stalks, each long enough with a cap big enough to be the top of a great tower. The cavern floor surrounding the stalk is covered by a carpet of fungi.
>
> An eerie luminescence pours through slitted windows carved into the trunk, with the same cacophony of atonal music heard earlier echoing within. A stench of rot and decay wraps around you, seemingly threatening to penetrate your flesh and pervade your soul.

Yestabrod's Garden of Welcome is a pale reflection of the true horrors surrounding Yggmorgus. A 20-foot-high crescent-shaped ledge hugs the cavern wall and gradually slopes down to the lower basin. The ledge is covered with a carpet of moss and fungi, scores of variously sized lumps, and pockmarks where pools of vile fluids suppurate and ooze, some drying out and scabbing over. The entire ledge is difficult terrain. Characters venturing this close to Yggmorgus must succeed on a DC 11 Wisdom saving throw or gain one level of madness (see "Madness" in chapter 2).

Characters can discern the shapes of writhing creatures inside each lump. Most of these are humanoids, though a few of the lumps are occupied by what appear to be gricks, nothics, and giant spiders. This is the Great Garden of Rot, nourished both by the creatures subsumed within it and the *faerzress* pervading this cavern.

As if on cue, one of the lumps closest to the characters bubbles up and bursts. A dense cloud of spores and dark, reeking fluid explodes outward, even as the characters hear a piercing scream of agony and terror. Inside the pockmark left behind by the burst is one of Xinaya's drow scouts—or at least what's left of him. Other than a face, long white hair, and a breastplate, it is impossible to distinguish where the drow ends, and the rot and fungi consuming him begins. The drow feebly thrashes, his screams rising ever higher in pitch, until he locks eyes with one of the characters and abruptly stops screaming. A brief moment of lucidity replaces his terror, even as his eyes roll back into his head in some kind of bizarre euphoria as he goes limp and slowly sinks back down into the fungal muck. Characters witnessing this must succeed on a DC 13 Wisdom saving throw or gain one level of madness.

Throughout the entire cavern, loud moans and cries of agony answer the drow's screams in a terrifying and deafening chorus, drowning out all other sounds until eventually winding down into a low susurration of groans and burbles. The entire stalk of the giant mushroom seems to shudder, almost as if in delight.

Characters who descend to the cavern's lower basin witness the next spectacle of unspeakable horror spawned by the Lady of Decay.

Mad Dance

Scores of deformed creatures dance around the base of the giant fungal tower. The revelers are a motley collection of humanoids and various other creatures, all sporting tumors, cankers, and putrid patches of flesh all over their bodies. They are joined by dancing fungi vaguely shaped and twisted into forms resembling humanoids. Some of these creatures are spore servants enthralled to the Demon Queen of Fungi. Others are myconids and other fungal life forms infested with Zuggtmoy's spores.

The dancing creatures pay no attention to trespassers unless they are attacked. In that event, 1d6 **drow spore servants** and 1d6 **hook horror spore servants** (see appendix C for both) stop dancing and turn on their attackers.

Voices can be heard cackling and chatting amiably about Sovereign Phylo's success at "bringing so many new guests to attend the party!" The characters see drow dancing as if their bones were melting, duergar roaring with mock merriment and vomiting slime, and even nothics laughing madly as they leap and caper.

If the characters observe the mad dance for a few rounds, they see a form rising up out of the fungal muck. It is the drow scout whose terrible end they just witnessed, wading out to join the other revelers in their mad dance. A character who witnesses this grotesque moment must succeed on a DC 15 Wisdom saving throw or gain one level of madness.

Great Palace

Yggmorgus is the home that Zuggtmoy, the Demon Queen of Fungi, has carved for herself inside the great mushroom. The general layout is simple enough, with the hollowed stalk of the mushroom making a towering central hall in which Zuggtmoy floats, surrounded by spiraling balconies where her growing number of bridesmaids attend her, singing as they weave her bridal gown to prepare for the fateful wedding day.

If the adventurers enter Yggmorgus, they come face to face with **Zuggtmoy** (see appendix D), attended by twelve **bridesmaids of Zuggtmoy** (see appendix C). Fortunately for them, Zuggtmoy is deep in meditation as her gown and veil are being prepared. She doesn't move, although she can speak and use her other abilities. Her bridesmaids attempt to chase off intruders, wailing and scolding them about how it is unlucky for them to see the bride before it is time. If the characters don't withdraw immediately, Zuggtmoy awakens and uses her Mind Control Spores ability to send them away, using her Infestation Spores only if the characters insist on engaging the demon lord here and now.

Dozens of spore servants and myconids respond to Zuggtmoy's telepathic call if their mistress is in danger, attacking the characters heedless of their own safety. Any attack that successfully deals damage to Zuggtmoy damages her gown, driving the demon queen into a rage to attack the intruders.

Leaving Neverlight Grove

Leaving the myconid enclave is easier than fi̵ Whether they politely avoid Phylo's invitation their lives and sanity from the Demon Queen the adventurers can easily receive the aid of S̵ Basidia and the circles still loyal to it. Where characters go next is up to them—a decision ̵ upon where they have been, the pursuing dro̵ whatever they have acquired (food, potions, tr̵ from the doomed drow patrol, and so on) duri̵ visit to the grove.

Depending on how the characters interacte̵ the myconids and what tasks they accomplish̵ their hosts, they might depart in the company̵ myconid guide, or even two whole circles of ̵ fleeing the grove before Zuggtmoy's madness̵ them. Sovereign Phylo doesn't stop the chara̵ or Sovereign Basidia from leaving, still convi̵ the cause it embraces is one of joy and prosp̵ its people.

In all probability, the characters leave the f̵ with dire and horrific news. They have witnes̵ effect a single demon lord can have on the M̵ Plane—and they realize far more and worse ̵ are coming.

Regardless of how many battles the charac̵ have had inside Neverlight Grove, discoverin̵ demon lord is on the loose on the Material Pl̵ major revelation. Moreover, if they were in Sl̵ to witness the rise of Demogorgon, they now̵ more than one demon lord is at large, hinting̵ magnitude of the threat.

If the adventurers simply passed through t̵ and enjoyed the hospitality of the doomed my̵ they leave with only suspicions about their o̵ which can help them later in piecing together̵ mystery in the Underdark.

If the adventurers learned nothing about th̵ presence of Zuggtmoy or her plans, you migh̵ information on to them by having a friendly ̵ such as Stool or Rumpadump come to them ̵ they are leaving. The myconid enters rapport̵ shows them a vision of the Garden of Welcor̵ Yggmorgus, saying these images come from ̵ of other myconids in the grove, and asking w̵ "strange dreams" mean.

Chapter 6: Blingdenstone

Blingdenstone, once called the City of Speaking Stones, is a deep gnome settlement founded more than two millennia ago. The deep gnomes, insular and secretive by nature, care little about histories and legacies, and thus most of the ruined city's past is lost to time.

For centuries, Blingdenstone remained hidden and isolated from the rest of the Underdark, thanks to a combination of misdirection and magic. It wasn't until they provided shelter to a drow exile named Drizzt Do'Urden that the deep gnomes began to take a more active interest in the world outside their caverns. Perceiving the threat the drow represented to all the peoples of the Underdark, the deep gnomes abandoned their isolation when they came to the defense of the dwarves of Mithral Hall, defeating an invading drow force from Menzoberranzan.

This alliance, however, would spell Blingdenstone's doom. The vengeful drow bided their time, rebuilt their forces, and sent their armies out to strike back hard against the svirfneblin, returning in great force to lay siege to Blingdenstone. The deep gnomes were no match for the drow army. Thousands of svirfneblin were slaughtered, and those survivors who didn't escape to Mithral Hall or the surface world were dragged back in chains to Menzoberranzan as slaves.

Within the past decade or so, the deep gnomes have returned to reclaim, resettle, and rebuild their city. The ultimate success of their efforts, however, hangs by a slender thread. Most of the ruined city is a dangerous place and remains closed off, with tunnels and chambers barricaded with gates or deliberately caused cave-ins. The svirfneblin must contend with incursions by wererat squatters, insane elementals, ghosts, and a plague of invading oozes controlled by the Pudding King—a mad deep gnome under the influence of the demon lord Juiblex. Before they can offer the party any help, the deep gnomes likely need some themselves.

Going to Blingdenstone

Blingdenstone is an obvious destination for characters seeking refuge from their drow pursuers and a way out of the Underdark. The deep gnomes continue to have regular dealings with the surface world.

Among the party's fellow escapees, the deep gnome Jimjar is the most enthusiastic about visiting Blingdenstone, and he can lead the adventurers there. Topsy and Turvy also know the way, but they are noticeably less willing to go to the settlement because of the fear and shame they feel regarding their lycanthropic affliction. The shield dwarf scout Eldeth Feldrun isn't sure how to reach the gnome settlement, but is in favor of going there if it offers a route to the surface or to Gauntlgrym. If the characters allow Glabbagool (the sentient gelatinous cube from "The Oozing Temple" in chapter 2) to accompany them, it feels a certain pull toward Blingdenstone, and is curious enough to guide the characters there.

DROW PURSUERS

The svirfneblin settlement is a haven for the characters. For good reason, the deep gnomes rarely allow drow into Blingdenstone, and only then with a heavily armed escort. A drow character must succeed on a DC 15 Charisma (Persuasion) check to enter escorted. However, if any deep gnomes are traveling with the party, having them vouch for the drow allows the escort to be waived at your discretion.

The party's drow pursuers won't attempt to follow the characters into Blingdenstone. The party's pursuit level (see "Drow Pursuit" in chapter 2) doesn't change while they are in the svirfneblin settlement.

If the party's pursuit level is 3 or higher when they arrive at Blingdenstone, Ilvara and her party are watching the tunnels leaving the settlement. The pursuit level increases to 5 when the characters leave Blingdenstone, possibly leading to a chase or straight into chapter 7, "Escape From the Underdark."

ARRIVING AT BLINGDENSTONE

Blingdenstone has a reputation for being a dangerous ruin inhabited only by monsters and other undesirables. Others think of it as a budding settlement well on its way to recovery. Once the characters reach the gates, they can see that the truth lies somewhere in between.

ROLEPLAYING THE SVIRFNEBLIN

Deep gnomes are a dour lot, reserved and careful in their dealings with outsiders. They make the assumption that every non-svirfneblin means to do them harm—which is understandable given their history. They speak softly in caves and tunnels where sound carries, eyes darting furtively, looking for signs of danger.

Despite their harsh outlook, svirfneblin are still gnomes, and many are as benevolent and joyful as their surface cousins. They reveal these aspects most easily among their own kind, and to those they come to trust.

The svirfneblin assign defined roles to each gender but hold females and males in equal standing. It is ancient custom for there to be both a king and a queen with equal responsibilities. Svirfneblin males are hunters, explorers, laborers, and warriors, while females are managers, judges, politicians, and caretakers. Deep gnomes sometimes forget this is not the case with other races, and that males are capable of careful thought just as much as females can fight.

The characters must prove their goodwil⟨...⟩ deep gnomes before they are allowed insid⟨...⟩ characters win the gnomes' trust, they are⟨...⟩ into Inner Blingdenstone, and to what fo⟨...⟩ the locals can readily provide.

CHANGING SVIRFNEBLIN ATTIT⟨...⟩

The general attitude of deep gnomes to⟨...⟩ hostile—not necessarily opposed, but dee⟨...⟩ This attitude can be shifted to indifferent a⟨...⟩ friendly as the characters help the svirfnebl⟨...⟩ (see "Social Interaction" in chapter 8 of the *Du⟨...⟩ Master's Guide*).

Some deeds in Blingdenstone reward the charact⟨...⟩ with an automatic attitude shift, while others require⟨...⟩ DC 15 group Charisma (Persuasion) check. If the group⟨...⟩ check succeeds, the attitude of the svirfneblin shifts by one. If characters are rude or act in a way to make the deep gnomes more suspicious toward them, they must also make another group check. If this group check fails, the deep gnomes' attitude worsens by one.

RANDOM ENCOUNTERS IN BLINGDENSTONE

Once per day while the characters are exploring the deep gnome settlement, roll a d20 and consult the Blingdenstone Encounters table to determine what, if anything, they encounter.

BLINGDENSTONE ENCOUNTERS

d20	Encounter
1–10	No encounter
11	1d4 + 1 animated drow statues
12	1d4 + 2 cave badgers
13	Dungeon hazard
14	Elemental vagabonds
15	1d4 + 2 fiendish giant spiders
16	1 **ghost**
17	Mephit gang
18	Roaming ooze
19	1d4 + 1 svirfneblin wererats
20	1 xorn

ANIMATED DROW STATUES

Once part of a expedition from Menzoberranzan, these drow were petrified by a medusa and later animated by Ogrémoch's Bane (see "Settlers, Squatters, and Invaders" later in this chapter). They have the statistics of **animated armor**, except they are elementals instead of constructs.

CAVE BADGERS

The svirfneblin use these beasts as part of their digging workforce. Cave badgers are **giant badgers** with AC 12 (natural armor), tremorsense out to a range of 60 feet, and a burrowing speed of 15 feet. When they burrow, they leave tunnels behind them.

DUNGEON HAZARD

The characters approach a section of Blingdenstone in horrible disrepair. If they explore the area, roll a d6 and consult the Dungeon Hazards table to determine what the characters encounter. See "Dungeon Hazards" in chapter 5 of the *Dungeon Master's Guide* for more information on each hazard.

DUNGEON HAZARDS

d6	Hazard
1–3	Patch of brown mold
4–5	Patch of green slime
6	Patch of yellow mold

ELEMENTAL VAGABONDS

A **dust mephit** guides an **earth elemental** through the caverns and passages of Blingdenstone. If approached peacefully, they can point the way to Entémoch's Boon (see "Blingdenstone Outskirts" later in this chapter).

FIENDISH GIANT SPIDERS

Former servants of the drow, these spiders burn with baleful energy. Treat them as **giant wolf spiders** with a challenge rating of 1/2 (100 XP), resistance to cold, fire, and lightning damage, and immunity to poison damage. They are also immune to the poisoned condition.

GHOST

Some of the svirfneblin who perished during the drow invasion didn't go easily, and their ghosts linger. When the characters encounter one of these ghosts, roll a d20 and consult the Ghost's Attitude table to determine the attitude of the ghost.

GHOST'S ATTITUDE

d20	Attitude
1–6	Indifferent and unaware of the characters until it is attacked by them
7–12	Indifferent but aware of the characters
13–17	Friendly
18–20	Hostile

MEPHIT GANG

A mephit gang consists of 1d4 **dust mephits** and 1d4 **mud mephits**. If encountered in Inner Blingdenstone or Rockblight, they are insane and attack immediately. Otherwise, they mock the party but don't fight except in self-defense.

ROAMING OOZE

The presence of the Pudding King (see "The Pudding Court" later in this chapter) is drawing oozes to Blingdenstone. Roll a d4 and consult the Roaming Ooze table to determine what appears.

ROAMING OOZE

d4	Encounter
1	1 black pudding
2	1 gelatinous cube
3	1d4 + 1 gray oozes, one of which is a psychic gray ooze variant (as described in the *Monster Manual*)
4	1d2 ochre jellies

SVIRFNEBLIN WERERATS

These wererats belong to Clan Goldwhisker and are searching for new places to settle within the ruins of the former city. They're always hostile and attack the party if they can't flee. Use the **wererat** stat block in the *Monster Manual* with a few modifications: svirfneblin wererats are Small and have the following additional features.

Gnome Cunning. The wererat has advantage on Intelligence, Wisdom, and Charisma saving throws against magic.

Innate Spellcasting. The wererat's innate spellcasting ability is Intelligence (spell save DC 11). It can innately cast the following spells, requiring no material components:

At will: *nondetection* (self only)
1/day each: *blindness/deafness, blur, disguise self*

Stone Camouflage. The wererat has advantage on Dexterity (Stealth) checks made to hide in rocky terrain.

XORN

This creature leaves the characters alone if they feed it as least 50 gp worth of gems or precious metals. Otherwise, it follows them around Blingdenstone, hoping that they leave behind something it can eat. The xorn is antisocial and doesn't help the party in any way.

IMPORTANT NPCs

When the characters visit Blingdenstone, they can meet one or more of the following svirfneblin.

BLINGDENSTONE NPCs

Dorbo Diggermattock	Leader of the mining expeditions
Senni Diggermattock	Leader of the settlers
Nomi Pathshutter	Earth elemental wrangler with a task for the party
Gurnik Tapfinger	Priest of Callarduran Smoothhands with a task for the party
Kazook Pickshine	Alchemist and ore specialist who receives and gives quests
Chipgrin Goldwhisker	Leader of the wererat colony
Burrow Warden Jadger	Undead leader of the burrow wardens
The Pudding King	Insane deep gnome enthralled by the demon lord Juiblex

CORNERED RATS

If they are with the party, Topsy and Turvy do their best to conceal and resist their lycanthropic curse if the adventurers have not already learned of it. In the time since they were imprisoned in Velkynvelve, the two have likely undergone their wererat transformation at least once. When the decision is made to go to Blingdenstone, the twins might come clean about leaving home because of their curse, or they could abandon the adventurers and strike out on their own. In any event, they might fall in with the Goldwhisker clan of wererats, either on their own or with the adventurers' help.

Settlers, Squatters, and Invaders

The current citizens of Blingdenstone are a different breed than their forebears. They aren't simply hard workers and resourceful miners, but also settlers, explorers, and—above all—survivors.

Leaders of Blingdenstone

By deep gnome tradition, Blingdenstone is governed jointly by a king and queen, but the svirfneblin have had no true sovereigns while living as refugees for the good part of a century. Dorbo and Senni Diggermattock are talented miners, but they have become even more capable as community leaders. They spent years planning an expedition to Blingdenstone, paying adventurers to scout and keep an eye on the territory while they organized their people across the dwarven holds and surface-world cities that had received them.

After a decade of careful and determined planning, the Diggermattocks led a force back to Blingdenstone to reclaim it. While they have not yet been crowned,

everybody treats them as the de facto rulers of the settlement.

Chief Dorbo oversees rebuilding industry, opening mines, and organizing patrols to explore parts of the ruined city that remain uninhabited by the svirfneblin. He is also responsible for rebuilding and commanding the new settlement's defenses. Like most svirfneblin, Dorbo is serious and aggressive when dealing with outsiders; for all of that, however, he is also a loving and caring husband and a thoughtful leader of his people, devoted to the vision that he and his wife share of a Blingdenstone rebuilt and reborn.

Quartermaster Senni takes the count and measure of everything, ensuring her husband's efforts are well supported and efficient. She oversees the trade efforts and caravans to Mithral Hall, Gauntlgrym, and Mantol-Derith. She manages and helps to maintain Blingdenstone's magical infrastructure, and is intimately familiar with security conditions across the settlement. As quartermaster, she assigns homes to the ever-increasing numbers of svirfneblin returning to Blingdenstone.

Miners' Guild

The svirfneblin base most of their economic subsistence on their ability to mine ores and gems. The settlement is largely self-sufficient, but it still relies on the duergar of Mantol-Derith for tools, weapons, and supplies.

Because the Blingdenstone economy depends on mining, the Miners' Guild holds a lot of power in Blingdenstone. Led by the Pickshine family, the Miners' Guild oversees all of Blingdenstone's mines, as well as the mining, cutting, and enchanting of *spell gems* (see appendix B), both for the settlement's defense and for trade export.

Stoneheart Enclave

This group of svirfneblin spellcasters once trained under the Emerald Enclave but eventually splintered off, choosing to focus solely on earth elemental magic. After doing so, they absorbed the surviving priesthood serving the deep gnome deities Segojan Earthcaller (the god of deep earth and nature) and Callarduran Smoothhands (the god of stone and mining).

The Stoneheart Enclave is in charge of summoning earth elementals to help defend Blingdenstone. They also use their magic to aid in various engineering tasks, such as widening burrows, closing off tunnels, or establishing *spell gem* emplacements and defensive measures. When needed, the spellcasters of the Stoneheart Enclave serve as extraplanar diplomats, forging occasional agreements with xorn and galeb duhr to aid Blingdenstone.

The enclave's leader is Yantha Coaxrock, a young female mage who splits her time and energy between conducting magical research in Blingdenstone, aiding the svirfneblin enclave in Mantol-Derith (see chapter 9), and working with the rest of the Stoneheart Enclave.

Burrow Wardens

Most of the honored protectors of the svirfneblin died during the drow invasion, and the rest perished while protecting their people during their flight from

Svirfneblin Ghosts

Blingdenstone to Mithral Hall. Only the memory of their valiant effort remains today—and even that is fading due to the deep gnomes' penchant for forgetting their own history.

In the last year, a handful of svirfneblin youths have been training in secret under the rather terrifying care of the veteran Burrow Warden Jadger, who lingers on as a ghost. In life, Jadger was an expert in the Underdark and its many denizens, as well as how to fight them. He is grooming his brightest student, Trisk Adamantelpiece, to command the new burrow wardens, who are preparing to announce their existence to the Diggermattocks and demand recognition as the new Burrow Wardens of Blingdenstone.

GHOSTS OF BLINGDENSTONE

Although not truly organized, the ghosts of the svirfneblin killed during the drow attack are an undeniable presence. The settlers have been wise enough to mark haunted burrows off from their reclamation plans. But as new svirfneblin arrive and need accommodation, space is starting to become a problem. There are far more ghosts in the ruined settlement than anyone expected, and each ghost is different. Some are harmless, appearing only as echoes of the event that led to their deaths. Others are fully aware—and often hostile and dangerous.

OGRÉMOCH'S BANE

Ogrémoch's Bane is a drifting cloud of transparent, magical dust that first appeared in Blingdenstone over a century ago. Believed to be sentient, it is found roaming the Rockblight section of the settlement. Elemental creatures touched by the cloud fall under its control.

The cloud's origin remains a mystery, but it is known to have something to do with Ogrémoch, Prince of Evil Earth. A medusa named Neheedra serves Ogrémoch's Bane and leads some of the elemental creatures that have become enslaved by the evil cloud (see the "Rockblight" section and area 19 in particular).

CLAN GOLDWHISKER

After Blingdenstone's fall, a gang of wererats tried to make a home in the ruined city. The last handful of svirfneblin hiding in Blingdenstone after the drow armies abandoned the city managed to kill or drive off the wererats, but many of the deep gnomes became infected with lycanthropy.

Today, deep gnome wererats claims a large chunk of the ruins under the name of Clan Goldwhisker, holding territory against new settlers and engaging in urban warfare against them. The pack leader is the cunning and charismatic Chipgrin, whose concern for his pack's safety has him hoping to negotiate a truce with the Diggermattocks and stop his svirfneblin cousins from seeing his people as dangerous monsters fit only for extermination. Chipgrin is all too aware of the threat posed by Ogrémoch's Bane and the oozes plaguing the settlement, and he hopes that making common cause against those threats will force the other svirfneblin to recognize Clan Goldwhisker's right to remain in Blingdenstone.

THE PUDDING KING'S "COURT"

The so-called Pudding King holds court in the deepest sections of Blingdenstone. He was part of the first settler mission led by the Diggermattocks, but the other svirfneblin soon shunned him for his many disturbing habits, among them his preoccupation with capturing and studying oozes, and his penchant for stealing and hoarding food until it rotted ... and then talking to it.

The shunned deep gnome eventually struck out on his own. He spent years living among the oozes of the region, eventually subjugating a black pudding he calls "Princess Ebonmire" and a gray ooze he calls "Prince Livid." When the demon lords arrived in the Underdark, he followed the oozes drawn by Juiblex's presence, immediately throwing himself down before the Faceless Lord and pledging his eternal loyalty. His previous name and existence ended in that moment, and now there is only the Pudding King.

Juiblex granted the Pudding King the power to summon and command oozes, then ordered him to return to Blingdenstone and claim it as part of the Faceless Lord's new domain. The Pudding King slipped back into the closed-off areas of Blingdenstone and set up court, summoning all manner of oozes along the way and rendering portions of the ruined city uninhabitable and dangerous to outsiders.

Utterly insane and channeling a terrible power, the Pudding King sits upon his throne with his "children" at his side, summoning ever more loyal subjects with each passing day. When he is ready, he will send them forth to cover and devour everything, transforming Blingdenstone and its people into one giant mound of slime and goo formed in the image of his master, the Faceless Lord.

BLINGDENSTONE OUTSKIRTS

The quarries, mines, mushroom fields, and forges of Blingdenstone are located outside the settlement, accessible by tunnels and passages beyond the main gate. Trade caravans headed toward Blingdenstone are either re-routed to the outlying mines, farms, and forges, or they are stopped at the city gate, where their cargo is searched, unloaded, and distributed by agents of Quartermaster Senni. This keeps unwanted riffraff out of the city proper and protects Blingdenstone's security.

The deep gnomes working in the mines, farms, and forges outside the settlement spend less time enjoying the leisure and company of their kin and friends back home. The rising madness of the demon lords affects these brave pioneers more than those who live within the relative security of the reclaimed parts of Blingdenstone.

Svirfneblin in the outskirts are more curt with strangers, and a few might even try to steal from them. Taskmasters at each location are now feeling themselves driven to the point of near tyranny, demanding that their workers toil ever harder. Some miners pocket gemstones they dig out, while others are drawn to possess things the adventurers are carrying.

ENTÉMOCH'S BOON

This large cavern is located west of Blingdenstone (see the map of Underdark regions and locations in chapter 2) and has always been a closely guarded secret. Most svirfneblin who knew of it perished during the drow invasion of Blingdenstone. A few members of the Stoneheart Enclave have heard of its existence, but have either dismissed it as legend or have simply been too preoccupied with the reclaiming and rebuilding of Blingdenstone to search for it.

The cave is two days' walk of the settlement, its entrance a small tunnel leading to a ledge high above the cavern floor. The cave is lined with stalagmites and stalactites, but the dominant feature is the summoning circle at its center. The circle was once used by the svirfneblin to summon Entémoch, a prince of elemental earth, and his energies suffused the entire cavern, empowering elemental summoning within its confines.

If the circle is used to cast a spell that summons an earth elemental, the spell's duration becomes 1d4 + 6 days and the spell requires no concentration. The summoned elemental never becomes hostile toward the spell's caster or its companions. To gain these benefits, the caster must provide material components in the form of gems with a total value of 10 gp per Hit Die of the elemental summoned.

FINDING ENTÉMOCH'S BOON

Locating the tunnel that leads to Entémoch's Boon is a great service for the svirfneblin, and might be a quest set for the adventurers (see "Uniting Blingdenstone" later in this chapter). Despite how close the cavern is to Blingdenstone, finding it is no easy task.

Characters can search for the tunnel by traveling at a slow pace in its general vicinity. Each day they search, have the characters make a DC 20 group Intelligence (Investigation) or group Wisdom (Survival) check. If the group check succeeds, the characters find a curious waymarker: a small pyramid of carefully stacked stones next to the mouth of an otherwise unassuming tunnel.

After locating the waymarker and following the tunnel next to it, the party can make a DC 20 group Intelligence (Investigation) or Wisdom (Survival) check. On a failure, the party wastes a day searching for the next waymarker. If the group check succeeds, the characters find their next lead after 2d6 hours: a tunnel whose entrance is flanked by the sculpted faces of a male and female deep gnome. This tunnel features many side tunnels concealed by rock formations. The party must make a DC 20 group Intelligence (Investigation), Wisdom (Perception), or Wisdom (Survival) check. If this group check succeeds, the party finds Entémoch's Boon; if the check fails, the characters waste a day of exploration searching for it.

Finding Entémoch's Boon allows the characters to make a check to improve the attitude of the deep gnomes (see "Changing Svirfneblin Attitudes").

Random Encounters. For each day of exploration, check for random encounters using the tables in chapter 2 and adjust the drow pursuit level as necessary.

THE BEASTS OF ENTÉMOCH'S BOON

Characters who explore the cavern find shattered bits of statuary. A successful DC 17 Intelligence (Investigation) check confirms that the stone bits are the remains of petrified cave vermin. Unless they leave the cavern immediately, the characters are accosted by a mated pair of **basilisks** that call Entémoch's Boon home.

Once the basilisks are defeated, characters can resume their exploration of the cave and find three basilisk eggs in a nest made of pulverized stone. Each egg is a 6-inch-diameter, 20-pound sphere with a pebbled-gray shell as hard as stone. Left alone, the eggs hatch in 1d4 + 1 months. An infant basilisk that emerges imprints on the first creature it sees. It thereafter follows that creature around like its parent, demanding to be fed. If the characters manage to keep the basilisk alive, it reaches adulthood after twelve months. Track its growth using the Basilisk Maturation table.

BASILISK MATURATION

Age	Size	Notes
Infant (up to 3 months)	Tiny	AC 11; 4 (1d4 + 2) hit points; speed 10 ft.; Str 10 (+0); no Petrifying Gaze; bite attack is +2 to hit and deals 1 piercing damage plus 1 poison damage on a hit; Challenge 0 (10 XP)
Young (3–12 months)	Small	AC 13; 22 (4d6 + 8) hit points; speed 15 ft.; Str 13 (+1); Petrifying Gaze has a range of 15 feet; bite attack is +3 to hit and deals 3 (1d4 + 1) piercing damage plus 2 (1d4) poison damage on a hit; Challenge 1 (200 XP)
Adult (12+ months)	Medium	See the *Monster Manual*

WHITESHELL MINE

Blingdenstone's largest salt mine is half a day's travel to the south. Like many of Blingdenstone's resource sites, the road to the mine is easy to miss by casual travelers, but sentries hiding along the way can recognize friendly visitors (such as those in the company of Jimjar, Topsy, or Turvy) and guide them along the proper tunnels.

Whiteshell Mine is an interconnected network of small caverns dug into the vast salt veins lining this area of the Underdark. The mine produces enough salt to supply both the Blingdenstone settlers and sell in the market hub of Mantol-Derith. The mine has a cavern devoted to keeping the giant cave lizards the svirfneblin use as beasts of burden.

The **deep gnome** Perigrog Scrapedust runs the mine with a fair but demanding hand. He believes that the more the mine produces, the more he can export, and the quicker Blingdenstone can be returned to its former glory.

PICKSHINE MINES

Renamed after the largest and most influential family in the Miners' Guild, the Pickshine Mines comprise several mines scattered in a wide circle around Blingdenstone. The deep gnomes have engineered the access tunnels in such a way that only one known entrance leads to the mine complex, and this entrance is defended by four **galeb duhr** disguised to look like ordinary boulders and a dozen **deep gnomes**.

The largest mine shafts include veins of common metals such as iron and copper, as well as many veins of rarer minerals such as mithral and adamantine. The mines also hold crystal caverns where the svirfneblin harvest all manner of gems.

All the main routes to Blingdenstone intersect near the mine complex's main entrance, meaning the characters are likely to pass it before arriving in Blingdenstone. If they stop there, they meet Dasco Pickshine, the **deep gnome** overseer in charge of general operations. Dasco is willing to let the characters tag along with a cargo of ores heading for Blingdenstone, happy to have the extra security.

STONEHEART QUARRY

The Stoneheart Enclave has its headquarters in this cavern suffused with *faerzress* and elemental energy. This quarry doesn't provide stone for construction, since Blingdenstone builders need only take a pick to any wall to find their building materials. Rather, this cavern provides the small army of earth elementals aiding the settlers, and its magical stone is used in the creation of items such as *earth elemental gems, rings of earth elemental command*, and *stones of controlling earth elementals*. Elementals entering into the Material Plane here, whether by spell or other means, have an additional 2 Hit Dice.

Normally, Yantha Coaxrock leads the operations in the quarry. While she is in Mantol-Derith (see chapter 9), her apprentice Nomi Pathshutter is in charge of the druids and wizards of the Stoneheart Enclave.

ELEMENTAL HEALING

Nomi Pathshutter is aware of Ogrémoch's Bane and has made it her life's work to protect elementals from its influence. She studies samples of corrupted elementals as part of her efforts, and rewards characters who bring her a sample from any out-of-control earth elemental creature found in the unexplored areas

of Blingdenstone. She pays 10 gp per Hit Die of the creature from which the sample was taken.

> ### DOORS OF BLINGDENSTONE
> Heavy stone doors reinforced with steel or adamantine are found throughout the deep gnome settlement. Unless otherwise indicated, a door in Blingdenstone has AC 18, 40 hit points, a damage threshold of 15, resistance to thunder damage, and immunity to poison and psychic damage.

OUTER BLINGDENSTONE

Everything in Outer Blingdenstone was designed to thwart would-be invaders.

1. STAIRS

Rising up to a broad terrace before the gate, these wide stairs are built for gnomish feet. They are difficult terrain for Medium and larger creatures.

1A. CART LIFT

At the top of the stairs is a large entrance on the west wall, where wagons are secured on stone sleds pulled by a chain up a steep slope. The hoisting mechanism is at the top of the lift is operated by an **earth elemental**, although any creature with a Strength of 20 or any group of creatures with the combined strength to lift 600 pounds can operate it.

The lift's tunnel is wide enough for the sleds but has little clearance above them. The floor is part of the mechanism and is difficult terrain. Climbing in and out of a sled costs 10 feet of movement.

2. MAIN GATE

The main gate of Blingdenstone is a door made of steel and mithral, inlaid with a secret magic-resistant alloy and plated with adamantine. The gate has AC 23, 60 hit points, a damage threshold of 20, resistance to thunder damage, and immunity to poison and psychic damage.

The terrace between the top of the stairs and the gate has a slight upward slope. The slope imposes disadvantage on checks made to ram the gate.

Eight **deep gnomes** guard the gate. One of them carries a *spell gem* (see appendix B) that contains a *see invisibility* spell and uses it to scan for invisible creatures when the party arrives. Arriving characters are questioned to determine their intentions. The guards are thorough but not threatening; as long as the characters seem benign, they are granted entry. Four of the guards escort them through the maze (area 3) and the gauntlet (area 4) to Inner Blingdenstone.

Having Jimjar, Topsy, or Turvy in the party helps smooth the characters' entrance to Blingdenstone. This is especially important if the party contains one or more drow, whose presence would otherwise demand an armed escort at all times within the settlement.

If the characters reveal that they are fleeing the drow, the guards decide that Chief Dorbo Diggermattock should hear their tale. The armed escort that brings the characters into the settlement leads them to an audience with the chief in area 14.

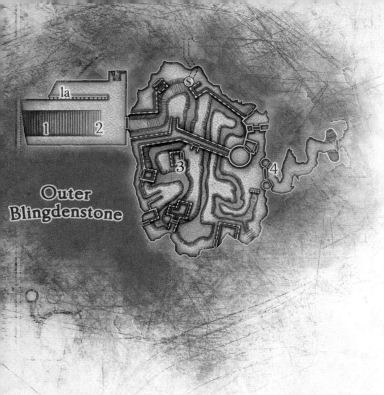

3. MAZE

Between the gate and Blingdenstone proper, the svirfneblin built the maze: a twisting and turning path that runs between 10-foot-high walls studded with nails. Climbing a nail-studded wall requires a successful DC 13 Strength (Athletics) check. Even with a successful check, a creature must succeed on a DC 13 Dexterity saving throw to avoid the nails, taking 1d4 piercing damage on a failed save. The path slopes up and down, so sections can be flooded or inundated with poisonous smoke. At certain points, the path narrows to allow Small creatures through; Medium creatures must squeeze, and Large creatures can't fit through at all unless they have an amorphous form.

A second path is inaccessible from the main gate, traveling above the winding path. This upper path is festooned with towers and battlements where defenders can fire freely at creatures attempting to make their way along the lower path. A paved road runs along the western wall of the cavern, onto which wagons and draft animals are hoisted so they can bypass the maze. The hoist mechanism can be destroyed with the single pull of a lever if invaders manage to hijack it.

4. GAUNTLET

Blingdenstone's last line of defense is a wide, winding tunnel behind a gate similar to the one in area 1.

GATE TOWERS

Flanking the gate are two stone towers embedded in the cavern walls. Peering through shuttered windows in each tower are four **deep gnomes**, eight in all. These gnomes operate winches that open and close the gate. If the characters are traveling with a deep gnome escort, the gates open as they approach, allowing access to the tunnel beyond. If the characters arrive here unescorted, the gnomes refuse to open the gate.

TUNNEL

The tunnel has a 30-foot-high ceiling, and embedded in its walls are *spell gems* spaced 30 feet apart and 15 feet above the rough-hewn floor. The gems are set in sockets and held in place with *sovereign glue*, and each gem contains a *symbol* spell. Any deep gnome who can see a gem can activate the spell within it by using its action to speak the proper command word. Any attempt to pry a *spell gem* from the wall destroys the gem.

At the north end of the tunnel is a smaller door made of stone reinforced with adamantine (see the "Doors of Blingdenstone" sidebar). Fifteen-foot-high ledges in alcoves flank the door. The ledges are currently unguarded, and the stone door opens easily to reveal the caves of Inner Blingdenstone beyond.

INNER BLINGDENSTONE

Population: 300 deep gnomes (svirfneblin)
Government: Work collective led by Dorbo and Senni Diggermattock
Defense: Militia, summoned earth elementals
Commerce: Salt, gemstones, and rare minerals
Organizations: The Miners' Guild, the Stoneheart Enclave

The defenses in Outer Blingdenstone paint a picture of a paranoid people under siege, but once past the final gates, the true character of the settlement is revealed. Warm, cozy, and welcoming, Blingdenstone is a rarity in the Underdark.

Read the following boxed text when the characters first arrive in Inner Blingdenstone, omitting the second paragraph if they arrive unescorted.

> You leave the dark tunnel behind and step into what looks like another world. These aren't sinister drow caverns or harsh, bare stone, but a subterranean land of warm colors and welcoming smells. The deep gnomes you see going about their business glance up at you with suspicion, but you instinctively understand that you face no threat here.
>
> One of the guards escorting you abandons his severe frown to give a deep nod as he prompts you past the inner gate. "Welcome to Blingdenstone, travelers."

5. RECEPTION HALL

This busy cavern welcomes visitors to Blingdenstone and connects the most important chambers of the new settlement. Two sealed tunnels here lead to the Goldwhisker Warrens. One is closed off by a deliberately caused cave-in to the south, and the other by reinforced, locked, and guarded gates.

6. BARRACKS

This chamber is above the main level of Blingdenstone, and houses off-duty svirfneblin currently assigned to defend the entrance.

7. Traders' Grotto

This cavern serves as Blingdenstone's central market. All manner of fungi once grew in the moist grotto, but a miscast spell turned them to stone centuries ago. Blingdenstone's merchants gather here in makeshift stalls amid the stone stalks to hawk their wares and barter with one another. Arriving caravans lower their cargo to warehouses carved out beneath the grotto.

Kazook Pickshine

If the characters accepted Werz Saltbaron's errand in Gracklstugh (see chapter 4), they can deliver Werz's sack of gems to Kazook Pickshine, who has a stall in the Traders' Grotto. Kazook is a **deep gnome**. If the characters approach him openly and present the sack to him, he muffles a gasp as he looks around, then quickly ushers the characters into the stall, admonishing them to talk quietly and not be so open. He inspects the gems, weighs them by hand while looking at the characters with suspicion, then pays them for the delivery with a zircon worth 50 gp.

Gelatinous Cube Incursion

The first time the characters visit the Traders' Grotto without an escort, a clanging bell sounds near the main entrance. When this happens, read the following boxed text to the players.

> The deep gnomes around you all draw weapons and retreat as you see a guard stumble back, then rise up in the air. A strange shimmer around him reveals the surface of the gelatinous cube that has engulfed him.

Two **gelatinous cubes** seep through a collapsed tunnel between the Traders' Grotto and area 24 of the Goldwhisker Warrens. Both cubes advance, attempting to engulf and consume any other creatures in their paths until they are destroyed.

The trapped svirfneblin is named Mev Flintknapper (use the **veteran** statistics in the *Monster Manual*, but also give Mev the Stone Camouflage, Gnome Cunning, and Innate Spellcasting features of a **deep gnome**). He has already taken 10 acid damage and takes another 21 (6d6) acid damage at the start of each of the cube's turns until pulled free with a successful DC 12 Strength check. The attempt requires an action, and any creature making the attempt takes 10 (3d6) acid damage is it reaches into the cube.

If Glabbagool is with the characters, it attempts to intimidate the other cubes by interposing itself between them and the characters. At your discretion, allow Glabbagool to use the Help action to assist the characters' attacks.

Treasure. Once destroyed, the hostile cubes spill their contents on the ground: 12 gp and a *+1 shortsword* of drow manufacture (see the "Drowcraft Items" sidebar in appendix B).

INNER BLINGDENSTONE: GENERAL FEATURES

Inner Blingdenstone covers the areas the svirfneblin have recovered from supernatural squatters and other dangers, now secured by mundane and magical means.

Chambers. Blingdenstone is not a single cavern, but a network of interconnected caves and pockets the svirfneblin have widened and worked for use as homes, workshops, vending stalls, places of worship, storerooms, and the like. Other than the private homes of svirfneblin families, all chambers are tall enough for Medium creatures to walk around without difficulty, and common areas are even larger.

It is rare for cavern walls to be bare in Blingdenstone. The walls of large caverns are studded with stairs and ramps leading to balconies and hollows serving as storage or shops. The largest caverns are crisscrossed by walkways allowing svirfneblin and visitors to reach connecting tunnels high above the floor.

Light. The caverns of Inner Blingdenstone are brightly lit with a mix of bioluminescent fungi, caged giant fire beetles, and magic. The light from these chambers spills into short connecting tunnels lacking their own illumination, creating areas of dim light. Longer tunnels have their own light, usually magically produced.

Connecting Tunnels. Svirfneblin and other Small races can walk through tunnels with ease, but Medium or larger creatures must duck and squeeze—a feature intended to control invaders' movements. Most tunnels have smooth floors, but those around the periphery of the reclaimed areas are strewn with rubble and debris.

Some of the connecting tunnels in Blingdenstone are trapped. The most common traps are collapsing roofs and spiked pits (see "Sample Traps" in chapter 5 of the *Dungeon Master's Guide*). Many tunnels slope down before rising up again, allowing the gnomes to flood them. All tunnel traps are inactive in Inner Blingdenstone, but the svirfneblin can quickly activate them in case of emergency.

Development

After the gelatinous cube encounter, svirfneblin inform the characters that incursions by oozes are becoming more frequent. In every case, it seems as though the oozes are trying to make their way toward the abandoned northwest section of the city (labeled "The Pudding Court" on the map of Blingdenstone).

XP Awards

The characters gain a special award of 100 XP each for delivering Werz's sack of gems to Kazook Pickshine.

If the characters managed to rescue Mev, or made a sincere effort to do so, award each of them 50 XP, and allow the characters to make a group Charisma check to improve the deep gnomes' attitude (see "Changing Svirfneblin Attitudes").

8. The Ruby in the Rough

The Stoneheart Enclave agreed to join the Diggermattock effort to resettle Blingdenstone in exchange for help reclaiming this temple known as the Ruby in the Rough. The temple is dedicated to Segojan Earthcaller, the svirfneblin god of deep earth and nature. The rituals and day-to-day duties of the temple are overseen by a deep gnome named Glyphic Shroomlight, a nervous young novice doing his best in a situation requiring a much older and more experienced

BLINGDENSTONE

BLANDO

cleric (use the **acolyte** statistics in the *Monster Manual*, but also give Glyphic the Stone Camouflage, Gnome Cunning, and Innate Spellcasting features of a **deep gnome**).

Despite the desecration of the drow invasion and the decades of scavenging and raiding in its aftermath,

THE WAY HOME

The svirfneblin know of routes from Blingdenstone to both the surface world and Gauntlgrym. If you want to keep the characters adventuring in the Underdark, Blingdenstone should either be their last destination after having explored the other areas in the initial chapters of the adventure, or they should be kept busy with other commitments and quests before returning to the surface world. These quests could come either from the deep gnomes or from earlier chapters of the adventure.

The svirfneblin won't help the party reach the surface world until their attitude toward the characters is friendly. The characters can achieve this through minor acts and services (see "Changing Svirfneblin Attitudes" earlier in this chapter), as certain svirfneblin ask for their help.

If the characters leave the svirfneblin without providing them assistance in dealing with their troubles, the deep gnomes' attitude toward the characters is hostile if they ever return to Blingdenstone.

the old city's honored dead still rest securely in the catacombs beneath the temple. A passage on the east side of the cavern leads down into this network of small linked caverns accessible only through the temple.

The catacombs are built along a mostly regular grid, making it easy for characters to find their way among standing statues and funerary niches. If the characters come here following rumors of ghosts, it's only a matter of time before they meet Burrow Warden Jadger, a ghost from the time of the drow invasion.

If the characters recovered Pelek's severed hand in the "Whorlstone Tunnels" section of chapter 4, they can lay Pelek's spirit to rest by placing his remains in the catacombs. If they do this, the ghost of Burrow Warden Jadger appears before them.

BURROW WARDEN JADGER

Jadger's **ghost** greets the characters but disappears through a wall if they attack. (Word quickly gets around the settlement of the adventurers' rudeness, negatively shifting the gnomes' attitude toward the characters.) Jadger speaks candidly about who he is and what happened to him. After gaining any sense that the characters are seeking information from the svirfneblin, he asks them to perform two tasks involving laying other svirfneblin spirits to rest:

- Destroy Vazuk, a deep gnome who is mad with grief and a threat to the other residents of Blingdenstone. His specter can be found haunting his old home in area 12a.
- Recover the remains of a deep gnome named Udhask and bring them to the catacombs. Jadger knows that the deep gnome died somewhere in Rockblight, the northeast section of Blingdenstone.

Jadger tells the characters he will answer one question for each ghost laid to rest (including Pelek from Gracklstugh, if the characters have returned his hand here). His knowledge of the Underdark is considerable, though somewhat outdated.

XP Awards
If the party returns Pelek's remains to the catacombs, each character gains a special award of 100 XP.

9. Cultivation Cave
This cavern complex is devoted to the cultivation of useful fungi the svirfneblin use in their cooking and crafting, including the following edible and exotic fungi:

- 3d6 barrelstalks
- 6d6 bluecaps
- 3d6 Nilhogg's noses
- 3d6 torchstalks
- 3d6 trillimacs

Two blocked-off tunnels lead north and northeast to areas that have not been resettled. All elementals are kept away from the passages because the Stoneheart Enclave believes they lead to the caverns where Ogrémoch's Bane lurks.

10. Staging Area
This cave is fortified with barricades and defended by eight **deep gnomes** and four **cave badgers** (see "Random Encounters in Blingdenstone"). There are no earth elementals reinforcing security here because the passage on the north wall—sealed at either end with a locked door—leads to areas where the deep gnomes have confirmed the influence of Ogrémoch's Bane.

Unseen Evil
The leader of the guards is a wryly cynical svirfneblin named Sark Axebarrel, who warns the characters of reports of a medusa lurking in the caverns beyond the doors, in a section of the old city that the gnome refers to as Rockblight. If they decide to explore Rockblight, Sark asks them to find out whatever they can about the medusa and kill her if they are able. He offers a payment of 50 gp per character for useful information, plus a diamond worth 1,000 gp if they bring back proof that the medusa is dead.

11. Caves of Clatter
This cluster of caverns on the eastern end of the settlement serves as a workspace for weaponsmiths and armorsmiths. Traditional svirfneblin arms, including picks, darts, and daggers, along with ring mail, scale mail, and chain mail shirts, are forged and traded here. Less common equipment such as swords and shields can be custom ordered. Prices for weapons and armor are double those listed in the *Player's Handbook*.

The passages leading to area 17 are sealed off by steel walls that can't be opened.

12. Residential Caves
These caverns branch off into smaller caves serving as hovels for families of svirfneblin. Tunnels lead to secondary chambers that branch out into more hovels. Deep gnome hovels have no doors.

The locals are willing to talk with the characters, pointing them toward a particular cave that was recently evacuated. A "ghost" manifested there and chased out a family trying to settle within (see area 12a).

12a. Vazuk's Home
Vazuk was a simple leatherworker who died in the drow invasion. His spirit awoke when a family moved into what used to be his home, then began to throw fits and terrorize any creatures coming near.

Vazuk is a **specter** (use the poltergeist variant). He can't be turned while inside his former home. He attacks the characters as soon as they enter the house, all the while screaming "Mine! My stuff! Not yours!"

Treasure. A character who searches the hovel and succeeds on a DC 15 Wisdom (Perception) check spots a concealed hole in the floor. The hole contains a small zurkhwood chest holding eight tiny rubies worth 250 gp each.

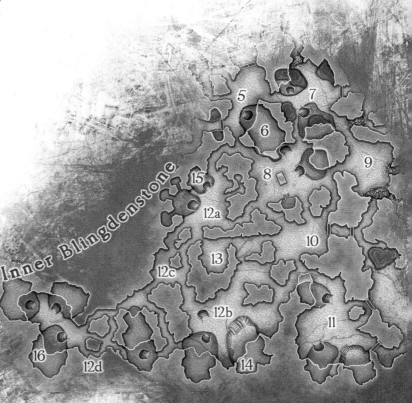

XP Awards

In addition to the XP earned for defeating Vazuk, each character earns 50 XP if they inform Burrow Warden Jadger (see area 8) that the spirit has been dealt with.

13. Speaking Stones

A circle of stone menhirs predating Blingdenstone stands at the center of this small cavern. The gnomes believe this henge is a cluster of truly ancient galeb duhr, venerated as manifestations of the gods. The more religious members of the Stoneheart Enclave cast *augury* and *commune* spells within the circle, interpreting the responses to their entreaties through subtle changes in the vibrations in the bedrock below.

Cleanse the Steadfast Stone

Gurnik Tapfinger, head priest of Callarduran Smoothhands in the Stoneheart Enclave, approaches the characters if they show any interest in the Speaking Stones (use the **priest** statistics in the *Monster Manual*, but also give Gurnik the Stone Camouflage, Gnome Cunning, and Innate Spellcasting features of a **deep gnome**). He asks them to undertake a task in a closed-off area of the old city known as Rockblight, where the temple of his god stands desecrated. If the characters agree, he gives them a ruby *spell gem* (see appendix B) containing the *hallow* spell and asks them to place the gem in the Steadfast Stone's menhir (see area 22).

Gurnik warns them that once they place the gem, Ogrémoch's Bane will send its servants to stop them. They must defeat these servants until the gem awakens three temple guardians, at which point the temple will be cleansed and the characters can leave. Once the characters accomplish this task, Gurnik channels the power of the cleansed temple, bestowing a *blessing of protection* or a *blessing of weapon* on each of the characters (each player's choice); see "Other Rewards" in chapter 7 of the *Dungeon Master's Guide* for more information on blessings.

14. Diggermattock Hall

This is the home of Dorbo and Senni Diggermattock as well as the "palace" of the provisional government of Blingdenstone. Characters are escorted here if they reveal to the guards in area 1 that they are fleeing from the drow.

> Two dozen or so svirfneblin occupy this well-lit cavern, some moving briskly with messenger pouches in hand while others huddle around several stone tables covered in maps and other papers, talking in hushed, serious tones. The back of the room is dominated by a dais carved from the rock of the cavern, atop which rest two stone desks facing each other. Two svirfneblin—one male, one female—sit behind the desks, conferring with advisers and each other. They turn their attention to you as you enter.

The de facto rulers of Blingdenstone are interested in everything the characters have to say about their adventures, especially if they've witnessed any events related to demonic influence in their visits to other parts of the Underdark.

The Diggermattocks offer characters a safe haven on the condition they cause no trouble in the community. If asked about reaching the surface, Dorbo says he'd like to help, but Blingdenstone is under severe pressure and he can't spare anyone to guide them. Moreover, the gnomes don't allow strangers to buy or borrow their maps. Both Dorbo and Senni become evasive and angry if the characters press the issue, at which point the characters must succeed on a group DC 15 Charisma check or have the attitude of the svirfneblin worsen.

If the adventurers offer to help the beleaguered settlement, the svirfneblin leaders mention things the characters can do to help take the pressure off the community and free up its resources. Each task the characters successfully undertake shifts the attitude of the svirfneblin (see "Changing Svirfneblin Attitudes").

"Operation: Ooze There?"

The Diggermattocks relay rumors that some monster or magic in the northwestern part of the settlement might be responsible for the growing number of oozes in Blingdenstone. If the characters return with information about the Pudding Court and the threat lurking therein, the Diggermattocks pay them with an empty *spell gem* of the highest spell level a spellcaster in the party can cast.

"Operation: Exterminate?"

The wererats of the Goldwhisker clan are a point of contention among the Diggermattocks. Dorbo wants them out of the warrens to free up living space for hard-working svirfneblin. He also wants to recover the House Center he believes is still in the wererats' grasp (see area 28). Senni argues that the wererats are descendants of Blingdenstone citizens and deserve to stay and rejoin their community.

Since the wererats are as territorial and defensive as the svirfneblin, any attempt to parley has been met with violence. Senni asks the characters to venture into the warrens and talk with whomever is in charge. The characters' report will determine whether the svirfneblin step up their efforts to eliminate the wererats or work toward an agreement.

If Topsy or Turvy are with the party, they want to learn more about the wererat community. If their own nature as wererats is revealed to the Diggermattocks or other deep gnomes, the twins are given the choice of going into the wererat-controlled part of Blingdenstone or being cast out of the settlement altogether, which might encourage the characters to meet and talk with the Goldwhisker clan.

15. Singing Stones

This elevated cavern near one of Blingdenstone's main residential areas holds a variety of rocks and crystals in the middle of its bowl-shaped floor. Svirfneblin minstrels skilled in the art of stone singing can alter the pitch of the vibrations emitted by the individual stones, creating an effect similar to an assemblage of harp-playing bards. When the characters initially come here, a **deep gnome** named Garra Songstone is playing the crystals for an appreciative audience of 3d4 deep gnome children (noncombatants).

16. The Foaming Mug

The Foaming Mug was built as an inn to house foreign guests visiting Blingdenstone. It was abandoned after the drow invasion but has recently reopened. While its supply of surface foods and beverages is meager, the rooms are sized for Medium guests, with comfortable beds and two separate hot springs used for bathing and relaxation. There are no other guests currently, so party members who stay here have the inn to themselves. Many svirfneblin frequent the inn's taproom after work, keeping the place lively. The tavern serves Darklake Stout, an ale that the svirfneblin purchase from duergar traders in Mantol-Derith (see chapter 9).

Tappy Foamstrap, a bored **deep gnome**, runs the inn. The characters' arrival is the most exciting thing that has happened in months, so she peppers them with questions about their lives and adventures, pushing free drinks and food on them.

Rumor and Hearsay

The svirfneblin community is tight-knit, so rumors spread quickly. Characters who engage with the tavern's patrons while the gnomes' general attitude is indifferent or friendly learn the following information.

- Blingdenstone's ghost problem is getting worse, and there are even spirits haunting the catacombs.
- There was a crazy svirfneblin back in the first days of reclamation who disappeared. Some of the scouts claim to have seen him, skulking around the unrecovered areas of the settlement. (The scouts don't know that this gnome is the Pudding King.)
- The Stoneheart Enclave is closing in on a solution to the threat of Ogrémoch's Bane (untrue). The gnomes call a large unclaimed area in the northeast of the settlement "Rockblight," as earth elementals go mad whenever they go near it.
- People are divided as to what to do about the wererats living in the southwest caverns. Some want them out, while others propose an alliance of mutual defense.
- A merchant from Gracklstugh says there's an influx of surface-world coins there, but nobody knows where they come from. (See chapter 4 for more information.)
- A svirfneblin caravan returning from Whiteshell Mines encountered a parade of dancing myconids. Through their rapport spores, the myconids told the gnomes about a "wedding celebration," which is strange considering that myconids don't celebrate or have weddings. (See chapter 5 for more information.)

The characters can spend a few hours socializing in the taproom of the Foaming Mug. If they do, they gain advantage on their next group Charisma check made to improve the deep gnomes' attitude.

Rockblight

When the drow attacked Blingdenstone, Ogrémoch's Bane retreated to the far corners of the ruined city, waiting for the time to reemerge and seek out earth elementals to corrupt. The malevolent entity didn't have to wait long, as the drow sent teams of scavengers to loot the treasures the deep gnomes left behind, bringing their own elemental creatures with them.

Ogrémoch's Bane haunted the drow with the same relentless cruelty it did the svirfneblin, turning their elemental servants against them. Eventually, the drow armies departed the city, but when they did, a drow priestess of Lolth named Neheedra Duskryn stayed behind. Neheedra was obsessed with collecting *spell gems* for their power and beauty, intent on making herself the regal and powerful master of her own underground realm. She commanded a force of drow servants and soldiers with unabashed cruelty, relentlessly driving them to seek out *spell gems* and increase her own wealth and power.

Overcome by her own greed and vanity, Neheedra engaged in dark rituals designed to secure her hold on power, imagining that Blingdenstone would one day become a drow enclave with her as its immortal leader. Unfortunately, the magical pacts she struck eventually transformed the vain priestess into a medusa.

Enraged by her fate, Neheedra turned her servants to stone and descended into madness. Over decades, she petrified any creature she encountered, eventually

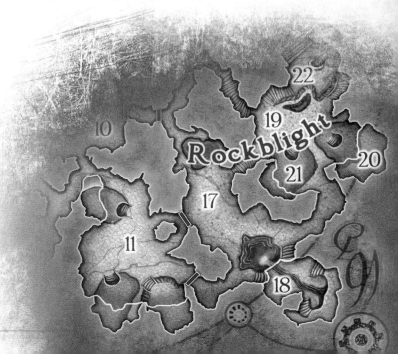

catching the attention of Ogrémoch's Bane. Now, the medusa works in concert with the fell entity, creating stone servants animated by its power.

Since the return of the svirfneblin to Blingdenstone, the deep gnomes have studiously avoided sections of the old city that Ogrémoch's Bane and Neheedra inhabit, blocking it off from the rest of the settlement and giving it the name "Rockblight."

17. Abandoned Residences

This large cavern mirrors the residential areas of Inner Blingdenstone, except there is no warmth or joy here— only darkness and signs of carnage.

> Every step echoes against walls beyond your circle of light. The air is cold and damp, and you can hear a waterfall somewhere in the blackness, along with faint echoes of battle.

The echoes of battle are always in the darkness beyond the range of the characters' light and darkvision. As characters move toward the apparent source, the echoes become more distant, as though originating somewhere else.

Unless the characters quickly retreat whence they came, the **ghost** of a svirfneblin named Udhask appears. It uses Horrifying Visage, then attacks with his Withering Touch. If it takes any damage, the ghost shouts "They are coming! Everyone must hide!" It then flees. The characters can follow the fleeing ghost to an old burrow, where it disappears. Within the burrow, Udhask's skeletal remains lie next to a stone bed. There's no evidence that he died a violent death. In fact, when the drow attacked Blingdenstone, Udhask had a heart attack and died while reaching for his loot (see "Treasure").

Pool and Waterfall
A waterfall fed by an underground freshwater stream pours into a 100-foot-diameter, 10-foot-deep pool that dominates the east end of the cavern. Flanking the pool are two wide, rough-hewn staircases that climb 30 feet to an overlooking cave filled crystals and fungi (area 18). The stream runs through the higher cave before pouring into this one.

Treasure
Udhask's skeleton appears to be reaching under the stone bed. A character who searches under the bed and succeeds on a DC 15 Wisdom (Perception) check finds a hidden compartment in the floor. Within the compartment is a rotted pouch containing six 100 gp gems and a *potion of invisibility*.

Development
Collecting Udhask's bones and taking them to Burrow Warden Jadger's ghost in area 8 completes one of Jadger's tasks.

18. Overlook

> A shallow, swiftly flowing stream bisects this cave. Crystalline formations sprout from the floor on both sides of the stream, and rough-hewn staircases at the back of the cave climb 30 feet to a barren stone ledge with a pair of winged statues perched atop it.

The "winged statues" on the ledge are two **gargoyles**. If the characters attack the gargoyles or move within 30 feet of them, the monsters swoop down and attack. In the second round of combat, an insane **earth elemental** rises from the stone floor and joins the fight.

The stream that flows through the cave originates from a naturally formed culvert in the northeast wall, beneath the ledge. The stream is only 3 feet deep.

The crystal formations growing throughout the cave are large enough for characters to hide behind, but they are neither magical more valuable.

Treasure
Among the remains of the earth elemental, the characters can find an *earth elemental gem*. Before they can use it, however, it must receive a *remove curse* spell from a priest of the Stoneheart Enclave. Otherwise, the elemental summoned by the gem is always hostile toward its summoner. The characters can also harvest samples from the bodies of the corrupted elemental and the gargoyles for Nomi Pathshutter (see "Stoneheart Quarry" in the "Blingdenstone Outskirts" section).

19. Crystal Garden

> Light from bioluminescent fungi refracts through large crystal formations erupting from the floor, creating a kaleidoscope of colors on the surrounding walls. The crystals are semitransparent, slightly distorting images seen through them. A statue of a gnome cowers near a crystal outgrowth, holding a broken crystal in its hands.

Six nightlights (see "Fungi of the Underdark" in chapter 2) illuminate this cave. Tunnels in this area climb up to area 20 and down to area 21, and two sets of stairs carved from the walls lead up to area 22.

The statue is actually a **deep gnome** named Vort, who was turned to stone by Neheedra the medusa. He tried to use one of the crystals to block the medusa's gaze but failed. Anyone examining the statue notices that the gnome seems to be raising the crystal toward his face, as if to look through it.

The crystals here can be used as countermeasures against Neheedra's gaze. A creature with one hand free can hold a crystal to its eyes, gaining advantage on the Constitution saving throw made against Neheedra's gaze. However, the creature makes attack rolls with disadvantage.

20. Neheedra's Lair

Neheedra Duskryn was part of the expedition sent to loot Blingdenstone of its *spell gems*. Her abode reflects the richness and elegance of the drow monarch she yearned to be.

> The adornments in this chamber would be more at home in a drow city. Spider-themed tapestries, fine zurkhwood furniture, and racks of expensive clothing fill the area, all of it old and rotted. At the center of the chamber, a female drow sits upon a zurkhwood throne. She stands, eyes closed and arms crossed as if in meditation or prayer. Then her white hair writhes, and you see it is formed of pale, hissing snakes.

The **medusa** attacks intruders without hesitation. Neheedra's curse has driven her mad, and reasoning with her isn't an option.

Treasure

Five of the dresses in Neheedra's rack are made of spider silk shaped by drow magic. They are worth 200 gp each if sold in the markets of the Underdark. The drow magic on a dress fades when the garment is exposed to sunlight, causing it to fall apart.

Development

If the characters divulge the medusa's location to Sark Axebarrel in area 10, they receive the promised reward of 50 gp each. If they deliver Neheedra's head to Sark, he also gives them the 1,000 gp diamond he promised them.

XP Awards

The characters gain 50 XP each if they successfully report back to Sark, whether they defeat the medusa or not. Upon earning this award, the characters can make a group Charisma (Persuasion) check to improve the gnomes' attitude (see "Changing Svirfneblin Attitudes").

21. Drow Statues

This cave is filled with thirty statues of drow warriors, all standing as if on guard. In her madness, Neheedra turned these warriors of her house to stone. Over long years, Ogrémoch's Bane has used its power to animate these statues, turning them into elemental creatures.

When the characters step inside the chamber, six of the statues animate and attack. The statues have the statistics of **animated armor**, except that they are elementals instead of constructs.

The statues attack until destroyed but don't leave this area. If the characters spend 1 round or longer in the chamber after defeating the last statue, six more statues animate. This process repeats until either all of the statues are destroyed or until the characters leave the cave. A statue also animates and attacks if touched or otherwise disturbed.

Ogrémoch's Bane

If every statue in this cave is destroyed, Ogrémoch's Bane appears.

> As the last statue crumbles, a cloud of dust erupts from its shattered remains and expands to fill the cave.

The cloud is Ogrémoch's Bane. Characters within the cloud can sense its malevolence, and a successful DC 15 Intelligence (Arcana) check confirms that the cloud is of extraplanar origin. The cloud has a flying speed of 20 feet and is impervious to all damage and spells except the following.

- A *gust of wind* spell or similar magic can forcibly move the cloud.
- Casting a *banishment* spell on the cloud sends it back to the Elemental Plane of Air if it fails its Charisma saving throw (it has a +4 modifier to the roll). A *dispel evil and good* spell is equally effective and doesn't require a successful attack roll; however, the caster must be in contact with the cloud.

Creatures native to the Elemental Plane of Earth (including earth elementals, galeb duhr, gargoyles, and xorn) that come in contact with Ogrémoch's Bane instantly fall under the cloud's sway. The effect lasts as long as the enslaved elementals and Ogrémoch's Bane are on the same plane of existence.

XP Awards

If Ogrémoch's Bane is banished back to the Elemental Plane of Earth, award each character 150 XP.

22. Steadfast Stone

Once a temple of Callarduran Smoothhands, the deep gnomes' god of stone and mining, this cavern was named after its long-lost galeb duhr protectors—the *dharum suhn* (the "Hearts of Steadfast Stone").

> The floor of this cavern is worn smooth, but the walls are rough. A great menhir carved from a stalagmite stands in the center of the chamber, pockmarked with dozens of empty sockets that might once have held gems.

Characters with a passive Wisdom (Perception) score of 14 or higher notice that the roughness of the walls outlines several large, vaguely humanoid shapes.

Cleansing the Temple

If the characters accepted Gurnik Tapfinger's task (see area 13), they can place the ruby *spell gem* he gave them into one of the sockets in the menhir. When they do so, the elementals in the walls begin to stir.

> As the ruby begins to glow against the menhir, the walls begin to rumble. Part of one wall shifts, detaches, and charges toward you.

An **earth elemental** materializes out of the wall and attacks. When the elemental is reduced to 0 hit points, it crumbles, and a **galeb duhr** emerges from the ground near the menhir in an unoccupied space. The galeb duhr faces outward in a guarding pose, but doesn't move or respond. Another earth elemental then emerges from the wall of the chamber and attacks, when it is destroyed, a second stoic galeb duhr appears. This summoning process repeats once more, until the third earth elemental appears and is destroyed. The elementals ignore the galeb duhr, which continue to stand motionless throughout the fight.

When the characters reduce three earth elementals to 0 hit points and summon three galeb duhr, a white light shines from the menhir, producing a *hallow* effect protecting the galeb duhr from the influence of Ogrémoch's Bane. The galeb duhr then animate and acknowledge the characters with a grave nod, before settling down in their boulder guise around the menhir.

Gurnik delivers his promised blessings when the characters return to notify him of their success in the temple. He can sense whether or not the temple has been restored to its former glory, so if the characters fail to cleanse the temple but tell him they succeeded, he knows they're lying, and the deep gnomes' attitude toward the party worsens. If the characters accomplish Gurnik's task, they can make a DC 15 group Charisma check to improve the gnomes' attitude, with all characters making the check with advantage.

DEVELOPMENT

A wide, descending staircase ends before a wall of collapsed stone that blocks access to the tunnels and caves that constitute the Pudding Court. The debris can be cleared with a few days of work. However, if the characters want to use this passage as an entry point to attack the Pudding King, they can use a volatile concoction brewed by Kazook Pickshine to quickly clear the debris (see "Battle for Blingdenstone" later in this chapter).

XP AWARDS

Each character gains 200 XP for restoring the temple.

GOLDWHISKER WARRENS: GENERAL FEATURES

One of the first things lycanthropy cost the svirfneblin was their fastidious tidiness. The wererat warrens are messy, with several areas smelling of mushrooms too ripe for any normal person to eat.

Light. The wererats light their warrens with nightlight fungi and torchstalks (see "Fungi of the Underdark" in chapter 5).

Traps. The wererats have rigged traps throughout the warrens. All wererats know where the traps are and how to avoid them. The traps are marked with russet squares on the map. The first time a party member enters one of these areas, he or she triggers a trap unless the trap has been detected and disarmed. Roll a d6 to determine the type of trap: 1–2, spiked pit (10 feet deep and lined with zurkhwood spikes); 3–4, collapsing roof; or 5–6, poison darts. See "Sample Traps" in chapter 5 of the *Dungeon Master's Guide* for information on each trap.

GOLDWHISKER WARRENS

The svirfneblin wererats of the Goldwhisker clan don't remember having lived anywhere but in the ruins of Blingdenstone. They descend from survivors of the drow invasion who became infected with lycanthropy after an unfortunate encounter with a pack of wererats.

For decades, the Goldwhisker svirfneblin have lived and thrived in these caverns, avoiding drow and crazed elementals, and securing their homes in cunning and vicious ways. They aren't willing to leave just because the cowards who fled Blingdenstone when it needed them most have now returned.

23. MAIN ENTRANCE

The svirfneblin installed locked doors to close off this section of the warrens. West of the doors, the wererats have installed a trap (see the "Traps" section in the "Goldwhisker Warrens: General Features" sidebar).

Four svirfneblin **wererats** (see "Random Encounters in Blingdenstone") attack when the characters trigger, disarm, or avoid the trap. The wererats avoid biting their enemies to minimize the risk of giving them the "gift" of wererat lycanthropy. If the characters kill two of the wererats, the survivors retreat to area 25.

DEVELOPMENT

Sounds of battle here alert every other wererat in the warrens. Thereafter, the wererats can't be surprised.

24. REFUSE PILE

The characters notice a foul stench as they approach this cave. This chamber used to be a small residential area, with homes dug into the walls at various heights, but no one dwells here now.

The pile of refuse dominates the cave. It contains decomposing matter, including a pair of slimy, partially digested svirfneblin corpses. A successful DC 12 Intelligence (Investigation) check reveals that the gnomes were victims of some kind of ooze.

25. HALL OF MINERS

During Blingdenstone's heyday, this cavern held the old city's smelters and marketplace for ore and uncut gems. It's now the main square of the wererat warrens.

> A small crowd has gathered here. Most of the assembled creatures are deep gnomes, but some have ratlike features—including a fat specimen standing in front of the others, smiling at you with jagged buckteeth. "Peace," the big wererat says. He takes a step forward, arms extended and hands open. "Chipgrin's the name. I'm chief of the Goldwhisker clan. Shall we talk?"

Forty svirfneblin **wererats** (see "Encounters in Blingdenstone") are gathered here, making combat a dangerous proposition and likely inspiring the characters to accept Chipgrin's peaceful parley. The wererat boss climbs a set of stairs to the top of a natural rise (area 26), bidding the characters to follow him.

Chipgrin is a svirfneblin **wererat** with 45 hit points and AC 14 (studded leather).

26. CHIPGRIN'S RISE

The leader of the Goldwhisker clan claims this plateau as his personal retreat and also entertains guests here.

> Stairs lead to the top of this rise, where the floor is covered with a soft and well-manicured carpet of green moss. The wererat chief sits on a stone chair flanked by two giant rats. Draped over the chair's back is a cave badger pelt.
>
> "Let's get down to brass hobnails, then. You were sent by the Diggermattocks 'cause they want us out, right? Right?! Well, they might get their wish soon enough, but in a way they ain't likely to cheer about."

The wererats face constant attacks by the oozes and are close to fleeing the settlement and leaving the other deep gnomes to fend for themselves. However, Chipgrin has learned of the mysterious figure controlling the oozes, and he hopes to use that information to strike a bargain. If the characters are willing to hear what he has to say, Chipgrin goes on to describe the creature he refers to as "the Pudding King."

> "I remember him from when he worked in the tunnels, and my kin saw him when he returned. I know who he is, what he's doing, and—most of all—where he can be found! If you and the Diggermattocks want, I can take you straight to him—he what calls himself the Pudding King."

The wererat leader remains civil, but he refuses to tell the characters anything more about the Pudding King until he has secured a meeting with the Diggermattocks. If there is any hint of violence, he calls for help.

If the characters decide to fight, all forty svirfneblin **wererats** in the surrounding cavern (area 25) rush to attack, in addition to Chipgrin and his two **giant rats**. Chipgrin orders his fellow wererats to take down clerics first, then any other spellcasters, and to keep melee combatants locked down. He doesn't kill the characters, but makes sure they are infected with wererat lycanthropy before dumping them in the maze in Outer Blingdenstone (area 3).

During any negotiation, Chipgrin is affable but firm in his demands. He also asks the characters if they've noticed anything odd among the svirfneblin. The wererats have noticed the greed and aggression growing among their cousins living outside Blingdenstone (see "Blingdenstone Outskirts"). However, they are unaffected by it themselves, given their bestial natures. Chipgrin doesn't know about demon lords, but he's

smart and can help the characters connect the dots if they've heard of Juiblex and its unending hunger.

If either Topsy or Turvy are with the characters, Chipgrin is pleased to welcome them to the Goldwhisker clan. The twins accept the offer unless their bond of friendship with the characters inspires them to remain with the party.

DEVELOPMENT

This encounter tests the characters' skills as diplomats and peacemakers. If they take Chipgrin's message to the Diggermattocks and arrange an audience, Chipgrin suggests that they stick around long enough to see what comes from "all this chit-chat and howdy-do!"

27. SECRET TUNNEL

The wererats use this secret tunnel to enter and leave their warrens. Oozes have also been using this route to enter Blingdenstone and join the Pudding King's court. The secret doors are well hidden and require a successful DC 18 Wisdom (Perception) check to spot.

THE PUDDING COURT

The Pudding King set up his court in the northwest corner of Blingdenstone, slipping through the wererat warrens with his beloved "children," Princess Ebonmire and Prince Livid (see the "Royal Oozes" sidebar). Since his return, the Pudding King has been using the power granted him by Juiblex to summon and command every ooze in the region.

28. HOUSE CENTER

This cavern was once the heart of Blingdenstone's government—a large space with a rocky sphere in its center. The sphere is hollowed out and contains the royal chambers from which the old kings and queens ruled. All of it has been transformed by the presence of the Pudding King.

ROYAL OOZES

Princess Ebonmire is a **black pudding** with an Intelligence of 6 (−2) and the ability to hurl blobs of its substance as a ranged weapon attack out to a range of 30 feet. This attack has the same attack bonus, damage, and effect as the black pudding's Pseudopod attack.

Prince Livid is a **gray ooze** with 30 hit points (use the psychic gray ooze variant).

> The walls of this great cavern are covered in slime—dripping, sickening green slime. Echoes of dripping water also fill the cave, in the center of which is a large spherical structure is held up off the floor by stone pillars. Around these pillars crawl dozens of living oozes, heaving forward while reaching out with grasping pseudopods. The sphere's surface, like the cave walls, is covered with slime. Black slime swirls with yellow and gray slime in a disgusting soup, the unearthly patterns in the movements of the slime straining your eyes and tugging at your mind.
>
> A disembodied voice fills the cave. "What's this, what's this? Visitors? Now? Not yet! We're not ready! Go away, pests! I will call upon thee and all of Blingdenstone to announce our glad tidings of the Faceless Lord to come at the proper time! Begone!"

Hundreds of ooze creatures congregate here, drawn by the will of the Pudding King. They include dozens of **black puddings**, **gray oozes**, and **ochre jellies**, as well as the occasional **gelatinous cube**. If the characters intend to rush this deadly tide, warn them that retreat is a better option, and that this is a fight they aren't likely to survive without strategy and aid. See the "Battle for Blingdenstone" section for the ways the characters can return here and have a chance to triumph.

If Glabbagool is with the party, it attempts to communicate with the other ooze creatures, telling the characters that others of its kind are calling for it to join them. The adventurers can convince the gelatinous cube not to go, but even if it does, Glabbagool might still serve as an ace in the hole during the battle for Blingdenstone.

The cavern is damp and has a 180-foot-high ceiling lined with dripping stalactites. The walls are covered with patches of green slime (see "Dungeon Hazards" in chapter 5 of the *Dungeon Master's Guide*). Any creature that comes into contact with a wall takes damage as normal.

Royal Sphere

The hollowed-out stone sphere is 150 feet in diameter and elevated 10 feet off the ground, such that the top of the sphere is 20 feet below the cave ceiling. Stone ramps without railings climb 30 feet to four small, open doorways in the sides of the sphere. A patch of green slime (see "Dungeon Hazards" in chapter 5 of the *Dungeon Master's Guide*) hangs above each door. The chambers the fill the sphere's interior have been scoured by the ooze creatures, leaving nothing but bare corridors and empty chambers. Even the metalwork has been corroded and eaten away. There is nothing of interest or value within.

29. Ruined Stockade

This cavern was once a shrine for Baervan Wildwanderer, the gnomish deity known as the Father of Fish and Fungus. Now it belongs to the Pudding King.

> The sound of dripping water fills this dark cave, and various oozes slither across the walls and floor. Some sort of fungal wall or partition once divided the cave, but that barrier has been destroyed. Beyond it lies more wreckage and debris scoured clean by the oozes.

This area once contained a stockade fashioned from zurkhwood and trillimac fungi. Here, the deep gnomes kept their deep rothé (Underdark cattle). The place was ransacked during the drow invasion, and the Pudding King's oozes have dissolved most of what the drow left behind, including the bones of the slaughtered rothé. Two freshwater pools form along the west wall.

Dozens of ooze creatures—**black puddings**, **gray oozes**, and **ochre jellies**—inhabit this cavern. However, they don't attack intruders unless they are harmed or commanded to do so by the Pudding King.

This cave is also home to a **gibbering mouther** that isn't under the sway of Juiblex or the Pudding King. It crept into this cave and hides among the oozes, occasionally feeding on them. It looks like a pool of reddish-brown slime in the middle of the cave until one or more characters touch it, whereupon it opens its eyes and attacks.

30. Throne Room

> Phosphorescent lichen illuminates this cave, the floor of which is covered with pools of green slime. More green slime clings to the ceiling and forms hideous drapes along the walls. In the middle of the cave, facing east, is a slime-covered throne.

The **Pudding King** (see appendix C) holds court here, attended by his royal "children," Princess Ebonmire and Prince Livid (see the "Royal Oozes" sidebar).

The Pudding's King's throne is made of chiseled stone and sculpted with lidless eyes and gaping mouths. A patch of green slime covers it (see "Dungeon Hazards" in chapter 5 of the *Dungeon Master's Guide*). More patches of green slime hang from the ceiling and form pools on the floor. The pools are easily avoided, while the patches on the ceiling don't fall unless the Pudding King commands them to. The Pudding King can use a bonus action to make a patch of green slime fall from the ceiling onto a creature below.

In front of the throne is a footstool made from a squat, petrified mushroom. The mushroom's cap can be removed, revealing a hollow compartment in the stem where the Pudding King hides his treasure.

Treasure

The hidden compartment in the Pudding King's fungal footstool contains 55 gp, 30 ep, a *potion of poison* in a gourd, two *spell scrolls* written on sheets of dried trillimac (*conjure minor elementals* and *speak with plants*), and a varnished nothic eye that functions as a *crystal ball of true seeing* that can be used only once.

BATTLE FOR BLINGDENSTONE

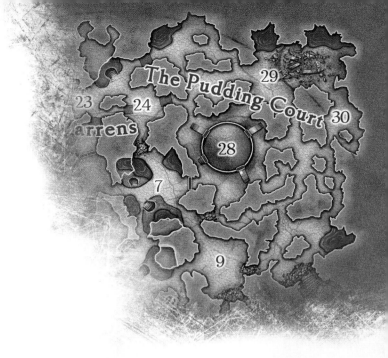

Once the characters see how overwhelming the opposition is inside the Pudding Court, they have little choice but to retreat and report their findings to the Diggermattocks. The deep gnome leaders grimly thank them for their efforts, asking them to wait and attend a council meeting the following day.

The council meeting takes place in Diggermattock Hall (area 14) and includes Chief Dorbo and Quartermaster Senni, Nomi Pathshutter and Gurnik Tapfinger representing the Stoneheart Enclave, Kazook Pickshine representing the Miners' Guild, and Burrow Warden Jadger's ghost or Trisk Adamantelpiece representing the Burrow Wardens. If the characters talked with Chipgrin Goldwhisker and agreed to take his offer to the Diggermattocks, Dorbo and Senni invite him to attend as well.

Senni asks the characters to inform everyone about what they saw, after which the council debates what to do. If nobody suggests it first, Jadger's ghost says that Blingdenstone has no hope to defeat this threat if the settlement stands divided. That means counting the Goldwhisker wererats as allies and recognizing their right to rejoin the community.

Give the characters a chance to ask questions of the svirfneblin regarding what each faction can bring to the table (see "Blingdenstone Factions").

BLINGDENSTONE FACTIONS

The following sections describe what each deep gnome faction has to offer in the Battle of Blingdenstone.

THE DIGGERMATTOCKS

If the characters don't suggest it, the deep gnome leaders note that fighting all the oozes might not be necessary. If the adventurers can get to the Pudding King and destroy him, the oozes might be reduced to their typically mindless and disorganized state. A large force can serve as a distraction, while the characters sneak in from an alternate route.

Dorbo Diggermattock wants the main force to attack from the temple of the Steadfast Stone. Before the battle can get underway, the temple must be cleansed (see area 22). Meanwhile, Senni Diggermattock gives Kazook Pickshine the materials he needs to create an alchemical concoction that can clear the debris blocking the way into the domains of the Pudding King.

THE GOLDWHISKER CLAN

Chipgrin doesn't know about the Pudding King's deal with Juiblex, but he knows the Pudding King can command the oozes as if they were intelligent. If the characters help convince Dorbo Diggermattock that the Goldwhisker clan belongs in Blingdenstone, the svirfneblin wererats participate in the battle and prove sturdier than the average deep gnome, taking point on any attack.

THE STONEHEART ENCLAVE

Stone is a resilient defense against oozes, making earth elementals the perfect force to combat them. Nomi Pathshutter suggests that if Entémoch's Boon could be found and its summoning circle put to use, the likelihood of victory would increase greatly.

Gurnik Tapfinger says that with Ogrémoch's Bane still lurking, any elemental brought to the battle runs the risk of being driven insane.

Nomi and Gurnik agree that if the Steadfast Stone is cleansed and Ogrémoch's Bane is banished, the Stoneheart Enclave can protect its elementals during the battle.

THE MINERS' GUILD

Kazook Pickshine can concoct an oil to protect weapons and armor from acid corrosion, but he needs a large quantity of ingredients from Neverlight Grove. If the characters have already been in Neverlight Grove and witnessed the horror of Zuggtmoy, they can discard this idea or brave a stealthy return to the corrupted myconid haven.

Another option is to send a shipment of salt to Gracklstugh to trade for high-quality weapons. The characters could escort the caravan if they have already visited the City of Blades and have unfinished business.

SVIRFNEBLIN SPIRITS

If the characters have not already completed Burrow Warden Jadger's tasks, doing so convinces Jadger's ghost to rally the other benevolent ghosts of Blingdenstone and join the battle.

TASK LIST

The success of any plan to rid Blingdenstone of the Pudding King and his minions is more likely if the characters complete the following tasks:

- Convince Dorbo Diggermattock that the Goldwhisker clan deserves to live in Blingdenstone.

- Find Entémoch's Boon.
- Cleanse the Steadfast Stone (area 22).
- Travel to Neverlight Grove and harvest a wagon load of ingredients among its fungal pools and fields.
- Escort a salt shipment to Gracklstugh to trade for duergar-made weapons.
- Complete one or both tasks set forth by the ghost of Burrow Warden Jadger (see area 8).

Let the players come up with other ideas that might help, such as asking for aid from the stone giants of Gracklstugh or stealing magic weapons from the drow. Some quests might take time to complete, since they require travel through the Underdark.

See the "Benefits for Completing Tasks" sidebar for benefits that the characters gain during the Battle of Blingdenstone if they complete certain tasks.

CRY HAVOC!

When the characters feel that they have attained their goals and secured their resources, the battle for Blingdenstone can begin.

Earth elementals under the control of the Stoneheart Enclave lead the charge, followed by the wererats of Clan Goldwhisker. Svirfneblin under Chief Dorbo Diggermattock form the rearguard and provide ranged support. If the ghosts participate, they attack from above and below. The plan is to get the characters to the Pudding King while the other factions hold the oozes at bay.

To reach the Pudding King, the characters must face 1d4 + 2 encounters, minus one encounter per goal achieved in the "Task List" section. Roll a d6 and consult the Battle of Blingdenstone Encounters table to determine each encounter.

BENEFITS FOR COMPLETING TASKS

Completing certain tasks in Blingdenstone can provide the characters with benefits and allies in the final battle.

- If the characters find Entémoch's Boon and share its location with the svirfneblin, or if they cleanse the temple of Callardurran Smoothhands (area 22), an **earth elemental** aids them. If the characters completed both tasks, the elemental has 15 additional hit points.
- If the characters fetch the ingredients from Neverlight Grove, their metal equipment is immune to the corrosive effects of oozes.
- If the characters procure weapons in Gracklstugh, they can call for ranged artillery support during the Battle of Blingdenstone. Each character deals 2 extra damage with each attack during the "Cry Havoc!" encounters, representing covering fire from svirfneblin using duergar-made crossbows.
- If the characetrs complete the tasks set before them by Burrow Warden Jadger, each character can reroll one attack roll or saving throw during the Battle of Blingdentone as a ghost emerges from the ground to distract foes.
- If the characters befriended Glabbagool and brought it to Blingdenstone, the intelligent **gelatinous cube** joins the battle as their ally. If Glabbagool left the party previously, it can reappear as a surprise ally during the battle.

BATTLE OF BLINGDENSTONE ENCOUNTERS

d6	Encounter
1–2	1 **black pudding** and 2 **gray oozes**
3	1 **gelatinous cube** and 1 **ochre jelly**
4–5	3 **gray oozes** and 1 **ochre jelly**
6	2 **black puddings**

During the battle, the voice of the Pudding King can be heard through the layers of oozing miasma, crying out "Fight for your king!" and "Glory to the Faceless Lord!"

OOZING ROYALTY

When the characters defeat the last group of oozes, but before they reach area 30, the Pudding King appears.

> The insane, slime-covered deep gnome points at you and cackles. "Devour them, my precious children! Make your father proud!" He then bolts as two oozes drop from the ceiling in front of you, their dark forms flowing in your direction with unsettling awareness and malevolence.

The characters must contend with Princess Ebonmire and Prince Livid (see the "Royal Oozes" sidebar). These dimly intelligent oozes defend their master to the death, blocking the characters from reaching the Pudding King as he retreats to his throne room (area 30).

Princess Ebonmire engages in melee, protecting Prince Livid as it uses its Psychic Crush attack. Prince Livid prefers to slink and hide while its Psychic Crush attack recharges.

TREASURE

When Princess Ebonmire dies, the black pudding disgorges a pair of spellbooks with covers made from troglodyte hide and pages made from trillimac fungus (see "Fungi of the Underdark" in chapter 2). The covers and pages are coated with a magical varnish that renders them immune to acid damage, protecting them from the pudding's digestive juices. The varnish also protects against water damage.

A svirfneblin archmage named Lesla Carrowil authored both spellbooks. The wizard spells contained in each book are listed below; feel free to swap out any spell with another of the same level.

The first spellbook, titled *Underland Magick*, contains the following spells:

1st level: *alarm, color spray, comprehend languages, find familiar, grease, identify, jump, Tasha's hideous laughter, unseen servant*
2nd level: *alter self, blur, crown of madness, gust of wind, invisibility, knock, magic weapon, phantasmal force, spider climb*
3rd level: *blink, dispel magic, gaseous form, major image, protection from energy, slow, tongues, water breathing*
4th level: *blight, fabricate, fire shield, hallucinatory terrain, locate creature, phantasmal killer, polymorph, stoneskin*

The second spellbook, titled *Magick from Beyond the Mirror*, contains the following spells:

5th level: *Bigby's hand, cloudkill, hold monster, legend lore, passwall, Rary's telepathic bond, telekinesis, wall of stone*

6th level: *chain lightning, disintegrate, Drawmij's instant summons, eyebite, flesh to stone, Otto's irresistible dance, true seeing*

7th level: *forcecage, mirage arcana, Mordenkainen's magnificent mansion, prismatic spray, reverse gravity, teleport*

8th level: *antimagic field, feeblemind, incendiary cloud, maze, power word stun, telepathy*

THE PUDDING KING

The mad svirfneblin waits for the characters in his disgusting throne room. If the characters haven't seen the throne room before, read the boxed text description of the room (see area 30) and add the following:

> The Pudding King cowers behind his slime-covered throne and chortles in his joy. "Callooh! Callay! Now you can join the party!" he cackles. "You can be one with the Faceless Lord. Just let yourselves be eaten and disgorged!"

The **Pudding King** (see appendix C) prefers to cast spells while using the throne for cover. As a bonus action on his turn, he commands a patch of green slime to drop from the ceiling onto one randomly determined party member (see "Dungeon Hazards" in chapter 5 of the Dungeon Master's Guide for the rules and effects of green slime).

When one or more of the characters close to within reach of the Pudding King, he laughs madly as he tears away his humanoid guise and transforms into an ooze. When he reaches 0 hit points, he shrieks as he dissolves into a dense puddle of goo. Read the following boxed text as he expires:

> "You haven't won! No! We will rise from our children! We will be reborn from the Faceless Lord! Juiblex will consume the banquet of the Queen of Fungi and we … will … all … grow … !"

With the Pudding King gone, the oozes lose their organization, but they are still too many and the svirfneblin sound the call to retreat. Three **galeb duhr** led by the ghost of Burrow Warden Jadger arrive to take the characters to safety. If the svirfneblin of Blingdenstone didn't already have a friendly attitude, they become friendly toward the characters after the battle.

DEVELOPMENT

Back in Diggermattock Hall, the gnome leaders make good on their promise, giving the characters a *stone of controlling earth elementals* along with the gratitude of their people.

XP AWARDS

If the characters participated in the battle, they gain a special award of 200 XP each.

LEAVING BLINGDENSTONE

The characters can leave Blingdenstone as heroes of the svirfneblin. If they express interest in visiting other Underdark locations, the deep gnomes give them whatever help they can, including placing them in a caravan to Gracklstugh or Neverlight Grove. If the characters ask for help reaching the surface world, the gnomes guiding them to a tunnel that leads there (eventually). They also provide enough food, water, and other basic supplies for the party's journey.

The characters achieve a great victory if they defeat the Pudding King, but their victory is incomplete. The Pudding King's death is a small setback for Juiblex, and the demon lord might send another minion to command the remaining oozes in Blingdenstone until they are destroyed.

The "banquet" the Pudding King referred to is the demonic rite of domination through which Zuggtmoy plans to transform the Underdark into her new abyssal domain. See chapter 16, "The Fetid Wedding," for more information.

THE PUDDING KING

Chapter 7: Escape from the Underdark

This chapter marks the midpoint of *Out of the Abyss* and sees the characters finally make their way out of the Underdark. Before their final push to freedom, however, the vengeful drow pursuing the adventurers catch up to them, intent on dragging them back to their domain of perpetual darkness.

If they survive this final confrontation, the characters reach the surface in a place of your choosing. After all their arduous adventures, they are finally safe to return to their homes, and must say goodbye to many of the NPCs who've been traveling with them. Though the characters don't yet know it, their exploits in the Underdark will bring them to the attention of the dwarves of Gauntlgrym, setting the stage for chapter 8 and a new call to adventure.

By the time they reach this point, the characters should be at least 7th level, having overcome countless challenges in their wild and dangerous journey through the locations described in chapters 1 through 6. They should also have reached a terrible conclusion: multiple demon lords of the Abyss are at large in the Underdark and could soon threaten the surface world.

The Way Out

Since their escape from Velkynvelve in chapter 1, the characters have sought a way out of the Underdark. Given the somewhat free-form nature of chapters 2 through 6, which the characters can undertake in any order, it's up to you to determine how and where the adventurers finally find their escape route, as best suits the story of their journey through the Underdark.

Finding the Way

Escaping the Underdark is no simple matter. Characters who try to find their own way out might wander for years without stumbling upon the right series of passages to take them to the surface. As the DM, you determine where and when they find the way out. The characters can visit the places described in chapters 3 through 6, using the interconnecting material in chapters 2 and 3, in virtually any order. This makes it problematic to put the way to the surface world in a particular place, since the adventurers could just as easily bypass it as stumble upon it prematurely. Instead, the characters' escape is made possible by a set of conditions that you can implement when the time is right.

Blingdenstone

The deep gnome settlement (see chapter 6) has the most dealings with the surface world of any community in this region of the Underdark, and the adventurers can find the resources there to guide them out. However, the deep gnomes are dealing with a number of looming threats to their settlement, and they can't afford to help the characters unless the characters help them first.

Since Blingdenstone is the most obvious and reliable location from which to find a way out of the Underdark, you might want to steer the campaign to other locations first. This can be done by treating the other chapters as side adventures to the characters' main journey, with many of those side adventures focused on the characters helping their NPC companions return to their homes in the Underdark.

Gracklstugh

The duergar of Gracklstugh have fewer dealings with the surface world compared to other Underdark races, relying more on trade flowing through Mantol-Derith (see chapter 9). The paranoid duergar are reluctant to share known routes to the surface world, so the adventurers need to cultivate considerable influence with the gray dwarves to earn such a prize.

The Wormwrithings

The drow of Menzoberranzan know of several tunnels in this region of the Underdark that lead to the surface world. Characters lucky enough to find one eventually emerge in the Lurkwood, a forest south of the Spine of the World mountains. For more information on the Wormwrithings, see chapter 13.

Farther Afield

Various other tunnels and passages wend their way to the surface in places around the Evermoors or even more remote locations. You can place these wherever you like, if an opportune time for the characters to depart comes along before exploring any of the previous options.

Portals

A number of ancient portals can be found in the Underdark. A functional portal is a magical doorway leading to some other specific location in Faerûn. If the characters' choices during the adventure leave them unable to secure escape with the help of the NPCs they meet, you could place a portal in or near one of the locations explored in chapters 2 through 6. If the portal is damaged, the characters might need to repair it. The characters also need to figure out how to activate the portal, or find the key or spell necessary to activate it. A portal can be one-way only and send the adventurers anywhere you want.

Gaining Access

By the time they have visited the locations detailed in the previous chapters, the characters should have knowledge of a route to the surface world and a map or guide to help them navigate it. These two goals should serve as tools to help motivate the players throughout the earlier chapters of the adventure. As a reward in one chapter, the characters might learn of the existence of a potential route out, leading them to another location in the Underdark where it is supposed to be. Then they need to find a map or guide for the potential route, which could involve them in what is happening in the new location. To complicate the search, they might then discover that a route or guide isn't all they had hoped for, but instead leads them to more promising options.

As an example, the characters might hear of a potential route to the surface from Gracklstugh. They go to the duergar city and become embroiled in events unfolding there, only to be denied access by the gray dwarves. However, meeting a group of wandering myconids in the city reveals that the myconids of Neverlight Grove know a great deal about the hidden ways of the Underdark.

Clues and leads should become more plentiful and substantial as the characters approach 7th level, leading them toward their eventual escape route—and with many adventures and encounters happening along the way. If you hand out these hints and opportunities carefully, the characters' path through the Underdark should feel like a smoothly escalating series of discoveries, no matter what order they chose to explore the locations and deal with the challenges of the previous chapters.

Bidding Farewell

When the characters finally reach the surface, it's likely that some of their subterranean companions will choose to remain in the Underdark rather than face the perils of the surface world.

Underdark Natives

Knowing that many of their NPC companions have homes in the Underdark can be an important part of the decision-making process that guides the characters through the early chapters of this adventure. The Underdark is a dangerous place, and characters might be reluctant to let their newfound friends fend for themselves. Helping some of them return home makes a good incentive to visit locations in the Underdark. Shuushar, Topsy, Turvy, Stool, Rumpadump, and Glabbagool would rather remain in the Underdark than suffer sunlight.

Surface Dwellers

Companions such as Eldeth and Ront, who prefer to live on or near the surface, gladly follow the characters all the way out if they can. Eldeth wishes to return to Gauntlgrym, and her presence there can provide a connection for the characters when they visit the dwarven settlement in chapter 8. If Eldeth didn't survive, she might have charged the characters with returning her body or effects to Gauntlgrym. Ront might wish to rejoin his tribe or seek a new home elsewhere, based on how the events in the earlier chapters of the adventure have influenced him. Depending on how he was treated, the orc most likely parts from the characters in peace—out of respect for their battle prowess, if nothing else.

With Friends Like These ...

Buppido, Prince Derendil, and Sarith might be gone well before the adventurers are ready to return to the surface, having already revealed their dark secrets and treacherous natures.

If Buppido or Sarith are still around, either NPC could go mad and attempt to kill the adventurers before they reach the surface world. Derendil might still hold to his delusion of being an elf prince wanting to return to his forest kingdom. However, the quaggoth is poorly suited to travel on the surface, needing shelter from the light during the day. He becomes increasingly irrational and erratic, seeing enemies and plots everywhere, until he eventually accuses the characters of colluding with his enemies and attacks in a mad fury.

Confronting the Drow

The drow from Velkynvelve have pursued their escaped prisoners throughout the first half of the adventure. Along the way, they might have engaged the characters in combat or set up a number of near-miss encounters. At times, the adventurers might have believed they had

Drow Chase Complications

d20	Complication
1	Uneven ground threatens to slow your progress. Make a DC 10 Dexterity (Acrobatics) check to navigate the area. On a failed check, the ground counts as 10 feet of difficult terrain.
2	A fissure, rocky outcropping, or debris threatens to trip you up. Make a DC 10 Dexterity (Acrobatics) check. On a failure, you fall prone.
3	You disturb a **swarm of bats** that makes one attack against you before quickly scattering.
4	A colony of **piercers** hangs 20 feet overhead. As you pass, one of them drops and makes an attack against you.
5	You have to dodge around stalagmites and columns. Make a DC 10 Dexterity (Acrobatics) check. On a failure, you take 1d4 bludgeoning damage from running into an obstacle.
6	A mass of webbing blocks your path. Avoiding it requires a successful DC 12 Dexterity (Acrobatics) check. On a failure, you are caught in the web and restrained. As an action, you can make a DC 12 Strength check, bursting the webbing on a success. The webbing can also be attacked (AC 10; hp 5; vulnerability to fire damage; immunity to poison and psychic damage).
7	A patch of green slime drops from the ceiling, requiring a successful DC 10 Dexterity saving throw to avoid. On a failure, you are struck and take 5 (1d10) acid damage. You take 5 (1d10) acid damage again at the start of each of your turns until the slime is scraped off or destroyed (see "Dungeon Hazards" in chapter 5 of the *Dungeon Master's Guide*).
8	The floor beneath you is smooth and slick with moisture, requiring a successful DC 10 Dexterity saving throw to navigate. On a failed save, you fall prone.
9	The floor beneath you is littered with sharp rocks and debris, and you must succeed on a DC 10 Dexterity saving throw to cross it. On a failure, you take 1d4 piercing damage and the ground counts as 10 feet of difficult terrain.
10	The chase kicks up a cloud of dust, sand, or spores. You must succeed on a DC 10 Constitution saving throw to pass through the cloud. On a failure, you are blinded until the end of your turn. While blinded in this way, your speed is reduced by half.
11–20	No complication.

shaken off their pursuers for good, only to have the drow show up unexpectedly. The characters' departure from the Underdark offers the final opportunity for them to confront their pursuers and settle the score.

The possibility that her prey might escape drives Ilvara onward. In turn, she relentlessly pushes those under her command to redouble their efforts to catch the characters. At this point, the pursuit level tracking set out in chapter 2 is no longer relevant. Ilvara and her warriors catch up to the adventurers just before they reach the uppermost level of the Underdark. The adventurers can choose to lead the drow on a risky chase, or stand and fight.

Drow Chase

If the adventurers flee from the drow, use the chase rules in chapter 8 of the *Dungeon Master's Guide* to play out the pursuit. The drow are on foot. If she gets close enough to do so, Ilvara tries to cut off the party's escape by casting *web* across the tunnel ahead. In addition to giving chase, the **drow** in the pursuit party pepper the characters with poisoned crossbow bolts, hoping to render some of them unconscious.

Chase Complications

Each participant in the chase rolls a d20 at the end of its turn and consults the Drow Chase Complications table. The result (if any) affects the next chase participant in initiative order.

If the characters escape from the drow, they can exit the Underdark unopposed. Ilvara returns in disgrace with nothing to show for her considerable efforts, although she and others from Velkynvelve might reappear when the adventurers return to the Underdark (see chapter 15, "The City of Spiders").

If you want to extend the chase, the drow could pursue the characters onto the surface, which places them at a disadvantage once the sun comes up (see "Evening the Odds").

If the drow catch up with the characters, the chase becomes a combat (see "Stand and Fight").

Stand and Fight

If the characters stand and fight, or if the drow catch them, they're in for a tough battle. Ilvara alone is a challenge for a group of 8th-level characters, and she is accompanied by her most powerful servants. The attacking drow force consists of the following:

- Ilvara, **drow priestess of Lolth**, armed with a *tentacle rod* in addition to the usual equipment
- Asha, junior drow priestess (use the **priest** stat block in the *Monster Manual*, but give Asha the Fey Ancestry, Innate Spellcasting, and Sunlight Sensitivity features of a typical **drow**)
- Shoor and Jorlan, **drow elite warriors** (Jorlan has disadvantage on attack rolls, Dexterity checks, and Dexterity saving throws)
- Four **drow** warriors

If any of the named drow were killed in chapter 1, they have been replaced by other drow with similar statistics.

On her first turn in combat, Ilvara casts *conjure animals* to summon two **giant spiders** to fight alongside the drow, while Asha casts *spirit guardians* on herself and concentrates to maintain it. The other drow cast *darkness* to hinder ranged attackers before closing to melee. Shoor protects Ilvara, while Jorlan makes no effort to protect his fellow drow. Ilvara prefers to strike from a distance with her *tentacle rod*, or cast spells such as *poison spray* and *ray of sickness*.

If Ilvara loses more than half her hit points, she attempts to summon a **yochlol** demon.

Evening the Odds

The characters might have a couple NPC companions around to help them defeat the drow (see "Bidding Farewell"), but if they need more assistance, consider the following options:

- Having pushed themselves to catch up to their prey, the drow all have one level of exhaustion.
- Ilvara and Asha have already expended some of their spell slots.
- The characters make it to the surface before being intercepted by the drow, and the dark elves follow them into daylight. Under the light of the sun, the drow have disadvantage on their attack rolls and on Wisdom (Perception) checks relying on sight. The drow can pursue the characters for 1 hour before their armor and weapons are destroyed by the sunlight.
- Asha chooses the confusion of combat as the moment to betray Ilvara, attacking while the elder priestess's back is turned. Ilvara instantly turns her attention to eliminating the traitor, distracting her and weakening the drow side if she succeeds.
- Wanting to deny Ilvara the triumph of recapturing the adventurers, Jorlan turns against his fellow drow, attacking them until he's slain. If he survives, he turns against the characters in his self-destructive fury once all the drow are dead.
- One or more NPC companions whom the characters left behind in the Underdark show up to help, having spotted the pursuing drow and followed them.

Treasure

The characters can claim any equipment and treasure carried by the drow, although drowcraft items don't survive exposure to sunlight (see the "Drowcraft Items" sidebar in appendix B). In addition, if the characters fled Velkynvelve without retrieving specific magic items or valuables, Ilvara can be carrying those items, allowing the adventurers to finally reclaim their property.

XP Awards

Each character earns 300 XP if the party makes it to the surface.

Further Adventures

The end of this chapter of *Out of the Abyss* forms a break between the first half of the adventure and the second half, which begins when the characters are summoned to an audience with King Bruenor Battlehammer of Gauntlgrym (see chapter 8). You can use the break between the two halves of the adventure to deal with any or all of the following.

Overland Travel

Once they reach the surface, the characters must still travel some distance to reach civilization. Most of the tunnels that connect to the Underdark in this region lie in or near the Evermoors or the Lurkwood—wild regions filled with ruins and monsters. You can choose to narrate as much of the party's overland travel as you wish, setting up encounters en route. If Eldeth is still with the characters, she wants to set off for Gauntlgrym as soon as possible. If the characters accompany her, this journey can easily form part of the bridging material between this chapter and chapter 8.

Recovery and Downtime

After their harrowing experiences in the Underdark, the characters might need time to recuperate, ridding themselves of madness and find the means to break curses and cure diseases. Other downtime activities are also possible (as determined by you, the Dungeon Master). For more information on downtime activities, see the "Downtime Activities" sections in chapter 8 of the *Player's Handbook* and chapter 6 of the *Dungeon Master's Guide*.

Resupply

Characters can visit a surface community or trading post to acquire proper equipment and supplies in exchange for some of the treasures they bring out of the Underdark. By the beginning of chapter 8, they should be properly and fully equipped for the first time since the start of the adventure.

Warnings

The events the characters have witnessed during their harrowing escape are likely to make them want to warn the world that demon lords have come to the Underdark. It's only a matter of time before these fiends find their own way out of the depths, threatening the existence of the surface world.

Characters belonging to factions might feel compelled to report to their superiors. Others can share what they've learned with well-connected NPCs who can get the word out. The attention gained by the characters as a result leads into the events of chapter 8.

Level Advancement

The characters should be 8th level by the start of the next chapter. If they're not there yet, plan additional encounters so that the characters can earn more experience points during their overland journey to Gauntlgrym.

If you'd rather skip the encounters and jump ahead to chapter 8, assume that the characters survive a few harrowing encounters en route (which you can describe or not) and gain enough XP to advance to 8th level by the time they reach Gauntlgrym.

Chapter 8: Audience in Gauntlgrym

After their escape from the Underdark in chapter 7, the adventurers have time to rest, recuperate, and reorient themselves back in the surface world from which they were taken. Some three months after their return, they receive a summons to the dwarf kingdom of Gauntlgrym in the North. King Bruenor Battlehammer desires an audience with them regarding their experiences in the Underdark. Representatives of several factions with an interest in what is happening in the Underdark will also be in attendance. Following the audience, Bruenor extends an offer to the characters, who are tasked with returning to the Underdark once more on a perilous mission.

Summoned by Bruenor

King Bruenor has learned of the characters' exploits from dwarf merchants and couriers recently returned from the Underdark. (If Eldeth Feldrun was part of the adventurers' successful escape and returned safely to Gauntlgrym, word of the party's heroics came to Bruenor through her. See "Gauntlgrym Connections.") King Bruenor's summons reaches the characters by whatever method best suits the story, depending on where they go and what they are doing following their return to the surface world. It can be in the form of a messenger carrying a handwritten letter bearing the king's seal, or even an *animal messenger* or *sending* spell focused on one or more of the adventurers. Regardless of how it gets to them, the message is simple and clear:

> Come at once to Gauntlgrym for an audience with King Bruenor Battlehammer, to discuss matters of grave importance concerning your experiences in the Underdark.

Characters belonging to any of the factions involved in the meeting at Gauntlgrym (see "Forging an Alliance") might receive a summons from their faction as well, and could even travel with the representative of that faction to the dwarf hold if circumstances permit. Otherwise, the choice to make the journey is up to the characters, although ignoring Bruenor's request leads the dwarf king to send ever more insistent messages.

Gauntlgrym Connections

If Eldeth Feldrun survived and escaped from the Underdark with the characters, she is eager to return home to Gauntlgrym, and does so at the first opportunity. In that case, King Bruenor's summons might come in the form of a personal message or a visit from her, and it's likely Bruenor has heard all about the Underdark exploits from Eldeth.

If Eldeth didn't survive, she might have charged the characters with returning either her remains or her warhammer and shield to her home. This errand can bring the characters to Gauntlgrym of their own volition even before Bruenor's summons.

Either aiding Eldeth's return or honoring her memory enhances the party's reputation with the dwarves of Gauntlgrym. It also reinforces King Bruenor's opinion that these adventurers are the right people to do the job of investigating the happenings in the Underdark.

Arrival

Once the characters arrive at the gates of Gauntlgrym, they are welcomed as the king's guests and escorted into the underground city, through the Vault of Kings (see below), and shown to guest quarters. The dwarves of Gauntlgrym take matters of hospitality seriously, ensuring that the adventurers are offered food, drink, and a chance to rest and refresh themselves before their audience with the king (see "Audience with Bruenor" under "Events in Gauntlgrym").

The characters' arrival is noteworthy, and the dwarves of Gauntlgrym treat them in a manner befitting great dignitaries. You can also have one or two of the faction representatives described under "Forging an Alliance" pass the characters in the corridors of the city, giving them curious looks—and perhaps even making a brief introduction—before moving on.

Gauntlgrym

In ages past, the subterranean city of Gauntlgrym was the capital of the ancient dwarven Delzoun Empire. Its cavernous halls—some large enough to contain entire surface villages—were carved with unerring precision, their ceilings soaring scores of feet overhead. Towering statues of dwarven gods and heroes stood vigil over chambers and thoroughfares, the least of which was wide enough to march fifty dwarves standing abreast.

The mines of Gauntlgrym produced endless tides of iron, silver, gold, and mithral, and booming trade brought goods and wealth to the city from across Faerûn. But it was the Great Forge that was the burning heart and true treasure of the city. Deep beneath the settled levels of Gauntlgrym, dwarven crafting and elven magic bound the slumbering primordial Maegera, a being of fire and destruction, harnessing its incredible powers to heat the forge. On anvils of adamantine blessed by priests of Moradin, great items of power were forged, their base material infused with a splinter of Maegera's essence. The unceasing wonders flowing from these forges helped make Gauntlgrym into one of the most magnificent cities Faerûn has ever known.

Relations between the great empires of the elves, dwarves, and humans soured as the centuries passed. And so when numberless hordes of orcs smashed into the north, each empire stood alone. The war was brutal and devastating. Gauntlgrym was swarmed by rampaging armies of orcs, and the empire of Delzoun was overrun in the terrible fighting. Ultimately, the dwarves of Delzoun drove back the orcs, but at great cost. The once-mighty dwarven empire was left crippled, never to recover, and the great city of Gauntlgrym was left in the control of an orc horde.

It was humans from nearby Illusk who finally drove the orcs from Gauntlgrym, but their hold on the city proved just as short-lived, as foul creatures from the Underdark swarmed from the depths to claim Gauntlgrym as their own. Over the next thousand years, history turned to legend, and mighty Gauntlgrym was all but forgotten on the surface world. Illithids, duergar, drow, and aboleths vied for control of the fallen city, its treasures, and the primordial still bound within its core. The drow House Xorlarrin eventually took Gauntlgrym, establishing a new city they called Q'Xorlarrin, producing weapons at the forge that they traded and used to pay tribute to Menzoberranzan.

In recent years, the dwarf hero Bruenor Battlehammer was able to seize the fabled city back from its drow masters. Bruenor, along with his companions Wulfgar, Cattie-brie, Regis, and Drizzt Do'Urden, gathered many allies from the surface world and nearby Underdark communities and retook the city. They prevented Maegera from being unleashed upon Faerûn, and set about attempting to restore the city to its former glory. Bruenor now sits upon the Great Throne of Moradin, working to rebuild the city and keep it safe—even as a new threat looms in the depths of the Underdark.

The following areas within Gauntlgrym might be of some importance during this part of the adventure, although they don't represent the full measure of the city by any means. A detailed description of every level, chamber, and vault of Gauntlgrym would take up an entire volume of its own, and the characters have limited time to see the wonders of the dwarven city.

The Vault of Kings

Large enough to enclose a small town, this high-ceilinged chamber rises above a network of bridges, stone towers, and sturdy walls carved from rock and sheathed in iron and mithral. Dozens of smaller chambers lead out from the Vault of Kings, including sprawling residential areas not yet filled by Gauntlgrym's new occupants.

The vault is on the same level as the city's main gates and can be reached from there, though a system of smaller gates and checkpoints has been set up to keep potential invaders from reaching as far as the throne room. That section of the vault, where the king spends a considerable amount of his time, is a large hall lined with pillars and benches, intended as a meeting place as much as a seat of rulership. The Great Throne of Moradin is protected by powerful magic, and forcefully ejects anyone but the rightful king who attempts to sit upon it. While so seated, Bruenor has advantage on all

Intelligence, Wisdom, and Charisma checks—a divine blessing granted to the king of Gauntlgrym by Moradin and the other dwarven gods.

The majority of the city's current inhabitants live and work within the vault, happy to share tales of the city's reclamation and praise Bruenor's leadership at any opportunity. This is where the characters reside as Bruenor's guests, and where the representatives of the five factions are likely to be found. Here, residents and guests alike enjoy access to well-lit passages, comfortable quarters, and substantial amounts of food and drink.

GAUNTLGRYM: GENERAL FEATURES

Gauntlgrym is a city carved out of the living rock, with halls and passages wide enough for the largest dragons to walk through. There are hundreds of levels, twisting stairs, functioning elevators, and a system of mine carts crossing in and out of the central hub of the Iron Tabernacle. The players should feel their characters are in a place of great antiquity, poised on the edge of reclaiming its ancient glory. By no means is the city fully occupied. Indeed, given the relatively small size of Bruenor's occupying force, keeping track of anyone within Gauntlgrym is nearly impossible.

Light. In the upper levels and around the Iron Tabernacle and Vault of Kings, Gauntlgrym is brightly lit. *Driftglobes*, phosphorescent fungi, and huge braziers and troughs of burning coals fill most hallways and chambers. Lights in many parts of the city are dimmed somewhat during the nighttime hours, so that its residents can mark the passage of time on the surface world. In the lower reaches, around the Great Forge, light isn't as ubiquitous. Farther down, and in parts of the city yet to be reclaimed from the ruins of the past, there is no light other than whatever visitors bring with them.

Mine Carts. Mining was one of Gauntlgrym's primary sources of wealth and materials. To facilitate the movement of ore, as well as the great quantities of stone used to construct and expand the city, the dwarves laid miles of track traversed by mine carts propelled by enchantments woven into their wheels. Even after thousands of years, the tracks remain largely intact and the magic of the carts has not faded. Where the carts trundle steadily throughout the city, Gauntlgrym's residents use them for travel, hopping on and off along the system's wide range of routes. While in Gauntlgrym, the characters can also make use of this convenient transportation system.

All tracks eventually lead to a switching station in the Iron Tabernacle. There, posted operators manipulate levers and gears to transfer carts from one track to another.

Ghosts. The shades of long-deceased inhabitants of the city, from the time of the Delzoun of old, haunt many of the tunnels and hallways of Gauntlgrym. These spectral remnants are seen passing through ruined sections of the city as if those sections were still intact, following habitual routes, engaging in silent conversation with one another, and generally keeping out of the way of the living. From time to time, the characters might run into a dwarven **ghost** who warns them away from a place of danger, or confront a less beneficial creature such as a **shadow** or **specter**. King Bruenor has decreed the restless dead be left alone for now unless they cause problems.

The Vault of Kings is heavily patrolled and guarded by shield dwarf **veterans** traveling in squads of six. It is the safest part of the city, and the characters can probably depend upon its security enough to rest without interruption in one of the guest suites provided to them, barring any unusual occurrences (see "Events in Gauntlgrym").

THE IRON TABERNACLE

The Iron Tabernacle is Gauntlgrym's spiritual and cultural heart as well as its physical center. More than a temple, the tabernacle is an entire section of the city larger than some surface towns, devoted to the faith of the former Delzoun Empire and of the dwarves who answered Bruenor's call to reclaim the city. Vast cathedrals of stone once echoed with the paeans of a thousand chanting voices. Great sculptures in honor of a multitude of gods gazed across an array of shrines and altars. Priests stood ready by night and day to tend to the spiritual needs of their people, and hundreds of stone tablets trumpeted the holy words of Moradin.

Like so much else of ancient Gauntlgrym, the Iron Tabernacle isn't what it once was. The intricate patterns and knotwork have faded from the walls, some of the statues have begun to crumble, and many passages are blocked with rubble. The devilish duergar, once in control of the mines below, took delight in defiling the holy icons of the absent dwarves. They defaced statues, tore down altars, and carved obscenities into the sacred tablets. Anything of value, such as silver or mithral trim, gold icons, and hallowed weapons, has been completely scavenged.

REBUILDING FAITH

Shield dwarf **priests** have begun the long task of rebuilding, revitalizing, and restoring the Iron Tabernacle to its former glory. The area is vast, and its halls are numerous and multileveled. The dwarf priests have restored many shrines and altars, and have cleared paths through the cracked and broken hallways to the Vault of Kings so that Bruenor can make personal visits to the main shrines and offer thanks to the gods. This procession often includes Bruenor's visitors or those ambassadors from the surface who come to Gauntlgrym to seek counsel with the king. Bruenor leads these processions not only to show off the city and its sheer size, but also to take measure of his guests' endurance and patience in matters of spirit.

ALL ROADS LEAD HERE

As the heart of Gauntlgrym, the Iron Tabernacle is the central hub of the city's passageways and railways. Broad corridors, winding stairs, iron rails, roadways carved into the earth—nearly all the city's major byways pass through the tabernacle. Every part of Gauntlgrym can be reached from this area, albeit sometimes indirectly. Notably, the Vault of Kings is about a mile to the north of the Iron Tabernacle, and the Great Forge is several hundred feet below it and a half mile to the south.

SLUMBER OF ANCIENTS

The lowest level of the Iron Tabernacle is a seemingly endless collection of crypts. Laid out according to patterns or traditions now lost to time, the tombs contain thousands of Gauntlgrym's honored dead. Some crypts are simple biers; others are intricate sarcophagi. All include names, titles, and lineage carved into the stone. A number of scholars have been drawn to Gauntlgrym in response to Bruenor's call, hoping to record a complete lineage of the great families of Gauntlgrym, including their possible connections to modern bloodlines, from an exhaustive study of the records carved in the crypt's stones.

Unlike the rest of the Iron Tabernacle, the tombs are unmarred. Spectral dwarves are common in this area, though their spirits remain quiet as long as visitors are respectful of the dead. If any creatures attempt to deface or steal from the sarcophagi, a mob of dwarven **ghosts** quickly attacks. Start with a total number of ghosts equal to the number of intruders present, then add two new ghosts for each ghost destroyed.

IRON TABERNACLE RANDOM ENCOUNTERS

The Iron Tabernacle is close enough to some of the lower reaches and fissures in the Underdark that monsters from below occasionally find their way in and set up lairs in one shrine or another. The dwarves impress upon the characters to be on their guard, or to take guards with them, if they visit. From time to time, the sound of combat rings through the tabernacle hallways, a contrast to the chanting voices of the priests and a sure sign that something unwelcome has made its way into this most sacred of places.

Check for a random encounter once every hour of travel in the Iron Tabernacle by rolling a d20 and consulting the table below to determine what, if anything, the characters meet.

IRON TABERNACLE ENCOUNTERS

d20	Encounter
1–12	No encounter
13	1 cloaker
14	1d2 driders
15	1 dwarf **ghost** (friendly unless attacked)
16	Patrol consisting of six shield dwarf **veterans**
17	1 shield dwarf **priest** and 1d4 + 1 shield dwarf **acolytes**
18	1d6 + 1 gargoyles
19	1 grick alpha and 1d4 + 1 gricks
20	1d4 rust monsters

THE GREAT FORGE

The Great Forge is a cavernous chamber divided into smaller sections housing furnaces and anvils. Some areas of the cavern are raised on daises of stone, while others stand in shallow pits. Layers of stone catwalks crisscross the chamber, providing not only vantage points but also anchors for pulleys transporting buckets of ore and water throughout the forge. The Great Forge is about a half mile south of the Iron Tabernacle and

several hundred feet below it, and can be reached by mine cart or on foot.

It was said of old that the Iron Tabernacle was Gauntlgrym's heart, the Vault of Kings its mind, and the Great Forge its mighty hands. Here, on adamantine anvils blessed by Moradin's priests, wonders were hammered from iron, mithral, silver, and steel. When Gauntlgrym thrived, the forge echoed with the hammering and songs of a hundred smiths working at once. In time, it might do so again.

It was the furnaces of the Great Forge that made this place the apex of the dwarf smiths' art, for those furnaces are driven by the power of Maegera the Dawn Titan—a primordial imprisoned below them. Slumbering within the stone, Maegera exudes an unnatural heat that the dwarves tap into by winding coils of copper and adamantine throughout the forge like webs and using them as conduits to transfer magical heat to their furnaces. Runes of power carved into the walls and etched into the coils allow them to withstand the intense energy. Metals melt almost instantly in the furnaces of the Great Forge, and tools cast from those metals are enchanted with motes of primordial essence.

When Maegera awoke in the last century, the earth shook, and many of the furnaces' conduits were severed. Today, lengths of twine-thin metal hang limp and broken throughout the rubble of the Great Forge, which lies upon the bones of those unable to escape the collapse of bridges and walls. Other coils remain in place, and the furnaces to which they are linked burn as hot today as they did in centuries gone by.

THE FIERY PIT

Heat and ruddy light emanate from a pit in the depths of Gauntlgrym. Chambers and tunnels lead away from this chasm at different heights. Despite channels built into the walls to carry water to the magma below, the heat from the pit is ferocious. Gouts of steam billow up through cracks in the stone to fill the chambers above this area, and the earth rumbles in a pulse like labored breathing.

The Fiery Pit is the prison of the primordial known as Maegera, who slumbers fitfully in its depths. The only sign of the entity's presence is a whirlpool of white-hot magma that resembles a great eye, set in the center of the lake of molten rock at the pit's bottom. Maegera sleeps and dreams, half conscious of its surroundings and half delirious with whatever dreams haunt a being of pure destruction.

When the mages of the Arcane Brotherhood first tapped into Maegera's power, they used water magic to bind elementals that cooled the primordial's rage and kept it asleep. This bond lasted for centuries until the channels of water were closed through trickery by agents of Thay. With the pit's cooling mechanism shut down, Maegera stirred in its slumber, and its dream of ruination was enough to destroy Gauntlgrym.

In the years following, Maegera groggily awoke from time to time, causing earthquakes throughout the region. Eventually, the primordial was returned to its slumber through the efforts of Bruenor, Drizzt

Do'Urden, Jarlaxle, and other heroes. Where Maegera sleeps now, the intense heat it generates once again fires the Great Forge of Gauntlgrym.

Back in Operation

Under Bruenor's watchful governance, the Great Forge has again begun to produce metalworks. If the characters are in the market for any metal goods (including arms and armor), or have any such goods in need of repair or replacement, the dwarves of the Great Forge are happy to help. No magic weapons or armor are available for sale, although damaged magic items can be repaired.

The king has left the day-to-day running of the Great Forge to a pair of experienced smiths: Helgrim Candlewick and Rollo Summergold (both shield dwarf **veterans**).

Great Forge Random Encounters

The Great Forge is always occupied by either Helgrim or Rollo, their apprentices and assistants (2d4 shield dwarf **commoners**), and shield dwarf **veterans** working in squads of six to guard the active furnaces. The characters might also encounter other creatures if they explore the unoccupied areas of the Great Forge. Check for such an encounter once per hour of travel or rest outside the protected areas of the forge by rolling a d20 and consulting the Great Forge Encounters table to determine what, if anything, comes out of the darkness. If the heroes call for help, four shield dwarf **veterans** arrive in 1d4 + 1 rounds to aid them.

Great Forge Encounters

d8	Encounter
1–14	No encounter
15	1d4 + 1 **doppelgangers** disguised as shield dwarves
16	1d2 **fire elementals** and 3d6 **magmins**
17	1 **salamander** and 1d4 + 1 **fire snakes**
18	1 **spirit naga**
19	3d6 **troglodytes**
20	1 **wraith** leading 1d6 + 1 **specters**

Events in Gauntlgrym

This chapter is dominated by negotiation, social activity, and diplomacy—first directed at the characters, then directed by them. The adventurers must first hear what King Bruenor has to say as he entreats them to head back into the Underdark to find out more about the rising threat of the demon lords. Then the characters must help convince the other factions summoned to Gauntlgrym to aid them on their mission. This section of the adventure has some opportunity for action, but players who enjoy plotting, making plans, and pitting NPCs against one another can shine here.

Take note of your players' preferences. If they're not much for long periods of conversation with NPCs, you might want to move things along a little more quickly. On the other hand, you can really bring to life not just the faction representatives and the dwarf king in this chapter, but also highlight the personalities and goals of the characters and any NPCs who remain with them.

Audience with Bruenor

After the characters arrive and are shown to guest accommodations, they are allowed some time to refresh and prepare themselves. They are then called to an audience with Bruenor Battlehammer, the king of Gauntlgrym. Read or paraphrase the following:

> You are taken to a mighty hall in which a red-haired dwarf of fierce and proud demeanor sits upon a massive stone throne, flanked by a number of guards and advisors. Although a long stone table has been set to one side, laid out with refreshments, there do not appear to be any other guests. "Welcome, friends," says the king. "I've a mind to know about the rumblings and rumors about goings-on in the depths outside my city. If ye relate to me what ye know, we can talk about what ye might want to do next."

King Bruenor listens carefully to what the adventurers have to say. Once the adventurers have told their tale, Bruenor might have a few questions, particularly concerning the threat of the demon lords. The dwarf king answers questions from the characters if they have any. However, if asked about his overall plans, he says simply that he must consider all the information presented to him and consult with advisors. With the audience at an end, Bruenor tells the characters he will consider all they have told him, and that they will speak again at a welcoming feast later that night.

Guests at the Feast

After the characters have had a chance to speak with Bruenor and take care of any personal business, the Vault of Kings plays host to a memorable feast. In attendance are representatives of different factions from the surface world, who have come to Gauntlgrym following rumors of bizarre events in the Underdark. If any of the adventurers belong to a faction, representatives of that faction might even be following up on information provided by the characters themselves. See "Forging an Alliance" for more information.

The celebration serves both to welcome the adventurers, who are seated at the high table with Bruenor, and to provide an opportunity for the representatives of the different factions to gather socially and be officially introduced to the adventurers. In addition to the king and his allies, a number of dwarves from Bruenor's court and important citizens of Gauntlgrym are also present. The feast is also an opportunity for you to include NPCs of your choice who might either be from or visiting Gauntlgrym, or part of the entourage of one of the representatives.

This is a free-form scene, which you can play out as best suits your group. It can range from a detailed roleplaying session, with characters mixing and mingling with their potential allies and members of Gauntlgrym society, or just a brief description of the event and the characters' initial impressions of the faction representatives, before their later efforts to negotiate with those representatives for the factions' aid.

If you want to add some intrigue or action, consider having one of the options from "Enemies Among Us" interrupt the feast, giving the characters an opportunity to demonstrate their abilities in front of their potential patron and allies. Rogue fire elementals roaring out of the hearth or a disguised assassin poisoning one or more of the representatives can completely change the scene.

BRUENOR'S PLAN

Once the feast winds down, Bruenor excuses himself as the guests depart. Shortly thereafter, a servant comes to collect the characters and takes them to a private chamber where the king of Gauntlgrym awaits them. His previously friendly manner has turned grave.

> "I've told the allies ye met tonight what ye told me," he says. "I invited them here to learn what is happening, to share what we know, and to get their backing for what it is I propose. Ye have braved the Underdark and lived to tell the tale. Ye know, better than anyone, what it is we face, but we need to know more.
>
> "The Zhentarim have a stake in a secret Underdark trading post called Mantol-Derith. If ye can get them on our side, they'll guide ye there, where ye can meet with one of their agents, Ghazrim DuLoc. He can provide ye with a map to Gravenhollow. It's a legendary place built by the stone giants long ago, said to contain all the knowledge of the depths. If there's answers to be found for what has happened, ye might find them there. If ye are willing to go back, that is.
>
> "I don't propose to send ye into the dark unprepared, and I hope ye make an impression on those gathered here so they'll support our cause and your mission. From all I've seen and heard, there's no one better to do what needs be done.
>
> "So, what say ye?"

Paraphrase Bruenor's speech as needed to handle interjections by the characters. The king provides honest answers to any questions. He truly does believe the characters represent the best option to find out more about the demonic threat, unless they've given him any reason to think otherwise.

Bruenor assures the adventurers they will have his gratitude and that of all Gauntlgrym—indeed, of all Faerûn—if they are successful. If the characters press for details or try to negotiate compensation for their service, the king points out that Gauntlgrym has considerable space, and he can offer them titles, property, and the products of the Great Forge as rewards. Such mercenary negotiation lowers Bruenor's opinion of the adventurers a bit, but he never loses his genial manner.

BRUENOR BATTLEHAMMER

The legendary Bruenor Battlehammer is a good dwarf and king, and always has the best interests of his people and home at heart. He is drawn to help characters who follow a strong moral and ethical code, and often seeks their help in return. Use his good humor and folksy demeanor to help endear him to the players. The more the players grow to like him, the easier it is for them to respect his advice and request—and to gain more resources and assistance from him in turn.

If the characters are agreeable, the king tells them the next step is to bring the various factions on board. One of the reasons he is looking to the adventurers to lead a new mission into the Underdark, apart from their experience, is that they can serve as brokers among all the various parties with an interest in the mission. They need to meet with the different faction representatives, emphasizing the importance of getting the Zhentarim to agree to grant access to Mantol-Derith. Otherwise,

BRUENOR BATTLEHAMMER

the journey to locate Gravenhollow is likely to be much longer and more difficult.

ENEMIES AMONG US

Even Gauntlgrym isn't entirely safe, nor is it immune to the influence of the demon lords. During the characters' time in the city, you can implement one or more of the following threats to challenge them—and to potentially disrupt their negotiations with the factions.

- One of the characters' traveling companions is revealed as a traitor or succumbs to madness. This NPC secretly serves one of the demon lords and turns against the adventurers.
- If any of the party's drow pursuers survived from the previous chapter, they might slip into Gauntlgrym and look to slay their quarry.
- A dwarf **assassin** belonging to a demon-worshiping cult steals into Gauntlgrym to kill one or more of the faction representatives. Hoping to cast suspicion onto the adventurers, the assassin frames them as demonic agents.
- A **doppelganger** spy poses as one of the faction representatives and tries to arrange a private meeting with one or more of the characters, hoping to discover additional information regarding the looming threat. The doppelganger might serve a faction of the Underdark or a surface world faction Bruenor didn't invite (such as the Arcane Brotherhood or the Red Wizards of Thay), or might simply be an opportunist looking to sell information to the highest bidder.
- Maegera roars within its prison, stirred by the madness and chaos growing within the depths of the Underdark. As a natural reaction to this new stress upon itself, the primordial spawns a trio of **fire elementals** that attack the Vault of Kings, setting fire to marketplaces and unleashing chaos upon the dwarven residents. If defeated or somehow convinced to return to the Fiery Pit, the elementals dissipate peacefully and Maegera falls dormant once again ... for now.

FORGING AN ALLIANCE

King Bruenor has called representatives of the Harpers, the Order of the Gauntlet, the Emerald Enclave, the Lords' Alliance, and the Zhentarim to Gauntlgrym to hear about the state of things in the Underdark and to court their aid in finding out more about the situation. The representatives of each faction receive a briefing on what the characters told Bruenor, and all have an opportunity to converse with the adventurers before making their decisions as to whether they will support Bruenor's plans.

To play out these meetings, use the social interaction rules provided in chapter 8, "Running the Game," of the *Dungeon Master's Guide*. Some representatives are fine with meeting the adventurers in the Vault of Kings, but you might have others request a private or even clandestine meeting—perhaps in the characters' quarters, in an out-of-the-way alcove of the Iron Tabernacle, or in the Great Forge.

King Bruenor is the original proponent of the adventurers returning to the Underdark to gather additional information, but he knows that success requires the support of the other factions—particularly the Zhentarim. He doesn't, however, have the power to command the factions to help—and in some cases, can't even openly negotiate with them. As King of Gauntlgrym, he can't be seen to favor one faction over another. He is therefore relying on the characters to do the legwork of getting the different factions on board.

If the characters are already involved with one or more factions, and especially if they have previously contacted the factions with news of developments in the Underdark, adjust the information presented below as needed.

THE HARPERS

Members of this clandestine network of spellcasters and spies pride themselves on being incorruptible defenders of the greater good and champions of the oppressed. Harper agents are trained to act alone and rely on their own resources. When they get into scrapes, they don't count on fellow Harpers to rescue them. Sometimes Harper agents must band together to face world-threatening foes, at which point the deep friendships between them forge the kind of fighting force needed to overthrow tyranny and eradicate evil.

Harper scouts engaged in charting and blocking off Underdark passages leading to the surface world have recently brought back the terrifying news of the demon lords' incursion into the Underdark. Word has spread quickly through their network, and the finest mages in their ranks are researching how to defeat the demon lords and their kind.

For long years, the Harpers have sworn to put an end to unbridled evil in all its forms—especially evil that wields dark magic. They know the demon lords seek to prey on the weak and corrupt the innocent. The Harpers feel this is the moment they have trained for, and their conscience now calls them to act.

LORD ZELRAUN ROARINGHORN
Lawful neutral male human wizard

Ideals: Freedom, opportunity, civilization
Personality: Proud, self-assured, fickle, spendthrift
Potential Resources: Shield guardian

Lord Roaringhorn hails from a Waterdhavian noble family, with all the self-assurance and pride that entails. He pursued his talent for the arcane arts, but never forgot his roots or lost his fondness for spending his family's considerable income on the finer things in life. He's a confident sort who likes to gamble. Winning over Roaringhorn requires a willingness to dine, drink, and potentially game with him.

Lord Roaringhorn is accompanied by a shield guardian and holds its control amulet. The shield guardian currently has a *lightning bolt* spell stored within it. A character can gain use of the shield guardian by winning a game of chess against the Harper wizard. Zelraun suggests a match after dinner.

A chess match takes 1 hour, and the outcome is determined by a best-of-three Intelligence check contest. Zelraun's experience gives him a +9 modifier to his Intelligence checks. Zelraun loans the shield guardian and its control amulet to the first character to beat him at the game. If Zelraun proves unbeatable, you can decide that Zelraun, ever the gracious winner, loans the shield guardian and amulet to the party on the provision that the characters vow to redeem themselves with a rematch upon their return from the Underdark.

If a character obtains Zelraun's shield guardian and control amulet, photocopy the **Shield Guardian** stat card at the end of this chapter and give it to the player whose character has the amulet. If the amulet changes hands, so too does the shield guardian and its stat card.

If the characters attack Zelraun, use the **archmage** statistics in the *Monster Manual* to represent him.

THE ORDER OF THE GAUNTLET

The Order of the Gauntlet is a dedicated, tightly knit group of holy-minded crusaders driven by a finely honed sense of justice and honor. Friendship and camaraderie are important to members of the order, and they share a trust normally reserved for siblings. They seek to uphold justice as best they can, and to continually test their mettle against the forces of evil. There are few, if any, lone operatives in this organization. Working in pairs and small groups reinforces the bonds of friendship and helps keep members from straying off the path of righteousness.

The Underdark has always been a proving ground for candidates of the order, as well as a frequent destination for veteran paladins, monks, and clerics looking to smite evil. It hasn't taken long for reports of new threats rising in the Underdark to reach the order.

The demon lords embody the kind of evil the Order of the Gauntlet is sworn to destroy. All members of the order see the evolving situation as an opportunity to deal a mighty blow to the forces of the Abyss. They want to send the demon lords howling back into the pit, proving the worth of the order as well as testing their own valor and bravery.

SIR LANNIVER STRAYL
Lawful good human fighter

Ideals: Faith, devotion, justice, duty
Personality: Patient, determined, witty
Potential Resources: Order of the Gauntlet veterans

A devout follower of Tyr and a member of the Order of the Gauntlet, Sir Lanniver is the most respected figure among the factions in Gauntlgrym. Little surprises him at this point in his life, and he accepts what comes with a wry wit and an unshakable faith that things will always work out—provided those of good intent do what must be done. If most of the characters in the party are of good alignment, Sir Lanniver is supportive of their mission and wants them to succeed. However, a party of mostly neutral or evil characters will need to work to gain his support.

If he's of a mind to provide aid, Sir Lanniver pledges five human veterans of the order to the party's mission. The veterans' names are Thora Nabal, Sylrien Havennor, Olaf Renghyi, Elias Drako, and Tamryn Tharke. Sir Lanniver can also offer a member of the party a *+1 warhammer*, one of a handful of treasures held in trust by the order. He prefers to bestow this weapon on a good- or neutral-aligned cleric or paladin. Feel free to swap this magic weapon with another magic item more useful to the adventurers.

If the veterans accompany the party, make five photocopies of the **Veteran of the Gauntlet** stat card at the end of this chapter. If you don't want to control the veterans yourself, you can distribute the stat cards among the players and let them run the NPCs.

Should Sir Lanniver come under attack, use the **knight** statistics in the *Monster Manual* to represent him. In addition to the veterans mentioned above, Sir Lanniver travels with a young but able squire (female human **guard**) named Rhiele Vannis.

THE EMERALD ENCLAVE

Members of the Emerald Enclave are spread far and wide across the Sword Coast and the North. They usually operate in isolation, relying on their own abilities and instincts to survive. Living deep in the wilderness demands great fortitude and the mastery of certain fighting and survival skills. Down in the Underdark, far from the wild lands, the Emerald Enclave must remain ever vigilant to avoid being blindsided by unnatural forces.

Some members of the enclave engage with the people of the world as protectors, emerging from the wilderness to help others survive its perils. Some are charged with defending sacred glades and preserving the natural balance. At times, however, all members of the order are called together to combat foes great enough to disrupt or destroy the natural order. The demon lords are one such threat.

Druids and scouts of the Emerald Enclave have recently witnessed the corruption spreading through of the flora and fauna of the Underdark. In particular, they have tracked this corruption back to Zuggtmoy and Juiblex, with the demon lords both infecting different parts of the subterranean realm.

The Emerald Enclave fights tirelessly against the corruption of nature. Its members are well aware that the newly seen demonic corruption will not be contained within the Underdark for long. Eventually it will break through to the surface and threaten all Faerûn—and by the time it does, it might be too late to stop it.

MORISTA MALKIN
Neutral good shield dwarf scout

Ideals: Loyalty, nature, the dwarven people
Personality: Stern, stubborn, insightful
Potential Resources: Emerald Enclave scouts and giant lizard mounts

Morista Malkin is the only faction representative who currently resides in Gauntlgrym. Originally from the Silver Marches, she heard Bruenor's call to reclaim the glory of the ancient line of Delzoun and followed him to Gauntlgrym. Here, she balances her work with the Emerald Enclave and her loyalty to her people and their cause. Stern and stubborn, Morista sees it as her duty to protect the people of Gauntlgrym from the often savage nature of the Underdark and to remind them of its natural beauty. She serves King Bruenor as an advisor and both admires and respects him.

Morista spends some of her time training elite scouts to reconnoiter the Underdark passages near the city. A few months ago, one of her scouts—a wood elf named Sladis Vadir—disappeared while on a mission in the Underdark. Hopeful that the characters might stumble upon Sladis and see him safely back to Gauntlgrym, Morista pledges a team of three shield dwarf scouts to accompany them, along with a giant lizard mount for each enclave scout and each player character. The scouts are named Brim Coppervein, Thargus Forkbeard, and Griswalla Stonehammer.

If the characters accept the Emerald Enclave's support, make three photocopies of the **Emerald Enclave Scout** stat card at the end of this chapter as well as photocopies of the **Giant Riding Lizard** stat card (one for each enclave scout and player character). If you don't want to control the scouts and giant lizards yourself, you can distribute their stat cards among the players and let them run the NPCs.

Should Morista come under attack, use the **scout** statistics in the *Monster Manual* to represent her.

THE LORDS' ALLIANCE

The Lords' Alliance is a political and economic coalition of cities spread throughout the North and the Sword Coast. The alliance owes its success to effective cooperation and diplomacy between its members, who work to align their separate settlements toward a mutual purpose. This cooperation is easier during times of crisis, making the Lords' Alliance a powerful force when threats require a united front. The agents of the Lords' Alliance work to maintain the delicate network

of information and diplomacy that sustains their order, alert for anything that might threaten the alliance's interests. Recent reports of unusual activity from the Underdark might mark one such threat.

The alliance has noted how many Underdark sites near their settlements have gone quiet. Routine forays and raids onto the surface world have come to a halt, as has the flow of trade and information. Rumors have reached the Lords' Alliance of demon-worshiping cults and chaos around places such as Blingdenstone and Menzoberranzan, though they have little confirmation.

The possibility that the demon lords of the Abyss are active in the Underdark is a threat the Lords' Alliance can't ignore.

LORD ERAVIEN HAUND
Lawful neutral half-elf noble

Ideals: Order, society, peace, stability
Personality: Charming, sly, worldly
Potential Resources: Lords' Alliance guards and spies

The representative of the Lords' Alliance is a noble of Tethyrian and moon elf heritage, his youthful looks belying his actual age and experience. Although he hails from Waterdeep, Lord Eravien often travels to other alliance settlements. He's a charming and sly courtier, able to immediately size up any social situation, but his fondness for socializing often distracts him from what's important. As a result, Eravien has heard relatively little of the recent events in the Underdark, and he is initially unconvinced of the importance of the party's mission.

If they can convince him otherwise, Lord Eravien arranges for some agents of the Lords' Alliance to join the expedition:

- Five dwarf guards from the alliance city of Mirabar. Their names are Nazrok Blueaxe, Kirsil Mantlehorn, Anzar the Brazen, Gargathine Truesilver, and Splinter Darkmorn.
- Three human spies from the alliance city of Yartar. Their names are Farryl Kilmander, Zilna Oakshadow, and Hilvius Haever.

If the party accepts these NPCs into its ranks, make five photocopies of the **Lords' Alliance Guard** and three photocopies of the **Lords' Alliance Spy** stat cards at the end of this chapter. If you don't want to control these NPCs yourself, you can distribute their stat cards among the players and let them run the NPCs.

Eravien knows that the Lords' Alliance has a deep-cover operative in the Underdark. Khelessa Draga, a high elf from Silverymoon, was sent to spy on the drow over a year ago. Eravien knows that Khelessa uses magic to disguise herself as a dark elf and warns the characters not to attack any drow they encounter until they can confirm the target isn't Khelessa in disguise. The Lords' Alliance lost contact with Khelessa months ago, so Eravien doesn't know where she is.

Should Lord Eravien come under attack, use the **noble** statistics in the *Monster Manual* to represent him. He travels with three servants (strongheart halfling **commoners**) and three well-paid human **guards**.

THE ZHENTARIM

Members of the shadowy Black Network consider themselves part of an extended family, and rely on the larger organization for resources and security. The Zhentarim recognizes and rewards ambition, granting its members autonomy to pursue their own interests and gain some measure of personal power or influence. In this way, the organization is a meritocracy. The Zhentarim welcomes dangerous times as opportunities. When a merchant caravan needs an escort, a noble needs bodyguards, or a city needs trained soldiers, the Zhentarim provides the best-trained fighting forces money can buy.

Zhentarim agents traveling to and from Mantol-Derith have recently passed on information and rumors concerning demonic activity in the Underdark. The organization's members have yet to realize the full extent of the threat, as corruption and madness have already infiltrated their secret outpost since those initial reports (see chapter 9). However, even the most cautious member of the Zhentarim knows that demons at large in the world are bad for business. The organization thus views the possible presence of the demon lords in the Underdark with the same concern as any other external threat to their way of life.

Zhentarim bonds of oath and honor hold the network together and galvanize its members in united purpose. More importantly, those bonds reflect the pattern of tight control that the leaders of the Zhentarim hope to one day see imposed across the North and beyond. The organization is thus willing to commit to stop the demon lords from breaching the surface—knowing that such a fate would destroy the Zhentarim's plans for control of Faerûn.

DAVRA JASSUR
Lawful evil human assassin

Ideals: Order, discipline, ambition
Personality: Driven, focused, ruthless
Potential Resources: Zhentarim thugs

Graceful and elegant as a blade, Davra Jassur ostensibly recruits promising new talent for the Zhentarim. But she also deals with internal problems, ensuring those problems are nipped in the bud before they can reveal any weakness within the organization. The pragmatic Davra values order and discipline as well as drive and ambition, and she embodies all those traits.

The Zhentarim's intelligence-gathering resources and access to an established Underdark outpost give the organization the strongest hand of any of the factions, and Davra knows it. Access to Mantol-Derith is key to the plan, and though she ultimately won't withhold that access from the adventurers, she intends to make sure it's not given away for free. Davra deals with the adventurers directly—and privately, if possible—asking for a full share of any treasure the characters claim during their next incursion into the Underdark, and a full reporting to her of all information given to Bruenor or the other faction leaders. If one of the characters is a member of the Zhentarim, Davra tries to make the deal for information with that character alone.

In addition to access to the hidden trading post of Mantol-Derith, Davra Jassur can provide Zhentarim mercenaries to fill out the expedition. These eight human thugs proudly wear the crest of the Black Network on their armor. If these NPCs join the party, make eight photocopies of the **Zhentarim Thug** stat card at the end of this chapter. If you don't want to control these NPCs yourself, you can distribute their stat cards among the players and let them run the NPCs. The thugs' names are Nero Kelvane, Lenora Haskur, Aligor Moonwhisper, Gorath Torn, Saliyra Dalnor, Primwin Halk, Iandro Alathar, and Lhytris Ilgarn. All of them know the route to Mantol-Derith.

Davra is an **assassin**. In addition to her weapons, she carries *dust of disappearance* and wears *goggles of night* while roaming the dark halls of Gauntlgrym.

THE WAY AHEAD

Depending on how negotiations go, the characters are either an advance force to scout and soften up opposition in the Underdark while looking for valuable strategic information, or a diversionary expedition meant to buy time for the surface world to organize a stronger response. Faction representatives not impressed by the adventurers' cause might return to their factions convinced that the characters have little chance of succeeding—or surviving. The others are confident that the characters can live up to the promise they demonstrated in escaping from the drow and the Underdark.

King Bruenor convenes a final gathering of his inner circle of advisors and the adventurers, giving the characters his thanks for their commitment to the fight against the demon lords.

> "Ye all know the dangers and threats of the world below, and have bought that knowledge with bravery and guile. Even more, in diplomacy have ye forged the first of the connections that will see the North prepared for what might come. If we survive the coming onslaught, we'll have ye to thank, and no dwarf of Gauntlgrym will soon forget it. Ye all have the courage and conviction of heroes. Aye, I'll even say ye remind me of other heroes I've known. From a previous life. ..."

The characters have at least a few days before they must venture into the Underdark again—time they can spend to shape their plans, gather resources, and prepare for the threats that stand ahead of them. When they are ready to brave the Underdark once again, they can start the long and dangerous journey to Mantol-Derith (see chapter 9).

Shield Guardian

Large construct, unaligned

Armor Class 17 (natural armor)
Hit Points 142 (15d10 + 60)
Speed 30 ft.

STR	DEX	CON	INT	WIS	CHA
18 (+4)	8 (–1)	18 (+4)	7 (–2)	10 (+0)	3 (–4)

Senses blindsight 10 ft., darkvision 60 ft., passive Perception 10
Damage Immunities poison
Condition Immunities charmed, exhaustion, frightened, paralyzed, poisoned
Languages understands commands given in any language but can't speak
Challenge 7 (2,900 XP)

Bound. The shield guardian is magically bound to an amulet. As long as the guardian and its amulet are on the same plane of existence, the amulet's wearer can telepathically call the guardian to travel to it, and the guardian knows the distance and direction to the amulet. If the guardian is within 60 feet of the amulet's wearer, half of any damage the wearer takes (rounded up) is transferred to the guardian.

Regeneration. The shield guardian regains 10 hit points at the start of its turn if it has at least 1 hit point.

Spell Storing. A spellcaster who wears the shield guardian's amulet can cause the guardian to store one spell of 4th level or lower. To do so, the wearer must cast the spell on the guardian. The spell has no effect but is stored within the guardian. When commanded to do so by the wearer or when a situation arises that was predefined by the spellcaster, the guardian casts the spell stored with any parameters set by the original caster, requiring no components. When the spell is cast or a new spell is stored, any previously stored spell is lost.

Actions

Multiattack. The guardian makes two fist attacks.

Fist. *Melee Weapon Attack:* +7 to hit, reach 5 ft., one target. *Hit:* 11 (2d6 + 4) bludgeoning damage.

Reactions

Shield. When a creature makes an attack against the wearer of the guardian's amulet, the guardian grants a +2 bonus to the wearer's AC if the guardian is within 5 feet of the wearer.

Name: _____

Veteran of the Gauntlet

Medium humanoid (human), lawful good

Armor Class 17 (splint)
Hit Points 58 (9d8 + 18)
Speed 30 ft.

STR	DEX	CON	INT	WIS	CHA
16 (+3)	13 (+1)	14 (+2)	10 (+0)	11 (+0)	10 (+0)

Skills Athletics +5, Perception +2
Senses passive Perception 12
Languages Common, Dwarvish
Challenge 3 (700 XP)

Actions

Multiattack. The veteran makes two longsword attacks. If it has a shortsword drawn, it can also make a shortsword attack.

Longsword. *Melee Weapon Attack:* +5 to hit, reach 5 ft., one target. *Hit:* 7 (1d8 + 3) slashing damage, or 8 (1d10 + 3) slashing damage if used with two hands.

Shortsword. *Melee Weapon Attack:* +5 to hit, reach 5 ft., one target. *Hit:* 6 (1d6 + 3) piercing damage.

Heavy Crossbow. *Ranged Weapon Attack:* +3 to hit, range 100/400 ft., one target. *Hit:* 5 (1d10) piercing damage.

Name: _____

Emerald Enclave Scout

Medium humanoid (dwarf), lawful neutral

Armor Class 16 (breastplate)
Hit Points 19 (3d8 + 6)
Speed 25 ft.

STR	DEX	CON	INT	WIS	CHA
11 (+0)	14 (+2)	14 (+2)	11 (+0)	13 (+1)	11 (+0)

Skills Nature +4, Perception +5, Stealth +6, Survival +5
Damage Resistances poison
Senses darkvision 60 ft., passive Perception 15
Languages Common, Dwarvish
Challenge 1/2 (100 XP)

Dwarven Resilience. The scout has advantage on saving throws against poison.

Keen Hearing and Sight. The scout has advantage on Wisdom (Perception) checks that rely on hearing or sight.

Actions

Multiattack. The scout makes two melee attacks.

War Pick. *Melee Weapon Attack:* +4 to hit, reach 5 ft., one target. *Hit:* 7 (1d8 + 3) piercing damage.

Heavy Crossbow. *Ranged Weapon Attack:* +3 to hit, range 100/400 ft., one target. *Hit:* 5 (1d10) piercing damage.

NAME:

LORDS' ALLIANCE GUARD
Medium humanoid (dwarf), chaotic good

Armor Class 16 (chain shirt, shield)
Hit Points 11 (2d8 + 2)
Speed 30 ft.

STR	DEX	CON	INT	WIS	CHA
14 (+2)	12 (+1)	12 (+1)	10 (+0)	11 (+0)	10 (+0)

Skills Perception +2
Damage Resistances poison
Senses darkvision 60 ft., passive Perception 12
Languages Common, Dwarvish
Challenge 1/4 (50 XP)

Dwarven Resilience. The guard has advantage on saving throws against poison.

ACTIONS

Halberd. *Melee Weapon Attack:* +4 to hit, reach 10 ft., one target. *Hit:* 7 (1d10 + 2) slashing damage.

NAME:

LORDS' ALLIANCE SPY
Medium humanoid (human), neutral

Armor Class 13 (leather armor)
Hit Points 27 (6d8)
Speed 30 ft.

STR	DEX	CON	INT	WIS	CHA
10 (+0)	15 (+2)	10 (+0)	12 (+1)	14 (+2)	16 (+3)

Skills Deception +5, Insight +4, Investigation +5, Perception +6, Persuasion +5, Sleight of Hand +4, Stealth +4
Senses passive Perception 16
Languages Common, Dwarvish
Challenge 1 (200 XP)

Cunning Action. On each of its turns, the spy can use a bonus action to take the Dash, Disengage, or Hide action.

Sneak Attack (1/Turn). The spy deals an extra 7 (2d6) damage when it hits a target with a weapon attack and has advantage on the attack roll, or when the target is within 5 feet of an ally of the spy that isn't incapacitated and the spy doesn't have disadvantage on the attack roll.

ACTIONS

Multiattack. The spy makes two melee attacks.

Shortsword. *Melee Weapon Attack:* +4 to hit, reach 5 ft., one target. *Hit:* 5 (1d6 + 2) piercing damage.

Hand Crossbow. *Ranged Weapon Attack:* +4 to hit, range 30/120 ft., one target. *Hit:* 5 (1d6 + 2) piercing damage.

NAME:

ZHENTARIM THUG
Medium humanoid (human), neutral

Armor Class 11 (leather armor)
Hit Points 32 (5d8 + 10)
Speed 30 ft.

STR	DEX	CON	INT	WIS	CHA
15 (+2)	11 (+0)	14 (+2)	10 (+0)	10 (+0)	11 (+0)

Skills Intimidation +2
Senses passive Perception 10
Languages Common
Challenge 1/2 (100 XP)

Pack Tactics. The thug has advantage on an attack roll against a creature if at least one of the thug's allies is within 5 feet of the creature and the ally isn't incapacitated.

ACTIONS

Multiattack. The thug makes two melee attacks.

Mace. *Melee Weapon Attack:* +4 to hit, reach 5 ft., one target. *Hit:* 5 (1d6 + 2) bludgeoning damage.

Heavy Crossbow. *Ranged Weapon Attack:* +2 to hit, range 100/400 ft., one target. *Hit:* 5 (1d10) piercing damage.

GIANT RIDING LIZARD
Large beast, unaligned

Armor Class 12 (natural armor)
Hit Points 19 (3d10 + 3)
Speed 30 ft., climb 30 ft.

STR	DEX	CON	INT	WIS	CHA
15 (+2)	12 (+1)	13 (+1)	2 (–4)	10 (+0)	5 (–3)

Senses darkvision 30 ft., passive Perception 10
Languages —
Challenge 1/4 (50 XP)

Spider Climb. The lizard can climb difficult surfaces, including upside down on ceilings, without needing to make an ability check.

ACTIONS

Bite. *Melee Weapon Attack:* +4 to hit, reach 5 ft., one target. *Hit:* 6 (1d8 + 2) piercing damage.

CHAPTER 9: MANTOL-DERITH

Mantol-Derith has endured for centuries as a neutral outpost where drow, duergar, svirfneblin, and surface dwellers can meet and trade without fearing for their lives. Despite its usefulness and the safety it enjoys, Mantol-Derith has never become a proper town. Those who maintain it as a trade hub have resisted any urge for expansion, apart from installing basic infrastructure to assist with commercial activities.

The Zhentarim took over the holdings where surface dwellers conducted business and quickly cornered the market for surface goods, gaining the organization a foothold in the Underdark. This presence grew into a power base that serves the Black Network well, and which is now being made available to the characters.

Upon arrival, however, the characters discover there is no safe haven anywhere in the Underdark with the demon lords running rampant. The safety of Mantol-Derith has been shattered by the demon lord Fraz-Urb'luu, who has turned the trading outpost's various factions against one another.

The characters must navigate and overcome the madness dominating Mantol-Derith in order to find their Zhentarim contact, Ghazrim DuLoc. He has the means for them to reach the stone giant library of Gravenhollow (see chapter 11), whose vast lore might provide some clue as to what has brought the demon lords to the Underdark.

FRAZ-URB'LUU'S GEM

Having previously been imprisoned for many mortal lifetimes on the Material Plane, Fraz-Urb'luu had taken steps to bind himself to his layer of the Abyss. As soon as he felt the tug of Gromph's spell, Fraz-Urb'luu transferred his evil life force to a specially crafted, magically protected receptacle—a black jewel. However, the spell proved irresistible, and the precious receptacle was cast into the Underdark. As a further indignity, Fraz-Urb'luu found himself trapped within the gem, unable to escape while on the Material Plane.

Anyone who touches the gem risks falling prey to delusional madness. A duergar ale merchant named Krimgol Muzgardt found the gem and took it to Mantol-Derith. By the time he arrived, Krimgol had succumbed to the delusion that he was a *calassabrak*—a duergar without honor. He paid Yantha Coaxrock, an honest svirfneblin mage, to appraise the jewel, hoping that he could use it to buy back the goodwill of his clan. Touched by the gem's madness, Yantha lied to Krimgol and told him the gem was worthless. She offered a lump of gold in exchange, whereupon Krimgol suspected treachery and demanded the gem's immediate return. While Krimgol and Yantha argued, one of Yantha's apprentices tried to hide the gem for his mistress but succumbed to its evil power. The apprentice, Flink, took the gem to the drow enclave, hoping to trade it for some rare spell components that he imagined Yantha needing to make Krimgol go away. A gargoyle assigned to watch for thieves spotted the gem and wrested it from Flink, who hid for fear of incurring Yantha's wrath. Soon thereafter, the delusional gargoyle laid eyes on a drow assassin named Kinyel Druu'giir and was instantly smitten by her. The gargoyle gave her the black gem as a token of its devotion, which she, in her madness, mistook as a payment from the drow enclave to assassinate Lorthuun, a maimed beholder allied with the Zhentarim.

Yantha's theft of the gem led Krimgol to leave and return with duergar reinforcements. They attacked the svirfneblin enclave and captured Yantha, triggering open conflict between the two enclaves. With the fragile truce in Mantol-Derith finally broken, the drow are preparing to take out the weakened duergar and svirfneblin forces. Meanwhile, Druu'giir has infiltrated a drow delegation sent to meet with representatives of the Zhentarim enclave to discuss how best to divvy up Mantol-Derith between them.

Finding and destroying the gem prevents others from falling prey to Fraz-Urb'luu's madness. While imprisoned inside the gem, Fraz-Urb'luu retains his alignment and senses (see appendix D), but loses all of his other attributes and can't take actions. The gem is as big as a human fist and has AC 10, 1 hit point, immunity to poison and psychic damage, and immunity to bludgeoning, piercing, and slashing damage from nonmagical weapons. It is also immune to any spell effect that requires a saving throw. While inside the gem, the demon lord can't be attacked, harmed, coerced, or heard. He can be contacted via telepathy, however. Shattering the gem releases Fraz-Urb'luu's life force, which instantly returns to the demon lord's body in the Abyss.

Any creature that touches the gem must succeed on a DC 23 Charisma saving throw or succumb to a form of indefinite madness, as determined by rolling on the Madness of Fraz-Urb'luu table in appendix D. A creature that succeeds on the saving throw is immune to the madness-inducing effect of the gem for the next 24 hours. The madness lasts until cured.

If the characters destroy Fraz-Urb'luu's gem, award each of them 1,000 XP.

REACHING MANTOL-DERITH

If the characters reached an agreement with Davra Jassur in chapter 8, they can travel to Mantol-Derith along one of the many routes the Zhentarim use to move merchandise to the trade hub from the surface world. The Black Network doesn't reveal the shortest route for security reasons. Instead, its representatives lead the adventurers to a remote cave in the Surbrin Hills, about 180 miles east of Gauntlgrym. Black Network sentries (six human **veterans**) guard the cave, which leads to a series of tunnels. These tunnels descend sharply as they wind their way east for another 200 miles. Check for random encounters as the party's expedition makes its way to Mantol-Derith, using the tables in chapter 2.

If the characters are traveling with faction representatives (see chapter 8), these NPCs help the characters overcome random encounters. Whenever a random encounter check yields a "no encounter" result, use that opportunity to roleplay some of these NPCs and develop their personalities as you see fit.

Mantol-Derith abuts the Darklake and is roughly six days' travel from Blingdenstone and Menzoberranzan, and 22 days from Gracklstugh via the Darklake locks (see the overview map of the Underdark in chapter 2). Characters accompanied by Zhentarim guides approach Mantol-Derith via a subterranean rift. A narrow trail winds up the side of the rift, ending at a secret door in the northwest corner of the trade hub (area 1a).

MANTOL-DERITH

Population: Approximately 140 (drow, duergar, humans, and svirfneblin)

Government: Informal council comprised of four chief negotiators (one per enclave), recently dissolved

Defense: Private guards

Commerce: Rare and exotic goods; see each enclave for information on the goods traded by the duergar, the drow, the svirfneblin, and the Zhentarim

Organizations: The drow, duergar, svirfneblin, and Zhentarim enclaves

Thousands of years' worth of trickling water carved out the cavern where the drow, the duergar, and the svirfneblin established Mantol-Derith. Four warehouses have been excavated at the corners of the cavern, each controlled by an enclave and containing offices and temporary lodgings for its merchants.

Few of Mantol-Derith's denizens are permanent residents. Even the chief negotiators of each enclave return to their centers of power periodically, leaving representatives to conduct business. Everyone in Mantol-Derith is there to trade, negotiate, and, of course, spy on their counterparts in the other enclaves.

The arrival of Fraz-Urb'luu has upset the balance of power in Mantol-Derith (see "Fraz-Urb'luu's Gem"), resulting in open conflict between the duergar and svirfneblin. The drow are poised to eliminate both, thus reducing by two the number of enclaves in Mantol-Derith. The drow are simultaneously hoping to preserve the truce with their Zhentarim neighbors. However, a delusional drow assassin threatens to turn the drow and Zhentarim enclaves against one another.

The location of Mantol-Derith is a well-guarded secret, and the influence and power merchants gain from access to it isn't something they want to share. Normally, life in Mantol-Derith is regulated by three simple covenants: no stealing of goods from fellow merchants, no disguising of goods by any means, and no use of magic during negotiations and haggling. The punishment for breaking any covenant is equally straightforward: the violator is wrapped in chains and tossed into the Darklake. Recent events in Mantol-Derith have rendered these rules moot.

IMPORTANT NPCs

The following NPCs have key roles in this chapter of the adventure.

MANTOL-DERITH NPCs

Sladis Vadir	High elf druid of the Emerald Enclave
Rystia Zav	Human spy for the Harpers
Peebles	Svirfneblin spy working for Xazax the Eyemonger
Zilchyn Q'Leptin	Drow mage and kleptomaniac
Yantha Coaxrock	Svirfneblin mage and leader of the Stoneheart Enclave
Flink Thunderbonk	Yantha's svirfneblin apprentice
Gabble Dripskillet	Svirfneblin chief negotiator
Ghuldur Flagonfist	Duergar and chief negotiator from Gracklstugh
Sirak Mazelor	Drow and chief negotiator from Menzoberranzan
Kinyel Druu'giir	Drow assassin
Ghazrim DuLoc	The characters' contact and chief negotiator of the Zhentarim
Lorthuun	Maimed beholder

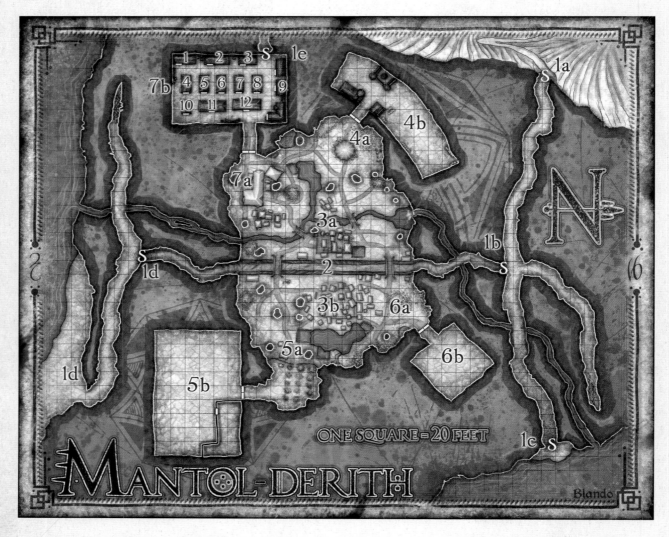

ONE SQUARE = 20 FEET

MANTOL-DERITH

Blando

KEYED ENCOUNTERS

The following encounters are keyed to the map of Mantol-Derith.

1. SECRET ENTRANCES

Mantol-Derith is hidden behind 10-foot-square secret doors carved to resemble walls of natural stone. A creature within 5 feet of a secret door can make a DC 15 Wisdom (Perception) check to spot it. Each secret door has an *arcane lock* spell cast on it. Speaking the proper password within 5 feet of a secret door opens it. Opening a secret door by any means other than the correct password triggers a magical disintegration trap on whichever side the door is opened from. Each creature in the 20-foot-square area directly in front of the secret door must succeed on a DC 15 Dexterity saving throw, taking 55 (10d10) force damage on a failed save, or half as much damage on a successful one. A creature reduced to 0 hit points by this trap is disintegrated, leaving only its possessions behind.

1A. NORTHWEST ENTRANCE

Characters guided by representatives of the Zhentarim arrive at Mantol-Derith via this route—a subterranean rift with a rough-hewn path carved into one wall. This entrance is also used by svirfneblin from Blingdenstone and drow from Menzoberranzan. The switchback path ends at the secret door whose password is "im'yat," a svirfneblin word meaning "darkness."

1B. NORTH ENTRANCE

The password to open this secret door is "belaern," a drow word meaning "wealth." If the characters are being guided by members of the Black Network, they are led through this secret door into the trench that bisects Mantol-Derith (area 2).

1C. NORTHEAST ENTRANCE

This secret door stands at the back of a naturally formed ledge overlooking the Darklake. The password to open it is "ssussun," a drow word meaning "light." When the characters first gaze upon the ledge, read the following boxed text to the players.

> An elf with long red hair and a backpack sits on a ledge overlooking a vast, water-filled cavern. The elf is dressed in the finest attire and is dipping his bare feet in the murky water. "Care to join me?" he asks with a wry smile.

The figure dipping his feet in the water is Sladis Vadir, a high elf druid and member of the Emerald Enclave. Use the **druid** statistics in the *Monster Manual* to represent him, with the following modifications:

- Sladis is neutral good.
- He has darkvision out to a range of 60 feet.
- He speaks Common, Elvish, and Undercommon.
- His fey ancestry gives him advantage on saving throws against being charmed, and magic can't put him to sleep.

RYSTIA ZAV

SLADIS VADIR

- He can cast the *prestidigitation* cantrip at will and uses it to make his dirt-stained garments look clean.

Sladis Vadir has always felt a strange attraction to the Underdark, but the demonic incursion has broken his sanity. He kills and eats other humanoids he encounters or, as he calls it, "culls the herd to maintain the natural order." This is considered a form of indefinite madness (see "Madness" in chapter 8 of the *Dungeon Master's Guide*).

Sladis happily accompanies the party and graciously offers his services as a guide. He knows how to get to Neverlight Grove, Blingdenstone, Gracklstugh, and Menzoberranzan, but not Gravenhollow. If the characters invite Sladis to accompany them, he thanks them by offering them some "food" (see "Treasure").

Treasure. In addition to his quarterstaff and spell components, Sladis carries a blood-caked flint knife that he uses to cut up his victims, as well as a *Heward's handy haversack* stuffed full of severed limbs and eviscerated organs—the uncooked remains of his svirfneblin, grimlock, quaggoth, and drow victims.

XP Awards. If the characters cure Sladis Vadir's madness, award each of them 100 XP. If he is safely returned to Morista Malkin in Gauntlgrym (see chapter 8), award each character 150 XP.

1D. SOUTH ENTRANCE AND SHORE

This secret door to Mantol-Derith lies halfway down a dead-end tunnel stemming from a rocky shoreline that hugs the Darklake. Duergar traders from Gracklstugh use this entrance. The password to open the secret door is "groht," an archaic Dwarvish word meaning "stone."

When the characters first gaze upon the shore, read the following boxed text to the players.

> Someone has pitched a small tent on this pebbled beach overlooking a vast underground lake. Above the sound of water lapping at the shoreline, you hear a soft, feminine voice humming an unfamiliar tune. The voice comes from inside the tent, which is illuminated from within.

The tent belongs to the figure inside it: a female human named Rystia Zav. Rystia is a chaotic good Harper

spy from Nesmé who descended into the Underdark two years ago to find Mantol-Derith and infiltrate the Zhentarim enclave there. She got lost in the depths and has no idea how close she's come to finding what she's been looking for. She also has no idea how to get to the surface. Fear, loneliness, and the demonic incursion have driven her mad. She now believes that everyone she encounters is out to kill her. This is considered a form of indefinite madness (see "Madness" in chapter 8 of the *Dungeon Master's Guide*).

Traps. Rystia has planted four spring-loaded hunting traps under the pebbles around her tent. A creature within 15 feet of the tent can spot the hidden traps with a successful DC 15 Wisdom (Perception) check. Any creature that approaches within 10 feet of the tent and is unaware of the traps steps on one (see chapter 5, "Equipment," in the *Player's Handbook* for hunting trap rules).

Treasure. In addition to her weapons and traps, Rystia possesses a satchel made from carrion crawler hide, inside which are ten pounds of edible fungi. She also carries a full waterskin and three torchstalks (see "Fungi of the Underdark" in chapter 2), one of which is already lit.

XP Awards. If the characters cure Rystia's madness, award each of them 100 XP.

1e. Zhentarim Secret Door

The password to open this secret door is "eyebite."

The tunnel leading away from Mantol-Derith winds steadily upward, and branches leading to other areas of the Underdark have been sealed off with *wall of stone* spells, leaving a single navigable passage. This passage is clear of monsters, but the Zhents have installed trip wires and pressure plates at irregular intervals. These are triggering mechanisms for collapsing roofs, poison darts, and rolling spheres (see "Sample Traps" in chapter 5 of the *Dungeon Master's Guide*). The passage ends at a dungeon complex under a ruined watchtower overlooking the Surbrin River, north of the Evermoors. The Zhentarim have guards stationed throughout the dungeon to keep surface dwellers from finding their way to Mantol-Derith via this route. If the characters find this secret door and use it to make their way back to the surface world, design and populate the Zhentarim dungeon as you see fit.

2. Trench

This 20-foot-wide, 50-foot-deep trench bisects Mantol-Derith from north to south, with a secret door at each end (areas 1b and 1d, respectively). A shattered platform of crystal sits in the middle of the trench—an old magic device once used to lift caravans up into the main cavern of the outpost and back down into the trench. It now lies broken, its magic spent.

The duergar and drow collaborated to replace the crystal lift with a system of four mechanical lifts, two on each side of the shattered platform. These lifts use magic to power their winches and lighten the loads on the lifts. Each lift is designed for easy use and can be operated as an action simply by pulling on a lever.

The trench's walls sport numerous handholds and can be climbed with a successful DC 10 Strength (Athletics) check.

3. Main Cavern

When the characters exit the trench, they find the normally quiet outpost in chaos.

> The trench bisects an enormous cavern with a 30-foot-high ceiling supported by naturally formed stone columns. *Continual flame* spells cast on stone lampposts reflect off crystals embedded in the walls and ceiling, illuminating myriad fountains, waterfalls, streams, and pools. Water drips from stalactites onto leather tarps covering clusters of merchant stalls west and east of the trench. Beyond these marketplaces are well-tended gardens of mold and fungi, crystal walkways, and stone bridges. The tranquil beauty of Mantol-Derith is undone by sounds of combat to the northeast, where you hear the thunderous boom of metal against stone and see panicked svirfneblin running from 8-foot-tall duergar.

The marketplaces of Mantol-Derith have been closed ever since the duergar attacked the svirfneblin. The duergar are killing any svirfneblin they encounter and breaking into the svirfneblin warehouse (see area 6a).

3a. West Marketplace

The drow and Zhentarim markets are clustered here, on the west side of the trench. However, the tents, stalls, and pens stand empty, the merchants having retreated to their respective enclaves with their goods and livestock. A stream runs nearby, crossed by two stone bridges leading to the drow and Zhentarim enclaves. The stream is 5 feet deep and fed by the Darklake. The water isn't fit for drinking.

3b. East Marketplace

The svirfneblin and duergar markets are clustered on the east side of the trench. Most of their tents and stalls have been knocked over, and various goods (see "Treasure") are strewn upon the cavern floor amid the slaughtered corpses of giant lizards and steeders. Characters approaching the market see two enlarged **duergar** chasing a pair of **deep gnomes** who have cast *blur* spells on themselves. A third unarmed **deep gnome** is hiding in plain sight under the wreckage of a zurkhwood stall. He has a pale leather bag tucked under one arm.

If the characters rescue the blurry svirfneblin, they reveal that more duergar are trying to smash into the svirfneblin warehouse (area 6b), and that Yantha Coaxrock, a svirfneblin mage, has been captured and taken to the duergar warehouse (area 5b). The svirfneblin don't know why the duergar broke the peace in Mantol-Derith. If a duergar is captured and interrogated, he or she reveals that Yantha stole a valuable gemstone from a duergar merchant and refused to return it.

Peebles. The svirfneblin holding the bag is Peebles. He came to Mantol-Derith to investigate rumors of a beholder living here. He claims to be fascinated by aberrations, beholders in particular. He has confirmed that there are no beholders in the duergar or svirfneblin enclaves, but he hasn't yet been able to explore the drow or Zhentarim enclaves.

Peebles is the deranged, neutral evil servant of Xazax the Eyemonger, a beholder that hunts other beholders, takes their eyestalks, and grafts them to its own body. Peebles is Xazax's private surgeon. Once he has confirmed the presence of a beholder in Mantol-Derith, Peebles plans to find his "master" and share the news of his discovery. He suggests that the characters take him to the drow or Zhentarim enclave, under the pretense of having information about the duergar attack. Once he has found Lorthuun the beholder, Peebles tries to leave Mantol-Derith at once. If the characters delay his departure, he gets angry at them and claims to be an expert Underdark guide, promising to lead them wherever they wish to go. If they accept his offer, he leads them to Xazax the Eyemonger (see chapter 10 for more information).

Peebles's bag is made from stitched quaggoth hide and contains a pair of sharpened flint knives, a spool of thread made from roper gut, a thin iron needle, two pounds of barrelstalk flesh, and a copper canteen containing a half gallon of water.

Pool. The large pool east of the market is fed by small waterfalls pouring through cracks in the cavern ceiling. The water is fresh and safe to drink. Growing along the shore are 3d6 waterorbs (see "Fungi of the Underdark").

Treasure. Characters who search the marketplace find a total of 2d6 50 gp gems scattered about.

4. Drow Enclave

The drow use Mantol-Derith to trade exquisite and exotic goods according to their rarefied tastes. Rare perfumes, potions, distilled beverages, and other alchemical products are some of their regular goods, as well as common and uncommon magic items. House Baenre controls the flow of merchandise here, placing and removing chief negotiators as their efficiency wanes.

Sirak Mazelor is the current drow representative. A sophisticated merchant, she deals in luxury items from drow artisans: gems of high value, incense, art objects, various magical treasures, and exotic spices and spirits exclusive to the Underdark.

4a. Drow Fungi Grove

This is where the drow cultivate edible and poisonous fungi. In the heart of the fungi grove is a stunted zurkhwood mushroom, 20 feet tall, with a thick stalk and a wide cap that forms a dome, keeping the area underneath dry. The dark elves use the mushroom as a pavilion, and this is where Sirak Mazelor conducts business with visiting traders.

Six **gargoyles** perch on natural ledges overlooking the fungi grove. They attack any creature unaccompanied by a drow that approaches the stone double doors leading to the drow warehouse (area 4b). Standing in front of

ZILCHYN Q'LEPTIN

PEEBLES

the double doors are two female **drow elite warriors** that do the same.

Zilchyn Q'Leptin. Sitting on a zurkhwood bench under the giant zurkhwood mushroom is a male **drow mage** named Zilchyn Q'Leptin. Trained as a wizard in Menzoberranzan, "Zilch" was forced to flee the drow city after a rash of spell component thefts was traced back to him. He can't control his kleptomania, which is considered a form of indefinite madness (see "Madness" in chapter 8 of the *Dungeon Master's Guide*). This madness befell Zilch long before the demon lords arrived, and has only gotten worse since.

Zilch lost his spellbook during his escape from Menzoberranzan, and an unfortunate encounter with a black pudding left him with acid scars covering the left side of his body, including his face. In addition to his staff, which doubles as a walking stick, the drow carries a purple bag made of kuo-toa skin that contains hand-drawn maps of the Underdark on sheets of trillimac, material components for all of Zilch's prepared spells, and 1d4 + 3 stolen trinkets (roll on the Trinkets table in chapter 5 of the *Player's Handbook*). Characters can use Zilch's maps to get to Menzoberranzan, Gracklstugh, or the Wormwrithings from Mantol-Derith.

Zilch doesn't know what caused the duergar to attack the svirfneblin, but he knows the drow merchants have withdrawn to the warehouse and that the drow are waiting to see how the violence plays out. If the characters seem approachable, Zilch offers to help them get inside the drow warehouse.

If the characters take a short or long rest and Zilch is with them, he attempts to steal something from one randomly determined party member. Far from being a skilled thief, Zilch must succeed at a Dexterity check contested by the passive Wisdom (Perception) scores of every character with line of sight to him. If he wins the contest, Zilch hides the stolen item in his bag and feigns innocence if questioned about the item's disappearance.

Flink Thunderbonk. Huddled against a stone column at the edge of the fungi grove is a cowardly **deep gnome** named Flink. He suffers from a form of indefinite madness (see "Madness" in chapter 8 of the *Dungeon Master's Guide*) that makes him want to please his mistress, Yantha Coaxrock, and also causes him to be deathly afraid of her. He uses his Stone Camouflage feature to blend in with the rocky terrain, afraid that the drow and the gargoyles might attack him. If he sees the characters, he runs toward them in a panic, babbling about a stolen gem. A successful DC 15 Charisma (Intimidation or Persuasion) check or *calm emotions* spell allows Flink to speak coherently, whereupon he reveals the following information:

- A duergar ale merchant named Krimgol Muzgardt asked Flink's mistress, Yantha Coaxrock, to appraise a large black gemstone. For reasons unknown to Flink, Yantha didn't want to give the gemstone back to the duergar and instead offered him a lump of gold in trade. An argument ensued.
- Yantha entrusted the gemstone to Flink. He took it to the drow enclave to buy an eyelash encased in gum arabic—the component for an *invisibility* spell, knowing that's what Yantha would want him to do. Before he could complete this task, a gargoyle snatched the gemstone from Flink's grasp. Flink is afraid Yantha will punish him for losing the gemstone.
- Flink has been spying on the gargoyles to find the one that took his gem, but that gargoyle isn't among the ones currently guarding the drow enclave.

4B. DROW WAREHOUSE

The drow warehouse is both a fortress and a residence. The stone double doors leading to it have an *arcane lock* spell cast on them, which only Sirak Mazelor and her elite warrior guards can bypass.

Characters who gain entry find the warehouse occupied by two female **drow elite warriors**, eighteen **drow** merchants, nine **quaggoth** slaves, and six **giant lizards** fitted with saddles (use the giant riding lizard statistics in chapter 8). The 30-foot-high ceiling of the warehouse is hidden with thick webs that conceal a dozen **giant spiders** loyal to the drow.

The warehouse's denizens attack the party unless the characters are accompanied by a drow. The merchants have been instructed to remain in the warehouse until Sirak Mazelor returns. The drow chief negotiator and her entourage have gone to the Zhentarim enclave (area 7) to meet with representatives of the Black Network, in the hopes of forging an alliance against the unruly duergar and svirfneblin enclaves.

The drow sleep in cots arranged in neat rows, while the merchants store their valuable wares in three stone buildings. The door to each building is protected by a *glyph of warding* (save DC 14) that triggers an explosive runes effect (5d8 thunder damage) when a creature other than a drow opens it.

Treasure. Each storage building contains 2d6 crystal vials of exotic perfume worth 100 gp each, 3d6 crystal bottles of distilled beverages worth 25 gp each, 1d4 magic items (determined by rolling on Magic Item Table A in chapter 7 of the *Dungeon Master's Guide*), and 2d6 vials of carrion crawler mucus (see "Poisons" in chapter 8 of the *Dungeon Master's Guide*). Characters also find 1d10 × 10 pounds of food and 1d10 × 5 gallons of water stored in each building.

5. DUERGAR ENCLAVE

The gray dwarves trade mostly in armor and weapons of superior craftsmanship, but their enclave also deals in other metalwork, raw ores, and uncut gemstones. The duergar chief negotiator is Ghuldur Flagonfist, who sells armor, arrowheads, locks, mining and smithing equipment, and smoked Darklake fish. Ghuldur is friends with Krimgol Muzgardt, a gray dwarf merchant who sells frothy Darklake Stout ale.

5A. DUERGAR FUNGI GROVE

An iron-wrought fence encloses this fungal grove, through which the duergar have carved narrow aisles. The grove contains a host of edible fungi and is illuminated by six nightlight mushrooms (see "Fungi of the Underdark" in chapter 2). A tunnel in the south wall leads to a set of double stone doors.

Guarding the fungi grove are four invisible **duergar** that attack intruders on sight. Four more invisible **duergar** stand in front of the double doors and attack any non-duergar that come into view.

5B. DUERGAR WAREHOUSE

The stone double doors to the warehouse are unlocked and open to reveal a 40-foot-high, rough-hewn chamber containing thirty **duergar** merchants and twelve male **steeders** (see appendix C) used as pack animals. These duergar aren't spoiling for a fight and parley with intruders, sharing the following information:

- A svirfneblin mage stole a gemstone from a duergar ale merchant named Krimgol Muzgardt. Krimgol is a good friend of Mantol-Derith's duergar chief negotiator, Ghuldur Flagonfist.
- When the svirfneblin mage refused to return the stolen gem, Flagonfist sent invisible duergar to the svirfneblin enclave to capture her and bring her to him for questioning.
- Other svirfneblin tried to free the mage, leading to the first of several armed confrontations. Flagonfist has since sent his duergar guards to storm the neighboring enclave and wipe out the deep gnomes.

A 20-foot-high stone building stands in the northeast corner of the warehouse. Inside this unlocked building, Ghuldur Flagonfist and Krimgol Muzgardt (a pair of male **duergar**) are interrogating Yantha Coaxrock, an unarmed female **deep gnome** suffering from a form of indefinite madness (see "Madness" in chapter 8 of the *Dungeon Master's Guide*) that makes her tell lies, even at the risk of harming herself and others. The duergar have dressed her in a robe sewn with gemstones (see "Treasure" below) and suspended her above the mouth of Ghuldur's "pet"—a hungry **xorn**. Ghuldur grasps the rope from which she hangs and is threatening to feed her to the xorn unless she divulges the location of the gem she stole from Krimgol.

Yantha Coaxrock. Yantha is the leader of the Stoneheart Enclave based in Blingdenstone (see chapter 6). She is bound with rope and spinning an elaborate lie about how the drow must've charmed her and taken Krimgol's gem. She has an Intelligence of 16 (+3) and the following additional feature:

Spellcasting. Yantha is a 5th-level spellcaster. Her spellcasting ability is Intelligence (spell save DC 13). She has the following wizard spells prepared:

Cantrips (at will): *dancing lights, friends, mending, prestidigitation*
1st level (4 slots): *comprehend languages, detect magic, Tenser's floating disk*
2nd level (3 slots): *detect thoughts, hold person*
3rd level (2 slots): *sending*

Treasure. The storage building contains 1d10 × 10 pounds of food, 1d10 × 5 gallons of water, thirty zurkhwood casks of Darklake Stout ale worth 50 gp each, and a plethora of finely crafted metalworks:

- 2d6 battleaxes
- 2d6 glaives
- 2d6 lances
- 2d6 longswords
- 2d6 morningstars
- 2d6 war picks
- 2d6 warhammers
- 1d6 suits of half-plate
- 1d6 suits of chainmail
- 1d6 suits of splint mail
- 1d6 suits of plate mail

An iron safe stands in a corner of the storage building. The safe weighs 1,000 pounds, is locked, and contains 1d4 magic items (determined by rolling on Magic Item Table B in chapter 7 of the *Dungeon Master's Guide*).

Ghuldur knows the combination to unlock the safe, which otherwise requires a *knock* spell or similar magic to open.

Yantha's gem-studded robe is worth 750 gp.

Development. If the characters cure Yantha's madness, she confesses to giving Krimgol's black gem to her apprentice, Flink Thunderbonk. She doesn't know Flink's current whereabouts but can use a *sending* spell to contact him, whereupon she learns that he's "trapped" in the drow enclave (area 4). She then asks the characters to rescue him.

Restoring Yantha's sanity doesn't placate Ghuldur or Krimgol. The characters can only appease Krimgol by finding his gem and returning it to him. If he and his pet xorn are defeated in combat, Ghuldur can be persuaded to call off the duergar attacking the svirfneblin enclave (see area 6a).

XP Awards. If the characters rescue Yantha, award each of them 100 XP. If they cure her madness, award an additional 150 XP to each character.

6. Svirfneblin Enclave

The deep gnomes look for any opportunity to corner the market on goods their competitors are in short supply of. Gabble Dripskillet, the svirfneblin chief negotiator, used to sell salt, gemstones, and rare minerals from a stall in the eastern market (area 3b), but she and several other svirfneblin merchants were forced to retreat to their warehouse (area 6b) when the duergar attacked.

6A. Svirfneblin Fungi Grove

The fungal grove in the deep gnome enclave has been left to grow wild. Strewn about the grove are the corpses of a dozen dead svirfneblin, all of whom were killed by duergar.

Set into the northeast wall is a set of stone double doors that the svirfneblin have barred from within. Four enlarged **duergar** are breaking through the doors with war picks, and it's only a matter of time before they reduce the doors to rubble. Eight more invisible **duergar** stand nearby, ready to storm the svirfneblin warehouse as soon as the doors crumble.

Treasure. Each dead svirfneblin carries a pouch that contains 1d4 50 gp gems.

In addition to species of edible fungi, the svirfneblin grove contains the following exotic fungi (as described in the "Fungi of the Underdark" section of chapter 2):

- 2d6 barrelstalks
- 3d6 bluecaps
- 3d6 Nilhogg's noses
- 2d6 tongues of madness
- 2d6 torchstalks
- 2d6 trillimacs

6B. Svirfneblin Warehouse

Twenty-two **deep gnomes**, including Gabble Dripskillet, are holed up in this chamber, which is shaped like a cube. The ceiling is 100 feet high, and the walls are lined with niches that serve as residences and storage spaces. Levitating crystal platforms throughout the warehouse allow the deep gnomes to reach these compartments. Each crystal platform can move up, down, or side-to-side on command, but only the deep gnomes know the command words to activate them.

Most of the svirfneblin have retreated to their residential niches. Gabble Dripskillet is the only one at floor level, and she's prepared to negotiate with whoever or whatever breaks through the doors. If the characters deal with the duergar, Gabble is grateful and offers them a reward (see "Treasure" below).

Gabble doesn't know what provoked the duergar into attacking her enclave, but she is friends with Yantha Coaxrock and would like to see the svirfneblin mage returned safely.

Treasure. Stored throughout the warehouse are sixty 10-pound sacks of salt worth 5 gp each, thirty sacks of precious minerals worth 25 gp each, twenty-four quartz gemstones worth 50 gp each, a dozen amethysts worth 100 gp each, and six peridots worth 500 gp each.

Half way up the southeast wall is a hidden compartment. Finding it requires a successful DC 19 Wisdom (Perception) check. The compartment contains 1d4 magic items (determined by rolling on Magic Item Table C in chapter 7 of the *Dungeon Master's Guide*).

Gabble keeps a crystal coffer in her niche. The coffer is worth 100 gp, and it contains a black sapphire pendant on a silver chain worth 5,000 gp. She offers the pendant as a reward to the party for saving her enclave.

7. Zhentarim Enclave

The Zhentarim found great profits in Mantol-Derith by bringing in products impossible to obtain in the Underdark. Items as innocuous as sugar and fresh spices are treasures in high demand here. The surface dwellers trade mostly in raw materials, including wood, fine fabrics, and leathers, but also maintain stocks of perfumes, alcoholic beverages, confectionery, paper, and clothing made by surface artisans with surface materials. The human Ghazrim DuLoc leads the Zhentarim enclave in Mantol-Derith and also holds the key to finding the library of Gravenhollow.

7A. Zhentarim Encampment

Zhentarim traders cut down most of the fungi grove outside the entrance of their warehouse, keeping only a few small gardens for decoration. In its place they erected a huge pavilion and several smaller tents. Water dripping from the ceiling runs off the tents to form puddles everywhere. The pavilion is where Ghazrim DuLoc conducts business, while the smaller tents are set aside for fifteen Black Network merchants (all human **commoners**).

Perched on a ledge overlooking the pavilion is a **gargoyle** touched by the madness of Fraz-Urb'luu's gem. Characters with a passive Wisdom (Perception) score of 13 or higher spot the creature. It's waiting for Kinyel Druu'giir, its "true love," to emerge from the pavilion.

Inside the pavilion are four drow: Sirak Mazelor (a female **drow mage** and the chief negotiator of the drow enclave), two **female drow elite warriors**, and a female drow **assassin** posing as another elite warrior. The assassin, Kinyel Druu'giir, has Fraz-Urb'luu's gem on her person. She also has the Fey Ancestry, Innate Spellcasting, and Sunlight Sensitivity features of a drow elite warrior. These drow await the arrival of the Zhentarim's chief negotiator, Ghazrim DuLoc. A table covered with food and wine stands in the middle of the pavilion, although the drow refuse to partake.

Development. If the characters keep their distance and spy on the Zhentarim enclave for a few minutes, Ghazrim DuLoc, Lorthuun, and six human **thugs** emerge from the nearby warehouse (area 7b) to meet with the drow delegation. Before Sirak can negotiate an alliance, Kinyel attacks the beholder. Unless the characters intervene, Kinyel escapes with 19 hit points remaining. Everyone else is killed in the crossfire.

If the characters confront the drow before Ghazrim and Lorthuun arrive, Sirak orders them to leave at once. If they refuse, she and her warriors attack as Kinyel cuts a gash in the back wall of the pavilion with her sword and finds a place to hide until the beholder appears. If the characters pursue Kinyel, the gargoyle attacks them to protect her. Ghazrim and his entourage arrive 1d4 + 2 rounds after the battle is joined.

Kinyel was forced to leave Menzoberranzan in disgrace after failing to assassinate a house rival. Fraz-Urb'luu's gem has afflicted her with a form of indefinite madness (see "Madness" in chapter 8 of the *Dungeon Master's Guide*). She is convinced that the gargoyle who gave her the gem is a messenger from House Druu'giir, and that killing Lorthuun will redeem her.

7b. Zhentarim Warehouse

The double doors leading to the Zhentarim warehouse are made of thick zurkhwood reinforced with iron bands. A window slit at eye level allows two human **veterans** stationed inside the doors to peer out into the cavern. They will not open the doors to strangers without Ghazrim DuLoc's permission. The doors are barred from the inside. They have AC 15, 80 hit points, and a damage threshold of 10. They can also be forced open with a DC 25 Strength check.

The Zhentarim warehouse contains a dozen iron storage sheds filled with neatly sorted merchandise. Two more sheds serve as quarters for Ghazrim DuLoc (a human **noble**) and his guards. Ten human **thugs** (minus any killed in area 7a) are asleep in their bunks but rise quickly if the warehouse comes under attack.

Lorthuun, a maimed **beholder**, also guards the warehouse. Years ago, Lorthuun got into a terrible fight with a behir and lost four of its eyestalks. Its spherical body is also covered with scars from the behir's claws and breath weapon. Lorthuun has the statistics of a normal beholder, except that it no longer has its sleep, petrification, disintegration, or death rays. The beholder's adjusted challenge rating is 9 (5,000 XP).

Ghazrim and Lorthuun both serve the Zhentarim, but they rarely see eye to eye. They bicker and insult each other like an old married couple, and only their dedication to the Black Network keeps them from turning against one another.

Born into a wealthy family, Ghazrim has the typically smarmy demeanor of the Amnian aristocracy coupled with a biting sense of humor that he uses to diffuse tense situations. He's not afraid of a good fight but is averse to attacking a superior force. If he realizes the characters are in league with the Black Network, he offers them food, wine, and whatever else they need to complete their mission (see "Treasure").

Ghazrim's Shed. The door to this shed is locked, and Ghazrim carries the only key. In addition to his comfortable bed, Ghazrim has a morbid collection of tiny, malformed creatures in pickle jars on a shelf.

Secret Door. A secret door in the west wall opens to reveal a wide tunnel beyond (area 1e). The secret door makes a lot of noise when opened, alerting the warehouse's occupants.

Storage Sheds. The contents of the twelve storage sheds are described below:

Shed 1 contains the Zhents' supplies, consisting of 2d10 × 10 pounds of food in the form of dried meats, plucked chickens, fresh fruit and vegetables, and loaves of baked bread. There are also six casks of wine worth 50 gp each.

Shed 2 holds 1d10 backpacks, 2d10 bedrolls, 2d10 blankets, 2d6 climber's kits, and 2d6 healer's kits.

Shed 3 contains 3d6 hooded lanterns, 3d6 flasks of oil, 3d6 50-foot coils of hempen rope, 3d6 grappling hooks, and 3d6 tinderboxes.

Shed 4 holds five crates, each one containing 1d20 days of rations.

Shed 5 contains 2d10 empty glass bottles, 2d6 scroll cases, 2d10 copper tankards, 2d10 iron pots, 2d10 empty sacks, and 2d10 empty waterskins.

KINYEL DRUU'GIIR

GHAZRIM DULOC

Shed 6 holds 2d10 empty wooden chests with iron fittings and 2d10 locks with keys.

Shed 7 contains 2d6 jars of ink, 3d12 blank pieces of parchment, 3d6 boxes of candles (12 candles per box), and 2d6 ink pens.

Shed 8 holds 3d6 crowbars, 3d6 hammers, and 3d6 miner's picks.

Shed 9 is locked, and Ghazrim DuLoc carries the only key. The lock is also trapped with a poison needle (see "Sample Traps" in chapter 5 of the *Dungeon Master's Guide*). The shed contains 250 pp, 1,800 gp, 3,300 sp, 6,000 cp, and thirty 100 gp gems in a loose pile.

Shed 10 contains 3d6 jars of spices worth 10 gp each, 2d6 10-pound sacks of cinnamon worth 20 gp each, and 3d6 boxes of soap (12 bars of soap per box).

Shed 11 holds four wooden chicken coops, each one containing 1d6 + 1 live chickens. Sacks of chicken feed are stored on a shelf above the coops.

Shed 12 is currently empty.

Treasure. Ghazrim carries a key that unlocks shed 9. He also wears a gold ring fitted with a star ruby (worth 1,000 gp). A *detect magic* spell reveals that the gem radiates a faint aura of divination magic. The gem's star-shaped core is a magical compass that guides the ring's wearer along the safest, shortest route to Gravenhollow. Ghazrim is aware of the ring's property and gives the ring to the characters if they claim to be headed that way.

LEAVING MANTOL-DERITH

If Ghazrim DuLoc dies, characters can remove the ring from his dead hand and use it to find their way to Gravenhollow.

If the characters deduce that Kinyel's gem is responsible for the havoc in Mantol-Derith and inform

---

BEHOLDER EYESTALKS

If Lorthuun is killed, 1d4 of its eyestalks survive intact. Should Peebles the svirfneblin happen upon the beholder's remains, he uses a flint knife to remove the intact eyestalks, then tucks them in his bag for safe delivery to Xazaz the Eyemonger (see "Follow-Up Encounters").

the chief negotiators of this fact, the ones who are still alive are thankful enough to share disturbing news from their home settlements of Blingdenstone, Gracklstugh, and Menzoberranzan, respectively (see chapter 10, "Descent into the Depths").

FOLLOW-UP ENCOUNTERS

Having Sladis Vadir (see area 1c), Peebles (see area 3b), or Zilchyn Q'Leptin (area 4a) join the party can lead to special follow-up encounters in the vicinity of Mantol-Derith, as described below.

CRICKET CATCHER

If Zilchyn Q'Leptin is with the party as it leaves Mantol-Derith, he insists on visiting a nearby cave to retrieve his secret stash of potions.

Zilch's cave lies one day's travel west of Mantol-Derith, along the same route the characters must travel to reach Gravenhollow. The cave is swarming with bats and infested with dozens of giant albino cave crickets that feed on the bat guano. The crickets are as big as halflings yet harmless. A happy-go-lucky **kuo-toa** named Ougalop is also here, trying to catch the giant crickets in a homespun net. When he sees other intruders, Ougalop waves at them and continues with his cricket catching. He poses no threat and has no interest in joining the party. The kuo-toa lives in Sloobludop (see chapter 3) and is blissfully unaware of recent events there.

Treasure. On a 30-foot-high shelf overlooking the cave is an old grick nest. Hidden here are three *potions of vitality*. Climbing the wall to reach the shelf requires a successful DC 10 Strength (Athletics) check.

AMARITH'S ZOO

If Sladis Vadir joined the party and is still around when the characters are ready to leave Mantol-Derith, he offers to guide them to a cavern roughly eight days' travel west of Mantol-Derith, along the same route the characters must travel to reach Gravenhollow. Sladis claims that the cave is home to another member of the Emerald Enclave: a dwarf named Amarith Coppervein. This news will interest characters searching for Amarith on behalf of Morista Malkin (see chapter 8).

Amarith Coppervein is a shield dwarf **veteran** with the following statistical modifications:

- Amarith's alignment is neutral good.
- She has darkvision out to a range of 60 feet.
- Amarith's dwarven resilience gives her advantage on saving throws against poison, and she has resistance against poison damage.

- She wields a warhammer instead of a longsword (1d8 + 3 bludgeoning damage on a hit, or 1d10 + 3 bludgeoning damage if using the weapon with two hands).

Amarith's cavern contains a dozen stalagmites which have been hollowed out and fitted with iron bars to serve as monster cages. Locked in three of these cages are a **rust monster**, a **winged kobold**, and a **fire snake**. Amarith charges 3 cp per person to tour her "zoo."

If the characters ask Amarith to join them, she gathers up her belongings and does just that, lamenting that "the zoo business is tough!" Her gear includes a backpack, a bedroll, a lantern with no oil, a tinderbox, an iron pot, ten days of rations (edible fungi), a pouch containing 3 cp, a 50-foot coil of hempen rope with a grappling hook tied to one end, a net, a miner's pick, and a 10-foot pole.

XAZAX THE EYEMONGER

If Peebles or the characters harvest Lorthuun's eyestalks (see the "Beholder Eyestalks" sidebar), Peebles asks to join the party as it leaves Mantol-Derith. After traveling with them for a tenday, Peebles urges the characters to deviate from their preferred route, claiming that they're dangerously close to a nest of purple worms. Peebles uses this lie to propose an alternate route. If the characters follow this detour, Peebles leads them to the cavern of Xazax the Eyemonger, a terrifying **beholder** that kills others of its kind and grafts their eyestalks to its body. Peebles heads to Xazax's cave regardless of whether the characters follow him or not.

Xazax's cavern has a 30-foot-high ceiling and is unremarkable save for a 20-foot-wide, 100-foot-deep shaft in the middle of the floor. Upon arriving, Peebles calls out, "Master! I've returned!" Moments later, Xazax rises up from the shaft. Xazax has eight extra eyestalks grafted to its body, giving it a total of eighteen, but it can't fire rays from the grafted eyes. If the characters took one or more of Lorthuun's eyestalks, Peebles demands that the characters surrender them at once. Whether they do or not, Xazax becomes enraged and attacks. Both Xazax and Peebles fight to the death.

Treasure. At the bottom of the beholder's shaft, buried among the shattered remains of petrified foes, is a *flame tongue* longsword. Scaling the shaft requires a successful DC 10 Strength (Athletics) check.

XAZAX THE EYEMONGER

AMARITH COPPERVEIN

OUGALOP

Chapter 10: Descent into the Depths

Having survived Mantol-Derith and obtained Ghazrim DuLoc's ring, the adventurers and their allies continue on into the Underdark. This time, rather than escaped prisoners looking for a way out, they are at the head of an expeditionary force ready to challenge whatever the Underdark has to offer.

Much of this middle section of the adventure is free-form, dictated largely by the characters' decisions and tactics. The adventurers' immediate destination is the legendary library of Gravenhollow (see chapter 11), where they gain information that likely takes them to the tower of Araj, home of the mysterious drow archmage Vizeran DeVir. However, the characters are free to explore and visit different places before and after they explore Gravenhollow and unlock its secrets.

The events described in chapters 13 through 16 can be interspersed among the material in this part of the adventure, as the characters work to fully understand the new menaces that have appeared in the Underdark, seek new allies and information, and ultimately attempt to create a plan to end the demon lord threat.

Character advancement through this section of the adventure is important. The journey from Mantol-Derith to Gravenhollow should involve sufficient encounters and challenges for the characters to reach 10th level by the time they visit the stone giant library. As the characters travel from place to place, check for random encounters as normal (see chapter 2), but swap out the creature encounters with ones presented in this chapter. Ideally, the characters should be 14th level by the time they crash Zuggtmoy's wedding (chapter 16, "The Fetid Wedding"), and 15th level for the final showdown against the demon lords (see chapter 17, "Against the Demon Lords").

Fellow Travelers

The characters initially traveled through the Underdark as a small group, perhaps joined by a few of their fellow prisoners from Velkynvelve and other allies they met along the way. Now, they return to the subterranean realm at the head of a group of allies that might outnumber the adventurers four-to-one, depending on how many NPCs were recruited from the factions in Gauntlgrym (see chapter 8). This changes some of the conditions described in "Underdark Travel" in chapter 2.

MARCHING ORDERS

The tunnels and passages of the Underdark aren't easy routes through which to lead a large group of NPCs. When the characters set out, have the players describe how their expeditionary force is arrayed while traveling in single file, two abreast, and in open formation in wide-open spaces. Also ask the players if any of the NPCs are scouting ahead or serving as a rear guard (see "Scouting," below) or if the larger party remains in close formation at all times.

The marching order affects where and how different encounters might occur, particularly if they happen while characters are marching single file or two abreast. A threat approaching from above, below, or the flank could strike the middle of the expanded party, making it difficult for the characters at either end to reach it. Likewise, spellcasters must be aware of the allies around them at all times when casting area spells that don't solely target enemies.

TRAVEL PACE

The pace of Underdark travel remains as outlined in chapter 2, and the characters move no slower for traveling with a larger party. Although a portion of the expeditionary force might be mounted on giant lizards, the lizards travel at the pace of the rest of the party unless they move out ahead.

As noted in chapter 2, a fast pace makes it harder for characters to spot ambushers or items of interest, and prevents characters from foraging. A slow pace improves chances of foraging. However, even while traveling at a slow pace, the characters and the NPCs can't use stealth, since they are too large a group to go unnoticed. Stealth is an option only for a smaller scouting party traveling away from the main force (see "Scouting").

NAVIGATING

While traveling as part of a larger group, the characters have an easier time navigating their way through the Underdark than they did during their initial escape. The characters' own experience, plus that of their followers, along with maps and other information they might have acquired in Gauntlgrym or elsewhere, give all members of the expanded party advantage on any Wisdom (Survival) checks to avoid becoming lost (see chapter 5, "Adventure Environments," of the *Dungeon Master's Guide*).

SCOUTING

A portion of the expanded party can break off in order to travel some distance ahead, scouting for the right path while remaining on the lookout for potential hazards. A smaller group might also lag behind, serving as a rearguard watching for threats coming up behind the characters as they travel. NPCs can serve as scouts or members of a rearguard as the players wish. Some of the adventurers might choose to do so as well.

A smaller scouting group can make use of stealth to travel unnoticed. If a random encounter occurs during the journey, characters in the scouting party discover it first and can choose whether to avoid or deal with the encounter. If characters in the scouting party notice the encounter without being seen themselves, they can retreat back to the main force to inform the other characters. Similarly, if a random encounter escapes the scouting characters' notice, the encountered creatures can lie in wait for the rest of the characters in order to ambush them.

IN COMMAND

No longer a ragtag band of survivors and prisoners, the adventurers are now in command of a dedicated force of NPC followers. In addition to the advantages that brings, the characters must assume leadership roles as they deal with allies who might not entirely trust or respect them—or each other. Add in the dangers of the Underdark, along with the unpredictable influence of demonic madness, and the characters have several new challenges that must be faced.

PERSONALITIES

Although the NPCs the characters lead are ostensibly allies, many belong to different factions, and old grudges and differences in ethos aren't easily set aside. Personality conflicts might arise among the followers in the expanded party, and the adventurers would be well advised to head off potential trouble. For example, having Lords' Alliance troops acting as scouts while keeping Zhentarim mercenaries close at hand will help keep those factions from fighting.

HEART OF DARKNESS

In this phase of the campaign, the characters are moving toward the demon lords and their influence rather than away from it, even as the Underdark sinks deeper into madness and chaos. The characters will make saving throws against acquiring levels of madness, as called for in different encounters and whenever you feel it is appropriate. (See chapter 2 of the adventure for more information on madness.)

The NPCs following the characters into the Underdark are just as vulnerable to demonic madness. However, rather than make saving throws or track madness levels for each individual NPC, use the Random Events table in this chapter to determine when madness appears among those followers.

When madness appears among the NPCs, use it not just for its mechanical effects but to create real complications for the adventurers. For example, if the Random Events table indicates that one member of the expanded party suffers long-term madness, you might decide to bestow extreme paranoia on that NPC. In addition to the effect of Wisdom and Charisma checks, that character might believe that the adventurers are actually agents of the demon lords, and are intent on leading the NPCs to their doom.

LOYALTY

Having the adventurers leading an expanded party gives you the opportunity to use the optional loyalty rules in chapter 4, "Creating Nonplayer Characters," of the *Dungeon Master's Guide.* You can track the loyalty scores of groups of NPCs, such as those belonging to each faction, rather than having to track NPCs individually. The characters must balance the goals and bonds of their followers in order to maintain and improve their loyalty.

PROVISIONS

The factions in Gauntlgrym see to it that the expeditionary force is well provisioned with whatever the characters' expeditionary force can carry. Food and water aren't easy to come by in the Underdark, as the characters know all too well, and supplies must be managed and safeguarded.

If the expeditionary force needs to supplement or replace supplies while traveling, the amounts that characters are able to find become more important with a larger group to support. See "Foraging" in chapter 5 of the *Dungeon Master's Guide,* as well as the guidelines in chapter 2 of this adventure.

TREASURE

Just as they must ensure sufficient supplies for all the NPCs, the characters need to think about how best to share the spoils of encounters and adventures with their followers. Although the NPCs all accompany the adventurers out of loyalty to their factions—and on orders from their superiors in Gauntlgrym—the characters' treatment of the NPCs influences the loyalty of those followers during the mission into the Underdark.

The characters should come up with some means for dividing any treasure taken on the expedition between the NPCs. As long as the division is reasonably fair, most of the followers will be content. However, the NPCs will complain if all the choice pieces of treasure go to the adventurers.

The characters might also need to contend with the problem of theft, whether NPCs stealing from spoils not yet divided, stealing from the adventurers, or stealing from each other. Such theft might be driven by sheer greed, or it could be a manifestation of madness. A bout of long-term madness could easily lead to obsession with particular items of treasure—especially magic items—with an obsessed NPC willing to steal or even kill to obtain them.

MAINTAINING ORDER

The adventurers are in command of their NPC followers, and that means they are responsible for welding together disparate forces and maintaining discipline. The characters have a bit of an advantage in this regard, in that the NPCs placed under their command are all well-trained faction operatives, not raw recruits or mercenaries. However, some of these seasoned personnel might question the right of a ragtag band of adventurers to command them, even if their superiors seem to trust the player characters. Likewise, though the individual factions are typically disciplined within their own ranks, members of any faction might bristle at having to work alongside (much less take orders from) members of other factions.

CHAIN OF COMMAND

In addition to deciding how the expeditionary force is organized and distributed (see "Marching Orders"), the players must also institute a clear chain of command. One or more of the adventurers might be the field commanders of the expanded party, while others serve as lieutenants. Likewise, the adventurers might appoint some of the NPCs to command positions. Without a clear chain of command, information might not go to the right people, and decisions might not get made quickly enough—or at all. Adding to the challenge of maintaining discipline is the ever-present threat of demonic madness growing among the ranks, creating problems even for seasoned and professional troops (see "Heart of Darkness").

If the expeditionary force is made up of diverse factions, the players also need to decide how much latitude to give those factions. For example, Zhentarim mercenaries might be eager to torture prisoners for information unless the characters put a stop to it, and members of the Emerald Enclave might place a higher priority on maintaining the balance of nature in the Underdark than on political struggles.

RANDOM EVENTS

The adventurers must contend with a variety of events as they lead their forces through the Underdark. Every other day of travel or camping in the Underdark, an event automatically occurs. Roll a d20 and consult the Random Events table, or choose a suitable event.

For the rules on madness, see chapter 2 of this adventure and chapter 8, "Running the Game," in the *Dungeon Master's Guide.*

SPLITTING THE PARTY

You can change up the feel of these later chapters of *Out of the Abyss* by allowing the players to take on the roles of their faction allies as well as their regular characters. This can range from letting each player control the overall actions of the NPCs in a single faction, to creating multiple subgroups so that characters can split off and have their own adventures. While this involves a good deal more coordination among the game group, it can add a lot of detail, intrigue, and interaction to the campaign.

RANDOM EVENTS

d20	Event
1–2	Battle aftermath
3–6	Creature encounter
7–9	Demon encounter
10–11	Discipline problem
12–13	Disease
14–15	Madness
16–17	Poisoned NPCs
18–19	Spoiled supplies
20	Vanishing NPCs

BATTLE AFTERMATH

The party stumbles upon the remains of one or more creatures slaughtered by rampaging demons. Roll a d10 and consult the Corpses table to determine what they find. A thorough search of the area yields no treasure.

CORPSES

d10	Corpse Present
1	1 dead behir
2–3	1d4 dead drow and 1d4 – 1 dead giant lizards
4–5	3d8 dead giant fire beetles (their glands are no longer glowing)
6–7	2d4 dead gricks
8–9	2d4 dead kuo-toa
10	1 dead purple worm

Roll a d6 and consult the Scavengers table to determine what scavengers, if any, are feasting on the remains.

SCAVENGERS

d6	Scavengers
1–2	1d3 **black puddings**
3–4	1d4 **carrion crawlers**
5	1d6 **gnolls** and 1d6 **hyenas**
6	1 **otyugh**

CREATURE ENCOUNTER

Roll on the Creature Encounters table in chapter 2 or the Darklake Creature Encounters table in chapter 3, depending on where the party is traveling.

DEMON ENCOUNTER

Roll a d20 and consult the Demon Encounters table to determine what appears. If the characters stumble upon Juiblex and flee immediately, the demon lord doesn't pursue or attack them.

DEMON ENCOUNTERS

d20	Encounter
1–4	1d4 **barlguras**
5–8	1d4 **chasmes**
9–10	1d2 **hezrous**
11–14	1d4 **shadow demons**
15–18	1d3 **vrocks**
19–20	**Juiblex** (see appendix D)

DISCIPLINE PROBLEM

A discipline problem is revealed among the NPCs. Roll a d6 and consult the Discipline Problems table to determine what transpires.

DISCIPLINE PROBLEMS

d6	Problem
1–2	A loud argument that has a 50 percent chance of attracting nearby monsters (roll on the Creature Encounters table in chapter 2)
3–4	Theft or dispute over the division of spoils
5–6	Brawl or other outbreak of violence

DISEASE

One or more NPC party members contract a disease. Roll a d4 to determine how many NPCs are affected, then roll a d6 and consult the Diseases table to determine which disease is contracted. See in chapter 8, "Running the Game," in the *Dungeon Master's Guide* for descriptions of cackle fever, sewer plague, and sight rot.

DISEASES

d6	Disease
1–2	Cackle fever
3–4	Sewer plague
5	Sight rot
6	Zuggtmoy's spores (see chapter 5, "Neverlight Grove")

MADNESS

One NPC party member goes mad. To determine the kind of madness, roll a d6 and consult the Madness table below. To determine the madness effect, roll percentile dice and consult the appropriate table in chapter 8 of the *Dungeon Master's Guide*.

MADNESS

d6	Madness
1–3	Short-term madness
4–5	Long-term madness
6	Indefinite madness

POISONED NPCs

One or more NPC party members are poisoned for 1d10 × 10 hours by eating tainted food or poisonous Underdark mushrooms. Roll a d12 to determine how many NPCs are poisoned in this way.

SPOILED SUPPLIES

The party's provisions become infested with Underdark vermin or infected with spores that render them poisonous. Unless the characters have access to *purify food and drink* or similar magic, the party must dispose of 3d6 days of rations.

VANISHING NPCs

One or more NPC party members go missing and are never seen again. Roll a d4 to determine how many NPCs vanish in this way. Efforts to find them or magically contact them turn up no trace.

Underdark Outposts

Characters can clear out Underdark areas and create defensible outposts where they and their followers can store supplies and take refuge. To ensure that an outpost isn't overrun and looted, guards must be assigned to the outpost while the characters are away.

Outposts not only allow scouts to easily backtrack through the Underdark, carrying messages and information to the characters' allies, but also allow additional supplies and reinforcements to reach the expeditionary force with relative ease. Characters without outposts must rely on magic to send messages or receive supplies and reinforcements once their expeditionary force is more than a tenday's travel away from Mantol-Derith.

New Downtime Activity: Establish an Outpost

Establishing an Underdark outpost is a new downtime activity available to characters in this adventure. An outpost requires a total of 150 hours of work to build, assuming its location is clear of creatures and hazards. Multiple characters can combine their efforts to reduce the completion time.

Each Underdark outpost is basically a fortified encampment. It can take one of the following forms:

- A small cave, roughly 20 feet square, with one or more gated or barricaded exits
- A walled compound, up to 20 feet square, within a much larger cavern
- A island with boats or rafts
- A hard-to-reach ledge, pinnacle, or promontory accessed by ladders and/or ropes

Retracing Steps

This section addresses what happens if the characters visit places they skipped during their escape from the Underdark, and what might have changed or shifted in their absence.

Blingdenstone

If the adventurers encountered the Pudding King and uncovered evidence of Juiblex's presence near Blingdenstone, they might want to return there to confirm that the svirfneblin settlement remains safe from the demon lord's influence.

Alternatively, if the characters didn't previously visit Blingdenstone, news of the challenges faced by the deep gnomes can reach them while they travel through the Underdark. Deep gnome merchants headed to Mantol-Derith bring word of oozes infesting the settlement, giving the characters an opportunity to face off against the Pudding King.

At some point after the Pudding King is dealt with, Juiblex and its servants make their way toward the caverns of Araumycos to crash Zuggtmoy's wedding (see chapter 16, "The Fetid Wedding"). If the Pudding King is among the survivors, he leads the mad march to confront Zuggtmoy and her fungal followers.

Reinforcements

The deep gnomes of Blingdenstone are valuable allies. In gratitude for the adventurers' aid, they offer to reinforce the party's expeditionary force with twelve **deep gnomes**. Chief Dorbo Diggermattock can also be persuaded to lend additional aid and troops, if the heroes present a compelling case. Use the information in chapter 6 to guide any negotiations or arrangements the adventurers attempt to make with the svirfneblin.

The Darklake

To move their expeditionary force across the Darklake, the characters must build rafts or coracles from Underdark materials, or seek out duergar or kuo-toa ferries for hire. Each ferry they find can transport up to eight members of the expeditionary force.

Chapter 3 contains information on navigating the Darklake. If the expeditionary force splits up, check for random encounters with each group separately.

Fallen Sloobludop

If the characters visit Sloobludop, they find the kuo-toa community in ruins. Demogorgon smashed and crushed many of the structures of the settlement, killing about half the kuo-toa community in the process. The survivors have fallen prey to madness and the predations of Underdark monsters in the time since.

Obscene altars and shrines are everywhere, many of them depicting elements of Demogorgon's twisted iconography—spirals and "Y" shapes, two-headed creatures, manta rays, and tentacles. Other shrines show the influence of other demon lords, including piles of skulls and bones, strange maze patterns, spore clouds, and fetid pools of ooze. Conflicts are rapidly rising between the various "sects" that have formed.

If Shuushar the Awakened (see chapter 1) was not killed in a previous chapter of the adventure, the characters find him among Sloobludop's survivors. He is the sole point of calm and reason in the ruined settlement, and the various factions of the kuo-toa show him respect. Shuushar mediates disputes between the kuo-toa and supervises the allocation of their dwindling resources. Even so, the kuo-toa monk isn't sure how long he can sustain his people and keep them from destruction.

Gracklstugh

If the characters visited Gracklstugh previously, the duergar response to their return is dictated by the gray dwarves' prior experience with the characters. The duergar are cautious—if not downright alarmed—at the sight of an armed expeditionary force from the surface world at their gates. They likely refuse entry to the full party, allowing only a select few characters into the Darklake District. Invisible duergar guards keep watch on characters in the city at all times, and might even infiltrate the expeditionary force, attempting to eavesdrop on conversations to learn the adventurers' intentions.

Chaos in the City

The influence of the demon lords grows ever stronger in Gracklstugh. Paranoia and fear are rampant, with duergar barricading themselves in their homes and strongholds, afraid to venture out into the streets—even invisibly. Rumors abound of creatures active in the Darklake, and of secret rituals and offerings made to the dark waters to appease them. A number of foreigners have disappeared, and incoming trade to the city has slowed as outsiders depart or stay away.

Conflict between the Keepers of the Flame and the Gray Ghosts thieves' guild comes to a boil. Each side blames the other for recent happenings in the City of Blades and believes it can use the situation to its advantage. Keepers turn up dead, murdered by mysterious assailants, while agents of that order use increasingly brutal methods to ferret out and eliminate the Gray Ghosts—or anyone believed to associate with them.

Whether due to the intervention of the adventurers, the recent events in the Underdark, or both, Themberchaud the Wyrmsmith knows that the Keepers are deliberately oppressing him, and he plots to thin their ranks and weaken their power. Though the dragon knows that he is effectively trapped in the caverns of Gracklstugh even if he wins his freedom, he hungers for it nonetheless, just as he hungers for revenge against those who oppose him.

Dark Plots

If the characters spend much time in Gracklstugh, they become caught up in a rush of destructive events. A secret alliance of factions within the Council of Savants and the Keepers of the Flame, driven by demonic madness, comes to the conclusion that Gracklstugh's salvation lies in eliminating Themberchaud before he becomes a bigger threat. In the process, both factions plan to acquire a new and far more powerful patron.

The duergar and derro hatch a scheme to sacrifice Themberchaud as an offering to Demogorgon, drawing the demon prince to their city and pledging themselves to the Prince of Demons. A few of them even have delusions that they can somehow bind or influence the demon lord's power, or that the demon lord will lead them in conquering the whole of the Underdark. Meanwhile, rumors mount that the drow of Menzoberranzan are behind the demonic incursion. Tales range from the drow raising a mighty army of demons to a summoning spell gone terribly wrong. A demonic rampage is said to have nearly destroyed the City of Spiders, and characters with knowledge of the situation in Menzoberranzan are of great interest to all the factions of Gracklstugh. Any evidence that the drow are responsible for the presence of the demon lords stokes the already blazing embers of animosity against the dark elves, with the more militant factions of Gracklstugh calling for a renewed war of vengeance against Menzoberranzan.

Menzoberranzan

The characters might decide to visit Menzoberranzan before heading to Gravenhollow, either to learn what the drow know about the arrival of the demon lords or to assess their involvement in recent events.

March on Menzoberranzan

If the characters advance their expeditionary force toward the drow city, word of their approach reaches Menzoberranzan two days before their arrival, and the drow dispatch a well-armed defense force to destroy the surface dwellers. Racing ahead of this drow force is a high elf from Silverymoon named Khalessa Draga. A deep cover agent of the Lords' Alliance, Khalessa has been spying on the drow for years—so long, in fact, that her superiors are beginning to wonder if she's a defector. Khalessa is a loyal alliance **spy** with the following statistical modifications:

- Khalessa's alignment is neutral.
- She has darkvision out to a range of 60 feet.
- She speaks Common, Elvish, and Undercommon.
- Khalessa's fey ancestry gives her advantage on saving throws against being charmed, and magic can't put her to sleep.
- She can cast the *dancing lights* cantrip at will.
- She owns a *hat of disguise*, which she uses to appear as a female drow while in the company of drow, and she wears a *piwafwi* (see appendix B).

Khalessa urges the characters to turn back. If they don't, she fears that the drow force will overwhelm them. Having blown her cover to warn the characters, she asks to stay with them until they reach Gauntlgrym or an alliance settlement.

The leaders of the drow force are a female **elite drow warrior** named Ryzliir Symryvvin and her consort, a male **drow mage** named Velgor Zolond. They are joined by a prisoner in manacles—an unarmed and unarmored male human **knight** of the Order of the Gauntlet named Aljanor Keenblade. Sir Aljanor was captured during a surface raid months ago, and the drow have beaten him such that he has only 3 hit points remaining. Members of the order traveling in the party's expeditionary force recognize Sir Aljanor instantly and are surprised; they assumed he had been killed.

Ryzliir vows to execute Aljanor unless the characters withdraw their expeditionary force immediately. Under no circumstances will she willingly release her prisoner. If the characters refuse to turn back, Ryzliir kills Aljanor and orders her own force to attack. If the characters leave Aljanor behind or allow him to die, members of the party's expeditionary force in league with the Order of the Gauntlet who make it back to Gauntlgrym report the incident to Sir Lanniver Strayl (see chapter 8).

Ryzliir and Velgor are mounted on **giant riding lizards** (see the end of chapter 8 for statistics), and Aljanor rides behind Velgor. Ryzliir commands a force of six **drow** warriors, twelve **bugbear** slaves, and sixty **goblin** slaves. If all the drow are killed, the goblinoids flee as their morale breaks.

Sir Aljanor has made his peace with Tyr and expects to die. He is disappointed if good lives are lost in a

KHALESSA DRAGA

ALJANOR KEENBLADE

foolish attempt to rescue him. If he survives, he accepts any offer to join the party's expeditionary force and is quick to assume a leadership role.

Neverlight Grove

If the characters return to Neverlight Grove, myconids loyal to Sovereign Basidia (including Stool and Rumpadump if they remained behind) try to intercept them before their arrival and warn them off. The myconids say that matters have become grave, and that the characters should avoid the grove at all costs.

If the adventurers don't leave immediately, six **myconid adults**, four **quaggoth spore servants**, and four **awakened zurkhwoods** (see appendix C) loyal to Sovereign Phylo cut off their retreat. They surround the characters and their followers, offering to escort them to Phylo as the sovereign's honored guests.

Sovereign Phylo is friendly and offers all visitors food and drink; however, his offerings are poisoned. Each creature that consumes the food or drink must succeed on a DC 13 Constitution saving throw or become poisoned for 8 hours. The creature is also unconscious while poisoned in this way. Any creature that remains unconscious in the grove for 1 hour or more is afflicted by Zuggtmoy's spores, as described in chapter 5.

If the characters take Basidia's advice and turn back, the myconid sovereign promises to contact them again when "the time is right to oppose Zuggtmoy" (as described in chapter 16, "The Fetid Wedding").

Velkynvelve

If the adventurers return to the drow outpost where they were imprisoned, they find Velkynvelve under the command of a **drow mage** named Servan Llarabbar. Six male **drow** report to him, while three more male **drow** and one female **drow elite warrior** have been locked in the slave pen. The prisoners are afflicted with various forms of indefinite madness (roll on the Indefinite Madness table in chapter 8 of the *Dungeon Master's Guide*). Even Servan is beginning to show heightened megalomania and paranoia, seeing enemies everywhere. He has delusions of grandeur and fantasies about declaring Velkynvelve independent of Menzoberranzan, rallying followers to his side and eventually toppling the matriarchs of the great houses.

Chapter 11: Gravenhollow

The library of Gravenhollow is a bastion of peace and order in an Underdark gone mad. Carved out long ago from the bones of the world and protected by ancient and potent magic, the library possesses a kind of awareness. It blocks and misdirects those unworthy of reaching its gates, even as it facilitates finding the way for those who need it.

The adventurers need to find the library in their quest to learn what has happened in the Underdark. Before obtaining the answers they seek, however, they must come to understand Gravenhollow and its keepers—three stone giants who reside within the library. These librarians are tasked with recording and maintaining the lore of their own kind, as well as all the echoes of the past, present, and future haunting the library's halls.

Gravenhollow is a place where visitors will most certainly find answers. However, those answers might not be the ones the characters wanted—or might even be things they never wanted to know.

Going to Gravenhollow

The objective of the adventurers' return to the Underdark is to find Gravenhollow. Ancient legends state that every event that has ever occurred in the Underdark is recorded on the countless tablets and cylinders in Gravenhollow's halls. As such, it might be the key to discovering the cause of the demon lords' arrival.

The stone library lies west of the Wormwrithings, 360 miles from Mantol-Derith and 120 miles from Gauntlgrym. Only one tunnel leads to the library, and the magic surrounding Gravenhollow can change where the tunnel's entrance appears among the surrounding passageways, even as that magic allows visitors to locate its entrance. Fortunately for the characters, the library's awareness—in tune with all events in the Underdark— knows that they are coming. As such, the ring obtained from the Zhentarim in Mantol-Derith (see chapter 9) allows them to find the secret site. The journey from Mantol-Derith to Gravenhollow takes 60 days. If the characters teleport back to Gauntlgrym and start there, the trip takes 20 days. See chapters 2 and 10 for information on traveling in the Underdark.

FINDING THE WAY

The characters can find the route to Gravenhollow using Ghazrim DuLoc's ring. If they don't have the ring, there are a couple other options available to them.

GHAZRIM'S RING

The star ruby in Ghazrim's ring has a white, star-shaped core that guides its wearer along the safest, shortest route to Gravenhollow.

SOCIETY OF BRILLIANCE

If one or more members of the Society of Brilliance are traveling with the party (see the "Society of Brilliance" random encounter in chapter 2), they can find the way to Gravenhollow, having found it once before. Any Society of Brilliance member who comes within a day's travel of the library can make a DC 15 Intelligence check to find the passage leading to Gravenhollow. If its check fails, it can try again after 8 hours of searching and contemplation.

STONE GIANT GUIDE

If the characters don't have the ring to guide them, a duergar NPC (for example, Ghuldur Flagonfist in Mantol-Derith) might suggest that they talk to Stonespeaker Hgraam in Gracklstugh. If the characters helped the stone giants by putting an end to the horrid derro rituals in the Whorlstone Tunnels (see chapter 4), Stonespeaker Hgraam is willing to assign them a guide—a **stone giant** named Jaal—who can lead them to Gravenhollow. As he guides the expeditionary force through the Underdark, Jaal periodically stops to press his hands against ancient stone, as though communing with the rock itself. His mystical connection to the Underdark allows him to find the safest, shortest route to the stone library.

VELDYSKAR THE BASILISK

When the characters are within a day's travel of Gravenhollow, they hear someone singing strange tunes in various languages, the voice echoing down adjacent tunnels. Approaching the sound reveals a **basilisk** named Veldyskar resting in an intersection. No ordinary basilisk, Veldyskar has an Intelligence of 10 (+0) and speaks Common, Dwarvish, Giant, and Undercommon.

A small group of characters scouting can sneak up on Veldyskar with a successful DC 10 group Dexterity (Stealth) check. Any characters who observe the basilisk can note that it keeps its eyes downcast, as if consciously trying to control its petrifying gaze. When Veldyskar becomes aware of the characters, he calls them over, speaking in all the languages he knows until he determines that the characters understand Common.

> A many-legged reptile stretches out as if it has been sitting for a long while, avoiding your eyes as it looks to the rocky floor at your feet. "About time you lot arrived! Come! The library bid me guide you to the gates, and I've waited too long for you already."

After his initial greeting, Veldyskar speaks only if spoken to, and his answers are brief. With the basilisk as their guide, it takes the characters another eight hours to reach the gates of Gravenhollow.

Untold years ago, a visiting stone giant druid presented the librarians with a gift: Veldyskar, an intelligent basilisk trained to serve the keepers as a guardian and general-purpose helper. The basilisk adapted readily to the timeless nature of the library and embraced his new duties with great dedication.

Veldyskar is committed to the protection of the library and its librarians. If trouble arises, his philosophy is to petrify first and ask questions later. Initially, this presented a problem for the stone giant librarians, as the basilisk had some difficulty reconciling his temper and bestial nature with the recognition of what trouble might actually look like. The stone giants taught Veldyskar how to cast *greater restoration*, which the basilisk can do once per day to restore anyone who crosses him.

GATES OF GRAVENHOLLOW

A pair of massive basalt doors mark the entrance to Gravenhollow, flanked by stone giant statues that are actually **stone golems**. The doors are opened simply by pushing, after which the entire expeditionary force can enter along with the characters. The golems turn their heads to watch new arrivals but otherwise remain still. The basilisk Veldyskar guides the characters in through the gates, instructs them to continue straight ahead, then quickly disappears down a side passage.

> Walking across the threshold of Gravenhollow is like stepping into another realm. The oppressive gloom of the Underdark is replaced by light and a sense of openness that brings back memories of the surface world.
>
> The corridor beyond the gates is wide enough for ten people to walk side by side, and the ceiling's height reminds you of the great halls of Gauntlgrym. The corridor opens into a central well, with walkways crossing its span to the opposite side. You can barely see the ends of the level to your right and left, with doors opening into so many rooms that you doubt you could explore them all in a single day.
>
> The ceiling is bright, with rainbows trapped in hundreds of crystal formations combining to create a warm and inviting illumination. Looking down is a dizzying experience. Staircases connect to different levels below, and you soon lose count of how far down they go.
>
> A stout, rocky creature detaches from the perfectly smooth wall to your left, leaving an imprint of its body in the wall that quickly smooths out and fades from sight. "Trravelerrrrsss. I am Hourm. The masterrrsss arre occupied. Therre arre rroomsss forr all of you. Choose yourr own. The rresourrcesss of Grravenhollow arre at yourr disssposssal. You need only asssk."

Hourm, a friendly **galeb duhr**, answers any questions the characters have about Gravenhollow to the best of its ability, including how navigate its levels, and how to access the library's knowledge. After leading the party to living quarters one level below the library's main level, it merges into another wall and disappears.

THE STONE LIBRARY

When the characters first enter Gravenhollow, the library appears to be a simple arrangement of great cavernous halls carved out from the stone of the Underdark. However, the library is suffused with magic that warps the space within it, and which makes navigating and exploration a unique challenge (see the "Gravenhollow: General Features" sidebar).

Each room on each level of Gravenhollow is part of either the Archives of the Past, the Archives of the Present, or the Archives of the Future. Galeb duhr

THE LIBRARIANS

assistants pick up tablets as Gravenhollow's three stone giant librarians carve and catalog them, but the classification system the giants use to organize the library's information is known only to them.

RESIDENTS

The library is quiet and peaceful, and visitors are free to move within it as they wish. If anyone has a need to find any other character within Gravenhollow (including one of the librarians), the library subtly directs the character toward its target within minutes.

The three **stone giants** who serve as Gravenhollow's librarians don't specifically welcome visitors—or even notice their comings and goings—unless the library directs them to do so. The characters need to seek the keepers out.

ULTHAR

Ulthar is the Keeper of the Past. He sorts and files ancient texts, maintaining the immeasurably vast catalog that organizes them. When not cross-referencing his expanding collection, he composes epic poetry and is responsible for curating and restoring wall carvings throughout the library.

Ulthar is infinitely patient, always welcoming any chance to discuss history with visitors. Of the three librarians, he is the most willing and likely to spend time with the library's guests. He treats surface dwellers as if they were figments out of dreams, but makes it obvious he believes that such dreams have wisdom to share.

URMAS

Urmas, the Keeper of the Present, is the busiest of all the librarians. He commands a vast network of magically augmented subterranean beasts, which he uses as messengers, bringing and sending news from giants throughout the Underdark and sometimes from the "dream" of the surface world. Urmas exchanges messages with Stonespeaker Hgraam (see chapter 4), keeping abreast of events as they pertain to the stone giant community in the duergar city of Gracklstugh.

Though Urmas is patient, it quickly becomes obvious that he suffers the characters' questions and presence out of duty and politeness, seeking to return to his work as soon as possible. The giant is distracted by the increasingly dire news brought in by his messengers, including reports from stone giant mystics, as well as elemental servitors such as galeb duhr and xorn. However, if the characters bring news about the demon lords in the Underdark, they have Urmas's immediate and full attention.

USTOVA

The Keeper of the Future, Ustova is a seer who spends most of her time in constant meditation, transcribing her visions onto stone tablets as she experiences them. Like Urmas, she focuses her efforts on the fate of the different giant communities and clans, sorting through the various threads of destiny and possibility for omens presaging the resurgence of the giants' once-great civilization.

The irruption of the demon lords into the Underdark has sent powerful ripples of indescribable chaos through Ustova's visions. All she sees of the future is fire, blood, and death, shot through with signs and portents based upon the natures of the demon lords—the bloody spirals and twin-forked symbols of Demogorgon, the excessive growth and rot of Zuggtmoy, visions obscured and clouded by the slime of Juiblex, and so on. She gladly helps any characters who can offer clarity in what she is seeing, treating such information as beneficial visions from the dream that is the world outside the Underdark.

Galeb Duhr Assistants

The library draws in elemental spirits to animate earth and stone, forming **galeb duhr** to serve as assistants for the keepers. These creatures are humorless but diligent.

Echoes

Gravenhollow "remembers" all who have walked its halls, as well as those who will visit the library in the future. As the characters explore the library, apparitions constantly flicker in and out of existence around them—the echoes of those who have come or will come to Gravenhollow in search of knowledge.

The time-displaced echoes in Gravenhollow are a prime opportunity to introduce great NPCs of Faerûn in a way that will not negatively impact the story you want to tell, nor steal the spotlight from the characters. The echoes offer characters the chance to receive advice from experienced adventurers and heroes, and for the players to interact with some of their favorite characters from the Forgotten Realms.

An echo is a quasi-real duplicate of the original creature, except it has 1 hit point and can't attack or cast spells. An echo reduced to 0 hit points vanishes.

It's impossible to tell at a glance whether an echo is from the past or the future. Clothing and equipment might help, or characters can simply ask. Interacting with an echo is the same as interacting with the original creature, but because most echoes are in the midst of their own search for knowledge, they prefer to be left alone.

Echoes appear so often that the characters find one every time they go looking for any information in the library. Use the Echoes in Gravenhollow table to determine who the characters encounter, or place echoes as you see fit.

Echoes in Gravenhollow

d20	Echo
1–2	Alustriel Silverhand
3–4	Andarin Zarith
5–6	Bruenor Battlehammer
7–8	Elminster
9–10	Graz'zt
11–12	Hgraam
13–14	Jalynfein Oblodra
15–16	Society of Brilliance
17–18	Xetzirbor
19–20	Yauln

Illustrious Visitors

The time-displaced echoes in Gravenhollow are a prime opportunity to introduce some of the great adventurers and personalities of Faerûn in a way that will not negatively impact the story you want to tell, nor steal the spotlight from the characters. The echoes offer them the chance to receive advice from experienced adventurers and heroes, and for the adventurers to meet some of their favorite characters from the world of the Forgotten Realms.

The echoes belong to those who managed to find Gravenhollow, coming there to seek knowledge for whatever all-important purpose or quest drove them there. Each echo is also from a specific point in time (possibly including the future).

Alustriel Silverhand

This legendary wizard and leader appears as a human female in her early twenties. She interacts with the characters with kindness and a certain whimsy, but doesn't disclose what time period she's from, admonishing characters who try to learn too much of the past or future.

Andarin Zarith

This human Red Wizard of Thay will visit Gravenhollow nearly a century in the future. He treats the characters as annoying apparitions and refuses to deal with them.

Bruenor Battlehammer

The dwarf king's red hair has turned mostly white, and he leans heavily on a thick crystal cane. He is old, frail, and quite senile, and he can't remember why he came to Gravenhollow or what he's looking for.

Elminster

This echo of the future claims to be searching for a long-forgotten spell. If the characters ask the venerable human archmage about the demonic incursion, Elminster reveals that the demonic incursion was the unintended result of a spell cast by Gromph Baenre, a former Archmage of Menzoberranzan. Elminster doesn't reveal what happened to Gromph, for he's reluctant to divulge too much information about the future. If the characters press him for details, Elminster says only that many great heroes were lost to the demonic tide, but several powerful demon lords were driven back to the Abyss.

Graz'zt

This echo of Graz'zt (see appendix D) is gathering all the information it can about the Underdark. The Dark Prince asks the characters what part of the Underdark they come from. If they mention the surface world, Graz'zt eyes widen as his curiosity is piqued.

Hgraam

This younger version of Stonespeaker Hgraam (see chapter 4, "Gracklstugh") treats the characters as spirits and asks them philosophical questions about the nature of dreams. If the characters engage him in conversation, he bids them farewell with the words, "I will remember you."

Jalynfein Oblodra

This young male drow was cast out of Menzoberranzan after he lost his sight, yet he survived and found his way here. The blind drow came to the library hoping to overcome his blindness and take revenge on his family. Characters familiar with drow lore or history know, with a successful DC 14 Intelligence (History) check, that House Oblodra was all but wiped out years ago.

Society of Brilliance

The characters encounter echoes of all five members of the Society of Brilliance (see the "Society of Brilliance" random encounter in chapter 2). Any members of the society traveling with the party know that these are echoes from the past.

The Society of Brilliance came to Gravenhollow years ago on a pilgrimage of enlightenment. If the characters mention the demonic incursion and postulate a theory of drow involvement, the Society of Brilliance echoes confirm that such an event is inevitable, "given the drow propensity for demon summoning and the inherent unpredictability of *faerzress*." These echoes don't have much else to offer, although they can explain how the library works (see the "Gravenhollow: General Features" sidebar).

Xetzirbor

This mind flayer regards the characters with interest. Xetzirbor refuses to disclose its timeline but hints that it knows about the demonic incursion. The mind flayer tries to entice the characters into telling it what they have discovered, but of its own purpose, Xetzirbor reveals only that it came to Gravenhollow to find a way to save a dying elder brain it calls Cyrog.

Yauln

A male stone giant from an ancient past, Yauln came to Gravenhollow to seek answers on whether his clan should enter an alliance with the bearer of the Cairngorm Crown (see chapter 4, "Gracklstugh").

Living Quarters

Each level of Gravenhollow features rooms reserved for habitation. The galeb duhr keep the rooms clean, and can provide food and drink magically created by the library if asked.

Librarians' Quarters

Urmas and Ustova live on the top level of the library, taking up all the living quarters at either end of that level. Their rooms reflect their duties and personalities. Urmas's quarters contain a collection of carved tablets, as well as actual books and scrolls found nowhere else in the library. Ustova's quarters feature a collection of musical instruments and divination tools, including crystal orbs, bags of bones, and a large mithral basin.

Ulthar lives on a lower level that he claims is "near the bottom of the library," though such a distinction is meaningless given how distorted distance and direction can be in the library (see the "Gravenhollow: General Features" sidebar). His quarters are a work of art, covered with murals and wall carvings of his own design, along with workshops where he engages in crafting.

Guest Quarters

The guest quarters appear bare until a visitor chooses a room. The next time that room is entered, it is fully furnished according to the character's taste and needs. Characters don't need to make any check to find their guest rooms after exploring the library: they need only wish to return, and the next set of stairs they come to leads them to the appropriate level.

Walkways

The walkways that surround the central well are wide and mostly empty, with the occasional galeb duhr or visitor echo wandering about. Each level consists of a well opening surrounded by a wide walkway connecting the rooms dug into the surrounding wall. Bridges cross the well at regular intervals, and also connect to stairs to the levels above and below. No matter how far down visitors go, there always appear to be more levels below.

Archives

Gravenhollow's records are organized by rooms attuned to the past, the present, or the future. Each level has a random number of rooms, arranged without any apparent system other than the library's intuitive ability to direct visitors to where they want to go—or to where the library thinks they need to go.

Accessing the Records

The library keeps its records on stone and crystal slabs, monoliths, and stelae fitting neatly in niches carved into the walls of every room. Thanks to the library's *comprehend languages* effect, anyone can easily decipher and understand the runes and glyphs carved into the stone.

These records contain only what the librarians were able to write down. Even with their network of messengers and informants, and the visions they receive using the powers of the library, the stone giants are still mortal creatures. As such, the giants' own understanding might limit the characters' ability to locate information in the library.

The library's written records deal only with events in the Underdark and the history of giants. Like most stone giants, the librarians consider the surface world a realm of dreams, and what happens there is deemed less important than events in the Underdark.

To acquire information not inscribed in the records (including any events outside the Underdark), the characters need a *stonespeaker crystal* (see appendix B), after which they must find an appropriate archive to query events in the past, present, or future.

Archives of the Past

Every room devoted to the records of the past has the same inscription carved above the doorway in runes that anyone who knows Dwarvish or Giant understands:

The past is a crystal, for it can be seen from many facets yet it always remains the same.

These rooms contain crystals of many colors. Ulthar and his assistants periodically move tablets, cylinders, and stelae from the Archives of the Present into these rooms. Some of the records here date back to the mythic times of the earliest giant gods.

Annals of History. Characters can research the backgrounds of the primary settlements of the Underdark and any well-known characters who dwell there. This lets them know what to expect if they visit those sites in the future, or to better understand some of the events that occurred during a previous visit. For example, they can learn more information about Themberchaud, about the drow siege and demonic assault of Blingdenstone, or any other part of the well-known history of Faerûn.

ARCHIVES OF THE PRESENT

The rooms that contain the works of Urmas have inscriptions carved above the doorway that anyone who knows Dwarvish or Giant can translate:

> *The present is like sand, ever flowing and escaping one's grasp without mercy or respite.*

The records in these rooms detail the current state of the Underdark and the giant kingdoms.

Current Affairs. Reading the tablets in these archives provides a good overview of what is going on in the Underdark at the present time. The latest news has a delay of a few days and is often incomplete, becoming more detailed as Urmas obtains more information from his messengers and informants. The reports about the demons' invasion are sketchy and incomplete, but characters can still get a rough idea about which demon lord arrived where. They can learn that Zuggtmoy might be on the move to an undisclosed location, or follow the ravaging paths of Yeenoghu and Baphomet as they gather and rally the races that worship them. Unlike the bits and pieces of news about the other demon lords, a significant amount of information is known about the cults of Demogorgon festering under Gracklstugh, as events there directly affect the resident stone giant clan.

ARCHIVES OF THE FUTURE

The rooms with Ustova's prophetic writings have inscriptions above the doorways that anyone who knows Dwarvish or Giant can decipher:

> *The future is a song we remember, but we cannot rush to its end lest we destroy the melody.*

Unlike the other rooms in the library, these archives echo with the sound of running water. The wall niches containing the stone cylinders Ustova favors for scribing are also fountains, where water shimmers over crystals as it falls.

Prophetic Visions. The information in the Archives of the Future is uncertain, not only because Ustova focuses on prophecies but also because her visions

GRAVENHOLLOW: GENERAL FEATURES

Not even the current librarians know who built Gravenhollow. All they know is that the library has existed since the dawn of giantkind.

Power Node. Gravenhollow was carved from a titanic geode whose crystals are imbued with magic that concentrates *faerzress*. The magic that suffuses the library profoundly affects time and space, altering the perceptions and reality of all beings within its walls.

Bigger on the Inside. The notion of space works strangely in Gravenhollow. The interior of the library continually expands as lore is added to it, but visitors can still traverse all its floors and chambers with ease. Only the most absentminded and scatterbrained become lost in Gravenhollow.

Universal Language. While in Gravenhollow, all creatures gain the benefit of the *comprehend languages* spell.

Hidden from Magic. Gravenhollow is a window into the passage of time and history, and the magic permeating the library blocks it off from the real world around it. Though divination magic works normally within the library, no divination effect used outside the library can discern any creature, object, or location within it.

A Place of Peace. Visitors to the library of Gravenhollow are expected to conduct themselves with decorum, and to refrain from arguments and violence. Creatures that incite conflict quickly draw the attention of the basilisk Veldyskar, who is quick to use his Petrifying Gaze on troublemakers. If a threat arises that Veldyskar can't handle, the library generates 3d6 galeb duhr to assist him.

Willful Navigation. Finding anything in Gravenhollow is an effort of will. Whenever a character seeks a specific location in the library (a particular floor or period of history, for example), the character must make a successful DC 14 Wisdom check to find that location. On a failure, the character takes a wrong turn and must make additional checks until successful. If led by one of the library's keepers, characters don't need to make checks to find the location they seek.

detail potential futures, not definite outcomes. Urmas and Ustova compare notes often to validate their visions. The prophecies in these rooms are limited to the future of giantkind—and the trials still to come for those once-great races—because this is Ustova's sole interest.

THE ENEMY OF OUR ENEMY

As the characters explore the library, ideally after encountering an echo or two, they meet the venerable drow archmage Vizeran DeVir, accompanied by Kleve, a **death slaad** bodyguard in its natural form. Vizeran is an **archmage** with the following statistical modifications:

- Vizeran's alignment is neutral evil.
- Vizeran's fey ancestry gives him advantage on saving throws against being charmed, and magic can't put him to sleep.
- Vizeran can innately cast the following spells, requiring no material components: *dancing lights* at will, *darkness* once per day, *faerie fire* once per day (spell save DC 15), and *levitate* (self only) once per day.
- While in sunlight, Vizeran has disadvantage on attack rolls, as well as on Wisdom (Perception) checks that rely on sight.

When the characters first encounter Vizeran and Kleve, read the following boxed text to the players.

> Two figures approach—a withered drow clad in dark flowing robes, and a hulking gray-skinned monster resembling a spiky humanoid toad, its wide mouth full of razor-sharp teeth. The drow's pinched and lined face speak to his great age, and his red eyes narrow and appraise you carefully as he approaches.

Vizeran greets the adventurers cautiously, introduces himself and his companion, and asks what business brings them to Gravenhollow. He remains cool and polite, trying to avoid any tension for fear of inciting violence in this place.

If the characters are willing to talk to him, Vizeran tells them he has opposed the tyranny of Lolth and her priestesses for centuries. He believes that some kind of demonic invasion of the Underdark is underway, and he has come to Gravenhollow to confirm his suspicions and make plans to combat it.

The drow archmage suggests that the adventurers make their own inquiries—and that they look in particular into Menzoberranzan and its archmage, Gromph Baenre. Vizeran then returns to his quarters, telling the adventurers how to seek the librarians if they don't already know how to do so.

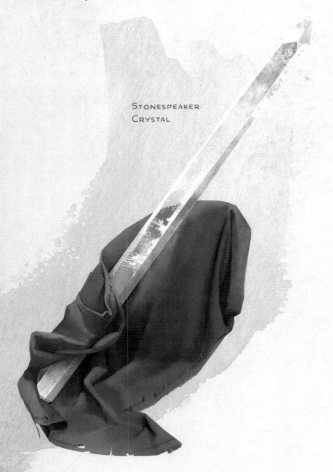

STONESPEAKER
CRYSTAL

During their time in the library, the characters can meet with Vizeran several times to exchange notes. The drow archmage already knows a lot of what has transpired since the demon lords arrived. He isn't, however, using the library to delve into specific events, so he welcomes the characters' input while remaining tight-lipped about his own intentions and goals.

If the characters threaten Vizeran, Kleve looms menacingly nearby even as the archmage tries to keep things civil, pointing out that there is nothing to be gained by fighting. If the adventurers attack him or Kleve, Vizeran casts *time stop* and departs before Veldyskar shows up (see "A Place of Peace" in the "Gravenhollow: General Features" sidebar). Kleve becomes invisible and follows his master out of Gravenhollow. Despite their attack upon him, the archmage contacts the characters again in an attempt to forge an alliance (see chapter 12, "The Tower of Vengeance").

APPROACHING THE LIBRARIANS

If the characters set out to find a librarian, Ulthar is the one they find first. He and Urmas agree that current events in the Underdark are a serious concern, but their roles as record keepers prevent them from acting in any way other than to provide information. Ulthar will speculate that this is likely why the library allowed Vizeran and the characters to find it so easily.

Urmas has been following recent events that might have led to the current crisis. He bids the characters to tell him about their own experiences in the Underdark—specifically, their encounters with the demon lords.

Ulthar offers the characters one of the library's *stonespeaker crystals* if they don't have their own, instructing them on how to attune to it. He warns the characters to not let themselves become lost in the visions they will experience.

STONESPEAKER CRYSTALS

A creature attuned to a *stonespeaker crystal* (see appendix B) gains the ability to peer through the veils of time and receive visions of the past, present, and future—but only while in Gravenhollow.

A creature attuned to a *stonespeaker crystal* gains the following additional benefits while in the library:

- While standing in the Archives of the Past with the crystal in hand, the creature can choose to experience a vision of the past. After receiving this vision, the creature can't experience another vision of the past until it finishes a long rest.
- While standing in the Archives of the Present with the crystal in hand, the creature can choose to receive a vision of something happening at that moment. After receiving this vision, the creature can't experience another vision of the present until it finishes a long rest.
- While standing in the Archives of the Future with the crystal in hand, the creature can choose to receive a glimpse of what might happen if the demon lords aren't stopped. After receiving this vision, the creature

can't experience another glimpse of the future until it finishes a long rest.

- While standing in the appropriate archive, the creature can expend 2 of the crystal's charges to ask a question pertaining to the past, present, or future and receive a truthful answer in the form of a vision.

Characters can expend charges to confirm suspicions, fill in gaps in their knowledge, and see for themselves the events that brought the demon lords into the world. Such research might take several days. Ulthar doesn't give them another *stonespeaker crystal* to speed up the process, but the characters can try to steal one, as the trusting librarian keeps them on a shelf in his quarters. The giant discovers the theft in 1d4 days, at which point the characters are confronted by Veldyskar and a host of galeb duhr, who politely ask them to leave Gravenhollow at once.

POSSIBLE VISIONS

The following are the most relevant visions the characters can receive as answers to their questions. Elaborate upon or modify these as needed, and improvise visions for other questions the characters ask based on the information in the adventure.

GROMPH'S FOLLY

If the characters inquire about Gromph Baenre or the arrival of the demon lords, they receive a vision of how everything started.

> An imperious drow archwizard in spider-silk robes casts a mighty conjuration spell. As the ritual draws toward its conclusion, a web of *faerzress* energy expands outward. The wizard seems alarmed by this, his efforts to complete the spell growing more crazed as he realizes he's lost control.
>
> And then, madness! Rifts open in the web of energy around him. These cracks stretch and widen, and through them come horrific fiends that scream, shriek, and howl as they are wrenched from the Abyss and cast into the Underdark.
>
> A woman's deep, dark laugh echoes in your mind as the drow wizard shrinks away from the demonic hordes he has unwittingly unleashed.

If a character receiving this vision has a passive Wisdom (Perception) score of 13 or higher, he or she sees a drow insignia on the wizard. If the character is a drow or otherwise familiar with the iconography of Menzoberranzan's drow houses, he or she recognizes the symbol as representing House Baenre. The character can also recall the symbol well enough to draw it, so that another more knowledgeable character can discern its significance.

ZUGGTMOY'S ARRIVAL

The characters can inquire about Zuggtmoy or the events in Neverlight Grove.

> A cavern of peculiar beauty opens up before you, with lights of every color shining from the pure essence of life, diffused and amplified by the glow of *faerzress*. The glow pulses, and you can feel the life in the cavern rotting away, bursting with infection. A mushroom grows in the center of the cave, ever larger and taller, pustules forming and seeping as its stem thickens and its cap reaches to the cavern's ceiling, forming a vast fungal tower.
>
> Two myconids approach the site in awe, not minding the carpet of rot under their feet. You sense their minds come alive in wonder, and as they kneel in worship, you know they are doomed. A voice sounds out within clouds of spores that fall like snow. The voice tells the myconids to prepare for a gift unlike any they have ever known.

If the characters visited Neverlight Grove, they recognize one of the myconids as Sovereign Phylo, while somehow knowing that the other is Yestabrod before it became mutated.

JUIBLEX AND THE PUDDING KING

As much as the characters learned from fighting the Pudding King in Blingdenstone, they might decide to seek more knowledge of the mad svirfneblin or his fiendish master, Juiblex the Faceless Lord.

> A deep gnome spurned by others of his kind weeps as he wanders the dark tunnels, talking to the things that crawl and seep from the walls. You see him adopt two slick patches of ooze, sensing his innate power over them. He plays with them as if they were children, chasing them through the gloomy depths.
>
> Something changes, and the oozes flow away. The deep gnome runs after them, fearful of being alone once again. You feel a great hunger seize him. He experiences visions that pass into your vision, showing what appears as a paradise to him but an oozing nightmare for all others. The great hunger speaks to him, his already broken mind a shield against the hunger's shattering power. That power seems to recognize and acknowledge something in the gnome that will serve it well.
>
> The great hunger has a name—Juiblex. And its power . . . oh, such great and terrible power! It grants the gnome the ability to command the little hungers—his children—so that they can return to the place that cast them out and devour it all!

SUNDERED BLADES

The corruption in Gracklstugh slowly rots duergar society from within, leading it toward a brutal fate.

You see a circle of small hooded figures, their forms hunched and emaciated. Their gestures and movements are jerky, indicative of the madness possessing them. They are chanting, swaying to their own words. And then they stop as the glow of *faerzress* rises around them, whispering to them in unintelligible sounds. The derro cackle and dance, their hands glowing with a power that isn't theirs. The vision shifts, and suddenly gray dwarves stare down at the red-hot metal on their anvils. The constant rhythm of their hammering falters. Suddenly, brother turns against brother as minds turn inward upon themselves. Sparks fly and a city burns.

DEMOGORGON'S ALTAR

One of the first brushes the characters might have had with the demon lords was in Sloobludop, where they witnessed the rise of Demogorgon, the so-called "Deep Father" of the mad kuo-toa.

You see a kuo-toa swimming in the gloomy depths of a dark, subterranean lake, uncertain. It turns left and right, trying to find something, even as it's surrounded by a fanged creatures resembling manta rays. The kuo-toa smiles, its needle teeth gleaming even in the darkness. It has seen something. It understands a new secret, and its already unhinged mind plunges further into madness.

The kuo-toa curls in on itself, arms extended in worship. Then from the circle of rays, two tentacles emerge—followed by two howling baboon heads.

FRAZ-URB'LUU AND THE GEM

Characters might be curious to know more about the source of the discord in Mantol-Derith, leading to a revelation about Fraz-Urb'luu.

A rift formed by *faerzress* opens wide, illuminating a dark tunnel. The rift spits out a black gem that clatters as it tumbles across the tunnel floor. The gem is picked up by a gray-skinned dwarf, who inspects it closely.

The vision shifts to a brightly lit cavern full of crude merchant stalls, where the duergar hands the gem to a svirfneblin for appraisal. The gnome refuses to return the gem, instead giving it to one of her svirfneblin apprentices. The young apprentice skulks away with the gem in his clutches, but is ambushed by a gargoyle. The gargoyle snatches the gem, flies away, and gives it to a female drow. The drow gazes into the black gemstone and sees a hideous demonic face looking back at her. Thoughts of murder and carnage fill her thoughts as she hides the gemstone on her person, draws her shortsword, and coats the blade with poison.

CYROG LIVES! HAIL ORCUS!

Although Orcus doesn't have a significant role in this adventure, players might wonder what the Demon Lord of Undeath is up to.

In the heart of a alien cavern glistening with slime, scores of mind flayers gather around an enormous brain resting in a pool. The brain is dead. You can hear the illithids' incomprehensible thoughts as they mourn its passing. One word echoes louder than the others: Cyrog.

Suddenly, *faerzress* bathes the dark and twisted hall in purplish light. A rift opens, and a hulking, horned figure that reeks of putrescence steps out. It raises a skull-tipped wand and points it at the dead elder brain. The elder brain begins to pulsate, and you see intermittent flashes of purple light under its rotting flesh. The mind flayers are aghast as the elder brain speaks to them once more, telling them that Orcus has saved Cyrog, and commanding them to follow it into undeath.

The librarians of Gravenhollow know that Cyrog is the name of distant mind flayer settlement. Vizeran DeVir and every member of the Society of Brilliance also knows that Cyrog is named after an ancient elder brain that commands the settlement, which lies deep in the Underdark, thousands of miles to the east.

BAPHOMET, THE HORNED KING

The demon lord Baphomet doesn't play a significant role in this adventure. However, a character seeking clues to the Horned King's whereabouts receive the following vision.

The smell of blood fills your nostrils as you wander a maze of Underdark tunnels, moving with purpose as your giant hooves crush stones underfoot. *Faerzress* light reveals that your shadow is monstrous, suggesting a hulking beast with a crown of horns. With your bloody glaive, you carve a swath through a forest of towering zurkhwood mushrooms that stands in your way. The tunnels beyond would confuse an ordinary mind, but you instinctively know the path you must walk. Every step brings you closer to a magma-filled chasm, lodged in which is an enormous contraption of metal and stone—a weapon capable of reshaping the Underdark itself.

This vision provides a brief glimpse of the Maze Engine, an arcane device located in the heart of the Labyrinth (see chapter 14).

SPAWN OF YEENOGHU

A character that tries to learn more about Yeenoghu, the Demon Lord of Gnolls, receives the following unsettling vision.

A hunched and rotting creature with the head of a fiendish hyena swings a triple-headed flail at a beholder, crushing it. As the eye tyrant falls to the floor, a pack of hyenas leaps onto the corpse and tears off its eyestalks while the demon lord licks the gore off his weapon. As the hyenas feed, they transform into slavering, cackling gnolls before your eyes.

Lolth, Demon Queen of Spiders

If the characters inquire about Lolth, they receive a vision of her home in the Demonweb Pits, confirming that at least one demon lord didn't escape the Abyss.

You behold the true form of the Demon Queen of Spiders—that of a black, bloated arachnid with the head of a female drow. Nestled in the webs all around her are thousands upon thousands of gray eggs. Lolth knows she is being scried, her fury tangible as her mind reaches out to find you. Her shriek of rage as she's shut out by the powerful wards of Gravenhollow echoes in your mind as the vision is suddenly torn away to darkness.

This vision offers a glimpse of Lolth's plan to drive her rivals out of the Abyss and repopulate its layers with her own demonic offspring. The character experiencing the vision must succeed on a DC 16 Wisdom saving throw or gain one level of madness (see "Madness" in chapter 2).

Other Visions

The other visions the characters might look for depend on what they experienced during their escape from the Underdark, and what you want the adventure to focus on (including the activities of other demon lords).

Returning to Vizeran

When the characters have discovered all they are looking to find out, they can go to Vizeran. If they don't, he seeks them out, having finished his own research.

"That fool Gromph brought the demon lords down upon us, with his demon queen pulling his strings all the while. He has given Lolth free reign in the Abyss. My own research leads me to believe Gromph used *faerzress* to achieve such a summoning, though I am sure he didn't intend this result. Imbecile!

"I can save you months of research—time we clearly don't have. The information I found here has confirmed my theories, and I know how to banish the demon lords back to the Abyss. We can do this only if we work together, if you are willing and daring enough to directly challenge the demon lords. Or perhaps foolhardy is the better word."

If the characters seem hesitant to work with Vizeran, he reminds them of the peril facing the surface world should the demon lords escape from the Underdark. If the characters accuse Vizeran of having ulterior motives, the drow smiles thinly and agrees. Still, he insists his goal is the same as the characters' own, and he doesn't ask them to involve themselves in his other plans. He points out that he is by far the most inconsequential of the many evils that the characters must contend with.

Vizeran invites the adventurers and their NPC followers to Araj, his tower and stronghold, where they can discuss the matter further. There, he can demonstrate what he intends to do and why he needs the heroes' help. He refuses to discuss plans in detail in Gravenhollow, saying, "The walls here literally have ears, and echoes linger forever." Only his home is secure enough to serve as the place from which to plan the demon lords' defeat.

Leaving Gravenhollow

As long as the characters remain respectful guests, the librarians don't mind them staying in Gravenhollow as long as they like. However, the library stops providing new visions after the characters learn the most essential information. If the players persist beyond that point, their efforts prove fruitless, and the librarians or their assistants suggest there is no more they can learn at this time.

The characters can travel with Vizeran, or he provides them with a map and precise directions to guide them to Araj if they want to deal with other matters in the Underdark first. He emphasizes that time is of the essence. Every day the characters tarry allows the demon lords' power and influence in the Underdark to grow. See chapter 12, "The Tower of Vengeance," for more information about Araj.

The last favor the library provides for the adventurers is to have the tunnel out directly connect with routes leading to the characters' desired destination, whether that destination is Araj, Blingdenstone, Menzoberranzan, Gracklstugh, Mantol-Derith, the edge of the Darklake, or somewhere else.

XP Awards

The characters should leave Gravenhollow with a clear picture of what is happening in the Underdark under the influence of the demon lords, and the roles that Gromph Baenre and Lolth have played in creating the crisis. Each character gains 5,000 XP for learning the truth.

Chapter 12: The Tower of Vengeance

Offered an alliance by the drow archmage Vizeran DeVir, the adventurers travel to his tower in the depths of the Underdark. There, they learn more about what he knows of the threat posed by the demon lords—and potentially forge a pact with him to deal with that threat. They must be cautious, however, as their potential ally has his own interests at heart and his own agenda where his fellow drow are concerned.

If the characters rebuffed Vizeran's overtures to an alliance in Gravenhollow (see chapter 11), the drow archmage subsequently sends Grin Ousstyl (see later in this chapter) as a peace envoy, renewing the offer and leading the characters to Araj if they accept it. Further exploration of the Underdark on their own might convince the adventurers to at least hear what Vizeran has to say. If they find the means to communicate his offer to their allies on the surface world, those allies encourage the characters to forge an alliance with the drow archmage.

Reaching the Tower

Vizeran's tower lies on the edge of the Wormwrithings, about ten days from Menzoberranzan. The map and directions the archmage provides the adventurers in chapter 11 allow them to find the cavern where the tower stands without getting lost. Use random encounters from chapter 13, "The Wormwrithings," on the way to the tower.

The final stretch to reach the tower is through a narrow passage off a side tunnel, concealed by a magically protected secret door. If Vizeran's map comes within 10 feet of the door, soft purple light outlines the word "Araj"—a drow word for "vengeance"—across its surface in spidery Elvish script. Touching the map to the door causes it to open for 1 minute or until the map is more than 100 feet away from it. If the characters travel with Vizeran, the secret door opens on his command.

The adventurers can travel to Araj with the full complement of their expeditionary force. Vizeran allows only the player characters within the tower, though the cavern around it offers space to camp and no risk of encounters. However, if the characters are riding giant lizards or other mounts, those mounts are unable to navigate the narrow route to the tower, and a separate camp farther from the tower will need to be established.

The passage behind the secret door is narrow enough that you need to move through it single file, occasionally turning sideways to squeeze. It takes about an hour to navigate its pitch-black darkness, and the journey is filled with a constant echo of distant sounds. The passage then widens, opening out into a cavern whose far walls and ceiling are out of sight in the darkness. Bits of quartz and mica in the stone glimmer as they catch the light, showing a footpath worn into the stone floor. At the end of that path, a vast, dark shape rises—an enormous stalagmite carved into a bleak, black tower.

Araj: Vizeran's Tower

Vizeran's tower is a enormous stalagmite, carved with a spiraling series of chambers leading up to its peak. The center of the stone spike is hollowed out to form an open vertical shaft. A stone staircase spirals around the shaft, with landings leading to chambers on the upper levels:

Level 1 has a broad antechamber and audience hall.
Level 2 contains kitchens, storage, and currently disused servants' quarters.
Level 3 houses guest bedchambers and a torture chamber for "special guests."
Level 4 contains Vizeran's library and laboratory.
Level 5 contains the archmage's private chambers.
Level 6 is Vizeran's sanctum at the tower's peak, where he spends his time in contemplation and study.

The sanctum features a permanent *teleportation circle* that Vizeran can use to return to his home if his need is great. (He uses it only as a last resort, however, given the risks involved in teleporting in the Underdark; see "*Faerzress*" in chapter 2.) Vizeran doesn't reveal this circle's existence to outsiders unless absolutely necessary, and he never gives away its sigil sequence.

Meeting with Vizeran

Assuming the adventurers arrive as Vizeran's guests, they find the door to the tower open to them. If they arrive under other circumstances, see "Stealing into Araj" at the end of this chapter.

> Past the heavy iron door that is the tower's only visible entrance, a short tunnel extends through five feet of solid rock into a cool, dark chamber. As you enter, a floating orb of pale violet light brightens before you, revealing an opening in the vaulted ceiling and a spiral stone staircase with no railing, climbing up into darkness.
>
> Around the stairs, the light reveals a circular audience chamber with cold, unlit lanterns hanging from brackets set into the stone wall, heavy carpets covering the smooth stone floor, and a throne-like stone chair on a raised dais to the left of the entrance.
>
> The ball of violet light floats to a stop beneath the center of the open shaft, beyond the foot of the stairs. It then hovers there as if waiting for you.

The orb of magical light attempts to guide the characters up the shaft to Vizeran's sanctum at the top of the tower. Characters can climb the stairs if they wish, but any creature that steps past the stairs and into the open shaft activates a magical levitation effect imbued into the shaft (see the "Vizeran's Tower: General Features" sidebar). If the adventurers arrive in Vizeran's company, he informs them of the command words for the levitation effect.

Vizeran DeVir

Vizeran DeVir is one of the greatest magical talents produced by the drow city of Menzoberranzan.

Unfortunately for him, his rise to power came at the same time as one of the other great arcane talents of the City of Spiders, Gromph Baenre. A scion of the First House and as gifted a schemer as he is a mage, Gromph engineered Vizeran's disgrace and exile as an unbeliever in Lolth. Ironically, this might have saved Vizeran's life, as House DeVir was wiped out not long thereafter by its rival, House Do'Urden.

Consigned to solitude in the Underdark, Vizeran didn't perish as most assumed he would. Instead, he put his arcane powers to work to create a safe haven for himself, and spent the following centuries in isolated study, furthering his mastery of the magical arts. He has watched from afar as countless events unfolded in the Underdark and across Faerûn, gathering information and making plans for his eventual return. After waiting for centuries, Vizeran now believes that time has come.

Vizeran harbors a thirst for vengeance against his only living rival—Gromph Baenre, the drow Archmage of Menzoberranzan. As a follower of the Elder Elemental Eye, Vizeran also despises Lolth and her influence over the drow. He would like nothing more than to show up Gromph and prove to the drow that Lolth has used them for her own gain. Of course, he also wants to learn whatever arcane secrets have allowed Gromph to tap into magic powerful enough to summon the demon lords to the Underdark.

Vizeran makes a powerful but dangerous ally. His plans and goals are entirely self serving, and he will sacrifice the characters without hesitation to further his schemes. Moreover, Vizeran isn't as immune as he believes to the demonic madness growing in the Underdark, which has been feeding his megalomania and his thirst for vengeance against his fellow drow.

Vizeran is an **archmage** with the following statistical modifications:

- Vizeran's alignment is neutral evil.
- Vizeran's fey ancestry gives him advantage on saving throws against being charmed, and magic can't put him to sleep.
- Vizeran can innately cast the following spells, requiring no material components: *dancing lights* at will, *darkness* once per day, *faerie fire* once per day (spell save DC 15), and *levitate* (self only) once per day.
- While in sunlight, Vizeran has disadvantage on attack rolls, as well as on Wisdom (Perception) checks that rely on sight.

Kleve

Vizeran holds the control gem of a **death slaad** he calls "Kleve." The slaad serves as the archmage's bodyguard, and is close by at all times. Kleve can change its form to appear as any Small or Medium humanoid, sometimes taking on the appearance of a deep gnome servant or a drow assistant to Vizeran if it wants to blend in. It can also cast *invisibility* to observe silently from hiding, and relies on its true form when it wants to intimidate other creatures. Although cruel by nature, Kleve takes no action to harm anyone without Vizeran's permission.

Kleve's control gem is a smoky crystal that Vizeran wears on a chain around his neck, beneath his robes.

As long as Vizeran possesses the gem, the death slaad must obey him and can't be charmed.

GRIN OUSSTYL

The only other person in Araj is Grin Ousstyl, Vizeran's **drow mage** apprentice. A clever troublemaker from an out-of-favor house, Grin worked his way into the outlawed alliance of drow mages known as the Council of Spiders, but was careless and nearly executed for his ambition. Exiled from Menzoberranzan, he was taken in by Vizeran, who plays the role of a shadowy patron of the council. The young drow has continued his magical training under the archmage's tutelage.

Grin is loyal to his master but not well suited to such a solitary existence. He longs for the opportunity to return to Menzoberranzan, supporting the notion of an uprising to overthrow the matron mothers and end their rule. He is less enthused about the potential of turning his old home into a battlefield for the demon lords, however, and he eventually betrays Vizeran's confidence

VIZERAN DEVIR

to the adventurers in an effort to prevent that outcome (see chapter 15, "The City of Spiders").

OTHER INHABITANTS

No other living creatures dwell in Araj, but the tower features a number of magical inhabitants the adventurers might interact with.

Each level of the tower has a permanent *unseen servant* in effect to attend to Vizeran, Grin, and the archmage's guests. Two dozen decorative suits of armor are also on display throughout the tower, all of which are suits of **animated armor** that move and fight at Vizeran's command. Between one and three suits guard each room and corridor of the tower. If Vizeran is threatened, he uses them to run interference, buying him time to escape or counterattack.

A character who pokes around the tower and succeeds on a DC 15 Wisdom (Perception) check notes signs that other humanoid creatures were recently present in Araj, including discarded clothing, moldering foodstuffs, and chains and manacles embedded into the walls in some of the tower's rooms. Vizeran dismisses any questions about such matters, but Grin Ousstyl confides to the characters that Vizeran once kept bound minor demons and humanoid slaves in his service. Vizeran banished the demons with the arrival of the demon lords in the Underdark, fearing some hidden connection between the creatures of the Abyss. The slaves held by the drow archmage (most of them acquired from Gracklstugh) are all dead—either lost to madness and killed by Vizeran, or sacrificed as part of the preparations for the archmage's dark ritual. Grin Ousstyl doesn't speak directly of that latter fate, saying only that Vizeran's work can be hard on his assistants.

VIZERAN'S TOWER: GENERAL FEATURES

The following features are found throughout the tower.

Light. The cavern outside the tower is dark, for the inhabitants of Araj require no light. Inside the tower, occasional *driftglobes* shed dim light, with the rest of the place in darkness.

Guards and Wards. The interior of the tower is under the effect of a permanent *guards and wards* spell to thwart intruders. Vizeran suspends the spell's effects for his guests, allowing them to enter unhindered, but those trying to sneak into the tower must deal with the spell's effects (see "Stealing into Araj"). Additionally, the tower is warded against scrying. Divination spells cast from outside cannot cross the tower's walls unless Vizeran allows it, and he immediately knows if the tower's wards thwart a divination spell.

Levitation Shaft. The central shaft of the tower has a permanent *levitate* spell in effect, such that any creature that steps into the shaft (or that falls off the stairs) is suspended in midair. A creature that speaks the command word *aluhal'kafion* ("descend") drops 20 feet per round until it reaches the bottom of the shaft. If the word *ku'lam* ("rise") is spoken, a creature rises 20 feet per round until reaching the top level. Movement stops immediately if the creature says *ilkalik* ("halt"). While in the tower, Vizeran can deactivate or reactivate the levitation effect as an action.

VIZERAN'S SCHEME

Vizeran DeVir invites guests to settle into his study while *unseen servants* bring trays of dried mushrooms, smoked rothé meat, and goblets of spicy liquor. The drow archmage takes a cup for himself and makes a point of drinking first, although he scoffs at any suggestion that he would try to poison his guests, given all the trouble he has taken to arrange their meeting.

Within the safe haven of his tower, Vizeran continues the discussion he began with the characters back at Gravenhollow, speaking more on what he knows of the demon lords.

> "The only one of my kind who could ever match me in the Art is Gromph Baenre. I think we knew from the moment we met that we were destined to be rivals. But where I sought only to master the Art, Gromph was also an astute political manipulator. No more devout than I in the service of the Spider Queen, he arranged for my disgrace and exile. Deprived of my considerable skills, my house fell to our rival, House Do'Urden. Gromph became the Archmage of Menzoberranzan under the auspices of his own house, the First House of the Ruling Council.
>
> "Gromph and I only ever had two things in common: our passion for the Art, and our hatred of the manner in which our fellow mages suffer at the hands of the matron mothers and mistresses of the drow. Gromph has always hungered for power, and not even becoming Archmage of Menzoberranzan was enough to satisfy him.
>
> "From this tower of exile, I kept watch on Gromph's activities. This was no easy task given his suspicious and circumspect nature. Nonetheless, my observations revealed that he was crafting a unique ritual—one that somehow drew on the energy of *faerzress* to channel incalculable arcane power. When Gromph performed this ritual, the walls between the planes shuddered. Then, as you have by now realized, the demon lords were wrenched from their layers of the Abyss and cast about here in the Underdark. What we all witnessed in Gravenhollow confirms this."

Vizeran answers questions from the characters as best he can, then makes his proposal. Use the points laid out in the following sections to play out the negotiations, utilizing whatever combination of ability checks and roleplaying you prefer. Vizeran is sincere in his willingness to help, even if his motives are entirely selfish. As such, he's inclined to reach an accord with the characters.

WHAT VIZERAN KNOWS

The characters can learn the following information from Vizeran by asking the right questions; he doles out information sparingly, but a successful DC 20 Wisdom (Insight) check might yield additional information if the archmage becomes cagey:

- Lolth is behind the plot to bring the demon lords to the Underdark through her manipulation of Gromph Baenre. The Spider Queen is using the drow as pawns in her schemes to dispose of her demonic rivals and seize power in the Abyss.
- The demon lords of the Abyss—along with many of their lesser servants and legions—have been set loose in the Underdark following Gromph's ritual.
- The presence of the demon lords is warping the fabric of the Underdark. The *faerzress* that permeates so much of the subterranean realm has become a conduit through which the insanity of the demon lords spreads.
- Gromph Baenre vanished following the ritual. Vizeran has not been able to detect any trace of his rival archmage using any of the resources at his command.
- Demogorgon, the Prince of Demons, arrived in the Claw Rift of Menzoberranzan and rampaged through the city before escaping into the wider Underdark.
- The intended purpose of Gromph's ritual is unclear, but Vizeran believes that his rival meant to summon and bind one specific demon lord. Vizeran finds it difficult to believe that even Gromph could be arrogant enough to think he could bind all the demon lords of the Abyss at once.
- The fact that the summoning originated in Menzoberranzan remains largely unknown. If the other races of the Underdark knew, they would have already moved against the drow. The dark elves almost certainly wish to keep this information a secret—assuming they even know it themselves.
- Vizeran knows of no means by which Gromph Baenre's ritual can be reversed. However, he believes there might be a different means of sending the demon lords back to the Abyss (see "Vizeran's Plan").

WHAT VIZERAN WANTS

Like any other sane creature, Vizeran has no wish to see the Underdark become home to the denizens of the Abyss. He points out that once the demon lords establish domains here, nothing will stop them from surging up to Faerûn to spread their madness and chaos. Indeed, such an outcome is inevitable given enough time.

Vizeran wants desperately to destroy his old rival. But even more so, the archmage dreams of thwarting Lolth and of having the Demon Queen of Spiders revealed to the drow as the treacherous creature she is. His deepest, burning desire is to watch Menzoberranzan destroyed by a demonic rampage. Then the ragged survivors of the drow will turn away from Lolth and her priestesses to seek Vizeran's guidance, letting him take his rightful place as a wise leader among his people.

WHAT VIZERAN OFFERS

Vizeran DeVir offers the adventurers his insight, his arcane power, and various magical resources that can help them deal with the demon lords. This includes the following benefits:

- Vizeran offers each character a drow *piwafwi* (see appendix B).
- Each character will be provided with an amulet that can be used one time as a *scroll of protection from fiends*.
- Vizeran offers the use of Araj as a safe haven in the Underdark, as long as his alliance with the characters lasts. The archmage won't countenance an army being housed within his home, but he opens it to the adventurers and their allies as they need it.
- Most important of all, Vizeran can offer a plan to defeat the demon lords—but he needs the adventurers' help to make it happen (see "Vizeran's Plan").

Vizeran is willing to negotiate other reasonable agreements, including tutoring wizards and providing them with opportunities to learn spells from his library. However, the archmage uses any such teaching opportunities to attempt to subtly corrupt his students.

VIZERAN'S PLAN

At the first sign that the adventurers are open to working with him, the drow archmage explains his plan.

> "Demons are creatures ruled by madness and hatred, even the greatest and most powerful of them. They war ceaselessly upon each other in the Abyss, and have already begun to do so here. We can play them against each other, and then deal with the weakened victors.
>
> "I believe I have the ability to devise and cast a ritual, similar to Gromph's but nowhere near as dangerous or foolish, that will draw the most powerful demon lords together to the site of the original summoning. Once they are brought together, they will try to destroy each other. But though the demon lords might destroy each other's physical manifestations here in our world, their essence cannot be extinguished. They will thus be cast back into the Abyss, as effectively as if they had been banished.
>
> "The ritual needs certain components to produce the talisman that will draw the demons. Then a rite to empower and activate it. Then blood and battle such as this world has never seen. Any survivors among the demon lords will be sorely weakened, and should be far easier to destroy.
>
> "All I need are the necessary ingredients," Vizeran says, "and, ideally, a look at Gromph's grimoires and notes from his sanctum." Where the drow archmage watches you, a thin smile curls one corner of his mouth.

The characters can refuse Vizeran at any time, at which point the archmage tells them to leave his home and wishes them good luck surviving in a world dominated by the demon lords. He says he will find other means to deal with the problem on his own.

If the adventurers are willing to ally with him, Vizeran further outlines his needs. He explains that the ritual is powered by a unique talisman he calls "the *dark heart.*" The talisman's creation requires a number of unique components:

- The intact and unhatched egg of a purple worm, for channeling great physical power.
- The central eye of a beholder, to break down magical resistance and overcome magical forces.
- Six feathers from six different angels—the authority of the celestial realms and a force to enrage fiendish creatures.
- The heart of a goristro, to reach and influence the hearts of other demons.
- Thirteen timmasks, also known as "devil's mushrooms," sprouted from the footprint of a marilith, a balor, or a goristro—a lure to draw demons in.
- A few drops of blood or ichor from a demon lord, to connect with the demons the ritual will call.
- Gromph Baenre's grimoires and notes on his ritual, to assist in better understanding the power that summoned the demon lords.

In his research, Vizeran has located potential sources for all these components, and he can direct the characters to retrieve them as detailed in subsequent chapters. The purple worm egg and the eye of the beholder can be found in the Wormwrithings (see chapter 13). The angel feathers and the demon heart can be claimed in the Labyrinth (see chapter 14). The grimoire is found in Menzoberranzan, the City of Spiders (see chapter 15). Being able to acquire the timmask mushrooms and blood from a demon lord depends on the adventurers' resourcefulness and on the opportunities found in other chapters of the adventure.

You can modify the components list if you wish, using the encounters in chapters 13 through 15 as guidelines and opportunities. Additional encounters can easily be inserted into chapters 13 and 14 for any other elements you want to add to the ritual.

Vizeran provides the means for the adventurers and their allies to gather the components for the talisman and encourages them to get started immediately. See chapters 13 through 15 for the sources Vizeran has found, then chapters 16 and 17 for the endgame battles against the demon lords.

Victory without Vizeran

It is up to you whether or not the adventurers can succeed against the demon lords without Vizeran's aid. They might be able to implement his plan on their own, particularly once he has supplied them with the necessary components and information. The *dark heart* talisman to be crafted for the ritual (see chapter 15) can be placed anywhere to draw the demons to it. Likewise, the ritual can be performed in any location in the Underdark imbued with *faerzress*. Vizeran has kept this information from the adventurers only because he sees the ritual as his chance to destroy Menzoberranzan and take his revenge on the drow who cast him out.

A player character spellcaster might be able to reproduce Vizeran's work to create and perform the ritual, setting up the scenario in chapter 17, "Against the Demon Lords." Regardless of how the plan unfolds,

though, the adventurers should get the opportunity to choose what they'll do about Vizeran when they learn that the drow archmage has not been entirely truthful with them. See chapter 15, "The City of Spiders," for details.

Stealing into Araj

If the characters don't take warmly to Vizeran's initial offer, they might want to enter Araj covertly instead of at the archmage's invitation. Likewise, once they realize that they are being used by Vizeran to advance his plan to destroy Menzoberranzan, the characters might decide to steal the archmage's secrets and resources to use against the demon lords—or even to slay him just for the sake of looting the place.

Wards

Getting to the tower undetected is all but impossible. Vizeran knows whenever the secret door accessing the passage to Araj opens, by way of a permanent magical effect similar to a powerful *alarm* spell. Intruders also have to deal with the *guards and wards* spell active within the tower, which places *arcane lock* spells on all the doors and sets *web* spells across the central shaft and stairways. Doors within the Tower of Vengeance (including the main door) have AC 16, 25 hit points, a damage threshold of 5, resistance to thunder damage, and immunity to poison and psychic damage.

A *magic mouth* spell at the entrance to the tower activates when intruders try to open the door, shouting: "You dare to enter here unbidden? Flee for your lives now, while you still can!" Another *magic mouth* placed outside Vizeran's sanctum repeatedly calls out: "Intruders! Beware!" when any intruder approaches within 20 feet of the sanctum door.

The tower's twenty-four suits of **animated armor** attack anyone who enters Araj without Vizeran's permission, and continue attacking until they are destroyed or he calls them off. At the first sign of trouble, the **death slaad** Kleve stalks intruders invisibly and attempts to attack with surprise. If Kleve is reduced to half its hit points, it retreats to its master's side.

Vizeran casts his protective spells before entering combat, along with *invisibility* (renewing the death slaad's *invisibility* as well if he has time). As a last-ditch escape, Vizeran casts *time stop* and uses the opportunity to flee or make a risky *teleport* attempt to a bolt-hole shelter he has hidden in another Underdark location of your choice.

In the event the characters have the opportunity to loot Araj, they find the items listed under "What Vizeran Offers," along with other treasure suitable for a foe of the archmage's power. See chapter 7, "Treasure," of the *Dungeon Master's Guide* for guidelines on creating Vizeran's treasury, keeping in mind that the wily drow has likely trapped his most powerful magic items. If he survives and escapes, Vizeran adds those who dare to threaten him and loot his home to the list of people who will suffer his revenge.

Chapter 13: The Wormwrithings

Two of the components that Vizeran needs to craft the talisman for his ritual (see chapter 12) can be found relatively close to the archmage's tower. The Wormwrithings are a honeycomb of tunnels spanning hundreds of miles in the northern reaches of the Underdark, carved from the rock by enormous purple worms. A purple worm nest in the Wormwrithings is an ideal place to find an unhatched purple worm egg. Additionally, Vizeran has heard rumors of a beholder living in the Vast Oblivium, a chasm deep within the Wormwrithings. If the characters didn't obtain the central eye from Lorthuun or Xazax (the beholders in chapter 9), they can search the Vast Oblivium for the beholder believed to lair there.

The Worm Tunnels

The nearest purple worm nesting area mapped out for the characters by Vizeran DeVir lies forty-eight miles west of the archmage's tower. The Vast Oblivium lies some twelve miles south of this nursery. Use the guidelines in chapters 2 and 10 as the party travels through the Underdark, but use the Wormwrithings Encounters table instead of the random encounter tables in chapter 2. Foraging is more difficult in the Wormwrithings, requiring successful DC 20 Wisdom (Survival) checks.

Faerzress permeates only the fringes of the Wormwrithings. While the party explores this region of the Underdark, spellcasters won't have to deal with the effects described under "*Faerzress*" in chapter 2.

The tunnels created by the purple worms are tubular and roughly 10 feet in diameter. A typical stretch of tunnel is 1d6 miles long before it intersects with another tunnel or a naturally formed cavern.

RANDOM ENCOUNTERS

As the characters explore the Wormwrithings, check for a random encounter once per day. Roll a d20 and consult the Wormwrithings Encounters table to determine what, if anything, the characters and their expeditionary force encounter.

When an encounter occurs, roll a d6 to determine how the area is illuminated. A roll of 1 indicates the area is dimly lit by phosphorescent lichen, while a 2–6 indicates the area is dark. The twisting tunnels of the Wormwrithings give creatures the opportunity to surprise the characters (see "Noticing Threats" in chapter 2).

WORMWRITHINGS ENCOUNTERS

d20	Encounter
1–10	No encounter
11	1 **drider**
12	Drow hunting party
13	3d6 dwarf **commoners**
14	1d6 **ettins**
15	3d6 **flumphs**
16	Grick nest
17	1 **purple worm**
18	2d6 **troglodytes**
19	1d4 **trolls**
20	1 **umber hulk**

DRIDER

This creature clings to the ceiling and prefers to make ranged attacks against the party. There is a 25 percent chance that the drider can cast spells (use the spellcasting variant in the *Monster Manual*). The drider flees if reduced to 30 or fewer hit points.

DROW HUNTING PARTY

A **drow mage** of House Melarn leads a group of 1d6 **drow** and 2d6 **bugbear** slaves through the tunnels in search of a purple worm nursery, where they hope to find a purple worm egg as a gift for their matron mother. If the characters have an egg clearly in their possession, the drow party tries to take it. Otherwise, the drow mage is happy to let the characters and their expeditionary force pass by unchallenged.

DWARF COMMONERS

There is a 75 percent chance that these shield dwarves are prospectors from Mithral Hall, hunting for precious stones and minerals. Otherwise, they are refugees who became lost in the Underdark after orcs attacked their stronghold and chased them underground. These dwarves are searching for a route to the surface.

Treasure. Each dwarf carries 1d10 pounds of food, 1d4 gallons of water (stored in canteens), and 1d6 gems worth 10 gp each.

ETTINS

These ettins used to be orogs until the *faerzress* and the corrupting influence of Demogorgon transformed them into two-headed giants. Their transformation can't be undone. They are starving and attack the party on sight.

FLUMPHS

A cloister of flumphs floats through the tunnels. These peaceful creatures have been disturbed by the powerful thoughts of the demon lords. They warn the characters that these evil thoughts have polluted the Underdark, and that kindness is the only response to such evil.

GRICK NEST

The characters stumble upon a naturally formed cyst in a tunnel wall. A **grick alpha** and 2d4 **gricks** are using the cyst as a nest, attacking anything that passes by.

Treasure. The walls of the cyst have precious crystals growing out of them. Characters can harvest these crystals, collecting 3d6 intact crystals worth 50 gp each.

PURPLE WORM

Roll a d6 and consult the Purple Worm Direction table to determine where the purple worm comes from.

PURPLE WORM DIRECTION

d6	Direction
1–2	The purple worm comes from behind the party, heading in the same direction and filling the entire tunnel. The party must either stay ahead of the worm or turn and fight it. If they stay ahead of the worm, the tunnel branches after 1d6 miles.
3–4	The purple worm is moving along the tunnel in the opposite direction as the party and appears in front of them. The party must either reverse course or fight the worm. If they reverse course, the tunnel branches after 1d6 miles.
5–6	The purple worm is burrowing through the solid rock on a path that intersects with the party's tunnel. The worm erupts from the tunnel wall behind the party, then continues on its way, leaving a new tunnel in its wake. The worm's passage triggers a rockfall in the party's tunnel, and each party member must succeed on a DC 13 Dexterity saving throw or take 10 (3d6) bludgeoning damage from falling debris.

TROGLODYTES

These troglodytes are heading toward their lair (see "Troglodyte Lair") and attack any other creatures they come across.

TROLLS

These ravenous, insane trolls attack the party on sight.

UMBER HULK

This creature is hidden behind a wall and uses its tremorsense to detect passing prey, bursting out of a nearby wall to attack the nearest party member. Randomly determine who is attacked, taking into account any NPCs traveling with the characters.

Troglodyte Lair

Approximately half way between Araj and the worm nursery, the characters' route is blocked by a looming battle between two factions of a troglodyte tribe.

> A foul stench and a cacophony of faint, hissing voices rises from ahead. The tunnel plunges sharply downward into a vast, open cavern dimly lit by luminous fungi and bisected by an underground stream. Tall reptilian humanoids stand on either side of the stream, waving makeshift weapons and howling threats at each other in a hissing language.
>
> The group of creatures closest to you has a captive lashed between two stalagmites atop a low rise in the cavern floor. That floor is some twenty feet below you, down a steep but navigable tunnel whose walls are piled high with rubble. The creatures are preoccupied with their conflict and haven't noticed you yet.

The reptilian humanoids are troglodytes that worship a lesser god called Laogzed—a reptilian horror that dwells in the Abyss. Although Laogzed isn't a demon lord (and so has not been summoned to the Underdark), troglodytes are being drawn across the Underdark to sites where the demon lords have manifested.

Any character who understands the troglodytes quickly learns what drives the conflict. Otherwise, a successful DC 13 Wisdom (Insight) check can provide a general sense of what's going on. The troglodytes ambushed and killed a drow scouting party whose leader wielded a magic sword that S'slaar, the troglodyte chieftain, claimed as a trophy. However, S'slaar's war marshal, H'slaat, was the one who killed the drow leader, and who now claims the right to wield the blade.

The disagreement blossomed into a full-fledged conflict, and the other troglodytes quickly chose sides. On one side of the stream, troglodytes loyal to H'slaat seized S'slaar's mate and are threatening her, hoping to force the chieftain to back down. On his side of the stream, S'slaar is wildly swinging the magic sword and screaming, as the troglodytes loyal to him shout insults and taunts at the other side.

The characters can turn back without being spotted and find an alternate route bypassing the troglodytes, but doing so adds forty-eight miles (and an increased chance of random encounters) to the distance they must travel before they reach the purple worm nursery. If the characters simply watch the standoff unfold, see "Resolving the Standoff" later in this section.

1. Entrance Tunnel

The worm tunnel the adventurers are traveling through opens up atop a steep slope leading 15 feet down into the open cavern. The slope is difficult terrain.

As long as the adventurers aren't calling attention to themselves, they can remain undetected here indefinitely. The troglodytes are too distracted by their standoff to notice them.

Rubble is piled up along the walls on either side of the tunnel. The rubble on the east side of the tunnel conceals a hidden passageway. Any character with a passive Wisdom (Perception) score of 15 or higher notices the hidden passage. Anyone actively searching the rubble finds it with a successful DC 10 Wisdom (Perception) check. Adventurers who head into the passage beyond the rubble discover the hidden entryway to area 5 at the end of the tunnel.

2. Cave Floor

H'slaat, a **troglodyte champion of Laogzed** (see appendix C), and twenty-two **troglodytes** are arrayed in a rough battle line along the south bank of a freshwater stream that nearly bisects the cavern. The stream runs west to east, tumbling down a short waterfall and forming a small pool (area 9). The stream is about 15 feet wide and 3 feet deep at its deepest point. It can be crossed on foot but is difficult terrain.

The troglodytes are so distracted that it's possible to sneak through this area undetected as long as the adventurers stay close to the cavern walls. Each character must succeed on a DC 10 Dexterity (Stealth) check or be noticed by the troglodytes.

Development

Any wounded creature entering the stream attracts the swarm of quippers from area 11.

3. Rise

This upthrust section of the cavern floor is edged by a steep slope to the southwest and a 6-foot-high cliff elsewhere. The cliff requires a successful DC 11 Strength (Athletics) check to climb.

Five **troglodytes** loyal to H'slaat are stationed here. In addition to their regular attacks, they are armed with javelins that they throw from a pile of twenty-five javelins on the cavern floor near them.

Javelin. *Melee or Ranged Weapon Attack:* +4 to hit, reach 5 ft. or range 30/120 ft., one target. *Hit:* 3 (1d6) piercing damage.

H'hoort, a **troglodyte** and Chieftain S'slaar's mate, is lashed between two stalagmites here. Another **troglodyte** stands guard next to her. Releasing H'hoort won't earn the adventurers a respite from the opportunistic troglodytes, but if the characters hold her captive, both sides are reluctant to attack them.

4. Basin

The area north of the stream is dominated by a 5-foot-deep basin. A 10-foot-wide furrow on the east side of the basin slopes down toward area 9.

The troglodyte chieftain has arrayed his forces along the narrow strip of high ground between the basin and the stream. Chieftain S'slaar is a **troglodyte** with 20 hit points and a *+2 longsword*. While he wields the sword, S'slaar gains the following action option:

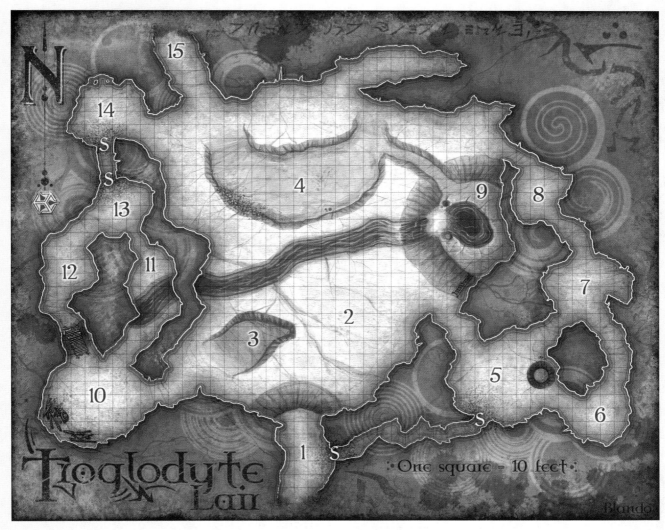

Troglodyte Lair

: One square = 10 feet :

Blando

+2 Longsword. Ranged Weapon Attack: +6 to hit, reach 5 ft., one target. *Hit:* 8 (1d8 + 4) slashing damage, or 9 (1d10 + 4) slashing damage if used with two hands.

S'slaar is accompanied by five **troglodytes** with 20 hit points each and three ordinary **troglodytes**.

Treasure

S'slaar's *+2 longsword* is of drow manufacture (see the "Drowcraft Items" sidebar in appendix B). It has a cross guard shaped like a stylized spider with tiny gems for eyes. Etched into its blade are the words *Oloth tlu malla*, which is a drow expression meaning "Darkness be praised."

5. Supplies and Captives

This area is held by H'slaat's forces. One **troglodyte** guards the cave. A character can sneak past the guard with a successful DC 12 Dexterity (Stealth) check.

The cave floor is strewn with gnawed bones—the remains of dead dwarves and drow. A circular pit, nine feet deep, holds six captives—two **drow** and four shield dwarf **commoners**. These unfortunates were separated from larger groups (see "Random Encounters" earlier in this chapter) and captured by the troglodytes. Every couple of days, one of them is eaten

by the tribe. The captives are filthy and weak; each has four levels of exhaustion and 1 hit point remaining. Any of the captives can explain the nature of the conflict between H'slaat and S'slaar. If freed, the drow immediately flee into the Underdark, but the dwarves offer to join the expeditionary force if the adventurers liberate them. The drow are male members of House Melarn and are named Rinil and Xol. The shield dwarves hail from the Silver Marches and are named Dauthorn Brightmantle (male), Traldak Xornbane

---

Troglodyte Lair: General Features

Characters notice commonly recurring features as they explore the troglodyte lair.

Light. Nightlights (see "Fungi of the Underdark" in chapter 2) and other luminous fungi dimly illuminate the caves and tunnels throughout the troglodyte lair.

Ceilings. The main cavern has a 90-foot-high ceiling. Smaller side caverns have 60-foot-high ceilings. Unless noted otherwise, all ceilings have stalactites hanging from them.

Stench. The troglodytes' foul musk can be smelled throughout the lair, although the stench is not strong enough to have any detrimental effect on visitors.

(male), Zulia Stonewhisper (female), and Hargritt Hammerhome (female).

Rubble is piled up along the south wall of the cavern, concealing a hidden passageway to area 1. Anyone with a passive Wisdom (Perception) score of 15 or higher notices the passage. Anyone actively searching the rubble must succeed on a DC 10 Wisdom (Perception) check to find it.

Treasure

Within the cave, four zurkhwood boxes hold a 50-foot length of spider-silk rope, four flasks of oil, twenty pounds of rancid food, a pile of moldy blankets, six maces and sixteen javelins (all battered but usable), four casks of unspoiled wine worth 10 gp each, and a locked tribute chest. It takes a successful DC 15 Dexterity check using thieves' tools to open the chest, which contains 180 gp (minted in Menzoberranzan and Gracklstugh), three gems each worth 50 gp each, a *potion of gaseous form*, and a *+1 dagger* with silvery, weblike filigree worked into the hilt. The dagger is of drow manufacture (see the "Drowcraft Items" sidebar in appendix B). The crude litters that the troglodytes use to bear these goods are propped up against the cave wall.

6. Steam Vent

A thick jet of hot steam spews forth from a crack in the floor near the east wall of this cavern. Growing around the steam vent is a patch of fire lichen (see "Fungi of the Underdark" in chapter 2).

Anyone with a passive Wisdom (Perception) score of 13 or higher notices a vein of precious gems embedded in the rock wall behind the steam vent. Anyone actively searching the cavern spots the gem deposit automatically. The gems can't be reached without entering a 10-foot-by-10-foot-by-10-foot cloud of hot steam. Any creature that enters the area or starts its turn there takes 1d8 fire damage. The litters in area 5 or a similar object can be used to block the steam emerging from the vent for 1 round before weakening and falling apart.

Treasure

For each round spent digging at the wall, a character has a 10 percent chance of extracting a gemstone worth 100 gp. The chance increases to 20 percent if the character has a mining background and a miner's pick. After ten such gems are extracted, the deposit is depleted. For each round that any number of characters dig at the wall, there is a 10 percent cumulative chance that the sound attracts the attention of any troglodytes remaining in areas 5 or 7.

7. Troglodyte Outpost

H'Slaat stationed four **troglodytes** here to watch for any of S'Slaar's forces that might try to make their way into attack position through the outer caverns. These guards are always on alert. One of them carries a horn that it sounds in the event of an attack. If the horn is blown, eight of the troglodytes in area 2 come through area 5 and into this cave to investigate and shore up the defenses.

8. Roper Lair

This small cavern is filled with stalactites and stalagmites, making the cave floor difficult terrain. No phosphorescent lichen grows here, so the cave is dark.

Two of the stalagmites are **ropers**, while four of the stalactites are **piercers** (the ropers' offspring). While lying in wait, the creatures are virtually undetectable. Any party member with a passive Wisdom (Perception) score of 20 or higher notices something unusual about the rock formations in the cave. Unless they are recognized, the ropers and piercers surprise anyone entering the area.

Treasure

Searching the cave reveals the remains of a half-eaten male drow lying against one wall. The drow carries a small pouch containing 30 gp and two *spell scrolls* (*shield* and *phantasmal force*) written on sheets of trillimac (see "Fungi of the Underdark" in chapter 2).

If the ropers are killed and cut open, the adventurers find 25 pp in the gizzard of one, and a *ring of protection* in the gizzard of the other.

9. Sunken Pool

Water from the stream pours into this 15-foot-deep grotto, forming a 10-foot-deep pool with a narrow crack in the bottom. The pool's water is safe to drink, and growing around the pool's edge are 3d6 waterorbs (see "Fungi of the Underdark" in chapter 2).

10. Ruins

This large cavern is strewn with zurkhwood beams—enough to make a raft. An old bridge made of moldy zurkhwood planks spans an underground stream in one of the tunnels to the north.

11. Spawning Pool

The underground stream passes through this cave, traveling west to east. The adventurers can hear something splashing in the water as soon as they enter this area. Any character who enters the stream is immediately attacked by the **swarm of quippers** that has spawned here.

12. Geothermic Vents

The adventurers feel the heat emanating from this area as they approach. Thick cracks, some as wide as 2 feet, crisscross the cavern floor, opening up to a pool of molten rock 25 feet beneath the cavern. The dull orange glow of the lava below bathes this area in dim light.

At the end of every minute the adventurers spend here, roll a d6. On a roll of 1, 1d4 **magma mephits** emerge from a crack in the floor and attack. No more than twelve mephits appear in a given 24-hour period.

13. Empty Cave

Rocks and small boulders are piled up along the north wall of this otherwise empty cave. The rubble conceals a passageway to area 14, buried during a rockslide. Anyone with a passive Wisdom (Perception) score of 15 or higher notices the hidden passage. Anyone actively searching the rubble must succeed on a DC 10 Wisdom (Perception) check to find it.

14. RALLY POINT

S'slaar's cavalry troops are gathered in this cavern, waiting for their master's order to attack. Six **troglodytes** are mounted on six **giant lizards**.

Rocks and small boulders are piled up along the south wall. The rubble conceals a tunnel to area 13. Anyone with a passive Wisdom (Perception) score of 15 or higher notices the hidden passage. Anyone actively searching the rubble must succeed on a DC 10 Wisdom (Perception) check to find it.

DEVELOPMENT

When the order comes to attack, S'slaar's cavalry bursts through the hidden passageway on the south wall of the cave (see "Resolving the Standoff").

15. EXIT TUNNEL

This purple worm tunnel leads back into the Wormwrithings. Unless they're being pursued, the characters can safely leave the troglodytes behind when they reach this area.

RESOLVING THE STANDOFF

H'slaat orders his followers to commence their attack 20 minutes after the characters arrive at area 1. Unless the characters intervene, the conflict plays out as follows:

- H'slaat orders his fellow troglodytes in area 2 to rush across the stream while the troglodytes in area 3 rain javelins down on the chieftain's forces. Meanwhile, H'Slaat grabs H'hoort from area 3.
- H'slaat crosses the stream, dragging her behind him. He threatens to kill her unless the chieftain meets him in battle.
- The troglodytes in areas 5 and 7 try to make their way through the side caverns to attack the chieftain's forces in area 4 from the rear. However, if the ropers and piercers in area 8 have not already been killed by the adventurers, the troglodytes are surprised and massacred.
- S'slaar's cavalry in area 14 makes its way through the western side caves and attack H'slaat's forces from behind.

If the adventurers don't intervene in any way, the battle lasts approximately 20 rounds and ends when H'slaat kills the chieftain in the basin at area 4. Half the troglodytes on both sides are killed in the conflict. Those who remain accept H'slaat as their new chieftain.

While the battle is underway, a character can sneak through an area occupied by troglodytes with a successful DC 10 Dexterity (Stealth) check.

As tense as the standoff between H'slaat and S'slaar might be, the troglodytes quickly forget their conflict and unite against common threats, such as the characters and their unwelcome expeditionary force.

VOICE IN THE DARK

After dealing with or avoiding the troglodytes, the adventurers can continue on toward the purple worm nursery. However, within six miles of the nursery they come across an unexpected presence in the darkness.

> The remnants of a rockfall have opened up a small vaulted cavern along the passageway. Apart from the occasional glowing insect scuttling along the walls, the cavern is dark.
>
> Suddenly, a loud voice booms out all around you in Undercommon: "Turn back or suffer a death so horrible you cannot imagine! You have been warned!"

The voice is actually a *minor illusion* cantrip. If no one in the party understands Undercommon, the dire warning is just loud gibberish to them. The cantrip was cast by Hanne Hallen, a young drow allied with House Mizzrym. Hanne has the statistics of a **drow**, with the following modifications:

- Hanne's AC is 12, or 15 with *mage armor*. She doesn't wear a chain shirt.
- Her Intelligence is 17 (+3).
- Add Arcana +5 and Investigation +5 to her skills.
- Add Common to her list of known languages.

Hanne also has the following Spellcasting feature:

Spellcasting. Hanne is a 1st-level spellcaster. Her spellcasting ability is Intelligence (spell save DC 13, +5 to hit with spell attacks). She has the following wizard spells prepared:

Cantrips (at will): *minor illusion, ray of frost*
1st Level (2 slots): *shield, mage armor*

Hanne's mother, Zhora Hallen, leads the Dark Hunters—drow explorers who steal purple worm eggs. These eggs are prized by wizards, who use them in various arcane rituals. Hanne was on her first egg run with her mother's team when a passing purple worm burst into the tunnel they were traveling through, separating her from the rest of the group. Convinced that her mother and the rest of the Dark Hunters were killed by the purple worm, the headstrong and half-starved young mage-in-training is attempting to make her way back to Menzoberranzan.

Hanne spotted the adventurers as they approached and tried to scare them away. She's hiding in the rubble along the cavern wall but can be spotted with a successful DC 15 Wisdom (Perception) check.

If the adventurers decide to turn back, finding another tunnel going in the right direction adds twenty miles to their journey to the worm nursery. If they press ahead, the voice shouts in Undercommon again: "Fools! Flee now! This is your final warning!" Once the adventurers enter the cavern, Hanne can be spotted with a DC 10 Wisdom (Perception) check. If spotted, Hanne threatens the party with her "powerful magic," but drops her hostile attitude if offered food and water. She can be convinced to tell her story with a successful DC 12 Charisma (Persuasion) check.

If the characters attack Hanne, she fights to the best of her ability. If the adventurers are friendly toward her, Hanne is willing to travel with them for safety.

Worm Nursery

As the characters near the nursery, they get a view of one of its guardians—and might take an unexpected fall.

> As you make your way through a long tunnel, everything around you begins to shake and rumble. Suddenly, the tunnel floor gives way at your feet.

The tunnel through which the characters travel is directly above area 1 of the nursery. The burrowing of a nearby purple worm weakens the tunnel floor, causing a 10-foot section of it to break apart and collapse. Any character in the area must make a successful DC 15 Dexterity saving throw or fall 25 feet into area 1 below.

1. Entry Cavern

Any characters dropped into this dark cave have time to recover, while characters who avoided falling can anchor ropes to the edge of the tunnel floor above, then climb down into the cave. In any event, the characters hear more rumbling off in the distance.

2. Fungus Cave

A variety of fungi blankets this dark, 15-foot-high cavern. Every 10 minutes spent foraging here yields 1d3 pounds of edible fungi per forager (to a maximum of 30 pounds).

Worm Nursery: General Features

The characters encounter the following features in the purple worm nursery.

Light. All tunnels and chambers are dark unless the text states otherwise.

Purple Worm Tunnels. The tunnels marked T1, T2, and T3 on the map do not exist when the characters first enter the nursery. They are created by purple worms after the party arrives, as noted here:

- Fifteen minutes after the party enters area 1, a purple worm digs into area 1, then travels through area 3 and creates tunnel T1 to enter area 8.
- Ten minutes after the first worm arrives, a second purple worm enters through the tunnel in area 7. It makes its way through the adjoining echo chamber, then into area 8. Then it digs tunnel T2 into the eastern echo chamber before exiting through the worm tunnel in area 14.
- Fifteen minutes after the second worm arrives, another purple worm enters through the tunnel in area 7, digs tunnel T3 from the southern echo chamber into the eastern echo chamber, then exits through the worm tunnel in area 14.

Visiting worms are heralded by a low rumbling sound 2 minutes before they appear. (The bats in area 9 also swarm and flee their roost 1 minute before a purple worm appears.) Purple worms ignore intruders except those in areas 5 or 8, but they won't pursue anyone fleeing from those areas.

The passage to area 3 is a steep slope leading 10 feet upward, and covered in small rocks and gravel. Moving up the slope requires a successful DC 12 Dexterity (Acrobatics) check. On a failed check, a character slips and tumbles down to the bottom of the slope, taking no damage. If someone at the top of the slope lowers a rope to help other characters climb, no check is necessary.

3. Ossuary

This 30-foot-high chamber is dimly lit by luminescent lichen. Thousands of bones carpet the cavern floor, including many recognizable as humanoid (primarily dwarf, elf, and goblin) and some belonging to strange and unidentifiable creatures. Exactly where the bones came from is a mystery. A crack in the south wall leads to area 4.

The tunnel marked T1 on the map doesn't exist until a purple worm creates it fifteen minutes after the party discovers area 1 (see the "Worm Nursery: General Features" sidebar). Thus, the characters won't be able to reach area 8 until the tunnel is formed.

4. Chasm

This 30-foot-high unlit cavern has a twenty-foot-wide pit in its center, which descends a thousand feet. Thirty feet down is a small ledge holding the skeletal remains of a moon elf adventurer clad in moldering leather armor.

Scaling the chasm walls without gear requires a successful DC 15 Strength (Athletics) check.

Treasure

The skeleton still wears a *ring of free action* on one bony finger.

5. Echo Chambers

These three 60-foot-high caverns, hollowed out and expanded by purple worms, are set around area 8 as a defensive measure. Using their saliva, the worms have created thick, resinous strands that stretch from wall to wall. These strands are 2 feet thick and suspended some 50 feet above the floor.

Any noise in one of these chambers (including a normal speaking voice or metal striking metal) causes the strands to reverberate, creating a loud humming that echoes throughout the surrounding caverns, alerting the purple worms to the presence of trespassers.

Development

If the adventurers set off a humming in one of these echo chambers, a distant rumbling can be heard and felt as a purple worm burrows toward the egg chamber, arriving there in 1d4 minutes (see area 8 for details).

6. Caretaker's Quarters

Phosphorescent lichen clings to the walls of this 30-foot-high cavern. Stronk, a brutish **fomorian**, lairs here. Somehow the giant formed a bond with the purple worms, becoming a caretaker of their eggs. He regularly checks the eggs, brushes fungus off them, and defends them against predators.

ONE SQUARE = 10 FEET

THE WORM NURSERY

BLANDO

Stronk is sleeping on a pile of skins and loudly snoring when the adventurers arrive. Characters looking around the room can see the remnants of the fomorian's grim meals—travelers lost in the Wormwrithings or egg-hunting adventurers.

Venturing into Stronk's lair without waking him requires a successful DC 12 Dexterity (Stealth) check. If awakened, the fomorian shouts out about "killing egg thieves" and "protecting my precious ones," then fights to defend the nesting area and protect the eggs. If Stronk is reduced to half his hit points or fewer, he charges into the adjoining echo chamber (area 5) and bellows to summon a purple worm before rejoining the battle.

TREASURE

All the treasure Stronk has taken from his victims has been placed under his sleeping skins for safekeeping: 40 pp, an electrum brooch worth 120 gp, six gems worth 50 gp each, two *potions of greater healing*, and a book of drow poetry worth 100 gp.

7. ENTRY CHAMBER

This cavern rises to a height of 50 feet and contains many stalagmites and stalactites. A purple worm tunnel leads out into the Wormwrithings through this area, but the tunnel's mouth is 40 feet above the cavern floor. Scaling the rock wall to reach the tunnel requires a successful DC 15 Strength (Athletics) check.

DEVELOPMENT

Zhora Hallen and her Dark Hunters enter the purple worm nursery by scaling down the rock wall here shortly after the adventurers arrive (see "Dark Hunters," below). Characters can also leave the nursery and return to the Wormwrithings via this route.

8. EGG CHAMBER

The ceiling of this cavern is 80 feet high. A pair of purple worms have laid their eggs here, cementing them together and anchoring them to the cavern walls with their resinous saliva. Seven clusters hold six eggs each, as noted on the map. Each egg is a silvery sphere 3 feet in diameter. Its shell is tough (AC 20), but an egg is destroyed if it takes any amount of damage.

Three of the four resin strands anchoring the network of egg clusters to the cavern walls feature stray threads that drop all the way down to the cave floor. It's possible to climb up to the strands at these points to reach the eggs. Traversing the strands is slow going; each 1 foot of distance costs 3 feet of movement. Anyone fighting or taking strenuous action atop a strand must succeed on a DC 10 Dexterity (Acrobatics) check to avoid falling off. An adventurer who reaches an egg cluster and has a suitable cutting tool (such as a dagger, sword, or axe) can carefully hack an egg out in 2d4 minutes.

The upper reaches of the egg chamber are covered in webs spun by the giant spiders in area 11. Some of these webs reach all the way down to the egg clusters.

For every five minutes the adventurers spend in this room, check for a random encounter by rolling a d20 and consulting the Egg Chamber Encounters table.

EGG CHAMBER ENCOUNTERS

d20	Encounter
1–15	No encounter
16–18	1 giant spider from area 11
19–20	1 purple worm

The giant spider walks on the ceiling and surprises the adventurers unless someone in the party has a passive Wisdom (Perception) score of 14 or higher.

If a purple worm appears, it enters the nursery through the tunnel in area 7 and circles the outside of the cavern. Any party member in the egg chamber can try to hide with a successful DC 10 Dexterity (Stealth) check. A failed check means the party member attracts the worm's attention.

The purple worm attacks anyone it detects in the chamber except the giant spiders from area 11 and the fomorian from area 6. It won't pursue fleeing characters anywhere except into the adjoining echo chambers (area 5) or the slop cave (area 10). If it doesn't detect any intruders, the purple worm exits the complex through the tunnel in area 7, passing through the nearest echo chamber along the way.

9. BAT CAVE

This cave is thick with stalactites and stalagmites, and home to thousands of bats. The cavern floor is covered in a thick layer of guano, making the floor difficult terrain. The bats spend most of their time clinging to the cavern's 60-foot-high ceiling, but the noise of the purple worms drives them into a shrieking, flapping frenzy.

Whenever a purple worm enters the area 8 (whether as a random encounter or in response to an alarm from area 5, or as noted in the "Worm Nursery: General Features" sidebar), a **swarm of bats** flies out of the cave 1 minute before the worm appears. Roll a d6 to determine which way the bats go. On a roll of 1–3, the

HANNE'S HELP

Educated by her mother, Hanne Hallen (see "Voice in the Dark") knows quite a bit about purple worms. If she's traveling with the characters, she realizes that they are in a worm nursery as soon as she enters area 8. She also recognizes the echo chambers (area 5) and understands their function.

Hanne won't want to leave the nursery without an egg of her own. If necessary, she'll sneak away from the rest of the party to try to obtain one.

bats take the shortest route to the tunnel in area 7 and exit through that tunnel. On a roll of 4–6, the bats take the shortest route to the tunnel in area 14 and exit through that tunnel.

The swarm doesn't attack unless threatened, but any creature that occupies an area the swarm passes through is buffeted by scores of bats, taking 1d4 bludgeoning damage.

DEVELOPMENT

When the purple worm that caused the bats to swarm exits the nursery, the bats return to this cave to roost 10 minutes later.

10. SLOP CAVE

The floor of this dark, 60-foot-high cavern is covered in a thick layer of viscous purple worm saliva. Consequently, the floor is difficult terrain. As they enter, adventurers notice dozens of glinting objects in the goo beneath their feet. Further inspection reveals the sparkling objects are precious gems.

For every minute the adventurers spend in this cave, there is a 25 percent chance they attract the attention of 1d4 giant spiders from area 11. The spiders scuttle along the walls and ceiling, avoiding the gooey floor.

TREASURE

If the adventurers take 10 minutes to search through the goo, they can retrieve a total of twenty 50 gp gems.

11. SPIDER NEST

Giant spiders enjoy a symbiotic relationship with purple worms and are frequently found lairing in purple worm nurseries. The multitude of predators that seek out the worms' eggs provide the spiders with easy prey, while the presence of the spiders provides additional protection for the hatchery.

The eastern half of this cavern floor is covered in webs stretching up to the ceiling. See "Dungeon Hazards" in chapter 5 of the *Dungeon Master's Guide* for rules about webs. Eight **giant spiders** lurk in the nest, minus any killed elsewhere in the nursery.

12. CHASM

A chasm cuts across this cavern, stretching from wall to wall. The chasm is 10 feet wide, 200 feet deep, and slopes down to the southwest at a sixty degree angle. The chasm's slope can be climbed with a successful DC 15 Strength (Athletics) check. A creature that fails the check by 5 or more goes tumbling down the slop to the bottom of the chasm, taking damage from the fall as normal.

TREASURE

At the bottom of the chasm lie the skeletons of two svirfneblin who tried to leap across the chasm while being chased by a purple worm. Lying near the remains are two miner's picks and a small leather pouch containing a *gem of brightness*.

13. Exit Tunnel

Characters can exit the worm nursery and return to the Wormwrithings via this purple worm tunnel.

The Dark Hunters

The Dark Hunters consist of Zhora Hallen (a **drow elite warrior**) and ten **drow**. Each carries adventuring equipment (bedroll, rope, a flask of oil), three days' worth of food and water rations, and 2d6 × 10 gp. Zhora and her comrades survived the purple worm attack that separated them from Hanne (see "Voice in the Dark"). Zhora believes that Hanne is dead.

Twenty minutes after the characters first enter the purple worm nursery through area 1, Zhora and her Dark Hunters enter these caverns through the tunnel in area 7, then scale down to the cavern floor. They spend a few minutes regrouping and making their way through the southern echo chamber, then arrive in area 8 and scale the resin strands to grab two purple worm eggs. If they encounter the adventurers and Hanne isn't present, the drow are hostile, though they might be convinced to enter a temporary truce with a successful DC 20 Charisma (Persuasion) check.

If Hanne is with the party and has been well treated, she and her mother have a quiet reunion. Zhora gravely promises the adventurers that she will repay the debt she owes them however she can.

Development

If the characters reunite Zhora and Hanne, this act of benevolence could lead to Zhora potentially aiding the adventurers in chapter 15, "The City of Spiders." See that chapter for details.

The Vast Oblivium

Following Vizeran's directions, the characters find the chasm known as the Vast Oblivium—the lair of the beholder Karazikar—twelve miles from the purple worm nursery.

The beholder created the Vast Oblivium using its disintegration eye ray. This lair consists of a central chasm known as "Karazikar's Maw," surrounded by ten vertical shafts. These are interconnected with horizontal tunnels resembling "spokes" and honeycombed with small caves used by the beholder's followers and slaves. A web of rope bridges crisscrosses the maw, connecting passages on different levels.

Inhabitants

Karazikar considers itself the master of all it surveys. The beholder doesn't live alone, though, keeping its lair well stocked with disposable servants.

Karazikar the Eye Tyrant

Like most of its kind, this beholder is hateful and paranoid, trusting no one. Its servants are keenly aware that failure to please their master means death or petrification.

Karazikar has goals beyond simply ruling over its domain. Long ago, the beholder heard rumors of an

---

arcane device known as the Maze Engine, capable of shifting the gears of reality. During the last Great Modron March, Karazikar captured a pentadrone and afterward became convinced the Maze Engine existed in the Underdark. Unfortunately, the modron's axiomatic mind couldn't be broken, and it perished rather than reveal anything. Since then, the beholder has made it known that it's interested in certain "curiosities," and it rewards anyone who brings it more modrons or hints about the existence or location of the Maze Engine (which is described in chapter 14).

Shedrak of the Eyes

The beholder's favorite slave is a human named Shedrak of the Eyes. As Karazikar's "high priest," he leads other slaves in worship of their master and carries out the beholder's commands.

Formerly an adventurer from the surface world, Shedrak and his companions delved too deeply into the Wormwrithings. His companions became Karazikar's playthings for a time, but Shedrak alone was able to resist and withstand all ten of the beholder's eye rays. Impressed by this feat of extraordinary luck, Karazikar made the human his acolyte after breaking his mind and his will. Shedrak is completely mad, considers Karazikar a god, and brooks no defiance or disrespect toward his "divine master."

Slaves

One hundred slaves of various humanoid races serve the beholder. Some were captured while wandering too far from their Underdark settlements, while others were purchased in the slave bazaars of Menzoberranzan. The youngest slaves were born in the Vast Oblivium and raised here, knowing no other life. Many of the beholder's slaves worship it, particularly those born here, their minds warped by the aberration's charm rays and their lifelong captivity.

All of the slaves fear Karazikar, and the notion of acting against the beholder seems impossible to them. However, witnessing the bravery of the adventurers has

a chance to sway them. If the characters demonstrate their willingness to challenge the beholder (including by killing Shedrak), surviving slaves can be convinced to aid them with a successful DC 16 Charisma (Persuasion) check. On a failed check, slaves either attack the characters or hide from them, waiting for Karazikar to deal with them.

ARRIVAL

When the characters come within a mile of the Vast Oblivium, they feel a growing sense of being watched. They catch glimpses of eyes peering out of the shadows. These eyes close and vanish when anyone tries to focus on them, and adventurers who search for signs of what caused them must succeed on a DC 11 Wisdom saving throw or gain one level of madness (see "Madness" in chapter 2).

The characters' tunnel ends at the top of one of the exterior shafts of the Vast Oblivium (see "The Vast Oblivium: General Features" sidebar). Characters can use the rope ladders to reach the bottom of the shaft, and from there make their way to the chasm known as Karazikar's Maw.

WELCOME TO KARAZIKAR'S MAW

Shedrak meets visitors at the chasm, greeting them in the name of his master, the great Karazikar, and asking their business. Use the **mage** statistics to represent Shedrak, with the following modifications:

- Shedrak is chaotic evil.
- He has ten small eyes tattooed on his bald head that allow him to see invisible creatures and objects as if they were visible.
- He carries a nonmagical staff topped with a varnished beholder eye. Karazikar can see through this eye and treats it as one of its own eyes for the purpose of using its eye rays. Breaking the staff renders the eye inert and prevents Karazikar from using this property.
- He carries a *potion of healing*, a *potion of poison*, and a *spell scroll* of *globe of invulnerability*.

As long as the adventurers are respectful toward Shedrak and his master—and particularly if they claim to carry messages or items of possible interest to the beholder—Shedrak agrees to lead them to Karazikar.

If the characters become hostile, Shedrak orders them to depart, lest they provoke the wrath of his all-powerful master. If attacked, he uses his *globe of invulnerability* scroll, casts *fly* on himself, and flies into the chasm.

Shedrak allows up to ten party members accompany him, demanding that the rest of the expeditionary force remain behind. Shedrak then leads the smaller group across a bridge into the middle of Karazikar's Maw.

AUDIENCE WITH KARAZIKAR

Whether they're escorted by Shedrak or make their own way into Karazikar's Maw, the adventurers first encounter the **beholder** as they cross the chasm. The beholder descends from the shadowy ceiling, staying at least 20 feet away from the bridge.

If the characters have come to talk, Karazikar hears them out. The beholder is supremely arrogant, and it speaks and understands only Deep Speech and Undercommon. If any of the characters bluff about having information of interest to the beholder, Karazikar mentions the Maze Engine, either to see if the adventurers know of it, or in a scoffing tone to suggest they can't possibly know anything that it has not already learned.

Killing Karazikar is the only way to claim the beholder's central eye for Vizeran. At the first hint of violence, the beholder uses its disintegration ray to disintegrate a 10-foot section of the bridge, hoping to plunge one of more party members into the chasm. It then targets enemies with its other eye rays and makes full use of its lair actions (see the *Monster Manual*). Against characters who attempt to hide from it, the beholder uses a lair action to cause an eye to open up on a wall with line of effect to a hiding creature, then attacks with one of its eye rays.

Karazikar's slaves fearfully scatter during any confrontation, but if Shedrak is alive, he protects his "god" as best he can. If the beholder is reduced to 45 or fewer hit points, it attempts to flee, ordering Shedrak (if he's still alive) to cover its retreat.

When the beholder is reduced to 0 hit points, its corpse slowly sinks, falling 10 feet at the start of every turn until it reaches the bottom of the chasm. A character within reach of the beholder can use an action to gouge out its central eye. There is also a 10 percent chance at the end of each turn that the beholder's corpse lands on a bridge.

Freed Slaves

If Karazikar and Shedrak are defeated, the beholder's slaves emerge from various tunnels, file out onto the bridges, and kneel in supplication, worshiping their liberators as gods. Each slave bears the brand of Karazikar on its forehead—a scar shaped like an open eye. The slaves are unarmed and include the following:

- 21 shield dwarf **commoners**
- 17 human **commoners**
- 11 moon elf **commoners**
- 8 female **drow** and 1 male **drow**
- 5 **deep gnomes**
- 23 **goblins**
- 15 **orogs**

All of the slaves have four levels of exhaustion (see appendix A of the *Player's Handbook*) and can't do much more than eat and follow simple instructions. They join the party's expeditionary force if urged or ordered to do so, but they aren't effective combatants until they've rested and reduced their exhaustion level.

The slaves know several intriguing bits of information:

- Karazikar hid its treasure in the uppermost reaches of the chasm. The only way to reach the treasury is by levitation or flight.
- The beholder was preoccupied with finding an arcane contraption called the Maze Engine.
- The beholder recently captured a strange mechanical creature that might know where the Maze Engine is

Lost Friends

The liberation of the Vast Oblivium makes a useful bit of backstory for introducing or reintroducing a character into the party. If an adventurer or NPC was lost in the Underdark, or if you want an NPC left behind at a settlement to put in a reappearance, have that character appear as a slave taken by Karazikar. Depending on the circumstances, the character might even join up with the adventurers during the final battle to defeat the beholder. Similarly, a new player character joining the party might start out as a prisoner of the beholder, now freed.

located (see "Modron Prisoner" below). The creature is locked in a room sealed with a rolling stone door. The beholder used its telekinesis eye ray to open and close the door.

Any slaves that don't join the party are anxious to make their way to the nearest peaceful Underdark settlement. The drow are eager to return to Menzoberranzan, the deep gnomes to Blingdenstone. If the characters urge the slaves to leave the Vast Oblivium and make their own way home, they are all killed while trying to escape from the Wormwrithings. If the characters assign members of their expeditionary force to lead the slaves out of the Wormwrithings, the slaves stand a much better chance of making it to safety.

Modron Prisoner

One or more slaves can lead characters to a small room on the uppermost level of the complex. The room is sealed off with a 6-inch-thick circular stone door that can be rolled aside with a DC 20 Strength check or opened with a *knock* spell or similar magic. The room holds a damaged **duodrone** that Karazikar recently captured in the hopes of unlocking more information about the Maze Engine.

The duodrone has 1 hit point remaining and speaks its own language of clicks and whirs, always referring to itself as "we" or "us." The demonic madness as scrambled its memory, but if a *greater restoration* spell is cast on it, the modron remembers two things:

- "We were part of a great march. We were separated. Then we were lost. Then we were captured. Then we started freaking out. Then you found us."
- "We know nothing about a 'Maze Engine.' However, we can detect an Orderer approximately 289 miles south of our present location." (The "Orderer," claims the modron, is a device that brings order to chaos. It is, in fact, what others refer to as the Maze Engine.)

Treasure

The beholder used its disintegration eye ray to carve a rough likeness of itself in the ceiling of Karazikar's Maw—a great stone beholder face glaring down upon the gaping chasm, its central eye a hollow shaft that leads up to a hemispherical vault where the beholder hides its considerable hoard: 15,000 gp, 1,300 pp, ten assorted gems worth 500 gp each, a *gem of seeing, a necklace of adaptation*, and a *robe of eyes*.

CHAPTER 14: THE LABYRINTH

More of the components needed for Vizeran's demon summoning ritual can be found in the depths of the Labyrinth—a snarl of twisting tunnels and caves extending approximately 240 miles from north to south and 120 miles east to west. Navigating the Labyrinth is a nightmare, since most tunnels follow a straight path only a short distance before doubling back on themselves or ending abruptly.

Baphomet the Horned King appeared in the Labyrinth when the demon lords were summoned to the Underdark. At the same time, Baphomet's rival Yeenoghu, Demon Lord of Gnolls, has taken to hunting the twisting passages of Baphomet's new domain.

Vizeran tells the characters to find the Gallery of Angels, a location in the heart of the Labyrinth lies some three hundred miles from Araj. It is the one place where Vizeran knows the characters can find the angel feathers required for his ritual's talisman. The Maze Engine lies forty-eight miles deeper into the Labyrinth if the characters choose to follow up on clues leading there (see the "March to Nowhere" and "Maze Engine" sections for details). The adventurers will also find a few unexpected opportunities to aid in the fight against the demon lords along the way.

Long ago, the Labyrinth was much like any other part of the Underdark, consisting largely of natural caverns connected by tunnels and underground rivers. The discovery of precious metals and gemstones led dwarves and others to excavate, extending its tunnels and expanding its caves. The results of those efforts saw an insignificant corner of the Underdark transformed into a vast, sprawling network of passages.

Abandoned settlements within the Labyrinth are common, marked out by rusting iron rails and scattered ore carts. Dark mine shafts descend into the unknown depths, while tunnels stretch off in random directions. Rifts both small and large also appear throughout. Many a tunnel ends abruptly at a rift, as if the way ahead was simply sheared off to leave a vast, yawning chasm. Some of these rifts run to depths of a few hundred feet. Others ascend and descend for miles. Many of the rifts show their age by the presence of carved switchback staircases along their walls, or weathered bridges spanning their gaps.

Characters in the Labyrinth can easily become lost. Traveling through this area follows the rules under "Navigating" in chapter 2, but it takes a successful DC 12 Wisdom (Survival) check to avoid becoming lost, rather than a DC 10 check. Spellcasters must contend with the effects of the *faerzress* for as long as they are in the Labyrinth, also as discussed in chapter 2.

LABYRINTH ENCOUNTERS

This chapter features a number of set encounters. Either as the characters journey to the Labyrinth or return to Vizeran's tower, you can run the "Adamantine Tower" encounter. Once the characters reach the edge of the Labyrinth, go to the "Spiral of the Horned Lord" encounter.

Within the Labyrinth, the characters take on the encounters "Filthriddens," "March to Nowhere," "Yeenoghu's Hunt," and "Gallery of Angels" (their intended destination). They might also take on "The Maze Engine" encounter, inspired by knowledge gained in chapter 13 and an encounter with some modrons in the Labyrinth.

RANDOM ENCOUNTERS

Twice each day that the party spends in the Labyrinth (whether traveling or resting), roll a d20 and consult the Labyrinth Encounters table to determine what, if anything, they encounter. This table replaces the random encounter tables in chapter 2 for as long as the party remains in the Labyrinth.

LABYRINTH ENCOUNTERS

d20	Encounter
1–10	No encounter
11	1 **behir**
12	2d4 **flumphs**
13	Gnoll pack
14	1d4 **grells**
15	1d4 **hezrous**
16	4d8 **manes**
17	2d4 **minotaurs**
18	1 **monodrone**
19	2d6 **quaggoths**
20	1d4 **shriekers**

BEHIR

This long-bodied reptile is either prowling a tunnel or resting in a cave when the characters encounter it. The behir retreats if reduced to 80 or fewer hit points.

FLUMPHS

This cloister of flumphs feeds on the psychic energy they detect from a nearby **mind flayer** that has enslaved 2d4 **quaggoths**. The flumphs warn adventurers who communicate with them about the nearby threats, but it is up to the characters whether they wish to engage those threats.

GNOLL PACK

A **gnoll fang of Yeenoghu** named Kurr made his way into the Labyrinth shortly after Yeenoghu was summoned to the Underdark. Kurr brought with him a pack of hyenas and had them feast on the corpses of his slain victims. This heinous act transformed the hyenas into ten **gnolls**. Kurr's pack now prowls the Labyrinth in search of Yeenoghu, slaughtering anything and anyone they happen upon.

KURR

Unknown to his gnoll progeny, Kurr has succumbed to a form of madness that quells his feral demeanor. He's lost his appetite for carnage and is overcome with guilt for all of the creatures he has slain. When his pack happens upon the party, he sends his gnolls into battle but doesn't partake of the violence, hoping that the characters slaughter his brethren. Once they are dead, Kurr bows his head solemnly, begs Yeenoghu's forgiveness (first in his own language and then in Abyssal), and then throws himself at the party's mercy.

Kurr is suffering from a form of indefinite madness (see "Madness" in chapter 8 of the *Dungeon Master's Guide*) which, if cured, reverts him to a typically feral gnoll. While afflicted with madness, Kurr can't bring himself to kill any living creature except in self-defense. If the characters spare his life, Kurr can act as a guide,

RANDOM ENCOUNTER LOCATIONS

Random encounters in the Labyrinth take place in one of the following environments, modified as you wish to suit the creatures in the encounter.

Caves. Most caves in the Labyrinth are small (up to 30 feet in diameter), with uneven floors featuring stalagmites, columns, or pools of standing water. A cave has a 10 percent chance of featuring luminescent growth on the walls that fill it with dim light. In addition to the tunnel through which the characters enter, there are 1d3 additional tunnels leading out. These tunnels can exit the cave through the floor, ceiling, or at odd angles.

Tunnels. Most tunnels in the Labyrinth are 5 to 10 feet wide, with ceilings 1d8 + 3 feet high. A tunnel follows a straight path for no more than 2d4 × 10 feet before it turns.

Rifts. The Labyrinth is shot through with rifts and chasms formed by upheavals in the earth. Blocks of stone thrust up in some places to hinder movement through passages and caverns, while other areas drop off suddenly, forming escarpments hundreds of feet high. In some places, the earth has shifted horizontally, creating tunnels that end suddenly only to continue hundreds of feet away.

Any rift the characters encounter has a 75 percent chance of featuring a bridge or staircase constructed to navigate it.

for he has explored a great deal of the Labyrinth and can lead the characters along a safe route to an Underdark shanty town (see "Filthriddens"). Characters have no random encounters if they follow Kurr along this route, although they periodically stumble upon the corpses and bones of Underdark creatures slain by his gnolls.

The encounter with Kurr's pack occurs only once. Any subsequent occurrence of this encounter is with a pack of 3d6 **gnolls**. These gnolls came to the Underdark with Yeenoghu. They cackle and scream the demon lord's name as they tear into their prey.

Grells

The grells drop from an overhead shaft to feed.

Hezrous

These demons are tearing apart an iron ore cart, a rusted section of mining track, or some other old fixture. Party members can attempt to slip past the demons without arousing their attention. Doing so requires a successful DC 11 Dexterity (Stealth) check. On a failed check, the demons detect the party member and attack.

Manes

Characters can hear the mewling of this vile mob long before it appears. The manes scour the Labyrinth for easy prey and move like a tide of putrid flesh.

Minotaurs

These minotaurs roams the Labyrinth, slaying creatures in the name of Baphomet.

Monodrone

This modron has become separated from its fellows (see "March to Nowhere"), and there is a 75 percent chance that it is looking to rejoin them. If the characters can understand its language, the monodrone repeatedly says, "We are on the march!"

A monodrone that doesn't want to rejoin its fellows is a rogue modron, made so by the chaotic energies suffusing the Underdark. This rogue monodrone gladly joins the party, saying "Down with Primus!" in its own language over and over. Its alignment is chaotic neutral, and it can only follow one simple task at a time.

Quaggoths

These quaggoths are hungry and attack the party regardless of its size. If there are five or more quaggoths in the group, one of them is a quaggoth thonot (see the "Variant: Quaggoth Thonot" sidebar in the "Quaggoth" entry of the *Monster Manual*). If the thonot dies, the other quaggoths immediately break off their attack and begin feasting on the thonot's remains, hoping to gain its psionic power.

Shriekers

The shriekers sound off when bright light or a creature is within 30 feet of them. Their shrieking has a 75 percent chance of attracting other monsters, in which case roll again on the Labyrinth Encounters table, treating another shrieker encounter as "no encounter."

Adamantine Tower

The adventurers come across a tower haunted by forces of darkness.

> Vaulted chambers bristle with stalactites and stalagmites, slowing your passage as you wend your way across uneven floors. Moving through a narrow passage, you enter a cavern dimly lit by phosphorescent fungi—and are met by the sight of a dark metal tower perched on the edge of a cliff that drops away into darkness.
>
> The square tower is twenty feet on a side and thirty feet high, with arrow slits in each wall. A battlement crowns its top, with a stone gargoyle peering over each side. Set into the middle of the wall facing you is a sturdy-looking door made of the same dark metal as the rest of the tower.

No ordinary structure, the tower is a *Daern's instant fortress* (see chapter 7, "Treasure," of the *Dungeon Master's Guide*). Made entirely of adamantine, the two-story tower has remained sealed since its last owner retreated inside and locked the door behind her—but not before a pair of shadow demons slipped in as well. The demons killed the owner and left her remains on the first floor. The tower can't be tipped over or otherwise moved from its position, and the arrow slits on each level are too narrow for anything bigger than a Tiny creature to squeeze through.

A character can learn the tower's command words by casting an *identify* spell on it. The command word to open the front door or the trap door on the roof is "mimsy." The command word to transform the tower into a one-inch metal cube is "brillig," but speaking it has no effect since the shadow demons are still inside. To return the tower to its cube form, the adventurers must first empty it of any creatures.

Four **gargoyles** perch atop the tower. They remain motionless as the characters enter the cavern, attacking only if anyone attempts to enter, climb, or damage the tower.

This cavern's rough floor has been flattened where the tower stands, while the floor behind the tower has collapsed into a shaft 300 feet deep and 100 feet in diameter. Several tunnels branch off from the rough-walled shaft at various points, allowing the characters to continue their journey after climbing down. They can move around the tower easily if they wish to ignore it.

First Floor

The first floor of the tower is an open room. A ladder affixed to the back wall leads up through a trapdoor to the floor above. A pile of bones and moldering clothes lies in the corner—the remains of the tower's former owner.

Treasure

Searching through the remains turns up two empty potion bottles and a *potion of mind reading*.

SECOND FLOOR

This empty chamber has a ladder affixed to one wall that climbs to an adamantine trap door leading to the roof. The trap door is closed and locked, though the proper command word ("mimsy") can open it.

The two **shadow demons** lurk in the darkness of this room and attack the first character who enters, likely taking their prey by surprise.

BATTLEMENTS

The top of the tower features an open space surrounded by a crenelated wall. If the four gargoyles have not yet attacked the adventurers, they do so here.

SPIRAL OF THE HORNED KING

Minotaurs have roamed the tunnels of the Labyrinth for ages, but as Baphomet's influence grows, so too has the ferocity of his chosen servants. The waxing of Baphomet's power has not gone unnoticed by the packs of gnolls rampaging through the Underdark. The gnolls have begun making inroads into minotaur territory. The latest battlefield in the ancient feud between Baphomet and Yeenoghu is a maze of passages that grant access to the deeper passages of the Labyrinth.

> The tunnel you have been following gradually widens until it opens into a cave with a high ceiling overhead. Patches of glowing fungi cling to the walls and fill the chamber with dim light. Columns of stone support the ceiling, the rock marbled with veins of glittering crystal. Across the chamber, a great cleft is ringed by a profusion of sigils and glyphs. Stacked to either side of the opening are two mounds of severed heads.

The cleft leads to the Spiral of the Horned King—a maze of tunnels and caves along the outer edge of the Labyrinth. Though other routes can be found into the Labyrinth, this entrance is the easiest to find.

Invocations to Baphomet, dire curses, and the inverted names of the gods are scrawled around the cleft in dried blood, and continue on down the tunnel walls. Anyone who can read the Abyssal tongue can tell that this place has been consecrated in the name of Baphomet, the Horned King and lord of minotaurs.

The minotaurs tear off their victims' heads, then leave them to "watch" the entrance for intruders. Most of the heads are from gnolls, though different Underdark races can be found if any character wants to sift through the piles.

GASH THE GNOLL

Minutes after the characters arrive, they hear the sounds of footsteps approaching. A few moments later, a gnoll slinks from the tunnel ahead.

> A gnoll creeps out of the shadows, glancing cautiously at the piles of heads to either side of it. Its filthy body is bent and covered with tatters of clothing and scraps of blood-crusted armor. The creature looks you over with one good eye, the other lost in a mass of scar tissue.

This wretched gnoll is named Gash. Thanks to treachery he committed against his kind, the minotaurs spared his life. However, their mercy comes with regular abuse and torment. The gnoll now sees himself as a loyal and willing servant of the brutes, and he is eager to lead gnolls and anyone else to his minotaur masters.

Gash is a **gnoll** with the following modifications:

- Gash has 11 hit points.
- He has a walking speed of 25 feet.
- He has disadvantage on Wisdom checks and Wisdom saving throws because of the physical and mental abuse he has suffered. A *lesser restoration* spell rids him of these effects.

Cringing and mewling, Gash approaches the party with arms out and head down. He speaks in both Gnoll and Abyssal. If the characters can't understand him, he pantomimes helpful gestures and beckons them to follow him.

> "Powerful masters," the gnoll whines. "You honor us by your presence. Seek you passage through the maze? The Spiral of the Great Horned King? I can help. Yes. Trust Gash and he will see you through the maze, he will."

Any aggressive action sends Gash skittering back into the maze and to his masters. If the characters capture him, he shrieks and screams, drawing one **minotaur** to investigate the racket.

Accepting Gash's offer transforms the cringing gnoll into a dutiful guide. He leads the characters through passage after passage, choosing directions seemingly at random until the characters encounter the minotaurs. If the battle turns against the minotaurs, Gash flees.

If the adventurers show pity or kindness, Gash becomes confused, as he has never experienced such things. A character can befriend the gnoll with a successful DC 20 Charisma (Persuasion) check. If any character uses magical healing on Gash, the check is automatically successful.

If the characters befriend Gash, he warns them to turn back, flee, and never return. He says his masters are vile minotaurs who wait in the maze, eager to kill all trespassers. If asked, Gash explains that the minotaurs spared his life in exchange for leading travelers into the maze. If the characters insist on entering the maze, Gash goes with them, trying to keep his new friends safe. If the characters defeat the minotaurs and move deeper into the Labyrinth, Gash can accompany them as a follower and guide, giving the characters advantage on Wisdom (Survival) checks to avoid becoming lost in the Labyrinth.

INTO THE MAZE

The minotaurs' maze fills a region of the Underdark one mile on each side. A network of corridors climbing up to higher levels and descending to lower ones by way of ramps, the maze requires time, attention, and patience to navigate. The corridors are 10 feet wide and tall, faced with stone blocks mortared into place. Bits of flesh and bone litter the floor, and splashes of blood cover the walls.

When the characters enter the maze, have them choose their pace (fast, normal, or slow). It takes 1 hour to navigate the maze at a fast pace, 2 hours at a normal pace, or 3 hours at a slow pace. Halfway through the journey, the navigator must make a DC 15 Wisdom (Survival) check. A fast pace imposes a −5 penalty to the check. A slow pace grants a +5 bonus. On a success, the characters find their way out. On a failure, the characters must start the journey from the beginning.

The longer it takes the characters to navigate through the maze, the greater the risk of encountering the creatures within it. Every 30 minutes the party spends in the maze, roll a d20 and consult the Maze Encounters table to see what, if anything, the characters meet.

If Gash was attacked by the characters and fled into the maze, he does his best to bring threats down on them, in which case roll two d20s and take the higher result. If Gash is friendly to the party and accompanying them, he tries to steer them away from danger, in which case roll two d20s and take the lower result.

GASH THE GNOLL

MAZE ENCOUNTERS

d20	Encounter
1–10	No encounter
11–12	Corpse
13–14	Gnawed bones
15–17	2d4 **gnolls**
18–20	1d6 **minotaurs**

CORPSE

The characters stumble upon the headless remains of a butchered corpse belonging to a dead dwarf, gnoll, human, or svirfneblin.

GNAWED BONES

A pile of cracked and gnawed bones is laid out around a pool of dried blood.

GNOLL PACK

A frenzied group of 2d4 **gnolls** is lost in the maze. The gnolls attack any creatures they see.

MINOTAURS

These bloodthirsty minotaurs are hunting gnolls but attack any other creatures they happen upon.

Treasure. The first time the characters fight the minotaurs, one of them carries 32 ep and 22 cp in a pouch made from a human face with the eyes and mouth sewn shut. The second time the characters encounter minotaurs, one of them wears silver caps (worth 25 gp each) on the ends of its horns.

FILTHRIDDENS

Filthriddens was, until recently, a shanty town of Underdark exiles and refugees. The greatest threat to inhabitants—apart from food shortages—was the minotaurs that raided the settlement from time to time, dragging off screaming prisoners to meet a grisly fate. The recent arrival of the demon lords changed things. A group of minotaurs was on its way to raid Filthriddens when Yeenoghu and a pack of his frenzied followers tore through this part of the Labyrinth, catching the minotaurs off guard and slaughtering them. The sole witness to this carnage was Grisha, an escaped human slave of the drow. Yeenoghu's intercession saved him from the minotaurs.

Yeenoghu and his pack moved on, but Grisha took the head of a slain minotaur and brought it back to Filthriddens. The skull became a talisman as Grisha named Yeenoghu as the new protector and patron of Filthriddens. Residents who opposed this dark worship were exiled or executed in short order. The cult of Yeenoghu now controls the settlement, and Grisha rules with an iron fist. He senses the power of Yeenoghu in all things—and particularly in the way in which cultists have begun to rise as undead ghouls after death.

GRISHA'S GREETING

Filthriddens lies 48 miles from the Spiral of the Horned King, deeper in the Labyrinth. Kurr (see "Random Encounters") or Gash (see "Gash the Gnoll") might lead the characters here if they don't find it on their own.

> The cavern that opens up ahead looks like a settlement, with tents and crudely built shanties lining its irregular walls. It appears deserted except for a lone human male kneeling within a circle of burning torchstalk mushrooms in the center of the cave and two ragged figures lurking near a zurkhwood door set into a wall thirty feet distant. The figure in the circle is praying over a rotting minotaur head but stands when he sees you. He's a thin human, and his face and arms are streaked with dry blood.
>
> "Friends," he says, "I have heard the call and I hope you have too. With my own eyes, I saw our Great Lord Yeenoghu slaughter the minotaurs that had plagued us. Now we are free and strong with his blessings. We feast while we live, and thanks to our lord, we will also feast when we are dead. If you've heard the call, come. Join my pack and feel the strength of Yeenoghu."
>
> The figure smiles as he speaks, revealing teeth filed to sharp points.

Filthriddens is contained within a cave roughly 100 feet long and 60 feet wide. The characters enter from a natural tunnel along one of the shorter walls, with another tunnel exiting on the opposite side. Much of the cave is taken up with crude shanties. Most of them stand empty, their inhabitants either exiled or dead.

Grisha (see appendix C) can recount the history of Filthriddens and how Yeenoghu saved its denizens from the oppression of the minotaurs. He can also reveal how he spent years as a slave of the drow. Grisha seeks new disciples to grow his cult's power.

Twelve **cultists** (a mix of shield dwarves, halflings, and humans) support Grisha if a fight breaks out. Ten of them are hidden in the shanties. Two more stand next to a zurkhwood door, beyond which lies a small side cave where cultists who have died and risen as undead are kept. If battle erupts, the cultists open the door and release six **ghouls**. The ghouls ignore the cultists as long as there are other creatures to feed on.

March to Nowhere

The Labyrinth is aptly named, for even the most resolute of explorers can become lost in its depths, as a number of modrons discovered to their dismay. Separated long ago from their fellows during the Great Modron March, these modrons have been wandering the Underdark for a long time.

As the party travels deeper into the Labyrinth, any character with a passive Wisdom (Perception) score of 15 or higher hears the sounds of marching feet off in the distance. To investigate the source of the noise, the characters must travel for 15 minutes through cramped tunnels requiring as much climbing as crawling. At the end of this time, the adventurers emerge onto a shelf 15 feet up the wall of a broad, straight tunnel some 20 feet high.

> A curious procession of creatures marches along the tunnel below your position. Twelve of the creatures are identical. Each has a round body, spindly arms and legs, a pair of fluttering wings rising above its arms, and a single eye staring out over a wide, smiling mouth. At the column's head stands a creature that looks like an inverted pyramid held up by six legs. It scuttles like a crab. On each side of its body, an eye is set above a mouth. Under the mouth, a single arm grips a spear in its hand.

Twelve **monodrones** and a **tridrone** have been wandering the Labyrinth since the last Great Modron March. The modrons became separated from their fellows and trapped here. Unable to find their way back to Mechanus, the modrons have been pressing on (and on), knowing that they must find their way back or be destroyed in the process.

The extended march has taxed the modrons to their limit. Most show signs of the frustration of being unable to fulfill their mission. The tridrone has managed to keep the group together, but it feels responsible for their collective fate and their failure to return home. Even if the characters have the ability to communicate with the modrons, the monodrones' ability to communicate is all but spent (see the "Roleplaying the Modrons" sidebar).

The tridrone can be very communicative—provided the characters have a way to speak with it and can allay its suspicions. A character can persuade the tridrone of the party's good intentions with a successful DC 15 Charisma (Persuasion) check. They have advantage on the check if the party includes one or more modrons.

Once convinced of the characters' friendly intentions, the tridrone tells them that it and its fellows are on a mission of supreme importance, though it doesn't reveal the nature of that mission. A character can puzzle out the reason why the modrons might be here by making a DC 20 Intelligence (Arcana) check. Success indicates that the character recalls stories about the Great Modron March, which occurs every 289 years and sees a vast army of modrons marching across the Outer Planes. If the check succeeds by 5 or more, the character also knows the last march happened over two

---

ROLEPLAYING THE MODRONS

Modrons have no sense of individuality. They are a collective and refer to themselves as "we" or "us." As a result, modrons don't understand individuality in others. When speaking to a group, the tridrone might focus its attention on the adventurer it believes to be at the top of the party's hierarchy even while talking to another.

Monodrones can normally relay messages up to forty-eight words long. However, years of wandering have degraded these creatures so that they can speak only a few words or phrases before sputtering off into clicking and popping noises. Among the words the monodrones repeat are "march," "Mechanus," "seventeen" (the number of cycles of the plane of Mechanus that mark the Great Modron March), and "lost."

hundred years ago, and that these modrons are likely remnants of that march. The tridrone doesn't admit this (not wanting to acknowledge its failure), though it might be convinced to follow the characters if they offer to lead the modrons out of the Labyrinth. Additionally, the tridrone knows the Labyrinth well, and befriending the modrons grants characters a +5 bonus to Wisdom (Survival) checks made to navigate the region.

The tridrone warns the characters to avoid the center of the Labyrinth, explaining that a malfunctioning "Orderer" is there. The characters might know the device by its other name: the Maze Engine. Because the device was built on Mechanus, its magical energy resonates with the modrons. The tridrone explains that an Orderer is designed to bring order to chaos by altering reality. A malfunctioning Orderer can be very dangerous, however, altering reality in unexpected ways. The tridrone knows exactly how far it is from the device. Because its knowledge of magic is limited and its focus on rejoining the Great Modron March is all-consuming, the tridrone has never thought about whether the Orderer might provide a solution to the modrons' predicament. If the characters express an interest in investigating this possibility, the tridrone leads the party to the center of the Labyrinth where the Maze Engine is found.

YEENOGHU'S HUNT

About twelve miles from their encounter with the modrons, as they travel through the Labyrinth, the characters hear sounds of howling in the distance off and on over the course of many hours. Sometimes the sounds get closer or fade away, echoing strangely through the surrounding tunnels.

Eventually, the characters enter a smaller tunnel leading upward. As they move forward, they can clearly hear the sound of fighting ahead. Bestial howls and yips can be heard, along with deeper roaring. A successful DC 13 Intelligence check recognizes the language of the battle cries as Gnoll. The characters can retreat

HUNTED BY YEENOGHU

If you'd like Yeenoghu to play more of a role in this chapter of the adventure, it's easy to do so. When the gnolls killed by the characters do not rejoin the hunt, the demon lord circles back to the site of the goristro's demise and discovers his slain minions—and also picks up the scent of the adventurers.

Later in the adventure, Yeenoghu hunts down the characters to make them pay for their impudence (ideally when they are much higher in level). Before the final confrontation, give the characters hints that they have become the demon lord's prey. They might face an increasing number of gnoll ambushes, for example. One or more of their attackers might refer to them as "prey of Yeenoghu," or otherwise taunt them by speaking of their impending doom.

The characters should have time to prepare for the fight they know is coming, and to think about tactics other than facing Yeenoghu in straight-up combat. For example, becoming the demon lord's quarry might work to their advantage later in the campaign, making them the perfect bait to lure Yeenoghu into a trap in chapter 17, "Against the Demon Lords."

away from the sounds of combat, but doing so means backtracking for six miles to find another route. If they continue ahead, they are confronted with a grisly scene. Though the characters likely have no firsthand experience of a goristro, they recognize the creature from the information provided to them by Vizeran DeVir.

> As you move forward, the sounds of furious battle grow louder. The tunnel ends at a ledge twenty feet above the floor of a large cavern, giving you a perfect view of the conflict below.
>
> On the shores of an underground lake, a pack of frenzied gnolls and hyenas surrounds a demon standing nearly twenty feet tall, with massive arms, clawed hands, cloven hooves, and the head of a bull. This is a goristro, whose heart Vizeran DeVir has instructed you to claim.
>
> Leading the gnolls is a figure of fearful countenance, twelve feet tall with the head of a snarling, amber-eyed hyena. He wields a massive triple flail, whose whirling heads smash into the larger goristro. The gnolls howl their master's name as he strikes swiftly, again and again: "Yeenoghu! Yeenoghu!"
>
> The larger demon roars, slashing with its bull's horns and flailing with its claws, but to no avail. Yeenoghu evades or shrugs off its attacks, even as gnoll archers pepper it with arrows. Then the gnolls swarm the goristro as it begins to falter, bringing it crashing to the ground.
>
> In less than a minute, the battle is won. The demon lord Yeenoghu pulls back the goristro's head by the horns and rips out its throat with his teeth. He throws back his head and his howl of triumph echoes through the chamber, shaking the stones themselves. Several hyenas nipping at Yeenoghu's heels leap onto the goristro's corpse and begin feasting on its flesh. As you watch, these hyenas transform into gnolls.

Any adventurer witnessing this horrible tableau must succeed on a DC 12 Wisdom saving throw or gain one level of madness (see "Madness" in chapter 2). If this causes the character to suffer a bout of indefinite madness, determine the nature of the madness using the Madness of Yeenoghu table in appendix D.

Yeenoghu (see appendix D) has been wandering the Underdark since he was first summoned, and the adventurers have run across him and his pack. The characters' only advantage at this moment is that they haven't yet been detected. Considering their level at this stage of the adventure, the players might be creating new characters quite soon if they dare confront the demon lord.

If the characters stay hidden and observe, Yeenoghu leaves in short order. He is restless and eager for new prey. Yeenoghu gathers up most of the gnolls and hyenas and leads them down a tunnel on the right side of the cavern. Eight **gnolls** led by a **gnoll pack lord** remain in the cavern, feasting on the goristro's corpse.

If the characters want to continue forward, the gnolls and hyenas need to be dealt with. Alternatively, if the characters are indecisive or spend too long debating the best course of action, the gnoll pack lord sniffs out the intruders. When it realizes that enemies are present, the pack lord howls to draw the attention of its followers.

DEVELOPMENT

Another tunnel on the opposite side of the cavern heads off in a different direction than where Yeenoghu led his pack. Characters who defeat the remaining gnolls can continue on their way without losing any more time.

The close brush with Yeenoghu pays dividends to the adventurers by delivering two components of Vizeran's ritual into their hands. The first is the heart of the goristro, which the characters can remove from its corpse. The massive heart is the size of a small trunk and weighs nearly one hundred pounds. Any characters close to it while it is being transported imagine that they can occasionally hear it beating. A character who carries the heart, even in a *bag of holding* or similar extradimensional space, makes saving throws against madness with disadvantage.

The second component takes the form of a few spatters of a demon lord's blood. A successful DC 10 Wisdom (Perception) check finds some of Yeenoghu's black blood on the fallen goristro's horns.

GALLERY OF ANGELS

This cavern lies deep inside the Labyrinth and contains another ritual component that Vizeran needs.

> The passage you follow climbs upward as it corkscrews through stone, finally emerging through the floor of a large cavern. The ceiling arches sixty feet overhead, bristling with stalactites that drip water onto stalagmites rising from the uneven and broken floor. Here and there between the stalagmites, several statues of winged humanoids are set in poses of suffering and anguish. Some cover their faces, while others claw at them. Others reach toward the ceiling, their faces twisted into expressions of longing.

This chamber houses the petrified remains of eight fallen angels, condemned by the gods to pass the ages in the dark depths. Each appears to have been carved from stone in some position of fear, suffering, hatred, or longing. Each statue is spotted with lichen and marred by mineral deposits, which have crystallized out of the water dripping from the ceiling over uncounted years.

Even though they are transformed into stone statues, the fallen angels remain very much alive, their petrified bodies having become prisons for their minds and souls. They remember who they were. They know what they did and why they are here. They know everything transpiring around them. Yet they can do nothing. They are trapped forever, and the isolation, darkness, and endless torment of their fate have driven them mad. No

spell can undo the angels' curse or free them from their petrified state.

FALLEN ANGELS

The angels can communicate, albeit in a limited fashion, with living creatures that touch them.

A character who makes physical contact with an angel (even through gloves or some other protective covering) knows that angel's name and experiences the effect described below. If you wish, you can roll a d8 to determine which angel a character touches, rerolling any repeat results. Unless specified otherwise, the effect is instantaneous. While there's no limit to the number of creatures that can touch an angel and be affected by it, a creature that touches an angel and triggers its effect can't trigger that particular angel's effect again until 24 hours have elapsed.

ANAYA

This angel reaches toward the ceiling, its face a mask of hatred. A creature that makes contact with this angel must make a DC 15 Wisdom saving throw, taking 3d6 psychic damage on a failed save or half as much damage on a successful one.

BAATRAL

This angel appears to be reaching out as if offering something. A character making contact with the angel must succeed on a DC 15 Charisma saving throw or become charmed for 1 minute.

While the character is charmed, the angel has a telepathic link with the character as long as it and the character remain on the same plane of existence. The angel issues commands to the character, and the character does its best to obey those commands if it is conscious. The angel typically commands a character to kill, maim, rob, or otherwise harm its companions.

Each time an affected character takes damage, he or she makes a new Charisma saving throw against the effect. If the saving throw succeeds, the effect on it ends.

HARAJIN

This angel points at a spot on the cavern wall, and its mouth hangs open in horror. A character who makes contact with the angel hears horrific screaming and must succeed on a DC 15 Wisdom saving throw or gain one level of madness (see "Madness" in chapter 2).

LORABELIOS

This angel stands feet apart, head downcast, arms at its sides. A character making contact with the angel hears a soft voice say in Common, "Do not lose hope." The character's next Wisdom saving throw is made with advantage.

NEMEVON

This angel holds its hands to its face, concealing its visage. Upon making contact with this angel, the character hears a soft voice repeating two words over and over in the Celestial language: "Kill me." There is no obvious way for the characters to do so, however. The voice persists even if the angel is shattered.

SILNIA

This angel covers its eyes with its arm but appears to be smiling. A character who touches the angel must make a DC 15 Wisdom saving throw. On a failed save, terrifying nightmares haunt the character's sleep during his or her next long rest. The character derives no benefits from that rest and, upon waking, takes 3d6 psychic damage.

TAMIEL

This angel kneels on the floor and buries its face in its arms. A character making contact with the angel hears a soft voice say in Common, "What would you know? Ask and I shall answer." The character must make a DC 15 Intelligence saving throw. On a failed save, the character takes 3d6 psychic damage and gains one level of madness. On a success, the character can ask two questions. The angel replies as if the character had successfully cast the *contact other plane* spell.

ZAROD

This angel claws at its eyes, and its face appears torn and rent. When a character makes contact with the angel, it invites the character to ask a single question concerning a specific goal, event, or activity to occur within seven days. The angel replies as if the character had successfully cast the *divination* spell.

DEVELOPMENT

The adventurers can chisel or break off stone feathers from the angels' wings. One each from six different angels fulfills the requirements for Vizeran's ritual, although characters can take more feathers if they want.

Other creatures in the Labyrinth avoid this cavern, making it a safe place for the party to take a long rest.

THE MAZE ENGINE

Deep within the Labyrinth lies the Maze Engine—a mechanical, magically powered device capable of altering reality. Modrons refer to the device as an Orderer because it was designed is to bring order to chaos. If the characters activate the Maze Engine, it has the potential to aid their fight against the demon lords.

The engine looks like a working model of the Great Wheel (see chapter 2, "Creating a Multiverse," in the *Dungeon Master's Guide*). It's a 20-foot-diameter sphere built of 1-foot-wide bands of magically hardened and shaped bronze, engraved with arcane symbols. Gaps in the bands show various gears and articulation arms within the sphere, which rotate and shift to represent the relationships between the various known planes of existence.

Characters might learn about the existence of the Maze Engine from the beholder Karazikar (see chapter 13) or from Vizeran, who has heard rumors about an ancient reality-altering device. Characters might also learn about the engine from Karazikar's modron prisoner or from the modrons lost in the Labyrinth (see "March to Nowhere").

Information about the Maze Engine can also be found in Gravenhollow (see chapter 11). The characters could

experience a vision of a journey to the Labyrinth in the library, or read an account of the device in its archives.

REACHING THE ENGINE

Located forty-eight miles southeast of the Gallery of Angels, the Maze Engine is wedged halfway down a 20-foot-wide, 100-foot-deep crevasse located in the middle of a large cavern. The bottom of the crevasse is filled with magma. A shimmering curtain of heat rises from the crevasse and makes the cavern hot and dry.

The roughly spherical engine is 40 feet below the top of the crevasse and 40 feet above the magma. It can be reached by magic or by climbing down to it. The sheer sides of the crevasse require a successful DC 12 Strength (Athletics) check to climb. On a failed check, a character makes no progress and dislodges loose stones that clatter down the crevasse into the magma. If the check fails by 5 or more, the climber falls into the magma. Any creature that enters the magma or starts its turn there takes 42 (12d6) fire damage. Every foot moved in the magma costs 5 feet of movement.

SLAUGHTERTUSK

Having just recently found the Maze Engine, Baphomet has set a **nalfeshnee** named Slaughtertusk to watch over the crevasse and prevent any creature from approaching the device. Slaughtertusk would rather be helping the Horned King track down and kill Yeenoghu. The nalfeshnee is bored with its assigned task, although it knows better than to disobey the Horned King. Still, rather than immediately destroying any intruders, it toys with them for as long as possible.

Slaughtertusk is happy to let a fight drag on, feasting on its enemies' pain before finally slaying them. If reduced to fewer than 100 hit points, it uses its Summon Demon feature (see the "Variant: Demon Summoning" sidebar in the "Demons" entry of the *Monster Manual*) and tries to summon 1d6 **vrocks**. It has a 50 percent chance of succeeding.

Slaughtertusk is a bully at heart and begs for its life if the adventurers have it at their mercy, promising to tell them the secrets of the Maze Engine or anything else they want. At the first opportunity, it teleports away, summoning demonic aid to cover its retreat if possible.

ACTIVATING THE ENGINE

A successful DC 15 Intelligence (Arcana) check is needed to activate the device by puzzling out its array of gears and levers. It then takes 12 rounds for the engine to "align itself" and activate its magical effect. If an initiative order hasn't already been established by the time the engine activates, have everyone in the party roll initiative.

If the tridrone from "March to Nowhere" accompanies the characters, it can instruct them how to activate the Maze Engine without a check and inform them of how long it takes for the magical effect to occur.

SHAKING LOOSE

The engine, which weighs two tons, is ordinarily set on a solid stone surface. Being wedged partway down a crevasse makes its operation more problematic. When the engine is activated, the vibration of its clacking gears sends showers of loose stones down the crevasse walls.

Once the engine has been activated, it "acts" on initiative count 15.

MEPHIT MADNESS

On the round after the Maze Engine activates, two **magma mephits** fly out of the magma on initiative count 10. Two more **magma mephits** emerge from the magma each round thereafter on the same initiative count, until a dozen mephits have appeared. The mephits attack anyone on or near the Maze Engine.

SHAKE, RATTLE, AND ROLL

At the end of its turn during round 3, the engine shifts. Any creature standing on it must make a DC 10 Dexterity saving throw. If the save fails by 5 or more, the creature is knocked off the engine into the magma. Otherwise, a creature failing its save slides down the spherical side of the engine but automatically grabs one of its bands before falling. The creature can use an action to try to climb back onto the engine, doing so with a successful DC 10 Strength (Athletics) check.

At the end of its turn during round 6, the engine shifts again. The effect is the same as described above, except that a creature hanging onto one of the engine's bands has disadvantage on the saving throw.

If a creature falls from the Maze Engine, another creature adjacent to the falling creature and hanging onto one of the engine's bands can attempt to use a free hand to grab the falling creature, doing so with a successful DC 10 Dexterity saving throw. A creature saved in this manner can use its action to try to climb back onto the engine, doing so with a successful DC 13 Strength (Athletics) check. If the check fails and the creature's weight exceeds the carrying capacity of the creature that grabbed it (see "Lifting and Carrying" in chapter 7 of the *Player's Handbook*), the creature grabbing it must succeed on a DC 15 Strength check at the start of its next turn or lose its grip on the fallen creature, which then plunges into the magma.

At the end of each of its turns starting on round 9, the Maze Engine slides down the crevasse, dropping 10 feet toward the magma each round. Any creature on the engine must make a successful DC 15 Dexterity saving throw each time it drops down to avoid being thrown off. Resolve the effects as described above. On its turn during round 13, the Maze Engine sinks into the magma and is destroyed.

SHUTTING DOWN THE ENGINE

The engine shuts down if any part of it comes into contact with an *antimagic field* or if it is targeted by a successful *dispel magic* (DC 19). Otherwise, it can only be shut down by a *wish* spell or divine intervention.

Maze Engine Effects

The Maze Engine was damaged when the crevasse opened underneath it and swallowed it up. The engine can't be repaired, and once activated, it does strange and unpredictable things on each of its turns until it is deactivated or destroyed.

On each of the engine's turns, roll a d100 and consult the Maze Engine Effects table to determine what the engine does.

Maze Engine Effects

d100	Effect
01	The engine emits a flash of golden light. All magic items within 300 feet of the engine are destroyed, except for artifacts, which are cast into the Astral Plane.
02–08	Arcs of white light play across the surface of the engine until the end of its turn.
09–10	The engine emits a bright flash of white light. All player characters are transported back in time, as they are now, to the moment when the adventure began. They appear in Velkynvelve's slave pen, unshackled and unbound, with all of their experience points, abilities, equipment, and memories.
11–15	The engine makes a loud "WHAAAH" sound until the start of its next turn. For as long as the sound lasts, the engine projects an *antimagic field* (as the spell) around itself.
16–19	The hollow interior of the engine flickers with crimson light until the end of its turn, whereupon one dead character or NPC of the DM's choice is restored to life, as though subjected to a *resurrection* spell. The revived creature appears in a safe, unoccupied space within 120 feet of the engine.
20–22	The engine spews slippery goo that splatters across its outer surface. Saving throws to avoid being knocked off the engine and ability checks made to climb the engine have disadvantage until the engine's next turn.
23–27	The engine crackles with lightning. All creatures within 30 feet of the engine must make a DC 18 Dexterity saving throw or take 10d6 lightning damage. A target made primarily of metal or wearing metal armor has disadvantage on its saving throw.
28–32	The engine hums until the end of its turn, at which point a **green slaad** appears in a safe space within 120 feet of the engine. The slaad rolls initiative and, on its turn, attacks any other creatures it sees.
33–35	The engine groans loudly and turns each creature within 120 feet of it invisible. A creature's invisibility lasts until it attacks or casts a spell.

d100	Effect
36–39	Loud whispers emanate from the hollow interior of the engine. Each character in direct contact with the engine can increase one ability score of his or her choice by 2, to a maximum of 24.
40–43	Multicolored arcs of light play across the surface of the engine, which casts a *polymorph* spell (save DC 18) on each creature within 20 feet of it. Any creature that fails the saving throw is polymorphed into a **flying snake**.
44–48	The engine spits out multicolored gemstones. Any character within 20 feet of the engine can use his or her reaction to catch a 500 gp gem with a free hand. The rest of the gemstones fall into the magma and are destroyed.
49–52	The engine emits a flash of yellowish-white light. A randomly determined magic item appears in a safe location within 120 feet of the engine. Roll on Magic Item Table G in the *Dungeon Master's Guide* to determine what appears.
53–57	The engine emits a flash of green light. Each creature in direct contact with the engine must succeed on a DC 18 Constitution saving throw or take 10d6 + 40 force damage. If this damage reduces the target to 0 hit points, it is disintegrated. A disintegrated creature and everything it is wearing and carrying, except artifacts, are reduced to fine dust.
58–60	The engine flickers with blue light and casts *faerie fire*, targeting all creatures within 20 feet of it (save DC 18). The spell's effect has a duration of 1 minute.
61–66	The engine spews harmless, multicolored sparks until the start of its next turn.
67–70	The engine emits a flash of violet light. Each creature within 20 feet of the engine must succeed on a DC 18 Constitution saving throw or be petrified until the engine's next turn.
71–76	The engine plays calliope music. The next time this result is rolled, the music stops.
77–80	The engine makes a horrible grinding noise. All lawful creatures within 30 feet of it regain all of their hit points.
81–00	The engine emits a flash of violet-white light. All extraplanar creatures within 100 miles of the engine instantly return to their native planes of existence.

Development

If you want to add tension to the end of this encounter, have the Maze Engine trigger a minor eruption after it sinks into the magma, causing the magma to bubble up out of the crevasse, spill into the cavern and nearby tunnels, and force the adventurers and their allies to stay ahead of the magma surge.

Chapter 15: The City of Spiders

The center of the chaos and madness now spreading throughout the Underdark is the great drow city of Menzoberranzan. Few of the city's drow residents know that the Demon Queen of Spiders is behind the summoning ritual that brought the demon lords to the Underdark—and that the reward for their faith in Lolth might well be their destruction.

Menzoberranzan was the site of Demogorgon's appearance in the Underdark, and the lash of his tentacles and the crushing tread of his clawed feet left a trail of broken buildings, bodies, and minds. Unfortunately for the drow, the worst may be yet to come if the renegade drow archmage Vizeran DeVir won the adventurers' support for his plan to use a powerful ritual to draw the demon lords and their fiendish servants out of the Underdark and set them against each other. As the demon lords destroy each other in the material world, their dark essences will be drawn back to the Abyss once more. But one of the key parts of Vizeran's plan involves the characters' making sure that the City of Spiders plays host to this final, devastating battle.

Goals

If the characters are working with Vizeran DeVir, they have two goals in the City of Spiders: obtain Gromph Baenre's demon summoning grimoire, and place Vizeran's talisman in Menzoberranzan to draw the demon lords there for an epic showdown.

Placing the "Dark Heart"

After their adventures in the Wormwrithings and the Labyrinth, the characters can return to Araj to deliver the components they have collected to Vizeran DeVir. Over ten days, the drow archmage uses those components to craft a talisman that looks and feels like a five-pound black heart carved of black stone. Imbued with arcane and fiendish power, the *dark heart* talisman acts as a beacon when Vizeran's ritual is performed, drawing all demons presently loose in the Underdark. The talisman radiates faint conjuration magic even before it is activated, but it's primarily a focus for the power of the ritual rather than a source of power itself.

Vizeran's plan calls for the adventurers to place the *dark heart* in Menzoberranzan. Vizeran would prefer for the *dark heart* to be left wherever the characters find Gromph Baenre's grimoire in Sorcere—the center of wizardly training in Menzoberranzan. However, Vizeran tells the characters that placing the talisman anywhere in the City of Spiders will do.

OBTAINING GROMPH'S GRIMOIRE

Gromph Baenre's grimoire contains notes and references for his ill-fated demon summoning. Vizeran knows from research at Gravenhollow that the grimoire is in Gromph's sanctum in the tower of Sorcere. To reach the grimoire, the characters need to penetrate one of the most important and well-protected places in the City of Spiders.

Fortunately for the characters, Vizeran isn't without allies in the city. The Council of Spiders is a secret alliance of drow mages who want to overthrow Lolth's priestesses. The council has infiltrated Sorcere, the city's academy for arcane magic, and has sympathizers among male drow wizards. Vizeran has already contacted his allies, who have agreed to help the party gain access to the tower and Gromph's sanctum (see "Sorcere" later in this chapter).

GOING TO MENZOBERRANZAN

Seventy-two miles of twisting passageways separate Araj from Menzoberranzan. Vizeran has a secret route between the two, which he allows the characters to use if they agree to follow his plan. Otherwise, the characters must travel to Menzoberranzan by commonly known routes monitored by drow scouts, patrols, and outposts. If the characters opt to use Vizeran's secret route, the drow archmage's apprentice, Grin Ousstyl (see chapter 12), accompanies the characters at Vizeran's behest, serving as their guide.

Vizeran strongly suggests that the characters leave their expeditionary force at Araj, asserting that a small team has the best chance of infiltrating the drow city.

STATISTICAL MODIFICATIONS FOR DROW NPCs

When using the generic stat blocks in appendix B of the *Monster Manual* to represent drow NPCs, assume that the drow are neutral evil and speak Elvish and Undercommon. Also give those NPCs the following additional features.

Fey Ancestry. The drow has advantage on saving throws against being charmed, and magic can't put the drow to sleep.

Innate Spellcasting. The drow's innate spellcasting ability is Charisma (spell save DC equal to 10 + the drow's Charisma modifier). The drow can innately cast the following spells, requiring no material components:

At will: *dancing lights*
1/day each: *darkness, faerie fire, levitate* (self only)

Sunlight Sensitivity. While in sunlight, the drow has disadvantage on attack rolls, as well as on Wisdom (Perception) checks that rely on sight.

VIZERAN'S SECRET ROUTE

Grin Ousstyl shows the characters a secret door in the cavern wall outside of Vizeran's tower. Beyond this door is a long and winding tunnel that took Vizeran centuries to create using stone-shaping spells. The passage, which is free of monsters and hazards, ends at a secret door at the bottom of the Westrift in Menzoberranzan. The trip from Araj to the city takes twelve days on foot, during which time Grin says very little. Any character who succeeds on a DC 15 Wisdom (Insight) check can tell that the drow mage is troubled by something, although he refuses to share his private thoughts and concerns.

If the characters read Grin's thoughts or compel him to speak using magic or torture, Grin reveals that he has misgivings about Vizeran's plan. Though he has no affection for the matron mothers and priestesses that govern Menzoberranzan, Grin has no wish to see his birthplace—and its people—destroyed. If Grin sees firsthand the destruction wrought by Demogorgon's rampage through the city, he becomes even more reluctant to see Vizeran's plan through (see "A Change of Heart" later in this chapter).

If the characters prod Grin for information about Menzoberranzan and what they can expect to find there, he relates the information contained in "The Way of Lolth" section. He can also describe the major districts of the city.

OTHER ROUTES

Characters who can't avail themselves of Vizeran's secret route or choose not to use it must find another way to Menzoberranzan. There are many routes to choose from, such that the party can approach the City of Spiders from literally any direction. However, all of these routes are known to the drow. The characters might have encountered a drow force on a previous attempt to reach the city (see "March on Menzoberranzan" in chapter 10). If so, they already know what they're up against. Even if they decline to use Vizeran's secret route, the drow archmage recommends that the characters take Grin Ousstyl with them, not so much as a guide but to help the party talk its way past drow patrols.

The demonic invasion has put Menzoberranzan's defenses on high alert, making it even harder than normal for non-drow to approach the city safely by any known route. While the characters are within 18 miles (three days' travel) of the city, use the Drow Patrols table to determine random encounters instead of using the tables in chapter 2. Once every hour, roll a d20 and consult the table to determine what, if anything, the party encounters.

DROW DEFENSES

d20	Encounter
1–10	No encounter
11–14	Drow patrol A
15–17	Drow patrol B
18–19	Drow patrol C
20	Drow patrol D

Drow Patrol A

The standard patrol consists of two drow **scouts** mounted on **giant riding lizards** (use the statistics at the end of chapter 8). Characters who can see out to a range of 120 or more and are moving at a normal pace spot the drow scouts with a successful DC 16 Wisdom (Perception) check. If the characters are moving at a fast pace, they take a −5 penalty to their checks.

Unless the characters are moving at a slow pace and being stealthy, the drow spot them with their darkvision and withdraw to an outpost located a mile away. Defending the drow outpost are a female **drow elite warrior** (the commander), a male **drow mage**, and sixteen **drow**. The outpost is a four-story tower carved out of a 60-foot-tall, 15-foot-wide column in the middle of a 75-foot-diameter cavern. Both the cavern and the outpost are unlit. A secret door in the column's base leads to the tower interior, but finding it requires a thorough search and a successful DC 20 Wisdom (Perception) check. Arrow slits on each floor allow the drow to cast spells and make ranged attacks in every direction while enjoying three-quarters cover against attacks from the cavern.

If the drow scouts escape and the characters don't follow them, the scouts report to the outpost commander, who organizes a hunting party consisting of her and eight drow (leaving the mage and eight drow to staff the outpost). Use the drow pursuit rules in chapter 2, and assume a pursuit level of 4.

Drow Patrol B

The characters encounter a **drow elite warrior** and 1d8 **drow** fighting a **hezrou** demon. The hezrou has 2d10 + 45 hit points remaining, while each drow has 2d6 hit points remaining. The drow elite warrior isn't wounded. Without interference, the drow slay the demon, with the drow elite warrior and 1d4 − 1 drow surviving the encounter. If the characters get involved, the encounter becomes a three-way fight, as neither the drow nor the demon are interested in forming an alliance.

Characters can keep their distance and avoid the altercation. However, any drow who survive the battle head to the nearest drow outpost 1d4 miles away. After hearing the survivors' report, the outpost commander organizes a hunting party to search for the characters, as described in "Drow Patrol A."

Drow Patrol C

The characters encounter a drow patrol consisting of a **drow mage**, 2d4 **drow**, and a group of slaves. Roll a d8 and consult the Drow Slaves table to determine what slaves are present. Trolls fight to the death; other slaves attempt to flee if all the drow are killed.

Drow Slaves

d8	Slaves
1–2	3d6 derro (see appendix C)
3–4	3d6 goblins
5–6	3d6 orcs
7–8	2d6 quaggoths
9–10	1d6 trolls

Drow Patrol D

The characters encounter a **drow mage** riding on the back of a **stone golem** carved from stone and shaped like a giant spider. The mage rides in a howdah that provides half cover against attacks from the ground. Escorting the mage are 2d4 **drow elite warriors** mounted on **giant riding lizards** (use the statistics at the end of chapter 8). These drow fight to the death to protect their territory.

Treasure. The spider golem's eight eyes are six-inch-diameter red crystal orbs worth 1,000 gp each.

Menzoberranzan

Population: 20,000 drow plus thousands of slaves (of various races)

Government: Matriarchal theocracy worshiping Lolth, the Demon Queen of Spiders

Defense: Large standing army of trained drow warriors and mages, bolstered by armed slaves and magical wards; the citizens of the city create a formidable militia

Commerce: Well-trained slaves; various fungi, molds, and exotic creatures for food; poisons, potions, oils, and elixirs; jewelry, perfume, and silk

Organizations: The Ruling Council (comprised of the matron mothers of the eight most powerful drow noble houses in the city), the Church of Lolth (based in Arach-Tinilith), Bregan D'aerthe (company of drow spies, mercenaries, and assassins)

The City of Spiders is carved out of and built within a great cavern the drow call *Araurilcaurak*, its vault soaring a thousand feet above the stone floor. Drow dwellings and strongholds are carved from massive stalagmites and stalactites, connected with delicate-looking bridges of hardened spider silk and lit with coldly glowing eldritch fires.

Menzoberranzan: General Features

The following features can be found throughout the City of Spiders.

Light. Most streets and buildings are lit by eldritch green, blue, and violet lights as bright as torches (created with *continual flame* spells). Other areas are dark.

Shielded City. The drow have locked down their city in the wake of Demogorgon's rampage. For the duration of this adventure, creatures can't teleport into or out of Menzoberranzan. In addition, creatures, objects, and spaces within the city can't be targeted by divination spells or perceived through scrying sensors created by divination spells.

The Stone Curse. The "stone curse" is an ancient enchantment woven by the wizards of Sorcere to protect the city from cave-ins. Any character casting *earthquake*, *move earth*, or similar magic within the city triggers a *reverse gravity* spell (save DC 18) centered on the caster, which takes effect before the triggering spell is completed. The *reverse gravity* lasts for 1 minute, and is accompanied by a peal of thunder that alerts everyone nearby. The caster of the triggering spell must make a successful DC 18 Constitution saving throw to maintain concentration. On a failed check, the triggering spell fails.

THE DARK DOMINION

The rock surrounding the city is honeycombed with tunnels and passageways forming the Dark Dominion, a territory claimed by the drow but not part of the city proper. Home to all manner of Underdark denizens, this maze forms part of Menzoberranzan's defenses as well as its underworld—a dangerous place for dark dealings and clandestine meetings.

The Dark Dominion is a great place for random encounters. When it suits you, roll a d20 and consult the Dark Dominion Encounters table to determine what the party encounters, or choose an encounter that you like.

DARK DOMINION ENCOUNTERS

d20	Encounter
1–2	2d4 **bugbears**
3–4	Clandestine meeting
5	1d4 **driders**
6–10	Drow patrol
11–12	1d4 + 1 **drow spore servants** (see appendix C)
13–14	Escaped slaves
15–16	1d4 + 1 **goblins**
17–19	*Glyph of warding*
20	1d4 **intellect devourers**

BUGBEARS

The bugbears are branded with the mark of a drow house, identifying them as slaves. They try to sneak up on the party and score an easy kill.

CLANDESTINE MEETING

The party happens upon a meeting between a **drow** house representative and some outside business interest. The drow is escorted by 1d4 − 1 **bugbear** bodyguards. The individual with whom the drow is meeting can be any of the following.

Duergar Alchemist. This **duergar** is trying to procure rare alchemical ingredients or equipment (see the "Duergar Alchemist" sidebar in chapter 4 for statistical modifications).

Duergar Spy. This **duergar** from Gracklstugh is trying to bribe a drow for information about who is responsible for the demonic invasion.

Human Assassin. This **assassin** does dirty work for the drow and is being hired to eliminate someone on the surface world.

Khalessa Draga. If the characters haven't already encountered this Lords' Alliance spy, Khalessa (see "March on Menzoberranzan" at the end of chapter 10) is in her drow disguise, buying information of value to the alliance. When she sees the party, she ends her meeting and tries to find out why the characters are here. If the party includes one or more members of the Lords' Alliance, she offers to help them complete their mission. Otherwise, she is unwilling to break her cover.

DRIDERS

These outcasts perch atop high ledges or cling to the high ceiling, attacking with their bows while staying out of the range of melee weapons. A drider retreats if reduced to 60 hit points or fewer.

DROW PATROL

The characters encounter a patrol consisting of 2d4 **drow** led by a **drow elite warrior**. The patrol stops and questions any non-drow who aren't slaves, as well as drow they deem suspicious. It might take roleplaying or a successful DC 15 Wisdom (Deception or Persuasion) check to convince the patrol not to attack the party. If Grin Ousstyl is with the party, he quietly suggests that the characters offer the drow a bribe of at least 50 gp. If they do, the characters gain advantage on checks made to talk their way past the patrol.

Any sign of a large, armed, and potentially hostile group causes the patrol to retreat and seek reinforcements. If the characters remain in the area, the patrol returns with two additional patrols 1d10 minutes later.

DROW SPORE SERVANTS

These drow became infected with Zuggtmoy's spores and have transformed into spore servants. They silently observe the party but don't attack the characters unless threatened.

ESCAPED SLAVES

A group of 1d4 **commoners** (of any race) attempts to hide from the approaching party. If spotted, they beg the characters for mercy, explaining that they have escaped from their drow masters following "the great demon's rampage" and have been hiding in the tunnels ever since. The slaves can provide the characters with a detailed description of the attack, confirming that the demon lord Demogorgon was behind the destruction. The slaves are desperate to escape from the drow and pitifully grateful for any aid offered.

GOBLINS

The goblins beg for food. If the characters give them food or otherwise treat the goblins well, they show the party a secret door that opens into a forgotten tunnel. Roll a d10 and consult the Goblin Tunnel table to determine where the tunnel leads.

GOBLIN TUNNEL

d10	Tunnel Destination
1–2	Kyorbblivvin (see "Kyorbblivvin")
3–4	A hidden cave containing 1d4 **mind flayers**
5–6	A hidden cave in which the party can rest without having to worry about random encounters
7–8	A hidden cave containing 4d8 **goblins** and a **goblin boss**, who will trade a magic item in its possession for the equivalent of 30 days of rations (to determine the item, roll once on Magic Item Table C in chapter 8 of the *Dungeon Master's Guide*)
9–10	A trap door near the Bazaar (see "The Bazaar")

GLYPH OF WARDING

Drow priestesses are fond of placing *glyphs of warding* in the tunnels surrounding Menzoberranzan. Such a

glyph allows drow to pass safely but triggers whenever a non-drow passes by it. A drow *glyph of warding* has a spell save DC of 13 and an explosive runes effect (see the spell's description in the *Player's Handbook*).

INTELLECT DEVOURERS

Mind flayers like to send intellect devourers into the Dark Dominion in search of hosts, using them as spies to keep an eye on the drow city. These intellect devourers creep up behind the party and use their Devour Intellect attack against party members in the rear of the marching order.

CITY LOCATIONS

Characters who infiltrate Menzoberranzan might find themselves in one or more of the following areas or districts.

THE BAZAAR

This 750-foot-wide circle of bare bedrock is a crowded, untidy labyrinth of stalls, many of which were flattened or torn asunder by Demogorgon. Merchants who survived the attack are slowly returning to the Bazaar

and cleaning up the mess, but little business is happening here at present. Drow commoners go quietly about their business, heads down and hoods drawn, as drow patrols brutally stamp down anything that resembles theft or looting.

Characters moving through the Bazaar have at least one encounter with a drow patrol consisting of two **drow** mounted on **giant riding lizards** (see the end of chapter 8 for statistics). If one or more party members appear to be anything other than drow or slaves in the company of its drow master, the patrol immediately calls for reinforcements, which arrive in 1d4 rounds. These reinforcements consist of 3d4 **drow** on foot and 2d4 **giant spiders** that scuttle down from nearby rooftops.

THE BRAERYN

The Braeryn (also known as "the Stenchstreets") is a shantytown of ramshackle structures overlooking garbage-choked alleyways, inhabited by the dregs of drow society. Fallen priestesses, bankrupt merchants, escaped slaves, and the homeless or maimed are common here, as are visitors to the city who wish to go unnoticed.

The population of the Stenchstreets has swelled in the wake of Demogorgon's rampage. Drow who have lost homes or businesses find what shelter they can here, scratching out a meager existence among the roughest folk in Menzoberranzan.

The Braeryn is a great place to find allies or meet an untimely end. Roll for random encounters as the characters explore this district. You can roll a d20 and consult the Encounters in the Braeryn table, or choose an encounter that you like. The party can avoid random encounters in the Braeryn by succeeding on a DC 15 Dexterity (Stealth) group check.

ENCOUNTERS IN THE BRAERYN

d20	Encounter
1–2	1d4 + 2 **bugbears**
3–8	Drow adolescents
9–10	Drow pickpocket
11–12	3d6 **giant wolf spiders**
13–14	Infected drow
15–16	Mad drow
17–18	1 shield dwarf **berserker**
19–20	Svirfneblin lure

BUGBEARS

These bugbears skulk through the streets, murdering lone travelers or small groups for food. If the party outnumbers them, they follow the characters in the hopes that one or more of them become separated from the larger group, whereupon the bugbears attack.

DROW ADOLESCENTS

This roving gang consists of 1d6 + 6 drow **bandits**. If the gang outnumbers the party, the drow attack. Otherwise, they make lewd hand gestures at the party but retreat if accosted.

DROW PICKPOCKET

This homeless drow **commoner** tries to pick the pockets of a random party member. The drow has a Sleight of Hand skill modifier of +2.

GIANT WOLF SPIDERS

These spiders are hungry and crawl out of buildings or descend from rooftops to attack the party.

INFECTED DROW

This drow has been infected with Zuggtmoy's spores (see chapter 5) and will succumb to the infestation in 1d12 hours. Strange fungi has already begun sprouting from the drow's head and limbs. The drow offers a 500 gp gemstone in exchange for the party's protection and tries to stay as close to the characters as possible, hoping to infect them with his or her spores when the time comes.

MAD DROW

This drow **commoner** suffers from a form of indefinite madness (see "Madness" in chapter 2 of the *Dungeon Master's Guide*). The drow believes he or she is the true voice of Lolth, tasked by the Demon Queen of Spiders to admonish everyone for their lack of devotion, warning that "Demons will consume you all!" The mad drow wears an amulet made from a dead spider.

SHIELD DWARF BERSERKER

This chaotic neutral dwarf—a former slave of the drow— sees nonexistent enemies everywhere, swinging his or her greataxe at the empty air. If a character engages the dwarf in battle or conversation, the dwarf attacks.

SVIRFNEBLIN LURE

A homeless **deep gnome** serves as host to an **intellect devourer**. It tries to lure one or more characters to a "secret enclave where enemies of the drow plot to overthrow Menzoberranzan." A successful DC 15 Wisdom (Insight) check reveals something indescribably odd or untrustworthy about the gnome. If the characters follow the possessed gnome, they are led to a cramped cave under a dilapidated building. The cave is the secret lair of another 2d4 **intellect devourers**.

DONIGARTEN

Donigarten is the name given a large lake and the surrounding farmland that dominates the eastern part of the cavern. Herds of rothé cattle graze the island at the center of the lake, whose northern and western shores hold broad stretches of slave-tended fungi fields that feed much of Menzoberranzan.

The dark, cold waters of the lake have a sinister reputation, dating back to days when notable leaders of the great houses and their honored heroes were cast into the lake, dressed in full regalia and weighed down with stone spars. Many less important drow have been sent by rivals to the bottom of the lake as well, whose depths are suffused with *faerzress* that makes them impenetrable to scrying and divination spells.

Donigarten was spared from Demogorgon's rampage. Although it is sparsely populated, the area is so vital to the city's survival that drow patrols are common here. Roll for random encounters as the characters cross this district. You can roll a d20 and consult the Donigarten Encounters table, or choose an encounter that you like. The party can avoid random encounters in Donigarten by succeeding on a DC 11 Dexterity (Stealth) group check.

DONIGARTEN ENCOUNTERS

d20	Encounter
1–5	Drow patrol
6–8	2d4 + 2 **drow spore servants** (see appendix C)
9–10	Escaped slaves
11–14	1d6 + 2 **giant wolf spiders**
15–20	Slave farmers

DROW PATROL

This patrol consists of two **drow** mounted on **giant riding lizards** (see the end of chapter 8 for statistics). If one or more party members appear to be anything other than drow or slaves in the company of its drow master, the patrol immediately calls for reinforcements, which arrive in 1d4 + 2 rounds. The reinforcements consist of 1d4 similar drow patrols.

DROW SPORE SERVANTS

These drow fell prey to Zuggtmoy's spores and were drawn to the fungi fields of Donigarten, where they now roam as a pack, attacking intruders on sight.

ESCAPED SLAVES

A group of 1d4 **commoners** (of any race) fled their masters when Demogorgon attacked and took refuge here. The characters find them hiding in the fields or a nearby building. The slaves can provide the characters with a detailed description of the attack, confirming that Demogorgon was behind the destruction. The slaves are desperate to escape from the drow and pitifully grateful for any aid offered.

GIANT WOLF SPIDERS

These spiders lurk in burrows under the spongy ground, leaping out to attack the party as it passes by. Party members with a passive Wisdom (Perception) score of 17 or higher aren't surprised by the spiders.

ORC SLAVE FARMERS

The drow use orc slaves to farm their fungi fields. The orcs pour water into carefully irrigated dung fields, renewing and expanding the fields with wagonloads of excrement brought in from the city proper. The orcs are so disciplined that they can be relied upon to perform their tasks with minimal or no supervision.

The characters encounter 3d6 orc **commoners**. The orcs are chaotic evil and have darkvision out to a range of 60 feet, but they don't attack drow or anyone accompanied by a drow. There's a 25 percent chance that 1d4 drow **guards** are standing within 120 feet of the orcs, quietly resenting the fact that they've been assigned to "watch orcs till our waste." If the orcs come under attack, the drow rush in to protect them.

DUTHCLOIM

Known commonly as "Manyfolk," the area surrounding the Bazaar and bordered by the Clawrift to the east is home to Menzoberranzan's merchants, tradesfolk, and crafters. Duthcloim features small inns, taprooms, and pleasure houses catering to locals, visitors, and high-status drow seeking distraction. Parts of Duthcloim were damaged or destroyed after Demogorgon emerged from the Clawrift. Nevertheless, business has been booming as drow celebrate the deaths of rivals.

If you want a random encounter to occur as the characters make their way through the Duthcloim district, roll a d20 and consult the Duthcloim Encounters table, or choose an encounter that you like. The party can avoid random encounters in Duthcloim by succeeding on a DC 13 Dexterity (Stealth) group check.

DUTHCLOIM ENCOUNTERS

d20	Encounter
1–4	Bregan D'aerthe spy
5–8	Drow foot patrol
9–12	Drow priestess of Lolth
13–16	Spider nest
17–20	Statue of Lolth

THE WAY OF LOLTH

Menzoberranzan's principle law is the Way of Lolth. Its tenets are as follows:

- There is no god or goddess other than Lolth. Any who follows the dictates of another entity will be slain, preferably as a sacrifice to Lolth.
- Ritual worship of any entity other than Lolth is forbidden within the city's vault. Non-drow who violate this tenet are fined and expelled from the city. Second offenders or any drow who do so are slain.
- Slaves have no rights, and there are no limits to the punishments or duties that can be set for them. Treatment of slaves is the affair of their owners. It is a capital offense for a slave to refuse any order from a drow of the house that owns the slave.
- A commoner or student of the Academy who refuses to obey a priestess can be punished as the offended priestess sees fit, up to and including death. If the offender is the property of another house and the noble of that house is present and objects, the two must agree on a punishment (usually flogging).
- Any drow who falsely wears the colors of another house or who deliberately alters his or her appearance to masquerade as one of a different station will be slain.
- Any non-drow who adopts the appearance of a particular drow, a drow of a noble rank, or a drow of a house other than his or her own will be slain.
- If it can be proved that two or more houses attacked another house, all the houses that participated in the attack will be destroyed jointly by the remainder.

BREGAN D'AERTHE SPY

A male drow **spy** takes an interest in the characters and begins shadowing them, attempting to remain unseen. Characters keeping an eye out for trouble spot the drow with a successful Wisdom (Perception) check contested by the drow's Dexterity (Stealth) check.

The drow is a member of Bregan D'aerthe (see "Unexpected Allies" later in this chapter) and reveals as much if the characters confront him. If the characters reveal that they're trying to banish the demon lords back to the Abyss, he offers Bregan D'aerthe's assistance. If they're amenable, he leads them to a Bregan D'aerthe safe house until a meeting with Jarlaxle, the leader of Bregan D'aerthe, can be arranged. While escorted by the spy, the characters have no hostile random encounters.

Development. The Bregan D'aerthe safe house is a three-story stone tower guarded by four members of Bregan D'aerthe (male **drow elite warriors**) and maintained by one or more freed slaves (use the **commoner** statistics). While in the safe house, the characters have no hostile encounters.

If the characters agree to a meeting with Jarlaxle, the Bregan D'aerthe spy tells them that a drow operative named Krilelyn H'Kar will fetch them when the time comes (see "Private Meetings"). The spy then leaves the characters alone.

DROW FOOT PATROL

This patrol consists of 2d4 **drow**. If one or more party members appear to be anything other than drow or slaves in the company of its drow master, the patrol confronts the party and starts asking questions. If any of the answers arouse suspicion or come across as insolent, the drow attack.

If combat erupts, reinforcements arrive every 1d4 rounds. Each wave of reinforcements consists of 2d4 **drow** plus 1d4 **giant spiders** that crawl down from rooftops.

Drow Priestess of Lolth

A **drow priestess of Lolth** accompanied by a **drow elite warrior** and 2d4 **drow** is out surveying damaged sections of the city. Merchants and crafters who confront the priestess, claiming to have lost everything in Demogorgon's attack, are banished to the Braelyn. Locals driven mad by the demonic invasion are brought before the priestess and put to death.

If the characters approach the priestess claiming to have vital information about the demon attack, they can, with a successful DC 20 Charisma (Persuasion) check, convince the priestess to escort them to Matron Mother Quenthel Baenre (see "Private Meetings" later in this chapter). If the check fails by 5 or more, the priestess and her escort attack the party.

Spider Nest

The characters stumble upon a spiders' nest containing 4d6 giant spider eggs with soft, sticky shells. Each egg weighs 20 pounds and has AC 6 and 1 hit point. Disturbing the eggs attracts 1d4 **giant spiders**, which descend from nearby rooftops to defend the nest.

Statue of Lolth

The characters stumble upon a 9-foot-tall statue of Lolth depicted in her drow form. There is a 25 percent chance that the statue was toppled during Demogorgon's rampage, in which case it lies in pieces on the ground.

If an intact statue is touched by a non-drow or otherwise defiled, the statue opens its mouth and disgorges a **swarm of insects** (spiders). These spiders crawl down the statue and attack whoever touched or defiled the statue. Once the statue disgorges a swarm, its mouth closes, and it can't release another swarm until 1 hour has passed.

Eastmyr

Eastmyr bridges the gap between prosperous Duthcloim and the down-and-out despair of the Braeryn. It is home to common merchants, tradesfolk, mercenaries, and crafters either making their way up the social ladder or trying to slow the downward descent of shifting fortunes. Though this area suffered relatively little damage during Demogorgon's rampage, its population has swelled with formerly high-profile drow forced out of their homes and holdings.

If you want a random encounter to occur as the characters make their way through the Eastmyr district, roll a d20 and consult the Eastmyr Encounters table, or choose an encounter that you like. The party can avoid random encounters in Eastmyr by succeeding on a DC 15 Dexterity (Stealth) group check.

Eastmyr Encounters

d20	Encounter
1–5	Bregan D'aerthe spy
6–10	Cult of "Y"
11–15	Drow foot patrol
16–20	Scroll from Narbondel's Shadow

Bregan D'aerthe Spy

See "Duthcloim" for more information.

Cult of "Y"

Eastmyr has become a haven for a group of drow driven mad by Demogorgon's rampage. These drow carve the symbol of Demogorgon—a Y with curled ends—into their palms and foreheads, and they can hear the twin voices of the Prince of Demons talking to them, telling them that they will rise from the dregs of drow society to greatness once the nobility is cast down.

The characters encounter a group of 1d4 + 4 drow **cultists** wearing cloaks and cowls in the midst of kidnapping a low-ranking drow **noble**. If the characters kill four or more cultists, the rest flee like rats. Sounds of combat attract the attention of a drow foot patrol (see "Duthcloim" for more information), which arrives in 1d6 rounds. Any cultists that escape flee to a crumbling tenement a block away that the cult has converted into a shrine to Demogorgon. The shrine contains 1d4 **shadow demons** as well as 2d4 drow **cultists**, each of whom has a "second head" (in the form of a severed drow head on a pole) that the cultist has lashed to his or her body. Painted in wet blood on the shrine's floor is a familiar "Y" symbol.

Development. The drow noble offers no reward to his or her rescuers and chastises the drow patrol for not arriving sooner. If the characters demand a reward, the noble frowns and gives them an insignia bearing the mark of his or her house, then instructs the characters to visit the noble's estate "when the light of Narbondel reaches its zenith" to receive their "reward." If the characters visit the noble's estate in Narbondellyn at the appointed time, they are set upon by the house guards, who have orders to eliminate them and dispose of the remains (see "Narbondellyn" for more information on drow noble estates).

Drow Foot Patrol

See "Duthcloim" for more information.

Scroll from Narbondel's Shadow

A cloaked half-drow **spy** named Shinzi approaches the characters when they are alone and gives them a scroll bearing an advertisement for Narbondel's Shadow, the "finest rooming house in Menzoberranzan." If the party includes non-drow, Shinzi says that non-drow are "more than welcome at the Shadow." The advertisement doesn't list any prices, but on the back of the scroll is a map marking the location of the rooming house in northeastern Eastmyr, near the Clawrift.

Development. Narbondel's Shadow, which wasn't damaged during Demogorgon's rampage, offers some of the best food and lodging money can buy, but the cost is high: 25 gp per night, per person. A strongheart halfling **commoner** named Dalfred Noakes owns and runs the establishment. Dalfred had a violent encounter with a young Hunzrin noble, which left him scarred and without his left ear. He has never forgotten nor forgiven the noble. To this day, he uses a small cave system that doesn't connect with the Dark Dominion to smuggle goods and hide people fleeing angry drow nobles. If the characters look like they could use his help, Dalfred does whatever he can to assist them.

The orphaned daughter of a drow merchant and a human slave, Shinzi was adopted by Dalfred and is one of his many spies. She has darkvision out to a range of 60 feet, as well as the Fey Ancestry and Innate Spellcasting features of a drow (see the "Statistical Modifications to Drow NPCs" sidebar). However, she doesn't have the Sunlight Sensitivity feature.

KYORBBLIVVIN

Kyorbblivvin is a spider-haunted forest of giant mushrooms that spreads across the northern portion of the Qu'ellarz'orl plateau. Members of the great houses use Kyorbblivvin as a private hunting domain. Drow warriors patrol the forest, alert for poachers and intruders. Check for random encounters in Kyorbblivvin once every hour. Roll a d20 and consult the Kyorbblivvin Encounters table to determine what, if anything, the characters encounter. The party can avoid random encounters in Kyorbblivvin by succeeding on a DC 15 Dexterity (Stealth) group check.

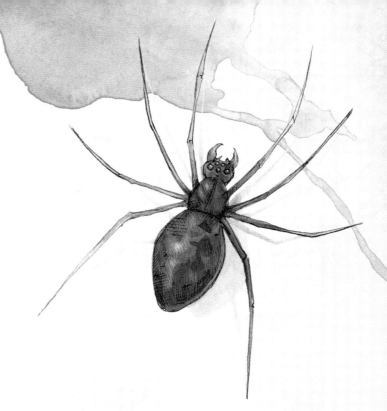

KYORBBLIVVIN ENCOUNTERS

d20	Encounter
1–10	No encounter
11	1 **black pudding**
12	3d6 **drow spore servants** (see appendix C)
13	Elite drow foot patrol
14	Exotic fungi
15	1d4 **giant spiders**
16	1d4 **gricks**
17	Hunting party
18	1 **shrieker**
19	3d6 **stirges**
20	1d4 + 1 **violet fungi**

BLACK PUDDING

Thanks to the growing influence of Juiblex, this ooze has an Intelligence of 6 (−2). It uses its newfound intelligence to hide inside a bloated, hollowed-out giant mushroom. Characters can see viscid black goo oozing from the mushroom's stalk. Disturbing the mushroom causes the pudding to burst forth and attack.

DROW SPORE SERVANTS

These drow fell prey to Zuggtmoy's spores and were drawn to the fungi fields of Kyorbblivvin, where they now roam as a pack, attacking intruders on sight.

ELITE DROW FOOT PATROL

This patrol consists of 2d4 **drow elite warriors**. If one or more party members appear to be anything other than drow belonging to one of the eight ruling houses, or slaves in the company of such a drow, the patrol attacks. Each drow carries a horn that it can blow (as an action) to summon reinforcements. The first wave of reinforcements arrives in 1d4 + 4 rounds and consists of another 2d4 **elite drow warriors**. The second wave arrives after ten minutes and consists of 3d6 **elite drow warriors** mounted on **giant riding lizards** (see the end of chapter 8 for statistics).

EXOTIC FUNGI

The characters find a patch of exotic fungi (see "Fungi of the Underdark" in chapter 2). Roll a d6 and consult the Exotic Fungi table to determine what they find.

EXOTIC FUNGI

d6	Fungi
1	1d6 nightlights (50 percent chance they are unlit)
2	2d6 Nilhogg's noses
3	1d6 patches of ormu
4	2d6 timmasks
5	1d6 tongues of madness
6	3d6 torchstalks

GIANT SPIDERS

There is a 50 percent chance that the giant spiders have a nest nearby (see "Duthcloim" earlier in this section). In addition to the eggs, characters find a 1d4 − 1 man-shaped cocoons containing the exsanguinated corpses of escaped slaves (of any race).

GRICKS

Drow nobles unleash these creatures in the forest and hunt them for sport. The gricks fight until slain.

HUNTING PARTY

The characters happen upon a group of 1d4 + 2 **drow** from one of the eight ruling houses that live atop the plateau. These "lesser nobles" wear the insignia of their house and are hunting gricks for sport. They try to make short work of any trespassers they encounter. Roll a d8 and consult the Drow Ruling Houses table to determine which house they belong to. If the result is House Do'Urden, the drow are actually Bregan D'aerthe initiates on a training exercise (see "House Do'Urden" later in this chapter).

DROW RULING HOUSES

d8	House
1	Baenre
2	Barrison Del'Armgo
3	Faen Tlabbar
4	Mizzrym
5	Fey-Branche
6	Melarn
7	Vandree
8	Do'Urden

SHRIEKER

The shrieking of this fungus might attract other nearby creatures, which arrive in 2d4 rounds. Roll again on the Kyorbblivvin Encounters table to determine what, if anything, shows up. Treat an "exotic fungi" encounter as "no encounter."

STIRGES

These bloodsucking pests lair in the cap of a giant mushroom, fluttering out to attack when they detect light or motion within 20 feet of their roost.

VIOLET FUNGI

These fungi extrude their branches and attack when the characters pass between them.

NARBONDEL

The most dominant feature within the city, Narbondel is a 1,000-foot-tall column of rock that helps support the cavern ceiling. At the same time each day, the city's Archmage (or a representative from Sorcere) magically heats Narbondel's base, causing the stone to glow. The band of warm light rises slowly up the column to mark the passage of time, taking twenty-four hours to reach the top. The Archmage of Menzoberranzan, Gromph Baenre, has fled the city in the wake of Demogorgon's attack, leaving the task of lighting Narbondel to a host of other wizards.

NARBONDELLYN

The estates of the various drow houses are clustered beneath the plateau of Qu'ellarz'orl in an area called Narbondellyn, allowing the superiors of those drow to literally look down upon them. Largely untouched during Demogorgon's rampage, the so-called "Broad Streets" district remains the bright center of Menzoberranzan, as the lesser houses vie to outdo each other in shows of wealth, power, and influence. Soaring stalagmite towers and great manors rise across the area, which is also home to luxury shops, pleasure houses, and discriminating merchants.

A noble estate in Narbondellyn maintains its own militia, consisting of fifty or more highly disciplined **drow** warriors and **drow elite warriors**, with one elite warrior for every ten drow warriors. In addition, an estate holds 3d6 drow **nobles** and scores of slaves, 6d6 of which can be pressed into defending the house. These fighting slaves are usually **bugbears**, **ogres**, **orcs**, or **quaggoths**. Doors and windows are protected with *glyph of warding* spells (spell save DC 13), and 2d6 **gargoyles** watch for trouble from ledges and rooftops.

If you want a random encounter to occur as the characters make their way through the Narbondellyn district, roll a d20 and consult the Narbondellyn Encounters table, or choose an encounter that you like. The party can avoid random encounters in Narbondellyn by succeeding on a DC 13 Dexterity (Stealth) group check.

NARBONDELLYN ENCOUNTERS

d20	Encounter
1–3	Beholder
4–7	Bregan D'aerthe mercenaries
8–12	Elite drow patrol
13–16	Noble entourage
17–20	Statue of Lolth

BEHOLDER

This monster is passing through the city. The drow give it a wide berth.

BREGAN D'AERTHE MERCENARIES

Bregan D'aerthe was instrumental in driving the demons out of Menzoberranzan. Since the incursion, Bregan D'aerthe mercenaries have taken to patrolling the streets of the wealthier districts, accepting payments from drow nobles for the added security.

The characters encounter a group of 3d4 male **drow elite warriors**—all members of Bregan D'aerthe. Unlike most drow patrols, this group is gregarious and jovial. The mercenaries stop the characters to ask their business, but more to alleviate boredom than to throw their weight around. Unless the characters brazenly declare their intention to attack a noble house, the Bregan D'aerthe leader flips them a platinum coin and cheerfully sends them on their way after concluding his "interrogation."

The Bregan D'aerthe leader carries a gem-studded minotaur horn. If the characters attack the mercenaries, the leader blows his horn, which can be heard throughout the district. All noble houses go on high alert as reinforcements arrive every round for the next 1d8 rounds. Each wave of reinforcements consists of an elite drow patrol (see below) and 1d4 **gargoyles**.

Treasure. The gem-studded horn carried by the Bregan D'aerthe leader is worth 2,500 gp. In addition, each drow mercenary has a pouch containing 2d10 pp.

ELITE DROW PATROL

This patrol consists of two **drow elite warriors** mounted on **giant riding lizards** (see the end of chapter 8 for statistics). If one or more party members appear to be anything other than drow or slaves in the company of its drow master, the patrol immediately calls for reinforcements, which arrive in 1d4 + 2 rounds. The reinforcements consist of 1d4 similar drow patrols.

NOBLE ENTOURAGE

The characters encounter a drow **noble** traveling with eight **drow** warriors bearing the symbol and colors of their noble house. There is a 25 percent chance that a **succubus** or **incubus** accompanies the noble in drow form, and a 75 percent chance that the noble is being carried around in a palanquin by unarmed slaves. Roll a d6 and consult the Drow House Slaves table to determine what kind of slaves and how many.

DROW HOUSE SLAVES

d6	Slaves
1–2	6 shield dwarf **commoners**
3–4	6 moon elf **commoners**
5–6	6 human **commoners**

Treasure. Each noble carries a pouch that contains 2d10 pp and wears 1d3 pieces of fine jewelry worth 250 gp each.

Development. If the characters do anything to antagonize the nobles, they order their guards to attack. If the guards are defeated, the nobles offer the party a bribe in exchange for their lives.

STATUE OF LOLTH

See "Duthcloim" for more information.

QU'ELLARZ'ORL

Untouched by Demogorgon's rampage, the high southern plateau of Menzoberranzan is home to many of the oldest and greatest noble houses, with House Baenre situated at the plateau's highest point, to the east. At the west end of Qu'ellarz'orl is a small cavern containing a sculpted stalagmite tower. Within this tower rests the Chamber of the Ruling Council, where the matron mothers of the eight great drow houses gather and meet.

Each noble estate in Qu'ellarz'orl maintains its own militia, consisting of several hundred highly disciplined **drow** warriors and **drow elite warriors**, with one elite warrior for every ten drow warriors. In addition, an estate holds 3d12 drow **nobles** and scores of slaves, 10d10 of which can be pressed into defending the house. These fighting slaves are usually **bugbears**, **ogres**, **orogs**, or **quaggoths**. Doors and windows are protected with *glyph of warding* spells (spell save DC 13), and either 3d6 **gargoyles** or 3d6 **giant spiders** watch for trouble from ledges and rooftops. These gargoyles and giant spiders have truesight out to a range of 120 feet, enabling them to spot invisible trespassers.

Roll for random encounters as the characters cross this district. You can roll a d20 and consult the Qu'ellarz'orl Encounters table, or choose an encounter that you like. The party can avoid random encounters in Qu'ellarz'orl by succeeding on a DC 15 Dexterity (Stealth) group check.

QU'ELLARZ'ORL ENCOUNTERS

d20	Encounter
1–5	Elite drow patrol
6–8	2d4 **gargoyles**
9–10	1d6 + 2 **giant wolf spiders**
11–14	Groundskeepers
15–20	Slave parade

ELITE DROW PATROL

This patrol consists of two **drow elite warriors** mounted on **giant riding lizards** (see the end of chapter 8 for statistics). If one or more party members appear to be anything other than drow of one of the eight ruling houses, or slaves in the company of such a drow, the patrol calls for reinforcements, which arrive in 1d4 + 2 rounds and consist of 1d4 similar drow patrols.

DROW RULING HOUSES OF MENZOBERRANZAN

Rank	House	Matron Mother	Notes
1	Baenre	Quenthel Baenre	Controls all three branches of the Academy (see "Tier Breche")
2	Barrison Del'Armgo	Mez'Barris Armgo	Has the largest number of trained wizards and mercenaries-for-hire
3	Faen Tlabbar	Vadalma Tlabbar	Fanatically devoted to Lolth
4	Mizzrym	Miz'ri Mizzrym	Dominates Menzoberranzan's slave trade
5	Fey-Branche	Byrtyn Fey	Skilled at forging alliances
6	Melarn	Zhindia Melarn	Devoted to rooting out drow apostates, particularly within the nobility
7	Vandree	Fiirnel'ther Vandree	Vicious and vindictive house determined to rise to the top
8	Do'Urden	Dahlia Sin'felle	Newly resurrected and disgraced vassal house under the firm control of House Baenre, with Dahlia (a moon elf prisoner) as its figurehead

OLD ENEMIES

It is possible that the adventurers' drow jailers or pursuers from Velkynvelve (chapter 1) managed to survive to this point in the campaign, and that they have returned to Menzoberranzan in the wake of Demogorgon's attack and the ongoing chaos. If so, they might be on hand for an unfortunate encounter with the party. If you are looking to throw a twist into the events in the City of Spiders, having an old foe turn up at the least opportune moment to denounce the characters as escaped prisoners and enemies of the drow could well be it.

GARGOYLES

These creatures are loyal to House Baenre and have magically bestowed truesight out to a range of 120 feet. As they fly over the plateau, they keep a watchful eye on everyone and everything. However, they don't attack unless House Baenre's holdings are in jeopardy.

If the characters drawn attention to themselves, the gargoyles fly back to House Baenre and report what they've seen. Matron Mother Quenthel Baenre, believing that the characters are potentially of use to her, dispatches eight elite drow patrols (see above) to bring them to her at once. If the characters allow themselves to be brought before the most powerful individual in the city, see the "Private Meetings" section for tips on how to roleplay the encounter with Matron Mother Quenthel.

GIANT WOLF SPIDERS

These spiders lurk in burrows beneath the gardens, leaping out to attack the party as it passes by. Party members with a passive Wisdom (Perception) score of 17 or higher aren't surprised by the spiders.

GROUNDSKEEPERS

The characters happen upon 1d8 drow **commoners** tending the decorative fungi fields and gardens that surround the various noble estates. These drow are low-ranking members of their house. They give strangers unpleasant looks but pose little threat.

There is a 25 percent chance that one of the drow groundskeepers is actually a young drow **noble** who's being punished for some infraction or political misstep. This noble is bold enough to approach the characters and demand to know their business. The noble also seizes any opportunity to reverse his or her recent misfortune, perhaps by rooting out enemy spies or using the characters to dispose of a rival. This noble is treacherous, however, and doesn't make good on any promises or bribes.

Slave Parade

To impress its neighbors and rivals, one of the ruling houses organizes a parade of its choicest slaves. The characters encounter the parade as it meanders along the boulevards of Qu'ellarz'orl.

Dozens of naked and chained slaves form the parade, their bodies painted with dyes and perfumes. Leading the slave parade is a drow **noble**, while order is maintained by 4d6 **drow** warriors in full ceremonial house regalia.

The Rifts

Three large chasms score the floor of the cavern of Menzoberranzan.

Clawrift

The Clawrift's uncharted depths have long been rumored to extend into the Abyss. This legend was seemingly proven true when the demon lord Demogorgon emerged from the Clawrift, obliterating the rope bridges that once extended across it. Bregan D'aerthe spies are assessing the damage from their base in a ruined drow compound overlooking the Clawrift. (The compound was once House Oblodra, a powerful drow house that was destroyed by Lolth over one hundred years ago during the Time of Troubles.)

Mistrift

This long gorge at the city's center earned its name from the rolling clouds of steam that forever billow up from below. A number of subterranean streams flow out of the Mistrift's vertical walls, their icy waters cascading down into the darkened void below. Half a mile down, the runoff collects in an ancient aquifer, its waters superheated by an adjacent magma flow. Arcane watermills collect water from the falls, diverting it to an underground cistern that the drow can tap into.

Westrift

The newest of the city's large clefts, Westrift swallowed up three drow houses and a score of lesser dwellings when it opened its yawning maw three centuries ago. In more recent years, the rift has become home to hundreds of giant arachnids, which have filled much of the cleft with their webs and nests—to the extent that anyone falling into the rift has a 75 percent chance of being caught in a web, taking no damage from the fall but attracting 1d4 + 1 hungry **giant spiders**. See "Dungeon Hazards" in chapter 5 of the *Dungeon Master's Guide* for rules on escaping webs.

Characters entering Menzoberranzan by means of Vizeran DeVir's secret tunnel come to a secret door that pulls open to reveal a narrow ledge 60 feet below the lip of the rift. Characters can scale the cleft wall with a successful DC 10 Strength (Athletics) check, as there are abundant handholds. Any character who fails the check by 5 or more falls.

Tier Breche

The Great Stair of Tier Breche rises from the floor of Menzoberranzan to the cavern housing the three branches of the Academy: Melee-Magthere,

a pyramid-shaped edifice where drow warriors are trained; Arach-Tinilith, a spider-shaped cathedral where drow priestesses worship their demon goddess; and Sorcere, a magnificent tower where drow mages learn to master the magical arts. Non-drow are forbidden from entering this part of the city.

The stone steps are some three hundred feet wide and rise nearly the same distance. A pair of giant jade spiders flanks the stairway at the top, ready to animate to attack non-drow that climb the steps. The two jade spiders have the statistics of **stone golems** with the following statistical modifications:

- The jade spiders have 250 hit points each.
- They have a climbing speed of 30 feet.
- They have truesight out to a range of 120 feet.

Roll for random encounters as the characters explore the Academy grounds. You can roll a d20 and consult the Tier Breche Encounters table, or choose an encounter that you like. The party can avoid random encounters by succeeding on a DC 17 Dexterity (Stealth) group check. Sounds of battle are common at the Academy; however, drow guards are trained to tell the difference between training exercises and the sound of real combat. The latter attracts reinforcements in the form of 1d4 **elite drow warriors** every round until the perceived threat is eliminated.

Tier Breche Encounters

d20	Encounter
1–6	Drow acolytes
7–12	Drow mages
13–20	Drow warriors

Drow Acolytes

The characters encounter 2d6 female drow **acolytes** out for a walk. There is a 25 percent chance that a **drow priestess of Lolth** is with them, filling the young devotees' heads with wisdom and instructing them on the Way of Lolth (see "The Way of Lolth" sidebar). If they come under attack, the acolytes withdraw to Arach-Tinilith while the priestess stands her ground.

Drow Mages

The characters encounter 1d3 **drow mages** out for a walk. There is a 50 percent chance that these mages are members of the Council of Spiders and of a mind to help the characters infiltrate Sorcere, should the characters reveal that they are in league with Vizeran DeVir. These mages offer to cast *greater invisibility* spells on visible characters and escort the party to Gromph's sanctum in the tower. As long as the characters are under the protection of these mages, they have no hostile encounters until they enter Gromph's sanctum (see "Sorcere" for details).

Drow Warriors

The characters encounter 4d6 **drow** warriors on a training exercise. There is a 50 percent chance that 1d4 **drow elite warriors** are with them, providing instruction and discipline. If they spot non-drow on Academy grounds, the drow try to kill any intruder.

West Wall

West Wall (also called "the Old Quarter") is a primarily residential neighborhood. Largely untouched by Demogorgon's assault on the city, West Wall is a quiet district, as its residents like to keep their dark schemes and vile indulgences behind closed doors. Amid the twisted streets and quiet mansions of West Wall stand scores of stone monuments dedicated to important figures and moments in the city's history, as well as numerous statues and graven images of Lolth.

Between West Wall and Narbondellyn is a residential neighborhood called Lolth's Web. Its residents built their homes upward, crafting streets of magically calcified strands of spider silk from the cavern floor to the vaulted roof above. Hollow, cocoon-like dwellings are constructed both above and below the layers of webbing.

Roll for random encounters as the characters cross this district. You can roll a d20 and consult the West Wall Encounters table, or choose an encounter that you like. The party can avoid random encounters in West Wall by succeeding on a DC 13 Dexterity (Stealth) group check.

West Wall Encounters

d20	Encounter
1–3	Bandersnatches
4–7	Bregan D'aerthe spy
8–14	Drow foot patrol
15–17	Slave abuse
18–20	Statue of Lolth

Bandersnatches

The characters draw the unwanted attention of the Bandersnatches, a gang of young, demon-worshiping drow who, in the wake of Demogorgon's attack, are eager to create further unrest in the city. Gang members send coded messages to one another by tapping hollow rocks together, creating eerie clicking sounds that echo throughout the otherwise quiet neighborhood. Initially, 1d4 drow **bandits** follow the party, scuttling through dark alleys and across web-strung rooftops while tapping their stones, urging more gang members to converge on the party's location. At the end of each round of clicking stones, another 1d4 drow **bandits** appear. If the number of gang members grows to twenty or more, the bandits surround the party and demand payment of 100 gp per party member for safe passage. If the characters kill four or more bandits, the rest flee before a drow patrol (see below) shows up.

Development. The consequence of killing one or more bandits is retaliation. The gang organizes a hunting party to find and kill one party member for every gang member slain. This hunting party is bold enough to leave the West Wall district, and you might have the Bandersnatches try to ambush the characters as they make their way out of Menzoberranzan. The hunting party consists of the gang's leader, her **quasit** advisor, and thirty drow **bandits**.

The leader of the Bandersnatches is a capricious and nihilistic female drow named Viln Tirin. She has the statistics of a **bandit captain** with the following modifications:

- Viln is chaotic evil and has drow features (see the "Statistical Modifications to Drow NPCs" sidebar).
- She wields a *scimitar of speed* and can make one attack with it as a bonus action on her turn. All of Viln's attacks with the weapon are +7 to hit and deal 8 (1d6 + 5) slashing damage on a hit.
- Viln carries four daggers coated with purple worm poison (see "Poisons" in chapter 8 of the *Dungeon Master's Guide*). The poison on a dagger's blade is good for one hit only, whether the poison takes effect or not.
- She has a challenge rating of 5 (1,800 XP).

Bregan D'aerthe Spy

See "Duthcloim" for more information.

Drow Foot Patrol

This patrol consists of 2d4 **drow**. If one or more party members appear to be anything other than drow or slaves in the company of its drow master, the patrol confronts the party and starts asking questions. If any of the answers arouse suspicion or come across as insolent, the drow attack.

Slave Abuse

The characters see a drow **noble** flogging one of a handful of slaves (**commoners** of any race) while 1d4 **bugbear** bodyguards keep an eye out for trouble. Unless the characters intervene, the merciless noble has the slave dragged to the Westrift and unceremoniously tossed into it. The poor slave falls 3d6 × 10 feet before being caught in a web and cocooned by a **giant spider** (to be devoured later). If the characters come to the slave's defense, the bugbears attack them.

Statue of Lolth

See "Duthcloim" for more information.

Unexpected Allies

As hostile as Menzoberranzan seems to outsiders, there are powerful figures within the city who want the demon lords expelled from the Underdark and are willing to help the characters accomplish this goal.

House Baenre

The matron mother of House Baenre is the voice of Lolth in Menzoberranzan, and despite recent events, maintains absolute control of the city. Quenthel knows how Demogorgon made his way from the Abyss to the City of Spiders. She wasn't surprised to learn that her brother Gromph—the Archmage of Menzoberranzan—was behind it, for she's seen evidence of his growing unhappiness in recent months, and she also knows that Lolth was behind it. Quenthel assumes that Lolth is making some sort of power play in the Abyss.

If Quenthel learns that adventurers are trying to rid the Underdark of its demon lord menace, she doesn't stand in their way (see "Private Meetings") and even allows them to travel through the city unmolested.

BREGAN D'AERTHE

Bregan D'aerthe is a mercenary company with more power and influence in Menzoberranzan than all the lesser noble houses combined. Bregan D'aerthe benefits from its close ties with House Baenre. The company's founder and leader, Jarlaxle, is brother to both Matron Mother Quenthel Baenre and Archmage Gromph Baenre, though this fact isn't widely known.

Jarlaxle doesn't care what the demon lords do in the Underdark, but he's worried about the future of Menzoberranzan as well as his secret holdings on the surface world. He wants to know how the demon lords arrived and how to send them back, and members of Bregan D'aerthe will support characters who claim to have those answers.

COUNCIL OF SPIDERS

Many drow wizards have long sought a means of increasing their power and influence, frustrated that the arcane arts are viewed as secondary to the divine magic of Lolth's priestesses. A secret cabal of noble wizards calling itself the Council of Spiders works to see wizards represented on the Ruling Council—overturning thousands of years of tradition while remaining true to Lolth's will.

The disappearance of Gromph Baenre and the involvement of Vizeran DeVir in fending off the demonic invasion offers wizards of the council an unparalleled opportunity to advance their agenda. Vizeran has cultivated his role as a patron and ally of the council to gain influence among its members—while giving them no hint of his desire to destroy the drow's obsessive worship of Lolth. Vizeran has told council members that adventurers are helping him banish the demon lords back to the Abyss, and that they might come to Menzoberranzan seeking lore from Gromph's sanctum in Sorcere. The council stands ready to disable the magical wards on the tower, should this come to pass.

PRIVATE MEETINGS

If House Baenre and Bregan D'aerthe get wind of the party's presence in the city, the characters are confronted by drow tasked with escorting them to a private meeting with the leader of each faction. Jarlaxle sends a devilishly charming and sarcastic male **drow elite warrior** named Krilelyn H'Kar, tasked with leading characters to the ruins of House Do'Urden in the West Wall district. Matron Mother Quenthel Baenre sends thirty dour **drow elite warriors** mounted on **giant riding lizards** (see the end of chapter 8 for statistics), with six **gargoyles** providing aerial support. They have orders to escort the party to House Baenre atop Qu'ellarz'orl.

MATRON MOTHER QUENTHEL BAENRE

Matron Mother Quenthel Baenre is absolutely loyal to Lolth, but she has suspected for some time that her brother Gromph is not. The archmage has been missing since the disastrous summoning ritual that pulled the demon lords into the Underdark, and no one claims

COUNCIL OF
SPIDERS MAGE

to know his whereabouts. The matron mother and her closest allies have carefully covered up the truth about Gromph's disappearance, proclaiming that the archmage is hard at work investigating the demonic invasion and seeking the means to send the demon lords back to the Abyss. Quenthel doesn't know if Gromph is alive or dead. She knows only that she can't hide his disappearance forever—even as she must ensure that no damage comes to her house as a result of his actions.

Quenthel doesn't care that the adventurers are fighting to send the demon lords back to the Abyss, or that Menzoberranzan might suffer under another demon lord assault. She's concerned only about House Baenre. By the matron mother's addled logic, Lolth is using the demon lords to test the strength of House Baenre and lay waste to the enemies of the drow. However, the matron mother doesn't want Gromph's spell or damning evidence of his actions falling into the wrong hands.

Whether the characters are brought in by force or arrive willingly, read the following when they meet Quenthel Baenre.

> A vast web of heavy metallic strands forms a kind of fence around a sprawling compound of structures laid out on the plateau at the top of Menzoberranzan's great cavern. Dozens of massive stalagmites and stalactites have been carved and shaped into towers, girded with balconies and walkways, and connected with delicate-looking ramps and bridges. All the compound is lit with blazing light in pale shades of violet, green, and blue. Dozens of drow warriors are stationed on the overlooks and walkways, ever vigilant as they watch your approach.

When the characters are taken into the compound, the matron mother welcomes them in her throne room—a massive chamber that occupies the entire fourth level of one tower. She sits upon a throne carved from a single black sapphire, with large diamonds set into its arms shedding light at the matron's command.

Quenthel doesn't know that Vizeran DeVir is still alive, and any mention of him piques her interest, although she doesn't consider him a threat. After Gromph disappeared, she sent underlings to Sorcere to rid his sanctum of any incriminating evidence. They found none. The matron mother doesn't know about Gromph's secret inner sanctum or the grimoire hidden there. If the characters explain the broad strokes of their goal to get the grimoire out of the city, Quenthel allows and supports their mission—even as she secretly plans to manufacture evidence that the adventurers were behind the ritual that brought the demon lords to the Underdark if they are caught with the grimoire in their possession. She grants permission for the characters to enter Sorcere and instructs the tower's inhabitants not to impede their investigation.

As a Chosen of Lolth, Quenthel Baenre is, by herself, a threat comparable to any demon lord. Surrounded by the well-trained guards and magical wards of House Baenre, she could annihilate the adventurers without breaking a sweat. If the characters attack her, use the statistics of the **drow priestess of Lolth** with the following modifications:

- Quenthel has an Armor Class of 19 (*+3 scale mail*) and 132 (24d8 + 24) hit points.
- She has an Intelligence of 18 (+4) and a Wisdom of 20 (+5). Her saving throw bonuses are as follows: Con +8, Wis +12, Cha +11. Her skill bonuses are as follows: Insight +12, Perception +12, Religion +11, Stealth +9.
- She's an 20th-level spellcaster who can cast any cleric spell up to 9th level at will (save DC 20, +12 to hit with spell attacks).
- She wields a *tentacle rod*.
- While seated on her throne, Quenthel can use an action on her turn to cast *disintegrate* (save DC 19). A target that fails its saving throw takes 10d6 + 40 force damage. If this damage reduces the target to 0 hit points, it is disintegrated.
- She has a challenge rating of 22 (41,000 XP).

XP Awards

If the party gains the support of Quenthel Baenre, award each character 2,000 XP.

JARLAXLE BAENRE OF BREGAN D'AERTHE

The dashing and dapper commander of the Bregan D'aerthe mercenary company, Jarlaxle Baenre is a drow warrior with centuries of experience. A nonconformist in a culture where failure to conform usually means death or exile, he has learned to walk the line between being too defiant to be part of drow society and being too useful to get rid of.

In addition to witnessing first hand the destruction wrought in Menzoberranzan, Jarlaxle understands the terrible implications of the demon lords' arrival in the Underdark, and he knows that his brother Gromph is

responsible. Jarlaxle knows that Gromph is hiding in the city of Luskan on the Sword Coast, but he doesn't share this information under any circumstances. Jarlaxle has eyes and ears everywhere in Menzoberranzan, and he takes an interest in the adventurers—particularly if they travel with Grin Ousstyl.

If the characters agree to meet with Jarlaxle in House Do'Urden, read the following when they first arrive.

> A drow house stands alone and forlorn with its back against the west wall of Menzoberranzan's great vault. Its towers are dark, its walls crumbling and in desperate need of repair. The old fortress has the countenance of a haunted ruin, but here and there you glimpse signs of life: drow in black leather armor standing guard in the shadows and magical flames dancing in the stone braziers that flank the entrance. As you are led inside, a pillared hall strewn with broken statuary looms all around you. Leaning against a cracked pillar is a drow with an eyepatch and a wide-brimmed hat. A saber hangs from his hip, and he cuts a dashing figure. "Well met!" he says with a smile.

When Matron Mother Quenthel Baenre resurrected House Do'Urden, she ordered her brother Jarlaxle to look after the long-abandoned Do'Urden estate. He now uses the ruined drow house as a Bregan D'aerthe base. Most of the house is off-limits to visitors, and Jarlaxle won't allow the characters to stay long.

Jarlaxle doesn't want the demon lords rampaging through the Underdark or making it to the surface world. If the characters reveal that their ultimate goal is to send the demon lords back to the Abyss, Jarlaxle gives them whatever aid he can short of doing their "dirty work" for them. If the characters mention Vizeran DeVir, Jarlaxle's interest is piqued, for he thought Vizeran was dead. He warns them not to trust that "relic of a bygone house." If the characters mention Vizeran's plan to make Menzoberranzan the site for the final showdown with the demon lords, Jarlaxle insists that the characters choose a different battleground, warning them that Bregan D'aerthe will oppose any effort to visit further destruction upon the city.

If the characters claim to be looking for a safe way into Sorcere, Jarlaxle arranges for a member of the Council of Spiders to visit the party at a Bregan D'aerthe safe house in West Wall. This male **drow mage** brings scrolls of *greater invisibility*—one for each party member—and also gives the characters a password that temporarily bypasses the tower's defenses. Characters who speak the password while inside the tower won't have to deal with the tower's *guards and wards* effect for a period of 1 hour (see "Sorcere" later in this chapter). Bregan D'aerthe makes sure that the characters have no hostile encounters as they make their way to the Academy.

Once he becomes aware of Gromph's grimoire, Jarlaxle does everything in his power to make sure the characters get the grimoire out of the city. Once

Vizeran's ritual is complete, Jarlaxle plans to send Bregan D'aerthe spies to find Vizeran and steal the grimoire, so that he has evidence he can lord over his brother.

Vizeran's plan is appealing to Jarlaxle because it doesn't cost him anything. As long as the adventurers are committed to driving the demon lords back to the Abyss, Jarlaxle keeps his Bregan D'aerthe forces on the sidelines, ready to defend Menzoberranzan.

XP Awards

If the party gains the support of Jarlaxle Baenre, award each character 1,500 XP.

A Change of Heart

At some point as the characters explore Menzoberranzan, Grin Ousstyl confesses that his master Vizeran has not been entirely truthful with the adventurers. (If Grin didn't accompany the characters to the city, he pursues and eventually catches up with them to share what he knows.)

Grin has studied Vizeran's work in crafting the *dark heart* talisman and its associated ritual to draw the demon lords together, and he believes that the ritual will have its intended effect regardless of where the talisman is placed. It doesn't need to be placed in Sorcere, or even in Menzoberranzan. Placing the talisman there only ensures that the drow city becomes the site of the demon lords' battle—and might well be laid waste in the process. If pressed, Grin admits that he isn't absolutely certain that Vizeran's ritual will work if the talisman is placed elsewhere. He's not as learned or powerful as his master.

Grin encourages the adventurers place the *dark heart* elsewhere and, in so doing, arrange a different battlefield for the demon lord showdown. He refuses to go along with any effort to leave the talisman in Menzoberranzan. If the characters intend to place the *dark heart* as planned, they need to find some way to convince Grin or ensure his silence. Alternatively, Grin can betray them to the nearest drow patrol, disclosing Vizeran's plan in the hope of saving the city.

Sorcere

The information the adventurers need to better understand the ritual that summoned the demon lords into the Underdark is in Gromph Baenre's sanctum within Sorcere, Menzoberranzan's academy of wizardry. The archmage's quarters have been declared off limits by Matron Mother Quenthel Baenre, who's trying to cover up Gromph's involvement in the devastating attack on Menzoberranzan.

The adventurers can safely enter Sorcere with the aid of Matron Mother Quenthel Baenre, Jarlaxle Baenre, or members of the Council of Spiders. Once inside, the characters on their own, as none of these NPCs or their agents want to be connected to the adventurers if things go awry.

Guards and Wards

The whole tower is protected by permanent *guards and wards* spells. The tower's drow residents are immune to the effects, but intruders are not. If the characters have the support of the Council of Spiders, members of the council give them a password which, when spoken aloud inside the tower, grants the speaker immunity to the spells' effect for 1 hour. After that, the password magically changes, and any characters still in the tower must deal with the *guards and wards* effect.

Random Encounters in Sorcere

Inside Sorcere, the characters might encounter drow wizards as well as their apprentices, familiars, and other magical creatures. If they enter with Quenthel Baenre's permission, they can avoid most trouble with the tower's inhabitants. Otherwise, stealth and caution will be important.

Have the characters make four DC 13 Dexterity (Stealth) group checks from the moment they enter the tower to when they reach the archmage's sanctum. Each failed group check results in an encounter from the Sorcere Encounters table. The characters make the same checks while exiting the tower.

If the tower goes on alert (as indicated in some of the encounter descriptions), all characters have disadvantage when making their group Dexterity (Stealth) checks.

Sorcere Encounters

d20	Encounter
1–6	1d4 **drow mages**
7–8	1 **giant spider**
9–10	1 invisible **quasit**
11–12	1 mad **drow mage**
13–14	1 **shadow demon**
15–18	1d4 slaves
19–20	1 **succubus** or **incubus**

Drow Mages

There is a 50 percent chance that these mages have been forewarned of the party's arrival, either by Vizeran DeVir or by Matron Mother Quenthel Baenre, in which case they let the characters pass. Otherwise, the drow mages assume the characters are intruders and attack unless Grin Ousstyl is with them. If the characters declare that they have Quenthel Baenre's permission to be here, they can convince the mages to stand down with a successful DC 12 Charisma (Deception or Persuasion) check.

If one or more mages fall in battle, the rest use *greater invisibility* spells to turn invisible and retreat, putting the tower on alert if it isn't already.

Giant Spider

This giant spider crawls along the walls or ceiling. It ignores the characters unless they take hostile action against it, in which case it attacks.

Invisible Quasit

A drow wizard's **quasit** familiar invisibly haunts the halls and chambers of the tower. It follows and observes the characters to find out what they're up to, leaving to alert its master (a **drow mage**) if they enter Gromph's sanctum or are seen leaving it. If the demon escapes, the tower goes on alert.

Mad Drow Mage

This drow is afflicted with a form of indefinite madness. Roll on the Indefinite Madness table in chapter 8 of the *Dungeon Master's Guide* to determine how the madness is expressed.

Shadow Demon

A bound servant of a drow mage, this demon attempts to hide from the characters, then follows to learn what they're up to. It fights the characters only if they attack it, fleeing if reduced to 10 or fewer hit points. If the demon escapes, the tower goes on alert.

Slaves

These **commoners** (your choice of race) are on an errand for their drow mage master when they run into the party by accident. If the characters state that they have legitimate business in Sorcere, the slaves answer questions about the tower if asked. If the slaves suspect the characters are trespassers, or if they're threatened or attacked, they flee and call for help. If any slaves escape the encounter, the tower goes on alert.

Succubus or Incubus

A sometime lover and ally of one of the tower's wizards, this fiend adopts the form of a slave (your choice of race). Curious to see the inside of Gromph's sanctum, the "slave" offers to guide the characters there, taking them along a route that avoids other random encounters. The fiend tries to steal Gromph's grimoire if the opportunity presents itself, first by using its Charm ability to convince a character to part with the book, and then by using Etherealness to disappear with it.

Gromph's Outer Sanctum

The black marble door to Gromph Baenre's chambers is etched with silvery runes around its edge and closed with an *arcane lock* keyed to him. Picking the lock requires a successful DC 23 Dexterity check using thieves' tools, while forcing the door open requires a successful DC 25 Strength check. A *knock* spell also opens the door, and Grin Ousstyl can have the spell prepared if none of the adventurers knows it.

> The chamber beyond the door is floored in black marble, lined with shelves laden with books and scrolls, and dominated by a broad desk of polished bone. A plush chair covered with lizard hide sits behind the desk, while a smaller and simpler zurkhwood chair sits facing it on the opposite side. A seven-foot-tall obsidian statue of a four-armed, sword-wielding drow warrior stands behind the desk against one wall. Burning red candles are set about the room in holders made from skeletal hands.

Continual flame spells have been cast on the dozen candles in the room, filling the area with bright light. If anyone other than Gromph enters the chamber without speaking the word *tyrnae* ("quench"), a **fire elemental** appears and attacks the intruders. Casting *dispel magic* (DC 15) on the door before it opens disables this trap, but the elemental can't be dispelled once it appears.

If anyone tampers with the desk or the shelves' contents, or attempts to remove anything from the room, the four-armed statue animates and attacks. It has the statistics of a **stone golem**, but replace its Multiattack and Slam action options with the following:

Multiattack. The golem makes four sword attacks.

Sword. *Melee Weapon Attack:* +10 to hit, reach 5 ft., one target. *Hit:* 10 (1d8 + 6) slashing damage.

Anyone speaking the statue's name (*Szashune*) aloud isn't attacked by it.

Trapped Secret Door

Any party member with a passive Wisdom (Perception) score of 20 or higher notices a secret door in the wall, while a character searching the room for secret doors must succeed on a DC 15 Wisdom (Perception) check to find it. Any creature with 12 Hit Dice or fewer that approaches within 5 feet of the secret door without speaking the word *khaless* ("trust") triggers an *imprisonment* spell (save DC 17). On a failed save, the creature is trapped in minimus containment inside a gemstone in Gromph's inner sanctum (described in the next section). The trap ceases to exist once a creature becomes imprisoned. A successful *dispel magic* (DC 19) cast on the secret door removes the trap.

Opening the secret door requires a *knock* spell or a successful DC 20 Intelligence (Arcana) check to assess and manipulate its magic. Beyond it lies a dark void that can't be dispelled or destroyed. Anyone or anything that touches the void is instantly transported to a labyrinthine demiplane similar to that created by a *maze* spell. A creature that succeeds on the DC 20 Intelligence check to escape the maze reappears in the middle of the outer sanctum. However, if a creature casts a spell of 5th level or higher while in the demiplane, all creatures and objects in the demiplane instantly appear in Gromph's inner sanctum instead.

TREASURE

The collection of rare books and scrolls in the archmage's chambers is worth 15,000 gp, assuming the characters have the means to haul it out. A character who spends 10 minutes poring over the collection can make a DC 15 Intelligence (Arcana) check. On a successful check, the character confirms that Gromph's grimoire isn't among the books in the collection and also identifies the collection's five most valuable tomes, worth 1,000 gp each. However, one of these valuable works is trapped with a *glyph of warding* that triggers the third effect of *bestow curse* (save DC 17), and which lasts until dispelled.

The drawers of the desk are sealed with *arcane lock* spells. Picking a drawer's lock requires thieves' tools and a successful DC 23 Dexterity check. A *knock* spell or a successful *dispel magic* (DC 15) cast on a drawer removes its magical lock. When opened, the drawers are empty. An effect similar to *Leomund's secret chest* shifts the drawers' contents into an extradimensional space when anyone other than Gromph opens them.

GROMPH'S INNER SANCTUM

Read the following text to players whose characters escape Gromph's demiplane (see "Gromph's Outer Sanctum") and appear in the archmage's inner sanctum.

> This circular chamber is lit by magic candles and floored in black stone, engraved and inlaid with magical diagrams in silver and gold. A female drow stands in the center of one magic circle, hands resting on her hips. Behind her, shelves and cabinets hold ceramic pots, glass vials, and other arcane paraphernalia, while a tome bound in black leather lies open on a lectern, its pages covered in spidery glyphs. The only exit appears to be an archway filled with a black void.

Any creature that touches the dark void is whisked away to the demiplane that separates Gromph's inner and outer sanctums (see the previous section for details).

A **yochlol** demon in drow form—Lolth's messenger to Gromph—is imprisoned within the magic circle. It pretends to be a drow priestess named Y'lara for as long as the disguise is useful, claiming to have been trapped in the circle by the archmage after failing to convince Gromph not to cast his spell (a lie). The demon tries to get the characters to free it by breaking the circle, whereupon it attacks and tries to kill them. As long as the circle is intact, the demon can't leave it and doesn't have line of effect to anything outside of the circle. The yochlol does whatever it can to prevent the adventurers from leaving with Gromph's grimoire (see "Treasure").

The characters can bargain with the trapped or defeated demon. It is reluctant to tell them what it knows, but angrily answers questions in exchange for its freedom. The demon tries to convince the characters to release it before it tells them what it knows, and any promises it makes are forgotten once it is freed.

The yochlol was sent by Lolth to "assist" Gromph with his ritual, knowing that it wouldn't work as intended. When Gromph lost control of the ritual, he fled the city, but not before trapping the yochlol. The yochlol knows that Gromph's inability to harness the *faerzress* is the reason why the ritual failed, but it doesn't know Gromph's present whereabouts. If the characters ask "Y'lara" what Lolth stands to gain from Gromph casting the ritual, the demon replies, "Chaos."

If the yochlol is killed, a character who investigates the grimoire can confirm beyond doubt that Gromph was responsible for bringing the demon lords to the Underdark.

TREASURE

Gromph's grimoire rests atop the lectern near the circle and bears the title *Zhaun'ol'leal* ("The Book of the Eight" in Elvish) and describes rituals for summoning and binding powerful demons. It's open to a chapter that talks about the summoning of Demogorgon.

The various arcane components and ritual items in the workroom are worth 1,000 gp total. A 6,000 gp diamond also sits on a small stand atop a workbench. It contains any creature trapped by the *imprisonment* spell that guards the secret door in Gromph's Outer Sanctum.

XP AWARDS

If the party acquires Gromph's grimoire, award each character 1,500 XP.

DEVELOPMENTS

By the end of this chapter, characters should have Gromph's grimoire and certain knowledge of the archmage's ritual in their possession. Given Grin Ousstyl's information, the characters are faced with a grim choice—place Vizeran's *dark heart* talisman in Menzoberranzan or in some other location. If they decide to leave it in Menzoberranzan, they must also decide how to deal with Grin, and possibly the wrath of Jarlaxle Baenre as well.

CHAPTER 16: THE FETID WEDDING

Zuggtmoy, Demon Queen of Fungi, plots to "wed" Araumycos, an enormous fungus occupying a large area of the Underdark. After uniting their powers in an unholy mockery of matrimony—in truth, a demonic rite of domination—Zuggtmoy will gain the power to transform the whole of the Underdark into her new Abyssal domain. The only things in her way are a core of resistance in the myconid community, the rage of her rival Juiblex, and the determination of the adventurers.

The characters receive a warning about Zuggtmoy's plans from Basidia, one of the myconid sovereigns of Neverlight Grove. After traveling to the caverns of Araumycos, they reach out to Araumycos's alien mind with the aid of Basidia's rapport spores, and try to free it from Zuggtmoy's demonic influence. Juiblex seizes the opportunity to crash the wedding, and the two demon lords do battle. When the characters sever Zuggtmoy's link with Araumycos, Juiblex destroys her material form, leaving the adventurers to face the remaining (and weakened) demon lord in battle.

WEDDING INVITATION

The adventurers become caught up in Zuggtmoy's plots when they experience a vision from the rebel myconids of Neverlight Grove, delivered by Sovereign Basidia. The characters know of Basidia and the myconids' struggles if they visited Neverlight Grove (see chapter 5). Otherwise, the myconids reach out to them if they sheltered Stool or Rumpadump for a time.

Basidia's vision can come at any point, whether the characters are asleep or awake. You can choose to have the vision affect all or some of the player characters, or to have some of their NPC followers affected as well. Read the following text aloud, making adjustments as necessary if the characters have not met Sovereign Basidia.

> A soft, glowing light rises from ahead, emanating from a vast cavern. The entire surface of the cave—floor, walls, and ceiling—is blanketed in moss and fungi, all in shades of white and soft pastels of pink, violet, green, and pale blue. The diffuse light the mushrooms shed makes the vista waver as if seen through mist.

> "Araumycos," a voice says in your mind. You turn and see a myconid sovereign standing beside you where there was no one before, recognizing Basidia of Neverlight Grove. "The largest and greatest being of our world," the myconid says sadly. "All that you see before you is Araumycos; all this and much more. All is in danger from the corruption that will claim the whole of the world if you do not help us."

Although myconids can normally use their rapport spores only over short distances, Basidia explains that Zuggtmoy has been spreading her own spores throughout the Underdark, channeling *faerzress*. By tapping into this growing presence, the myconid sovereign can rapport over great distances to ask the characters for their help.

Zuggtmoy, the demon queen who has corrupted the myconids, has made her intentions clear. She is leading her new followers to the vast cavern complex occupied by Araumycos, the largest life-form in the Underdark and perhaps in all the world. There, the two will be bonded in a demonic ceremony, giving Zuggtmoy dominion over a fungal kingdom larger and greater than any surface-world realm. To that end, she and her followers have been performing rituals and releasing spores to lull the great Araumycos into a kind of charmed sleep. The full implications are unclear to Basidia and the myconids, but as Araumycos is the oldest and most powerful being known to them, they greatly fear what Zuggtmoy's corruption of it will bring.

Fortunately, there is hope. Basidia believes it can assist in creating a rapport between the adventurers and Araumycos's vast, sleeping mind. The characters can help to awaken it and aid its struggle against the demon queen's influence. Or, if there's no other choice, they can destroy Araumycos before Zuggtmoy can claim the great creature as her own.

If Stool or Rumpadump have met the characters and are still alive, they join the rapport between Basidia and the characters, offering their support and encouragement as they implore the adventurers to intervene. If the characters saw the hideous Garden of Welcome in Neverlight Grove—or, worse yet, glimpsed the horrors of Yggmorgus—the myconids remind them that the whole world might become like that if Zuggtmoy unites Araumycos's power with her own.

Basidia proposes that the characters travel quickly to Araumycos, where the myconid sovereign will temporarily immunize them against the effects of the demon-tainted spores released by myconids under Zuggtmoy's influence. Basidia will then initiate a rapport with Araumycos while Zuggtmoy and her followers are preoccupied with the wedding ceremony.

Basidia and its followers can meet the adventurers within Araumycos's vast cavern complex. The sovereign is too closely watched to slip away and meet them before that, and it recommends that the characters avoid contact with other myconids on their travels. Basidia can use the extended rapport link to fix on the characters' location, and promises to find them when they are near the center of Araumycos. The vision then ends.

Myconid March

Shortly after the party receives Basidia's vision and warning, myconids and fungal creatures throughout the Underdark fall under the influence of Zuggtmoy's spreading spores, making a slow and steady march toward Araumycos, their "queen's betrothed." Thousands are on the move, and the procession has a bizarrely festive air, the fungi capering, dancing, and skipping as they celebrate the impending nuptials.

That behavior alone is alarming enough. However, under the demon queen's influence, the myconids and other fungi release clouds of spores as they move through the tunnels of the Underdark. Strange perfumes and scents fill the air. The marching myconids sow chaos as they move through the Underdark, passing around the Darklake. Other intelligent Underdark creatures give the procession a wide berth.

Characters making their way toward Araumycos can avoid much of the risk by following Basidia's advice and staying away from the myconid march. If not, they run the risk of falling under Zuggtmoy's sway (see "Random Encounters" in this chapter).

Uninvited Guests

The fungi of the Underdark aren't the only ones on the move. Juiblex the Faceless Lord has caught wind of its rival Zuggtmoy's intentions and mobilized an army of oozes now making its way toward Araumycos. The demon lord wants to slow Zuggtmoy's progress toward her goal. More importantly, though, Juiblex seeks the opportunity to appear at the ceremony, either to thwart its rival's intentions, take advantage of Araumycos's vulnerability, or both. Though Araumycos represents the perfect mate to Zuggtmoy, Juiblex sees it only as a living feast of tremendous proportions.

With both forces on the move, outbreaks of violence between oozes and fungi become more common, although the followers of Zuggtmoy outnumber the Faceless Lord's creatures.

Araumycos: General Features

The domain of Araumycos is a bizarre fungal realm in the heart of the Underdark.

Light. Araumycos's tunnels and caverns are dimly lit by phosphorescent fungi.

Terrain. Fungal life fills the caverns and passageways in the region, with visitors literally walking upon and within Araumycos upon entering its domain. The floor is carpeted with thick mold and fungus, creating patches of difficult terrain throughout. In some tunnels and caves, fungi growths obstruct passage. Characters either have to climb or hack their way through the fungal growth. In other places, the fungus covering the floor is soft enough that characters can sink into it with no warning. Use the quicksand rules in chapter 5, "Adventure Environments," of the *Dungeon Master's Guide* for such areas. Creatures that fail to escape become food for Araumycos.

ARAUMYCOS

Some forty miles southeast of the Darklake lies the vast territory of Araumycos (see the Underdark overview map in chapter 2).

RANDOM ENCOUNTERS

As the characters travel toward Araumycos, use the Creature Encounters table in this section rather than the Creature Encounters table in chapter 2.

Once the characters enter Araumycos's territory, use the Araumycos Encounters table instead of the random encounter tables in chapter 2. While the characters are in Araumycos's domain, check for a random encounter twice per day: once while they are traveling, and again while they are camped or resting.

CREATURE ENCOUNTERS

d20	Encounter
1	Death tyrant
2–6	Demons
7–8	Gnoll pack
9–10	Gricks
11–14	Myconid parade
15–18	Oozes
19–20	Two-headed trolls

ARAUMYCOS ENCOUNTERS

d20	Encounter
1–5	No encounter
6–10	Fungi
11–14	Mold pit
15–17	Myconid parade
18–20	Oozes

DEATH TYRANT

Characters within 1 mile of the death tyrant's lair feel as if they're being watched even when they aren't. While defending its cavernous lair, the tyrant avails itself of its lair actions.

Treasure. If the characters defeat the death tyrant, they can plunder its hoard: 4d6 × 1,000 gp, 5d6 × 100 pp, 3d6 500 gp gems, and 1d6 magic items (determine each one by rolling on Magic Item Table C in chapter 8 of the *Dungeon Master's Guide*).

DEMONS

One or more demons encounter the party and attack. Roll a d12 and consult the Demons table to determine what the characters meet.

DEMONS

d20	Demons
1–2	2d4 barlguras
3–4	2d4 chasmes
5–6	1d4 hezrous
7–8	1d100 manes
9–10	1 nalfeshnee
11–12	2d4 vrocks

FUNGI

This encounter occurs only while the characters are traveling; otherwise, treat it as "no encounter."

The party happens upon a cave overgrown with fungi. Roll a d6 and consult the Fungi table to determine what special type of fungi can be found here.

If this encounter takes place in Araumycos's domain, an overabundance of fungi cover all of the other cave exits, requiring the characters to hack or blast their way through (or find a route around).

FUNGI

d6	Fungi
1	1d6 gas spores
2	1d6 violet fungi
3–4	3d6 edible fungi (choose from the varieties in "Fungi of the Underdark" in chapter 2)
5–6	3d6 exotic fungi (choose from the varieties in "Fungi of the Underdark" in chapter 2)

GNOLL PACK

A hunting pack consisting of one **gnoll pack lord** and 3d6 **gnolls** has been driven into a frenzy by the presence of Yeenoghu in the Underdark. The characters can't be surprised by the gnolls, whose incessant cackling gives them away.

GRICKS

A **grick alpha** and 1d4 + 2 **gricks** lair in a cave. They spring out from hiding to attack any creature that stumbles into their territory.

MOLD PIT

One party member (determined randomly) steps on a pit of soft mold hidden beneath a thin carpet of moss, and sinks into it. The effect is identical to that of quicksand (see chapter 5, "Adventure Environments," of the *Dungeon Master's Guide*).

MYCONID PARADE

The characters stumble upon 1d4 **myconid adults**, 2d6 **myconid sprouts**, and one or more spore servants. Roll a d8 and consult the Spore Servants table to determine what kind of spore servants are present.

SPORE SERVANTS

d8	Spore Servants
1–2	1d6 chuul spore servants (see appendix C)
3–4	1d6 drow spore servants 1d6 duergar spore servants (see appendix C for both)
5–6	1d6 drow spore servants (see appendix C) and 1d6 quaggoth spore servants
7–8	1d6 hook horror spore servants (see appendix C)

Subjects of Zuggtmoy, the myconids and their spore servants caper and dance madly to music only they can hear. The myconids insist that all other creatures they meet join them, releasing a cloud of spores if anyone refuses to do so. They can release this cloud once, and any creature within 30 feet of one or more of the myconids when the cloud is released must succeed on a DC 11 Constitution saving throw or become charmed. While charmed in this way, a creature can do nothing other than dance and use its movement to follow the myconid parade. The creature can repeat the saving throw at the end of each hour, ending the effect on itself on a success. Casting *lesser restoration*, *greater restoration*, *remove curse*, or similar magic on a creature also ends the effect on it.

The myconids and their spore servants attack only if they're attacked or prevented from continuing on their march.

Oozes

The characters encounter one or more oozes. Roll a d4 and consult the Oozes table to determine what kinds of oozes the characters encounter.

Oozes

d4	Oozes
1	1 black pudding and 1d6 gray oozes
2	1 black pudding and 1d4 ochre jellies
3	3d6 black puddings
4	2d4 gelatinous cubes

If the encounter occurs en route to Araumycos, the oozes are slithering toward the giant fungus. Otherwise, the oozes are feasting on Araumycos itself. In either event, the oozes fight only in self-defense.

Two-Headed Trolls

Warped by Demogorgon's presence in the Underdark, these trolls have each grown a second head. As part of its Multiattack routine, a two-headed troll can make a Bite attack as a bonus action on its turn. The party encounters 1d4 + 1 of these hungry creatures, which otherwise have the statistics of a normal **troll**.

Enter the Groom

In the time it takes the characters to reach Araumycos's caverns after receiving Basidia's message, Zuggtmoy and her fungal entourage arrive at the site of the ceremony, near the center of those caverns. The entourage includes hundreds of **myconid adults** and **myconid sprouts**, accompanied by **awakened zurkhwoods** and **bridesmaids of Zuggtmoy** (both from appendix C), as well as ambulatory fungi such as **violet fungi** and **gas spores**. Various spore servants fill out Zuggtmoy's entourage (see the "Myconids" entry of the *Monster Manual* and appendix C of this adventure).

Basidia's Aid

As the characters approach the center of Araumycos's great cavern complex, Basidia meets them with a small detachment of loyal myconids. The myconid sovereign explains that it can infuse the characters with rapport spores and neutralized servitor spores, enabling them to blend in with the fungal servitors accompanying Zuggtmoy. The characters then have a few hours to make their way to the center of Araumycos's territory where Zuggtmoy's ritual is set to take place.

When they are sufficiently close to the epicenter of the ritual, the characters will be able to enter rapport with Araumycos. Basidia's rapport spores help facilitate the process, but Araumycos's sleeping mind isn't in full control of the defenses of its body, and might interpret the characters' presence as an attack. Basidia warns the characters that they must be on their guard for a reaction from the vast fungus.

Once the characters have entered rapport, they must seek out Araumycos's sleeping mind and awaken it to the danger it faces. Basidia doesn't know if Zuggtmoy will become aware of what the characters are doing, but if she does, they will have only a limited amount of time before the demon queen tries to stop them.

Ooze Spies

Once Basidia has explained the plan to the characters, read the following boxed text aloud to the players.

> Even as the myconid sovereign's thoughts fill your mind, you become aware of a faint hissing and fizzing sound. The fungus around you dissolves to a formless goo as something moves in the undergrowth to surround you!

A pair of regenerating **black puddings**, spies for Juiblex, slither through the undergrowth to attack the party. The characters' myconid allies fall back from the fray, desperate to protect Sovereign Basidia and pleading for the adventurers' aid through the telepathic rapport they share.

Empowered by Juiblex, these regenerating black puddings have an Intelligence of 6 (−2) and the following feature, which increases each pudding's challenge rating to 5 (1,800 XP).

Regeneration. The pudding regains 10 hit points at the start of its turn. If the pudding takes fire damage, this trait doesn't function at the start of the pudding's next turn. The pudding dies only if it starts its turn with 0 hit points and doesn't regenerate.

Across the Fungal Fields

Once the characters receive Basidia's spores and overcome Juiblex's black pudding spies, they should set out at once for the depths of Araumycos as the rapport takes hold. Unfortunately, they have no means of assuring the slumbering fungal entity of their intentions, and the growing threat posed by Zuggtmoy and the demon lords has roused Araumycos's defenses.

> The pastel colors of fungi transform the caverns you pass through into softly glowing meadows. The floor is spongy, and the myconid spores are making you start to feel drowsy—at least, you hope that's what's behind this strange sensation. Then you feel the ground beneath you shift as something moves—a number of a thick, spiky tendrils bursting from the ground.

Two fungal creatures resembling **otyughs** rise up and attack the characters. Created by Araumycos to perfectly duplicate the abilities, traits, and actions of otyughs, these creatures are plants rather than aberrations. They attack until slain, whereupon each bursts into a cloud of sweet-smelling spores as its body dissolves back into the larger mass of fungi filling the cavern.

Read the following to the players when the final creature is defeated.

> The creature bursts like an overfull wineskin, releasing a clear ichor and a cloud of dusty spores. The deflating bulk of its body sinks back beneath the shimmering fungal field where you stand. Your vision starts to swim, and you feel dizzy and faint. Your limbs are numb and your legs no longer support you.

A successful DC 13 Intelligence (Arcana or Nature) check confirms that the characters are in no physical danger but are entering rapport with Araumycos. The adventurers are paralyzed as the myconid spores fully take effect. Even creatures immune to sleep and paralysis are affected as the spores seep into mind and body. The characters collapse harmlessly to the soft surface of Araumycos, its fungus quickly spreading across them as the rapport begins. When this happens, continue with "Into the Gray Dream."

INTO THE GRAY DREAM

The rapport with Araumycos affects the adventurers like an *astral projection* spell, sending their astral bodies out into the Astral Plane where Araumycos's vast, dreaming mind resides. Their bodies remain unconscious in suspended animation while they are projected into the Astral Plane. Read the following aloud to the players.

> You are floating, weightless, adrift. A gray, silvery light spreads around you like the dawn of a cloudy day, illuminating a peculiar realm. All of you are floating in a silvery haze that shimmers with swirls of color. Objects drift past in the distance, but whether they are small stones or rocks the size of mountains, you can't say for certain. Your moment of reverie is broken by the sound of Basidia's voice in your mind. "It begins."

The adventurers, now psychically linked with both the myconid sovereign and Araumycos, are aware of the demon queen and her minions performing Zuggtmoy's demonic ritual.

> Through your link with Basidia, you sense that Zuggtmoy's wedding ceremony has begun. Receiving the myconid's impressions, you become aware of a huge crowd of fungal creatures and spore servants—hundreds, perhaps thousands of them—watching as a grotesque procession makes its way through them. Myconids of all sizes caper madly before a troupe of giant animated mushrooms, bearing a mossy litter upon which sits the Demon Queen of Fungi in all her terrible splendor.
>
> Zuggtmoy is draped and veiled in molds and fruiting mushrooms woven into a grotesque gown. Vaguely humanoid figures set with clusters of luminescent lichen and tumescent fungal growths follow her like bridesmaids, carrying a veil and train of lacy mycelia. Stepping off the litter as her followers set it down, the Demon Queen of Fungi rises to tower above all the creatures around her. "My betrothed," she intones, the meaning of her words clear within the vision. "I am here at last."

THE MIND OF ARAUMYCOS

Navigating on the Astral Plane is largely a matter of thought and perception. The characters feel a psychic "pull" in the right direction as they seek out the consciousness of Araumycos with their own minds. A creature flies through the Astral Plane at a speed in feet equal to 3 × its Intelligence score, but a feeling of timelessness on the plane makes it difficult to judge the length of the journey.

The characters' thoughts draw them toward a distant, floating object. It appears to be a hemisphere, until its slow rotation reveals its true form: a giant skull missing its jawbone, formed out of some kind of pale rock. As the characters draw closer, the skull reveals itself to be the size of a small mountain. Its surface is covered in lichens and broad patches of mold, the colors resembling those of Araumycos on the Material Plane.

Through the empty eye sockets of the skull, the adventurers can see that its interior is hollow and filled with a bewildering variety of giant fungi. Tendrils and growths extend outward, twining together to form a mass suspended in the middle of the open space—a brain-shaped fungus the size of a castle.

The closer the characters come to the floating skull, the more strongly they feel a presence—the mind of Araumycos, to which they are linked. That consciousness is largely unaware of them, lulled by the insidious influence of Zuggtmoy's spores and unable to resist the demon queen's presence.

Wedding Crashers

When any character enters the skull or touches its surface, the mind of Araumycos stirs—and the Demon Queen of Fungi senses it. Read the following to the players as Zuggtmoy uses the connection of the rapport spores to push into Araumycos's mind.

> "Who dares?" a voice shouts in your mind. "Who dares disturb my intended nuptials?" Spores and tendrils erupt from the surface of the skull, coalescing before your eyes into the image of the Demon Queen of Fungi, her dead eyes glaring with inhuman fury.

Zuggtmoy projects her psychic presence to confront the characters, while at the same time maintaining limited control over her material form. She intends to complete the ritual necessary to grant her full power over Araumycos, needing only to delay or destroy the intruders in order to succeed. The split in the Demon Queen's attention works in their favor, as Zuggtmoy's demonic rival Juiblex chooses that moment to launch its attack and claim Araumycos for its own.

Before Zuggtmoy acts against the adventurers, the demon queen is distracted, turning away to glance at something they can't see. She hisses the name "Juiblex" like a curse, then recoils as if struck. Her image then vanishes.

The Sleeper Wakes

As the psychic din awakens Araumycos from its trance, the shimmering colors piercing the silver of the Astral Plane flare even brighter. The following round, Araumycos enters into full rapport with the characters and their myconid allies. The entity reveals that Zuggtmoy has already infected its mind with her demonic influence, which Araumycos can feel growing in strength. It's only a matter of time before it falls to the demon queen's will. Focused but fearful, the entity asks the adventurers to cut out and destroy the diseased part of its mind before it's too late.

The characters are guided to the far side of the suspended fungus cluster inside the skull, where a dark mass is spreading. The first time any character comes within 20 feet of the dark mass, it erupts with the effect of an *Evard's black tentacles* spell. The infected area of Araumycos's mind has AC 13, 100 hit points, and vulnerability to necrotic and psychic damage.

When the infected area first takes damage, Zuggtmoy senses it and turns her attention away from Juiblex in an attempt to stop the characters. As she exerts her will over Araumycos, a burst of spores spreads out in a cloud from the infected area. Any creature within 20 feet of the infected area must make a successful DC 19 Constitution saving throw or take 3d6 poison damage and become poisoned. While poisoned in this way, the creature takes 3d6 poison damage at the start of each of its turns. A poisoned creature can repeat the saving throw on each of its turns, ending the effect on itself on a success.

As the characters destroy more of the infected area, the view beyond the bounds of the skull chamber begins to darken. When the area reaches 0 hit points, a powerful psychic wind howls through the area. Each character must make a successful DC 15 Intelligence saving throw to avoid the mental effect of a psychic wind (see "The Astral Plane" in chapter 2 of the *Dungeon Master's Guide*). This psychic wind has no location effect, as the rapport ends thereafter and the characters awaken back in their physical bodies. Physical damage and ongoing effects suffered by their astral forms aren't carried over to the characters' physical bodies.

Let Them Speak Now …

If the characters free Araumycos from Zuggtmoy's influence, they weaken the power of the Demon Queen of Fungi, fatally distracting her. With the loss of many of her fungal minions and the amount of power she has expended to perform her ritual, Zuggtmoy is weakened to the point that Juiblex overwhelms her, destroying and consuming her material form and casting her essence back into the Abyss.

Characters reduced to 0 hit points in the battle on the Astral Plane are catapulted back to their bodies on the Material Plane. Their rapport with Araumycos is broken, and they are helpless to intervene further in the conflict going on within the entity's mind. You can have a group of oozes or spore servants from the Araumycos Encounters table appear in the cavern where the adventurers entered into rapport with Araumycos, so that characters shunted out of that rapport can defend their compatriots' helpless bodies while the fight continues.

If all the characters are defeated on the Astral Plane, the awakened Araumycos remains conscious enough to resist Zuggtmoy with a final effort, sufficient to distract the Demon Queen of Fungi and thereby allowing Juiblex to overwhelm her. In any event, the characters can hear the battle between Juiblex and Zuggtmoy unfolding in the ritual cavern just a few minutes ahead of them.

Retreat!

If the adventurers retreat from the sounds of battle, they barely escape from a partial collapse of their local section of Araumycos's cavern complex. They race ahead of a small horde of Zuggtmoy's minions, which are crushed by falling rock that also seals off the characters' escape route. Basidia and some of the myconid rebels survive, and will accompany the adventurers out of Araumycos's caverns before returning to Neverlight Grove to root out any remainder of the demon queen's infestation.

To Battle!

If the adventurers head toward the battle between the two demon lords after awakening from their rapport, they arrive just in time to see the grotesque display of the Faceless Lord slurping up the defeated Zuggtmoy into the mass of its body, enveloping and dissolving her before turning its attention toward the newcomers.

FIGHTING THE FACELESS LORD

Under normal circumstances, **Juiblex** (see appendix D) would be an overwhelming foe. Fortunately for the adventurers, the Faceless Lord's battle with Zuggtmoy has weakened it. The characters might also have aid from allies, the newly freed myconids, and Araumycos in overcoming the demon lord.

Apply the following penalties to Juiblex:

- Its current hit points are 200.
- It has no more uses of Legendary Resistance for the day.
- Its Eject Slime action has been used and must recharge.
- It has no lair actions or regional effects.

Basidia rallies thirty **myconid adults** and thirty-two **drow spore servants** (see appendix C) to fight alongside the characters. Their attacks are incapable of harming Juiblex. However, as they swarm around the demon lord, one time per round (as agreed upon by the players), a character who would be hit by an attack can have a myconid or a spore servant hit by the attack instead. The myconids can also fight off oozes, allowing the adventurers to focus their attention on the demon lord.

If the adventurers freed it from Zuggtmoy's influence, Araumycos aids them by releasing spores into the cavern, granting all living creatures in the area immunity to poison damage and the poisoned condition.

VICTORY OR DEFEAT

The characters might overcome two demon lords if they are successful in this chapter. If they fail, terrible consequences unfold for the myconids and other creatures of the Underdark, though the adventurers will get another chance to take the fight to Zuggtmoy, Juiblex, and all the other demon lords in chapter 17.

ESCAPING DEFEAT

If the characters lose their battle against Juiblex, their best hope lies in Vizeran DeVir's ritual. In the worst-case scenario where one or more heroes fall in the fight against the Faceless Lord, their allies might be able to carry them to safety so that they can be healed or restored to life.

If the adventurers flee from Juiblex, the demon lord pursues them. However, Araumycos (or its death throes) triggers a cave-in, allowing defeated characters to barely escape. Juiblex then turns its attention to feeding on Araumycos and is one of the demon lords drawn into battle by Vizeran's ritual in chapter 17.

ACHIEVING VICTORY

If the adventurers succeed, they achieve a great victory with two demon lords banished back to the Abyss. The creatures under the demon lords' influence eventually return to normal. Neither Zuggtmoy nor Juiblex is truly destroyed, however. Each demon lord reforms on its layer of the Abyss, never forgetting those responsible for its defeat.

The elimination of the Demon Queen of Fungi wins the adventurers the eternal gratitude of the surviving myconids of Neverlight Grove. Basidia quickly assumes leadership of the grove, taking steps to heal the minds of those myconids afflicted by demonic corruption. The myconids also declare their intention to cleanse their home of Zuggtmoy's lingering influence.

The removal of Juiblex from the Underdark causes most oozes and related creatures to revert to their normal state. If the Pudding King survived this long, he retreats to Blingdenstone, but it's a far easier matter for the deep gnomes to deal with him and his oozing minions without Juiblex around.

DEVELOPMENTS

Even if Araumycos survives, its fate is unclear. The entity's mind has clearly been damaged by both the necessity of cutting away its corruption and the buffeting force of the psychic wind that followed. Basidia and the myconids offer to meld with Araumycos to try to heal it and guide it back to wholeness. Though not as serious as death, the trauma still causes a significant amount of fungal die-off in areas of the creature's domain, potentially uncovering lost ruins or other hidden sites.

In addition to possible victory over one or two demon lords, the adventurers receive one last bequest from the mind of Araumycos. A puff of rapport spores or a lingering psychic connection informs them of one or more of the secrets of the Underdark gathered during the entity's vast existence. If you want to provide the players with any remaining information about virtually anything in the adventure, this is an excellent opportunity to do so.

TREASURE

In addition to (or instead of) providing information to the adventurers, the last connection to the surviving Araumycos can bestow a *charm of heroism* to all the player characters (see "Other Rewards" in chapter 7 of the *Dungeon Master's Guide*).

Additionally, the thirteen timmask mushrooms on the list of required components that Vizeran needs to create his *dark heart* talisman (see chapter 12) can be found in the aftermath of the failed wedding ceremony, sprouting in locations touched by Zuggtmoy or Juiblex.

If the characters didn't collect traces of Yeenoghu's blood from the fallen goristro in chapter 14, any successful weapon attack against Juiblex in this chapter leaves traces of the Faceless Lord's blood on a character's weapon. Collecting this blood for Vizeran DeVir provides another component he needs to craft his *dark heart* talisman.

XP AWARDS

If the characters rid Araumycos's mind of its demonic infection, award each of them 2,000 XP. If the party delivers to Vizeran all of the components he needs to craft his *dark heart* talisman, award each character an additional 2,500 XP.

Chapter 17: Against the Demon Lords

In the culmination of *Out of the Abyss*, the heroes implement Vizeran DeVir's scheme to take on the demon lords. The archmage's ritual draws the demon lords together to fight to the death, leaving Demogorgon victorious but weakened as the adventurers face off against the Prince of Demons. Even wounded and weakened, though, Demogorgon is a legendary foe, and the fate of the Underdark and all Faerûn rests on the adventurers' final battle.

Readying the Plan

Over the course of their adventures, the characters have collected the components needed to create the talisman at the center of Vizeran DeVir's summoning ritual:

- The intact and unhatched egg of a purple worm (from the worm hatchery in chapter 13)
- The central eye of a beholder (from Karazikar in the Vast Oblivium in chapter 13, or some other source).
- Six feathers from six different angels (from the petrified angels in the Labyrinth in chapter 14)
- The heart of a goristro (from the demon slain by Yeenoghu in chapter 14)
- Thirteen timmasks sprouted from the footprint of a greater demon (from Araumycos's cavern in chapter 16, or elsewhere)
- Gromph Baenre's grimoire (from Sorcere in chapter 15)

- A few drops of blood or ichor from a demon lord (from Yeenoghu's battle with the goristro in chapter 14, or from fighting Juiblex in chapter 16)

After Vizeran DeVir uses these components to create the talisman known as the *dark heart* to draw forth the exiled demon lords from across the Underdark, he expects the adventurers to plant it in Menzoberranzan. Having learned from Vizeran's apprentice Grin Ousstyl of the archmage's secret goal to see the city destroyed, the characters might decide to place the *dark heart* talisman elsewhere, determining the battlefield for their confrontation with the demon lords (see "Let This Be Their Battlefield").

Enacting the Plan

Once the *dark heart* is in place, the ritual can begin. The adventurers and their allies take up a position not far from the *dark heart*, close to where the demons will appear. Where exactly depends on the placement of the talisman and the adventurers' own tactics and plans. They can use a *sending* spell to signal Vizeran to begin the ritual once the talisman is in place. (If none of the characters can cast *sending*, Vizeran can provide the spell on a *spell scroll*).

Vizeran (assisted by Grin if the apprentice is available), performs the complex ritual in the sanctum of his tower. The ritual causes the *dark heart* to radiate a summons throughout the Underdark using the *faerzress*—an irresistible call drawing the demons toward it. When the ritual reaches its conclusion at the end of nine hours, portals of *faerzress* form. All the

demons and demon lords in the Underdark are drawn through those portals, appearing together in the area around the *dark heart* talisman.

Enraged by being forcibly summoned yet again by a ritual, the demons fly into a frenzy once they see each other, beginning a battle to the death. As each demon's material form is destroyed, its essence is banished back into the Abyss. The task of the adventurers is to be close at hand but not get caught up in the battle until one demon lord is left standing, weakened and spent from the conflict. That becomes the adventurers' cue to attack and destroy the last demon lord, banishing it to the Abyss if they succeed.

LET THIS BE THEIR BATTLEFIELD

The players can choose where their characters confront the demon lords by deciding where to set the *dark heart* talisman. Vizeran's preference is anywhere in Menzoberranzan, because he wants all drow to see the poisoned fruits of their misplaced worship of Lolth. However, from what Grin Ousstyl tells them in chapter 15, the adventurers should learn that the talisman can be placed in any location.

Wherever the players decide to place the talisman, their characters must travel to that location while Vizeran makes his final preparations for the ritual. Given their experiences in the Underdark, the adventurers should be able to think of a number of likely sites for the final battle. A few likely options are discussed here.

ARAUMYCOS

At the center of the network of caves and passages inhabited by Araumycos, the cavern where Juiblex and Zuggtmoy battled in chapter 16 is a good potential site. If the vast fungal colony is already dead or badly damaged by its abuse at Zuggtmoy's hands, it's in no position to object. Otherwise, it opposes becoming a battlefield out of a sense of self-preservation. Unleashing the demons within Araumycos does considerable damage to the fungal colony, but doesn't destroy it.

Broken Heart

If the characters lose or destroy the *dark heart*, they either have to go through the process of gathering the necessary components to make a replacement, or abandon Vizeran's plan. See "Loose Threads" later in this chapter for ideas about what to do if the plan never gets off the ground.

Neverlight Grove

If the characters inform the myconids of their need for a place to stage a daring last battle, Sovereign Basidia or another myconid representative might offer Neverlight Grove. The ranks of the myconids have been decimated by Zuggtmoy's depredations and the fetid wedding, and many fear their beloved caverns are corrupted. They are willing to seek a new home (perhaps in the caverns of Araumycos) and grateful enough to the heroes that they will sacrifice their old home to help them.

Sloobludop

The ruins of the kuo-toa settlement (see chapter 3) could become the site of the final fight against the demon lords. Shuushar the Awakened can be convinced to help evacuate the remaining inhabitants if asked. The nearby Darklake creates its own challenges, particularly given the presence of ixitxachitl loyal to Demogorgon.

Araj

Characters looking to double-cross Vizeran—or those with a sense of poetic justice—might hide the *dark heart* somewhere in the drow archmage's tower or the surrounding cavern. This reduces the number of bystanders, contains the demons and their battle, and ensures Vizeran's enmity.

Confronting the Demon Lords

The demon lords are some of the most powerful foes a party of adventurers could face. Indeed, any one of them at full strength could wipe out a group of 15th-level characters with ease. Fortunately for the heroes, the goal of Vizeran's plan isn't to fight multiple demon lords, but to turn them against each other. With the right combination of preparation, timing, and execution, the characters set the trap that Vizeran springs with his ritual—and hope whichever demon lord survives is weakened enough for them to destroy it.

Allied Forces

Vizeran is needed to perform the ritual, placing him far from the battle and leaving him with three levels of exhaustion (see appendix A of the *Player's Handbook*) once the ritual is completed. He is thus unwilling to aid the characters during the fight. The archmage prefers to keep Grin Ousstyl to assist him, so the drow mage is likewise unable to assist. However, the adventurers have a number of other allies willing to fight alongside them in this last battle.

Most of the heroes' allies are of limited use against the demon lords—creatures immune to many forms of attack, including nonmagical weapons. Rather than dealing with the ineffectual attacks of allies or a dozen or more additional actions each round, give characters backed up by a group of allies the following benefits.

Option: Jimjar's Last Gamble

If the adventurers need some extra help in their epic final battle at the end of the campaign, consider the following option involving Jimjar, the deep gnome gambler they met in the drow slave pen in chapter 1 of the adventure.

"Jimjar" isn't at all who he appears. He is, in fact, a god or other great power in disguise—or the Chosen of such a power—and has been watching the heroes since their first encounter in Velkynvelve. His reasons for doing this are his own, but when push comes to shove, he can give the heroes some help in overcoming the demon lords.

At an opportune moment, Jimjar shows up (even returning from death if he appeared to perish earlier in the adventure) and gives the characters a vote of encouragement, telling them, "I bet you can do this." Each character gains inspiration and a *blessing of wound closure* (see "Other Rewards" in chapter 7 of the *Dungeon Master's Guide*). Jimjar disappears afterward, potentially putting in one last appearance at the end of the adventure to hint as to his true nature before vanishing into the Underdark.

Who is Jimjar really? That depends on your characters and the campaign, but one of the characters' patron deities is a good possibility. He might also be a gnomish god such as Garl Glittergold or Callarduran Smoothhands, known tricksters and shapeshifters, and foes of demons and their ilk. The more important thing is that he serves as a "lucky charm" for the characters when they need him. This option works particularly well if the adventurers have been kind to the sometimes annoying deep gnome over the course of the campaign, earning his respect and gratitude.

Healing Support. A character regains 2d6 hit points at the end of each of his or her turns, provided the character has at least 1 hit point remaining.

Tactical Losses. Once each round, when a player character would be hit by an attack, a supporting ally is hit by the attack instead. The adventurers can use this option ten times before their allies are too weakened or depleted to provide assistance.

Heroic Sacrifice

Players should never have to think about sacrificing their characters, but you should be prepared for the possibility of one or more of the heroes giving up their lives in order to defeat the evil that has arisen in the Underdark. It's up to you how to handle such a high-stakes event, but consider treating it as an extreme variation of "Success at a Cost" from chapter 8 of the *Dungeon Master's Guide*. At the very least, a player deliberately sacrificing his or her character's life in a final, selfless heroic effort—the antithesis of the selfishness and evil of the Abyss—should grant all the character's allies inspiration. The sacrifice might not be enough to win the day on its own, but it can help turn the tide.

Rage of Demons

Once the *dark heart* talisman is placed and the characters signal Vizeran, there's no turning back.

> The waiting is the hard part. Time seems to drag as you remain alert, weapons drawn, every nerve singing with the tension in the air all around you.
>
> Finally, a swirling light begins to flare in the darkness. A barely audible humming shakes you to the core, rising and falling like a vast heartbeat in the depths. The glow of *faerzress* gathers and brightens, creating swirling pools like holes torn in the air. A roar sounds from far away as shadows move in the depths of those pools of light. The demons are coming.

The demon lords described in appendix D of this adventure all appear in the final battle, with the following exceptions:

- If Fraz-Urb'luu was not sent back to the Abyss in chapter 9, his gemstone is hurled into the fray by Vizeran's ritual. Unless the characters retrieve it, another demon lord steps on the gem, destroys it, and sends Fraz-Urb'luu's spirit back to the Abyss.
- If Juiblex and Zuggtmoy were sent back to the Abyss in earlier parts of the adventure, they are not present.
- Baphomet and Yeenoghu are absent if the characters activated the Maze Engine (see chapter 14) and the 81–100 result on the Maze Engine Effects table came up.

Numerous other demons also pour through the portals. For a brief moment, all of the demons and demon lords are disoriented as they attempt to get their bearings after being pulled across the Underdark. Then as their gazes fall upon each other, they roar, bellow, or shriek with a hatred too deep for mortals to truly comprehend, and the terrible battle begins.

Option: Playing Out the Battle

Rather than focusing on the adventurers biding their time and dealing with the fallout of the titanic battle between the demon lords, you can shift focus for this part of the adventure. Consider having the players take control of the various demon lords from appendix D, then play out the conflict between them.

Assign each player an available demon lord, or allow players to choose one demon lord to control during the battle. You manage any of the remaining demon lords. If there aren't enough demon lords for all the players, you can use **balors** or other powerful demons to round out their numbers.

The players control the demons in their battle to the death, with the only restriction being that they can't withdraw from the combat. Brief tactical retreats are permissible, but Vizeran's ritual has filled the demon lords with the rage to do battle.

The demonic victor of this battle, its hit points and other resources sufficiently depleted, is the foe that the adventurers must overcome in the final confrontation.

Demon Showdown

Ideally, the adventurers and their allies remain hidden from the battling demons, letting them fight it out among themselves. Still, there are challenges for the characters to overcome as they wait. Feel free to include as many of the following as you wish while narrating the struggle between the demon lords and their minions, keeping in mind that the characters will have no time for even a short rest before taking on the main challenge of this encounter—a fight with the sole remaining demon lord.

Demon Sortie

Rampaging lesser demons discover one or more of the characters where they wait out the battle, attacking at once. Roll a d4 to determine the demons involved.

Demon Sortie Force

d4	Demon Sortie
1	4 barlguras
2	4 chasmes
3	2 hezrous
4	3 vrocks

Demon Thief

An invisible **quasit** tries to steal a small, valuable item from a party member. The target must succeed on a DC 13 Wisdom (Perception) check to notice the theft as it happens. On a failed check, the quasit makes off with the item undetected. You can make the search for the item a loose thread for the conclusion of the adventure. Alternatively, have the quasit killed during the battle, with the stolen item turning up in the aftermath.

Endangered Allies

If any of the player characters' allies are accompanying them, a demon sortie (see above) attacks the NPCs. The characters must decide whether or not to break cover to aid their allies against the demons. If they do, another demon sortie attacks them 1d4 rounds later.

Near Miss

The battle between the demon lords shifts dangerously close to the characters. Roll a d6 and consult the Near Miss table to determine the result.

Near Miss

d6	Event
1–2	**Explosion.** Each creature within 20 feet of a point you choose must make a DC 13 Dexterity saving throw. On a failure, the creature takes 3d6 fire damage, or half as much damage on a success.
3–4	**Flying Debris.** Each creature within 30 feet of a point you choose must make a DC 13 Dexterity saving throw, taking 3d6 bludgeoning damage and falling prone on a failure.
5–6	**Close Call.** A character you choose must make a successful DC 13 Dexterity saving throw to dodge a stray attack. On a failed save, the character takes 3d6 bludgeoning damage.

Threatened Bystanders

If the battle takes place in a populated area such as Menzoberranzan, the characters spot bystanders under attack by lesser demons that prefer to take on easy prey rather than fighting against their own kind. A dozen **dretches** or **manes** (50 percent chance of either) attack, killing and consuming their mortal victims unless the adventurers intervene.

Against Demogorgon

After running any events you wish from "The Battle," the struggle between the demon lords comes to an end as Demogorgon proves why he is known as the Prince of Demons.

> The sounds of battle finally die away, the ground before you stained black and red with demonic blood and ichor. In the terrible grip of Demogorgon, even the mighty Orcus looks almost small. Tentacles hold the Demon Prince of Undeath in a crushing grip, slithering across the maggot-riddled flesh of the horned demon, as they tighten inexorably. A strangled gasp issues from the demon lord's throat as a horrific crunching sound echoes throughout the cavern and his skull-topped wand clatters onto the floor.
>
> Demogorgon casts aside the limp form, which melts away as Orcus returns to the Abyss that spawned him. The Prince of Demons throws back his two heads and roars his triumph. As he does, his nearer head turns, burning eyes raking across the battlefield. Filled with bloodlust and battle rage, the demon lord searches for another target.

Determine the characters' starting positions based on their actions during the battle. Demogorgon should be at least 80 feet away from them initially, unless the players specifically stated they were remaining close to the demon lord.

Demogorgon has been wounded during the fight, giving the characters an edge in the battle to come. Apply the following penalties to the **Demogorgon** stat block in appendix D:

- Demogorgon has 290 hit points remaining and can't regain hit points due to the disruptive nature of Vizeran's *faerzress*-empowered ritual.
- He has only one use of Legendary Resistance remaining for the day.
- His *feeblemind* innate spell is expended, as are all but one use each of *dispel magic*, *fear*, and *telekinesis*.
- With all the other demon lords banished back to the Abyss, Demogorgon becomes the focus of the disruptive power of Vizeran's ritual. This imposes a −5 penalty to his attack rolls, ability checks, and saving throws.

Even in his weakened state, the demon lord remains a terrifying opponent, attacking the adventurers in a howling fury as battle is joined.

Alternative Showdown

If you prefer, a demon lord other than Demogorgon could be the victor of the demonic showdown and the final foe of the campaign. This is particularly appropriate if the adventurers earned the ire of a specific demon lord during the adventure (including Juiblex or Yeenoghu). Alternatively, one or more of the characters' backgrounds might be tied to a particular demon lord.

Wand of Orcus

When Orcus is defeated, he drops the *Wand of Orcus* (see chapter 7 of the *Dungeon Master's Guide*), which falls to the ground. A party member can try to grab the wand before Demogorgon seizes it as a trophy, but any such theft draws the attention and ire of the Prince of Demons. Angry at its master's defeat, the *Wand of Orcus* tries to attune itself to the first willing creature other than Demogorgon that touches it. The attunement is instantaneous, allowing the wand's properties to be used during the battle.

Destroying Demogorgon

If the characters reduce the Prince of Demons to 0 hit points, they disrupt and destroy his material form. Shrieking and gibbering, the Prince of Demons disintegrates as his foul essence is cast back into the Abyss, ending the demonic threat to the Underdark.

If the characters fail to destroy Demogorgon, see "Demon Lords Triumphant."

Loose Threads

The conclusion of *Out of the Abyss* can be relatively quick and straightforward if Vizeran's scheme is successful and the heroes are victorious. The survivors of the battle against the demon lords can make their way out of the Underdark to report to a grateful alliance of surface-world factions that the threat is ended.

Major loose threads left hanging at the end of the final battle include the following.

Gromph's Grimoire

After recovering Gromph Baenre's grimoire from Sorcere in chapter 15, the characters might think about what to do with the dark tome once the threat of the demon lords is ended. The knowledge and power the book represents are dangerous in anyone's hands—especially Vizeran DeVir's, given what the characters know of him. However, the drow archmage doesn't give up the grimoire willingly.

Finding a means to get rid of Gromph's grimoire once and for all could be the basis for continued adventures, perhaps even leading characters into the Abyss (see "Into the Demonweb Pits"). Alternatively, if you arrange for the book to be stolen from Vizeran before the characters can deal with it, they might need to recover it to ensure its powers are never misused again.

If you prefer to tie up loose ends concerning the grimoire, you can have it banished into the Abyss along with the demon lords. It might be reclaimed by Lolth or lost somewhere within the infinite depths of that plane, at least until it resurfaces again.

LINGERING EVIL

One or more of the demon lords might remain in the Underdark or on the Material Plane by the end of the campaign, having managed to avoid being drawn into Vizeran's trap. Graz'zt is a good possibility. In this case, a continuing campaign might be necessary for the high-level heroes to acquire the resources they need to take on any remaining demon lords, since the trick with the *dark heart* isn't going to work a second time.

The characters' continuing adventures could involve further cooperation with Vizeran DeVir (if he survives) or delving deeper into the Underdark for legendary weapons or magic. The characters might even venture out into the other planes of existence with the aid of Araumycos or the librarians of Gravenhollow, seeking allies, lore, and resources to combat the demon lords and return them to the Abyss.

INTO THE DEMONWEB PITS

Ambitious adventurers might decide to take the fight to Lolth, seeking to punish her for what she unleashed on the Material Plane and to undo whatever her scheme might have gained her. Vizeran will be inclined to help them find a way to reach the Demonweb (Lolth's layer of the Abyss), since the drow archmage hates the Demon Queen of Spiders and her subjugation of his race.

As they travel through the Abyss, the characters might discover that the demon lords they defeated in the Underdark are potential allies in this new quest. Those demon lords want their own revenge upon Lolth for her scheme, and it might suit their mad whims to use the adventurers as their agents to achieve it.

If and when the characters confront Lolth, they find her pregnant and surrounded by thousands of eggs—her unborn young. When the eggs hatch, the Demon Queen of Spiders plans to send her offspring throughout the Abyss, creating a new generation of demon lords under her sway. How the heroes thwart Lolth's mad scheme remains to be seen!

DEMON LORDS TRIUMPHANT

In the event the heroes were not successful, a potential new campaign could take place in a Faerûn threatened—or even ruled—by demon lords with access to the surface world. In addition to their summoned armies of demons and fiendish creatures, they gather worldly forces of chaos and evil to their banners to launch a war against all civilized lands. A world under the assault or rule of the demon lords is a world in need of heroes.

GROMPH BAENRE

The fate of Gromph Baenre, instigator of chaos and Vizeran's rival, remains a mystery. If he yet lives, his role in recent events earns him many new enemies. Matron Mother Quenthel Baenre handpicks a new Archmage of Menzoberranzan to replace her troublesome brother, knowing Gromph will not be found until he chooses to reappear.

MENZOBERRANZAN

If the City of Spiders is the site of the demon lords' battle, it is damaged even more than it was by Demogorgon's arrival. Word of the city's misfortune spreads throughout the Underdark, with other races and factions trying to claim some of the power long held by the drow.

Despite Vizeran's best efforts, not all drow believe that Lolth is responsible for the disaster, instead blaming a lack of faith in the Demon Queen of Spiders, as well as the power of the wizards. Chaos and agitation for change embroil the city, forcing the already weakened ruling houses to put down challenges to their power even as they make concessions to their rivals.

A civil war between the drow isn't likely to remain contained within Menzoberranzan—or even the Underdark—as different sides look for resources and advantages. The adventurers could get involved on either side of the conflict, or might aid surface-world factions intent on containing the war in the Underdark until it eventually winds down.

GAUNTLGRYM

Even if the heroes eliminate the threat the demon lords represent to Gauntlgrym, the Underdark remains in a state of chaos. The defenders of Gauntlgrym need aid to rebuild and strengthen the city's defenses, and to remain vigilant for new threats gathering in the dark depths of the world. King Bruenor might offer the triumphant heroes noble titles and positions of power in his kingdom in the hope of enlisting their aid against the troubles to come. The adventurers might get the opportunity to earn those titles all over again when an Underdark army marches on the dwarf kingdom, determined to claim Gauntlgrym and the power of the primordial bound within its Great Forge.

VIZERAN DEVIR

Although he's nominally the party's ally during much of this adventure, Vizeran DeVir can't be underestimated. Once the immediate threat is dealt with, the drow archmage turns his attention to other goals—claiming what he considers his rightful place of power among the drow, and overthrowing the tyrannical rule of Lolth and her priestesses. Vizeran might start a civil war among the dark elves—one that could easily drag in the other civilizations of the Underdark and parts of Faerûn as well.

Although Vizeran won't immediately turn against his former allies, the adventurers would be fools to trust him. He seizes any opportunity to increase his own power and prestige, including holding on to Gromph's grimoire and any ritual components or trinkets the adventurers might have acquired for him.

If the adventurers thwarted Vizeran's revenge scheme by placing the *dark heart* talisman somewhere other than Menzoberranzan, they earn the drow archmage's enmity. Vizeran's plots expand to include the adventurers as well as his own people, and the next great challenge the heroes face might come from the archmage as he plans his revenge.

APPENDIX A: MODIFYING BACKGROUNDS

This appendix provides alternative background features and bonds for player characters, with options that are strongly connected to the NPCs, themes, and events of this adventure.

SUBSTITUTE FEATURES

A player can choose one of the following features to replace the feature normally granted by his or her character's background.

OPTIONAL FEATURE: DEEP DELVER

You have a knack for making your way in the deep places of the world. You can recall the twists and turns of passageways and tunnels such that you can always retrace your steps underground. You're also well acquainted with foraging and survival in the Underdark, and can determine when sources of food and water are safe to consume. You can always find sufficient food and water for yourself and up to five other people in the Underdark, as long as sustenance is available in the area.

OPTIONAL FEATURE: UNDERDARK EXPERIENCE

You are no casual visitor to the Underdark, but instead have spent considerable time there learning its ways. You are familiar with the various races, civilizations, and settlements of the Underdark, as well as its major routes for travel. If you fail an Intelligence check to recall some piece of Underdark lore, you know a source you can consult for the answer unless the DM rules that the lore is unknown.

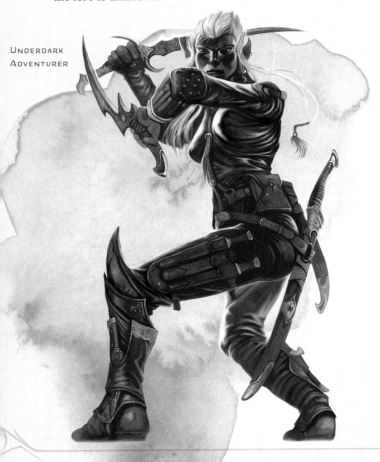

UNDERDARK ADVENTURER

SUBSTITUTE BONDS

This table provides alternative bonds that characters can have instead of the bonds from their backgrounds.

SUBSTITUTE BONDS

d10	Bond
1	You were once lost in the Underdark, and a group of kuo-toa helped you find your way out. You learned that there are kindly folk even among that otherwise mad race, and remain indebted to them for their aid.
2	You once had the opportunity to meet a circle of myconids—the mushroom folk of the Underdark. They offered you shelter and a chance to "meld" using their telepathic spores, and you have yearned ever since to repeat that experience.
3	One of your best friends in your youth was Morista Malkin, a shield dwarf and member of the Emerald Enclave. Though you haven't seen her in years, you heard she found her way to the reclaimed dwarf hold of Gauntlgrym.
4	You once worked for Davra Jassur, a Zhentarim "troubleshooter" recruiting promising new talent for the Black Network. She helped you get your start as an adventurer, and you owe her for that.
5	You have long had a curious recurring dream about visiting a vaulted stone library in the depths of the Underdark, and becoming lost in the endless lore it holds.
6	You studied with a deep gnome alchemist and miner named Kazook Pickshine, who saved your life once when a magical experiment went awry. Last you heard, his family controlled some of the largest mines in the deep gnome settlement of Blingdenstone.
7	What little you know about the Underdark, you learned from living and fighting alongside the Feldrun clan of dwarves. You swore an honor debt to the clan before they joined the forces retaking Gauntlgrym and established themselves there.
8	Years ago, a vicious noble named Ghazrim DuLoc was implicated in the death of someone you cared about. The crime was covered up, though, and DuLoc disappeared. Rumor has it the Zhentarim aided his escape, but you've sworn to find him one day.
9	Years ago, you lost people you loved in a raid by creatures from the Underdark. They disappeared without a trace, either slain or taken into the depths, and you've always wondered whether they might still be alive and held as prisoners.
10	You know the dwarf hold of Gauntlgrym well, having fought alongside the dwarves to help reclaim it. King Bruenor Battlehammer congratulated you on your valor, and you know the price the dwarves paid in blood to regain their home.

APPENDIX B: MAGIC ITEMS

Player characters can find a number of unusual magic items over the course of this adventure, including creations of the drow, the deep gnomes, and other inhabitants of the Underdark.

DAWNBRINGER

Weapon (longsword), legendary (requires attunement by a creature of non-evil alignment)

Lost for ages in the Underdark, *Dawnbringer* appears to be a gilded longsword hilt. While grasping the hilt, you can use a bonus action to make a blade of pure radiance spring from the hilt, or cause the blade to disappear. *Dawnbringer* has all the properties of a *sun blade* (see chapter 7, "Treasure," of the *Dungeon Master's Guide*).

While holding the weapon, you can use an action to touch a creature with the blade and cast *lesser restoration* on that creature. Once used, this ability can't be used again until the next dawn.

Sentience. *Dawnbringer* is a sentient neutral good weapon with an Intelligence of 12, a Wisdom of 15, and a Charisma of 14. It has hearing and darkvision out to a range of 120 feet.

The sword can speak, read, and understand Common, and it can communicate with its wielder telepathically.

PIWAFWI

DAWNBRINGER

Its voice is kind and feminine. It knows every language you know while you're attuned to it.

Personality. Forged by ancient sun worshipers, *Dawnbringer* is meant to bring light into darkness and to fight creatures of darkness. It is kind and compassionate to those in need, but fierce and destructive to its enemies.

Long years lost in darkness have made *Dawnbringer* frightened of both the dark and abandonment. It prefers that its blade always be present and shedding light in areas of darkness, and it strongly resists being parted from its wielder for any length of time.

PIWAFWI (CLOAK OF ELVENKIND)

Wondrous item, uncommon (requires attunement)

This dark spider-silk cloak is made by drow. It is a *cloak of elvenkind* (see chapter 7, "Treasure," of the *Dungeon Master's Guide*). It loses its magic if exposed to sunlight for 1 hour without interruption.

PIWAFWI OF FIRE RESISTANCE

Wondrous item, rare (requires attunement)

This cloak is a *cloak of elvenkind* (see chapter 7, "Treasure," of the *Dungeon Master's Guide*). It also grants you resistance to fire damage while you wear it. It loses its magic if exposed to sunlight for 1 hour without interruption.

Spell Gem

Wondrous item, rarity varies (attunement optional)

A *spell gem* can contain one spell from any class's spell list. You become aware of the spell when you learn the gem's properties. While holding the gem, you can cast the spell from it as an action if you know the spell or if the spell is on your class's spell list. Doing so doesn't require any components and doesn't require attunement. The spell then disappears from the gem.

If the spell is of a higher level than you can normally cast, you must make an ability check using your spellcasting ability to determine whether you cast it successfully. The DC equals 10 + the spell's level. On a failed check, the spell disappears from the gem with no other effect.

Each *spell gem* has a maximum level for the spell it can store. The spell level determines the gem's rarity and the stored spell's saving throw DC and attack bonus, as shown in the Spell Gem table.

You can imbue the gem with a spell if you're attuned to it and it's empty. To do so, you cast the spell while holding the gem. The spell is stored in the gem instead of having any effect. Casting the spell must require either 1 action or 1 minute or longer, and the spell's level must be no higher than the gem's maximum. If the spell belongs to the school of abjuration and requires material components that are consumed, you must provide them, but they can be worth half as much as normal.

Once imbued with a spell, the gem can't be imbued again until the next dawn.

Deep gnomes created these magic gemstones and keep the creation process a secret.

Stonespeaker Crystal

Wondrous item, rare (requires attunement)

Created by the stone giant librarians of Gravenhollow, this nineteen-inch-long shard of quartz grants you advantage on Intelligence (Investigation) checks while it is on your person.

The crystal has 10 charges. While holding it, you can use an action to expend some of its charges to cast one of the following spells from it: *speak with animals* (2 charges), *speak with dead* (4 charges), or *speak with plants* (3 charges).

> **DROWCRAFT ITEMS**
>
> Magic items crafted by the drow—and often other races of the Underdark—use components and rites never meant to see the light of day. Many such items, including drow armor, weapons, and *piwafwi* cloaks, permanently lose their magic if they are exposed to sunlight for 1 hour without interruption. Charged items such as a *wand of viscid globs* are destroyed after 1 hour's exposure to sunlight.

When you cast a divination spell, you can use the crystal in place of one material component that would normally be consumed by the spell, at a cost of 1 charge per level of the spell. The crystal is not consumed when used in this way.

The crystal regains 1d6 + 4 expended charges daily at dawn. If you expend the crystal's last charge, roll a d20. On a 1, the crystal vanishes, lost forever.

Wand of Viscid Globs

Wand, rare (requires attunement)

Crafted by the drow, this slim black wand has 7 charges. While holding it, you can use an action to expend 1 of its charges to cause a small glob of viscous material to launch from the tip at one creature within 60 feet of you. Make a ranged attack roll against the target, with a bonus equal to your spellcasting modifier (or your Intelligence modifier, if you don't have a spellcasting ability) plus your proficiency bonus. On a hit, the glob expands and dries on the target, which is restrained for 1 hour. After that time, the viscous material cracks and falls away.

Applying a pint or more of alcohol to the restrained creature dissolves the glob instantly, as does the application of *oil of etherealness* or *universal solvent*. The glob also dissolves instantly if exposed to sunlight. No other nonmagical process can remove the viscous material until it deteriorates on its own.

The wand regains 1d6 + 1 expended charges daily at midnight. If you expend the wand's last charge, roll a d20. On a 1, the wand melts into harmless slime and is destroyed.

A *wand of viscid globs* is destroyed if exposed to sunlight for 1 hour without interruption.

Spell Gem

Max. Spell Level	Gemstone	Rarity	Save DC	Attack Bonus
Cantrip	Obsidian	Uncommon	13	+5
1st	Lapis lazuli	Uncommon	13	+5
2nd	Quartz	Rare	13	+5
3rd	Bloodstone	Rare	15	+7
4th	Amber	Very rare	15	+9
5th	Jade	Very rare	17	+9
6th	Topaz	Very rare	17	+10
7th	Star ruby	Legendary	18	+10
8th	Ruby	Legendary	18	+10
9th	Diamond	Legendary	19	+11

Appendix C: Creatures

This appendix presents new monsters and NPCs encountered in this adventure.

Monsters and NPCs by Challenge Rating

Monster	Challenge
Bridesmaid of Zuggtmoy	1/8
Drow spore servant	1/8
Derro	1/4
Ixitxachitl	1/4
Male steeder	1/4
Duergar spore servant	1/2
Duergar soulblade	1
Female steeder	1
Awakened zurkhwood	2
Chamberlain of Zuggtmoy	2
Droki (NPC)	2
Duergar darkhaft	2
Duergar kavalrachni	2
Duergar Keeper of the Flame	2
Duergar Stone Guard	2
Duergar xarrorn	2
Grisha (NPC)	2
Narrak (NPC)	2
Vampiric ixitxachitl	2
Derro savant	3
Hook horror spore servant	3
Troglodyte champion of Laogzed	3
Chuul spore servant	4
The Pudding King (NPC)	4
Yestabrod (NPC)	4

Derro

The derro are degenerate Underdark humanoids that resemble small dwarves. Cruel and insane, they take delight in tormenting others—even their own kind.

Derro have blue-gray skin and straight hair that is white or yellow in color. Their uniformly pale white eyes lack both irises and pupils.

Unnatural Origin. Derro believe they were created by their god, Diirinka, but they are actually the result of cruel experiments on dwarves by mind flayers. Like duergar, the derro were a slave race to the mind flayers, but eventually freed themselves.

Born to Madness. The process of their creation rendered the derro irrevocably insane. They cooperate with each other only out of necessity and when riled up by a charismatic leader.

Life of Attrition. Derro can live to be one hundred and fifty years old, but they mature and breed quickly. When their elders deem that their numbers are becoming unmanageable, the derro declare war on some other race and surge forth in a reckless horde, fighting until their population dwindles to a tolerable size. These ghastly purges weed out the weak among the derro and are referred to as "Uniting Wars."

Second-Class Citizens. Derro create no settlements of their own. Instead, they form small, isolated enclaves in non-derro settlements throughout the Underdark, where they are treated as vermin or slaves. Their own cutthroat politics prevent the derro from mounting any effective resistance against such exploitation.

Derro Weapons. The derro wield special weapons. They use a hooked shortspear, which is a martial melee weapon that deals 1d4 piercing damage, weighs 2 pounds, and has the light weapon property (see chapter 5, "Equipment," of the *Player's Handbook*). It doesn't possess the thrown or versatile weapon properties of a normal spear. On a hit with this weapon, the wielder can forgo dealing damage and attempt to trip the target, in which case the target must succeed on a Strength saving throw or fall prone. The DC is 8 + the wielder's Strength modifier + the wielder's proficiency bonus.

The derro also use a light repeating crossbow fitted with a cartridge that can hold up to six crossbow bolts. This weapon is similar to a light crossbow except that it has half the range (40/160 feet) and doesn't have the loading property. It automatically reloads after firing until it runs out of ammunition. Reloading the cartridge takes an action.

Derro

Small humanoid (derro), chaotic evil

Armor Class 13 (leather armor)
Hit Points 13 (3d6 + 3)
Speed 30 ft.

STR	DEX	CON	INT	WIS	CHA
9 (−1)	14 (+2)	12 (+1)	11 (+0)	5 (−3)	9 (−1)

Skills Stealth +4
Senses darkvision 120 ft., passive Perception 7
Languages Dwarvish, Undercommon
Challenge 1/4 (50 XP)

Insanity. The derro has advantage on saving throws against being charmed or frightened.

Magic Resistance. The derro has advantage on saving throws against spells and other magical effects.

Sunlight Sensitivity. While in sunlight, the derro has disadvantage on attack rolls, as well as on Wisdom (Perception) checks that rely on sight.

Actions

Hooked Shortspear. *Melee Weapon Attack:* +2 to hit, reach 5 ft., one target. *Hit:* 1 (1d4 − 1) piercing damage. If the target is a creature, the derro can choose to deal no damage and try to trip the target instead, in which case the target must succeed on a DC 9 Strength saving throw or fall prone.

Light Repeating Crossbow. *Ranged Weapon Attack:* +4 to hit, range 40/160 ft., one target. *Hit:* 6 (1d8 + 2) piercing damage.

DERRO SAVANT

IXITXACHITL

Ixitxachitl (pronounced ick-*zit*-zah-chit-ul) are aquatic creatures resembling manta rays, with small, clawed hands at the ends of their "wings" and black eyes gleaming with sinister intelligence. Many creatures mistake ixitxachitl for common manta rays, but this can prove a deadly mistake. The ixitxachitl are as evil as they are cunning, leading to their common nickname "demon rays." They inhabit bodies of fresh and salt water, but their violent nature means that little is known of them.

Struggle for Survival. Ixitxachitl emerge from eggs as tiny creatures little more than a hand span in width. From that time onward, they struggle to survive at all costs, growing throughout their lives. Those ixitxachitl that master the secrets of survival gain powers of regeneration and feed on the life force of other creatures.

All Consuming. Ixitxachitl hollow out coral reefs or other natural aquatic formations to create labyrinthine dens, often compelling aid from captured aquatic species they enslave. They typically strip an area bare before moving on to new fertile grounds, leaving their abandoned dens behind. Schools of ixitxachitl often war on other aquatic creatures to claim feeding grounds and territory.

Demon Worshipers. The ixitxachitl venerate and serve various demons, particularly Demogorgon, whom they consider their patron and creator. They have an intense rivalry with the merrow over which of them are the greatest and most favored servants of the Prince of Demons.

IXITXACHITL

Small aberration, chaotic evil

Armor Class 15 (natural armor)
Hit Points 18 (4d6 + 4)
Speed 0 ft., swim 30 ft.

STR	DEX	CON	INT	WIS	CHA
12 (+1)	16 (+3)	13 (+1)	12 (+1)	13 (+1)	7 (−2)

Senses darkvision 60 ft., passive Perception 11
Languages Abyssal, Ixitxachitl
Challenge 1/4 (50 XP)

ACTIONS

Bite. *Melee Weapon Attack:* +3 to hit, reach 5 ft., one target. *Hit:* 4 (1d6 + 1) piercing damage.

REACTIONS

Barbed Tail. When a creature provokes an opportunity attack from the ixitxachitl, the ixitxachitl can make the following attack instead of using its bite. *Melee Weapon Attack:* +5 to hit, reach 5 ft., one target. *Hit:* 7 (1d8 + 3) piercing damage.

VARIANT: DERRO SAVANT

Derro savants have an affinity for arcane magic. A derro savant has the same statistics as a **derro**, except that it has 49 (11d6 + 11) hit points, a Charisma of 14 (+2), and a challenge rating of 3 (700 XP). The savant also gains the following additional feature.

Spellcasting. The derro is a 5th-level spellcaster. Its spellcasting ability is Charisma (save DC 12, +4 to hit with spell attacks). The derro knows the following sorcerer spells:

Cantrips (at will): *acid splash, light, mage hand, message, ray of frost*
1st level (4 slots): *burning hands, chromatic orb, sleep*
2nd level (3 slots): *invisibility, spider climb*
3rd level (2 slots): *blink, lightning bolt*

VAMPIRIC IXITXACHITL
Medium aberration, chaotic evil

Armor Class 16 (natural armor)
Hit Points 44 (8d8 + 8)
Speed 0 ft., swim 30 ft.

STR	DEX	CON	INT	WIS	CHA
14 (+2)	18 (+4)	13 (+1)	12 (+1)	13 (+1)	7 (−2)

Senses darkvision 60 ft., passive Perception 11
Languages Abyssal, Ixitxachitl
Challenge 2 (450 XP)

Regeneration. The ixitxachitl regains 10 hit points at the start of its turn. The ixitxachitl dies only if it starts its turn with 0 hit points.

ACTIONS

Vampiric Bite. *Melee Weapon Attack:* +4 to hit, reach 5 ft., one target. *Hit:* 6 (1d8 + 2) piercing damage. The target must succeed on a DC 11 Constitution saving throw or its hit point maximum is reduced by an amount equal to the damage taken, and the ixitxachitl regains hit points equal to that amount. The reduction lasts until the target finishes a long rest. The target dies if its hit point maximum is reduced to 0.

REACTIONS

Barbed Tail. When a creature provokes an opportunity attack from the ixitxachitl, the ixitxachitl can make the following attack instead of using its bite. *Melee Weapon Attack:* +6 to hit, reach 10 ft., one target. *Hit:* 9 (1d10 + 4) piercing damage.

CREATURE VARIATIONS

This section introduces variations of monsters that are described in the *Monster Manual*.

DUERGAR

The *Monster Manual* provides statistics for the typical armed **duergar**. However, characters meet other kinds of duergar in the course of this adventure.

DUERGAR DARKHAFT

The darkhafts are the members of the Deepking's secret corps of psionic agents. The duergar darkhaft has the same statistics as the **duergar** in the *Monster Manual*, except that its challenge rating is 2 (450 XP) and it has the following additional feature.

Innate Spellcasting (Psionics). The darkhaft's innate spellcasting ability is Intelligence (spell save DC 10). It can innately cast the following spells, requiring no components:

At will: *friends, mage hand*
1/day each: *disguise self, sleep*

DUERGAR KAVALRACHNI

The vicious kavalrachni are the duergar cavalry of Gracklstugh, riding giant tarantulas known as steeders (see the **female steeder** stat block in this appendix). The duergar kavalrachni has the same statistics as the **duergar** in the *Monster Manual*, except that its challenge rating is 2 (450 XP) and it has the following Cavalry Training feature and Heavy Crossbow action.

Cavalry Training. When the duergar hits a target with a melee attack while mounted on a female steeder, the steeder can make a melee attack against the same target as a reaction.

Heavy Crossbow. *Ranged Weapon Attack:* +4 to hit, range 100/400 ft., one target. *Hit:* 5 (1d10) piercing damage.

DUERGAR KEEPER OF THE FLAME

The Keepers of the Flame is a well-respected order of psionic clerics that serves the red dragon Themberchaud in Gracklstugh, and whose members are advisors to the Deepking.

The duergar Keeper of the Flame uses the same statistics as the **duergar** in the *Monster Manual*, except that its challenge rating is 2 (450 XP) and it has the following additional features.

Innate Spellcasting (Psionics). The Keeper of the Flame's innate spellcasting ability is Wisdom (spell save DC 12). It can innately cast the following spells, requiring no components:

At will: *friends, message*
3/day: *command*

Spellcasting. The Keeper of the Flame is a 3rd-level spellcaster. Its spellcasting ability is Wisdom (spell save DC 12, +4 to hit with spell attacks). The Keeper of the Flame has the following cleric spells prepared:

Cantrips (at will): *guidance, mending, sacred flame*
1st level (4 slots): *bane, inflict wounds, shield of faith*
2nd level (2 slots): *enhance ability, spiritual weapon*

Duergar Soulblade

Duergar soulblades are assassins with the ability to manifest blades of psionic energy.

Duergar Stone Guard

The Stone Guards are veteran warriors who serve the Deepking as bodyguards, elite troops, and secret police.

Duergar Xarrorn

The xarrorn are duergar warriors of Clan Xardelvar trained to wield lances that spew alchemical fire.

Duergar Soulblade
Medium humanoid (dwarf), lawful evil

Armor Class 14 (leather armor)
Hit Points 18 (4d8)
Speed 25 ft.

STR	DEX	CON	INT	WIS	CHA
11 (+0)	16 (+3)	10 (+0)	11 (+0)	10 (+0)	12 (+1)

Damage Resistances poison
Senses darkvision 120 ft., passive Perception 10
Languages Dwarvish, Undercommon
Challenge 1 (200 XP)

Duergar Resilience. The duergar has advantage on saving throws against poison, spells, and illusions, as well as to resist being charmed or paralyzed.

Innate Spellcasting (Psionics). The duergar's innate spellcasting ability is Wisdom (spell save DC 12, +4 to hit with spell attacks). It can innately cast the following spells, requiring no components:

At will: *blade ward, true strike*
3/day each: *jump, hunter's mark*

Sunlight Sensitivity. While in sunlight, the duergar has disadvantage on attack rolls, as well as on Wisdom (Perception) checks that rely on sight.

Actions

Enlarge (Recharges after a Short or Long Rest). For 1 minute, the duergar magically increases in size, along with anything it is wearing or carrying. While enlarged, the duergar is Large, doubles its damage dice on Strength-based weapon attacks (included in the attacks), and makes Strength checks and Strength saving throws with advantage. If the duergar lacks the room to become Large, it attains the maximum size possible in the space available.

Create Soulblade. The duergar creates a visible, shortsword-sized blade of psionic energy. The weapon appears in the duergar's hand and vanishes if it leaves the duergar's grip, or if the duergar dies or is incapacitated.

Invisibility (Recharges after a Short or Long Rest). The duergar magically turns invisible for up to 1 hour or until it attacks, it casts a spell, it uses its Enlarge, or its concentration is broken (as if concentrating on a spell). Any equipment the duergar wears or carries is invisible with it.

Soulblade. Melee Weapon Attack: +5 to hit, reach 5 ft., one target. *Hit:* 6 (1d6 + 3) force damage, or 10 (2d6 + 3) force damage while enlarged. If the soulblade has advantage on the attack roll, the attack deals an extra 3 (1d6) force damage.

Duergar Stone Guard
Medium humanoid (dwarf), lawful evil

Armor Class 18 (chain mail, shield)
Hit Points 39 (6d8 + 12)
Speed 25 ft.

STR	DEX	CON	INT	WIS	CHA
18 (+4)	11 (+0)	14 (+2)	11 (+0)	10 (+0)	9 (−1)

Damage Resistances poison
Senses darkvision 120 ft., passive Perception 10
Languages Dwarvish, Undercommon
Challenge 2 (450 XP)

Duergar Resilience. The duergar has advantage on saving throws against poison, spells, and illusions, as well as to resist being charmed or paralyzed.

Phalanx Formation. The duergar has advantage on attack rolls and Dexterity saving throws while standing within 5 feet of a duergar ally wielding a shield.

Sunlight Sensitivity. While in sunlight, the duergar has disadvantage on attack rolls, as well as on Wisdom (Perception) checks that rely on sight.

Actions

Enlarge (Recharges after a Short or Long Rest). For 1 minute, the duergar magically increases in size, along with anything it is wearing or carrying. While enlarged, the duergar is Large, doubles its damage dice on Strength-based weapon attacks (included in the attacks), and makes Strength checks and Strength saving throws with advantage. If the duergar lacks the room to become Large, it attains the maximum size possible in the space available.

King's Knife (Shortsword). Melee Weapon Attack: +6 to hit, reach 5 ft., one target. *Hit:* 7 (1d6 + 4) piercing damage, or 11 (2d6 + 4) piercing damage while enlarged.

Javelin. Melee or Ranged Weapon Attack: +6 to hit, reach 5 ft. or range 30/120 ft., one target. *Hit:* 7 (1d6 + 4) piercing damage, or 11 (2d6 + 4) piercing damage while enlarged.

Invisibility (Recharges after a Short or Long Rest). The duergar magically turns invisible for up to 1 hour or until it attacks, it casts a spell, it uses its Enlarge, or its concentration is broken (as if concentrating on a spell). Any equipment the duergar wears or carries is invisible with it.

Duergar Xarrorn

Medium humanoid (dwarf), lawful evil

Armor Class 18 (plate mail)
Hit Points 26 (4d8 + 8)
Speed 25 ft.

STR	DEX	CON	INT	WIS	CHA
16 (+3)	11 (+0)	14 (+2)	11 (+0)	10 (+0)	9 (−1)

Damage Resistances poison
Senses darkvision 120 ft., passive Perception 10
Languages Dwarvish, Undercommon
Challenge 2 (450 XP)

Duergar Resilience. The duergar has advantage on saving throws against poison, spells, and illusions, as well as to resist being charmed or paralyzed.

Sunlight Sensitivity. While in sunlight, the duergar has disadvantage on attack rolls, as well as on Wisdom (Perception) checks that rely on sight.

Actions

Enlarge (Recharges after a Short or Long Rest). For 1 minute, the duergar magically increases in size, along with anything it is wearing or carrying. While enlarged, the duergar is Large, doubles its damage dice on Strength-based weapon attacks (included in the attacks), and makes Strength checks and Strength saving throws with advantage. If the duergar lacks the room to become Large, it attains the maximum size possible in the space available.

Fire Lance. *Melee Weapon Attack:* +5 to hit (with disadvantage if the target is within 5 feet of the duergar), reach 10 ft., one target. *Hit:* 9 (1d12 + 3) piercing damage plus 3 (1d6) fire damage, or 16 (2d12 + 3) piercing damage plus 3 (1d6) fire damage while enlarged.

Fire Spray (Recharge 5–6). From its fire lance, the duergar shoots a 15-foot cone of fire or a line of fire 30 feet long and 5 feet wide. Each creature in that area must make a DC 12 Dexterity saving throw, taking 10 (3d6) fire damage on a failed save, or half as much damage on a successful one.

Invisibility (Recharges after a Short or Long Rest). The duergar magically turns invisible for up to 1 hour or until it attacks, it casts a spell, it uses its Enlarge, or its concentration is broken (as if concentrating on a spell). Any equipment the duergar wears or carries is invisible with it.

Myconids

Myconids that embrace Zuggtmoy can develop new, more destructive kinds of spores. Myconid adults can have two of the following spore effects. Myconid sovereigns have all these spore effects.

Caustic Spores (1/Day). The myconid releases spores in a 30-foot cone. Each creature inside the cone must succeed on a Dexterity saving throw or take 1d6 acid damage at the start of each of the myconid's turns. A creature can repeat the saving throw at the end of its turn, ending the effect on itself on a success. The save DC is 8 + the myconid's Constitution modifier + the myconid's proficiency bonus.

Infestation Spores (1/Day). The myconid releases spores that burst out in a cloud that fills a 10-foot-radius sphere centered on it, and the cloud lingers for 1 minute. Any flesh-and-blood creature in the cloud when it appears, or that enters it later, must make a Constitution saving throw. The save DC is 8 + the myconid's Constitution modifier + the myconid's proficiency bonus. On a successful save, the creature can't be infected by these spores for 24 hours. On a failed save, the creature is infected with a disease called the spores of Zuggtmoy and also gains a random form of indefinite madness (determined by rolling on the Madness of Zuggtmoy table in appendix D) that lasts until the creature is cured of the disease or dies. While infected in this way, the creature can't be reinfected, and it must repeat the saving throw at the end of every 24 hours, ending the infection on a success. On a failure, the infected creature's body is slowly taken over by fungal growth, and after three such failed saves, the creature dies and is reanimated as a spore servant if it's a type of creature that can be (see the "Myconids" entry in the *Monster Manual*).

Euphoria Spores (1/Day). The myconid releases a cloud of spores in a 20-foot-radius sphere centered on itself. Other creatures in that area must each succeed on a Constitution saving throw or become poisoned for 1 minute. The save DC is 8 + the myconid's Constitution modifier + the myconid's proficiency bonus. A creature can repeat the saving throw at the end of each of its turns, ending the effect early on itself on a success. When the effect ends on it, the creature gains one level of exhaustion.

Spore Servants

Statistics for four new kinds of spore servants are presented here.

Chuul Spore Servant

Large plant, unaligned

Armor Class 16 (natural armor)
Hit Points 93 (11d10 + 33)
Speed 30 ft., swim 30 ft.

STR	DEX	CON	INT	WIS	CHA
19 (+4)	10 (+0)	16 (+3)	2 (−4)	6 (−2)	1 (−5)

Damage Immunities poison
Condition Immunities blinded, charmed, frightened, paralyzed, poisoned
Senses blindsight 30 ft. (blind beyond this radius), passive Perception 8
Languages —
Challenge 4 (1,100 XP)

Actions

Multiattack. The spore servant makes two pincer attacks.

Pincer. *Melee Weapon Attack:* +6 to hit, reach 10 ft., one target. *Hit:* 11 (2d6 + 4) bludgeoning damage. The target is grappled (escape DC 14) if it is a Large or smaller creature and the spore servant doesn't have two other creatures grappled.

Drow Spore Servant

Medium plant, unaligned

Armor Class 15 (chain shirt)
Hit Points 13 (3d8)
Speed 20 ft.

STR	DEX	CON	INT	WIS	CHA
10 (+0)	14 (+2)	10 (+0)	2 (–4)	6 (–2)	1 (–5)

Condition Immunities blinded, charmed, frightened, paralyzed
Senses blindsight 30 ft. (blind beyond this radius), passive Perception 8
Languages —
Challenge 1/8 (25 XP)

Actions

Shortsword. *Melee Weapon Attack:* +4 to hit, reach 5 ft., one target. *Hit:* 5 (1d6 + 2) piercing damage.

Duergar Spore Servant

Medium plant, unaligned

Armor Class 16 (scale armor, shield)
Hit Points 26 (4d8 + 8)
Speed 15 ft.

STR	DEX	CON	INT	WIS	CHA
14 (+2)	11 (+0)	14 (+2)	2 (–4)	6 (–2)	1 (–5)

Damage Resistances poison
Senses blindsight 30 ft. (blind beyond this radius), passive Perception 8
Condition Immunities blinded, charmed, frightened, paralyzed
Languages —
Challenge 1/2 (100 XP)

Actions

War Pick. *Melee Weapon Attack:* +4 to hit, reach 5 ft., one target. *Hit:* 6 (1d8 + 2) piercing damage.

Hook Horror Spore Servant

Medium plant, unaligned

Armor Class 15 (natural armor)
Hit Points 75 (10d10 + 10)
Speed 20 ft., climb 20 ft.

STR	DEX	CON	INT	WIS	CHA
18 (+4)	10 (+0)	15 (+2)	2 (–4)	6 (–2)	1 (–5)

Senses blindsight 30 ft. (blind beyond this radius), passive Perception 8
Condition Immunities blinded, charmed, frightened, paralyzed
Languages —
Challenge 3 (700 XP)

Actions

Multiattack. The spore servant makes two hook attacks.

Hook. *Melee Weapon Attack:* +6 to hit, reach 10 ft., one target. *Hit:* 11 (2d6 + 4) piercing damage.

Troglodyte

The *Monster Manual* provides statistics for the typical **troglodyte**. Once in a while, a troglodyte tribe produces an unusually smart and strong specimen that can spew acid—what many troglodytes consider blessings from Laogzed, their demonic god. These hulking troglodyte champions make excellent chieftains.

Troglodyte Champion of Laogzed

Medium humanoid (troglodyte), chaotic evil

Armor Class 14 (natural armor)
Hit Points 59 (7d8 + 28)
Speed 30 ft.

STR	DEX	CON	INT	WIS	CHA
18 (+4)	12 (+1)	18 (+4)	8 (–1)	12 (+1)	12 (+1)

Skills Athletics +6, Intimidation +3, Stealth +3
Senses darkvision 60 ft., passive Perception 11
Languages Troglodyte
Challenge 3 (700 XP)

Chameleon Skin. The troglodyte has advantage on Dexterity (Stealth) checks made to hide.

Stench. Any creature other than a troglodyte that starts its turn within 5 feet of the troglodyte must succeed on a DC 14 Constitution saving throw or be poisoned until the start of the creature's next turn. On a successful saving throw, the creature is immune to the stench of all troglodytes for 1 hour.

Sunlight Sensitivity. While in sunlight, the troglodyte has disadvantage on attack rolls, as well as on Wisdom (Perception) checks that rely on sight.

Actions

Multiattack. The troglodyte makes three attacks: one with its bite and two with either its claws or its greatclub.

Bite. *Melee Weapon Attack:* +6 to hit, reach 5 ft., one target. *Hit:* 6 (1d4 + 4) piercing damage.

Claw. *Melee Weapon Attack:* +6 to hit, reach 5 ft., one target. *Hit:* 6 (1d4 + 4) slashing damage.

Greatclub. *Melee Attack:* +6 to hit, reach 5 ft., one target. *Hit:* 8 (1d8 + 4) bludgeoning damage.

Acid Spray (Recharge 6). The troglodyte spits acid in a line 15 feet long and 5 feet wide. Each creature in that line must make a DC 14 Dexterity saving throw, taking 10 (3d6) acid damage on a failed save, or half as much damage on a successful one.

Miscellaneous Creatures

This section contains statistics for various weird creatures and critters that appear in the adventure.

Plant Creatures

Zuggtmoy has several fungal bridesmaids and a chamberlain to help her prepare for her wedding to Araumycos. Meanwhile, her myconid servants use awakened zurkhwoods to guard their fungal groves.

Awakened Zurkhwood

This creature is an ordinary zurkhwood mushroom (see "Fungi of the Underdark" in chapter 2) given sentience and mobility. An awakened zurkhwood can be created by casting the *awaken* spell on a normal zurkhwood mushroom. A myconid sovereign can create one by performing a lengthy ritual.

An awakened zurkhwood has the same statistics as an **awakened tree** (see appendix A of the *Monster Manual*), with the following modifications:

- The awakened zurkhwood has darkvision out to a range of 120 feet.
- If the awakened zurkhwood was created by a myconid sovereign, it can't speak.
- The awakened zurkhwood's False Appearance feature allows it to be mistaken for a normal zurkhwood mushroom (instead of a tree).

Bridesmaid of Zuggtmoy

Medium plant, chaotic evil

Armor Class 13 (natural armor)
Hit Points 22 (5d8)
Speed 20 ft.

STR	DEX	CON	INT	WIS	CHA
14 (+2)	11 (+0)	11 (+0)	14 (+2)	8 (−1)	18 (+4)

Senses darkvision 60 ft., passive Perception 9
Languages understands Abyssal but can't speak
Challenge 1/8 (25 XP)

Fungus Stride. Once on its turn, the bridesmaid can use 10 feet of its movement to step magically into one living mushroom or fungus patch within 5 feet and emerge from another within 60 feet of the first one, appearing in an unoccupied space within 5 feet of the second mushroom or fungus patch. The mushrooms and patches must be Large or bigger.

Actions

Hallucination Spores. The bridesmaid ejects spores at one creature it can see within 5 feet of it. The target must succeed on a DC 10 Constitution saving throw or be poisoned for 1 minute. While poisoned in this way, the target is incapacitated. The target can repeat the saving throw at the end of each of its turns, ending the effect on itself on a success.

Infestation Spores (1/Day). The bridesmaid releases spores that burst out in a cloud that fills a 10-foot-radius sphere centered on it, and the cloud lingers for 1 minute. Any flesh-and-blood creature in the cloud when it appears, or that enters it later, must make a DC 10 Constitution saving throw. On a successful save, the creature can't be infected by these spores for 24 hours. On a failed save, the creature is infected with a disease called the spores of Zuggtmoy and also gains a random form of indefinite madness (determined by rolling on the Madness of Zuggtmoy table in appendix D) that lasts until the creature is cured of the disease or dies. While infected in this way, the creature can't be reinfected, and it must repeat the saving throw at the end of every 24 hours, ending the infection on a success. On a failure, the infected creature's body is slowly taken over by fungal growth, and after three such failed saves, the creature dies and is reanimated as a spore servant if it's a type of creature that can be (see the "Myconids" entry in the *Monster Manual*).

The bridesmaids of Zuggtmoy are plant creatures with vaguely humanoid forms. Their frail bodies are covered with clusters of luminescent lichen and crusty, tumescent growths.

Chamberlain of Zuggtmoy

Large plant, chaotic evil

Armor Class 13 (natural armor)
Hit Points 45 (6d10 + 12)
Speed 20 ft.

STR	DEX	CON	INT	WIS	CHA
17 (+3)	7 (−2)	14 (+2)	11 (+0)	8 (−1)	12 (+1)

Damage Resistances bludgeoning, piercing
Senses darkvision 60 ft., passive Perception 9
Languages Abyssal, Undercommon
Challenge 2 (450 XP)

Mushroom Portal. The chamberlain counts as a mushroom for the Fungus Stride feature of the bridesmaid of Zuggtmoy.

Poison Spores. Whenever the chamberlain takes damage, it releases a cloud of spores. Creatures within 5 feet of the chamberlain when this happens must succeed on a DC 12 Constitution saving throw or be poisoned for 1 minute. A creature can repeat the saving throw at the end of each of its turns, ending the effect on itself on a success.

Actions

Multiattack. The chamberlain makes two slam attacks.

Slam. Melee Weapon Attack: +5 to hit, reach 5 ft., one target. *Hit:* 10 (2d6 + 3) bludgeoning damage.

Infestation Spores (1/Day). The chamberlain releases spores that burst out in a cloud that fills a 10-foot-radius sphere centered on it, and the cloud lingers for 1 minute. Any flesh-and-blood creature in the cloud when it appears, or that enters it later, must make a DC 12 Constitution saving throw. On a successful save, the creature can't be infected by these spores for 24 hours. On a failed save, the creature is infected with a disease called the spores of Zuggtmoy and also gains a random form of indefinite madness (determined by rolling on the Madness of Zuggtmoy table in appendix D) that lasts until the creature is cured of the disease or dies. While infected in this way, the creature can't be reinfected, and it must repeat the saving throw at the end of every 24 hours, ending the infection on a success. On a failure, the infected creature's body is slowly

slowly taken over by fungal growth, and after three such failed saves, the creature dies and is reanimated as a spore servant if it's a type of creature that can be (see the "Myconids" entry in the *Monster Manual*).

A chamberlain of Zuggtmoy looks like a vaguely bipedal mass of blue mold with the barest hint of a face nested deep inside a mossy cowl. It pummels enemies with its mossy fists.

STEEDERS

Duergar breed and train these giant Underdark-dwelling tarantulas. Male steeders are as big as ponies and used by the duergar as beasts of burden. The larger females are trained and used as mounts.

Steeders don't spin webs, but they exude a sticky substance from their legs that lets them walk on walls and ceilings without trouble, as well as snare prey.

FEMALE STEEDER
Large beast, unaligned

Armor Class 14 (natural armor)
Hit Points 30 (4d10 + 8)
Speed 30 ft., climb 30 ft.

STR	DEX	CON	INT	WIS	CHA
15 (+2)	16 (+3)	14 (+2)	2 (−4)	10 (+0)	3 (−4)

Skills Stealth +7
Senses darkvision 120 ft., passive Perception 10
Languages —
Challenge 1 (200 XP)

Spider Climb. The steeder can climb difficult surfaces, including upside down on ceilings, without needing to make an ability check.

Leap. The steeder can expend all its movement on its turn to jump up to 90 feet vertically or horizontally, provided that its speed is at least 30 feet.

ACTIONS

Bite. *Melee Weapon Attack:* +5 to hit, reach 5 ft., one creature. *Hit:* 7 (1d8 + 3) piercing damage, and the target must make a DC 12 Constitution saving throw, taking 9 (2d8) acid damage on a failed save, or half as much damage on a successful one.

Sticky Leg (Recharges when the Steeder Has No Creatures Grappled). *Melee Weapon Attack:* +5 to hit, reach 5 ft., one Medium or smaller creature. *Hit:* The target is stuck to the steeder's leg and grappled until it escapes (escape DC 12).

MALE STEEDER
Medium beast, unaligned

Armor Class 12 (natural armor)
Hit Points 13 (2d8 + 4)
Speed 30 ft., climb 30 ft.

STR	DEX	CON	INT	WIS	CHA
15 (+2)	12 (+1)	14 (+2)	2 (−4)	10 (+0)	3 (−4)

Skills Stealth +5
Senses darkvision 120 ft., passive Perception 10
Languages —
Challenge 1/4 (50 XP)

Spider Climb. The steeder can climb difficult surfaces, including upside down on ceilings, without needing to make an ability check.

Leap. The steeder can expend all its movement on its turn to jump up to 60 feet vertically or horizontally, provided that its speed is at least 30 feet.

ACTIONS

Bite. *Melee Weapon Attack:* +4 to hit, reach 5 ft., one creature. *Hit:* 7 (1d8 + 2) piercing damage, and the target must make a DC 12 Constitution saving throw, taking 4 (1d8) acid damage on a failed save, or half as much damage on a successful one.

Sticky Leg (Recharges when the Steeder Has No Creatures Grappled). *Melee Weapon Attack:* +4 to hit, reach 5 ft., one Small or Tiny creature. *Hit:* The target is stuck to the steeder's leg and grappled until it escapes (escape DC 12).

NONPLAYER CHARACTERS

This section presents statistics for several unique NPCs encountered in the adventure.

DROKI
Small humanoid (derro), chaotic evil

Armor Class 15 (studded leather)
Hit Points 31 (7d6 + 7)
Speed 30 ft. (60 ft. with *boots of speed*)

STR	DEX	CON	INT	WIS	CHA
11 (+0)	16 (+3)	13 (+1)	10 (+0)	5 (−3)	16 (+3)

Skills Stealth +5
Senses darkvision 120 ft., passive Perception 7
Languages Dwarvish, Undercommon
Challenge 2 (450 XP)

Special Equipment. Droki wears *boots of speed*.

Insanity. Droki has advantage on saving throws against being charmed or frightened.

Innate Spellcasting. Droki's innate spellcasting ability is Charisma (spell save DC 13). He can innately cast the following spells, requiring no material components:

At will: *minor illusion*
1/day each: *darkness, fear, shatter*

Magic Resistance. Droki has advantage on saving throws against spells and other magical effects.

Sneak Attack (1/Turn). Droki deals an extra 7 (2d6) damage when he hits a target with a weapon attack and has advantage on the attack roll, or when the target is within 5 feet of an ally of Droki that isn't incapacitated and Droki doesn't have disadvantage on the attack roll.

Sunlight Sensitivity. While in sunlight, Droki has disadvantage on attack rolls, as well as on Wisdom (Perception) checks that rely on sight.

ACTIONS

Multiattack. Droki makes two attacks with his shortsword.

Shortsword. Melee Weapon Attack: +5 to hit, reach 5 ft., one target. *Hit:* 6 (1d6 + 3) piercing damage. The sword is coated with serpent venom that wears off after the first hit. A target subjected to the venom must make a DC 11 Constitution saving throw, taking 10 (3d6) poison damage on a failed save, or half as much damage on a successful one.

REACTIONS

Parry. Droki adds 3 to his AC against one melee attack that would hit him. To do so, Droki must see the attacker and be wielding a melee weapon.

GRISHA

Medium humanoid (Damaran human), chaotic evil

Armor Class 18 (chain mail, shield)
Hit Points 33 (6d8 + 6)
Speed 30 ft.

STR	DEX	CON	INT	WIS	CHA
14 (+2)	12 (+1)	12 (+1)	11 (+0)	14 (+2)	16 (+3)

Saving Throws Wis +4, Cha +5
Skills Persuasion +5, Religion +2
Senses passive Perception 12
Languages Common, Undercommon
Challenge 2 (450 XP)

Spellcasting. Grisha is a 6th-level spellcaster. His spellcasting ability is Wisdom (spell save DC 12, +4 to hit with spell attacks). He has the following cleric spells prepared:

Cantrips (at will): *guidance, light, sacred flame, thaumaturgy*
1st level (4 slots): *cure wounds, divine favor, inflict wounds, protection from good, shield of faith*
2nd level (3 slots): *continual flame, hold person, magic weapon, spiritual weapon*
3rd level (3 slots): *bestow curse, dispel magic, spirit guardians*

ACTIONS

Multiattack. Grisha makes two attacks with his *+1 flail.*

+1 Flail. Melee Weapon Attack: +5 to hit, reach 5 ft., one target. *Hit:* 7 (1d8 + 3) bludgeoning damage.

NARRAK

Small humanoid (derro), chaotic evil

Armor Class 12 (15 with *mage armor*)
Hit Points 40 (9d6 + 9)
Speed 30 ft.

STR	DEX	CON	INT	WIS	CHA
9 (−1)	14 (+2)	13 (+1)	14 (+2)	5 (−3)	16 (+3)

Saving Throws Dex +4, Cha +5
Skills Arcana +4, Stealth +4
Senses darkvision 120 ft., passive Perception 7
Languages Dwarvish, Undercommon
Challenge 2 (450 XP)

Insanity. Narrak has advantage on saving throws against being charmed or frightened.

Magic Resistance. Narrak has advantage on saving throws against spells and other magical effects.

Spellcasting. Narrak is a 5th-level spellcaster. His spellcasting ability is Charisma (save DC 13, +5 to hit with spell attacks). Narrak has two 2nd-level spell slots, which he regains after finishing a short or long rest, and knows the following warlock spells:

Cantrips (at will): *eldritch blast, friends, poison spray*
1st level: *armor of Agathys, charm person, hex*
2nd level: *hold person, ray of enfeeblement, spider climb*

Sunlight Sensitivity. While in sunlight, Narrak has disadvantage on attack rolls, as well as on Wisdom (Perception) checks that rely on sight.

ACTIONS

Armor of Shadows (Recharges after a Short or Long Rest). Narrak casts *mage armor* on himself.

Shortsword. Melee Weapon Attack: +4 to hit, reach 5 ft., one creature. *Hit:* 5 (1d6 + 2) piercing damage.

One with Shadows. While he is in dim light or darkness, Narrak can become invisible. He remains so until he moves or takes an action or reaction.

The Pudding King

Small humanoid (gnome, shapechanger), chaotic evil

Armor Class 13 (16 with *mage armor*)
Hit Points 49 (9d6 + 18)
Speed 30 ft.

STR	DEX	CON	INT	WIS	CHA
10 (+0)	16 (+3)	14 (+2)	12 (+1)	8 (−1)	17 (+3)

Saving Throws Con +5, Cha +6
Skills Arcana +4, Perception +2, Stealth +6, Survival +2
Damage Resistances acid, poison
Condition Immunities poisoned
Senses darkvision 60 ft., passive Perception 12
Languages Abyssal, Gnomish, Terran, Undercommon
Challenge 4 (1,100 XP)

Stone Camouflage. The Pudding King has advantage on Dexterity (Stealth) checks made to hide in rocky terrain.

Gnome Cunning. The Pudding King has advantage on Intelligence, Wisdom, and Charisma saving throws against magic.

Innate Spellcasting. The Pudding King's innate spellcasting ability is Intelligence (spell save DC 12). He can innately cast the following spells, requiring no material components:

At will: *nondetection* (self only)
1/day each: *blindness/deafness, blur, disguise self*

Insanity. The Pudding King has advantage on saving throws against being charmed or frightened.

Spellcasting. The Pudding King is a 9th-level spellcaster. His spellcasting ability is Charisma (spell save DC 14, +6 to hit with spell attacks). The Pudding King knows the following sorcerer spells:

Cantrips (at will): *acid splash, light, mage hand, poison spray, prestidigitation*
1st level (4 slots): *false life, mage armor, ray of sickness, shield*
2nd level (3 slots): *crown of madness, misty step*
3rd level (3 slots): *gaseous form, stinking cloud*
4th level (3 slots): *blight, confusion*
5th level (1 slot): *cloudkill*

Actions

War Pick. *Melee Weapon Attack:* +3 to hit, reach 5 ft., one target. *Hit:* 4 (1d8) piercing damage.

Change Shape. The Pudding King magically transforms into an ooze, or back into his true form. He reverts to his true form if he dies. Any equipment he is wearing or carrying is absorbed by the new form. In ooze form, the Pudding King retains his alignment, hit points, Hit Dice, and Intelligence, Wisdom, and Charisma scores, as well as this action. His statistics and capabilities are otherwise replaced by those of the new form.

Create Green Slime (Recharges after a Long Rest). The Pudding King creates a patch of green slime (see "Dungeon Hazards" in chapter 5 of the *Dungeon Master's Guide*). The slime appears on a section of wall, ceiling, or floor within 30 feet of the Pudding King.

Yestabrod

Large monstrosity, chaotic evil

Armor Class 15 (natural armor)
Hit Points 75 (10d10 + 20)
Speed 30 ft.

STR	DEX	CON	INT	WIS	CHA
12 (+1)	10 (+0)	14 (+2)	13 (+1)	15 (+2)	10 (+0)

Damage Immunities poison
Condition Immunities poisoned
Senses darkvision 120 ft., passive Perception 12
Languages Abyssal, telepathy 60 ft.
Challenge 4 (1,100 XP)

Legendary Resistance (1/Day). If Yestabrod fails a saving throw, it can choose to succeed instead.

Actions

Slam. *Melee Weapon Attack:* +3 to hit, reach 5 ft., one target. *Hit:* 8 (3d4 + 1) bludgeoning damage plus 7 (3d4) poison damage.

Caustic Spores (1/Day). Yestabrod releases spores in a 30-foot cone. Each creature in that area must succeed on a DC 12 Dexterity saving throw or take 1d6 acid damage at the start of each of Yestabrod's turns. A creature can repeat the saving throw at the end of each of its turns, ending the effect on itself on a success.

Infestation Spores (1/Day). Yestabrod releases spores that burst out in a cloud that fills a 10-foot-radius sphere centered on it, and the cloud lingers for 1 minute. Any flesh-and-blood creature in the cloud when it appears, or that enters it later, must make a DC 12 Constitution saving throw. On a successful save, the creature can't be infected by these spores for 24 hours. On a failed save, the creature is infected with a disease called the spores of Zuggtmoy and also gains a random form of indefinite madness (determined by rolling on the Madness of Zuggtmoy table in appendix D) that lasts until the creature is cured of the disease or dies. While infected in this way, the creature can't be reinfected, and it must repeat the saving throw at the end of every 24 hours, ending the infection on a success. On a failure, the infected creature's body is slowly taken over by fungal growth, and after three such failed saves, the creature dies and is reanimated as a spore servant if it's a type of creature that can be (see the "Myconids" entry in the *Monster Manual*).

Legendary Actions

Yestabrod can take 2 legendary actions, choosing from the options below. Only one legendary action option can be used at a time and only at the end of another creature's turn. Yestabrod regains spent legendary actions at the start of its turn.

Corpse Burst. Gore, offal, and acid erupt from a corpse within 20 feet of Yestabrod. Creatures within 10 feet of the corpse must succeed on a DC 12 Dexterity saving throw or take 7 (2d6) acid damage.

Foul Absorption. Yestabrod absorbs putrescence from a corpse within 5 feet of it, regaining 1d8 + 2 hit points.

Appendix D: Demon Lords

Here are game statistics for the demon lords who have roles to play in this story. Beware! They are formidable opponents.

Baphomet

Civilization is weakness and savagery is strength in the credo of Baphomet, the Horned King and the Prince of Beasts. He rules over minotaurs and others with savage hearts. He is worshiped by those who want to break the confines of civility and unleash their bestial natures, for Baphomet envisions a world without restraint, where creatures live out their most savage desires.

Cults devoted to Baphomet use mazes and complex knots as their emblems, creating secret places to indulge themselves, including labyrinths of the sort their master favors. Bloodstained crowns and weapons of iron and brass decorate their profane altars.

Over time, Baphomet's cultists become tainted by his influence, gaining bloodshot eyes and coarse, thickening hair. Small horns eventually sprout from the forehead. In time, a devoted cultist might transform entirely into a minotaur—considered the greatest gift of the Prince of Beasts.

Baphomet himself appears as a great, black-furred minotaur, 20 feet tall with six iron horns. An infernal light burns in his red eyes. Although filled with bestial bloodlust, there lies within a cruel and cunning intellect devoted to subverting all of civilization.

Baphomet wields a great glaive called Heartcleaver. He sometimes casts this deadly weapon aside so that he can charge his enemies and gore them with his horns, trampling them into the earth and rending them with his teeth like a beast.

Baphomet's Lair

Baphomet's lair is his palace, the Lyktion, which is on the layer of the Abyss called the Endless Maze. Nestled within the twisting passages of the plane-wide labyrinth, the Lyktion is immaculately maintained and surrounded by a moat constructed in the fashion of a three-dimensional maze. The palace itself is a towering structure whose interior is as labyrinthine as the plane on which it resides, populated by minotaurs, goristros, and quasits.

Lair Actions

On initiative count 20 (losing initiative ties), Baphomet can take a lair action to cause one of the following magical effects; he can't use the same effect two rounds in a row:

- Baphomet seals one doorway or other entryway within the lair. The opening must be unoccupied. It is filled with solid stone for 1 minute or until Baphomet creates this effect again.
- Baphomet chooses a room within the lair that is no larger in any dimension than 100 feet. Until the next initiative count 20, gravity is reversed within that room. Any creatures or objects in the room when this happens fall in the direction of the new pull of gravity, unless they have some means of remaining aloft. Baphomet can ignore the gravity reversal if he's in the room, although he likes to use this action to land on a ceiling to attack targets flying near it.
- Baphomet casts *mirage arcane*, affecting a room within the lair that is no longer in any dimension than 100 feet. The effect ends on the next initiative count 20.

BAPHOMET

REGIONAL EFFECTS

The region containing Baphomet's lair is warped by his magic, creating one or more of the following effects:

- Plant life within 1 mile of the lair grows thick and forms walls of trees, hedges, and other flora in the form of small mazes.
- Beasts within 1 mile of the lair become frightened and disoriented, as though constantly under threat of being hunted, and might lash out or panic even when no visible threat is nearby.
- If a humanoid spends at least 1 hour within 1 mile of the lair, that creature must succeed on a DC 18 Wisdom saving throw or descend into a madness determined by the Madness of Baphomet table. A creature that succeeds on this saving throw can't be affected by this regional effect again for 24 hours.

If Baphomet dies, these effects fade over the course of 1d10 days.

MADNESS OF BAPHOMET

If a creature goes mad in Baphomet's lair or within line of sight of the demon lord, roll on the Madness of Baphomet table to determine the nature of the madness, which is a character flaw that lasts until cured. See the *Dungeon Master's Guide* for more on madness.

MADNESS OF BAPHOMET

d100	Flaw (lasts until cured)
01–20	"My anger consumes me. I can't be reasoned with when my rage has been stoked."
21–40	"I degenerate into beastly behavior, seeming more like a wild animal than a thinking being."
41–60	"The world is my hunting ground. Others are my prey."
61–80	"Hate comes easily to me and explodes into rage."
81–00	"I see those who oppose me not as people, but as beasts meant to be preyed upon."

BAPHOMET

Huge fiend (demon), chaotic evil

Armor Class 22 (natural armor)
Hit Points 333 (23d12 + 184)
Speed 40 ft.

STR	DEX	CON	INT	WIS	CHA
30 (+10)	14 (+2)	26 (+8)	18 (+4)	24 (+7)	16 (+3)

Saving Throws Dex +9, Con +15, Wis +14
Skills Intimidation +17, Perception +14
Damage Resistances cold, fire, lightning
Damage Immunities poison; bludgeoning, piercing, and slashing that is nonmagical
Condition Immunities charmed, exhaustion, frightened, poisoned
Senses truesight 120 ft., passive Perception 24
Languages all, telepathy 120 ft.
Challenge 23 (50,000 XP)

Charge. If Baphomet moves at least 10 feet straight toward a target and then hits it with a gore attack on the same turn, the target takes an extra 22 (4d10) piercing damage. If the target is a creature, it must succeed on a DC 25 Strength saving throw or be pushed up to 10 feet away and knocked prone.

Innate Spellcasting. Baphomet's spellcasting ability is Charisma (spell save DC 18). He can innately cast the following spells, requiring no material components.

At will: *detect magic*
3/day each: *dispel magic, dominate beast, hunter's mark, maze, wall of stone*
1/day each: *teleport*

Labyrinthine Recall. Baphomet can perfectly recall any path he has traveled, and he is immune to the *maze* spell.

Legendary Resistance (3/Day). If Baphomet fails a saving throw, he can choose to succeed instead.

Magic Resistance. Baphomet has advantage on saving throws against spells and other magical effects.

Magic Weapons. Baphomet's weapon attacks are magical.

Reckless. At the start of his turn, Baphomet can gain advantage on all melee weapon attack rolls during that turn, but attack rolls against him have advantage until the start of his next turn.

ACTIONS

Multiattack. Baphomet makes three attacks: one with Heartcleaver, one with his bite, and one with his gore attack.

Heartcleaver. *Melee Weapon Attack:* +17 to hit, reach 15 ft., one target. *Hit:* 24 (4d6 + 10) slashing damage.

Bite. *Melee Weapon Attack:* +17 to hit, reach 10 ft., one target. *Hit:* 19 (2d8 + 10) piercing damage.

Gore. *Melee Weapon Attack:* +17 to hit, reach 10 ft., one target. *Hit:* 21 (2d10 + 10) piercing damage.

Frightful Presence. Each creature of Baphomet's choice within 120 feet of him and aware of him must succeed on a DC 18 Wisdom saving throw or become frightened for 1 minute. A frightened creature can repeat the saving throw at the end of each of its turns, ending the effect on itself on a success. These later saves have disadvantage if Baphomet is within line of sight of the creature.

If a creature succeeds on any of these saves or the effect ends on it, the creature is immune to Baphomet's Frightful Presence for the next 24 hours.

LEGENDARY ACTIONS

Baphomet can take 3 legendary actions, choosing from the options below. Only one legendary action option can be used at a time and only at the end of another creature's turn. Baphomet regains spent legendary actions at the start of his turn.

Heartcleaver Attack. Baphomet makes a melee attack with Heartcleaver.
Charge (Costs 2 Actions). Baphomet moves up to his speed, then makes a gore attack.

DEMOGORGON

Prince of Demons, the Sibilant Beast, and Master of the Spiraling Depths, Demogorgon is the embodiment of chaos, madness, and destruction, seeking to corrupt all that is good and undermine order in the multiverse, to see everything dragged howling into the infinite depths of the Abyss.

The demon lord is a meld of different forms, with a saurian lower body and clawed, webbed feet, as well as suckered tentacles sprouting from the shoulders of a great apelike torso, surmounted by two hideous simian heads, named Aameul and Hathradiah, both equally mad. Their gaze brings madness and confusion to any who confront it.

Similarly, the spiraling Y sign of Demogorgon's cult can inspire madness in those who contemplate it for too long. All the followers of the Prince of Demons go mad, sooner or later.

DEMOGORGON'S LAIR

Demogorgon makes his lair in a palace called Abysm, found on a layer of the Abyss known as the Gaping Maw. Demogorgon's lair is a place of madness and duality; the portion of the palace that lies above water takes the form of two serpentine towers, each crowned by a skull-shaped minaret. There, Demogorgon's heads contemplate the mysteries of the arcane while arguing about how best to obliterate their rivals. The bulk of this palace extends deep underwater, in chill and darkened caverns.

DEMOGORGON
Huge fiend (demon), chaotic evil

Armor Class 22 (natural armor)
Hit Points 496 (34d12 + 272)
Speed 50 ft., swim 50 ft.

STR	DEX	CON	INT	WIS	CHA
29 (+9)	14 (+2)	26 (+8)	20 (+5)	17 (+3)	25 (+7)

Saving Throws Dex +10, Con +16, Wis +11, Cha +15
Skills Insight +11, Perception +19
Damage Resistances cold, fire, lightning
Damage Immunities poison; bludgeoning, piercing, and slashing that is nonmagical
Condition Immunities charmed, exhaustion, frightened, poisoned
Senses truesight 120 ft., passive Perception 29
Languages all, telepathy 120 ft.
Challenge 26 (90,000 XP)

Innate Spellcasting. Demogorgon's spellcasting ability is Charisma (spell save DC 23). Demogorgon can innately cast the following spells, requiring no material components:

At will: *detect magic, major image*
3/day each: *dispel magic, fear, telekinesis*
1/day each: *feeblemind, project image*

Legendary Resistance (3/Day). If Demogorgon fails a saving throw, he can choose to succeed instead.

Magic Resistance. Demogorgon has advantage on saving throws against spells and other magical effects.

Magic Weapons. Demogorgon's weapon attacks are magical.

Two Heads. Demogorgon has advantage on saving throws against being blinded, deafened, stunned, and knocked unconscious.

ACTIONS

Multiattack. Demogorgon makes two tentacle attacks.

Tentacle. Melee Weapon Attack: +17 to hit, reach 10 ft., one target. *Hit:* 35 (4d12 + 9) bludgeoning damage. If the target is a creature, it must succeed on a DC 23 Constitution saving throw or its hit point maximum is reduced by an amount equal to the damage taken. This reduction lasts until the target finishes a long rest. The target dies if its hit point maximum is reduced to 0.

Gaze. Demogorgon turns his magical gaze toward one creature that he can see within 120 feet of him. That target must make a DC 23 Wisdom saving throw. Unless the target is incapacitated, it can avert its eyes to avoid the gaze and to automatically succeed on the save. If the target does so, it can't see Demogorgon until the start of his next turn. If the target looks at him in the meantime, it must immediately make the save.

If the target fails the save, the target suffers one of the following effects of Demogorgon's choice or at random:

1. **Beguiling Gaze.** The target is stunned until the start of Demogorgon's next turn or until Demogorgon is no longer within line of sight.
2. **Hypnotic Gaze.** The target is charmed by Demogorgon until the start of Demogorgon's next turn. Demogorgon chooses how the charmed target uses its actions, reactions, and movement. Because this gaze requires Demogorgon to focus both heads on the target, he can't use his Maddening Gaze legendary action until the start of his next turn.
3. **Insanity Gaze.** The target suffers the effect of the *confusion* spell without making a saving throw. The effect lasts until the start of Demogorgon's next turn. Demogorgon doesn't need to concentrate on the spell.

LEGENDARY ACTIONS

Demogorgon can take 2 legendary actions, choosing from the options below. Only one legendary action option can be used at a time and only at the end of another creature's turn. Demogorgon regains spent legendary actions at the start of his turn.

Tail. *Melee Weapon Attack:* +17 to hit, reach 15 ft., one target. *Hit:* 31 (4d10 + 9) bludgeoning damage plus 22 (4d10) necrotic damage.
Maddening Gaze. Demogorgon uses his Gaze action, and must choose either the Beguiling Gaze or the Insanity Gaze effect.

DEMOGORGON

Lair Actions

On initiative count 20 (losing initiative ties), Demogorgon can take a lair action to cause one of the following effects; Demogorgon can't use the same effect two rounds in a row:

- Demogorgon creates an illusory duplicate of himself, which appears in his own space and lasts until initiative count 20 of the next round. On his turn, Demogorgon can move the illusory duplicate a distance equal to his walking speed (no action required). The first time a creature or object interacts physically with Demogorgon (for example, hitting him with an attack), there is a 50 percent chance that it is the illusory duplicate that is being affected, not Demogorgon himself, in which case the illusion disappears.
- Demogorgon casts the *darkness* spell four times at its lowest level, targeting different areas with the spell. Demogorgon doesn't need to concentrate on the spells, which end on initiative count 20 of the next round.

Regional Effects

The region containing Demogorgon's lair is warped by his magic, creating one or more of the following effects:

- The area within 6 miles of the lair becomes overpopulated with lizards, poisonous snakes, and other venomous beasts.
- Beasts within 1 mile of the lair become violent and crazed—even creatures that are normally docile.
- If a humanoid spends at least 1 hour within 1 mile of the lair, that creature must succeed on a DC 23 Wisdom saving throw or descend into a madness determined by the Madness of Demogorgon table. A creature that succeeds on this saving throw can't be affected by this regional effect again for 24 hours.

If Demogorgon dies, these effects fade over the course of 1d10 days.

Madness of Demogorgon

If a creature goes mad in Demogorgon's lair or within line of sight of the demon lord, roll on the Madness of Demogorgon table to determine the nature of the madness, which is a character flaw that lasts until cured. See the *Dungeon Master's Guide* for more on madness.

Madness of Demogorgon

d100	Flaw (lasts until cured)
01–20	"Someone is plotting to kill me. I need to strike first to stop them!"
21–40	"There is only one solution to my problems: kill them all!"
41–60	"There is more than one mind inside my head."
61–80	"If you don't agree with me, I'll beat you into submission to get my way."
81–00	"I can't allow anyone to touch anything that belongs to me. They might try to take it away from me!"

Fraz-Urb'luu

All demons are liars, but Fraz-Urb'luu is the Prince of Deception and Demon Lord of Illusions. He uses every trick, every ounce of demonic cunning, to manipulate his enemies—mortal and fiend alike—to do his will. Fraz-Urb'luu can create dreamlands and mind-bending fantasies able to deceive the most discerning foes.

Once imprisoned for centuries below Castle Greyhawk on the world of Oerth, Fraz-Urb'luu has slowly rebuilt his power in the Abyss. He seeks the pieces of the legendary *staff of power* taken from him by those who imprisoned him, and commands his servants to do likewise.

The Prince of Deception's true form is like that of a great gargoyle, some 12 feet tall, with an extended, muscular neck and a smiling face framed by long, pointed ears and lank, dark hair, and bat-like wings are furled against his powerful shoulders. He can assume other forms, however, from the hideous to the beautiful. Often the demon lord becomes so immersed in playing a role that he loses himself in it for a time.

Many of the cultists of Fraz-Urb'luu aren't even aware they serve the Prince of Deception, believing their master is a beneficent being and granter of wishes, some lost god or celestial, or even another fiend. Fraz-Urb'luu wears all these masks and more. He particularly delights in aiding demon-hunters against his demonic adversaries, driving the hunters to greater and greater atrocities in the name of their holy cause, only to eventually reveal his true nature and claim their souls as his own.

Fraz-Urb'luu's Lair

Fraz-Urb'luu's lair lies within the Abyssal lair known as Hollow's Heart, a featureless plain of white dust with few structures on it. The lair itself is the city of Zoragmelok, a circular fortress surrounded by adamantine walls topped with razors and hooks. Corkscrew towers loom above twisted domes and vast amphitheaters, just a few examples of the impossible architecture that fills the city.

The challenge rating of Fraz-Urb'luu is 24 (62,000 XP) when he's encountered in his lair.

Lair Actions

On initiative count 20 (losing initiative ties), Fraz-Urb'luu can take a lair action to cause one of the following effects; he can't use the same effect two rounds in a row:

- Fraz-Urb'luu causes up to 5 doors within the lair to become walls, and an equal number of doors to appear on walls where there previously were none.
- Fraz-Urb'luu chooses one humanoid within the lair and instantly creates a simulacrum of that creature (as if created with the *simulacrum* spell). This simulacrum obeys Fraz-Urb'luu's commands and is destroyed on the next initiative count 20.

Fraz-Urb'luu

Large fiend (demon), chaotic evil

Armor Class 18 (natural armor)
Hit Points 350 (28d10 + 196)
Speed 40 ft., fly 40 ft.

STR	DEX	CON	INT	WIS	CHA
29 (+9)	12 (+1)	25 (+7)	26 (+8)	24 (+7)	26 (+8)

Saving Throws Dex +8, Con +15, Int +15, Wis +14
Skills Deception +15, Perception +14, Stealth +8
Damage Resistances cold, fire, lightning
Damage Immunities poison; bludgeoning, piercing, and slashing that is nonmagical
Condition Immunities charmed, exhaustion, frightened, poisoned
Senses truesight 120 ft., passive Perception 24
Languages all, telepathy 120 ft.
Challenge 23 (50,000 XP)

Innate Spellcasting. Fraz-Urb'luu's spellcasting ability is Charisma (spell save DC 23). Fraz-Urb'luu can innately cast the following spells, requiring no material components:

At will: *alter self* (can become Medium-sized when changing his appearance), *detect magic*, *dispel magic*, *phantasmal force*
3/day each: *confusion*, *dream*, *mislead*, *programmed illusion*, *seeming*
1/day each: *mirage arcane*, *modify memory*, *project image*

Legendary Resistance (3/Day). If Fraz-Urb'luu fails a saving throw, he can choose to succeed insteady.

Magic Resistance. Fraz-Urb'luu has advantage on saving throws against spells and other magical effects.

Magic Weapons. Fraz-Urb'luu's weapon attacks are magical.

Undetectable. Fraz-Urb'luu can't be targeted by divination magic, perceived through magical scrying sensors, or detected by abilities that sense demons or fiends.

Actions

Multiattack. Fraz-Urb'luu makes three attacks: one with his bite and two with his fists.

Bite. *Melee Weapon Attack:* +16 to hit, reach 10 ft., one target. *Hit:* 23 (4d6 + 9) piercing damage.

Fist. *Melee Weapon Attack:* +16 to hit, reach 10 ft., one target. *Hit:* 27 (4d8 + 9) bludgeoning damage.

Legendary Actions

Fraz-Urb'luu can take 3 legendary actions, choosing from the options below. Only one legendary action option can be used at a time and only at the end of another creature's turn. Fraz-Urb'luu regains spent legendary actions at the start of his turn.

Tail. *Melee Weapon Attack:* +16 to hit, reach 15 ft., one target. *Hit:* 31 (4d10 + 9) bludgeoning damage. If the target is a Large or smaller creature, it is also grappled (escape DC 24). The grappled target is also restrained. Fraz-Urb'luu can grapple only one creature with his tail at a time.

Phantasmal Killer (Costs 2 Actions). Fraz-Urb'luu casts *phantasmal killer*, no concentration required.

- Fraz-Urb'luu creates a wave of anguish. Each creature he can see within the lair must succeed on a DC 23 Wisdom saving throw or take 33 (6d10) psychic damage.

REGIONAL EFFECTS

The region containing Fraz-Urb'luu's lair is warped by his magic, creating one or more of the following effects:

- Intelligent creatures within 1 mile of the lair frequently see hallucinations of long-dead friends and comrades that vanish after only a brief glimpse.
- Roads and paths within 6 miles of the lair twist and turn back on themselves, making navigation in the area exceedingly difficult.
- If a humanoid spends at least 1 hour within 1 mile of the lair, that creature must succeed on a DC 23 Wisdom saving throw or descend into a madness determined by the Madness of Fraz-Urb'luu table. A creature that succeeds on this saving throw can't be affected by this regional effect again for 24 hours.

If Fraz-Urb'luu dies, these effects fade over the course of 1d10 days.

MADNESS OF FRAZ-URB'LUU

If a creature goes mad in Fraz-Urb'luu's lair or within line of sight of the demon lord, roll on the Madness of Fraz-Urb'luu table to determine the nature of the madness, which is a character flaw that lasts until cured. See the *Dungeon Master's Guide* for more on madness.

MADNESS OF FRAZ-URB'LUU

d100	Flaw (lasts until cured)
01–20	"I never let anyone know the truth about my actions or intentions, even if doing so would be beneficial to me."
21–40	"I have intermittent hallucinations and fits of catatonia."
41–60	"My mind wanders as I have elaborate fantasies that have no bearing on reality. When I return my focus to the world, I have a hard time remembering that it was just a daydream."
61–80	"I convince myself that things are true, even in the face of overwhelming evidence to the contrary."
81–00	"My perception of reality doesn't match anyone else's. It makes me prone to violent delusions that make no sense to anyone else."

FRAZ-URB'LUU

Graz'zt

The appearance of the Dark Prince is a warning that not all beautiful things are good. Standing nearly nine feet tall, Graz'zt strikes the perfect figure of untamed desire, every plane and curve of his body, every glance of his burning eyes, promising a mixture of pleasure and pain. A subtle wrongness pervades his beauty, from the cruel cast of his features to the six fingers on each hand and six toes on each foot. Graz'zt can also transform himself at will, appearing in any humanoid form that pleases him, or his onlookers, all equally tempting in their own ways.

Graz'zt surrounds himself with the finest of things and the most attractive of servants, and he adorns himself in silks and leathers both striking and disturbing in their workmanship. His lair, and those of his cultists, are pleasure palaces where nothing is forbidden, save moderation or kindness.

The dark Prince of Pleasure considers restriction the only sin, and takes what he wants. Cults devoted to him are secret societies of indulgence, often using their debauchery to subjugate others through blackmail, addiction, and manipulation. They frequently wear alabaster masks with ecstatic expressions and ostentatious dress and body ornamentation to their secret assignations.

Although he prefers charm and subtle manipulation, Graz'zt is capable of terrible violence when provoked. He wields the greatsword Angdrelve, the Wave of Sorrow, its wavy, razor-edged blade dripping acid at his command.

Graz'zt's Lair

Graz'zt's principal lair is his Argent Palace, a grandiose structure in the city of Zelatar, found within his Abyssal domain of Azzatar. Graz'zt's maddening influence radiates outward in a tangible ripple, warping reality around him. Given enough time in a single location, Graz'zt can twist it with his madness. Graz'zt's lair is a den of ostentation and hedonism. It is adorned with finery and decorations so decadent that even the wealthiest of mortals would blush at the excess. Within Graz'zt's lairs, followers, thralls, and subjects alike are forced to slake Graz'zt's thirst for pageantry and pleasure.

Lair Actions

On initiative count 20 (losing initiative ties), Graz'zt can take a lair action to cause one of the following effects; he can't use the same effect two rounds in a row:

- Graz'zt casts the *command* spell on every creature of his choice in the lair. He needn't see each one, but he must be aware that an individual is in the lair to target that creature. He issues the same command to all the targets.
- Smooth surfaces within the lair become as reflective as a polished mirror. Until a different lair action is used, creatures within the lair have disadvantage on Dexterity (Stealth) checks made to hide.

Graz'zt

REGIONAL EFFECTS

The region containing Graz'zt's lair is warped by his magic, creating one or more of the following effects:

- Flat surfaces within 1 mile of the lair that are made of stone or metal become highly reflective, as though polished to a shine. These surfaces become supernaturally mirrorlike.
- Wild beasts within 6 miles of the lair break into frequent conflicts and coupling, mirroring the behavior that occurs during their mating seasons.
- If a humanoid spends at least 1 hour within 1 mile of the lair, that creature must succeed on a DC 23 Wisdom saving throw or descend into a madness determined by the Madness of Graz'zt table. A creature that succeeds on this saving throw can't be affected by this regional effect again for 24 hours.

If Graz'zt dies, these effects fade over the course of 1d10 days.

MADNESS OF GRAZ'ZT

If a creature goes mad in Graz'zt's lair or within line of sight of the demon lord, roll on the Madness of Graz'zt table to determine the nature of the madness, which is a character flaw that lasts until cured. See the *Dungeon Master's Guide* for more on madness.

MADNESS OF GRAZ'ZT

d100	Flaw (lasts until cured)
01–20	"There is nothing in the world more important than me and my desires."
21–40	"Anyone who doesn't do exactly what I say doesn't deserve to live."
41–60	"Mine is the path of redemption. Anyone who says otherwise is intentionally misleading you."
61–80	"I will not rest until I have made someone else mine, and doing so is more important to me than my own life—or the lives of others."
81–90	"My own pleasure is of paramount importance. Everything else, including social graces, is a triviality."
91–00	"Anything that can bring me happiness should be enjoyed immediately. There is no point to saving anything pleasurable for later."

GRAZ'ZT

Large fiend (demon, shapechanger), chaotic evil

Armor Class 20 (natural armor)
Hit Points 378 (36d10 + 180)
Speed 40 ft.

STR	DEX	CON	INT	WIS	CHA
22 (+6)	15 (+2)	21 (+5)	23 (+6)	21 (+5)	26 (+8)

Saving Throws Dex +9, Con +12, Wis +12
Skills Deception +15, Insight +12, Perception +12, Persuasion +15
Damage Resistances cold, fire, lightning
Damage Immunities poison; bludgeoning, piercing, and slashing that is nonmagical
Condition Immunities charmed, exhaustion, frightened, poisoned
Senses truesight 120 ft., passive Perception 22
Languages all, telepathy 120 ft.
Challenge 24 (62,000 XP)

Shapechanger. Graz'zt can use his action to polymorph into a form that resembles a Medium humanoid, or back into his true form. Aside from his size, his statistics are the same in each form. Any equipment he is wearing or carrying isn't transformed.

Innate Spellcasting. Graz'zt's spellcasting ability is Charisma (spell save DC 23). He can innately cast the following spells, requiring no material components:

At will: *charm person, crown of madness, detect magic, dispel magic, dissonant whispers*
3/day each: *counterspell, darkness, dominate person, sanctuary, telekinesis, teleport*

1/day each: *dominate monster, greater invisibility*

Legendary Resistance (3/Day). If Graz'zt fails a saving throw, he can choose to succeed instead.

Magic Resistance. Graz'zt has advantage on saving throws against spells and other magical effects.

Magic Weapons. Graz'zt's weapon attacks are magical.

ACTIONS

Multiattack. Graz'zt attacks twice with the Wave of Sorrow.

Wave of Sorrow (Greatsword). *Melee Weapon Attack:* +13 to hit, reach 10 ft., one target. *Hit:* 20 (4d6 + 6) slashing damage plus 14 (4d6) acid damage.

Teleport. Graz'zt magically teleports, along with any equipment he is wearing or carrying, up to 120 feet to an unoccupied space he can see.

LEGENDARY ACTIONS

Graz'zt can take 3 legendary actions, choosing from the options below. Only one legendary action option can be used at a time and only at the end of another creature's turn. Graz'zt regains spent legendary actions at the start of his turn.

Attack. Graz'zt attacks once with the Wave of Sorrow.
Dance, My Puppet! One creature charmed by Graz'zt that Graz'zt can see must use its reaction to move up to its speed as Graz'zt directs.
Sow Discord. Graz'zt casts *crown of madness* or *dissonant whispers*.
Teleport. Graz'zt uses his Teleport action.

Juiblex

Called the Faceless Lord and the Oozing Hunger in ancient grimoires, Juiblex is demon lord of slime and ooze, a noxious creature that doesn't care about the plots and schemes of others of its kind. It exists only to consume, digesting and transforming living matter into more of itself.

Juiblex

A true horror, Juiblex is a mass of bubbling slime, swirling black and green, with glaring red eyes floating and shifting within it. It can rise up like a 20-foot hill, lashing out with dripping pseudopods to drag victims into its bulk. Those consumed by Juiblex are obliterated.

Only the truly insane worship Juiblex and tend to its slimes and oozes. Those who offer themselves up to the demon lord are engulfed by it and become vaguely humanoid, sentient oozes. The bodies of these former flesh-and-blood creatures form Juiblex's extended physical body, while the demon lord slowly digests and savors their identities over time.

Juiblex's Lair

Juiblex's principal lair is known as the Slime Pits, a realm which Juiblex shares with Zuggtmoy. This layer of the Abyss, which is also known as Shedaklah, is a bubbling morass of oozing, fetid sludge. Its landscape is covered in vast expanses of caustic and unintelligent slimes, and strange organic forms rise from the oceans of molds and oozes at Juiblex's command.

Lair Actions

On initiative count 20 (losing initiative ties), Juiblex can take a lair action to cause one of the following effects; it can't use the same effect two rounds in a row:

- Juiblex slimes a square area of ground it can see within the lair. The area can be up to 10 feet on a side. The slime lasts for 1 hour or until it is burned away with fire. When the slime appears, each creature in that area must succeed on a DC 21 Strength saving throw or become restrained. When a creature enters the area for the first time on a turn or ends its turn there, that creature must make the same save.

  A restrained creature is stuck as long as it remains in the slimy area or until it breaks free. The restrained creature, or another creature who can reach it, can use its action to try to break free and must succeed on a DC 21 Strength check.

  If the slime is set on fire, it burns away after 1 round. Any creature that starts its turn in the burning slime takes 22 (4d10) fire damage.

- Juiblex slimes a square area of ground it can see within the lair. The area can be up to 10 feet on a side. The slime lasts for 1 hour or until it is burned away with fire. When the slime appears, each creature on it must succeed on a DC 21 Dexterity saving throw or fall prone and slide 10 feet in a random direction determined by a d8 roll. When a creature enters the area for the first time on a turn or ends its turn there, that creature must make the same save.

  If the slime is set on fire, it burns away after 1 round. Any creature that starts its turn in the burning slime takes 22 (4d10) fire damage.

- A green slime (see the *Dungeon Master's Guide*) appears on a spot on the ceiling that Juiblex chooses within the lair. The slime disintegrates after 1 hour.

Regional Effects

The region containing Juiblex's lair is warped by its magic, creating one or more of the following effects:

- Small bodies of water, such as ponds or wells, within 1 mile of the lair turn highly acidic, corroding any object that touches them.
- Surfaces within 6 miles of the lair are frequently covered by a thin film of slime, which is slick and sticks to anything that touches it.
- If a humanoid spends at least 1 hour within 1 mile of the lair, that creature must succeed on a DC 18 Wisdom saving throw or descend into a madness determined by the Madness of Juiblex table. A creature that succeeds on this saving throw can't be affected by this regional effect again for 24 hours.

If Juiblex dies, these effects fade over the course of 1d10 days.

MADNESS OF JUIBLEX

If a creature goes mad in Juiblex's lair or within line of sight of the demon lord, roll on the Madness of Juiblex table to determine the nature of the madness, which is a character flaw that lasts until cured. See the *Dungeon Master's Guide* for more on madness.

MADNESS OF JUIBLEX

d100	Flaw (lasts until cured)
01–20	"I must consume everything I can!"
21–40	"I refuse to part with any of my possessions."
41–60	"I'll do everything I can to get others to eat and drink beyond their normal limits."
61–80	"I must possess as many material goods as I can."
81–00	"My personality is irrelevant. I am defined by what I consume."

JUIBLEX
Huge fiend (demon), chaotic evil

Armor Class 18 (natural armor)
Hit Points 350 (28d12 + 168)
Speed 30 ft.

STR	DEX	CON	INT	WIS	CHA
24 (+7)	10 (+0)	23 (+6)	20 (+5)	20 (+5)	16 (+3)

Saving Throws Dex +7, Con +13, Wis +12
Skills Perception +12
Damage Resistances cold, fire, lightning
Damage Immunities poison; bludgeoning, piercing, and slashing that is nonmagical
Condition Immunities blinded, charmed, deafened, exhaustion, frightened, grappled, paralyzed, petrified, poisoned, prone, restrained, stunned, unconscious
Senses truesight 120 ft., passive Perception 22
Languages all, telepathy 120 ft.
Challenge 23 (50,000 XP)

Foul. Any creature, other than an ooze, that starts its turn within 10 feet of Juiblex must succeed on a DC 21 Constitution saving throw or be poisoned until the start of the creature's next turn.

Innate Spellcasting. Juiblex's spellcasting ability is Charisma (spell save DC 18, +10 to hit with spell attacks). Juiblex can innately cast the following spells, requiring no material components:

At will: *acid splash* (17th level), *detect magic*
3/day each: *blight*, *contagion*, *gaseous form*

Legendary Resistance (3/Day). If Juiblex fails a saving throw, it can choose to succeed instead.

Magic Resistance. Juiblex has advantage on saving throws against spells and other magical effects.

Magic Weapons. Juiblex's weapon attacks are magical.

Regeneration. Juiblex regains 20 hit points at the start of its turn. If it takes fire or radiant damage, this trait doesn't function at the start of its next turn. Juiblex dies only if it starts its turn with 0 hit points and doesn't regenerate.

Spider Climb. Juiblex can climb difficult surfaces, including upside down on ceilings, without needing to make an ability check.

ACTIONS

Multiattack. Juiblex makes three acid lash attacks.

Acid Lash. *Melee Weapon Attack:* +14 to hit, reach 10 ft., one target. *Hit:* 21 (4d6 + 7) acid damage. Any creature killed by this attack is drawn into Juiblex's body, and the corpse is obliterated after 1 minute.

Eject Slime (Recharge 5–6). Juiblex spews out a corrosive slime, targeting one creature that it can see within 60 feet of it. The target must make a DC 21 Dexterity saving throw. On a failure, the target takes 55 (10d10) acid damage. Unless the target avoids taking any of this damage, any metal armor worn by the target takes a permanent –1 penalty to the AC it offers, and any metal weapon it is carrying or wearing takes a permanent –1 penalty to damage rolls. The penalty worsens each time a target is subjected to this effect. If the penalty on an object drops to –5, the object is destroyed.

LEGENDARY ACTIONS

Juiblex can take 3 legendary actions, choosing from the options below. Only one legendary action option can be used at a time and only at the end of another creature's turn. Juiblex regains spent legendary actions at the start of its turn.

Acid Splash. Juiblex casts *acid splash*.
Attack. Juiblex makes one acid lash attack.
Corrupting Touch (Costs 2 Actions). *Melee Weapon Attack:* +14 to hit, reach 10 ft., one creature. *Hit:* 21 (4d6 + 7) poison damage, and the target is slimed. Until the slime is scraped off with an action, the target is poisoned, and any creature, other than an ooze, is poisoned while within 10 feet of the target.

ORCUS

ORCUS

Orcus is the Demon Prince of Undeath, known as the Blood Lord. He takes some pleasure in the sufferings of the living, but far prefers the company and service of the undead. His desire is to see all life quenched and the multiverse transformed into a vast necropolis populated solely by undead creatures under his command.

Orcus rewards those who spread death in his name by granting them a small portion of his power. The least of these become ghouls and zombies who serve in his legions, while his favored servants are the cultists and necromancers who murder the living and then manipulate the dead, emulating their dread master.

Orcus is a bestial creature of corruption with a diseased, decaying look. He has the lower torso of a goat, and a humanoid upper body with a corpulent belly swollen with rot. Great bat wings sprout from his shoulders, and his head is like the skull of a goat, the flesh nearly rotted from it. In one hand, he wields the legendary *Wand of Orcus*, which is described in chapter 7, "Treasure," of the *Dungeon Master's Guide*.

ORCUS'S LAIR

Orcus makes his lair in the fortress city of Naratyr, which is on Thanatos, the layer of the Abyss that he rules. Surrounded by a moat fed by the River Styx,

Naratyr is an eerily quiet and cold city, its streets often empty for hours at a time. The central castle of bone has interior walls of flesh and carpets made of woven hair. The city contains wandering undead, many of which are engaged in continuous battles with one another.

LAIR ACTIONS

On initiative count 20 (losing initiative ties), Orcus can take a lair action to cause one of the following effects; he can't use the same effect two rounds in a row:

- Orcus's voice booms throughout the lair. His utterance causes one creature of his choice to be subjected to *power word kill* (save DC 23). Orcus needn't see the creature, but he must be aware that the individual is in the lair.
- Orcus causes up to six corpses within the lair to rise as skeletons, zombies, or ghouls. These undead obey his telepathic commands, which can reach anywhere in the lair.
- Orcus causes skeletal arms to rise from an area on the ground in a 20-foot square that he can see. They last until the next initiative count 20. Each creature in that area when the arms appear must succeed on a DC 23 Strength saving throw or be restrained until the arms disappear or until Orcus releases their grasp (no action required).

REGIONAL EFFECTS

The region containing Orcus's lair is warped by the Orcus's magic, creating one or more of the following effects:

- Dead beasts periodically animate as undead mockeries of their former selves. Skeletal and zombie versions of local wildlife are commonly seen in the area.
- The air becomes filled with the stench of rotting flesh, and buzzing flies grow thick within the region, even when there is no carrion to be found.
- If a humanoid spends at least 1 hour within 1 mile of the lair, that creature must succeed on a DC 23 Wisdom saving throw or descend into a madness determined by the Madness of Orcus table. A creature that succeeds on this saving throw can't be affected by this regional effect again for 24 hours.

If Orcus dies, these effects fade over the course of 1d10 days.

MADNESS OF ORCUS

If a creature goes mad in Orcus's lair or within line of sight of the demon lord, roll on the Madness of Orcus table to determine the nature of the madness, which is a character flaw that lasts until cured. See the *Dungeon Master's Guide* for more on madness.

MADNESS OF ORCUS

d100	Flaw (lasts until cured)
01–20	"I often become withdrawn and moody, dwelling on the insufferable state of life."
21–40	"I am compelled to make the weak suffer."
41–60	"I have no compunction against tampering with the dead in my search to better understand death."
61–80	"I want to achieve the everlasting existence of undeath."
81–00	"I am awash in the awareness of life's futility."

ORCUS
Huge fiend (demon), chaotic evil

Armor Class 17 (natural armor), 20 with the *Wand of Orcus*
Hit Points 405 (30d12 + 210)
Speed 40 ft., fly 40 ft.

STR	DEX	CON	INT	WIS	CHA
27 (+8)	14 (+2)	25 (+7)	20 (+5)	20 (+5)	25 (+7)

Saving Throws Dex +10, Con +15, Wis +13
Skills Arcana +12, Perception +12
Damage Resistances cold, fire, lightning
Damage Immunities necrotic, poison; bludgeoning, piercing, and slashing that is nonmagical
Condition Immunities charmed, exhaustion, frightened, poisoned
Senses truesight 120 ft., passive Perception 22
Languages all, telepathy 120 ft.
Challenge 26 (90,000 XP)

Wand of Orcus. The wand has 7 charges, and any of its properties that require a saving throw have a save DC of 18. While holding it, Orcus can use an action to cast *animate dead*, *blight*, or *speak with dead*. Alternatively, he can expend 1 or more of the wand's charges to cast one of the following spells from it: *circle of death* (1 charge), *finger of death* (1 charge), or *power word kill* (2 charges). The wand regains 1d4 + 3 charges daily at dawn.

While holding the wand, Orcus can use an action to conjure undead creatures whose combined average hit points don't exceed 500. These undead magically rise up from the ground or otherwise form in unoccupied spaces within 300 feet of Orcus and obey his commands until they are destroyed or until he dismisses them as an action. Once this property of the wand is used, the property can't be used again until the next dawn.

Innate Spellcasting. Orcus's spellcasting ability is Charisma (spell save DC 23, +15 to hit with spell attacks). He can innately cast the following spells, requiring no material components:

At will: *chill touch* (17th level), *detect magic*

3/day each: *create undead*, *dispel magic*
1/day: *time stop*

Legendary Resistance (3/Day). If Orcus fails a saving throw, he can choose to succeed instead.

Magic Resistance. Orcus has advantage on saving throws against spells and other magical effects.

Magic Weapons. Orcus's weapon attacks are magical.

Master of Undeath. When Orcus casts *animate dead* or *create undead*, he chooses the level at which the spell is cast, and the creatures created by the spells remain under his control indefinitely. Additionally, he can cast *create undead* even when it isn't night.

ACTIONS

Multiattack. Orcus makes two *Wand of Orcus* attacks.

Wand of Orcus. *Melee Weapon Attack:* +19 to hit, reach 10 ft., one target. *Hit:* 21 (3d8 + 8) bludgeoning damage plus 13 (2d12) necrotic damage.

Tail. *Melee Weapon Attack:* +17 to hit, reach 10 ft., one target. *Hit:* 21 (3d8 + 8) piercing damage plus 18 (4d8) poison damage.

LEGENDARY ACTIONS

Orcus can take 3 legendary actions, choosing from the options below. Only one legendary action option can be used at a time and only at the end of another creature's turn. Orcus regains spent legendary actions at the start of his turn.

Tail. Orcus makes one tail attack.
A Taste of Undeath. Orcus casts *chill touch* (17th level).
Creeping Death (Costs 2 Actions). Orcus chooses a point on the ground that he can see within 100 feet of him. A cylinder of swirling necrotic energy 60 feet tall and with a 10-foot radius rises from that point and lasts until the end of Orcus's next turn. Creatures in that area are vulnerable to necrotic damage.

YEENOGHU

The Beast of Butchery appears as a great battle-scarred gnoll, towering 14 feet tall. Yeenoghu is the Gnoll Lord, and his creations are made in his twisted image. When the demon lord hunted across the Material Plane, packs of hyenas followed in his wake. Those that ate of great Yeenoghu's kills became gnolls, emulating their master's ways. Few others worship the Beast of Butchery, but those who do tend to take on a gnoll-like aspect, hunched over, and filing their teeth down to points.

Yeenoghu wants nothing more than slaughter and senseless destruction. The gnolls are his instruments, and he drives them to ever-greater atrocities in his name. Yeenoghu takes pleasure in causing fear before death, and he sows sorrow and despair through destroying beloved things. He doesn't parlay; to meet him is to do battle with him—unless he becomes bored. The Beast of Butchery has a long rivalry with Baphomet, the Horned King, and the two demon lords and their followers attack one another on sight.

The Gnoll Lord is covered in matted fur and taut, leathery hide, his face like a grinning predator's skull. Patchwork armor made of discarded shields and breastplates is lashed onto his body with heavy chains, decorated by the flayed skins of his foes. He wields a triple-headed flail called the Butcher, which he can summon into his hand at will, although he is as likely to tear his prey apart with his bare hands before ripping out its throat with his teeth.

YEENOGHU'S LAIR

Yeenoghu's lair in the Abyss is called the Death Dells, its barren hills and ravines serving as one great hunting ground, where he pursues captured mortals in a cruel game. Yeenoghu's lair is a place of blood and death, populated by gnolls, hyenas, and ghouls, and there are few structures or signs of civilization on his layer of the Abyss.

LAIR ACTIONS

On initiative count 20 (losing initiative ties), Yeenoghu can take a lair action to cause one of the following effects; he can't use the same effect two rounds in a row.

- Yeenoghu causes an iron spike—5 feet tall and 1 inch in diameter—to burst from the ground at a point he can see within 100 feet of him. Any creature in the space where the spike emerges must make a DC 24 Dexterity saving throw. On a failed save, the creature takes 27 (6d8) piercing damage and is restrained by being impaled on the spike. A creature can use an action to remove itself (or a creature it can reach) from the spike, ending the restrained condition.
- Each gnoll or hyena that Yeenoghu can see can use its reaction to move up to its speed.

YEENOGHU

- Until the next initiative count 20, all gnolls and hyenas within the lair are enraged, causing them to have advantage on melee weapon attack rolls and causing attack rolls to have advantage against them.

REGIONAL EFFECTS

The region containing Yeenoghu's lair is warped by his magic, creating one or more of the following effects:

- Within 1 mile of the lair, large iron spikes grow out of the ground and stone surfaces. Yeenoghu impales the bodies of the slain on these spikes.
- Predatory beasts within 6 miles of the lair become unusually savage, killing far more than what they need for food. Carcasses of prey are left to rot in an unnatural display of wasteful slaughter.
- If a humanoid spends at least 1 hour within 1 mile of the lair, that creature must succeed on a DC 17 Wisdom saving throw or descend into a madness determined by the Madness of Yeenoghu table. A creature that succeeds on this saving throw can't be affected by this regional effect again for 24 hours.

If Yeenoghu dies, these effects fade over the course of 1d10 days.

MADNESS OF YEENOGHU

If a creature goes mad in Yeenoghu's lair or within line of sight of the demon lord, roll on the Madness of Yeenoghu table to determine the nature of the madness, which is a character flaw that lasts until cured. See the *Dungeon Master's Guide* for more on madness.

MADNESS OF YEENOGHU

d100	Flaw (lasts until cured)
01–20	"I get caught up in the flow of anger, and try to stoke others around me into forming an angry mob."
21–40	"The flesh of other intelligent creatures is delicious!"
41–60	"I rail against the laws and customs of civilization, attempting to return to a more primitive time."
61–80	"I hunger for the deaths of others, and am constantly starting fights in the hope of seeing bloodshed."
81–00	"I keep trophies from the bodies I have slain, turning them into adornments."

YEENOGHU

Huge fiend (demon), chaotic evil

Armor Class 22 (natural armor)
Hit Points 348 (24d12 + 192)
Speed 50 ft.

STR	DEX	CON	INT	WIS	CHA
29 (+9)	16 (+3)	23 (+8)	15 (+3)	24 (+7)	15 (+2)

Saving Throws Dex +10, Con +15, Wis +14
Skills Intimidation +9, Perception +14
Damage Resistances cold, fire, lightning
Damage Immunities poison; bludgeoning, piercing, and slashing that is nonmagical
Condition Immunities charmed, exhaustion, frightened, poisoned
Senses truesight 120 ft., passive Perception 24
Languages all, telepathy 120 ft.
Challenge 24 (62,000 XP)

Innate Spellcasting. Yeenoghu's spellcasting ability is Charisma (spell save DC 17, +9 to hit with spell attacks). He can innately cast the following spells, requiring no material components:

At will: *detect magic, spiritual weapon* (8th-level spell, 4d8 + 2 force damage on a hit, appears as a flail)
3/day each: *dispel magic, fear, invisibility*
1/day each: *teleport*

Legendary Resistance (3/Day). If Yeenoghu fails a saving throw, he can choose to succeed instead.

Magic Resistance. Yeenoghu has advantage on saving throws against spells and other magical effects.

Magic Weapons. Yeenoghu's weapon attacks are magical.

Rampage. When Yeenoghu reduces a creature to 0 hit points with a melee attack on his turn, Yeenoghu can take a bonus action to move up to half his speed and make a bite attack.

ACTIONS

Multiattack. Yeenoghu makes three flail attacks. If an attack hits, he can cause it to create an additional effect of his choice or at random (each effect can be used only once per Multiattack):

1. The attack deals an extra 13 (2d12) bludgeoning damage.
2. The target must succeed on a DC 17 Constitution saving throw or be paralyzed until the start of Yeenoghu's next turn.
3. The target must succeed on a DC 17 Wisdom saving throw or be affected by the *confusion* spell until the start of Yeenoghu's next turn.

Flail. *Melee Weapon Attack:* +16 to hit, reach 15 ft., one target. *Hit:* 22 (2d12 + 9) bludgeoning damage.

Bite. *Melee Weapon Attack:* +16 to hit, reach 10 ft., one target. *Hit:* 31 (4d10 + 9) piercing damage.

LEGENDARY ACTIONS

Yeenoghu can take 3 legendary actions, choosing from the options below. Only one legendary action option can be used at a time and only at the end of another creature's turn. Yeenoghu regains spent legendary actions at the start of his turn.

Charge. Yeenoghu moves up to his speed.
Swat Away. Yeenoghu makes a flail attack. If the attack hits, the target must succeed on a DC 24 Strength saving throw or be pushed 15 feet in a straight line away from Yeenoghu. If the saving throw fails by 5 or more, the target falls prone.
Savage (Costs 2 Actions). Yeenoghu makes a bite attack against each creature within 10 feet of him.

ZUGGTMOY

ZUGGTMOY

The Demon Queen of Fungi, Lady of Rot and Decay, Zuggtmoy is an alien creature whose only desire is to infect the living with spores, transforming them into her mindless servants and, eventually, into decomposing hosts for the mushrooms, molds, and other fungi that she spawns.

Utterly inhuman, Zuggtmoy can mold her fungoid form into an approximation of a humanoid shape, including the skeletal-thin figure depicted in grimoires and ancient art, draped and veiled in mycelium and lichen. Indeed, much of her appearance and manner, and that of her servants', is a soulless mockery of mortal life and its many facets.

Zuggtmoy's cultists often follow her unwittingly. Most are fungi-infected to some degree, whether through inhaling her mind-controlling spores or being transformed to the point where flesh and fungus become one. Such cultists are fungal extensions of the Demon Queen's will. Their devotion might begin with the seemingly harmless promises offered by exotic spores and mushrooms, but quickly consumes them, body and soul.

Sharing a layer of the Abyss with Juiblex, plus their mutual insatiable hunger, has made the two demon lords mortal enemies, each devoted to destroying and ultimately devouring the other.

ZUGGTMOY'S LAIR

Zuggtmoy's principal lair is her palace on Shedaklah. It consists of two dozen mushrooms of pale yellow and rancid brown. These massive fungi are some of the largest in existence. They are surrounded by a field of acidic puffballs and poisonous vapors. The mushrooms themselves are all interconnected by bridges of shelf-fungi, and countless chambers have been hollowed out from within their rubbery, fibrous stalks.

LAIR ACTIONS

On initiative count 20 (losing initiative ties), Zuggtmoy can take a lair action to cause one of the following effects; she can't use the same effect two rounds in a row.

- Zuggtmoy causes four gas spores or violet fungi (see the *Monster Manual*) to appear in unoccupied spaces that she chooses within the lair. They vanish after 1 hour.
- Up to four plant creatures that are friendly to Zuggtmoy and that Zuggtmoy can see can use their reactions to move up to their speed and make one weapon attack.
- Zuggtmoy uses either her Infestation Spores or her Mind Control Spores, centered on a mushroom or other fungus within her lair, instead of on herself.

REGIONAL EFFECTS

The region containing Zuggtmoy's lair is warped by her magic, creating one or more of the following effects:

- Molds and fungi grow on surfaces within 6 miles of the lair, even where they would normally find no purchase.

- Plant life within 1 mile of the lair becomes infested with parasitic fungi, slowly mutating as it is overwhelmed.
- If a humanoid spends at least 1 hour within 1 mile of the lair, that creature must succeed on a DC 17 Wisdom saving throw or descend into a madness determined by the Madness of Zuggtmoy table. A creature that succeeds on this saving throw can't be affected by this regional effect again for 24 hours.

If Zuggtmoy dies, these effects fade over the course of 1d10 days.

MADNESS OF ZUGGTMOY

If a creature goes mad in Zuggtmoy's lair or within line of sight of the demon lord, roll on the Madness of Zuggtmoy table to determine the nature of the madness, which is a character flaw that lasts until cured. See the *Dungeon Master's Guide* for more on madness.

MADNESS OF ZUGGTMOY

d100	Flaw (lasts until cured)
01–20	"I see visions in the world around me that others do not."
21–40	"I periodically slip into a catatonic state, staring off into the distance for long stretches at a time."
41–60	"I see an altered version of reality, with my mind convincing itself that things are true even in the face of overwhelming evidence to the contrary."
61–80	"My mind is slipping away, and my intelligence seems to wax and wane."
81–00	"I am constantly scratching at unseen fungal infections."

ZUGGTMOY

Large fiend (demon), chaotic evil

Armor Class 18 (natural armor)
Hit Points 304 (32d10 + 128)
Speed 30 ft.

STR	DEX	CON	INT	WIS	CHA
22 (+6)	15 (+2)	18 (+4)	20 (+5)	19 (+4)	24 (+7)

Saving Throws Dex +9, Con +11, Wis +11
Skills Perception +11
Damage Resistances cold, fire, lightning
Damage Immunities poison; bludgeoning, piercing, and slashing that is nonmagical
Condition Immunities charmed, exhaustion, frightened, poisoned
Senses truesight 120 ft., passive Perception 21
Languages all, telepathy 120 ft.
Challenge 23 (50,000 XP)

Innate Spellcasting. Zuggtmoy's spellcasting ability is Charisma (spell save DC 22). She can innately cast the following spells, requiring no material components:

At will: *detect magic, locate animals or plants, ray of sickness*
3/day each: *dispel magic, ensnaring strike, entangle, plant growth*
1/day each: *etherealness, teleport*

Legendary Resistance (3/Day). If Zuggtmoy fails a saving throw, she can choose to succeed instead.

Magic Resistance. Zuggtmoy has advantage on saving throws against spells and other magical effects.

Magic Weapons. Zuggtmoy's weapon attacks are magical.

ACTIONS

Multiattack. Zuggtmoy makes four pseudopod attacks.

Pseudopod. *Melee Weapon Attack:* +13 to hit, reach 10 ft., one target. *Hit:* 15 (2d8 + 6) bludgeoning damage plus 9 (2d8) poison damage.

Infestation Spores (3/Day). Zuggtmoy releases spores that burst out in a cloud that fills a 20-foot-radius sphere centered on her, and it lingers for 1 minute. Any flesh-and-blood creature in the cloud when it appears, or that enters it later, must make a DC 19 Constitution saving throw. On a successful save, the creature can't be infected by these spores for 24 hours. On a failed save, the creature is infected with a disease called the spores of Zuggtmoy and also gains a random form of madness (determined by rolling on the Madness of Zuggtmoy table) that lasts until the creature is cured of the disease or dies. While infected in this way, the creature can't be reinfected, and it must repeat the saving throw at the end of every 24 hours, ending the infection on a success. On a failure, the infected creature's body is slowly taken over by fungal growth, and after three such failed saves, the creature dies and is reanimated as a spore servant if it's a type of creature that can be (see the "Myconids" entry in the *Monster Manual*).

Mind Control Spores (Recharge 5–6). Zuggtmoy releases spores that burst out in a cloud that fills a 20-foot-radius sphere centered on her, and it lingers for 1 minute. Humanoids and beasts in the cloud when it appears, or that enter it later, must make a DC 19 Wisdom saving throw. On a successful save, the creature can't be infected by these spores for 24 hours. On a failed save, the creature is infected with a disease called the influence of Zuggtmoy for 24 hours. While infected, the creature is charmed by her and can't be reinfected by these spores.

REACTIONS

Protective Thrall. When Zuggtmoy is hit by an attack, one creature within 5 feet of Zuggtmoy that is charmed by her must use its reaction to be hit by the attack instead.

LEGENDARY ACTIONS

Zuggtmoy can take 3 legendary actions, choosing from the options below. Only one legendary action option can be used at a time and only at the end of another creature's turn. Zuggtmoy regains spent legendary actions at the start of her turn.

Attack. Zuggtmoy makes one pseudopod attack.
Exert Will. One creature charmed by Zuggtmoy that she can see must use its reaction to move up to its speed as she directs or to make a weapon attack against a target that she designates.

Afterword

In the Rage of Demons story, demon lords invade the Underdark and spread madness throughout the subterranean realm. (As if the Underdark wasn't dangerous enough already!) The Underdark is home to some of the D&D game's most iconic monsters, as well as cultures both alien and wondrous.

To bring the Underdark to life, Richard Whitters and his concept artists created amazing imagery tied to various Underdark races: kuo-toa waymarkers, illithid "brain urns" and domiciles, duergar architecture, drow costuming, and much, much more. Their concept art was featured a "story bible" that we gave to our licensed partners. That story bible served as inspiration for miniatures, digital projects, and print products like the adventure you hold in your hands.

This appendix contains a sampling of the concept art we commissioned for the Rage of Demons story. We hope that this art further inspires you to run *Out of the Abyss* or create your own Underdark encounters.

—Chris Perkins

DERRO
THE SMALL, DEGENERATE DWARVES WERE ONCE SLAVES OF MIND FLAYERS. ENSLAVEMENT DROVE THE DERRO MAD.

DEEP GNOMES (SVIRFNEBLIN)
DEEP GNOMES ARE SECRETIVE AND INDUSTRIOUS. THE MINING OF GEMS AND PRECIOUS MINERALS FORMS THE FOUNDATION OF THEIR ECONOMY.

KUO-TOA CREATIONS
Kuo-toa archpriests fashion holy staffs and waymarkers that incorporate images of their made-up gods.

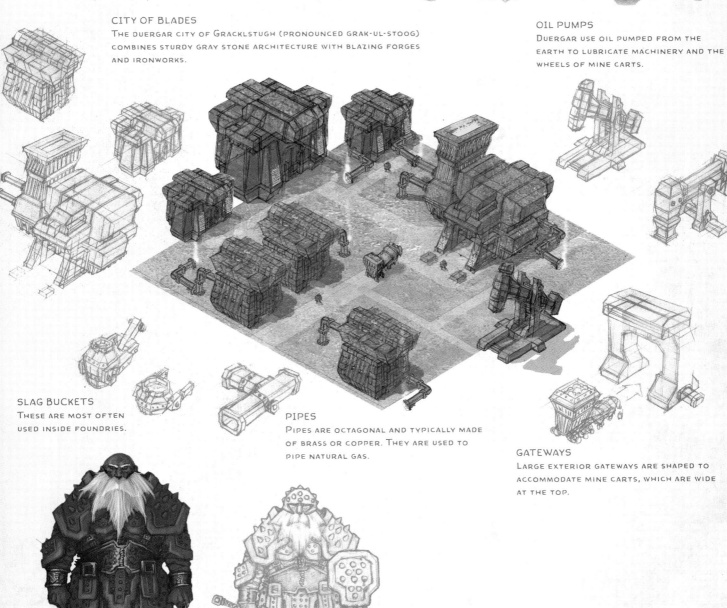

CITY OF BLADES
The duergar city of Gracklstugh (pronounced grak-ul-stoog) combines sturdy gray stone architecture with blazing forges and ironworks.

OIL PUMPS
Duergar use oil pumped from the earth to lubricate machinery and the wheels of mine carts.

SLAG BUCKETS
These are most often used inside foundries.

PIPES
Pipes are octagonal and typically made of brass or copper. They are used to pipe natural gas.

GATEWAYS
Large exterior gateways are shaped to accommodate mine carts, which are wide at the top.

DUERGAR ARMOR
Duergar armor is heavy without feeling restricting and cumbersome. The armor combines gold elements with crimson-dyed leather and iron trim.

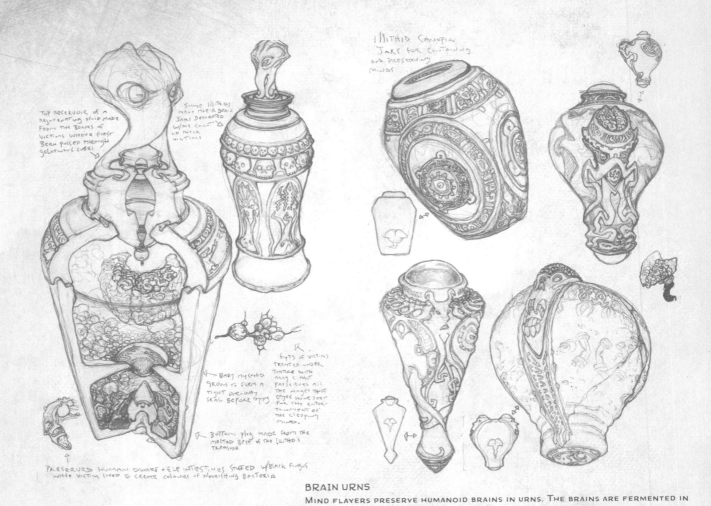

BRAIN URNS

MIND FLAYERS PRESERVE HUMANOID BRAINS IN URNS. THE BRAINS ARE FERMENTED IN SPECIAL BRINES OR DUSTED WITH FUNGAL SPORES FOR ADDED FLAVOR.

DROW FASHION

DROW MALES ARE SMALLER THAN THE FEMALES. THEIR ARMOR IS SNUG, FLEXIBLE, AND QUIET. WEB SHAWLS AND CLOAKS MADE FROM GIANT SPIDER HIDE ARE POPULAR ADORNMENTS.

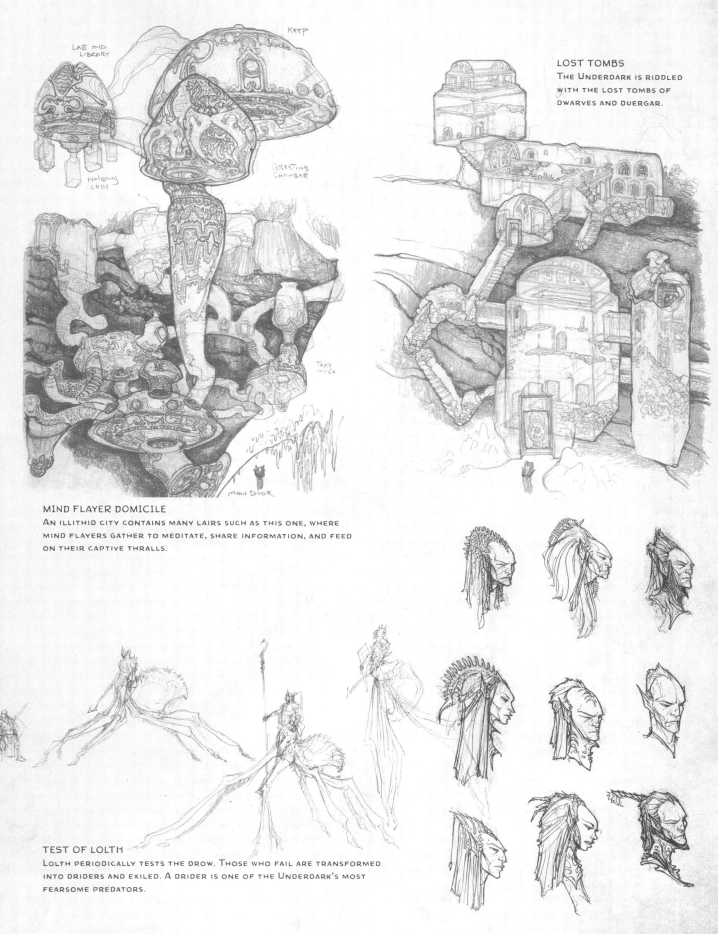

LOST TOMBS
The Underdark is riddled with the lost tombs of dwarves and duergar.

MIND FLAYER DOMICILE
An illithid city contains many lairs such as this one, where mind flayers gather to meditate, share information, and feed on their captive thralls.

TEST OF LOLTH
Lolth periodically tests the drow. Those who fail are transformed into driders and exiled. A drider is one of the Underdark's most fearsome predators.

VIZERAN DEVIR

House DeVir was attacked and destroyed by House Do'Urden on the day that Drizzt Do'Urden was born. The drow archmage Vizeran DeVir survived the destruction of his house because he wasn't in Menzoberranzan when the attack happened. Most other drow assume Vizeran was killed in the attack, allowing him to go into hiding.

Vizeran detests Lolth and her priestesses. Despite his dour disposition, he is ready to help adventurers banish the demon lords back to the Abyss, and he wants Lolth and her worshipers to suffer in the process.

ZELLIX

Zellix is the founder and administrator of a subterranean insane asylum. The mind flayer captures creatures afflicted with demonic madness so that he can feed on their deranged brains, which are far more succulent and tasty than sane ones. He also uses the juice from mad brains as a serum, injecting it into other creatures to make them crazy.

Zellix sends out intellect devourers in host bodies to lure new subjects to his asylum, which is built inside a network of spiraling tunnels.

DROW SPORE SERVANT

Zuggtmoy plans to marry the gigantic fungus Araumycos. As she prepares for her wedding, she casts her spores throughout the Underdark. These spores infect drow and other creatures, eventually turning them into her thralls. Through them, word of the impending marriage spreads to every corner of the Underdark.

The final stage of infestation causes a thrall's head to burst open, transforming it into a spore servant.

DEMOGORGON

Demogorgon figures prominently in the Rage of Demons story. When creating a three-dimensional plastic miniature or a model for a digital game or marketing video, it helps to have front, back, and side views that clearly show the demon prince's anatomy.

WHAT HAPPENS NEXT?

CONTINUE YOUR DESCENT INTO THE Underdark with *Sword Coast Legends*™, an isometric action roleplaying game on PC, Mac, Linux, and consoles. Embark on an epic quest—on your own or with friends—to discover a mysterious enemy that threatens your guild. Or you can summon your allies in DM mode, a first-of-its-kind experience in which a Dungeon Master uses campaign tools to guide players through adventures customizable in real-time.

Continue your journey in the D&D tabletop roleplaying game by playing in the D&D Adventurers League™ worldwide. Heroic characters meet up weekly at D&D Encounters to thwart the evil threatening the Forgotten Realms. Then level up your character with ongoing, convention-style play with D&D Expeditions. Contact your local store for dates and times.

For tabletop players who want to go beyond the adventure, bring Rage of Demons to life with miniatures, gameplay accessories, and apparel by Ultra PRO, Gale Force Nine, WizKids Games, and We Love Fine.

Finally, experience the depth of the Rage of Demons story with new novels by Erin M. Evans, Troy Denning, and *New York Times* best-selling author R.A. Salvatore.

Dare to Descend at DungeonsandDragons.com

DEMONS RAMPAGE THROUGH THE UNDERDARK, SPREADING INSANITY AND TERROR IN THEIR WAKE. A SEETHING MADNESS THREATENS TO CONSUME YOU. AND UNLESS YOU CAN STOP THE MONSTERS, THEY'LL BOIL UP FROM THE DEPTHS AND SPREAD ACROSS ALL FAERÛN.

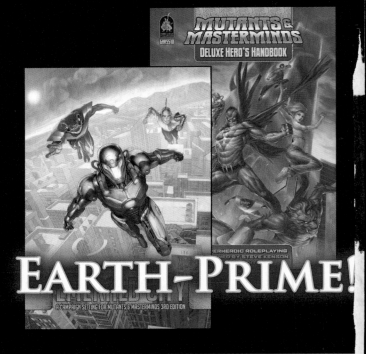